Visual Basic 5 Power OOP

Martin Rinehart

Visual Basic 5 Power OOP

Martin Rinehart

IDG Books Worldwide, Inc.
An International Data Group Company

Foster City, CA ♦ Chicago, IL ♦ Indianapolis, IN ♦ Southlake, TX

Visual Basic 5 Power OOP

Published by
IDG Books Worldwide, Inc.
An International Data Group Company
919 E. Hillsdale Blvd.
Suite 400
Foster City, CA 94404
http://www.idgbooks.com (IDG Books Worldwide Web site)

Library of Congress Catalog Card No.: 97-070948

ISBN: 0-7645-3029-1

Printed in the United States of America

10 9 8 7 6 5 4 3 2 1

1E/RZ/QV/ZX/FC

Distributed in the United States by IDG Books Worldwide, Inc.

Distributed by Macmillan Canada for Canada; by Transworld Publishers Limited in the United Kingdom and Europe; by WoodsLane Pty. Ltd. for Australia; by WoodsLane Enterprises Ltd. for New Zealand; by Longman Singapore Publishers Ltd. for Singapore, Malaysia, Thailand, and Indonesia; by Simron Pty. Ltd. for South Africa; by Toppan Company Ltd. for Japan; by Distribuidora Cuspide for Argentina; by Livraria Cultura for Brazil; by Ediciencia S.A. for Ecuador; by Addison-Wesley Publishing Company for Korea; by Ediciones ZETA S.C.R. Ltda. for Peru; by WS Computer Publishing Company, Inc., for the Philippines; by Unalis Corporation for Taiwan; by Contemporanea de Ediciones for Venezuela. Authorized Sales Agent: Anthony Rudkin Associates for the Middle East and North Africa.

For general information on IDG Books Worldwide's books in the U.S., please call our Consumer Customer Service department at 800-762-2974. For reseller information, including discounts and premium sales, please call our Reseller Customer Service department at 800-434-3422.

For information on where to purchase IDG Books Worldwide's books outside the U.S., please contact our International Sales department at 415-655-3023 or fax 415-655-3299.

For information on foreign language translations, please contact our Foreign & Subsidiary Rights department at 415-655-3021 or fax 415-655-3281.

For sales inquiries and special prices for bulk quantities, please contact our Sales department at 415-655-3200 or write to the address above.

For information on using IDG Books Worldwide's books in the classroom or for ordering examination copies, please contact our Educational Sales department at 800-434-2086 or fax 817-251-8174.

For press review copies, author interviews, or other publicity information, please contact our Public Relations department at 415-655-3000 or fax 415-655-3299.

For authorization to photocopy items for corporate, personal, or educational use, please contact Copyright Clearance Center, 222 Rosewood Drive, Danvers, MA 01923, or fax 508-750-4470.

is a trademark under exclusive license to IDG Books Worldwide, Inc., from International Data Group, Inc.

ABOUT IDG BOOKS WORLDWIDE

Welcome to the world of IDG Books Worldwide.

IDG Books Worldwide, Inc., is a subsidiary of International Data Group, the world's largest publisher of computer-related information and the leading global provider of information services on information technology. IDG was founded more than 25 years ago and now employs more than 8,500 people worldwide. IDG publishes more than 275 computer publications in over 75 countries (see listing below). More than 60 million people read one or more IDG publications each month.

Launched in 1990, IDG Books Worldwide is today the #1 publisher of best-selling computer books in the United States. We are proud to have received eight awards from the Computer Press Association in recognition of editorial excellence and three from *Computer Currents'* First Annual Readers' Choice Awards. Our bestselling *...For Dummies®* series has more than 30 million copies in print with translations in 30 languages. IDG Books Worldwide, through a joint venture with IDG's Hi-Tech Beijing, became the first U.S. publisher to publish a computer book in the People's Republic of China. In record time, IDG Books Worldwide has become the first choice for millions of readers around the world who want to learn how to better manage their businesses.

Our mission is simple: Every one of our books is designed to bring extra value and skill-building instructions to the reader. Our books are written by experts who understand and care about our readers. The knowledge base of our editorial staff comes from years of experience in publishing, education, and journalism — experience we use to produce books for the '90s. In short, we care about books, so we attract the best people. We devote special attention to details such as audience, interior design, use of icons, and illustrations. And because we use an efficient process of authoring, editing, and desktop publishing our books electronically, we can spend more time ensuring superior content and spend less time on the technicalities of making books.

You can count on our commitment to deliver high-quality books at competitive prices on topics you want to read about. At IDG Books Worldwide, we continue in the IDG tradition of delivering quality for more than 25 years. You'll find no better book on a subject than one from IDG Books Worldwide.

John Kilcullen
CEO
IDG Books Worldwide, Inc.

Steven Berkowitz
President and Publisher
IDG Books Worldwide, Inc.

Eighth Annual Computer Press Awards ≥ 1992

Ninth Annual Computer Press Awards ≥ 1993

Tenth Annual Computer Press Awards ≥ 1994

Eleventh Annual Computer Press Awards ≥ 1995

IDG Books Worldwide, Inc., is a subsidiary of International Data Group, the world's largest publisher of computer-related information and the leading global provider of information services on information technology. International Data Group publishes over 275 computer publications in over 75 countries. Sixty million people read one or more International Data Group publications each month. International Data Group's publications include: **ARGENTINA:** Buyer's Guide, Computerworld Argentina, PC World Argentina; **AUSTRALIA:** Australian Macworld, Australian PC World, Australian Reseller News, Computerworld, IT Casebook, Network World, Publish, Webmaster; **AUSTRIA:** Computerwelt Österreich, Networks Austria, PC Tip Austria; **BANGLADESH:** PC World Bangladesh; **BELARUS:** PC World Belarus; **BELGIUM:** Data News; **BRAZIL:** Annuário de Informática, Computerworld, Connections, Macworld, PC Player, PC World, Publish, Reseller News, Supergamepower; **BULGARIA:** Computerworld Bulgaria, Network World Bulgaria, PC & MacWorld Bulgaria; **CANADA:** CIO Canada, Client/Server World, ComputerWorld Canada, InfoWorld Canada, NetworkWorld Canada, WebWorld; **CHILE:** Computerworld Chile, PC World Chile; **COLOMBIA:** Computerworld Colombia, PC World Colombia; **COSTA RICA:** PC World Centro America; **THE CZECH AND SLOVAK REPUBLICS:** Computerworld Czechoslovakia, Macworld Czech Republic, PC World Czechoslovakia; **DENMARK:** Communications World Danmark, Computerworld Danmark, Macworld Danmark, PC World Danmark, Techworld Danmark; **DOMINICAN REPUBLIC:** PC World Republica Dominicana; **ECUADOR:** PC World Ecuador; **EGYPT:** Computerworld Middle East, PC World Middle East; **EL SALVADOR:** PC World Centro America; **FINLAND:** MikroPC, Tietoverkko, Tietoviikko; **FRANCE:** Distributique, Hebdo, Info PC, Le Monde Informatique, Macworld, Reseaux & Telecoms, WebMaster France; **GERMANY:** Computer Partner, Computerwoche, Computerwoche Extra, Computerwoche FOCUS, Global Online, Macwelt, PC Welt; **GREECE:** Amiga Computing, GamePro Greece, Multimedia World; **GUATEMALA:** PC World Centro America; **HONDURAS:** PC World Centro America; **HONG KONG:** Computerworld Hong Kong, PC World Hong Kong, Publish in Asia; **HUNGARY:** ABCD CD-ROM, Computerworld Szamitastechnika, Interneto online Magazine, PC World Hungary, PC-X Magazin Hungary; **ICELAND:** Tolvuheimur PC World Island; **INDIA:** Information Communications World, Information Systems Computerworld, PC World India, Publish in Asia; **INDONESIA:** InfoKomputer PC World, Komputek Computerworld, Publish in Asia; **IRELAND:** ComputerScope, PC Live!; **ISRAEL:** Macworld Israel, People & Computers/Computerworld; **ITALY:** Computerworld Italia, Macworld Italia, Networking Italia, PC World Italia; **JAPAN:** DTP World, Macworld Japan, Nikkei Personal Computing, OS/2 World Japan, SunWorld Japan, Windows NT World, Windows World Japan; **KENYA:** PC World East African; **KOREA:** Hi-Tech Information, Macworld Korea, PC World Korea; **MACEDONIA:** PC World Macedonia; **MALAYSIA:** Computerworld Malaysia, PC World Malaysia, Publish in Asia; **MALTA:** PC World Malta; **MEXICO:** Computerworld Mexico, PC World Mexico; **MYANMAR:** PC World Myanmar; **NETHERLANDS:** Computer! Totaal, LAN Internetworking Magazine, LAN World Buyers Guide, Macworld Netherlands, Net, WebWereld; **NEW ZEALAND:** Absolute Beginners Guide and Plain & Simple Series, Computer Buyer, Rapport, Kursguide Norge, Macworld Norge, Multimediaworld Norge, PC World Ekspress Norge, PC World Nettverk, PC World Norge, PC World ProduktGuide Norge; **PAKISTAN:** Computerworld Pakistan; **PANAMA:** PC World Weekly, Game Software, PC World China, Popular Computer Week, Software Weekly, Software World, Telecom World; **PERU:** Computerworld Peru, PC World Profesional Peru, PC World SoHo Peru; **PHILIPPINES:** Click!, Cerebro/PC World, Computerworld/Correio Informático, Dealer World Portugal, Mac*In/PC*In Portugal, Multimedia World; **PUERTO RICO:** PC World Puerto Rico; **ROMANIA:** Computerworld Romania, PC World Romania, Telecom Romania; **RUSSIA:** Computerworld Russia, Mir PK, Publish, Seti; **SINGAPORE:** Computerworld Singapore, PC World Singapore, Publish in Asia; **SLOVENIA:** Monitor; **SOUTH AFRICA:** Computing SA, Network World SA, Software World SA; **SPAIN:** Communicaciones World España, Computerworld España, Dealer World España, Macworld España, PC World España; **SRI LANKA:** Infolink PC World; **SWEDEN:** CAP&Design, Computer Sweden, Corporate Computing Sweden, Internetworld Sweden, it.branschen, Macworld Sweden, MaxiData Sweden, MikroDatorn, Nätverk & Kommunikation, PC World Sweden, PCaktiv, Windows World Sweden; **SWITZERLAND:** Computerworld Schweiz, Macworld Schweiz, PCtip; **TAIWAN:** Computerworld Taiwan, Macworld Taiwan, NEW ViSiON/Publish, PC World Taiwan, Windows World Taiwan; **THAILAND:** Publish in Asia, Thai Computerworld; **TURKEY:** Computerworld Turkiye, Macworld Turkiye, Network World Turkiye, PC World Turkiye; **UKRAINE:** Computerworld Kiev, Multimedia World Ukraine, PC World Ukraine; **UNITED KINGDOM:** Acorn User UK, Amiga Action UK, Amiga Computing UK, Apple Talk UK, Computing, Macworld, Parents and Computers UK, PC Advisor, PC Home, PSX Pro, The WEB, **UNITED STATES:** Cable in the Classroom, CIO Magazine, Computerworld, DOS World, Federal Computer Week, GamePro Magazine, InfoWorld, I-Way, Macworld, Network World, PC Games, PC World, Publish, Video Event, THE WEB Magazine, and WebMaster; online webzines: JavaWorld, NetscapeWorld, and SunWorld Online; **URUGUAY:** InfoWorld Uruguay; **VENEZUELA:** Computerworld Venezuela, PC World Venezuela; and **VIETNAM:** PC World Vietnam.   3/24/97

CREDITS

Software Acquisitions Editor
Tracy Lehman Cramer

Development Editor
Hugh Vandivier

Copy Edit Coordinator
Barry Childs-Helton

Editorial Assistant
Timothy Borek

Production Coordinators
Katy German
Ben Schroeter

Technical Reviewer
Larry VanDerJagt

Production Page Layout
Mario F. Amador
Jude Livinson
Christopher Pimentel
Dina F Quan
Andreas F. Schueller

Quality Control Specialist
Mick Arellano

Proofreader
Mary C. Oby

Indexer
Lori Lathrop

Cover Design
Liew Design

ABOUT THE AUTHOR

Martin Rinehart

This is Martin Rinehart's eighth book. He's lost count of the articles he's published. Marty, as he's known among friends, learned BASIC from its co-inventer, Professor John Kemeny, at Dartmouth College in 1965. He's been programming ever since.

Languages he's used professionally include BASIC, PL/I, Fortran, APL, Xbase, C, PC assembler, C++, and Java.

He's worked as a freelance programmer, manager of the Quantitative Analysis group at a major investment bank, Product Marketing Manager at a timesharing company, founder and DEO of a PC software company, and, most recently, as an independent author and consultant specializing in object-oriented, client/server applications.

When Marty is not at the computer keyboard, you can find him at his piano keyboard or out on a local soccer field. If you can't find him around home — and it's warm out — he's probably backpacking in the mountains, and when it snows, he'll be skiing down them.

This book is dedicated to Jane Rinehart, who has been a pillar of strength in difficult times.

— Martin Rinehart

ACKNOWLEDGMENTS

Ah, picture the solitary writer staring into his computer, working late into the night. What greater single achievement...

Forget it. Picture a football team taking the field and you're nearer the truth. The author's at left guard.

Acquisition editor Greg Croy put this book together with my agent, Matt Wagner. That's the head coach and owner, though I never figured out which was which.

At quarterback, editor Hugh Vandivier managed the project and edited the copy. If any of the words are correctly spelled or arranged in coherent sentences, thank Hugh.

At wide receiver, Larry VanDerJagt did the technical edit. If some of the code actually runs, thank Larry.

Offensive coordinator and Managing Editor Andy Cummings kept the project on track. If it weren't for Andy the team wouldn't get to the stadium on the same day as the fans.

On defense, the entire production crew at IDG Books. If any of the Listings and Figures land somewhere near appropriate spots, thank them.

For allowing those drive-killing sacks, as well as programming all the bugs and abusing the language, blame the left guard.

Finally, as all the screaming fans in the stands are the ones that make the game great, take a bow, readers. Without you it wouldn't mean a thing.

CONTENTS AT A GLANCE

TABLE OF CONTENTS

INTRODUCTION

This is a book for Visual Basic programmers who want to learn to build object-oriented systems. Begin with this equation:

ActiveX = Objects

To build ActiveX .DLLs, .EXEs, and components; you need to be able to program Visual Basic objects. If you can program Visual Basic objects, ActiveX is as simple as clicking on a dropdown list, but it starts with objects.

You'll find that the .BAS module (classic BASIC) is dying on the vine. I'll use a few in Part I of this book, but you won't find any in Part II. (That's where we build the MyTime system, a totally object-oriented system, the size of real systems in which you might be involved.)

Why Objects?

Every programmer knows that ten small programs are a lot easier to debug than one ten-times-larger program. The primary benefit of objects is that they break up large programs into collections of smaller, easier to program and debug, objects.

Of course, if you want to do ActiveX, you need to program objects. If you want to write modeless systems that your users will enjoy using, you need to program objects. In fact, if you want to move forward into the next century, you need to program objects.

Object-oriented programming will not, to be honest, live up to all the hype. If you think it will make all programming automatic, all systems slick, all problems a thing of the past, you'll be disappointed.

Object programming is a significant advance, however. Every programmer I've met has become better and more productive with an understanding of object orientation.

Is Visual Basic Object-Oriented Enough?

If you're an object purist, Visual Basic is absolutely not a candidate for object-oriented programming. If you have work to do, you can do it with Visual Basic.

In the second part of this system, we'll design and build a serious, completely object-oriented system for personal time management. It will incorporate to do lists; projects that break down into a tree of subprojects, sub-subprojects, and so on; appointments scheduled on a slick, zoomable schedule; critical path charting; time-management summaries; and more. It's the system your author uses for his personal time management. It's a serious piece of system building, created entirely from objects.

The system is serious enough to settle any argument about whether you can do real object-oriented programming in Visual Basic. The purists can go right on arguing while we finish our work. That's the good news.

The bad news is that Visual Basic's object muddle (not an object *model*, an object *muddle*) needs to be sorted out before you can complete that work. Sometimes it will work for us, sometimes we'll work in spite of it. Visual Basic is still the best tool I know if you want to do Windows programming. With native code compilation, you have very little reason to use Visual C++, even though the latter sports a true object model, not just a muddle.

Why This Book?

This is a learn-by-doing book. Chapter 1 introduces the concepts. In Chapter 2, you'll start writing code. We'll start with a cute little sample system, but by Chapter 3 we'll be working on serious, reusable objects.

In the first half of the book, you'll learn some theory in each chapter and then put the theory to use by working on objects. We'll be working on very useful objects, too:

- A calendar that is adept at date data entry
- A schedule that shows your daily grind
- An object database that can save 3MB in your executable file

I don't believe in little examples that illustrate a point but don't do anything very useful. Real objects raise real issues. Programming real objects teaches you to program real objects. It's like tennis: a little instruction is helpful, but most of your learning has to be out on the court, hitting balls.

From time to time, we'll play with the occasional toy object, too. Even serious programmers need to have some fun. We'll be serious most of the time, though.

Why This Author?

OK. I know you. You're a Visual Basic programmer who wants to learn object-oriented programming. Who am I?

I'm a programmer who started writing BASIC as a teenager. That was over 30 years ago. Since then I've programmed in most major languages and a host of minor ones. I can't even remember how many languages I've forgotten.

In the '80s I launched my own software company and built it from scratch to over a million dollars a year. We made programmers' tools. At the end of the '80s I sold out and retired to doing contract programming and writing books.

I try to keep up with the latest tools. Certainly Visual Basic is one of the most important. If you really want to learn C++, I'll recommend my own *Learn C++ Today*, also from IDG Books. (I've written on Java, too, though that's been for IDG Books' arch rivals. You can use the author index of *Books in Print* at your favorite bookstore.)

I've heard from many readers who have thanked me for making difficult topics clear. Of course, you'd never hear from the readers who put your books down, would you? On that you'll have to judge for yourself.

How Do I Get the Most Out of This Book?

It's like real estate. Three things are important in getting the most out of any good computer programming book:

- Make a plan
- Make a plan
- Make a plan

You will not become an object-oriented programmer by putting this book under your pillow. You'll become an object-oriented programmer by using this book alongside your keyboard. For that you need a plan.

Read Chapter 1 first (it's pure reading — you won't need your computer). Then sit down at the computer for Chapter 2. Time yourself as you work out all the examples. Multiply Chapter 2's time by 20 and that's your remaining time.

Then block out the 20 units of time in your schedule. Do it by getting up early for 20 days in a row or by locking your office door for two units each evening for ten days or by doing five units each Saturday or Sunday for four weeks straight, but do it on a schedule. At the end of that time, you'll be a confident, knowledgeable object-oriented programmer.

You'll also have one slick, personal time-management program to show for it, too, along with a bunch of reusable objects that you can just drop right into your other work.

LEARNING
OBJECT-
ORIENTED
PROGRAMMING

USING THE OBJECT MUDDLE

1

Welcome to *Visual Basic 5 Power OOP*. Most of you paid your own money to be here and are investing your own time. I appreciate that, and I'll try to help you make the most of your investment.

You're here to learn about object-oriented programming in Visual Basic. Before we begin, let me explain the plan of each chapter and the overall plan of this book.

Each chapter begins with an introduction that tells you where we'll be going. Each ends with a summary that wraps up where we've been. The introduction should help you focus on the important points. The summary gives you a chance to mentally tick off what you've learned.

Almost every chapter includes code listings. The first is in Chapter 2, Listing 2-1. On disk that code is found in 02-01.ZIP. Don't unzip these until I tell you. Don't unzip them at all until Chapter 16 if you really want to master this stuff. Remember, typing code is what programmers do. Typing means learning.

Because this is the the first chapter, this introduction will tell you where the whole book is going. The last chapter, Chapter 22, closes with a summary of the whole book.

This book has two parts. In Part I, you'll learn all about Visual Basic's object-oriented tools and techniques. Except for this chapter, you'll meet a batch of theory, and then we'll put the theory into use in programming working objects. You'll need your fingers on the keyboard to squeeze the most out of Part I. Near the end of Part I, we'll create ActiveX .DLLs, .EXEs, and controls. For those with the Standard edition, we'll do them without ActiveX, too. You'll see that programming objects *is* programming ActiveX.

In Part II, we'll build the MyTime system. That's a medium-sized system, built with nothing but objects. It's a nice system for personal time management. I use it every day. Because you'll learn it from the inside out, you should be able to tailor it to your own needs. In Part II, you'll begin coding at the keyboard in Chapter 15 and finish in Chapter 22 at the keyboard. In the intervening chapters, you can just study the code and use the disk files to customize MyTime to suit yourself.

Because MyTime is a personal product, it won't have every feature every possible customer on the planet might ever want. That means it will load promptly when we ask it to. (I sign my e-mail, WSSITO. That stands for *Whales Should Swim In The Oceans.* I'm not a member of Greenpeace. Got it?)

In this chapter, I'll introduce the MyTime system. I think you'll agree that it's a slick system with enough complexity to show you how real, object-oriented systems are put together. MyTime doesn't just argue that you can do real, object-oriented programming in Visual Basic, it proves it.

After looking at MyTime, I'll cover the Visual Basic object model. I'm not high on object theory, by the way. I wasted too much of my time on theory when I was new to object-oriented programming (OOP). I learned OOP by doing it. When I could do it, the theory didn't prove valuable. We'll have just enough so that we're all on the same page for basic terminology.

Then I'll dive right in to the Visual Basic object muddle. The bad news is that Visual Basic's been built with some objects this way, some that way. Newer ones make sense, although they're incomplete. Older ones don't match the newer ones. It's a mess.

We'll start with MyTime because it proves that once you sort out the muddle, you can do really nice work in Visual Basic OOP.

MyTime: A Slick, Object-Oriented System

MyTime is a personal time-management system. I use it to keep track of my own time and my regular overbooking thereof. Keeping your time organized is about half of what it takes to get a lot done. (Staying focused is the other half. That's an excellent topic for another book.)

We'll look at the MyTime design in depth in Chapter 14. Here we'll have the slick, whiz-bang, ain't-that-neat-stuff tour. While you're looking, keep thinking about the main point: This is completely object-oriented code written in Visual Basic. It doesn't even use the ActiveX technology. (We'll cover ActiveX for you Professional and Enterprise edition folks, but we have Standard edition owners here, too. MyTime is 100 percent Standard edition code.)

If any of this stuff looks so slick that you just have to try it, unzip 22-01 into a working directory and run the MyTime project. It won't look as good as what you see here until you enter some data, of course.

MyTime's Main Menu

Figure 1-1 shows the standard main menu.

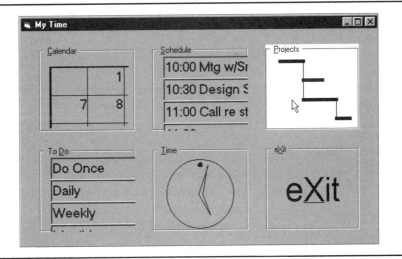

Figure 1-1
MyTime's main menu.

The main menu is a slick piece of work. It's a launcher for the components of the MyTime system. Like a browser, as your mouse pointer wanders over the half dozen panels, a highlight follows you around. Unlike a browser, it reorganizes itself any way you ask it to. In Figure 1-2, I've launched MyTime four times to show you how you can resize this tool any way you like.

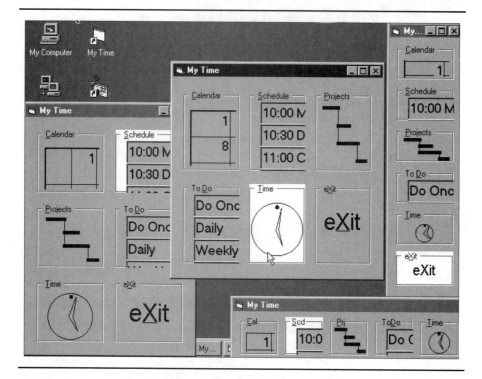

Figure 1-2
Main menu resized ridiculously.

Note the little details. Study the calendar. See how it's appearance changes to fit the best suggestion of a calendar into the available space?

The version of this that lives on my machine is the little menu on the bottom-right. See how I've slid the eXit pad off the edge of the world? At just 400K, I keep MyTime loaded all day long. Then there's about a zero-point-nothing delay between clicking a panel and seeing the tool appear. This makes it very handy for adding an item to your to do list or whatever.

By the way, these screen shots are taken at VGA resolution (640×480). This fits this book's requirements. At a higher resolution, that main menu eats only a tiny chunk of your screen's real estate after you shrink it down.

Launching the Projects' Cascade

Let's click that project chart panel on the main menu and see what it launches. Figure 1-3 shows the result.

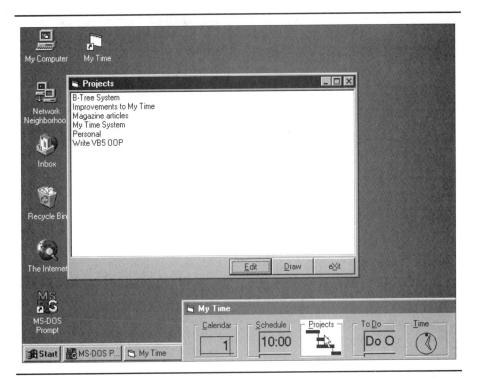

Figure 1-3
My main projects are listed.

I call this a project board. Let's double-click the MyTime System item. Figure 1-4 shows the new display.

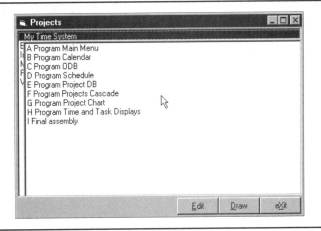

Figure 1-4
Cascading a detail board.

As you see, a new board is launched slightly down and to the right of the first. It shows the details of the MyTime System project. Above the board, you see the drilldown that brought you to this board.

Figure 1-5 shows what happens when you double-click item G.

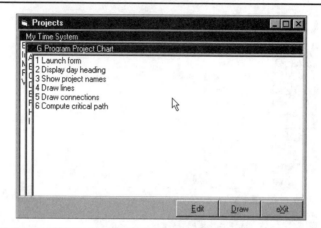

Figure 1-5
A third board cascades.

Now you're looking at the steps involved in programming the project chart. Click above the third board where you see the selected item in the second board. That will return to the second board, where you can click Draw and see what a project chart looks like (Figure 1-6).

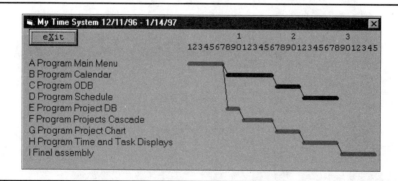

Figure 1-6
Drawing a project chart.

Vividly on the screen (though I imagine less so in black and white in this book) the critical path in this project is drawn in red.

Clicking Edit on any of these boards brings up a data entry panel (shown in Figure 1-7). Here I'll single-click item G Program Project Chart and then click Edit.

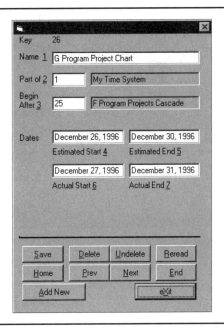

Figure 1-7
Data entry panels support these surfaces.

By the way, those data entry panels are not built with the Data Access Object, they're built with a custom Object Database Object (ODB) we'll program in the middle of Part I. Creating our own saves about 3MB in the size of the executable file. (That's WSSITO, pronounced *wuh-ZEE-toe*. Your computer should wait for you, not the other way around.)

An Appointment Schedule

How's your schedule? Booked? MyTime will track all those meetings reliably, although it can't help if you're booking too many. Figure 1-8 shows a sample.

This shows that overlapping your appointments is possible, if you really must.

The underlying data entry is slick, too. In Figure 1-9, I've clicked on Tom's call from the airport and clicked Edit. To change the day, click the date TextBox and the calendar pops up. Click the date you want, click OK, and the date is reset. This is a painless way to enter dates.

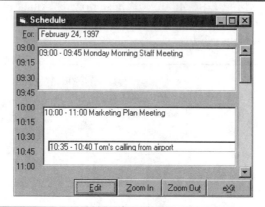

Figure 1-8
Zoomed in on a busy morning.

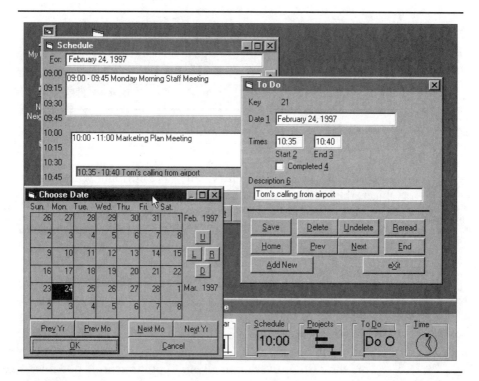

Figure 1-9
Clicking a calendar to enter a date.

That calendar object is the first one we'll build, by the way. We'll start it in Chapter 2.

There Is More

That's enough for now. MyTime also gives you a to do list for each day. It lets you establish chores. (Spend an hour a day on your e-mail? Enter that once and it generates a daily to do item.) It also summarizes your time. The time summary pulls the projects scheduled today together with your appointments, to do list items, and chores. It totals your time commitment, which is often a discouraging reminder.

The entire system is built from objects. No line of code is outside the realm of an object's methods. You can build your own version with nothing but the Visual Basic, Standard edition, too.

An Object Model

Visual Basic shares the object model used in both C++ and Java. (In the next section, we'll look at the exceptions, which sometimes seem to outnumber the places where it follows the model. This section is about what's supposed to be. The next section is about what is.)

You should know that this terminology is not universal. At its worst, other languages use the term *object* for the thing we call a *class*. If you meet programmers from other backgrounds, define your terms before you get too far into the conversation.

To begin, we have *classes* and *objects*. The class defines objects. The objects are called *instances* of the class. An object is said to *encapsulate* both code and data. The code defines an object's *methods*, those things it can do.

Let's look more closely at classes and objects because in spite of what you've heard, objects *do not* encapsulate code and data.

Classes

A class provides two essential things. First, it defines the data that each object will contain. Second, it holds the code. (Third, it should provide classwide data, but Visual Basic doesn't.)

Data Members Defined

Each object actually contains its own data. The class defines the data that the object will contain. A person class in Visual Basic would define data such as this:

```
' data declarations in Person.cls

    Public first_name As String
    Public last_name As String

    Private date_of_birth As Date
    ' etc.
```

Data is declared Private, Public, or Friend. This is called its *protection*. Public data can be read or written by any code that has access to the object. Private data can only be read and written by the object's own methods. (That is, by the methods the object's class provides.)

Friend protection is a complication that Java's designers wisely dropped when they discarded the less useful parts of C++. It's handy in C++ when you use multiple inheritance. It's a ridiculous complication in Visual Basic, which doesn't even support single inheritance.

Visual Basic calls data members *properties* of the object.

Methods Defined

The definition of a method is its code. The code is part of the class that's in RAM when your system runs. You may have one person object or a thousand. If there is an age() method (the trailing parentheses identify code), it lives in RAM just once.

The data definitions are used by the compiler to compile methods and to add the code that allocates and recovers space when you create and destroy objects. It's not in RAM when your system runs.

Methods are also given a Public or Private protection. Private methods can only be run by other methods in the class. Public methods can be run by outside objects.

Methods, like other Visual Basic code, can be subroutines (no return value) or functions with a defined return type.

There is an *abstract class* that declares, but does not define, methods. We'll talk about that in Chapter 13, where you'll have the rest of this stuff down pat. Ignore it until then.

Objects

Suppose your person class defines a private variable called date_of_birth. It might provide a public age() method. The age() method would compute and return the person's age based on the current date and the person's date of birth. Both are accessed by object.property syntax, like this:

```
person.date_of_birth ' a date variable
person.age           ' a method returning a number
```

This gives the appearance that the age method is attached to the person object just as it's data is part of the object. That's appearance only. The age method is part of the class. The individual object only holds data members.

A class can define special code that is run when an object is created. This is called a *constructor* method. Typical constructor jobs include assigning default values to variables and creating any arrays or objects that are *contained* as data members of the object being built.

C++ features *destructor* methods that are called when the object is being destroyed. Java and Visual Basic take charge of allocating and freeing memory for you, so they don't need destructors. Visual Basic doesn't properly release form-based objects, however, so you need to write your own destructor code for any object that contains other form-based objects. Building MyTime will show you how to handle these correctly.

Inheritance

When you create a form, you actually create a class that *inherits* the characteristics of the general form class. It can be moved, resized, and respond to mouse and keyboard events, for examples. You don't need to provide any code for these behaviors.

It also inherits all the data members of the underlying class. For a form, that includes Caption, Height and Width, border and other appearance characteristics, and so on.

You can provide additional data properties and methods. In Java, you say that the inheriting class *extends* the inherited class. The extending object contains the set of data members defined by the parent class, and it adds the others defined by the extending class. Similarly, the object can use the methods of the parent class as well as methods defined by its own class.

Unfortunately, most object literature speaks of the extending class as a *subclass*. The extending class is a superset of the extended class. Your form-based classes are a superset of the basic form, for example. I won't use the term *subclass* again. If you see it elsewhere, substitute the word *superset*, and you'll have a sound mental image.

VISUAL BASIC'S OBJECT MUDDLE

Visual Basic predates object orientation. It started with forms and controls, both of which have many object-like characteristics. Visual Basic 4 added user-defined classes (which I call *programmer-defined*). These are partly like your form modules. In other ways, they're different.

This section should leave you confused. In Chapter 2, we'll begin to sort this mess out.

Forms

When you create a form at design time, it feels like you're creating an object of the form class. You're not. You're creating a new class of form that inherits from the general form class.

You can run your form object by pressing F5 or clicking start, which will bring it alive. Again, this is an illusion. When you press F5, Visual Basic provides stub code that does this (substitute your form's name for Form1):

```
Dim f as Form1    ' Form1 is a class!
Set f = New Form1 ' create a Form1 class object
f.Show            ' Call its show() method
```

The .FRM file is a type of class. I call it a form-based class. Programmer-defined classes are similar, but they do not inherit from the form class.

In fact, Visual Basic doesn't support inheritance, although your form-based classes definitely enjoy all the benefits of inheriting from and extending a generic form class. Unfortunately, you cannot extend your own form class by inheriting from it.

Programmer-Defined Classes

When you don't need a form, you define your own class. In Java, this clearly inherits from an original source class, which Java calls Object. The basic object behaviors include allocating needed space on creation, freeing the space on destruction, responding correctly when asked its class's name, and so on. Your Visual Basic classes also inherit all these behaviors, though their source is never defined.

After the general confusion, the worst defect of Visual Basic's implementation is its lack of support for your classes to inherit from each other. We'll often work around this problem by having an object that should inherit from a parent class simply include a data member that is an object of the parent class.

That `age` method (return age by looking at `date_of_birth` and today's date) would work for any animal, so you might put it into an `animal` class. `person` should inherit from this class, so you could write:

```
person.age ' returns age
```

In Visual Basic, you have to include an `animal`-class object as a data member of the person. You obtain the age this way:

```
person.animal.age
```

At rock bottom, we'll kludge our way around the lack of inheritance by making multiple copies of our code and editing them in different ways. It's ugly, but if that's the best you can do, you do it.

Visual Basic's classes also lack classwide data. Our calendar class, for example, would like to have data like this:

```
Public month_names(1 to 12) As String
    month_names(1) = "January"
    month_names(2) = "February"
    ' etc.
```

This is typical of the type of data that you'll want to attach to the class, not to every object instantiated from the class. In Visual Basic, you kludge around the lack of classwide data by having a method, this way:

```
Public Function month_names(num as Integer) As String

    Select Case num
        Case 1: month_names = "January"
        Case 2: month_names = "February"
        ' etc.
```

It's highly inefficient, but it does the job. Other than these points, Visual Basic's programmer-defined classes provide the services of the object model we discussed in a consistent, regular way.

Unfortunately, the same can't be said of controls.

Controls

When you drop a control onto your form, it feels like you are putting a button object (or whatever) into a form object. The button inherits its behavior from a button class.

Don't you wish! You're defining a button data member of your form class. There's no accessible button class. You can't instantiate a button object from the `CommandButton` class at run time. An individual button has the data and methods defined by the `CommandButton` class, but that class doesn't otherwise exist.

For example, if a button object with a click method were attached to your `Form1` object, it would be accessed this way:

```
Form1.button.click
```

It's not, of course. The button click method is a method of the form, named this way:

```
Button_Click()
```

Internally, Visual Basic deciphers the name to mean "call this routine when the button is clicked." In other ways, however, the control *is* an independent object with its own methods and properties. These work

```
' call a button's method
    button.SetFocus

' assign a button's property
    button.Visible = False
```

Control Arrays

If that's not weird enough, you can attach methods to arrays of controls, so an array of controls can work like a class, with each control in the array being like an object of that class.

You can't do this with any other type of array, of course. It's totally outside any organized object model, but it works and sometimes its a good substitute for the lack of a better approach.

Remember MyTime? Once you sort this mess out you can make it work for you. In spite of this mess, your object-oriented Visual Basic will be easier to code and more robust than non–object-oriented code. In spite of this mess, I still prefer Visual Basic for Windows programming.

SUMMARY

We started this chapter with an introduction that explains the organization of the chapter. This being Chapter 1, we also looked at the whole book's organization.

In Part I (Chapters 1 through 13), we'll study object-oriented theory and then put it into practice building objects. In Part II (Chapters 14 through 22), we'll build our objects into a personal time-management system called MyTime.

We took a look at the MyTime system. It's a slick and useful tool. I use it throughout the day, and it's an example that proves that object-oriented Visual Basic programming really works.

Then we defined the object model that Visual Basic shares with Java and C++. A class defines the data structure of each object and holds the code for the methods that those objects can use. The objects themselves are data structures. In code, it looks like the object has both data and code members. In implementation, the code exists once at the class level. The data exists separately for each object in the class.

In the third and final section of the chapter, we looked at the Visual Basic object muddle. Forms are a type of class, although they feel like objects. User-defined classes are consistent with the model except that they lack inheritance and classwide data. Controls like buttons seem to be objects, but their classes only half exist. Sometimes they have methods, and sometimes the form has what should be their methods. Control arrays are weird structures that provide some of the features of a class.

Fear not. Once you sort all this out, you can do real object-oriented programming. The MyTime system proves that. In Chapter 2, we'll begin with a cute little tugboat class, but before we're done. We'll start serious coding in Chapter 3.

CREATING YOUR FIRST CLASS

2

*I*n this chapter, we'll begin our Visual Basic 5 object-oriented programming with a simple demonstration class. It won't do anything useful, but this won't become a habit. Starting in Chapter 3 and continuing for the rest of the book, we will do all our work on live classes that we can use in your applications. We'll combine our classes into the sample MyTime time-management system in the second part of this book, but this chapter is an exception.

We'll start by setting up a test bed. We'll use a standard (.BAS) module and a class (.CLS) module. The standard module will contain the `main()` subroutine that creates an object.

Then we'll write a *class constructor* and a *class destructor*. These are the routines that Visual Basic calls automatically when an object is created and when it is discarded. You'll see that you can inadvertently omit the destructor logic if you're not careful.

Then we'll go on to writing *methods*. These are the code members of the class. We'll call these methods from our `main()` routine.

With methods running, we'll continue to add and use *properties*, or data members. This will be simple, straightforward object-oriented programming. If you follow the examples, you'll master the basics quickly. If you've already built your own classes, you can skim through this material and just enter the source code.

Finally, we'll make our simple life complex by adding a Form object as a data member. You'll see that its constructor and destructor create interesting timing issues.

Let's get started by setting up our test bed.

CREATING A TEST BED

Begin by creating a working subdirectory anywhere that you find convenient. You'll see in the figures that I'm working in the chp02 subdirectory under C:\vbbk1\code.

After creating a place for your work, create a new shortcut to Visual Basic. Figure 2-1 shows me setting up my shortcut to start Visual Basic in the working subdirectory. Set up your working path to use the directory you've chosen.

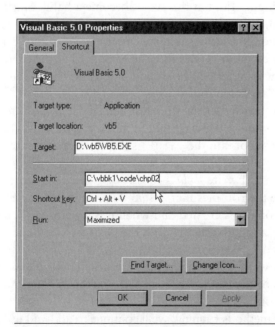

Figure 2-1
Setting the shortcut's default directory.

By the way, all the figures in this book were shot at standard VGA resolution (640×480). This is a good choice for screen shots but not for actually programming in Visual Basic. If you want to be productive, do whatever it takes to obtain at least a 17-inch monitor, which works well with 1,024×768 resolution. If you'll be doing a lot of programming, moving up to 21 inches will really help. You'll want as many open windows available as you can reasonably fit on your screen.

Now use your new shortcut to launch Visual Basic. You should see the New Project dialog box, shown in Figure 2-2.

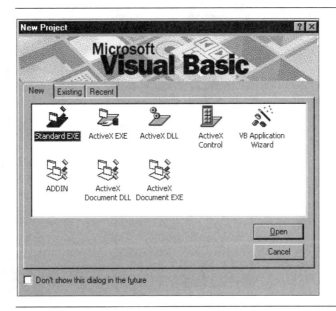

Figure 2-2
Creating a new standard .EXE project.

Use this dialog box to create a new standard executable file. If you've turned this dialog box off (checked the "Don't show..." box) you'll probably be reaching the next step automatically. If you didn't see it, choose File⇨New. You can also control this dialog box from the Environment tab of the Tools⇨Options dialog box.

Begin with the Default Project

Figure 2-3 shows Visual Basic launched with a new default project. This is a Form-based project, of course. This is a sensible default choice, but it doesn't suit our immediate needs. We want to build a standard module to launch an object from a class module.

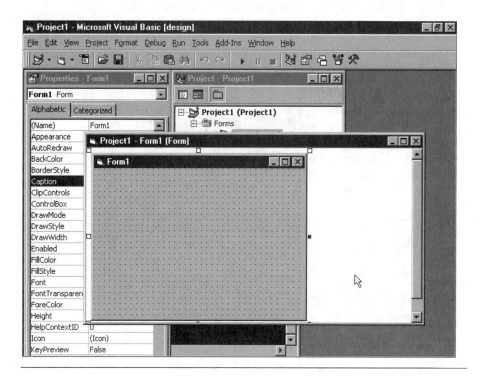

Figure 2-3
The default project is created.

The first thing to do is name the project. Right-clicking the project in the Project Explorer window sends you to the project's property sheet, as Figure 2-4 shows.

I'm deliberately avoiding long file names, here. As I write this, key utilities such as PKZip don't yet support them. By the time you read this, I'll bet that long file names will be a lot closer to universally used because they're so useful. Use longer names for your own projects and classes if you like.

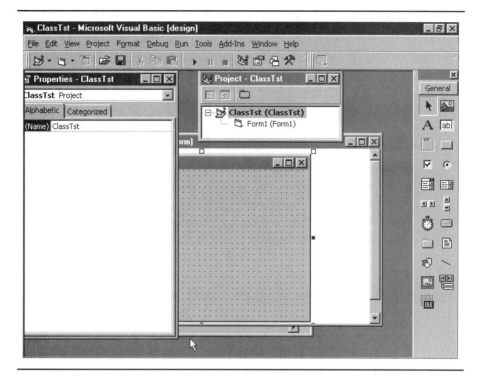

Naming the project.

You can use long project names and short project file names, too, but I find this becomes confusing. In Java, for example, the file and class names have to match exactly. Keeping them the same keeps your life simple.

Add a Class Module

Next, create a new class module by choosing Project⇨Add Class Module. This launches the dialog box shown in Figure 2-5.

When you choose the default new module, your code editor is launched with the new class, as shown in Figure 2-6. Before you begin entering code, give the class a name.

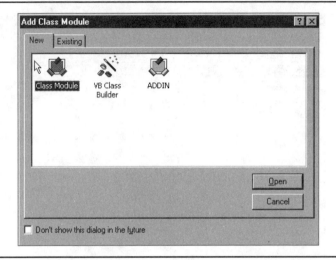

Figure 2-5
Creating a new class module.

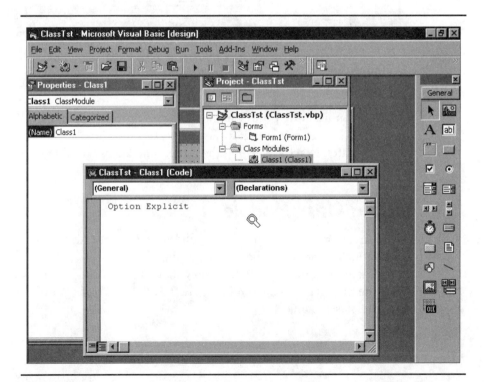

Figure 2-6
The new class is launched in the code editor.

Does your editor begin with "Option Explicit"? This statement requires variable declarations (public, private, dim, etc.) for all variables. Every Visual Basic book I've ever seen recommends that you always use Option Explicit. I agree completely. Check the "Require Variable Declaration" box on the Editor page of the Tools⇨Options dialog box to get this automatically. (I've checked every box on the whole page. It all helps.)

Memo To Bill Gates

Does "Require Variable Declaration" really belong on the Editor page, Bill? And since we all agree that you always ought to declare variables, shouldn't this be the default? The alternative is defaulting to variants, which are slow and let simple typos pass the compile phase and lurk as runtime bugs. Ugh.

Oh, yes. I just remembered, Bill, that your online docs suggest that you put all variable declarations at the top of the routine. Unfortunately, some authors simply repeat that bad advice without giving it any thought. It's dumb.

C++ didn't just add objects to C, it made a lot of other improvements. C required all declarations first. C++ (like Java and Visual Basic) lets you put your declarations anywhere you want. Put your declarations as close as you can to the variables' actual use. If you use a pair of variables in one section of a routine, declare them right at the start of that section this way:

```
Sub whatever ' code here
   ' other code here
   ' this section uses these vars:
      Dim count As Integer
      Dim amount As Single
      ' code here uses count and amount
   ' more code here
End Sub ' whatever
```

Sometimes you'll use a variable throughout a routine. In that case, you'll want to declare it at the top, but only when that's the case. Putting all your declarations at the top makes the code harder to write, and it makes it harder to read. But I'm digressing. Let's get back to work.

Again, use the Project Explorer to choose the new class and enter the name in the property sheet, as Figure 2-7 shows.

I'm building a tugboat class. Name yours after something you like. Before we start programming this class, we'll need a main line to create new tugboat objects. You can do this from a Form, but a little extra work now will make the rest of our job easier.

We'll use a standard module with a `main()` routine to start this project.

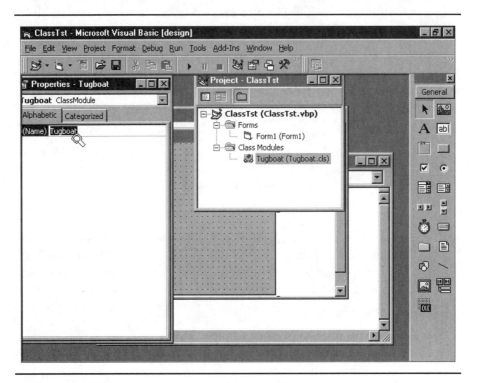

Figure 2-7
Naming the new class.

Add a Standard Module

Use the Project menu to add a standard (not class) module, as Figure 2-8 shows. Choose a new module from the Add Module dialog box, and you'll again be dropped into the code editor, this time for a standard module. Again, the very first thing to do is choose the new module in the Project Explorer and use the property sheet to give it a name. Mine's called "Tugger."

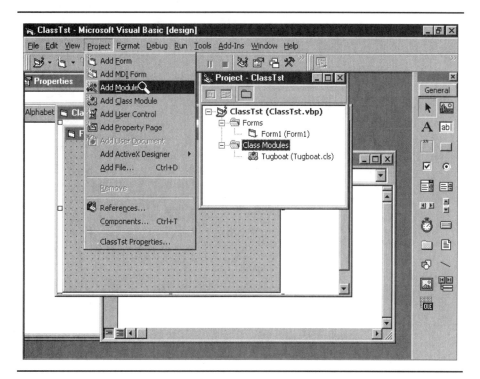

Figure 2-8
Adding a standard module.

Eliminate the Form

We're just about set. We won't need the Form any longer, so eliminate it. Figure 2-9 shows this step. I've selected Form1 in the Project Explorer, and then the appropriate Remove option appears in the Project menu. Now we're ready to program the `main()` routine.

Before you write the code, check that your work will be automatically saved before your program runs. This is on the Environment tab of the Tools⇨Options dialog box, shown here in Figure 2-10.

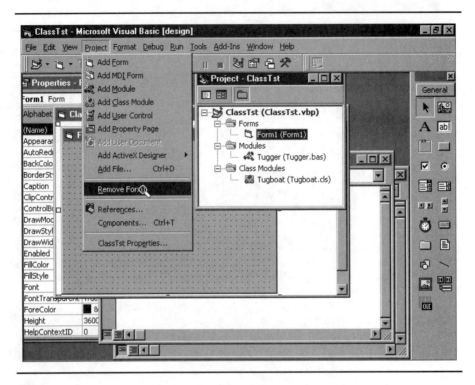

Figure 2-9

Removing the Form from the project.

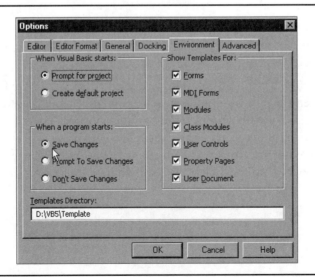

Figure 2-10

Running a program can automatically save your files.

Launch a Tugboat

Now we're ready to code. You need a main line in a subroutine named `main()` in the .BAS module. (The trailing parentheses after the name identify code, as they do in actual code.)

Listing 2-1 shows the four lines that you'll need.

Listing 2-1
Launching a tugboat object

```
Sub main()
Dim t As Tugboat
Set t = New Tugboat 'launch one
End Sub
```

When you run this program (press F5 or click the right-pointing triangle), you'll see a series of save file dialog boxes. These will save the project file (.Visual BasicP), the standard module (.BAS), and the class module (.CLS) using whatever names you've provided for the respective items.

Then nothing happens.

At least nothing apparent happens. Actually, your first tugboat object is created and then properly disposed of before the program ends. We'll make this process visible in the next section.

For now, note that the disk has all the necessary files corresponding to this listing in file 02-01.ZIP. If you expand it you'll find Classtst.vbp, Tugboat.cls and Tugger.bas.

Now lets add a constructor and destructor.

CONSTRUCTORS AND DESTRUCTORS

Constructors are the C++ and Java functions that the system automatically calls when you create a _new_ object. *Destructors*, which Java left out, are called when the system destroys an object.

Constructors and Destructors Defined

In practice, you'll often need constructors and seldom need destructors. This is because of the amount of work Visual Basic handles automatically.

Constructors

When you use the _new_ operator to create an object, Visual Basic automatically allocates the space it needs for your object's data members (properties). You write any other initialization code in the constructor (if you need any). Common operations for constructors include

- Assigning default properties
- Asking the user for additional data (for instance, a file name)

In C++, it's common to allocate space in a constructor. Like Java, Visual Basic takes care of this job for you. Visual Basic does its work before calling your constructor, so all properties exist and are ready for your code to manipulate.

Destructors

In C++, the common task of the destructor is to free the space that you allocated in the constructor. Because Visual Basic takes care of space allocation for you, as in Java this job is handled automatically when the object is destroyed.

When is an object destroyed? In the simple case, it happens when the routine that creates the object runs to completion. Consider this pseudocode:

```
MAIN
    x = new foo ' a foo object is created here
    call subr
end MAIN ' x destroyed here, before exit
SUBR
    y = new bar ' a bar object is created here
    ' the bar is open here
end SUBR ' y destroyed here, before return
```

This code shows the common case. More fully, an object is destroyed when the last reference to that object goes out of scope. If you assign an object to a static or a global variable, it will stay for the life of the program. If you create an object as a property of another object, it will live as long as the containing object.

An object is destroyed by first running its destructor, if any, and then by freeing its allocated space. The one type of object that you'll usually provide

destructor code is the object that has data the user might want to save.
Dialog boxes of this variety are common: "Data changed, save it?"

Now let's put theory into practice.

Coding a Tugboat Constructor and Destructor

All of this is simpler to do than to explain. Go to your class's code editor.
You'll be looking at the General Declarations section. Switch from General
to Class and you'll see the Sub and End Sub statements for a routine named
Class_Initialize. Add a msgbox() call that tells you you're in the
constructor, like this one:

```
MsgBox "Building a tugboat"
```

Run this program, and you'll see the message box that says "Building a
tugboat" (or whatever you put in your class).

If you click the dropdown list on the right, you'll see that besides
Initialize you have a Terminate choice. That's the destructor, of course.
Click Terminate, and you'll obtain the Sub and End Sub statements for the
destructor. Add another informative MsgBox() call, like this one:

```
MsgBox "Sinking the tug"
```

Now when I run, I see the "Building" message first and then the
"Sinking" message, which is exactly what you'd expect.

Listing 2-2 shows the complete class program. Disk file 02-02.ZIP
contains this class file as well as the associated .VBP and .BAS files.

Listing 2-2
Class with visible constructor and destructor

```
Option Explicit
Private Sub Class_Initialize()
   MsgBox "Building a tugboat"
End Sub
Private Sub Class_Terminate()
   MsgBox "Sinking the tug"
End Sub
```

Now let's create a second tugboat. Add another declaration and _new_
call to your main() in the .BAS as Listing 2-3 shows.

Listing 2-3

Building two tugboats

```
Option Explicit
Sub main()
   Dim t As Tugboat
   Set t = New Tugboat 'launch one

   Dim t2 As Tugboat
   Set t2 = New Tugboat ' launch another
End Sub
```

When you run this version, you'll see two "Building" messages followed by two "Sinking" messages, but you don't know which is which. Was the first tugboat sunk first or last?

To answer this question, we'll need to add a property.

Before we do this, though, there's one more point to make about destructors. You can count on them being run, unless your code says otherwise. Insert an End statement in the main line, so it looks like this:

```
Sub main()
   Dim t As Tugboat
   Set t = New Tugboat 'launch one

   Dim t2 As Tugboat
   Set t2 = New Tugboat ' launch another
   End ' ADD THIS ONE!
End Sub
```

When you run it, what will you see? Right. Your program ends at the End statement without calling the destructors. Good object-oriented programming avoids End statements.

Delete that End and let's go on to add object properties.

ADDING DATA MEMBERS

Our tugboats don't have any useful things in them yet. Like a big diesel engine, a hull, or a name. Because building diesel engines and tugboat hulls is complicated, let's just give them names. To create a data member for every object in a class, you just declare the data member in the General Declarations section of the class module. Use the Public or Private keyword to start the declaration. Figure 2-11 shows the one-line addition you need to give our tugboats names.

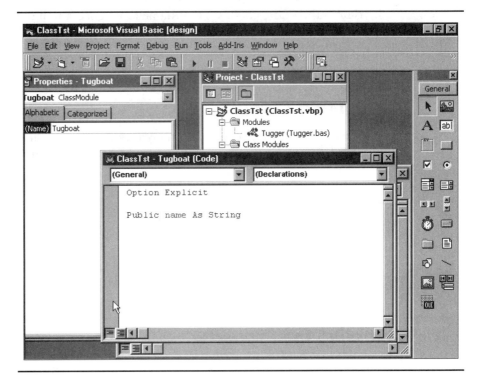

Figure 2-11

Adding the name property.

Visual Basic uses initial capitals for the properties of its intrinsic objects. I use all lowercase for properties of my own objects to make it easy to tell which is which:

```
Form1.Name ' Visual Basic intrinsic object
tugboat.name ' my class's object
```

Public data members are accessible where the object is accessible. If you want to assign and use names simply, public access works well. Let's begin by modifying our constructor and destructor messages to incorporate the name property. Mine now look like this:

```
' constructor:
MsgBox "Building a tugboat named " & name
' destructor:
MsgBox "Sinking the tug named " & name
```

If you run this code, you'll see that name is assigned a null string, which doesn't make these message box messages look very good. Having a default name would be nice.

Assigning a Default

The constructor can assign a default. Simply pick a name you like and assign it. This is a version of the constructor that assigns a default name:

```
Private Sub Class_Initialize()
    name = "Tuggy"
    MsgBox "Building a tugboat named " & name
End Sub
```

That's pretty simple, no? Run this version and all your message boxes will report that they are building or sinking Tuggy.

Accessing the Property

We still don't know which tugboat floated the longest. To find out, they'll need unique names. I'm going to name mine "Tooter One" and "Tooter Two." Listing 2-4 shows a new main line that assigns names after it creates the objects.

Listing 2-4
Adding names for the tugboats

```
Option Explicit
Sub main()
    Dim t As Tugboat
    Set t = New Tugboat 'launch one
    t.name = "Tooter One"

    Dim t2 As Tugboat
    Set t2 = New Tugboat ' launch another
    t2.name = "Tooter Two"
End Sub
```

Now when you run the program, your constructors report that they are building Tuggy, but the destructors report that they are sinking Tooter Two and Tooter One. The objects are in a Last In, First Out (LIFO) stack.

I've never seen this documented, by the way. That means that the LIFO stack in Visual Basic 5 could become a FIFO stack in Visual Basic 6. This simple tugboat class helps me find out lots of details about how Visual Basic 5 really works, but I try not to write code that depends on the discoveries I make.

If you care which tug goes down first, set the variable to Nothing. That will call the destructor (if there are no other references to the object). Listing 2-5 sinks the tugs in the order they were created.

Listing 2-5
Sinking the first tugboat

```
Option Explicit
Sub main()
   Dim t As Tugboat
   Set t = New Tugboat 'launch one
   t.name = "Tooter One"

   Dim t2 As Tugboat
   Set t2 = New Tugboat ' launch another
   t2.name = "Tooter Two"

   Set t = Nothing ' Sinks Tooter One, first
End Sub
```

The destructor for Tooter One is called when the last reference to it (the variable t was the only reference) is eliminated. The other tug lives on until the routine ends.

Now you've noticed that in the constructor we used name while in main() we used t.name and t2.name. What gives?

Property Access in the Class

A class has access to its own properties, of course. If you want to always refer to objectname.propname, within a class method the object is always named "Me." You could refer to Me.name in the constructor, for example. Referring to name is the same as referring to Me.name.

When the constructor, or any other method, is called, the Me reference is passed to the method automatically. In our example, Me is the variable t at first, and Me becomes t2. You can say Me.name in your methods, but no one does. It's implied.

Property Access Outside the Class

Outside the class, it's another story. You can't refer to "name" without using an object first, like t.name or t2.name. By itself, "name" would just confuse Visual Basic (whose name? what name?).

All the Visual Basic intrinsic objects have a Name property, too. Visual Basic wouldn't know what class you were referring to when you said "name." If it did know which class, it wouldn't know which object's name. You have to refer to the property of a specific object.

Remember that even in the class, the method never runs until called by a particular object. Someone is always Me in the method.

Now let's teach our tugboats to be happy.

PUTTING METHODS IN THE MADNESS

I'd like my tugboats to toot on command. Because this is a book, I'll settle for a visual toot. You can play a .WAV in your version, if you like.

Writing the Toot Method

The only trick to adding a method to a class file is to know what to click. For no particular reason that I can think of, you find the Add Procedure choice on the Tools menu. Therefore, select your class's code editor and then click Tools⇨Add Procedure. That launches the simple Add Procedure dialog box shown in Figure 2-12.

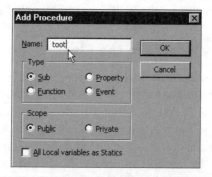

Figure 2-12
Adding a toot method.

Remember that a method is a procedure in a class module.

Memo To Bill Gates

Bill, do you know how long I looked for that Add Procedure choice? What's it doing on the Tools menu?

When you add the procedure, you'll see that the General section now has two choices: Declarations and toot.

My toot will just be a message box that says "toot," but I'll have a little fun, throwing in a parameter that let's you get as many toots as you like. Here's the code I added:

```
Public Sub toot(ntimes As Integer)
    Dim i As Integer
    Dim s As String
    For i = 1 To ntimes
        s = s + "toot "
    Next i
    MsgBox s & " says " & name
End Sub
```

Using the Toot Method

Now I have a method that I can call. Listing 2-6 shows the new main line that uses both the available syntaxes for calling the method. It's just like calling any other subroutine except that the object variable prefixes the method name.

Listing 2-6
Calling Object methods

```
Option Explicit
Sub main()
    Dim t As Tugboat
    Set t = New Tugboat 'launch one
    t.name = "Tooter One"

    Dim t2 As Tugboat
    Set t2 = New Tugboat ' launch another
    t2.name = "Tooter Two"

    t.toot 1
    t2.toot 1
```

(continued)

Calling Object methods

```
Call t.toot(2)
Call t2.toot(3)

Set t = Nothing ' Sinks Tooter One, first
End Sub
```

Figure 2-13 shows the final happy blast from Tooter Two.

Figure 2-13
Tooter Two responds to a "toot 3" message.

This is simple, right? What's the big deal?

We'll come to building a real class in the next chapter. It will be more work than our tugboats, but it will use all these concepts. You'll see how these pieces fit in real application building. Before we leave our tugboat class, however, we have two more items to cover.

ADDING PROTECTED DATA MEMBERS

Try changing the declaration of name in the class module from `Public` to `Private`. When you run your program, it halts with an error on the assignment to t.name in `main()`. The constructor runs correctly because class modules have access to both public and private properties. Outside the class, however, access is only provided to `Public` properties. Change name back to `Public` so that your program will run again.

Sometimes you want your data to be private, and sometimes you don't. Some object purists argue that all data members should be private. You should provide methods that let outsiders set and examine these methods. If we were doing this with name, we could declare name `Private` and then provide methods like these:

```
' methods for accessing a Private name property
Public Sub set_name(NewName As String)
    name = NewName
End Sub
```

```
Public Function get_name() As String
    get_name = name
End Function
```

Then your main line code would use these routines to access the name property. It would assign a name this way, for example:

```
' code in main line
    Dim t As tugboat
    Set t = New tugboat
    t.set_name("Tooter One")
```

You'll hear and read that this is the *best* way to provide access to all your properties. Horsefeathers!

When Do You Protect Your Data?

In the example I just gave using the tugboat name property, the protected access through methods is no different from direct public property access. It's just more bother. It's more of a bother for you to code and it's more of a bother for your program to process at run time.

The set_name() routine does not provide any sort of "protection" for the name property. It lets anyone who calls it set the name to anything he or she pleases. This is identical to leaving the property public.

Public is Perfect for Public Properties

If you place no restrictions on the values that others can assign to the name property, you might as well just let them assign it directly. Public access is very often precisely what you want. Freedom is a good thing.

Remember that Public access doesn't really apply to the general public. It applies to other Visual Basic programs that will set and read the Public property. Very often, you'll find that this is ideal.

Other times, however, you'll have reason to do some processing, to ensure that values are acceptable.

Protecting Private Properties

In Visual Basic, for example, the name property of the intrinsic objects is used in code. The Form object Form1 is the first one that every Visual Basic programmer meets. Thus the name assigned here must be a valid Visual

Basic variable name. It must start with a letter and continue with letters or digits or underscores (no spaces or punctuation, please).

When you enter a name in the property sheet, it is checked against these rules and rejected if it doesn't conform. Go ahead and try to enter a two-word name property for a Form, if you don't remember making this mistake.

This is where you want to provide `Private` properties. When a property is `Private`, you force access to it through a routine that you write which does any necessary checking.

Tugboats being my class, I'll make up my own rules for their names and then enforce the rule with restricted access. Here's the rule:

Tugboat names must start with the letter *T*.

Now we'll modify the class and calling program to enforce this rule.

How Do You Protect Your Data?

To make sure that our name property is always set correctly, you need three things in the class:

- The property must be `Private`.
- An assign method must enforce correct values.
- A retrieve method function provides read access.

With these three things, the code outside the class must assign and read the property through the methods you supply because it won't be able to access a `Private` property.

Inside the Class Code for Protection

You'll seldom need protection in the data retrieval function, but, if you make the property `Private`, you need to provide a public method if code outside the class will need to use the property. There's no way to say, "Read Public, Write Private," for a property.

Occasionally, of course, you'll want some read protection, such as a function to check user permissions for accessing sensitive data. Most of the time, however, the protection is in the property assignment code.

The critical point is that it's not enough for your assignment function to reject bad data. It should almost always provide for the correction of the data, as well. Otherwise the calling routine will be assuming that all is well when important data is missing.

If you're coding components to be used by others, you should return an appropriate message to the calling routine when you reject bad data. Leave the user interface programming (to correct the data) to the calling program. When programming a part of your own system, let the assignment function do as much as it can to correct the data.

Listing 2-7a shows public methods that provide access to the `Private` name property in the tugboat class module. (When you see a Listing number like 2-7a you can be sure there's at least a 2-7b coming up. These, and any other 2-7x will all be found in the 02-07 disk file.)

Listing 2-7a
Public access to a Private property

```
Public Function get_name() As String
   get_name = name
End Function
Public Sub set_name(nm As String)
   While Left(nm, 1) <> "T"
      nm = InputBox( _
         "Name must start with 'T'", _
         "Name the Tugboat", nm)
         'prompt, dialog box title, default value
   Wend
   name = nm
End Sub
```

The `get_name()` method simply provides universal public access to a `Private` name property. The `set_name()` method is more interesting. It uses a `While/Wend` loop to repeatedly ask for new data until it sees correct input. Then it assigns the correct input to the `Private` name property.

Add similar protection code to your own class. Note that the `While/Wend` loop is top tested. You'll never see this dialog box unless there is an invalid name supplied as the argument to `set_name()`.

Outside the Class Code for Protection

Your code outside the tugboat class can no longer access `tugboat.name`. It needs to use `tugboat.set_name()` and `tugboat.get_name()` to assign and read the property, respectively. Listing 2-7b shows new main line code that sets and accesses the name. (Look carefully! I've been sure to make an error in one of the `set_name()` calls to check out the error-handling code.)

Listing 2-7b
Accessing Private property

```
Sub main()
    Dim t As Tugboat
    Set t = New Tugboat 'launch one
    Call t.set_name("Tooter One")

    Dim t2 As Tugboat
    Set t2 = New Tugboat ' launch another
    t2.set_name "Hooter Two" 'OOPS!
    MsgBox (t2.get_name + " is OK")
    t.toot 1
    t2.toot 1

    Call t.toot(2)
    Call t2.toot(3)

    Set t = Nothing ' Sinks Tooter One, first
End Sub
```

I've used both syntaxes for calling `set_name`, just to show that they both work. I'd suggest you adopt one or the other and stick to it.

One More Alternative

For reasons that I don't understand, Visual Basic provides another syntax for achieving protected data access. It doesn't do anything that we haven't just seen, but it does it with brand new syntax. If you want to look at it, use the Class Builder tool to generate code for a class with new public and private data members.

Memo To Bill Gates

Visual Basic has about ten times as many different statements as Java. Why in the world are you adding more statements when the current bunch do the job perfectly?

Chapter 8 covers this syntax because you'll see it generated by Visual Basic. Rest assured, though, that if you can write simple routines like `set_name()` and `get_name()`, you already have mastered the functionality.

Visual Basic 5 also adds the `Friend` access protection. It lets you make object members generally `Private` but `Public` for their `Friends`. The "What's New" literature claims that this is a neat new feature from Java. Actually, the `Friend` concept was a later addition to C++ that the Java designers felt was an unnecessary complication and didn't include in Java.

Less is more. Language designers should pay close attention to this backpackers' maxim: When in doubt, leave it out.

USING A FORM OBJECT MEMBER

Any valid Visual Basic variable type is acceptable as a data member. Even variants work, but you really shouldn't use them. (As soon as I write that, I see some guy with more gray in his beard than I have showing me an example where a variant doesn't just work, but is, in fact, the best way to accomplish the job. Let rules guide you, but don't forget that you're the boss.)

You can also use arrays as members. You use them just as you do other property variables:

```
' class foo declares array bar
  public bar(10) as integer

' main line uses bar
  foo.bar(1) = 10
  foo.bar(2) = foo.bar(1) + 5
  . . .
```

You can't use user-defined types (DefType) in classes. In general, classes are superior to user-defined types, and it appears that Microsoft is steering us away from DefTypes toward classes. Therefore, instead of defining a type — one that includes this, that and the other — define a class and have it include the same variables.

You can use objects as data members of objects, so the lack of types is really no restriction. Once you have a tugboat class, for example, tugboat is a valid data type. Suppose you'll want an array of tugboats in your harbor object. Define the harbor class this way:

```
' class harbor, needs some tugboats
    public tooters(10) as tugboat
```

All this is very regular, and you'll find that it's surprisingly powerful as we build classes throughout this book and as you go on to do your own.

Where it becomes irregular is when we use the intrinsic objects, and the most irregular of the intrinsics is the Form. In this section we're going to use a Form object as a property of the tugboat.

Is it an Object or a Class?

When you first used Visual Basic, you saw a default form. We all dropped some controls onto the form, and we clicked the run icon or pressed F5, and our form sprang to life!

It was pretty slick. Then we went back and added this control, deleted that one, and moved some other stuff around. Press F5 again, and you've got instant program.

If we'd been looking ahead, though, we might have wondered about the problems we'd meet down the road.

The problem is that our Form is about half object and half class.

The .FRM file is very similar to the .CLS file. In fact, you can use a .FRM in lieu of a .CLS when you want a class that includes Form capabilities. In the next chapter, we'll start on a calendar class where our calendar will pop up in a Form. We'll use the .FRM just as we've used the .CLS in the tugboat class.

You don't really have a Form class available to your application. You can't say

```
Set f = new Form ' ERROR!
```

Your project includes one or more Form-based classes, each with its own name. You have to pick one of these Form-based classes (you were probably thinking of them as Form objects, instances of the Form class, weren't you?) to instantiate a new one, like this:

```
Set f = New Form1 ' OK. Uses a named Form.
```

If your application has a half dozen Forms, you can think of them as a half dozen objects of the Form class. More exactly, you have a half dozen classes which inherit from the Form class. Visual Basic will take care of instantiating one object of each of these classes.

This metaphor almost works, and might be the road Visual Basic could take to resolve some of the inconsistencies. Don't think too much about assigning the name property, though. Is that the name of a class or the name of an object? Here's a hint: include c) both of the above and d) none of the above as possible answers.

Memo To Bill Gates
Bill, are we all confused? I don't think so. I think that it's Visual Basic that's confused!

To minimize the confusion that Visual Basic creates, think of Form1 (assuming you accept the default name) as a class from which Visual Basic instantiates a single object at run time. When you take over the startup process by providing your own main() routine, instantiating an object from the Form1 class is under your control. You can instantiate a dozen Form1 objects, if you like.

Let's do this in Visual Basic so that you can see how to control it. (As much control as possible, that is.)

Launching the Tugboat's Form

You cannot instantiate an object of the Form class until you have one to serve as a class, so to obtain a Form, you need a Form in your project. You can choose Add Form from the Project menu, or click the taskbar icon (it's the second one from the left in the default setup). You'll see the Add Form dialog box shown in Figure 2-14.

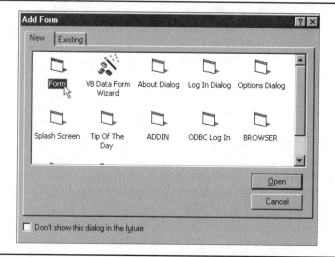

Figure 2-14
Adding a Form object (or is it a class?)

Immediately give it a name. Mine's "tugform." Then you can shrink it down to little more than the size of a postage stamp and move it off to an unused corner of your desktop.

You've now created a new class — tugform in my case — from which you can instantiate objects. Add another property to your class module, this way:

```
Option Explicit
Private name As String
Public tform As tugform ' Add this one
```

Next, eliminate all references to t2 in the main() routine. You'll see the Form issues more clearly from the deck of just one tugboat.

Then add the new line to your constructor that creates the tform property. (Declaring tform As tugform doesn't actually create a new object. The New operator is the one that creates the object.) Set any Form properties that you like. If you don't set the dimensions, they'll be left as you last sized it at design time.

This is my new tugboat constructor:

```
Private Sub Class_Initialize()
    name = "Tuggy"

    Set tform = New tugform
```

```
        tform.Height = 3000
        tform.Width = 5000
        tform.Caption = "Greetings from " & name

        MsgBox "Building a tugboat named " & name
    End Sub
```

With that constructor, you're ready to use this new tugboat property. Listing 2-8 shows my new main line that eliminates t2 and launches the tugboat's tugform.

Listing 2-8
Launching a tugboat's tugform

```
Sub main()
    Dim t As Tugboat
    Set t = New Tugboat 'launch one
    Call t.set_name("Tooter One")

    t.toot 1

    t.tform.Show

    Call t.toot(2)

    Set t = Nothing ' Sinks Tooter One, first
End Sub
```

When you run this code, the call to t.tform.Show launches the form and gives it focus. You may not see that it has focus because it lives in parallel with the launching application. The call to t.toot(2) triggers the message box that takes control from the tugform. When you click OK in this box, the tugform takes over again, only to be superseded by the message box from the destructor.

Maybe it's a Runaway Kite

When you click OK in the destructor, the tugform gets focus again, and this time gets to hold onto it. You can minimize it, maximize it, drag it around, and resize it.

You can also click Visual Basic or another application, which will take control. If your Visual Basic entirely covers the tugform, the latter will appear to have disappeared. You can still see it if you minimize Visual Basic.

You can also see if a subordinate Form is still active by looking at your Visual Basic taskbar. When your application is done, the square box icon that ends an application is grayed. If the box is still active, something is still floating around. You can kill it by clicking the tugform's close button. If you can't see the tugform, click the Visual Basic application-ending box icon. That will also kill any forms the application has launched.

Figure 2-15 shows the tugform after it has received focus for the last time. The important point here is that the destructor for t, the tugboat object, has already run. (It was the last message box to steal focus from the tugform.)

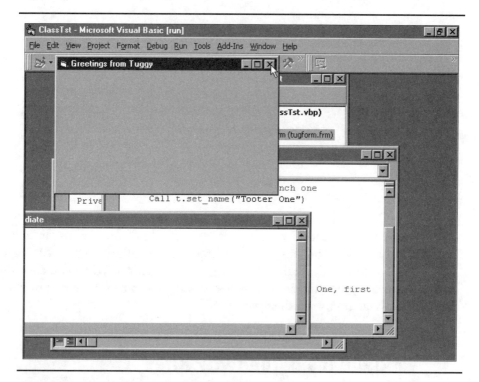

Figure 2-15

The tugform flying on its own.

This form is like a runaway kite. It's owner was flying the kite at the beach, but perhaps the string broke. The owner got in the car and went home. (Your tugboat was deleted when your application finished.) Now the kite is flying all on its own without any owner. It was a property of the tugboat, but the tug sank.

Actually, it's still attached to your application. Until you close this form, your application's still active.

You can experiment with the tugform's methods. In your tugform's code editor window, you can add methods, or attach code to existing methods.

Try launching appropriate message boxes out of the `paint()` and `resize()` methods. Try to predict, before launch, which order the messages will appear.

Have some fun with it. In the next chapter, we're going to become intimate with the `resize` method as we begin building our first useful object. While we do that, we'll take a closer look at Form-based classes.

SUMMARY

We started by creating a platform for object-oriented programming. You're probably used to starting with the Form, but we started with a new class module and a standard module, and we eliminated the form. We used the project's properties sheet to choose starting from a `main()` routine.

Then we programmed simple constructors and destructors. You saw that the constructor is called when you create a _new_ object and the destructor is called when the object goes out of scope. (The destructor isn't called at all if you use an ill-advised `End` statement.)

After the constructor and destructor, we went on to our first data member. We added a name property. You saw that you can address this as just "name" in the class, but you need an object, like `t.name`, to access the property outside the class. (In the class, you're really accessing `Me.name`.)

After properties, we added a code member, or method. These take parameters and generally behave like all other subroutines except that they are accessed with `object.method` syntax, as in `t.toot`.

Then we went on to using `Private` properties. These are useful when you want to control the values that can be assigned to properties or to control the access to the properties. You assign and access them through methods like `set_name()` and `get_name()`. The method that assigns values should not only check for valid data but it should also provide for correcting bad data.

Finally, we went on to add a `Form` object as a data property. We added constructor code to create (new) and assign values to the properties of the `Form` object. In the main line code, we called methods of this object, just as before except that we had to include the owner: `t.tform.show`, for instance. You also saw that the `Form` object can even outlive the object to which it was attached.

Now that you've got the basics well in hand, let's go on to begin our PIM project by creating our first useful class. In Chapter 3, we start on a calendar that you can use whenever you want the user to enter a date. Your users will enjoy it!

BUILDING THE FORM-BASED CALENDAR CLASS

3

*I*n this chapter we're going to build our first useful class: a calendar. We'll use this calendar in our MyTime project, and you can use its class in several other ways. I like to pop up a calendar whenever any form needs a date entry. Clicking on a calendar is a natural action, and it makes typos impossible.

In our MyTime application, we'll use this class for desk calendars. With a slight modification to the days, you could write notes on it. You'll want a larger size than for date entry, but our calendar will be resizable, so this won't be a problem.

You'll see that making the calendar resizable adds quite a bit of work to the project, but when we start creating our own ActiveX controls to extend the Visual Basic toolbox, programming the resize event is a key element.

Our programming will happen one step at a time, following a design effort. (Design is the hard part, but I've already done a design for you. Improving someone else's design is always more fun.)

After settling on a design, we'll create the calendar and then draw a grid for six weeks, seven days each. Then we'll make the grid resizable.

Following the grid we'll add features one at a time:

- Labels for the columns
- Labels for each day

■ Changing days on mouse clicks

■ Labels for month and year

Along the way you'll see how the .FRM module resembles the class module and how your Form object is really more of a Form class. You'll also see the ways in which the .FRM is not like a class module and how your Form class isn't really like the other classes you build.

Let's begin with the design.

DESIGNING YOUR CALENDAR

Figure 3-1 shows my completed calendar being used for data entry. (I've selected a big party day.)

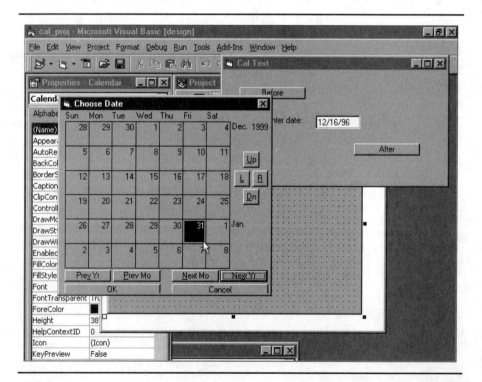

Figure 3-1

Using the completed calendar.

To choose a day, click whatever day you want. You can also click the diamond arrangement of buttons on the right, but it's really there to provide keyboard access (press U for Up, L for Left, and so on). Well-designed programs should support both alternatives. (Picture the user in seat 17C who finds, at 30,000 feet, that her mouse stayed home.)

Look very critically at this calendar. How would you do it better? If English isn't your native language, you'll certainly want to change the labels. Perhaps you can think of more important changes.

I've done all the work so far. Your job will be easy, so challenge yourself to make your second-generation calendar better than my first-generation one.

CREATING THE CALENDAR

Ready to start on the code? You can just read the rest of this chapter, but you'll get a lot more out of it if you work out your own code and make improvements (or just add personal touches) while you go along.

Begin by picking or creating a working location for the project. Think about developing a collection of .FRM and .CLS files that you'll use in other projects. Once you've made up your mind, create the subdirectory and modify your Visual Basic 5 shortcut to access your chosen subdirectory. You'll see that I'm working in C:\vbbk1\code\chp03, which is a choice that probably won't make sense for anyone but me.

Next, use your shortcut to launch Visual Basic and create a standard .EXE project. Then do the following:

- Change the Form's name from Form1 to Calendar
- Name the project Cal_proj
- Make the Form's Caption "Choose Date"
- Save the project (accept the suggested file names)

Now we're ready to go to work. Our first job will be to draw a grid.

PREPARING A GRID

If you check Figure 3-1, you'll see that the calendar has rows for six weeks. In December, 1999, the month could be shown in just five weeks: the entire last row is in January, 2000.

Suppose, however, that a 31-day month starts on Friday or Saturday. In that case, the 31st or both the 30th and the 31st of the month will be pushed into the sixth week. (Of course, when February begins on Sunday and it is 28 days long, the whole month fits in four weeks, but this doesn't happen often!)

The easy way to build a calendar is always to have space for six weeks and to start the month in the first row. So our first job is to draw the six by seven grid.

Drawing the Grid

If you experimented with the resize() and paint() methods in Chapter 2, you saw that resize() is called before paint(). This is sensible, of course: the user drags a corner to a new size, and your resize() routine is called to reposition the affected controls.

We're going to have a resizable calendar so that we'll be able to use the calendar for different purposes. This means that we'll position everything on the calendar in the resize() method. In turn, that means that the calendar you draw at design time is not the calendar that will be displayed at run time, so don't waste a lot of design time positioning things. The real positioning will happen at run time.

Drawing Horizontal Lines

Begin by double clicking the line tool or by dragging one onto your form. Leave enough space above it to write in the day names. Start near the left, but don't go all the way to the right. (Refer to Figure 3-1 or to your own, better design.)

On the properties sheet, make these changes:

- Change the name to Hlines (yes, plural)
- Change Visible to False

This step is shown in Figure 3-2.

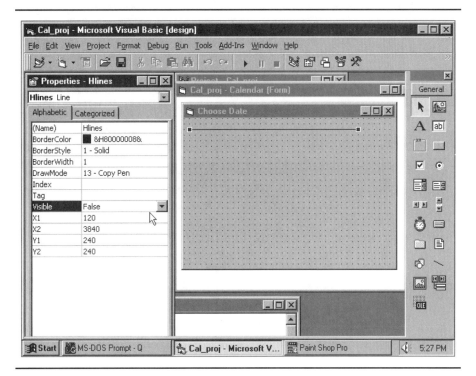

Figure 3-2
Setting up the first of the Hlines array.

Next, copy this line to the clipboard and paste a second line onto your Form. Visual Basic will respond with the "You already have a control named Hlines..." dialog box shown in Figure 3-3. Tell it, "Yes" you do want a controls array.

Once this array is created, subsequent paste operations will add to the array without the dialog box. Paste five more lines. This will give you a stack of six at the top of the form. The first Hlines became Hlines(0). The next one (your first pasted line) is Hlines(1). It's at the bottom of the stack. Hlines(6) is at the top of the stack.

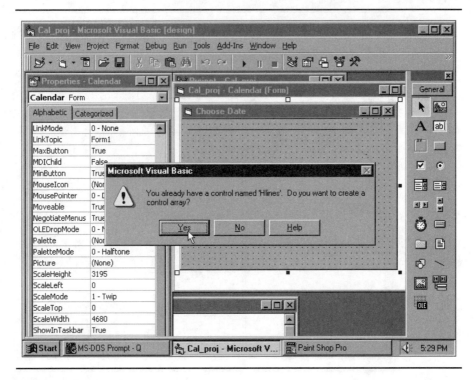

Figure 3-3
Creating the controls array.

Position the lines roughly: the resize() method will do the real positioning. Drag Hlines(6) down to the bottom of the grid. Drag Hlines(5) down not quite so far. Continue until you've spread the lines out so that they look something like the ones in Figure 3-4.

Actually, you could have left all these in the stack where the paste process dumped them, but I think putting them in place helps you visualize the code's result.

Drawing Vertical Lines

Now it's time to do the same for the vertical lines. We'll want eight lines this time (for seven days). Add a new line on the left. On its properties sheet, make these changes:

- Change its name to Vlines
- Change Visible to False

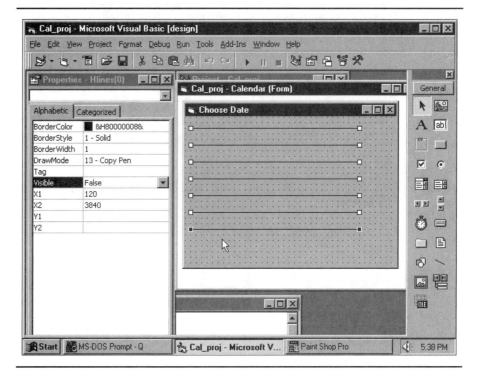

Figure 3-4
The Hlines array is in position.

Now copy and paste a second line onto your form. Again say "Yes" to the "Do you want a controls array?" question. Paste six more lines for a total of eight. Drag them into position, starting Vlines(7) on the right and working back to the left.

Figure 3-5 shows me positioning my final line. I've done a nice, neat job since it's posing for this portrait. You shouldn't waste time making it this neat. Remember, these are only for our form building; the resize() method will do the real positioning.

That's our next step in this project.

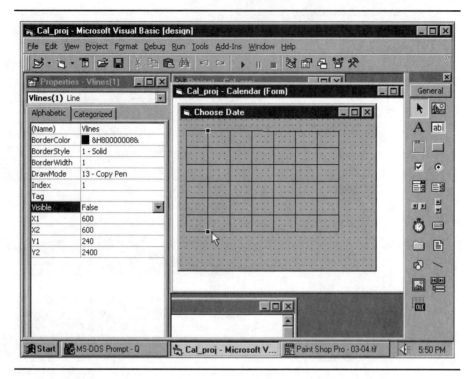

Figure 3-5
Positioning a grid line.

Resizing the Grid

Here's where we make the `resize()` event our friend. We'll begin with the design. I use fixed space surrounding the grid for labels and buttons. These elements stay the same size as the user resizes (or maximizes/normalizes) the calendar. I put all the flex in the grid.

Don't Resize if Minimized

First, `resize` is called whenever the Form's size changes, including when the user clicks the minimize button (or chooses to minimize the window from its system menu). I don't need to do any of the `resize()` method work in this case, so I start with a line that beats a hasty retreat when this is the case:

```
If WindowState = vbMinimized Then Exit Sub
```

As you see here, the `WindowState` property is set to minimize before the `resize()` method is called, which is just what you need. This line offends structured code purists who want every subroutine to have just one exit point. I think it's a case where breaking that rule is cleaner than following the rule. To follow the rule, you'd write the routine this way:

```
Public Sub Form_Resize

    If WindowState <> vbMinimized

        ... all the code goes here

    End If

End Sub
```

Do you see any advantage in that?

Limit the Minimum Size

Next, I put a lower limit on the minimum size of this form. This limits what the user can do, but it also makes the user's task simpler. If I want a tiny calendar, I just drag a corner quickly down to a very small size and the limits in the code spring it out to the working minimum. You can use a lower minimum than mine if you think even smaller is better. Just leave enough space for the buttons and a tiny grid. This is my code:

```
Const min_wd = 3500
Const min_ht = 3500

If Width < min_wd Then Width = min_wd
If Height < min_ht Then Height = min_ht
```

Calculating the Grid Size

My code uses constants to reserve the border space:

```
Const tp_space = 220
Const lf_space = 100
Const bt_space = 940
Const rt_space = 1000
```

Then the code divides the available space into six parts vertically and seven horizontally. It's direct except for one small point. After calculating the day's width, for example, I recompute the grid's width as seven times the day's width. This eliminates roundoff error. (For example, assume the grid width was 705. The day's width is 100, and the grid width is recomputed as 700.)

The code looks like this:

```
Dim grid_ht As Integer, grid_wd As Integer
grid_ht = Height - tp_space - bt_space
grid_wd = Width - lf_space - rt_space

Dim day_ht As Integer, day_wd As Integer
day_ht = grid_ht / 6
day_wd = grid_wd / 7

grid_ht = 6 * day_ht ' correct for roundoff
grid_wd = 7 * day_wd
```

Positioning the Lines

The last step is to position the lines. I start with Hlines(0), positioning it based on the space constants. Then I position Hlines(1) through Hlines(6) based on the Hlines(0). This is the code:

```
Dim i As Byte ' Loop Counter
' Place horizontal lines
    With Hlines(0)
        .X1 = lf_space
        .X2 = lf_space + grid_wd
        .Y1 = tp_space
        .Y2 = .Y1
        .Visible = True
    End With

    For i = 1 To 6
        With Hlines(i)
            .X1 = Hlines(0).X1
            .X2 = Hlines(0).X2
            .Y1 = Hlines(i - 1).Y1 + day_ht
            .Y2 = .Y1
            .Visible = True
        End With
    Next
```

The logic is substantially similar for the vertical lines, except that Vlines(0) can be positioned from the coordinates of Hlines(0) (top and left) and Hlines(6) (bottom). You can write it yourself before you look at the listing.

Memo To Bill Gates

Bill, I hope you give a really big stack of stock options to the person who invented `With/End With`. There's nothing like it in Java or C++, which makes them a lot tougher to type and tougher to read, too.

The complete grid code is in Listing 3-1. When you run this version, your calendar form will have a nice, stretchy calendar grid on it.

Listing 3-1
A stretchy calendar grid

```
Option Explicit

Private Sub Form_Resize()

' Exit immediately if the calendar is minimized
    If WindowState = vbMinimized Then Exit Sub

' Don't let it get too tiny
    Const min_wd = 3500
    Const min_ht = 3500


    If Width < min_wd Then Width = min_wd
    If Height < min_ht Then Height = min_ht

' Leave border space

    Const tp_space = 220
    Const lf_space = 100
    Const bt_space = 940
    Const rt_space = 1000

' Compute grid size
    Dim grid_ht As Integer, grid_wd As Integer
    grid_ht = Height - tp_space - bt_space
    grid_wd = Width - lf_space - rt_space

    Dim day_ht As Integer, day_wd As Integer
    day_ht = grid_ht / 6
    day_wd = grid_wd / 7

    grid_ht = 6 * day_ht ' correct for roundoff
    grid_wd = 7 * day_wd
```

(continued)

A stretchy calendar grid

```
    Dim i As Byte ' Loop counter

' Place horizontal lines
    With Hlines(0)
        .X1 = lf_space
        .X2 = lf_space + grid_wd
        .Y1 = tp_space
        .Y2 = .Y1
        .Visible = True
    End With

    For i = 1 To 6
        With Hlines(i)
            .X1 = Hlines(0).X1
            .X2 = Hlines(0).X2
            .Y1 = Hlines(i - 1).Y1 + day_ht
            .Y2 = .Y1
            .Visible = True
        End With
    Next

' Place vertical lines
    With Vlines(0)
        .X1 = Hlines(0).X1
        .X2 = .X1
        .Y1 = Hlines(0).Y1
        .Y2 = Hlines(6).Y1
        .Visible = True
    End With

    For i = 1 To 7
        With Vlines(i)
            .X1 = Vlines(i - 1).X1 + day_wd
            .X2 = .X1
            .Y1 = Vlines(0).Y1
            .Y2 = Vlines(0).Y2
            .Visible = True
        End With
    Next

End Sub
```

Adding Appropriate Comments

I always start and end listings with comments that clearly show where the
file starts and ends, who wrote the code, and when it was written. This
would be minimal:

```
' FOO.BAS — Program to compute FOO's vital statistics
' Copyright 1997, Martin L. Rinehart

    ... code goes here

' end of FOO.BAS
```

Other header standards include time and date (not just year), revision history, more detailed descriptions, and other similar information. Go ahead and add comments that meet your own standards.

Memo To Bill Gates

Bill, your code editor really makes it tough to have an end of file comment that stays at the end of the file. Also, it doesn't let me really write at the beginning of the file, either. Maybe you could have somebody give us an open/close comment feature where we could template in our names, time and date stamps, and version/revision numbers. TIA.

LABELLING THE COLUMNS

With the grid nicely positioned, adding labels over each day of the week is simple. We'll add controls and then do just a touch of programming.

Adding the Controls

Double-click (or drag, if you prefer) a text label onto your form and position it over the first column. The properties to adjust are thus:

- Name it col_labels
- Caption is "Sun."
- Top is 0
- Height is 200
- Width is 500

I presume that those of you who aren't building English calendars will substitute something equivalent for "Sun."

Then use copy and paste so you can tell Visual Basic that you want a controls array. You'll need seven labels. Drag them in position (Saturday first) and adjust the caption property appropriately.

Programming the Controls' Positions

Then add code like this to the `resize()` routine:

```
' Position column labels
    For i = 0 To 6
        col_labels(i).Left = Vlines(i).X1
    Next
```

Figure 3-6 shows my calendar, nicely enlarged, at this point in its development.

It looks like we're about ready to tell our calendar about its real job. Next we'll give it dates.

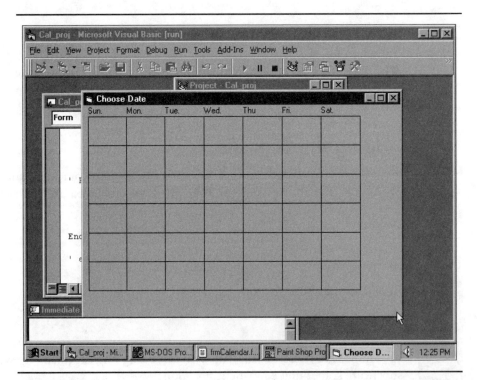

Figure 3-6
Calendar dragged to large size.

LABELLING THE DAYS

We're going to want to select a date by clicking it. One way to do that would be to write a `Form_Click` event-handling method. That would look at the location of the mouse pointer at the last click and do some math to figure out which date was clicked.

There's a much easier way using objects. We can drop a label object over each day, sizing it to fit just inside the grid. Then we can write a method that handles clicks in these label objects.

So far we've been writing methods for the Form. This parallels writing methods in a class module. You can also write methods for individual objects on the Form. You're probably used to writing methods that handle individual button clicks.

The .FRM is Not a .CLS in Disguise

When you write a button click method, you are creating a method for a single object. In all other object-oriented programming, methods are created for classes, not for individual objects. In the .FRM file, though, you have methods for the Form, which are like methods in a class module, and you have methods for other individual objects.

Actually, your .FRM has methods for individual objects, and it can have methods for control arrays. Our `col_labels` array, for example, can have event-handling methods for clicks, double clicks, mouse movement, and so on. The possibilities are the same as for an individual control except that a parameter is added to the method that identifies the individual control, this way:

```
Public Sub col_labels_Click(Index As Integer)

    If Index = 2 Then
        ' Tuesday was clicked
    End If

End Sub
```

The `Index` parameter varies from `0` (the first array element) to `n-1`, where `n` is the number of controls in the array. It identifies the control in which the event happened.

You can think of the control array methods as methods of a class. The objects of that class are the individual array elements. The `Index` parameter identifies the individual control, as the implicit `Me` parameter identifies objects in the classes you create.

Now you have the theory, or, perhaps I should say you have the facts. (There doesn't appear to be an excess of theory here.) Form modules are like class modules except that they contain methods that apply to individual objects, not to a class. When they contain control arrays, methods apply to the array as if the elements were members of a class.

Do you think the word *elegant* belongs in this discussion, or are you inclined to use less complimentary terms?

Whatever descriptive terms you want to use, we can make all this work for us.

Adding the Control Array

Begin by adding a label. Make it roughly fill a single day rectangle. Change its Name to day_labels, set Alignment to Right Justify, make Caption "0," and set Visible to False.

Copy and paste to create the control array, and then keep right on pasting until you have 42 day labels. If you watch the name in the Properties window, you can stop pasting when the name says day_labels(41).

I've just left my labels in a pile in the upper-left, where the paste operation put them. If you have more patience than I do, I suppose you could drag all these out where they belong. That's not helpful, though, because our resize() method will do the real positioning.

If you'd like to rescue your Sunday column label, use the dropdown list at the top of the Properties window to choose col_labels(0), and then choose Format⇨Order⇨Bring to Front.

Memo To Bill Gates

Do you really think having the Properties window sort an array by alphabetical sort is smart, Bill? We're going 1, 10, 11, ... 19, 2, 20, 21, ... Duh.

Programming the Control Array

Now we're ready to write some code. Let's start by putting these labels into position. Then we can go on to assigning real days, and then we can use the mouse to choose a particular day.

Positioning the Day Labels

I've made day labels slightly smaller than the day's rectangle so that clicks on or near a calendar grid line are ignored. My code, added to the resize() method, looks like this:

```
' Size and position day labels
    Const inset = 20 ' space around label within day
    Dim ht As Integer, wd As Integer

    ht = day_ht - (2 * inset) ' top and bottom inset
    wd = day_wd - (2 * inset) ' left and right

    Dim week As Byte, day As Byte, dnum As Byte

    For week = 0 To 5
        For day = 0 To 6
            dnum = day + (week * 7)
            With day_labels(dnum)
                .Top = Hlines(week).Y1 + inset
                .Left = Vlines(day).X1 + inset
                .Height = ht
                .Width = wd
                .Visible = True
            End With
        Next day
    Next week
```

With that addition, I have the result shown in Figure 3-7.

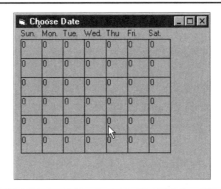

Figure 3-7
Properly positioning the day labels.

Of course, we don't want all the days to claim they are day zero. We're ready to get to real date intelligence.

Assigning Real Days

Here we're going to keep track of which day is highlighted (the days are numbered 0 through 41) and what date it is (12/31/99, for example). We'll also need to know what date to use for day 0. We want the calendar to start on the Sunday of the week that includes the first day of the month.

Once we have those items, assigning correct captions to the day labels will be easy. Visual Basic and Java, by the way, are very similar in that both use an eight-byte date item that includes both date and time.

Begin by adding `Private` variables to record the important date facts. These go in the General Declarations section:

```
Private hi_date As Date ' highlighted date
Private hi_day As Byte ' day 0 to 41

Private start_date As Date ' Sunday of week 0
```

Then add a routine that accepts a date and sets these values. As in a class module, that's Tools⇨Add Procedure. (You'll have to move your end-of-file comment to keep the comment at the end.) While you're there, also add a routine that sets the captions of the day labels.

These two routines will work:

```
Public Sub set_hi_date(dt As Date)

' first approximation: 1st of the month
    start_date = Str(Month(dt)) + "/1/" + Str(Year(dt))

' now find Sunday
    start_date = start_date - WeekDay(start_date) + 1

' set highlighted day and date
    hi_date = dt
    hi_day = hi_date - start_date

    set_day_captions

End Sub

Private Sub set_day_captions()

    Dim i As Byte
    For i = 0 To 41
        day_labels(i).Caption = Str(day(start_date + i))
    Next

End Sub
```

The first of these is Public and the other is Private. You'll want programs that use a calendar to be able to set the highlighted date, but the day label captions are internal to the calendar.

To make this work, you'll need to call this code. Later on we'll change this, but for now, let's choose today's date when the Form is initialized. Add a line to the Form_Initialize event handler, like this:

```
Private Sub Form_Initialize()
    set_hi_date (Date)
End Sub
```

Now run the code, and you'll see something beginning to look very much like a calendar. Mine's shown here in Figure 3-8.

Figure 3-8
The days are now labelled.

If you don't have a very fast machine, you'll see when you run this code that your formerly sparkling performance has turned dog slow. That's because Windows assumes that when you change a visual property it ought to redraw whatever you changed. In the resize routine you're changing Top, Left, Height, and Width of each day label, which is 168 (4×42) changes, triggering as many repaints.

Did you see that the first display was fast? That's because we set the Visible property to False. Windows doesn't have to redraw anything when Visible is False, so add a loop near the top of the resize() method that sets all 42 days' Visible properties to False. Your performance will be sparkling again.

Answering the Call of the Mouse

Are you ready to put in a highlighted day and use mouse clicks to move the highlight? I am. First, though, this is a good point to include a complete listing. My program thus far is shown in Listing 3-2.

Listing 3-2
Calendar with day labels

```
' Calendar.Frm — Form-based Calendar Class
' Copyright 1997, Martin L. Rinehart

Option Explicit

Private hi_date As Date ' highlighted date
Private hi_day As Byte ' day 0 to 41

Private start_date As Date ' Sunday of week 0

Private Sub Form_Initialize()
    set_hi_date (Date)
End Sub

Private Sub Form_Resize()

' Exit immediately if the calendar is minimized
    If WindowState = vbMinimized Then Exit Sub

' Don't let it get too tiny
    Const min_wd = 3500
    Const min_ht = 3500

    If Width < min_wd Then Width = min_wd
    If Height < min_ht Then Height = min_ht

' Leave border space

    Const tp_space = 220
    Const lf_space = 100
    Const bt_space = 940
    Const rt_space = 1000

' Compute grid size
    Dim grid_ht As Integer, grid_wd As Integer
    grid_ht = Height - tp_space - bt_space
    grid_wd = Width - lf_space - rt_space

    Dim day_ht As Integer, day_wd As Integer
```

```
        day_ht = grid_ht / 6
        day_wd = grid_wd / 7

        grid_ht = 6 * day_ht ' correct for roundoff
        grid_wd = 7 * day_wd

        Dim i As Byte ' Loop counter

' For performance, hide the day labels
        For i = 0 To 41
            day_labels(i).Visible = False
        Next


' Place horizontal lines
        With Hlines(0)
            .X1 = lf_space
            .X2 = lf_space + grid_wd
            .Y1 = tp_space
            .Y2 = .Y1
            .Visible = True
        End With

        For i = 1 To 6
            With Hlines(i)
                .X1 = Hlines(0).X1
                .X2 = Hlines(0).X2
                .Y1 = Hlines(i - 1).Y1 + day_ht
                .Y2 = .Y1
                .Visible = True
            End With
        Next

' Place vertical lines
        With Vlines(0)
            .X1 = Hlines(0).X1
            .X2 = .X1
            .Y1 = Hlines(0).Y1
            .Y2 = Hlines(6).Y1
            .Visible = True
        End With

        For i = 1 To 7
            With Vlines(i)
                .X1 = Vlines(i - 1).X1 + day_wd
                .X2 = .X1
                .Y1 = Vlines(0).Y1
```

(continued)

Calendar with day labels

```
                    .Y2 = Vlines(0).Y2
                    .Visible = True
            End With
        Next

    ' Position column labels
        For i = 0 To 6
            col_labels(i).Left = Vlines(i).X1
        Next

    ' Size and position day labels
        Const inset = 20 ' space around label within day
        Dim ht As Integer, wd As Integer

        ht = day_ht - (2 * inset) ' top and bottom inset
        wd = day_wd - (2 * inset) ' left and right

        Dim week As Byte, day As Byte, dnum As Byte

        For week = 0 To 5
            For day = 0 To 6
                dnum = day + (week * 7)
                With day_labels(dnum)
                    .Top = Hlines(week).Y1 + inset
                    .Left = Vlines(day).X1 + inset
                    .Height = ht
                    .Width = wd
                    .Visible = True
                End With
            Next day
        Next week

End Sub

Public Sub set_hi_date(dt As Date)

' first approximation: 1st of the month
    start_date = Str(Month(dt)) + "/1/" + Str(Year(dt))

' now find Sunday
    start_date = start_date - WeekDay(start_date) + 1

' set highlighted day and date
    hi_date = dt
    hi_day = hi_date - start_date

    set_day_captions
```

```
End Sub

Private Sub set_day_captions()

    Dim i As Byte
    For i = 0 To 41
        day_labels(i).Caption = Str(day(start_date + i))
    Next

End Sub

' end of Calendar.Frm
```

If you've looked in any .FRM files, you know that this really isn't the complete contents of Calendar.frm. It's just the part that shows in the code editor. Visual Basic writes the rest of the file to record all the objects and objects' properties on your form.

Now let's highlight a day. We'll need a routine that both highlights and removes the highlight from a day. (To switch from one day to another, you'll unhighlight the old day and then highlight the new day.) The issue you'll want to think about is which colors to use.

You want colors to look good and that are available on the user's computer. The safe (if boring) way to choose colors is to use colors that the user has chosen for his or her Windows setup.

I'm using white on a black background for the highlight and `ButtonText` and `ButtonFace` colors (these are also the window's background) for the plain days.

If you want to be really thorough, you should check to be sure that the user hasn't used white on black for his or her regular windows' colors. (Is this check worth the extra bytes? You decide.)

My routine for highlighting and unhighlighting days is this:

```
Private Sub hilite_day(day_num As Byte, _
    is_hi As Boolean)

    With day_labels(day_num)
        If is_hi Then
            .ForeColor = vbWhite
            .BackColor = vbBlack
        Else
            .ForeColor = vbButtonText
            .BackColor = vbButtonFace
        End If
    End With

End Sub
```

I call that routine when I set the `hi_day` property. You have to be sure to always call it twice: first to unhighlight the current selection and then to highlight the new selection. Those calls are added to the `set_hi_date()` method, this way:

```
Public Sub set_hi_date(dt As Date)

' first approximation: 1st of the month
    start_date = Str(Month(dt)) + "/1/" + Str(Year(dt))

' now find Sunday
    start_date = start_date - WeekDay(start_date) + 1

' unhilite current one
   Call hilite_day(hi_day, False)

' set highlighted day and date
    hi_date = dt
    hi_day = hi_date - start_date
    Call hilite_day(hi_day, True)

    set_day_captions

End Sub
```

If you're worried about what happens on the first call, I'm glad. You've not set any value for `hi_day`, and no day is highlighted. It turns out, though, that you don't need to add logic to handle this. Visual Basic sets `hi_date` to a default zero, and your code then specifies normal colors for `day_labels(0)`, which is fine.

When you run this, you'll have the current day highlighted. Mine's shown in Figure 3-9.

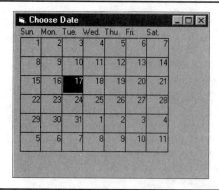

■ **Figure 3-9**
■ *Highlighting today's date.*

Now all that remains is responding to the mouse click. This is the method that we'll add to our `day_labels` array. (No, there is no such thing in object theory as attaching methods to arrays, but if it works, use it!)

One more routine brings this to life. Select the `day_labels` from the left-hand dropdown list on your code editor. It defaults to creating a `day_labels_Click` routine, which is just what you want. Add this code:

```
Private Sub day_labels_Click(Index As Integer)

' Do nothing if the current day was clicked
   If Index = hi_day Then Exit Sub

   Call hilite_day(hi_day, False)

   hi_day = Index
   hi_date = start_date + hi_day
   Call hilite_day(hi_day, True)

End Sub
```

When you run this, the highlight will move in response to mouse clicks. Simple, no?

Now look very critically at my code. Does that first line earn its keep? I'm not sure. It adds zero functionality for a cost of however many bytes, but try clicking a property in the Properties window. Now click it again. See the window blink as it's repainted? My calendar won't blink. If you skip that check, your calendar will be a bit smaller. Suit yourself.

LABELLING THE MONTHS

Only one more chore remains, and we're done with this phase of our object's development. That's to tell you what month and year. I do this with two labels. One is for the month that starts in the top week and the other is for the next month, when it starts.

Add the Controls

Begin by adding two label controls. I've named mine `top_mo_label` and `bot_mo_label`. Mine are 800 twips wide and 250 high.

Position the top one next to the top week. I've aligned the top of the label with the top line. Put the lower one down near the fifth or sixth week.

We'll have the program set the Top property to align with the week in which the new month starts. We'll also set the Left so that it is to the right of the rightmost grid line.

The caption will be set by the program to the appropriate month and year, in this format: "Mon. YEAR".

Program the Positions

There are two programming steps. We'll need to set the captions and to set the location. I'll begin with the caption using the design time locations for the moment.

Captions for the Month Labels

We'll show both labels next to the week in which the month starts. We can grab the month and year from the value in Saturday of that week. We'll always start a month in the top week. The next month will start in week five or six.

We'll want a function that tells us which week to use. Checking the day in the fifth Saturday will tell you: if it's less than 8, a new month has started. This is the routine I've added:

```
Private Function change_week() As Byte

' new month starts in week 5 or 6

    If day(start_date + 34) < 8 Then
        change_week = 5
    Else
        change_week = 6
    End If
End Function
```

You'll also need a function that returns an appropriate abbreviation for the name of the month. This is mine:

```
Private Function month_name(mo As Byte)
    month_name = Mid( _
        "Jan.Feb.Mar.Apr.May JuneJulyAug.Sep.Oct.Nov.Dec.", _
        (mo * 4) - 3, _
        4)

End Function
```

This function isn't as clear as it would be if you used an array and just returned the appropriate array element, but that would use more bytes in the executable file. I generally prefer the plainest possible code, but this time I let my byte-saving nature take over. Suit yourself. If you use my trick, be sure to include that space after `May`.

With that function available, you can write a function that actually sets the label's caption. This works:

```
Private Sub set_mo_caption(lbl As Label, wk As Byte)
    Dim dt As Date ' Saturday in the specified week
    dt = start_date + ((wk * 7) - 1)

    lbl.Caption = month_name(Month(dt)) + " " + Str(Year(dt))
End Sub
```

That uses a temporary date variable to hold the date value for Saturday in the appropriate week. Then it concatenates the name of that Saturday's month, a space, and the string form of the year.

The one remaining step is to call these functions. Because the `set_day_captions` method is called whenever the start date is changed, that's a convenient place to put the call. My revised version of that function adds these lines:

```
' label week 1
    Call set_mo_caption(top_mo_label, 1)

' label next week where month changes
    Call set_mo_caption(bot_mo_label, change_week)
```

Positioning the Month Labels

With the month labels correctly captioned, our final job is to position these labels. This is another addition to the growing `resize()` method.

This is the code I added:

```
'Position month labels
    top_mo_label.Left = Vlines(7).X1 + 40
    ' top, height and width as per design time

    bot_mo_label.Left = top_mo_label.Left
    bot_mo_label.Top = Hlines(change_week - 1).Y1
    ' height and width as per design time
```

I try to program in very small pieces. I like little routines because the small ones can be made to work, always. Big routines tend to have bugs, but there's one exception, and the `resize()` method is the perfect example.

Sometimes a job has a lot of little steps that always have to be done one after the other. You can make each little step a separate routine and then drive the steps from a caller, like this:

```
Sub caller()
    first_step
    next_step
    ...
    last_step
End Sub
```

Then the individual steps are all small routines, but this just forces the work to fit a preconceived notion (small routines are good). It's no more robust than including all the steps in place in the calling routine, as you see in `resize()`. Note how I use extended comments, though, to give a visual clue to the structure of the routine. This single-routine approach is somewhat smaller and faster, though probably not meaningfully so.

When you run this program, you should get a result like the one you see in Figure 3-10.

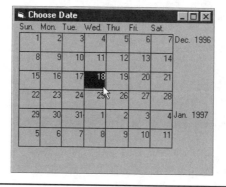

Figure 3-10
Our calendar masters dates.

We finally have a real calendar going that knows all about dates. At least it understands the current month. In Chapter 4, we'll teach it how to change months and years.

THE FINISHED CALENDAR CLASS

For those of you who have borrowed this book from the library long after someone else kept the disk (or those who own the book but the kids used the disk for a frisbee), Listing 3-3 shows the complete program to this point.

Listing 3-3
Calendar with labelled dates

```
' Calendar.Frm — Form-based Calendar Class
' Copyright 1997, Martin L. Rinehart

Option Explicit

Private hi_date As Date ' highlighted date
Private hi_day As Byte ' day 0 to 41

Private start_date As Date ' Sunday of week 0

Private Sub day_labels_Click(Index As Integer)

' Do nothing if the current day was clicked
    If Index = hi_day Then Exit Sub

    Call hilite_day(hi_day, False)

    hi_day = Index
    hi_date = start_date + hi_day
    Call hilite_day(hi_day, True)

End Sub

Private Sub Form_Initialize()
    set_hi_date (Date)
End Sub

Private Sub Form_Resize()

' Exit immediately if the calendar is minimized
    If WindowState = vbMinimized Then Exit Sub

' Don't let it get too tiny
    Const min_wd = 3500
    Const min_ht = 3500
```

(continued)

Calendar with labelled dates

```
        If Width < min_wd Then Width = min_wd
        If Height < min_ht Then Height = min_ht

' Leave border space

        Const tp_space = 220
        Const lf_space = 100
        Const bt_space = 940
        Const rt_space = 1000

' Compute grid size
        Dim grid_ht As Integer, grid_wd As Integer
        grid_ht = Height - tp_space - bt_space
        grid_wd = Width - lf_space - rt_space

        Dim day_ht As Integer, day_wd As Integer
        day_ht = grid_ht / 6
        day_wd = grid_wd / 7

        grid_ht = 6 * day_ht ' correct for roundoff
        grid_wd = 7 * day_wd

        Dim i As Byte ' Loop counter

' For performance, hide the day labels
        For i = 0 To 41
            day_labels(i).Visible = False
        Next


' Place horizontal lines
        With Hlines(0)
            .X1 = lf_space
            .X2 = lf_space + grid_wd
            .Y1 = tp_space
            .Y2 = .Y1
            .Visible = True
        End With

        For i = 1 To 6
            With Hlines(i)
                .X1 = Hlines(0).X1
                .X2 = Hlines(0).X2
                .Y1 = Hlines(i - 1).Y1 + day_ht
                .Y2 = .Y1
                .Visible = True
            End With
        Next
```

```
' Place vertical lines
    With Vlines(0)
        .X1 = Hlines(0).X1
        .X2 = .X1
        .Y1 = Hlines(0).Y1
        .Y2 = Hlines(6).Y1
        .Visible = True
    End With

    For i = 1 To 7
        With Vlines(i)
            .X1 = Vlines(i - 1).X1 + day_wd
            .X2 = .X1
            .Y1 = Vlines(0).Y1
            .Y2 = Vlines(0).Y2
            .Visible = True
        End With
    Next

' Position column labels
    For i = 0 To 6
        col_labels(i).Left = Vlines(i).X1
    Next

' Size and position day labels
    Const inset = 20 ' space around label within day
    Dim ht As Integer, wd As Integer

    ht = day_ht - (2 * inset) ' top and bottom inset
    wd = day_wd - (2 * inset) ' left and right

    Dim week As Byte, day As Byte, dnum As Byte

    For week = 0 To 5
        For day = 0 To 6
            dnum = day + (week * 7)
            With day_labels(dnum)
                .Top = Hlines(week).Y1 + inset
                .Left = Vlines(day).X1 + inset
                .Height = ht
                .Width = wd
                .Visible = True
            End With
        Next day
    Next week
```

(continued)

Calendar with labelled dates

```
'Position month labels
    top_mo_label.Left = Vlines(7).X1 + 40
    ' top, height and width as per design time

    bot_mo_label.Left = top_mo_label.Left
    bot_mo_label.Top = Hlines(change_week - 1).Y1
    ' height and width as per design time

End Sub

Public Sub set_hi_date(dt As Date)

' first approximation: 1st of the month
    start_date = Str(Month(dt)) + "/1/" + Str(Year(dt))

' now find Sunday
    start_date = start_date - WeekDay(start_date) + 1

' unhilite current one
    Call hilite_day(hi_day, False)

' set highlighted day and date
    hi_date = dt
    hi_day = hi_date - start_date
    Call hilite_day(hi_day, True)

    set_day_captions

End Sub

Private Sub set_day_captions()

    Dim i As Byte
    For i = 0 To 41
        day_labels(i).Caption = Str(day(start_date + i))
    Next

' label week 1
    Call set_mo_caption(top_mo_label, 1)

' label next week where month changes
    Call set_mo_caption(bot_mo_label, change_week())

End Sub

Private Sub set_mo_caption(lbl As Label, wk As Byte)
    Dim dt As Date ' Saturday in the specified week
    dt = start_date + ((wk * 7) - 1)
```

```
        lbl.Caption = month_name(Month(dt)) + " " + Str(Year(dt))
End Sub

Private Function month_name(mo As Byte)
    month_name = Mid( _
        "Jan.Feb.Mar.Apr.May JuneJulyAug.Sep.Oct.Nov.Dec.", _
        (mo * 4) - 3, _
        4)

End Function

Private Sub hilite_day(day_num As Byte, _
    is_hi As Boolean)

    With day_labels(day_num)
        If is_hi Then
            .ForeColor = vbWhite
            .BackColor = vbBlack
        Else
            .ForeColor = vbButtonText
            .BackColor = vbButtonFace
        End If
    End With

End Sub

Private Function change_week() As Byte

' new month starts in week 5 or 6

    If day(start_date + 34) < 8 Then
        change_week = 5
    Else
        change_week = 6
    End If
End Function

' end of Calendar.frm
```

SUMMARY

We started to build a form-based calendar class in this chapter. You can use the .FRM as you use a class module. You can add data properties and methods. You also can write methods for individual objects, and you can write class-like methods for control arrays. These capabilities are irregular, to say the least, but because they're there, you might as well take advantage of them.

We began here by designing a calendar. I short-circuited this by just showing you the finished product and then inviting you to make improvements.

Programming started with a grid of lines. Because we want a calendar that can be resized, we used the `resize()` method to position the lines (as opposed to placing them at design time).

Then we added column labels and a bit of code to position them correctly.

After the labels were placed over the columns, we used a control array to hold 42 individual day labels. Programming an event handler for a control array is like programming an event handler for a class. The method will be called appropriately with an `Index` parameter that lets you identify which object (array member) triggered the event. We used this capability to move a highlight in response to mouse clicks.

We completed this phase by adding month labels. Private function methods made this job easier.

Now we have a real calendar, but it only shows the current month. In Chapter 4, we'll teach it to change months and years, and we'll teach it to respond to the keyboard as well as the mouse.

COMPLETING THE CALENDAR

4

*I*n Chapter 3, we completed a calendar page for the current month. It has programmed flexibility so that you can set your system's date to any day you like and you'll see a calendar for that month. Of course, setting your system date to turn the page of a calendar isn't exactly convenient. In this chapter, we're going to fix that.

We'll be using Visual Basic's built-in events to obtain input from buttons and from the keyboard. In Chapter 10 we'll start programming our very own events, but for now we'll be working with the ones that are inherent in Visual Basic. (You'll see when we reach Chapter 10 that what you learn here is the main part of what you'll need to know to create your own events.)

We'll begin working with the keyboard. This will let us use navigation keys to move the highlighted day. You'll find that the simple KeyPress event isn't as powerful as its more complex cousin, the KeyDown event. Eventually both will prove disappointing, sorry to say.

Then we'll add a command button diamond that moves the highlighted day as well. You'll see that this will be our long-term solution for keyboard access.

After the button diamond, we'll go on to the scrolling functions. These will let us turn the page forward or backward a month at a time or a year at a time.

Once our calendar becomes smart about turning pages, we'll modify our general-purpose calendar to serve as a data entry popup box. We'll try to simplify its use as much as possible.

We'll begin with the keyboard.

EXPERIMENTING WITH THE KEYBOARD

I'd like to move that highlighted day around the calendar by pressing the arrow keys. PgUp and PgDn might be good choices for changing the month, too. Let's start by doing some testing.

Select the Form with the left dropdown menu at the top of your code editor. Then use the other dropdown list to see what capabilities the form has for handling keystrokes. You'll see interesting events such as KeyDown, KeyUp, and KeyPress. Start with the KeyPress event.

The KeyPress Event

When you click KeyPress, the outer lines of the following event-handling method are prepared for you. Add the middle line:

```
Private Sub Form_KeyPress(KeyAscii As Integer)
    MsgBox "keypress " & Str(KeyAscii)
End Sub
```

Figure 4-1 shows me looking at a keypress report as I ran this version of the calendar.

Try various keys. You'll see that the K key, for example, is 107 in lowercase and 75 in uppercase. Try Enter and Esc. You should get 13 for Enter and 27 for Escape.

Now for the bad news. Test the navigation keys (arrows, PgUp, PgDn, and so on). What do you see? I see absolutely nothing. They aren't considered keypresses by the KeyPress event.

Therefore, we're not going to use the KeyPress event to program responses to the arrow keys. Let's try again.

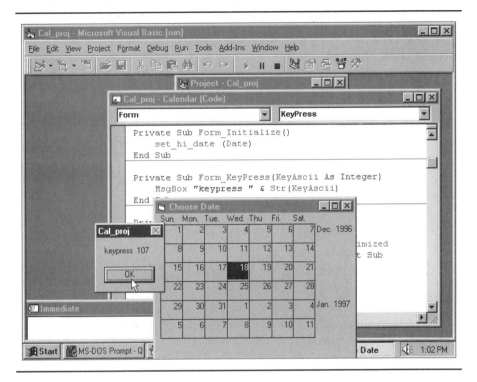

Figure 4-1
Examining a keypress.

The KeyDown Event

KeyDown is interesting. It reports whenever a key is pressed down. It also reports the shift status (all the shifts: left and right regular shift, Ctrl, and Alt). Click Form and KeyDown in the left and right dropdown lists of your code editor, and then add the middle of this function:

```
Private Sub Form_KeyDown(KeyCode As Integer, _
    Shift As Integer)

    Debug.Print "keydown " & Str(KeyCode) _
        & " " & Str(Shift)

End Sub
```

The Debug object's print method sends output to the Immediate window. It's there for situations like this. (Try to use a message box for this report, and you'll see why Debug.Print is useful here.)

You'll find that the shift is 0 when no shift key is held down. It's 1 when either regular shift key is pressed, 2 for the Ctrl key, and 4 for the Alt key. You can also use these in combinations. Alt+shift is 5, for example. Pressing the K key generates a keycode of 75 for any shift status.

When you hold a shift key, it's typematic feature generates repeated reports that it was pressed, which are interrupted when you add another key. KeyPress events are still triggered by the basic typewriter keys.

The keycodes for the arrows are 37 through 40 for left, up, right, and down, respectively.

PROGRAMMING THE ARROW KEYS

Now that you have found the arrow keys, it's not hard to implement them. A switch in the KeyDown event-handling method and a simple function to change days is all you need.

Changing Days

This is a simple function, but it has to worry about validity. I've chosen to have it do the checking, rather than the calling routines. Here's the code:

```
Private Sub change_day(delta As Integer)

    Dim new_day As Integer
    new_day = hi_day + delta

' exit on invalid delta
    If new_day < 0 Then Exit Sub
    If new_day > 41 Then Exit Sub

' change the day
    Call hilite_day(hi_day, False)
    hi_day = new_day
    hi_date = start_date + hi_day
    Call hilite_day(hi_day, True)

End Sub
```

Although the values of delta will be small, you need to use an integer. Bytes are unsigned (0 to 255, only) so they won't allow a negative delta.

Handling the Arrow Events

The KeyDown switch is similarly simple:

```
Private Sub Form_KeyDown(KeyCode As Integer, _
    Shift As Integer)

    Select Case KeyCode
        Case 37 ' left
            change_day (-1)
        Case 38 ' up
            change_day (-7)
        Case 39 ' right
            change_day (1)
        Case 40 ' down
            change_day (7)
    End Select

End Sub
```

Add this code, and you'll be able to use the arrow keys.

ADDING THE BUTTON DIAMOND

For an immediately apparent alternative means of moving the highlight, I've provided a diamond of command buttons. By prefixing the appropriate letters with ampersands, this gives the user another keyboard alternative: Alt+U, Alt+D, Alt+L, and Alt+R.

Adding the Buttons

Begin by placing four command buttons on your Form so that your design looks similar to the one in Figure 4-2.

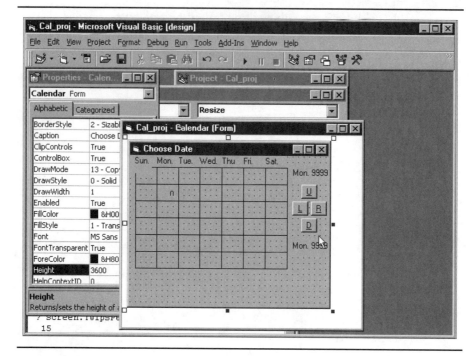

Figure 4-2
Placing the button diamond.

I've named my buttons `btnUp`, `btnDown`, `btnLeft`, and `btnRight`. A size of around 300 twips square works for me. Prefix each caption letter with the ampersand, so Alt+*letter* will work.

Programming the Buttons

Ready to program the buttons? It's trivial, especially because it's Visual Basic writing two of every three lines for you. Listing 4-1 shows the four new methods you see by double-clicking the buttons and adding the middle line.

Listing 4-1
Diamond button methods

```
Private Sub btnDown_Click()
    change_day (7)
End Sub
```

```
Private Sub btnLeft_Click()
    change_day (-1)
End Sub

Private Sub btnRight_Click()
    change_day (1)
End Sub

Private Sub btnUp_Click()
    change_day (-7)
End Sub
```

Resize() Positions the Buttons

As the buttons stand now, they are at a fixed distance from the left of your Form. They need to be a fixed distance from the right, so Resize() needs to set their Left properties.

This is the code I've added to Resize():

```
' position the diamond buttons
    btnUp.Left = Width - 700
    btnLeft.Left = Width - 900
    btnRight.Left = Width - 500
    btnDown.Left = btnUp.Left
```

You'll see the best result if your design positions the buttons so that they are already at the exact locations your initial call to Resize() computes. Otherwise, you'll notice annoying little button movements when the Form is first painted. (Windows appears to do its own paint before calling Resize().)

And Now the Bad News

Test your arrow keys again. They're gone.

When you have controls on your form that can gain focus, Windows uses the arrow keys to move focus. With these buttons, the KeyDown event is not fired for an arrow key. Your application will never know that they're being pressed.

> ### Memo To Bill Gates
>
> Bill, this is really, really poor. When I build an app, I want to build it the way I want to build it. I don't want someone in Redmond, Washington, deciding what's best for an application that he or she hasn't even thought about. I want to decide for myself, thank you.

Oh well. You can't always get what you want. You might as well delete that `KeyDown` event handler. It's useless.

SCROLLING

Our next project is to teach the calendar how to turn its pages. Begin by adding all the bottom buttons to your form.

Adding Buttons

Begin by adding the full set of bottom buttons you see in Figure 4-3.

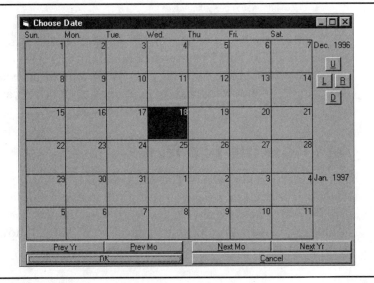

Figure 4-3
Bottom buttons added to the Form.

I've set the height of each button to 240. Don't worry too much about the horizontal positioning — our `Resize()` method will handle that.

But do worry about the `TabIndex` order. I've set mine so that OK has focus initially (`TabIndex 0`) and that the other buttons go in left-to-right, top-to-bottom order.

My button names are: `btnOK`, `btnCancel`, `btnPrevYr`, `btnPrevMo`, `btnNextMo`, and `btnNextYr`.

Positioning the Buttons

You have to set the buttons' `Visible` property to `False` near the start of the `Resize()` method. Then you can return `Visible` to `True` after each button is positioned. There's one exception, though.

If a button has focus when its `Visible` property is changed to `False`, focus moves to the next control in the `TabIndex` order. If all the buttons are invisible, none has focus. When the first button is made visible again, it will have focus. I want to keep focus on the OK button, so I don't turn its `Visible` property to `False`.

I'll let you turn the button's `Visible` property to `False` on your own. Put the code near the top of the `Resize()` method. Listing 4-2 shows the new additions to the `Resize()` method that I've made for positioning these buttons.

Add this at the bottom of your `Resize()` routine. Don't worry about the `TwipsPerPixelX` property. I'm going to explain that next.

Listing 4-2
Positioning the bottom buttons

```
' position the bottom buttons
    Dim bsize As Integer, hbsize As Integer
    hbsize = ((Width - 50) / 4) - lf_space
        ' half buttons

    ' Eliminate twips->pixel roundoff problems
        hbsize = hbsize / Screen.TwipsPerPixelX
        hbsize = hbsize * Screen.TwipsPerPixelX

    bsize = 2 * hbsize                    ' full buttons

    With btnOK
        .Top = Height - 640
        .Left = lf_space
        .Width = bsize
```

(continued)

Positioning the bottom buttons

```
      ' .Height as per design
      ' .Visible stays True to keep focus
End With

With btnCancel
    .Top = btnOK.Top
    .Left = btnOK.Left + btnOK.Width + _
        2 * lf_space
    .Width = bsize
    .Visible = True
End With

With btnPrevYr
    .Top = Height - 900
    .Left = btnOK.Left
    .Width = hbsize
    .Visible = True
End With

With btnPrevMo
    .Top = btnPrevYr.Top
    .Left = btnPrevYr.Left + btnPrevYr.Width
    .Width = hbsize
    .Visible = True
End With

With btnNextMo
    .Top = btnPrevYr.Top
    .Left = btnCancel.Left
    .Width = hbsize
    .Visible = True
End With

With btnNextYr
    .Top = btnPrevYr.Top
    .Left = btnNextMo.Left + btnNextMo.Width
    .Width = hbsize
    .Visible = True
End With
```

When I first wrote this code, my wide buttons never seemed to line up correctly with the two half-wide buttons that sat on top of them. I stared at the code for entirely too long, trying to find the bug. I stepped through it carefully in the debugger, but nothing looked wrong.

The problem was that my calculations were correct, but the way they translated in pixels was causing problems. For instance, suppose the half-wide button was 100.3 pixels wide. It would be drawn 100 pixels wide. The full-width button would be 200.6 pixels wide, which would be drawn as 201 pixels. Thus, nothing would quite line up, unless you happened to pick a lucky size when you resized.

Two properties, `TwipsPerPixelX` and `TwipsPerPixelY`, are available for these sorts of problems. They are properties of the global objects `Screen` and `Printer`. They report the appropriate ratio in both dimensions, of course.

If you're dealing with integers, dividing by a number and then multiplying by the same number effectively rounds down to the nearest multiple of the divisor. For example:

```
twips = 610
twips per pixel = 15

610 / 15 =  40 (remainder discarded)
 40 * 15 = 600 (original rounded down)
```

All of which is to say that sometimes it can take a little work to line everything up neatly.

The other little trick in this code is dividing `Width-50` by 4. Why discard 50? The `Width` of the Form includes a pixel or two for the borders. I picked 50 by experimenting.

Memo To Bill Gates

In Java, Bill, there's a nice property called `Insets` that tells you exactly how much to allow for a Form's borders. You don't want us to all go code Java, do you? How about giving us an `Insets` property?

With all our buttons nicely laid out, it's a little frustrating that they don't do anything when you click them. That's our next job.

Scrolling by Month

You have two things to consider when you scroll the calendar. First, if I click `PrevMo`, it's pretty obvious what I want to happen. I want the top line to show the start of the previous month.

The other question is what I want to do with the highlighted day. The currently highlighted one will be off the page most of the time. Should you highlight the same day of the new month?

That idea quickly gets complicated! Suppose March 30 is highlighted when you click PrevMo. There is no February 30, of course. I experimented with lots of solutions to this problem, all of them taking quite a bit of code and none really making me happy.

Then I changed my mind entirely. I just left the highlight alone. If the third Wednesday was highlighted, the third Wednesday stays highlighted. It's simple, and it looks good, too. With that in mind, let's change months.

With that decision, the code becomes simple. Start with a routine that will take an input date that is the first of the target month. From there it adjusts to start on Sunday and sets our start_date and hi_date values. Then it calls set_day_captions to take care of updating the visible calendar. This is the code:

```
Private Sub reset_start(dt As Date)

    ' resets the start date, but doesn't move highlight

    start_date = dt - WeekDay(dt) + 1

    hi_date = start_date + hi_day

    set_day_captions

End Sub
```

Now it's up to the button click handlers to figure out what the first of the month they want is. The only minor complication is that if you're backing up, you go from month 1 to month 12 of the previous year; if you're going forward month 1 of next year follows month 12 of this year.

Listing 4-3 shows the new event handlers.

Listing 4-3
Handling button clicks

```
Private Sub btnNextMo_Click()

    Dim dt As Date, mo As Byte
    dt = start_date + 6 ' Saturday, 1st week
    mo = Month(dt)

    If mo < 12 Then
        dt = Str(mo + 1) & "/1/" & Str(Year(dt))
    Else
        dt = "1/1/" & Str(Year(dt) + 1)
    End If

    reset_start dt
```

```
End Sub

Private Sub btnPrevMo_Click()

    Dim dt As Date, mo As Byte
    dt = start_date + 6 ' Saturday, 1st week
    mo = Month(dt)

    If mo > 1 Then
        dt = Str(mo - 1) & "/1/" & Str(Year(dt))
    Else
        dt = "12/1/" & Str(Year(dt) - 1)
    End If

    reset_start dt

End Sub
```

Scrolling by Year

Go right ahead and write the handlers for the next and previous years.
Then give your calendar a really good workout to be sure that it understands
dates completely.

Figure 4-4 shows me using these new routines to get in a party mood.

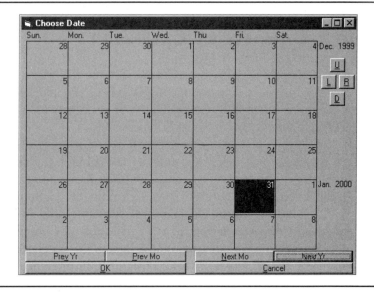

■ **Figure 4-4**
The calendar runs to the end of the century.

My version of the code is here:

```
Private Sub btnNextYr_Click()

    Dim dt As Date, new_date As Date
    dt = start_date + 6

    new_date = Str(Month(dt)) + "/1/" + Str(Year(dt) + 1)

    reset_start new_date

End Sub

. . .

Private Sub btnPrevYr_Click()

    Dim dt As Date, new_date As Date

    dt = start_date + 6

    new_date = Str(Month(dt)) + "/1/" + Str(Year(dt) - 1)

    reset_start new_date

End Sub
```

MAKING A DATA ENTRY CALENDAR

We've created a perpetual calendar at this point. If you want a perpetual calendar for yourself, you can compile this to pcode or to native code. In pcode, mine is just 20K. Compiled to native code (which bundles in all the necessary support routines) it's still only 30K.

To do this yourself, use Projects⇨Properties to select the type of output and then use File⇨Make Cal_proj to do the build. If you're creating native code, turn off most of the advanced optimizations. You can ignore the warning you see in Figure 4-5 if you're confident that your code has no bugs.

The online reference page you'll see if you click Help has a very clear example explaining aliasing, by the way. Unlike the bounds checking, for instance, you may use aliasing inadvertently. I don't check this option because it doesn't appear to make a significant difference in code size.

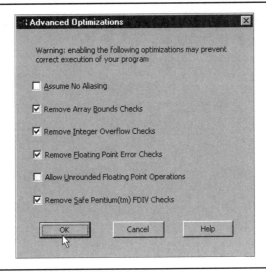

■ **Figure 4-5**
You might ignore this warning.

If you want a perpetual calendar utility, change the title and do something with the OK and Cancel buttons. You might have the OK button end the program and replace Cancel with Today, which would turn the calendar back to today. You could also just delete both buttons and give the others a bit more space.

A perpetual calendar utility is one nice freebie outgrowth of this project, but it wasn't my goal. I want a popup calendar that I can use in other projects for entering dates. The nice small size of this project suggests that it will do well in that role.

Now we have to make it convenient to drop into other programs.

Creating a Data Entry Form

Begin by creating a data entry form, like the one you see in Figure 4-6.

I want to have the date box display a default date. When focus moves to this box, I want the calendar to pop up, set to the default date. After the user sets a date and clicks OK (or presses Enter), I want the user's selected date to be displayed in the date box, and I want the focus to move to the next control. (I don't actually want the user to be able to type into the date box. That opens the possibility of bad dates.)

Use Project⇨Properties to set this new form as the project's startup.

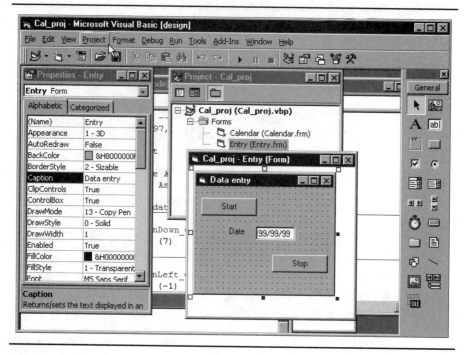

Figure 4-6
Designing a sample data entry form.

I don't want achieving this to be a lot of trouble. Now let me give you some advice concerning the mistakes I made when I started trying to achieve this result.

Beware of GotFocus and LostFocus Events

For my first try, I used `GotFocus` and `LostFocus` events in the `TextBox` control. I successfully programmed several infinite loops, each of which required pressing the hardware reboot button. If that's not your idea of fun, study this sequence carefully:

- `TextBox` gains focus

- `TextBox.GotFocus` launches calendar

- `TextBox` loses focus

- `TextBox.LostFocus` event triggered!

- User enters date, drops calendar
- `TextBox.GotFocus` is called again
- Focus moves to next control
- `TextBox.LostFocus` is called again

If you run your form as it stands now, the `TextBox`'s `GotFocus` is called when control passes to it. Then its `LostFocus` is called when control leaves for the next stop. If you add a calendar popup, you add two new events. The `TextBox` loses focus when the calendar pops up and gets focus back when the calendar drops down.

The GotFocus Solution

What works is code like this in the `GotFocus` event handler:

```
Static running As Boolean ' Initial value = False

If running Then
    running = False
Else
    running = True
    ' pop up the calendar and get date
End If
```

The `Static` variable retains its value for the life of the program. Visual Basic initializes it to a `False` value.

HIGH RISK PROGRAMMING

This program depends on Visual Basic intitializing the `Static` variable to a `False` value, and it's not documented.

Memo To Bill Gates

Java and C++ let us initialize our statics explicitly. Don't you think that's a good idea, Bill?

The first time focus moves to the date field, this event is trigerred. Running is `False`, so the `Else` portion of the logic executes. This sets running to `True` and pops up the calendar. (This control loses focus; the calendar gets it.)

When the user selects a date and drops the calendar, this control regains focus. The second time, running is `True`, so all we need to do is reset running to its initial `False` state, ready for the user to come back to this field.

Of course, that skips a lot of details. Let's start by programming the Start and Stop buttons.

The Start and Stop Buttons

I've included these buttons so that you can clearly see the issues involved with focus. When the user clicks Start, I want the focus to move to the date (`TextBox`) control. Unfortunately, the `Form` property that keeps track of focus isn't directly available to us.

Memo To Bill Gates

Wouldn't it be nice, Bill, if we could control focus directly and simply? All we need is to be able to set the Focus property, which you already have anyway.

You can use the `SendKeys` statement to stuff a tab character into the keyboard buffer, this way:

```
SendKeys "{tab}" ' presses the tab key
```

A slightly better approach — what happens above if the user has also typed? — is to turn the `Visible` property off and on. When it turns off, focus moves to the next control that can receive it. Turning it back on won't bring focus back, but if you do it immediately, you won't even see a blink. This is my event handler for the Start (`Command1`) button:

```
Private Sub Command1_Click()
    Command1.Visible = False ' Remove focus
    Command1.Visible = True
End Sub
```

Next let's program the Stop button (`Command2`) to live up to its name. To stop the main form, you use the `Unload` statement. This is the code:

```
Private Sub Command2_Click()
    Unload Me
End Sub
```

What would be consistent with everything else we're writing is this:

```
Private Sub Command2_Click()
    Me.Unload ' ERROR, no Unload method

        ' or just

    Unload ' ditto
End Sub
```

You can't do this because there's no `Unload` method. If you've been wondering, "Why Me?" you now see a case where Me is necessary.

Memo To Bill Gates

Bill, why a separate statement? An `Unload` method would be consistent with all the other methods, wouldn't it? That's what Java does. That's what keeps Java's language tiny compared to Visual Basic.

If it's OK

Now let's turn our attention to the calendar form-based class. We still need to program the OK and Cancel buttons. The OK button is trivial and Cancel isn't much harder. For OK, all we need to do is turn the Visible property off:

```
Private Sub btnOK_Click()
    Visible = False
End Sub
```

This is the same as calling the `Hide` method, by the way.

Did you notice that on the `Entry` form I left the default button names, `Command1` and `Command2`, but here I've taken the trouble to give the buttons proper (descriptive) names? The `Entry` form is throwaway code. It's just there to check out the `Calendar` class. The `Calendar`, on the other hand, is permanent code.

I guess you're probably wondering now if there's any method in my occasional use of Hungarian notation (that's using type-descriptive prefixes, like `btn`, on variable names). Microsoft is Hungarian happy! It was invented by their language guru, Charles Simonyi, who was born in Hungary.

These prefixes group all like-prefixed variables together. All the btnXxxx variables come together on the object (left) dropdown list in the code editor, and on the dropdown list at the top of the Properties window, for examples. In the case of form controls, that's exactly what I want, so I use consistent prefixes.

Other times, that's not what I want, so I don't use prefixes. For most variable names, I prefer long, descriptive names. I use underscores and all lowercase to distinguish my variables from Visual Basic's names. If you see first_name and last_name used in code, do you need another clue to the fact that they're String variables?

My last convention is to use tiny — one or two letters — names when a variable comes and goes in a tiny section of code. My personal rule is that this is acceptable if you can see the variable's declaration within a few lines (say, a modestly-sized code editor window's worth) of every use of the variable.

Now let's move on.

If it's Cancelled

The user might flip the pages of the calendar and then decide that he or she was better off originally. On a Cancel button click, I want to reset the date to its initial state.

What you expect the order of these events (listed alphabetically, here) is this:

- Activate
- Initialize
- Load

Drop a msgbox() or debug.print() call into each one and then launch your form. It's probably not what you would guess. Never make assumptions about event order. Always test.

What we need to do is trap the hi_date in another Private date variable. I've called mine initial_hi_date (another good example of a name that doesn't need a prefix to identify its type). Go ahead and add one of your own in the General Declarations section.

Then in Activate, drop in this line:

```
Private Sub Form_Activate()
    initial_hi_date = hi_date ' used for Cancel click
End Sub
```

Putting this in `Activate` (not `Load` or `Initialize`) lets the code that creates the calendar call the `set_hi_date` method. You'll trap the last value of `hi_date` before the form actually appeared for the user, which is just what you want.

With that preparation, the Cancel button's code is simple:

```
Private Sub btnCancel_Click()
    set_hi_date (initial_hi_date)
    Visible = False
End Sub
```

While you're in the `Calendar.frm` code add a routine to retrieve the highlighted date, like this:

```
Public Function get_hi_date()
    get_hi_date = hi_date
End Function
```

Now everything's in place for us to code the `GotFocus` method.

In Entry.frm

First, set the `Text1.text` to a valid date. You can do this by setting the property at design time. A better solution is to use the `Load` or `Initialize` event in `Entry.frm`, this way:

```
Text1.Text = Date
```

Now add the code in Listing 4-4 to your `Text1`'s `GotFocus` event handler:

Listing 4-4
The Form gets the job done

```
Private Sub Text1_GotFocus()
    Static running As Boolean ' initially False

    If running Then

        running = False
    Else

        running = True

        Dim c As New Calendar
        c.set_hi_date Text1.Text
```

(continued)

The Form gets the job done

```
        c.Show 1 ' Modal
        Text1.Text = CStr(c.get_hi_date)

        ' note c goes out of scope immediately

    End If

    Text1.Visible = False ' lose focus
    Text1.Visible = True

End Sub
```

I mentioned that setting `Visible` to `False` was the same as calling the `Hide` method. The opposite isn't quite true. Setting `Visible` to `True` is the same as calling `Show` with a zero or no parameter, which launches a nonmodal form. Be sure to launch a modal calendar — `Show(1)` — or your calendar `Form` will live forever.

I think it's a bug, but Visual Basic 4 worked the same way. Even when your last reference to a nonmodal form is released and it's not `Visible`, the `Form` lives on. Even when you explicitly `Unload` it, the `Form` lives on. You need to do something brutal (using the `End` statement works) to kill a nonmodal `Form`.

Memo To Bill Gates

Bill, the nice thing about Java, not to mention the rest of Visual Basic, is that when you stop using an object, it's automatically released. Memory is returned to the free pool. What's the point in breaking this rule for nonmodal forms?

When you run this code, you'll see exactly the effect we discussed. Clicking the Start button launches the calendar. When you select a date and click OK or Cancel, the `TextBox` control is updated and focus moves to the Stop button.

This means that simply tapping Enter accepts the initial, default date. This is important for fast data entry.

There's only one problem with this code. You had to write a big event handler to launch the calendar. Wouldn't it be nicer to encapsulate all this logic elsewhere?

A Classy Solution

When you see the word *encapsulate*, I hope you immediately thought class! A new class will handle this job nicely. Go ahead and add one (Project⇨Add Class Module). I've named mine PopCal because its job is to pop up a calendar.

Try this on your own. If you have trouble, look ahead to Listing 4-5. What you want to do is move the code from the GotFocus event handler of Text1 to a get_date() method of the new PopCal class. Have this method accept a TextBox parameter. Then use that parameter's name where we were using Text1 in the GotFocus method.

Then at the top of your Entry Form, add a new variable, like this:

```
Dim popup_calendar As New PopCal
```

That let's you reduce the code in your GotFocus event handler to just this:

```
Private Sub Text1_GotFocus()
    popup_calendar.get_date Text1
End Sub
```

From now on, when you want a popup calendar over a text box, you'll need to declare one and add exactly that one line. If you need three dates in an entry form, each additional date requires another line of code. That's just about as simple a solution as you could find.

The Unified Field Theory

Of course, using a class module and a form module means that you need to add both to your project. An even better solution would be to have just a single module.

After discovering relativity, Einstein spent the rest of his life looking for the theory that would unify forces like magnetism and gravity. He didn't find it. I'm not as smart as Einstein. I've spent a little time trying to reduce this to just one module, but I've not been able to do it. I know that some of you are smarter than I am. Maybe you can do it.

Teachers just swell up with pride when they see their students go on to pass their own knowledge. So help me out, here. As a hint, in Java you can attach methods to the class, so you don't need an object to call them. In Visual Basic you might be able to do the same.

I know that you can put a public method in `Calendar.frm` and call it this way:

```
' With object:
    dim c as new calendar
    c.method()

' Without object:
    Calendar.method()
```

I also know that this isn't documented and seems to create one of those unkillable ghost Forms. Good luck.

THE FULL PROGRAM

For those of you whose kid's bubble gum has ruined this book's disk, these are the full listings for the finished calendar project.

On disk these are in 04-05.ZIP. Listing 4-5a is the test form; 4-5b is the PopCal class, and 4-5c is the Calendar class. The portion of `Calendar.frm` not visible in the code editor is listed in Appendix A.

The Test Entry Form

Listing 4-5a
Entry.frm is throwaway code

```
Option Explicit

Dim popup_calendar As New Popcal

Private Sub Command1_Click()
    Command1.Visible = False ' Remove focus
    Command1.Visible = True
End Sub

Private Sub Command2_Click()
    Unload Me
End Sub
```

```
Private Sub Form_Initialize()
    Text1.Text = CStr(Date)
End Sub

Private Sub Text1_GotFocus()
    popup_calendar.get_date Text1
End Sub
```

The PopCal Class

Listing 4-5b
PopCal.cls links TextBoxes to popup calendars

```
'PopCal.cls — cover method for calling calendar form
'Copyright 1997, Martin L. Rinehart

Option Explicit

Public Sub get_date(tb As TextBox)
    Static running As Boolean ' initially False

    If running Then

        running = False

    Else

        running = True

        Dim c As New Calendar
        c.set_hi_date tb.Text
        c.Show 1 ' Modal
        tb.Text = CStr(c.get_hi_date)

        ' c goes out of scope immediately

    End If

    tb.Visible = False ' Lose focus
    tb.Visible = True

End Sub

' end of PopCal.cls
```

The Form-Based Calendar Class

Listing 4-5c
The general calendar

```
' Calendar.Frm — Form-based Calendar Class
' Copyright 1997, Martin L. Rinehart

Option Explicit

Private hi_date As Date ' highlighted date
Private hi_day As Byte ' day 0 to 41

Private start_date As Date ' Sunday of week 0
Private initial_hi_date As Date

Private Sub btnCancel_Click()
    set_hi_date (initial_hi_date)
    Visible = False
End Sub

Private Sub btnDown_Click()
    change_day (7)
End Sub

Private Sub btnLeft_Click()
    change_day (-1)
End Sub

Private Sub btnNextMo_Click()

    Dim dt As Date, mo As Byte
    dt = start_date + 6 ' Saturday, 1st week
    mo = Month(dt)

    If mo < 12 Then
        dt = Str(mo + 1) & "/1/" & Str(Year(dt))
    Else
        dt = "1/1/" & Str(Year(dt) + 1)
    End If

    reset_start dt

End Sub

Private Sub btnNextYr_Click()
    Dim dt As Date, new_date As Date
```

```vbnet
        dt = start_date + 6

        new_date = Str(Month(dt)) + "/1/" + Str(Year(dt) + 1)

        reset_start new_date

End Sub

Private Sub btnOK_Click()
    Visible = False
End Sub

Private Sub btnPrevMo_Click()

    Dim dt As Date, mo As Byte
    dt = start_date + 6 ' Saturday, 1st week
    mo = Month(dt)

    If mo > 1 Then
        dt = Str(mo - 1) & "/1/" & Str(Year(dt))
    Else
        dt = "12/1/" & Str(Year(dt) - 1)
    End If

    reset_start dt

End Sub

Private Sub btnPrevYr_Click()

    Dim dt As Date, new_date As Date

    dt = start_date + 6

    new_date = Str(Month(dt)) + "/1/" + Str(Year(dt) - 1)

    reset_start new_date

End Sub

Private Sub btnRight_Click()
    change_day (1)
End Sub

Private Sub btnUp_Click()
    change_day (-7)
End Sub
```

(continued)

The general calendar

```
Private Sub day_labels_Click(Index As Integer)

' Do nothing if the current day was clicked
    If Index = hi_day Then Exit Sub

    Call hilite_day(hi_day, False)

    hi_day = Index
    hi_date = start_date + hi_day
    Call hilite_day(hi_day, True)

End Sub

Private Sub Form_Activate()
    initial_hi_date = hi_date ' used for Cancel click
End Sub

Private Sub Form_Initialize()
    set_hi_date (Date)
End Sub

Private Sub Form_Resize()

' Exit immediately if the calendar is minimized
    If WindowState = vbMinimized Then Exit Sub

' Don't let it get too tiny
    Const min_wd = 3500
    Const min_ht = 3500

    If Width < min_wd Then Width = min_wd
    If Height < min_ht Then Height = min_ht

' Leave border space

    Const tp_space = 220
    Const lf_space = 100
    Const bt_space = 940
    Const rt_space = 1000

' Compute grid size
    Dim grid_ht As Integer, grid_wd As Integer
    grid_ht = Height - tp_space - bt_space
    grid_wd = Width - lf_space - rt_space

    Dim day_ht As Integer, day_wd As Integer
    day_ht = grid_ht / 6
```

```
        day_wd = grid_wd / 7

        grid_ht = 6 * day_ht ' correct for roundoff
        grid_wd = 7 * day_wd

        Dim i As Byte ' Loop counter

' For performance, hide the day labels
    For i = 0 To 41
        day_labels(i).Visible = False
    Next

' And the buttons
    btnUp.Visible = False
    btnLeft.Visible = False
    btnRight.Visible = False
    btnDown.Visible = False
    ' btnOK.Visible should get focus
    btnCancel.Visible = False
    btnPrevYr.Visible = False
    btnPrevMo.Visible = False
    btnNextMo.Visible = False
    btnNextYr.Visible = False

' Place horizontal lines
    With Hlines(0)
        .X1 = lf_space
        .X2 = lf_space + grid_wd
        .Y1 = tp_space
        .Y2 = .Y1
        .Visible = True
    End With

    For i = 1 To 6
        With Hlines(i)
            .X1 = Hlines(0).X1
            .X2 = Hlines(0).X2
            .Y1 = Hlines(i - 1).Y1 + day_ht
            .Y2 = .Y1
            .Visible = True
        End With
    Next

' Place vertical lines
    With Vlines(0)
        .X1 = Hlines(0).X1
        .X2 = .X1
```

(continued)

The general calendar

```
                .Y1 = Hlines(0).Y1
                .Y2 = Hlines(6).Y1
                .Visible = True
        End With

        For i = 1 To 7
            With Vlines(i)
                .X1 = Vlines(i - 1).X1 + day_wd
                .X2 = .X1
                .Y1 = Vlines(0).Y1
                .Y2 = Vlines(0).Y2
                .Visible = True
            End With
        Next

    ' Position column labels
        For i = 0 To 6
            col_labels(i).Left = Vlines(i).X1
        Next

    ' Size and position day labels
        Const inset = 20 ' space around label within day
        Dim ht As Integer, wd As Integer

        ht = day_ht - (2 * inset) ' top and bottom inset
        wd = day_wd - (2 * inset) ' left and right

        Dim week As Byte, day As Byte, dnum As Byte

        For week = 0 To 5
            For day = 0 To 6
                dnum = day + (week * 7)
                With day_labels(dnum)
                    .Top = Hlines(week).Y1 + inset
                    .Left = Vlines(day).X1 + inset
                    .Height = ht
                    .Width = wd
                    .Visible = True
                End With
            Next day
        Next week

    'Position month labels
        top_mo_label.Left = Vlines(7).X1 + 40
        ' top, height and width as per design time

        bot_mo_label.Left = top_mo_label.Left
```

```
    bot_mo_label.Top = Hlines(change_week - 1).Y1
    ' height and width as per design time

' position the diamond buttons
    btnUp.Left = Width - 700
    btnLeft.Left = Width - 900
    btnRight.Left = Width - 500
    btnDown.Left = btnUp.Left

    btnUp.Visible = True
    btnLeft.Visible = True
    btnRight.Visible = True
    btnDown.Visible = True

' position the bottom buttons
    Dim bsize As Integer, hbsize As Integer
    hbsize = ((Width - 50) / 4) - lf_space
        ' half buttons

    ' Eliminate twips->pixel roundoff problems
        hbsize = hbsize / Screen.TwipsPerPixelX
        hbsize = hbsize * Screen.TwipsPerPixelX

    bsize = 2 * hbsize                  ' full buttons

    With btnOK
        .Top = Height - 640
        .Left = lf_space
        .Width = bsize
        ' .Height as per design
        ' .Visible stays True to keep focus
    End With

    With btnCancel
        .Top = btnOK.Top
        .Left = btnOK.Left + btnOK.Width + _
            2 * lf_space
        .Width = bsize
        .Visible = True
    End With

    With btnPrevYr
        .Top = Height - 900
        .Left = btnOK.Left
        .Width = hbsize
        .Visible = True
    End With
```

(continued)

The general calendar

```
With btnPrevMo
    .Top = btnPrevYr.Top
    .Left = btnPrevYr.Left + btnPrevYr.Width
    .Width = hbsize
    .Visible = True
End With

With btnNextMo
    .Top = btnPrevYr.Top
    .Left = btnCancel.Left
    .Width = hbsize
    .Visible = True
End With

With btnNextYr
    .Top = btnPrevYr.Top
    .Left = btnNextMo.Left + btnNextMo.Width
    .Width = hbsize
    .Visible = True
End With

End Sub

Public Sub set_hi_date(dt As Date)

' first approximation: 1st of the month
    start_date = Str(Month(dt)) + "/1/" + Str(Year(dt))

' now find Sunday
    start_date = start_date - WeekDay(start_date) + 1

' unhilite current one
    Call hilite_day(hi_day, False)

' set highlighted day and date
    hi_date = dt
    hi_day = hi_date - start_date
    Call hilite_day(hi_day, True)

    set_day_captions

End Sub

Private Sub set_day_captions()

    Dim i As Byte
    For i = 0 To 41
```

```
            day_labels(i).Caption = Str(day(start_date + i))
    Next

' label week 1
    Call set_mo_caption(top_mo_label, 1)

' label next week where month changes
    Call set_mo_caption(bot_mo_label, change_week())

End Sub

Private Sub set_mo_caption(lbl As Label, wk As Byte)
    Dim dt As Date ' Saturday in the specified week
    dt = start_date + ((wk * 7) - 1)

    lbl.Caption = month_name(Month(dt)) + " " + Str(Year(dt))
End Sub

Private Function month_name(mo As Byte)
    month_name = Mid( _
        "Jan.Feb.Mar.Apr.May JuneJulyAug.Sep.Oct.Nov.Dec.", _
        (mo * 4) - 3, _
        4)

End Function

Private Sub hilite_day(day_num As Byte, _
    is_hi As Boolean)

    With day_labels(day_num)
        If is_hi Then
            .ForeColor = vbWhite
            .BackColor = vbBlack
        Else
            .ForeColor = vbButtonText
            .BackColor = vbButtonFace
        End If
    End With

End Sub

Private Function change_week() As Byte

' new month starts in week 5 or 6

    If day(start_date + 34) < 8 Then
        change_week = 5
```

(continued)

The general calendar

```
    Else
        change_week = 6
    End If

End Function

Private Sub change_day(delta As Integer)

    Dim new_day As Integer
    new_day = hi_day + delta
' exit on invalid delta
    If new_day < 0 Then Exit Sub
    If new_day > 41 Then Exit Sub

' change the day
    Call hilite_day(hi_day, False)
    hi_day = new_day
    hi_date = start_date + hi_day
    Call hilite_day(hi_day, True)

End Sub

Private Sub reset_start(dt As Date)

    ' resets the start date, but doesn't move highlight

    start_date = dt - WeekDay(dt) + 1

    hi_date = start_date + hi_day

    set_day_captions

End Sub

Public Function get_hi_date()
    get_hi_date = hi_date
End Function

' end of Calendar.frm
```

Summary

Congratulations! You have a professional calendar class and a PopCal class that makes it trivial to pop up a calendar anytime your applications want a date. Let's review how we got here.

We started looking at the keyboard events. `KeyPress()` is simple, but it doesn't report the navigation keys, such as arrows. `KeyDown` is more sophisticated. It reports both the key and the shift status (shift, Ctrl, and Alt keys).

We used the `KeyDown` method to move the date in response to arrow key presses.

Then we went on to add a diamond of buttons that provided an alternate method for moving the day highlight from both the keyboard and with mouse clicks. To our chagrin, we discovered that adding buttons makes Visual Basic take the arrow keys out of the `KeyDown` event class. The arrow keys are reserved by Visual Basic for moving focus. Our button diamond provides the only keyboard access to the date highlight.

Then we added buttons that would turn the pages on our calendar a month or a year at a time. A little date logic in the event-handling methods of our calendar class turned our calendar into a full-fledged, professional tool.

Finally, we programmed the OK and Cancel buttons of the calendar and mastered calling it from the `GotFocus` event of a `TextBox` on a sample data entry form. The logic here was not trivial. As a last step, we added a class that took over this logic. Through that class, the complications are nicely hidden from our applications.

In these early chapters we've covered most of the basics and put them into use. You've mastered the fundamentals, and you should be able to go off and build your own classes, from forms or otherwise. In the rest of this book, we'll create lots more useful objects, and we'll tie them together, including our calendar, in our object-oriented MyTime application.

AN OBJECT-
ORIENTED
DATABASE DESIGN

5

*R*eal applications need data. Visual Basic features the very powerful Data control, Microsoft's potent Jet database engine, and through ODBC, access to data in every major relational DBMS.

So we're going to write our own object database.

Crazy? I don't think so. When you write even the simplest Visual Basic application, you're using your own code plus code in the Dynamic Link Libraries (DLLs) that Microsoft supplies. The minimum set of DLLs — just for launching a "Hello, World!" form — tips the scales at about 3MB. This is an approximation of the RAM you'll be using at run time.

Of course, Windows features memory management, so it can work with less than the full application in memory. But as you know, when Windows needs to swap portions of your code in and out of RAM frequently, performance starts to degrade. It can degrade precipitously if the RAM needed seriously exceeds the RAM available. This becomes a serious problem on even well-equipped hardware as users run more than one program.

So adding code size, even if your program might fit into available RAM, is a negative. Dropping a Data control into your form approximately doubles the 3MB minimum. That's right, the Data control costs about 3MB in added code size! The power comes at a price.

If you're even thinking about ActiveX controls that your users will be downloading over the Web, the cost here can become prohibitive. Megabytes of download are out of the question for Web browsing.

We're going to build a tiny object database that you can drop into an application at almost no cost. I have pedagogical and practical purposes in mind.

First, the pedagogical pupose: it will teach you about *polymorphism*. You've already read about it as a theoretical topic. The simple database we'll build is an extreme example of the power of polymorphism. It will really show you just what tremendous power, flexibility, and simplicity this can bring to your classes. You'll want to use polymorphism all over after you see how this works.

On the practical side, I want to achieve two goals. First, I want our OODB to be tiny. Tiny size means minimal features. That means that this object database will only meet modest needs. That's OK. Just because something doesn't solve all your problems doesn't mean it's not useful. And because you'll know the code completely, you'll be able to add a feature or two that will extend it just enough to meet lots of your applications' requirements.

My second goal is to make it convenient. I'll settle for just a little more trouble than dropping in a Data control, but I won't accept a lot more trouble. This object database should be useful when you're writing a small application that needs modest data storage (your "to do" list or your personal phone manager). It should fit in larger applications when a small portion of the application has modest database needs. In both cases, it's critical that you can just drop it in and let it work without needing to invest any serious programming time.

In this chapter we'll begin by looking at RAM size. Although it's almost impossible to measure directly, the Setup Wizard does a very nice job of collecting all the .DLLs an application requires and telling us how big they are. It's a crude approximation — like counting MIPS, *Millions of Instructions Per Second*, or, as some say, *Meaningless Indication of Processor Speed* — but it's a readily available measure, good for order-of-magnitude approximations.

Then we'll take a close look at early and late binding. You'll see why early binding is preferred for runtime speed, but sometimes you'll use late binding for code flexibility.

Then we'll go on to the design of our object database, or ODB, class. This will take advantage of polymorphism in a way that makes an otherwise dauntingly complex job a simple, straightforward proposition.

MEASURING SIZE WITH THE SETUP WIZARD

As I noted in the introduction of this topic, we'll be using executable size as a crude measure of RAM requirements. This is a meaningful order-of-magnitude approximation if you're careful about its use.

Within a single product (for examples, in Visual Basic, Visual C++, or Visual J++), this measurement will give you a feel for code size. It would be completely invalid across products (comparing a Visual Basic application to a Visual J++ app, for example). I'll start with a quick tour of the Visual Basic Application Setup Wizard. We'll use it to measure a trivial application's size and then to check the size added when we invoke the Jet database engine through a Data Access Object.

A Sample Project

To use the Setup Wizard, you need an application. Figure 5-1 shows mine. To duplicate it, create a new, standard .EXE project. Drop a text box control on the form and set these properties:

- The Form's Name
- The Form's Caption
- The TextBox's Text

To be consistent with our other work, I'll show its code in Listing 5-1, which is one of the files in 05-01 on your disk. As you can see, I've done this for thoroughness because the code I've added is null.

Listing 5-1
A null program for size testing

```
' frmSzTst.frm — a size-testing project
' Copyright 1997, Martin L. Rinehart

Option Explicit

' there is no code in this project!

' end of frmSzTst.frm
```

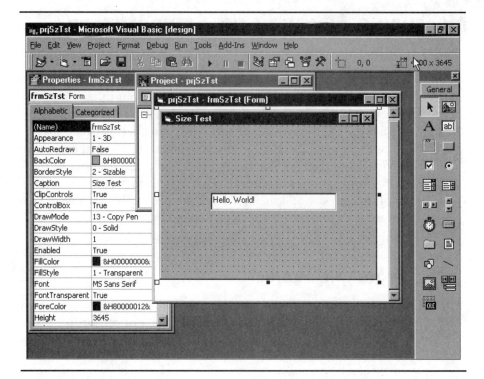

Figure 5-1
A trivial, Hello, World! project.

Using the Application Setup Wizard

If you're comfortable with this Wizard, skip this section. If you haven't used the Setup Wizard, it's a delight.

Collecting all the files you need for an application is a nuisance at best. How do you know what .DLLs are required for your application? Without the Setup Wizard, you probably don't, but the Wizard knows!

In this section, we'll use the Setup Wizard to collect the necessary information to make a setup program for the SzTst project we just created. You'll find this Wizard in the program group that Visual Basic creates, available on your Programs menu (Start⇨Visual Basic 5⇨Application Setup Wizard). It launches the screen shown in Figure 5-2.

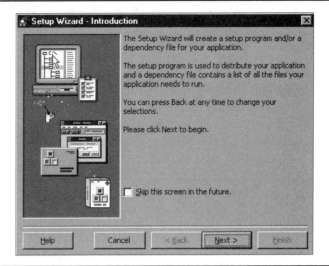

Figure 5-2
Starting the Application Setup Wizard.

Those of you who are using Visual Basic (as opposed to your author, who's writing this book *about* it) will probably want to take advantage of many of those checkboxes that agree not to bother you with these introductory screens after one or two viewings.

Memo To Bill Gates
I have to admit, Bill, those, "Don't show this screen...," options are great! They let us go slow the first time and get the beginners' stuff out of the way. As soon as I finish this book, I'm going to go check 'em all!

Figure 5-3 shows the second screen in the Setup Wizard. Here is where you specify the project and the output. If you don't specify a valid project, the Next button is not available. (The Wizard starts in the Visual Basic installed location, not in the default directory you've specified in your Visual Basic shortcut.)

I've asked for a dependency file only. The other outputs are too time consuming to create, and they're not necessary for size testing.

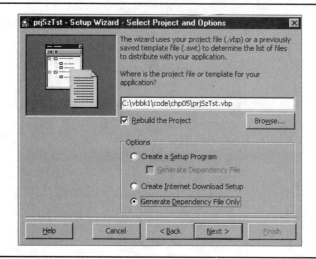

Figure 5-3
Specifying the input project and Wizard output.

The next step, shown in Figure 5-4, has the Wizard working hard (it takes a few seconds) to figure out all the ActiveX components that you use. It lists them for you (our trivial project doesn't use any) and lets you add or remove items from the list. For size testing, leave this list alone!

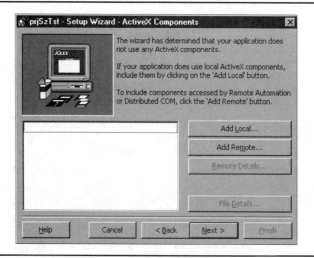

Figure 5-4
Our trivial project has no ActiveX components.

As Figure 5-5 shows, the next screen lists additional dependent files. Again, for size testing you want to leave the Wizard's results exactly as it provides them.

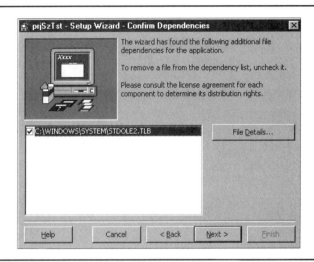

Figure 5-5
Additional files found by the Wizard.

In Figure 5-6 you see the file summary. This list includes all the files that are needed for you to distribute an application that does not require Visual Basic to be loaded on the machine that will run the application.

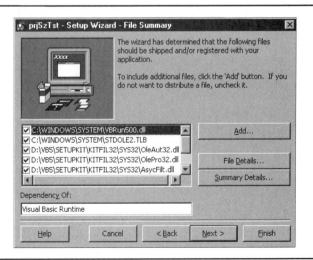

Figure 5-6
The Wizard gives you a complete file list.

Don't press Next at this point! You see that this screen also lets you request file and summary details. The summary details are what we're after. First, though, let's just look at one file's detail. Figure 5-7 shows the data for VBRun500.DLL, a key .DLL in the Visual Basic runtime system.

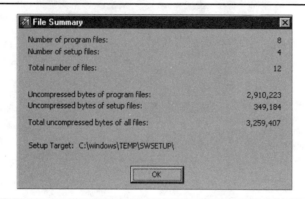

Figure 5-7
The full truth about VBRun500.DLL.

If you've looked at all the individual files of interest, let's go on to the summary data. Figure 5-8 shows the summary report. It may surprise you that such a tiny project requires almost 3MB of executable files.

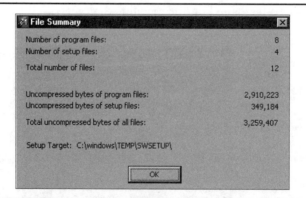

Figure 5-8
There are 2,910,233 bytes in the sample project.

When you read this data, ignore the bytes of setup files. The Wizard very nicely creates the setup program you need to install your application, but you don't want to include its size in the size of the installed program.

You could cancel immediately because you have all the information you need. However, we'll run to completion just so you can see what's next. Figure 5-9 announces that the Wizard is done, although this isn't strictly true.

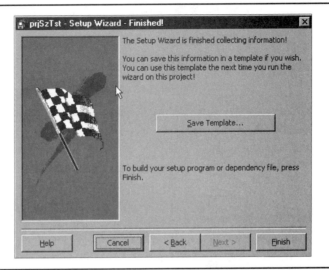

Figure 5-9
The Wizard is almost finished.

I've not found the template offered here to be helpful, although you might want to try it for yourself.

A final screen, which is also graced by a "Don't show this in the future..." checkbox, advises you that you should scan your distribution media for viruses. This is, of course, a good idea, though I'm not sure that we needed to be told.

If you've selected output of a setup program, it will be written at this point. As you can see, sending even a minimal application to floppy disks will take some time.

Adding a Data Access Object

For those of you who skipped the last section, the bottom line was that our Wizard needed 2,910,233 bytes for the uncompressed program files in our minimal application. Let's drop in a Data Access Object and link it to a database so that we can see how much code that adds.

Begin by dragging a Data Access Object control onto your size-testing form. Then choose Database Name on the Properties list. Select any handy database file, here. I'm grabbing the first one I see in the \VB5\Samples directory, as Figure 5-10 shows.

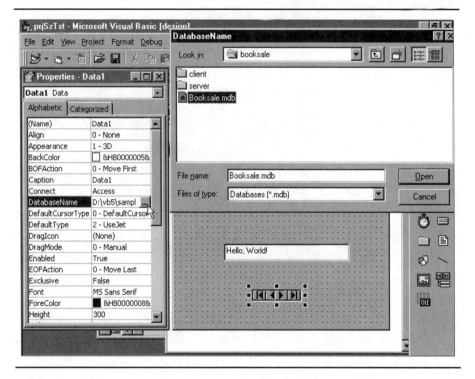

Figure 5-10
Connecting a Data Access Object to a database.

Again, Listing 5-2, included for completeness, shows the null code I've added. Disk listing 05-02 includes the complete details of the data connection, but I've done nothing other than adding the control and choosing a Database Name property.

Listing 5-2
Again, the code is null

```
' frmSzTst.frm — a size-testing project
' Copyright 1997, Martin L. Rinehart

Option Explicit

' there is no code in this project!
' second size test includes DAO control

' end of frmSzTst.frm
```

Of course, the statement that "there is no code in this project!" isn't really true. The code shown here in the listing is the part you normally edit. The full code includes Begin/End blocks describing the properties of all your controls. In this case, the DAO looks like this:

```
Begin VB.Data Data1
    Caption         =   "Data1"
    Connect         =   "Access"
    DatabaseName    =   _
       "D:\vb5\samples\clisvr\booksale\Booksale.mdb"
    DefaultCursorType=  0  'DefaultCursor
    DefaultType     =   2  'UseODBC
    Exclusive       =   0    'False
    Height          =   300
    Left            =   1680
    Options         =   0
    ReadOnly        =   0  'False
    RecordsetType   =   1  'Dynaset
    RecordSource    =   ""
    Top             =   2400
    Width           =   1140
End
```

(The long line — for DatabaseName — has been reformatted manually to fit this book. I'm not sure that this will actually work. If it does, I have no guarantee that it will work in the next release because none of this is documented.)

In the disk copy, I've used the Make option on the File menu to create an .EXE. It's an admirably compact 7K. Let's take a look at the whole story with the Setup Wizard.

Checking Size with the Setup Wizard

With that DAO control in place, it's time to return to the Setup Wizard and find out how much additional runtime support is needed. Launch the Application Setup Wizard again and run it as before.

After the preliminary screens, where you pick your project and output, you'll see a new screen, shown here in Figure 5-11.

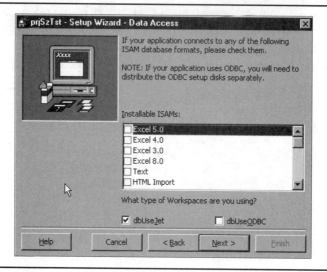

Figure 5-11
The DAO control triggers a new Wizard screen.

Here you can check specific, product-dependent choices. You also select Jet or ODBC connectivity. (Use Jet for local database work, ODBC for remote SQL databases.)

The next screen lists two files, whereas it only listed one for the simpler project. Then the screen with *Working* in the title stares at you while the Wizard tracks down everything the program needs to run. You'll see that it works on items like Database Drivers that it didn't do in our first run.

When it's done, you'll have another chance to order a summary. Mine is shown in Figure 5-12.

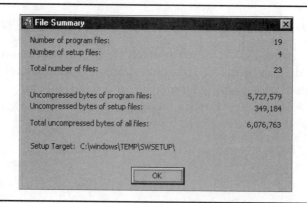

Figure 5-12
Summary details with Jet DAO control.

As you can see, this time we have 5,727,579 bytes of program files. That's almost doubled from the minimum. Adding the innocent-looking DAO control added almost 3MB to the executable files.

The .DEP File Output

The output of the Application Setup Wizard is a dependency file: an ASCII text file that shows key data, including necessary Windows Registry data, for each file needed by your application. It's name is your project (.VBP) file's name with a .DEP extension. The Wizard writes it in the directory where it finds the .VBP. This is a sample:

```
[VBRUN500.DLL <0009>]
Register=$(DLLSelfRegister)
Dest=$(WinSysPath)
Date=10/1/1996
Time=0:00:00
Version=5.0.33.30
CABFileName=VBRun500.cab
CABDefaultURL=
CABINFFile=VBRun500.inf
Uses1=

[STDOLE2.TLB <0009>]
Register=$(TLBRegister)
Dest=$(WinSysPathSysFile)
Date=9/30/1996
Time=0:00:00
Version=2.20.4054.1
CABFileName=
CABDefaultURL=
CABINFFile=
Uses1=OleAut32.dll
Uses2=OlePro32.dll
Uses3=AsycFilt.dll
Uses4=

[OLEAUT32.DLL <0009>]
Register=$(DLLSelfRegister)
Dest=$(WinSysPathSysFile)
. . .
```

The Wizard will also create, per your specification, a setup program, a set of floppy disks (or a directory, if you'll be distributing on CD-ROM) ready for installation, or an Internet-ready directory for users to download your application.

Much as I like the Setup Wizard's untiring willingness to do a very dull job, I don't like what it's telling me. Clearly, 3MB of additional executable files is more than I want for simple database applications.

Before you go on, try a little experiment. We're going to write a trivially simple object-oriented database. It will be able to store and retrieve simple objects. A "simple" object for our purpose will be one that does not include variable-length arrays or other items that cannot be written to a fixed-format record.

I'd like you to write down your estimate of the size of our project after we add our little OO database. We'll be able to read and write objects to the database and navigate (next object, previous object, first/last, and so on) among our stored objects. It won't be fancy, but for small uses it will serve nicely.

Before we get to programming, we'll look at a subject that sometimes confuses object newcomers.

Binding: Better Early than Late

We're going to use polymorphism in a way that makes this code so simple it will seem like we're cheating. We're also going to use *late binding*, which is actually cheating. It's relatively inefficient compared to *early binding*, which I'll explain in just a bit.

First, though, I want to assure you that the cheat is *not* in our use of polymorphism. If we took the trouble to change from using the generic Object data type to using an interface and the *implements* keyword we could use our polymorphism with early (efficient, non-cheating) binding. In fact, we wouldn't have to change our code more than a very little bit and we'd be truly elegant.

Java uses this technique in an almost identical way, including the *implements* keyword, but the concepts would get ahead of ourselves. For now, we'll use late binding so that we can focus on polymorphism.

When do You Want to be Bound?

Early and *late*, when used with *binding*, refer to compile time and run time, respectively. An object may be bound at compile time, which saves the work of binding at runtime.

Binding, in this usage, means matching a call to an actual subroutine (object method) to a specific bit of code. If the compiler does this matching, the work needn't be done at runtime, when it slows things down.

So the answer is simple: you always prefer early binding. Late binding is used only when you don't have a choice.

When are we Bound?

Let's look at an example of early binding. In Java, all the Java-supplied objects have a toPrint() method. Sun recommends that you write a toPrint() method for your objects, too. The toPrint() routine is loosely specified.

A toPrint() method provides a human-readable string version of an object. This is an excellent idea for debugging. It works as well in Visual Basic as it does in Java. In Visual Basic, it lets you poke in simple statements like this:

```
Dim foo As whatever
Set foo = New whatever
    ' whatever has a toPrint() method

. . . other code manipulates foo

Debug.Print foo.toPrint ' take a look!
```

You'll see that I've stolen this idea for our OO database, too.

The previous fragment shows an example of early binding. The compiler knows that foo is an object of the whatever class. The compiler knows where the whatever.toPrint() method is located, so it can replace the call to foo.toPrint with an actual subroutine address.

Now let's look at a routine that does debugging output for any object you throw at it. It assumes that you've coded toPrint() methods for all the classes it will be given:

```
Public Sub dumper(o As Object)

    Debug.Print ""
    Debug.Print "-------------=x13"
    Debug.Print "Object is:"
    Debug.Print o.toPrint

End Sub
```

This routine provides a little separation between objects in your Immediate window. It relies on the object's toPrint() method to do the heavy lifting. Presumably your toPrint() methods include at least a name, class name, and values of key properties.

The call to `toPrint()` here must be late bound. The compiler only knows that it will get an object variable. It might be some object that the user picks by clicking, for example. The compiler has no way of binding the `o.toPrint()` call to a specific bit of code.

At runtime, a particular object is passed to this routine. The line that does the `toPrint()` begins by calling a routine that knows about what's where. It asks, "Does `o` have a `toPrint()` routine? Where's it located?" When it has the answers to these questions it can actually call the routine (or raise an error).

I don't know how long the late binding process takes. In most C++ compilers, this was a double pointer dereferencing that didn't take much more time than the actual subroutine call. (Again, in my youth I always hacked in to take a look and answer questions like this. Now I know that even with an answer valid for today, I won't have an answer I can depend on tomorrow.)

Microsoft's documentation implies that the late binding process is quite slow. I doubt it, but I'm still going to use early binding whenever I can.

Except, that is, for right now, when I want you to concentrate on the power of polymorphism. We'll let the late binding go by because we know that we can replace it later, via the *implements* concept.

DESIGNING THE DATABASE

At first glance, designing a general-purpose database to store and retrieve objects seems a daunting proposition. If you're in the mood for being intimidated, try to absorb any general-purpose object specification, such as ActiveX, CORBA, or Java Beans. It's complicated!

I'm going to simplify the problem by specifying simple objects only. *Simple* means that the object must be convertible to a fixed-length record. This rules out, for example, variable-length arrays as potential data properties. Still, it leaves a huge universe of design possibilities. In fact, the number of combinations of data properties is infinite.

If we were to restrict ourselves to the Visual Basic intrinsic data types (byte, integer, long, float, boolean, date, string, and so on), we could invent some sort of descriptor record that the class could provide and build from there. But that would eliminate objects and other interesting data member types.

Because Visual Basic depends on object containment as a substitute for inheritance, we're going to need to store objects with other objects as data properties.

What are we going to do?

Polymorphism to the Rescue

Well, it turns out that we can swipe a little bit of Java, add a symetric idea, and reduce the enitre problem down to almost zero. Actually, we'll have our database delegate the problem back to the individual classes, which can handle it easily because they won't worry about a general-case solution. They'll just fend for themselves.

Assume that you can write a `toPrint()`-type routine that formats your object's properties in some regular manner. The `toPrint()` routine will return a string that contains the values of your object's properties. It will be a fixed-length string, and you'll start each value at a fixed position in the string. (Actually, you could get fancier and accommodate some degree of variability in string lengths, for instance, but that's up to you. Our database won't care.)

Next assume that you can also write a `fromPrint()` routine, which will accept a string in whichever format `toPrint()` creates. It will break that string apart into individual property values.

To make a class storable, you'll have to write a `toPrint()` and a `fromPrint()` method. You can get fancy and embed binary data in your string; you can keep it simple and convert numbers and everything else into their ASCII (human-readable) representations. Our ODB won't care. It will know that when it gets an object, it's getting a corresponding `toString()`, so all it has to store is a fixed-length string.

On the return trip, our ODB will retrieve the string and hand it back to the class's `fromPrint()` routine. That will properly stuff the string's information back into the object's properties. Here's a simplified example:

```
' Person object contains:
'     Name As String
'     Address As String
'     Date_of_Birth As Date

' Method code includes:

Public Function to_string()

    to_string = _
        fix_len(Name, 40) & _
        fix_len(Address, 40) & _
        date_to_MMDDYYYY(Date_of_Birth)

End Function
```

```
Public Sub from_string(s As String)
    Name = Left(s, 40)
    Address = Mid(s, 41, 40)
    Date_of_Birth = date_from_MMDDYYYY(Right(s,6))
End Sub
```

Writing a Fixed-Length String

You'll need some support routines, such as `fix_len()`, which forces a
string to a particular length, and date handlers. To fix a string's length you
can first pad it out with blanks and then chop off the piece you want. (This
works for strings of any length, starting at zero).

```
Public Function fix_len(s As String, n As Integer)

    fix_len = Left(s & Space(n), n)

End Function
```

By the way, that's an old APL trick — thinking up an algorithm that doesn't
need `If/Else` logic. APL was invented by IBM's Ken Iverson as a very
compact mathematical notation. It's still used extensively by actuaries and
on Wall Street. APL programmers' code avoids branching.

Converting Dates to String

Dates are a little more trouble but not much. A trick for forcing a day or
month number to two and only two digits is to add 100 and then take the
right two characters:

```
' d is a Date

right(str(Day(d)+100),2) ' returns "01" thru "31"
```

You could convert a date to `MMDDYYYY` this way:

```
Private Function date_to_MMDDYYYY(d As Date)
    date_to_MMDDYYYY = _
        fix_two(Month(d)) & _
        fix_two(Day(d)) & _
        Right(Str(Year(d)),4)
End Function
Private Function fix_two(n As Byte)
    ' returns "00" thru "99" — no error checking!
    fix_two = Right(Str(100+n), 2)
End Function
```

The `fix_two()` routine here is a good example of one that *must* be `Private`. It will function flawlessly for day and month values, but it will fail miserably for any negative value, and it truncates any number over 99. As a `Private` in this context it's good, error-free code. As a `Public`, it's an invitation to disaster.

Retrieving Dates from String

A convenient feature of `Date` variables is that you can put almost anything that looks like a date on the right side of an equal sign and Visual Basic will correctly assign a proper date to the variable. So your `MMDDYYYY_to_date()` function can return a date-holding string, this way:

```
Private Function MMDDYYYY_to_date(s As String)
    MMDDYYYY_to_date = _
        Left(s,2) & "/" & _
        Mid(s,3,2) & "/" & _
        Right(s,4)
End Function
```

Other Conversions

I'll leave it up to you to work up similar routines for time, floats, booleans, and whatever other data types you need. You should always think about the limitations of these routines when you design your whole application. For example, if you're storing 40 characters for the `Name` property, your data entry form should be limited to accepting about 40 characters. If it's critical data, have the `toString()` function carefully query the user when truncation is necessary.

Did you know that the correct name of the United States' large long-distance company is "The American Telephone and Telegraph Company, Inc."? It won't fit in 40 characters. You lawyers may need to allow enough space to fit the whole name, exactly as it appears on the corporate charter. Most of us, though, can find lots of readable abbreviations.

Remember, you don't want a complete set of conversion routines. You want a set exactly fitted to a particular class. If you don't normally use floating-point data, don't encumber your business applications with code that correctly handles IEEE floating-point forms.

Also, go with your own national standards. MMDDYYYY is a natural date for us here in America, but YYYYMMDD has a lot of advantages. An alphabetic sort on YYYYMMDD sorts dates in order, for instance.

A Simple, .DBF-like Structure

Back in the late 1970s, Wayne Ratliff wrote the product that became dBASE II on a primitive, 8-bit microprocessor with a grand total of 48K of RAM. You'd be correct in assuming that he had to find simple ways to do virtually everything. One of his simple designs was the .DBF (DataBase File) structure.

The essence of that structure is a fixed-format header followed by zero or more fixed-length data records. The records have a brief prefix (Wayne used a single byte!), followed by the actual data.

Though our current computers are far more capable, good design is good design. I've essentially borrowed Wayne's .DBF design, simplifying it even further because we'll store just a single string for each object's data. (In a bow to modernity, I've expanded the record prefix from one byte to a wasteful four, though.)

The Database Header

I'll use the extension .ODB to identify my object database files. We'll use one .ODB for each object type that we're storing. The .DBF file stores just one type of record. More sophisticated file structures, such as Microsoft's .MDB, store multiple record types in a single file. This is a valuable improvement, but it's costly in code size.

Critics of the .DBF structure say that you really can't call it a database file; it's really a single table file and multiple tables are required to make a database. You could say the same about our .ODB files with equal justice. I'll not argue, but I'll not let it bother me, either. Simple code works for many needs.

In the header, I've assigned the first 8 bytes as a signature. I'm using *mrVB5odb* as my signature. If you use my format, go ahead and use my signature. If you make even a slight format change, however, use a different signature. The idea is that when your code opens the file it will check the signature before it tries to use the data. If it sees the right signature in a file with the .ODB extension, it's probably the right type of file.

Following the signature I use 32 bytes for the name of the class. (You could use more characters if you needed them.) Finally, I'm using 8 bytes for the record length. That lets me write the length in human-readable ASCII digits. This imposes a very slight runtime cost, but only when the object database file is opened.

The Object Record

The file's header is followed by zero or more records, each holding the toString() representation of an individual object. I'm using a four-byte prefix in front of each object record.

The first two bytes are a carriage return and linefeed pair. If you think about the debugging process, you'll see that this lets us look at our .ODB using a simple tool such as Notepad. Each object will start on a new line of the file.

Then I use a byte as the deleted flag. If an object is deleted, we'll set a flag in this byte. (Physically deleting the object would require rewriting the entire file from the point of deletion to the end. This becomes slow in a large file.) When we read the file, we'll just pass over records that are flagged as deleted.

Finally, I add a single space character, padding the prefix to four bytes, which is a nice, round number. This may improve efficiency if the toString() record is also a multiple of four bytes. It will certainly improve readability if we use a text editor to examine the file's contents.

With the .ODB structure designed, it's time to think about our API.

Our Database API

The *API*, *Application Programming Interface*, is the set of methods that access the data, along with any public properties. The best API is the simplest one that does the job. We can design ours in two parts. We'll have ODB operations (like create and open), and we'll have object-specific (store and retrieve) operations.

A very good procedure is to program just the API before you actually write a single line of code. It will look something like this:

```
Public Sub open_odb(pn As String)

' open the .ODB file

End Sub


Public Sub add_obj(o As Object)

' append an object

End Sub
```

```
Public Sub del_obj(num As Integer)

' delete a specified object

End Sub


Public Sub get_obj(num As Integer, obj As Object)

' retrieve a specified object

End Sub
```

This is not just a good design practice; it's the abstract base class that you'll use in implementing interfaces. Those concepts, interfaces, and abstract base classes are getting ahead of our current work. For now, remember that when your design is done, you'll be well-advised to store the result in a separate file before you begin adding code.

The ODB Interface

We'll need three operations at the ODB level:

- Create an ODB
- Open an ODB
- Close an ODB

To create an ODB, you'll need an object of the target class, so I'll combine creation with appending the first object. For opening an ODB, we'll need a valid path and name.

The API can look like this:

```
Public Sub close_odb()

End Sub


Public Sub create_odb(first As Object)

End Sub


Public Sub open_odb(pn As String)

End Sub
```

With this is done, we're ready to go on to the individual objects.

The Object Interface

For individual objects, we'll need four operations:

- Add an object to the ODB
- Get an object from the ODB
- Delete an object in the ODB
- Replace an object in the ODB

These are simple methods of the ODB class:

```
Public Sub add_obj(o As Object)

End Sub


Public Sub del_obj(num As Integer)

End Sub


Public Sub get_obj(num As Integer, ByRef obj As Object)

End Sub


Public Sub rep_obj(num As Integer, obj As Object)

End Sub
```

We are passing `Object` variables, not any specific kind of object. This lets us use our ODB class to manipulate any kind of object that supplies the required methods: `to_string()` and `from_string()`. (We'll add another, but it's a small bookkeeping detail. These are the key ones.)

Our ODB object won't know or care about the contents of the string that the object creates. It will trust the constituent class to provide the `to_string()` and `from_string()` methods that are appropriate for the class's objects.

The reason for using an object parameter passed by reference in the `get_obj()` method is that we need the object's `from_string()` method. (We wouldn't have access to this method if we used a function that returned an object.)

As a matter of style, I specify passing ByRef when I intend to return values through a parameter. This should be the exception, not the rule.

A good argument is made for explicitly declaring every other parameter as ByVal, but that will complicate your life when you start writing out-of-process ActiveX classes. This is way ahead of our current programming, but you'll see when we get there that the object-oriented work we're doing here is almost all you need for ActiveX programming.

To complete the API, we'll need to add the data members. Here I'll show both the Public and Private properties. These will include an enum. If you're not familiar with this tool, it's the very first topic we'll take up in the next chapter.

Although we're including Private data members in the design, we're excluding Private methods. Most Private data members have consequences for the design of the Public methods. For example, we'll record the file's path and name when we create or open the ODB.

On the other hand, the Private methods are just implementation details that we can leave for later. For example, we'll need a method to locate a particular object in the file. We'll implement this as a separate method because both the object get and the object delete processes will need its capability. For the class's interface, though, it doesn't matter that we've separated this algorithm out into its own method.

The ODB Class's Data Members

```
Const signature = "mrVB5odb"
Const header_len = 48

' Errors:
    Public Enum err_types
        err_freefile = 0
        err_open
        err_seek
        err_close
        err_getdel
        err_badrec
        err_notgot
        number_of_errors
    End Enum

' Data members
    Public default_drive As String
    Public default_path As String

    Private file_number As Integer
```

```
Private rec_len As Integer
Private rec_buf As String
Private path_name As String
Private num_objects As Integer
Private current_object_num As Integer
```

THE FULL DESIGN

Listing 5-3 shows the full design, including the ODB file design. Remember that a class design built to this point should be saved separately before you go on to add the working portions of the code. This is the abstract base class that you would use to replace our late-bound version with an equivalent early-bound class.

Listing 5-3

The complete ODB design

```
' ODB.cls — Object DataBase class
' Copyright 1997, Martin L. Rinehart

' Creates a data file which holds objects of a single
' class.

' The class must provide a get_name() function returning
' a String, suitable for use as a file name.
' It must also provide a to_string() function that returns
' a fixed-length string containing all the property values
' that will be stored. And it must provide a from_string()
' method that extracts the property values from the string
' created by the to_string() operation.

' Format of the ODB file is:
'    Header
'    Object 0 record
'    Object 1 record
'    ...
'    Object n-1 record

' Format of the header is
'    Signature (8 bytes) = "mrVB5odb"
'    Object type name (32 bytes)
'    Record length (8 bytes)

' Format of the object record is
'    CR byte (chr(13))
'    LF byte (chr(10))
'    Deleted flag byte ("*" if deleted, " " otherwise)
'    unused byte (pad to dword boundary)
```

```
'    obj.to_string()

Option Explicit

Const signature = "mrVB5odb"
Const header_len = 48

' Errors:
    Public Enum err_types
        err_freefile = 0
        err_open
        err_seek
        err_close
        err_getdel
        err_badrec
        err_notgot
        number_of_errors
    End Enum

' Data members
    Public default_drive As String
    Public default_path As String

    Private file_number As Integer
    Private rec_len As Integer
    Private rec_buf As String
    Private path_name As String
    Private num_objects As Integer
    Private current_object_num As Integer


Public Sub close_odb()

End Sub


Public Sub create_odb(first As Object)

End Sub


Public Sub open_odb(pn As String)

End Sub


Public Sub add_obj(o As Object)

End Sub
```

```
Public Sub del_obj(num As Integer)

End Sub

Public Sub get_obj(num As Integer, ByRef obj As Object)

End Sub

Public Sub rep_obj(num As Integer, obj As Object)

End Sub

' end of ODB.CLS
```

SUMMARY

We began this chapter with a look at the Application Setup Wizard. This tool not only creates setup programs and the associated directories or disks, it also gives you a summary of the size of the executable file you'll need for an application. This lets you see that adding a Data Access Object control calls in almost 3MB of additional executable files.

To eliminate these megabytes, we're designing and programming a very simple replacement for the DAO control. Our design depends on polymorphism and uses late binding, which means the method references are resolved at runtime, not at compile time.

There's an available Visual Basic technique for replacing the late binding with early (compile time) binding, but we're going to keep this code focused on the essential polymorphism and ignore the *implements* keyword and the interface concept at this point.

Lastly, we used the power of polymorphism, having multiple classes supply externally identical methods as the fundamental part of our ODB design. We designed a file structure that depends on each class providing a to_print() and a from_print() method.

The to_print() method, a concept borrowed from Java, creates a fixed-length string from the object's property values. This is a useful debugging tool and is also our fundamental storage unit. The companion from_print() method reverses the to_print() process, taking the values from the string and assigning them to the object's properties.

In Chapter 6, we'll explain the strengths and weaknesses of Visual Basic's enum and usc it as we begin to implement the design of our ODB class.

IMPLEMENTING THE ODB CLASS

*I*n this chapter we're going to implement the ODB-related methods. We'll be able to create, open, and close ODBs. In Chapter 7 we'll go on to add, retrieve, and delete objects in our ODBs. We'll strike a balance between theory and practice as we do this.

In this chapter, we'll begin with a look at the new Enum statement, which is very useful in object-oriented programs but isn't quite implemented correctly. If you know its weakness, you can avoid problems and benefit from it. We'll be using enums from this point on.

After looking at the Enum statement we'll put it to use in handling errors in the ODB class. Actually we'll divide the error handling between a live part in the class and a one-time intialization in the global library. We'll do this when we create the `close_odb()` method, which is trivial except for the error handling.

To round out our set of ODB methods, we'll finish with `open_odb()`, which is not really complex but exercizes our error handling. You'll see that the Enum eliminates a lot of the problems that you might have had in this method.

We'll begin by looking at the Enum statement.

USING AND MISUSING ENUMERATIONS

Visual Basic 5 adds the Enum statement to the language. This is a valuable tool lifted straight from C++ and implemented in almost the same way as C++ handles it. Unfortunately, there's a huge flaw in the implementation. As with Visual Basic's object-oriented techniques, you can make Enum work for you if you understand its idiosyncrosies.

Enums are Useful Constants

In Visual Basic you can hard-code constants or use named constants. Here are examples:

```
' hard-coded constant:
    my_func = 2 ' the "2" is hard-coded

' named constants:

    ' create list of named constants:
    const ok_return = 0
    const bad_param = 1
    const null_value = 2

    ' use a named constant:
    my_func = null_value
```

In many cases, a list of named constants is preferable to hard-coded constants. The Enum statement provides an excellent method of organizing these names. I've included an Enum to organize the error constants in our ODB class. This solves some problems.

Hard-Coded Constants are Problematic

Our ODB class provides an example of code where several types of errors could occur. This is typical in file handling code. The disk might not be available, the disk might not have space, the file might not exist, and so on. We'll write a routine that pops up an appropriate message box. Omitting details, it would look like this with hard-coded constants:

```
Public Sub PopErrMsg(msg_number As Byte)

    Dim emsgs(15) As String
        emsgs(0) = "Drive not available"
```

```
            emsgs(1) = "Disk full"
            emsgs(2) = "File not found"
            . . .

        msgbox emsgs(msg_number)

    End Sub
```

In pseudocode, the calling routine would look like this:

```
' test: drive available?
    If Not drive_available
        PopErrMsg(0)
    End If
    . . .

' test: space available?
    If Not space_available
        PopErrMsg(1)
    End If
    . . .

' test: file found?
    If Not file_found
        PopErrMsg(2)
    End If
    . . .


    . . .
```

The problem is that you have to constantly look into the PopErrMsg() code to find the appropriate error message number. Then you need to test every error condition to be sure that the correct message pops up. Inevitably, you'll need to switch around a couple of message numbers to get it right. There's a better way.

Named Constants to the Rescue

The beginning of an elegant solution comes when you use named constants. Give each error a name and assign the names consecutive numbers. This is the module-level definition of the constants:

```
' file errors:
    const ferr_no_drive = 0
    const ferr_no_space = 1
    const ferr_no_file  = 2
    . . .
```

Then you do all your coding with the names not the values. The error array is defined this way:

```
Public Sub PopErrMsg(msg_number As Byte)

    Dim emsgs( 15 ) As String
        emsgs( ferr_no_drive ) = "Drive not available"
        emsgs( ferr_no_space ) = "Disk full"
        emsgs( ferr_no_file  ) = "File not found"
        . . .

    msgbox emsgs(msg_number)
End Sub
```

Memo to Bill Gates

Bill, I'd love to have control over my horizontal whitespace so I could line things up, as I did in the last code fragment. The code editor won't let me, though. Doesn't it look nice this way?

The calling code also uses the names, so it makes sense, and everything is correctly matched:

```
' test: drive available?
    If Not drive_available
        PopErrMsg(ferr_no_drive)
    End If
    . . .

' test: space available?
    If Not space_available
        PopErrMsg(ferr_no_space)
    End If
    . . .

' test: file found?
    If Not file_found
        PopErrMsg(ferr_no_file)
    End If
    . . .

    . . .
```

This is an almost elegant solution. Looking at `ferr_no_file` makes it simple to match the calling routine correctly to the message array. About the worst thing you can do is misspell one of the constant's names, and the compiler will be happy to point that out. Runtime mistakes are almost impossible.

Enums are provided to make this truly elegant.

Enums Make It Elegant

Enums let you eliminate all constants, entirely. After all, counting is something computers can do very well. You can replace all those public constants with an enumeration, this way:

```
Public Enum file_errors
    ferr_no_drive
    ferr_no_space
    ferr_no_file
    . . .
End Enum
```

That way no constants are in your source code. (Actually, the compiler's view is that the code is full of constants, but that's what compilers are supposed to do. You'll write **ferr_x** and the compiler will replace it with an appropriate number.)

In addition to the obvious convenience and organization that the Enum brings, you'll find some other advantages. For example, you inevitably add to the list of errors as you code. With constants, you either added at the end of the list, or you went to a lot of trouble renumbering. With an enum, you stick the new message name into the list anywhere you like. The compiler will renumber everything automatically.

One more advantage is that you can even eliminate the array size constant. (We all inevitably forget to increase it when we add another item.) Just stick a non-error constant at the end of the list, this way:

```
Public Enum file_errors
    ferr_no_drive
    ferr_no_space
    ferr_no_file
    . . .
    number_of_errors ' Automated count!
End Enum
```

Then your error message array is declared this way:

```
Dim emsgs(number_of_errors-1) As String
. . .
```

This is an elegant solution. You still have to test every error, but it's almost impossible to receive the wrong message, or to have any of the other problems that come from hard-coded constants.

Class Enums are Global

When you put a Public Enum in a class, you're adding named constants to the global name space. Your class can use them and all the other classes can use them. This is very handy, but it does open the potential for name conflicts.

Have you thought about Microsoft's use of *vb* as a prefix for all the Visual Basic built-in constants (`vbModal`, for example)? It's a nuisance to type, but it prevents any conflict with your own constant names. (At least it does if you don't use the *vb* prefix for your own names.)

If you give your constants an identifying prefix (I've used *ferr* for the `file_errors` Enum), you'll avoid name conflicts. This is one area where I think the prefix naming convention earns its keep.

Enums provide elegant, global names that clarify your code and prevent numerous errors that can occur with simple constants. That's the good news. The other news it that there's an additional feature here, which unfortunately is implemented so badly you don't want to use it.

The Type is Less Than Useless, Bill

Memo to Bill Gates
Bill, you'd better read this whole section. I wish I didn't have to say it, but somebody has to point it out.

In addition to creating a handy list of named constants that organizes (and lets you reorganize) your constants, the Enum also creates a new data type. In the previous example, I used the name `file_errors` to identify it. You can now use this name as a new data type. If you follow Microsoft's examples, you would use it this way:

```
' Change the parameter type:

Public Sub PopErrMsg(msg_number As file_errors)

    Dim emsgs(15) As String
        emsgs(ferr_no_drive) = "Drive not available"
        emsgs(ferr_no_space) = "Disk full"
        emsgs(ferr_no_file)  = "File not found"
        . . .

    msgbox emsgs(msg_number)
End Sub
```

You *can* do that, but don't! It hurts, not helps.

Bytes Are Good Bytes

You've probably noticed that I declare variables as Byte whenever that fits the number. (Remember, bytes are unsigned, 8-bit integers; 0 through 255.) There's a good reason for this.

In the Intel 80×86 instruction set, the opcode for moving a byte into the low eight bits of a register is a single byte. In 32-bit mode, the opcode for moving a long into all 32 bits of a register is also a single byte.

The byte-sized move, however, requires a byte-sized constant to move into the register. The 32-bit instruction requires a 32-bit constant. Thus, the full size of the instruction is two bytes (opcode plus a data byte) for assigning a Byte and 5 bytes (opcode plus four data bytes) for assigning a Long.

I used to fire up my debugger to check the actual code generated by a compiler. That way I'd be sure that, for instance, Visual Basic took advantage of the smaller data size. I don't do that any more because it's not really very smart. If one iteration of any compiler doesn't do a particular optimization, the next version may add it.

The smart way is to tell your compiler as much as you can and then trust it to behave intelligently. If you won't be needing all 32 bits, tell the compiler. If you assign a small value to a Long, for example, the compiler won't know that you don't intend to assign a much larger value at a later time, so it will have to use the larger instructions.

For reasons that completely elude me, the Enum is defined not as a Byte or an Integer but as a Long.

There is an excuse for this in the books online, which claims that 32-bit values are more efficient in 32-bit operating systems. This was obviously written by someone with no direct knowledge of the 80×86 architecture or instructions — it's mostly dead wrong. (To find this misinformation in Books Online, the drilldown is Component Tools Guide, Creating ActiveX Components, General Principles of Component Design, Providing Named Constants for Your Component.)

Longs are Bigger than Integers

If you tell an Intel chip that you'll be working with 32-bit values, you can still work directly with bytes, but 16-bit values become a special case. The opcode that would move a 32-bit value into a register needs a one-byte instruction prefix to move a 16-bit value.

Of course, the constant that is needed is 32 or 16 bits, as specified by the instruction. If you're using a 16-bit constant in 32-bit code, adding the one-byte prefix lets you save two bytes in constant size, so you still have a net saving in using Integer data instead of Long data.

Unfortunately, someone in Redmond, Washington, was 32-bit happy when the Enum was added. The vast majority of all Enum uses fit happily in byte-sized constants. I can't even think of an example where the Integer type *wouldn't* be adequate. You might need Integers when you use the capability to assign specific Enum values to include negatives, this way:

```
Public Enum return_values
    ret_normal
    ret_better
    ret_best

    ret_error = -1
End Enum
```

That lets the normal Enum machinery start counting at 0 but overrides it for your ret_error value. The error is assigned minus one.

Why anyone would need Long values in an Enum isn't readily apparent, however. Maybe you can think of an example in your applications. I don't think this exceptional use (if there is one) should be allowed to fatten all of our executable files, but it does.

An elegant redefinition would have the compiler pick the smallest integer size that fits the values in the Enum. Then the vast majority would be Bytes, a handful would be Integers, and perhaps one in a million would be Long.

I object to the sloppy use of bytes in the executable file, but Enums are so generally helpful in coding that I use them anyway. When it comes to saving a few bytes versus clearer code, I go for clearer code almost every time.

So what's wrong with using the Enum as a data type?

The Useless Data Type

What's wrong is that the type feature is useless. It's not really implemented. What we have now is just a synonym for Long. Consider this complete program:

```
Public Enum etest
    foo
    bar
End Enum

Public Sub main()

    test foo
    test bar
    test -1
    test 3.6

End Sub

Public Sub test(e as etest)

    debug.print str(e)

End Sub
```

The bad news is that this compiles as if it were correct code. The results of the four tests are 0, 1, –1, and 4, respectively. Clearly the latter two are not members of the etest Enum. These should generate errors, not values.

In fact, use of a nonmember value in an Enum type should generate a compile-time error, and use of a float should certainly trigger a compile-time error, but they don't! The compiler thinks that your Enum data type is just a synonym for Long, so it treats all values accordingly.

To my eyes, using the Enum type promises a benefit that isn't realized. I think this is dangerous, so I continue to state Byte (or Integer, if necessary) explicitly as my data type. Using Byte in place of etest as the data type in the test() parameter in the last code example at least triggers an overflow error on –1.

Memo to Bill Gates

Next time you have a minute, Bill, would you please see about moving constant type checking to compile time? As it is now, passing −1 to a Byte compiles correctly and fails at run time.

You could use my other principle to argue in favor of using the Enum type as your data type: tell the compiler as much as you can and trust that it will act intelligently. We know that it doesn't act intelligently right now, but the folks in Redmond, Washington, are hard at work improving it.

I accept that as an alternative — an equally valid alternative — way to go, provided that you (and everyone in your organization) recognize that the promise of a real data type is *not* met in the current implementation.

Memo to Bill Gates

Sorry about all my carping, Bill. I hope everyone knows that I'm darned glad we have Enums, and I use them whenever I can. These are definitely a nice addition to the language, and you know that I'm not generally in favor of adding to the language.

Now let's get on to implementing the ODB class.

CREATING THE DATABASE FILE

When we implemented our calendar, the debugging process and the implementation process were one and the same. The secret was that the calendar is a visual object. When you press F5 or click the run icon, you look at your latest improvement or addition. What you see is what you coded.

Unfortunately, bits on a hard disk are not so simple to see. I've already anticipated this problem at the design stage by using simple, printable text, wherever it was possible. We can pretty much check our work with Notepad or any handy text file reader. Still, you have to think through the debugging process as a key part — perhaps I should say *the* key part — of the implementation process.

We'll start with a utility program that will create our first .ODB file.

Begin by creating a new standard .EXE project. Name the project prjODB. Add a new class module, and type or copy Listing 5-3 from the end of the last chapter into it. Name it just ODB. Delete the Form and save the project using the default names supplied by Visual Basic.

Because we can't create an ODB without a class that implements the to_string() and from_string() methods, let's create one. While we're at it, we'll need a third method that retrieves the class name, called get_name().

The ODB class depends on these three methods, so you have to use these names for Public methods. In Chapter 13 we'll use Visual Basic's *Implements* capability to do this more formally. Using Implements lets the compiler check your interface.

The People Class

The People class uses a straightforward set of Public properties, all String types. These are as follows:

```
Const class_name = "People"

' Public data members
    Public first_name As String
    Public last_name As String

    Public addr1 As String
    Public addr2 As String
    Public city As String
    Public state As String
    Public postal_code As String
```

By the way, this isn't a very well-designed class for People. You don't have a proper form of address (Mr., Ms., Dr., or whatever is appropriate), the address won't handle international addresses well, and so on. I've deliberately simplified the design so we could concentrate on the code. Feel free to do better!

The get_name() routine is trivial:

```
Public Function get_name()
    get_name = class_name
End Function
```

I've already mentioned that there is a Visual Basic alternative syntax for retrieving a value, such as the name. We'll introduce that in Chapter 8. It doesn't do anything you don't see here.

The `to_string()` method just fixes the lengths of all these strings. In practice you'll want to check for truncation, although not necessarily in this routine. (You could check the lengths when the Text controls get data entry.) This is another simple routine:

```
Public Function to_string() As String

    to_string = fix_len(first_name, 16) & _
        fix_len(last_name, 24) & _
        fix_len(addr1, 40) & _
        fix_len(addr2, 40) & _
        fix_len(city, 20) & _
        fix_len(state, 10) & _
        fix_len(postal_code, 10)

End Function
```

We'll cover the `fix_len()` library routine in the next section.

Because we're only dealing with strings, the `from_string()` method is also straightforward. The only problem is that you have to be very careful to pick the string apart precisely as you constructed it. This does the job:

```
Public Sub from_string(s As String)

    last_name = Left(s, 16)
    first_name = Mid(s, 17, 24)
    addr1 = Mid(s, 41, 40)
    addr2 = Mid(s, 81, 40)
    city = Mid(s, 121, 20)
    state = Mid(s, 141, 10)
    postal_code = Right(s, 10)

End Sub
```

I've dropped the `fix_len()` routine into a global library module, ODB_LIB.BAS. This bothers object purists, but it doesn't bother me.

The Library File

In Java, for example, all routines are either object or class methods. Some people think this is an advantage. I'm not one of them.

Some routines perform globally useful functions. Fixing a string's length is a function that many different classes can use, so placing it in a library of globally accessible functions makes sense.

In Java, you could produce the same effect by declaring a class (call it the `Global` class, if you like) and attaching routines to the class not to objects. If this class were `Public`, it would have precisely the same usefulness as a library of routines in a .BAS module. If you're going to do that, why not be completely straightforward about it? Maintaining the purity of the object paradigm doesn't provide any useful benefit to your code.

The Visual Basic solution is more straightforward. Simple is good! This is the first routine I've added to ODB_LIB.BAS:

```
Public Function fix_len(s As String, _
    num_chars As Integer)

' returns s padded or truncated to num_chars length

    fix_len = Left(s & Space(num_chars), num_chars)

End Function
```

The Creator Main Program

Creating the ODB file is often a job done once by a utility program you write just for that purpose (mine's called Creator.bas). It's a trivial job. You create an object of your intended class (`People`, in our case) and then you pass that object to the `create()` method of an `ODB` object.

As you can see, most of the code in this `main()` just fills in values for the `People` properties:

```
Public Sub main()

' Create sample object
    Dim p As New People

    p.first_name = "John"
    p.last_name = "Johnson"
    p.addr1 = "123 Main St."
    p.city = "Anytown"
    p.state = "XX, USA"
    p.postal_code = "12345"
```

```
' Create ODB
    Dim od As New ODB
    od.create_odb p

End Sub
```

With this cast of supporting players, we're ready to take a look at the star, the ODB class itself.

The Create() Method

Our last job is actually to write a Create() method in the ODB class. Mine is a little short on error checking, but it does the main job. It looks like this:

```
Public Sub create_odb(first As Object)

    file_number = FreeFile

    path_name = first.get_name
    path_name = _
        default_drive & _
        default_path & _
        path_name & ".odb"

    If Len(Dir(path_name)) Then Kill path_name

    Open path_name For Binary As file_number

    rec_buf = Chr(13) & Chr(10) & "  " & first.to_string
    rec_len = Len(rec_buf)
    Dim header As String

    Dim nm As String
    nm = first.get_name

    header = signature & _
        fix_len(nm, 32) & _
        Right(Space(8) & Str(rec_len), 8)

    Put file_number, , header
    Put file_number, , rec_buf
    current_object_num = 1

End Sub
```

When I run this code, I create an ODB file, People.odb, in my working directory. Figure 6-1 shows me using the Object Browser (launch it with F2 or by clicking its icon) to look at the structure of the `People` class and examining the People.odb file with Notepad loaded on top.

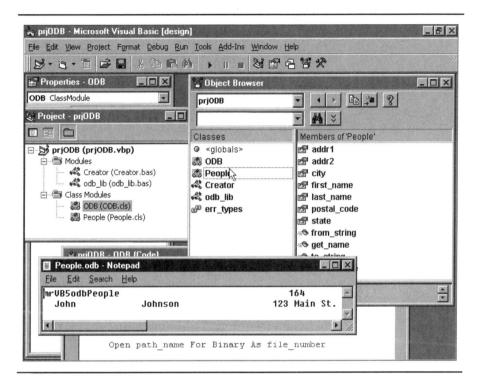

Figure 6-1
Checking with Notepad and the Object Browser.

If you're going to create your .ODB files using utility programs such as Creator.bas, the lack of error checking here is acceptable. (Presumably you'll create the file and use an editor like Notepad to check your work.) If you wanted a more flexible, end-user system, you'll need to add good error checking.

If you're not familiar with using binary files, I'll mention their capabilities as we go along. The feature that the `Create()` method exploits is that they write exactly what you tell them. No more; no less. `Chr(13)` and `Chr(10)` are a carriage return and linefeed pair — the standard DOS delimiter used between lines of text files.

That's a DOS-based standard. The Macintosh and Unix computers, for examples, use different delimiters in text files.

The Full Listings for Creating the ODB

If you've not been successful in doing this on your own, the listings here show the full files' editable portions. They're on disk along with the project file and the resultant .ODB in 06-01.

The Mainline File

Creator.bas has the main() routine that drives this program. It's shown in Listing 6-1a.

Listing 6-1a

Creator.bas is the main program

```
' Creator.bas — utility to create Object DataBase file
' Copyright 1997, Martin L. Rinehart

Option Explicit

Public Sub main()

' Create sample object
    Dim p As New People

    p.first_name = "John"
    p.last_name = "Johnson"
    p.addr1 = "123 Main St."
    p.city = "Anytown"
    p.state = "XX, USA"
    p.postal_code = "12345"

' Create ODB
    Dim od As New ODB
    od.create_odb p

End Sub

' end of Creator.bas
```

The Subroutine Library File

The odb_lib.bas file, shown here in Listing 6-1b, will hold our utility routines. At this juncture, it's holding just the fix_len() function.

Listing 6-1b
A global file holds global routines

```
'odb_lib.bas — Object DataBase library routines
'Copyright 1997, Martin L. Rinehart

Option Explicit


Public Function fix_len(s As String, _
    num_chars As Integer)

' returns s padded or truncated to num_chars length

    fix_len = Left(s & Space(num_chars), num_chars)

End Function

' end of odb_lib.bas
```

The People Class Module

The People.cls file defines the properties and methods that we'll use in the ODB. The Create() routine already used the to_string() method to write the initial object record. It's shown here in Listing 6-1c.

Listing 6-1c
The People class is used for testing

```
' People.cls — basic data about a person
' Copyright 1997, Martin L. Rinehart

Option Explicit

Const class_name = "People"

' Public data members
    Public first_name As String
    Public last_name As String

    Public addr1 As String
    Public addr2 As String
    Public city As String
    Public state As String
    Public postal_code As String
```

(continued)

People class is used for testing

```
Public Function get_name()
    get_name = class_name
End Function

Public Function to_string() As String

    to_string = fix_len(first_name, 16) & _
        fix_len(last_name, 24) & _
        fix_len(addr1, 40) & _
        fix_len(addr2, 40) & _
        fix_len(city, 20) & _
        fix_len(state, 10) & _
        fix_len(postal_code, 10)

End Function

Public Sub from_string(s As String)

    last_name = Left(s, 16)
    first_name = Mid(s, 17, 24)
    addr1 = Mid(s, 41, 40)
    addr2 = Mid(s, 81, 40)
    city = Mid(s, 121, 20)
    state = Mid(s, 141, 10)
    postal_code = Right(s, 10)

End Sub

' end of People.cls
```

The ODB Class Module

We've begun to extend the ODB class module past its design into implementation. Listing 6-1d shows it at this point in our development of the ODB class.

Listing 6-1d
The ODB class with Create() code added

```
' ODB.cls — Object DataBase class
' Copyright 1997, Martin L. Rinehart

' Creates a data file which holds objects of a single
' class.
```

```
' The class must provide a get_name() function returning
' a String, suitable for use as a file name.
' It must also provide a to_string() function that returns
' a fixed-length string containing all the property values
' that will be stored. And it must provide a from_string()
' method that extracts the property values from the string
' created by the to_string() operation.

' Format of the ODB file is:
'    Header
'    Object 0 record
'    Object 1 record
'    ...
'    Object n-1 record

' Format of the header is
'    Signature (8 bytes) = "mrVB5odb"
'    Object type name (32 bytes)
'    Record length (8 bytes)

' Format of the object record is
'    CR byte (chr(13))
'    LF byte (chr(10))
'    Deleted flag byte ("*" if deleted, " " otherwise)
'    unused byte (pad to dword boundary)
'    obj.to_string()

Option Explicit

Const signature = "mrVB5odb"
Const header_len = 48

' Errors:
    Public Enum err_types
        err_freefile = 0
        err_open
        err_seek
        err_close
        err_getdel
        err_badrec
        err_notgot
        number_of_errors
    End Enum

' Data members
    Public default_drive As String
    Public default_path As String
```

(continued)

The ODB class with Create() code added

```
Private file_number As Integer
Private rec_len As Integer
Private rec_buf As String
Private path_name As String
Private num_objects As Integer
Private current_object_num As Integer


Public Sub close_odb()

End Sub


Public Sub create_odb(first As Object)

    file_number = FreeFile

    path_name = first.get_name
    path_name = _
        default_drive & _
        default_path & _
        path_name & ".odb"

    If Len(Dir(path_name)) Then Kill path_name

    Open path_name For Binary As file_number

    rec_buf = Chr(13) & Chr(10) & "  " & first.to_string
    rec_len = Len(rec_buf)
    Dim header As String

    Dim nm As String
    nm = first.get_name

    header = signature & _
        fix_len(nm, 32) & _
        Right(Space(8) & Str(rec_len), 8)

    Put file_number, , header
    Put file_number, , rec_buf
    current_object_num = 1

End Sub


Public Sub open_odb(pn As String)
```

```
End Sub


Public Sub add_obj(o As Object)

End Sub


Public Sub del_obj(num As Integer)

End Sub


Public Sub get_obj(num As Integer, ByRef obj As Object)

End Sub


Public Sub rep_obj(num As Integer, obj As Object)

End Sub

' end of ODB.CLS
```

Now we're ready to go on to implement the rest of the class, beginning with `open_odb()` and `close_odb()`.

IMPLEMENTING THE OTHER ODB METHODS

Now that we can create an ODB file, we need to be able to open and close it. Let's start with the `close_odb()` method. It's simple, so it's a good opportunity to add and test our error handling, keyed by our `enum` values.

Implementing the close_odb() Method

The `close_odb()` method is almost trivial. If no possibility of error existed, this would work:

```
Public Sub close_odb ()

    Close file_number

End Sub
```

Adding a Class_Initialize Event Handler

Actually, I want to use `file_number` to signal when no file is open. Conveniently, the default value is zero, which will serve nicely as a *no file open* flag. Although it's a default, I'm going to add a `class_initialize()` method that sets up defaults explicitly. It looks like this:

```
Private Sub Class_Initialize()

    default_drive = ""
    default_path = ""
    file_number = 0 ' 0 = no file open

End Sub
```

Completing close_odb() with Error Handling

Now, if we had an error message mechanism, the full `close_odb()` routine could look like this:

```
Public Sub close_odb()

    If file_number = 0 Then
        err_msgs (err_close)
        Exit Sub
    End If

    Close file_number
    file_number = 0 ' signal no file open

End Sub
```

Adding an Error Message Reporting Method

You'll recall that `err_close` is a defined constant, declared in our `enum`. Here's an `err_msgs` routine that you can add to ODB.cls:

```
Private Sub err_msgs(errno As Byte)

    Static msgs_initialized ' defaults to False

    If Not msgs_initialized Then
        init_ferr_msgs
        msgs_initialized = True
```

```
        End If

        Call MsgBox(ferr_msgs(errno), vbCritical, "ODB Error")

End Sub
```

Assigning Error Messages Globally

I've moved the actual assignment of error messages to the array into the
ODB_LIB file. This lets us do the assignment once, not every time an error
occurs. The additions to ODB_LIB are these:

```
Public ferr_msgs(number_of_errors - 1) As String

Public Sub init_ferr_msgs()

    ferr_msgs(err_freefile) = _
        "No more file numbers available"
    ferr_msgs(err_open) = "Cannot open file"
    ferr_msgs(err_seek) = "Cannot perform seek"
    ferr_msgs(err_close) = "Cannot close — no file open"
    ferr_msgs(err_getdel) = "Cannot get — record deleted"
    ferr_msgs(err_badrec) = "Cannot get — record damaged"
    ferr_msgs(err_notgot) = _
        "Cannot get — invalid object number"

End Sub
```

Testing the Close and Error Routines

With these improvements, you're ready to test your `close_odb()` method.
You can do this conveniently in Creator.bas. I'm going to try to close the
ODB before it's created. That should generate the appropriate error message
for an attempted close without an open file.

Then we can go ahead and create the file and then correctly close it.
These are the modified lines in Creator.bas:

```
' Create ODB
    Dim od As New ODB
    od.close_odb ' Error! No file open.

    od.create_odb p
    od.close_odb ' Success
```

The attempted close shows the critical error message, as Figure 6-2 shows.

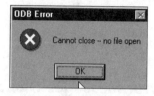

Figure 6-2
Displaying a critical error message.

Our last ODB-related method to implement is open_odb().

Opening an ODB

As is common in file opening code, our job is mostly to check for possible errors and then do a small amount of real setup work if everything goes as planned. The first job is to obtain a file number and exit with an appropriate message if none are available:

```
' check that a file number is available
    file_number = FreeFile
    If file_number = 0 Then
        err_msgs (err_freefile)
        Exit Sub
    End If
```

If we get a number, go on to open it. The Open statement will correctly open a nonexistent file. It will be zero bytes long, so we can check for both null and nonexistent files by looking at the length with the internal LOF() function:

```
' open the file - if it's 0-long, its new
    Open pn & ".odb" For Binary As file_number
    If LOF(file_number) = 0 Then ' not an ODB!
        Close file_number
        err_msgs (err_open)
        Exit Sub
    End If
```

You might want to separate out the various open errors by adding more error types. With the enum working for you, this is simply a matter of adding a new constant name in the enum and a new string in the error message array.

With a possibly valid open file, the next job is to create a buffer for input and read the header into it. The Get statement for a binary file uses exactly as much space as you provide to it in a string. It doesn't matter what is in the string when you do the Get; it will be replaced entirely by data from the file. This code reads the header:

```
' create buffer for header, then read header
    Dim header As String
    header = Space(header_len)

    Get file_number, , header
```

The omitted parameter in the Get statement specifies the record number. For binary files, this is a byte number. It defaults to zero, which is exactly what you want for reading the file header.

You can go on to check the file's signature. Again, we'll exit with an appropriate message if this isn't valid:

```
' check for a valid signature
    If Left(header, 8) <> signature Then
        Close file_number
        err_msgs (err_open)
        Exit Sub
    End If
```

Finally, you're reasonably safe in guessing that this file is OK when you've seen the signature match. Now we can go ahead and use the values we've accumulated to set up our Private properties to be ready to manipulate individual objects in the file. This is the working code:

```
' set up private data members
    rec_len = Val(Right(header, 8))
    rec_buf = Space(rec_len)
    path_name = pn

    num_objects = (LOF(file_number) - header_len) / rec_len
    current_object_num = 0
```

We could have done several more checks, which would give us a better assurance of file integrity. For example, if we record the file's size in the header we can match it against the LOF() value to be sure we haven't lost any.

It's your code. Add as much (or as little) checking as makes sense for your work. Do you back up regularly? Are the files in your applications on a server that is backed up automatically? What's the cost of a fatal error in reading an object?

Don't go and construct a bulletproof version of this code if you don't really need to. Bulletproof is nice, but light and quick is nice, too. Armor plating gets you a tank, not a sports car.

I suggest that you replace the create_odb() call in Creator with an open_odb() call and use F8 to step through the code, checking the values. If you just put the cursor over your Private data members after their values are assigned, you won't even need a watch window.

The Full Library and ODB Class Files

On disk the listing file is 06-02, which includes the project file as well as the sources. Here Listing 6-2a shows the new odb_lib.bas, and Listing 6-2b shows ODB.cls with all the ODB-related methods fully implemented.

Listing 6-2a
The global library code

```
'odb_lib.bas — Object DataBase library routines
'Copyright 1997, Martin L. Rinehart

Option Explicit

Public ferr_msgs(number_of_errors - 1) As String

Public Sub init_ferr_msgs()

    ferr_msgs(err_freefile) = _
        "No more file numbers available"
    ferr_msgs(err_open) = "Cannot open file"
    ferr_msgs(err_seek) = "Cannot perform seek"
    ferr_msgs(err_close) = "Cannot close — no file open"
    ferr_msgs(err_getdel) = "Cannot get — record deleted"
    ferr_msgs(err_badrec) = "Cannot get — record damaged"
    ferr_msgs(err_notgot) = _
        "Cannot get — invalid object number"
End Sub
```

```vbnet
Public Function fix_len(s As String, _
    num_chars As Integer)

' returns s padded or truncated to num_chars length

    fix_len = Left(s & Space(num_chars), num_chars)

End Function

' end of odb_lib.bas
```

Listing 6-2b
The ODB class module

```vbnet
' ODB.cls — Object DataBase class
' Copyright 1997, Martin L. Rinehart

. . . Comments omitted — see Listing 6-1d

Option Explicit

Const signature = "mrVB5odb"
Const header_len = 48

' Errors:
    Public Enum err_types
        err_freefile = 0
        err_open
        err_seek
        err_close
        err_getdel
        err_badrec
        err_notgot
        number_of_errors
    End Enum

' Data members
    Public default_drive As String
    Public default_path As String

        Private file_number As Integer
    Private rec_len As Integer
    Private rec_buf As String
    Private path_name As String
    Private num_objects As Integer
    Private current_object_num As Integer
```

(continued)

The ODB class module

```
Public Sub close_odb()

    If file_number = 0 Then
        err_msgs (err_close)
        Exit Sub
    End If

    Close file_number
    file_number = 0 ' signal no file open

End Sub


Public Sub create_odb(first As Object)

    file_number = FreeFile

    path_name = first.get_name
    path_name = _
        default_drive & _
        default_path & _
        path_name & ".odb"

    If Len(Dir(path_name)) Then Kill path_name

    Open path_name For Binary As file_number

    rec_buf = Chr(13) & Chr(10) & "  " & first.to_string
    rec_len = Len(rec_buf)
    Dim header As String

    Dim nm As String
    nm = first.get_name

    header = signature & _
        fix_len(nm, 32) & _
        Right(Space(8) & Str(rec_len), 8)

    Put file_number, , header
    Put file_number, , rec_buf
    current_object_num = 1

End Sub


Public Sub open_odb(pn As String)
```

```vb
' check that a file number is available
    file_number = FreeFile
    If file_number = 0 Then
        err_msgs (err_freefile)
        Exit Sub
    End If

' open the file — if it's 0 long, its new
    Open pn & ".odb" For Binary As file_number
    If LOF(file_number) = 0 Then ' not an ODB!
        Close file_number
        err_msgs (err_open)
        Exit Sub
    End If

' create buffer for header, then read header
    Dim header As String
    header = Space(header_len)

    Get file_number, , header

' check for a valid signature
    If Left(header, 8) <> signature Then
        Close file_number
        err_msgs (err_open)
        Exit Sub
    End If

' set up private data members
    rec_len = Val(Right(header, 8))
    rec_buf = Space(rec_len)
    path_name = pn

    num_objects = (LOF(file_number) - header_len) / rec_len
    current_object_num = 0

End Sub


Public Sub add_obj(o As Object)

End Sub


Public Sub del_obj(num As Integer)

End Sub
```

(continued)

The ODB class module

```
Public Sub get_obj(num As Integer, ByRef obj As Object)

End Sub


Public Sub rep_obj(num As Integer, obj As Object)

End Sub


Private Sub err_msgs(errno As Byte)

    Static msgs_initialized ' defaults to False

    If Not msgs_initialized Then
        init_ferr_msgs
        msgs_initialized = True
    End If

    Call MsgBox(ferr_msgs(errno), vbCritical, "ODB Error")

End Sub

Private Sub Class_Initialize()

    default_drive = ""
    default_path = ""
    file_number = 0 ' 0 = no file open

End Sub

' end of ODB.CLS
```

SUMMARY

We've implemented the ODB-handling methods. In Chapter 7, we'll go on to add the object-handling methods, and we'll add another technique that Visual Basic provides: working on multiple projects simultaneously.

In this chapter, we first talked about the strength of the Enum statement — it lets you create a set of named constants but completely frees you from actually thinking about the constants' values. The compiler takes over this bookkeeping chore. This is a powerful tool for avoiding mistakes with, for example, error codes.

We also saw that the Enum appears to create a new data type, which should be another powerful tool. Unfortunately, the current implementation simply uses the Enum name as a synonym for the Long type, which is distinctly unhelpful. I'm continuing to use the Byte type whenever I can because it's most efficient when it fits. You might choose to use the Enum type because Microsoft may improve its use of this type over time.

We used the Enum statement to organize the numerous error messages that are associated with our ODB-handling work. We implemented the close_odb() routine first, along with the error-handling code. We divided error handling into three pieces: the Enum in the class declarations section, a runtime error message routine as a Private method of the class, and a Public message array initialization routine in our global library.

After we had both file closing and the error message system running, we added the open_odb() method. This is a long list of error checks (mine could be made much longer without being wasteful) followed by a short bit of work when we were confident that we had correctly opened a real ODB file.

In Chapter 7, we'll finish the ODB job with the addition of the object-handling methods. While we do this, we'll stop working with a single project and start working with multiple, simultaneous projects.

You'll be surprised how simple this is. (This is one of the finest features of Visual Basic 5.) Actually, you'll probably wish we'd covered it earlier, as it would have helped in this chapter, too.

STORING OBJECTS IN THE ODB

*A*s you've seen, we're working on useful code and learning more about object-oriented programming at the same time. In this chapter, we're going to complete the ODB class, and we're going to begin taking advantage of Visual Basic 5's capability to work on multiple projects simultaneously.

When I first read about the multiple-project capability I thought, "Oh no, another complication." When I tried it, though, I found out that it simplified development, especially when you're building useful classes, and that is, of course, exactly what we're doing. Once you start working with project groups, you'll never go back to single-project development.

When we convert to multiple-project development, you'll also be doing ActiveX development. You'll see that this can be as simple as selecting ActiveX from a menu and setting appropriate switches.

Once we're working on multiple projects simultaneously, we'll go back to our ODB to complete the individual object-related methods. We'll teach it to add, delete, get, and replace objects.

When we write the get_obj() method, we'll dive into the Visual Basic debugger for our testing. If you're not familiar with it yet, you'll see that it's simple and very helpful.

Now let's start on multiple-project work.

MULTIPLE-PROJECT DEVELOPMENT

Visual Basic 5 brings us a big advance in its capability to work on multiple projects simultaneously. Microsoft pitches this for ActiveX development. It's correct to say that using multiple projects simplifies ActiveX development, but it's more correct to say that it simplifies object-oriented development. (When we talk about ActiveX in Chapter 11, you'll see that it's just a way of packaging the OOP work we're doing already.)

When you develop a generally useful class (as opposed to a project-specific class), you automatically create multiple projects. The class is one project, but you need to create a test environment. For our ODB work, we created a main line standard module and a `People` class module. Neither of these are part of the generic ODB project.

In Chapter 6, I had to force myself not to use a multiple-project development style. We should have put the `ODB` class, along with the supporting library file, into one project. The driving software that uses this class should have been a second project. That's the structure we'll be using in many different ways as we develop additional objects.

When we implement the object storage methods of the `ODB` class, we'll create a test program that will create objects automatically, along with a front-end form that we'll use to test our `ODB` class. These items will serve as a project in themselves. You'll see that this is a powerful but simple-to-use technique for organizing your work.

Memo To Bill Gates

Bill, this one's great! When I build Java classes, I really miss not being able to handle multiple projects. Visual Basic makes it simple to keep your work organized.

To see just how simple this is, let's restructure our ODB project into individual projects.

ELIMINATING GLOBAL LIBRARIES

Before we reach the easy part, however, we have to face the not-quite-so-easy part. Our global library has to go. Using multiple projects simultaneously implies that they will link together somehow. The straightforward way to do this is by compiling your class as an ActiveX .DLL. Later on we'll learn about in-process and out-of-process ActiveX programming, but for now we'll just tell Visual Basic that we want an ActiveX .DLL and then go right on with our normal object-oriented programming.

You do have to know that you can't include standard modules. This is unfortunate because we're about to discover another problem with Visual Basic: it has no provision for attaching data to a class instead of to individual objects.

Our error messages are a perfect example of the occasional need for classwide, static data. You don't want to attach a duplicate message array to every ODB object you create; you want the message array to exist once, and once only. Using a global array in a standard module worked nicely, but an even better solution would be an array in the class so that we could keep everything related to our class neatly encapsulated. (You don't want ODB error messages conflicting with other class's error messages.)

Static about Class Statics

C++ uses the keyword `static` class declarations to indicate that members (data and code) are attached to the class, not to objects instantiated from the class. These members aren't really static, but C++ follows C's long tradition of being miserly with its keywords. Because `static` almost fits, it was used again, rather than adding a more descriptive term, such as `classwide` members.

Unfortunately, the Visual Basic Books Online also uses the term *class static* to describe classwide data members. It explains that you actually can't have them, but that you can use `Property Get` functions to simulate them. We'll get to `Property Get` syntax in the next chapter. This function does the same thing:

```
Public Function classwide_name() As String
    classwide_name = "Some Nice Name"
End Function
```

This is simple, if somewhat kludgy, for a single value, and it's a nuisance when you have an array. We have an array.

Memo To Bill Gates

Bill, don't copy C++'s bad habits. Let's call classwide members something descriptive. I'd vote for `classwide members` as my candidate. The word *static* doesn't really describe them. (To be fair, Java picked up this bad habit from C++; it calls classwide members `static`, too.) You really have to add real classwide members, as soon as you have a spare minute.

Converting a Constant Array to a Function

The one mechanism that is available to attach something to the class, not to individual objects, is to use code. Methods occur only once in each class, not once for each object. That means that a method can be used, and it will do the job correctly, even though we would prefer a more direct approach. This method implements the equivalent of a classwide array of error messages:

```
Public Function ferr_msgs(msg_num As Byte)

    ' pseudo class static array

    Select Case msg_num
        Case err_freefile:
            ferr_msgs = "No file number available"

        Case err_open:
            ferr_msgs = "Cannot open file"

        Case err_seek:
            ferr_msgs = "Cannot perform seek"

        Case err_close:
            ferr_msgs = "Cannot close — no file open"

        Case err_getdel:
            ferr_msgs = "Cannot get — record deleted"

        Case err_badrec:
            ferr_msgs = "Cannot get — record damaged"

        Case err_notgot:
            ferr_msgs = _
                "Cannot get — invalid object number"
    End Select

End Function
```

Enter this function as a method of the ODB class. It gives you a passable substitute for a global array. It's not really what you want, but it does let you eliminate the initialization logic from your err_msgs() method. Reduce the err_msgs() logic to just this:

```
Private Sub err_msgs(errno As Byte)

    Call MsgBox(ferr_msgs(errno), vbCritical, "ODB Error")

End Sub
```

(Eliminate the check for initialization and the call to the initialization routine.)

Global Library Routines

One more routine in our ODB_lib.bas module has to be addressed: fix_len(). As you may recall, both the ODB class and the People class use fix_len(). If you move it into your main line standard module (right now it's Creator.bas), you'll have it available when you need it, but you'll have a poorly designed class.

A class shouldn't depend on support routines in the code that uses the class. It should be able to stand on its own two feet. It should be in the business of providing functionality, not consuming functionality.

Fortunately, Visual Basic now lets you place global routines in a class and call them from outside the class. You don't need to create an object to do this. Here's the hard way:

```
' The Hard Way:
    Dim foo as ODB
    Set foo = New ODB ' Create an instance

    Dim s As String
    s = foo.fix_len("Some String", 20)
```

In the case of a utility routine, such as fix_len(), what we really want is to let outsiders use the routine without requiring access through an object, this way:

```
' All You Really Want:
    Dim s As String
    s = fix_len("Some String", 20)
```

Fortunately, Visual Basic lets us do exactly what we want. You'll see that we need to throw a switch for permission to do this, but that's not much trouble.

Unfortunately, it provides the syntax we want but not the functionality. C++ and Java let you access class static methods with the name of the class, in place of using an object, this way:

```
' The C++/Java Solution — ERROR in VB
    Dim s As String
    s = ODB.fix_len( "Some String", 20)
```

(That's Visual Basic's, not C++ or Java's, syntax, of course.)

This code calls the method without creating an object. Visual Basic gets the calling syntax better, but internally Visual Basic instantiates an object. At least the documentation says it does. I don't know why it should, but the object doesn't seem to get in the way, so we can forget about the phantom object.

Memo To Bill Gates

What we really need, Bill, is a straightforward mechanism for classwide data and code members. While you're at it, allowing constant arrays as class members would really be just the thing for items like error messages, wouldn't it?

With all that said, the immediate solution to the `fix_len()` problem is just to move it from the ODB_lib.bas file into the ODB.cls file. Go ahead and use the clipboard to move `fix_len()`. I have one switch to throw, but I'll leave that undone until you see the error that's caused by not throwing it.

SEPARATING ODB INTO PROJECTS

Now that you've moved the library standard module's contents into the ODB class, you're ready for the easy part.

Begin by creating a new working subdirectory for the ODB development work. Copy into it the .BAS and two .CLS modules we've been using. We want to put ODB.cls into an ODB project and put Creator.bas and People.cls into a separate project.

Before you begin, shut down Visual Basic and modify your shortcut so that it specifies your new directory as the working directory. (Visual Basic will default to opening and saving all its files in the working directory, which becomes a real nuisance if the working directory isn't the one you want.) If you've forgotten, right-click the shortcut and then select Properties. The working directory is specified on the Shortcut tab of the attached properties sheet.

Once the source is available, building the projects is a simple matter. I'll give it to you step by step.

Step 1: Create a prjOtest Project

From the File menu, choose New Project. Double-click the standard .EXE icon to start a new, standard project. As Figure 7-1 shows, select the Form1.frm file on the Project Explorer and use the Project menu to remove the form. (You can also remove the form by right-clicking it in the Project Explorer and using the popup menu.)

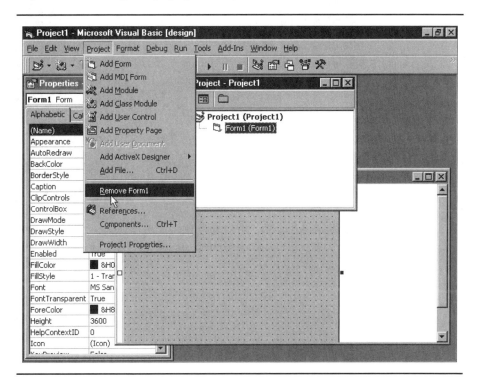

Figure 7-1
Removing Form1.frm with the Project menu.

Use the Properties window to change the name to prjODB. You've now created the testing project.

Step 2: Add the Project's Files

The easy way to add files is to press Ctrl+D at the keyboard and then select your file from the Add File dialog box. You can also access this menu by right-clicking the project in the Project Explorer, by clicking the dropdown arrow to the right of the Add Class Module icon on the toolbar, or from the Project menu. Figure 7-2 shows the toolbar route.

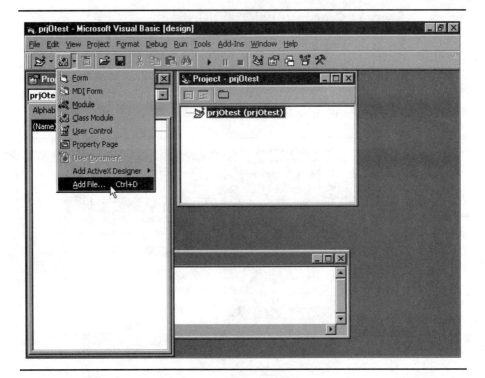

Figure 7-2
Navigating to the Add File... dialog box.

Add the Creator.bas file and then add the People.cls file. When Visual Basic reads the files, it sees that they are a standard module and a class module, respectively.

Step 3: Add Another Project

The leftmost icon on the standard toolbar shows the Tooltip "Add Standard EXE Project" if that was what you last used this button to add. If you click the dropdown arrow to its right, you'll see a menu of other project types. Choose to add an ActiveX.DLL. Use the Property window to change its name to prjODB.

When you add the project, you'll get a new class module, which you don't want. Remove it just as you removed Form1, and go to the Add File dialog box (anyway you like) and add ODB.cls. Figure 7-3 shows me finding Add File by the popup menu (right-click) from the Project Explorer.

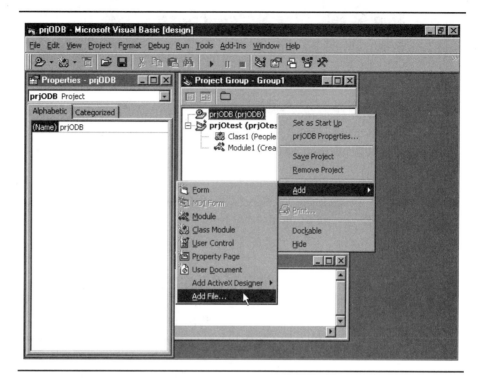

■ Figure 7-3
Another route to the Add File... dialog box.

This isn't an exhaustive treatment of ActiveX programming (we'll get there in Chapters 11 and 12), but for now you should be happy to know that simply placing a standard class in an ActiveX project is enough to program an ActiveX .DLL.

Just a year ago, programming ActiveX .DLLs was a complex challenge for C++ programmers. This is a beautiful change for the better.

Watch Your Project Explorer!

When you're working with multiple projects, be sure to look at the Project Explorer to see which one is selected. Adding a file, for instance, adds the file to the currently selected project.

If you make a mistake, just go ahead and delete the file from one project and then add it to another.

Step 4: Select the Startup Project

By default, the startup project is the first standard .EXE project you add. In this case that's the prjOtest project with Creator.bas, which is exactly what we want, so this really isn't a step at all, but this is a good time to learn to control this.

Right-click on prjODB in the Project Explorer. The first choice on the popup menu is Set As Startup. Click that choice, and then click one of the files in the Project Explorer list. You'll see that prjODB is in boldface and prjOtest is not. This tells you that prjODB is the startup project, whereas Visual Basic will look for subroutine Main(). This is wrong, of course.

Right-click prjOtest and choose Set As Startup. It is now boldfaced and prjODB reverts to the normal font.

RUNNING THE MULTIPLE-PROJECT SYSTEM

We've now established a new, multiple-project development environment. You'll be delighted to know that there's just that additional setting to choose and you're back in business. First, though, be sure that your Creator.bas is in the ODB-creating business. It's working code should be something like this:

```
Public Sub main()

' Create sample object
    Dim p As New People

    p.first_name = "John"
    p.last_name = "Johnson"
    p.addr1 = "123 Main St."
    p.city = "Anytown"
    p.state = "XX, USA"
    p.postal_code = "12345"

' Create ODB
    Dim od As New ODB

    od.create_odb p ' OK
    od.close_odb ' Success

End Sub
```

(Mine was saying, od.open_odb..., which is not what we want at the moment.)

Now you can save your work. If you pull down the file menu, you'll see that you've added commands for saving a Group. If you just click the save icon, you'll be asked for a name (the default is Group1.grp) for your group. I've called mine grpOtest.vbg.

The Instancing Property of ActiveX Projects

If you've saved and your Creator is ready, click the run icon or press F5. You'll die on a "User-defined type not defined" error at the line:

```
Dim od As New ODB
```

Visual Basic doesn't know what an ODB is. Why? Because the default instancing property for an ActiveX module is Private. At this point, you'll need to stop your program to fix the problem.

When you've stopped the program, click ODB.cls on the Project Explorer and look at the Property window. A normal class module has only a Name property. An ActiveX class module adds the Instancing property, which defaults to Private.

Private Instancing means the class is only available within the project. You need to give Creator.bas access to the ODB class, so change Instancing to 5 — MultiUse.

MultiUse Instancing and References

With the Instancing property set to MultiUse, run again, and you'll hang on the exact same error! (Go ahead and try it.) What's wrong?

The prjOtest project doesn't know that it should reference your ActiveX project. (Is this a feature or a bug? If this is a feature, I think it has six legs.) Stop the program again and choose References... from the Project menu.

As you see in Figure 7-4, Visual Basic has added your new ActiveX project to the References list, right below the four that it checks by default. You still have to check it, however.

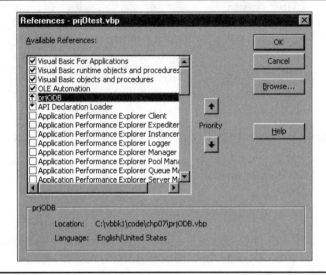

Figure 7-4
Telling Visual Basic that you want to use your project.

Memo To Bill Gates

Uh, Bill, maybe you could explain to me why I'd include an ActiveX project as one of my projects, but I wouldn't want to reference it. I'd sure like to know why I'd do that. I've never added a project I didn't intend to use.

Once you have checked the prjODB entry in the References list, try to run your project again. This will be our last failure (at least for now).

MultiUse and Global MultiUse

This time, as Figure 7-5 shows, we've pushed past the ODB problem and are hanging at our old friend, fix_len(). Visual Basic doesn't know where to find this routine.

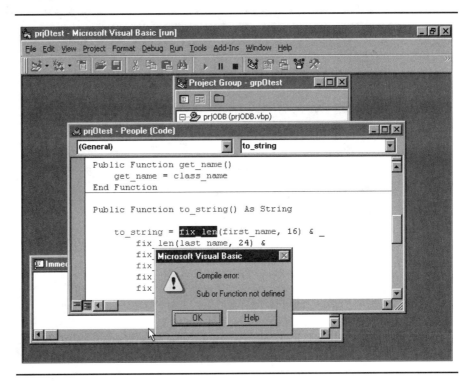

Figure 7-5
Visual Basic can't find `fix_len()`.

This is the difference between `MultiUse` and `Global MultiUse`. `MultiUse` makes your class available outside its project. `Global MultiUse` makes your class's methods available, too, as if they were global subroutines and functions.

For the last time, stop your project and go to the Property window to select Global MultiUse for Instancing. Before you get there, you may see the problem dialog box shown in Figure 7-6.

I'm not sure you'll see this dialog box because it's not correct. You're attempting to close the only program that's using this class, so you won't cause any problems. On the other hand, I'm not sure that Visual Basic can be sure that this is the case. It's fundamental to the nature of .DLLs that many programs can use them simultaneously.

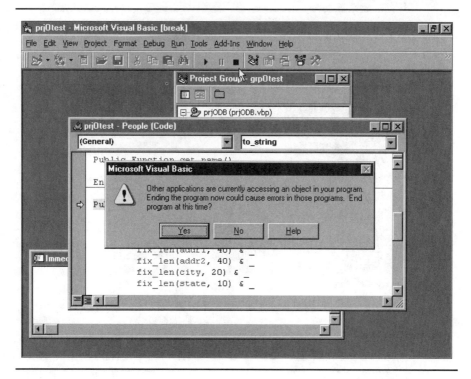

Figure 7-6
An erroneous error dialog box.

If Microsoft can't change this dialog box, go ahead and tell Visual Basic that you really do want to proceed. Then, as Figure 7-7 shows, select `Global MultiUse` for the `Instancing` property.

Now run again and you won't see a thing. More exactly, your program will run to completion successfully without any interruptions. Go ahead and use Notepad or your favorite text file editor to look at the newest member of your development directory's family: People.odb. It should be just the file you hoped to see.

THE LISTINGS

If you're not getting my results yet and your roommate has used this book's disk as a drink coaster, Listings 7-1a and 7-1b should help. Listing 7-1a shows Creator.bas, and Listing 7-1b shows ODB.cls. People.cls is also part of this project, but it's unchanged. Refer back to Listing 6-1c if you need to see People.cls.

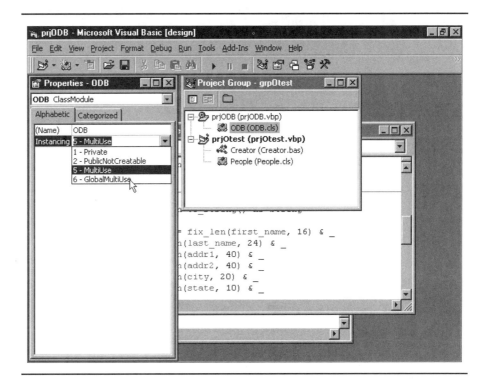

prjODB - Microsoft Visual Basic [design]

Figure 7-7
Choosing Global MultiUse Instancing.

Listing 7-1a
The main line test program

```
' Creator.bas — utility to create Object DataBase file
' Copyright 1997, Martin L. Rinehart

    Option Explicit

    Public Sub main()

    ' Create sample object
        Dim p As New People

        p.first_name = "John"
        p.last_name = "Johnson"
        p.addr1 = "123 Main St."
        p.city = "Anytown"
        p.state = "XX, USA"
        p.postal_code = "12345"
```

(continued)

The main line test program

```
' Create ODB
        Dim od As New ODB

        od.create_odb p ' OK
        od.close_odb ' Success

    End Sub

' end of Creator.bas
```

Listing 7-1b
The revised ODB class

```
' ODB.cls — Object DataBase class
' Copyright 1997, Martin L. Rinehart

' Creates a data file which holds objects of a single
' class.

' The class must provide a get_name() function returning
' a String, suitable for use as a file name.
' It must also provide a to_string() function that returns
' a fixed-length string containing all the property values
' that will be stored. And it must provide a from_string()
' method that extracts the property values from the string
' created by the to_string() operation.

' Format of the ODB file is:
'   Header
'   Object 0 record
'   Object 1 record
'   ...
'   Object n-1 record

' Format of the header is
'   Signature (8 bytes) = "mrVB5odb"
'   Object type name (32 bytes)
'   Record length (8 bytes)

' Format of the object record is
'   CR byte (chr(13))
'   LF byte (chr(10))
'   Deleted flag byte ("*" if deleted, " " otherwise)
'   unused byte (pad to dword boundary)
'   obj.to_string()
```

```
Option Explicit

Const signature = "mrVB5odb"
Const header_len = 48

' Errors:
    Public Enum err_types
        err_freefile = 0
        err_open
        err_seek
        err_close
        err_getdel
        err_badrec
        err_notgot
        number_of_errors
    End Enum

' Data members
    Public default_drive As String
    Public default_path As String

    Private file_number As Integer
    Private rec_len As Integer
    Private rec_buf As String
    Private path_name As String
    Private num_objects As Integer
    Private current_object_num As Integer

Public Sub close_odb()

    If file_number = 0 Then
        err_msgs (err_close)
        Exit Sub
    End If

    Close file_number
    file_number = 0 ' signal no file open

End Sub


Public Sub create_odb(first As Object)

    file_number = FreeFile

    path_name = first.get_name
    path_name = _
        default_drive & _
        default_path & _
        path_name & ".odb"
```

(continued)

The revised ODB class

```
    Open path_name For Binary As file_number

    rec_buf = Chr(13) & Chr(10) & "  " & first.to_string
    rec_len = Len(rec_buf)
    Dim header As String

    Dim nm As String
    nm = first.get_name

    header = signature & _
        fix_len(nm, 32) & _
        Right(Space(8) & Str(rec_len), 8)

    Put file_number, , header
    Put file_number, , rec_buf
    current_object_num = 1

End Sub


Public Sub open_odb(pn As String)

' check that a file number is available
    file_number = FreeFile
    If file_number = 0 Then
        err_msgs (err_freefile)
        Exit Sub
    End If

' open the file — if it's 0 long, its new
    Open pn & ".odb" For Binary As file_number
    If LOF(file_number) = 0 Then ' not an ODB!
        Close file_number
        err_msgs (err_open)
        Exit Sub
    End If

' create buffer for header, then read header
    Dim header As String
    header = Space(header_len)

    Get file_number, , header

' check for a valid signature
    If Left(header, 8) <> signature Then
        Close file_number
```

```
          err_msgs (err_open)
          Exit Sub
      End If

' set up private data members
    rec_len = Val(Right(header, 8))
    rec_buf = Space(rec_len)
    path_name = pn

    num_objects = (LOF(file_number) - header_len) / rec_len
    current_object_num = 0

End Sub


Public Sub add_obj(o As Object)

End Sub


Public Sub del_obj(num As Integer)

End Sub


Public Sub get_obj(num As Integer, ByRef obj As Object)

End Sub

Private Sub err_msgs(errno As Byte)

    Call MsgBox(ferr_msgs(errno), vbCritical, "ODB Error")

End Sub

Private Sub Class_Initialize()

    default_drive = ""
    default_path = ""
    file_number = 0 ' 0 = no file open

End Sub

Public Function ferr_msgs(msg_num As Byte)

    ' pseudo class static array

    Select Case msg_num
```

(continued)

The revised ODB class

```
            Case err_freefile:
                ferr_msgs = "No file number available"

            Case err_open:
                ferr_msgs = "Cannot open file"

            Case err_seek:
                ferr_msgs = "Cannot perform seek"

            Case err_close:
                ferr_msgs = "Cannot close — no file open"

            Case err_getdel:
                ferr_msgs = "Cannot get — record deleted"

            Case err_badrec:
                ferr_msgs = "Cannot get — record damaged"

            Case err_notgot:
                ferr_msgs = _
                    "Cannot get — invalid object number"

        End Select

End Function


Public Function fix_len(s As String, _
    num_chars As Integer)

' returns s padded or truncated to num_chars length

    fix_len = Left(s & Space(num_chars), num_chars)

End Function

' end of ODB.CLS
```

Congratulations. You've built your first ActiveX-based, object-oriented Visual Basic system. Now let's go on to finishing our ODB class. You'll see that once we have the mechanics squared away, you can forget that we're in multiple projects and just get back to work.

Memo To Bill Gates

Hey, Bill, did I mention that the way you've integrated the debugger right across ActiveX projects is slicker than black ice in a rainstorm? You just punch old, trusty F8 and step right through your work. It doesn't even hiccup as you cross into and out of the ActiveX code. Really, nice!

Adding Objects to the ODB

Let's go on to populate our ODB. I'm going to do this with a routine that creates `People` objects that we can add to the ODB file. It will look a little silly, but it will be handy for testing. Then we can modify our main line to use this routine and finally we can actually write the `add_obj()` method.

A PEOPLE GENERATOR

I'm going to fill in properties in a `People` object with values like `"Aaaa..."` and `"Bbbb..."`. The capital letters will show where each property starts and using different letters will show that we're correctly adding objects. Add this code to your People.cls file to create these instant People objects:

```
Public Sub fill_in(b As Byte)

    ' if b is 1, fills in with "Aaaaa..."
    ' if b is 2, fills in with "Bbbbb...", etc.

    Dim uchar As String, lchar As Byte

    uchar = Chr(Asc("A") - 1 + b)
    lchar = Asc("a") - 1 + b

    first_name = uchar & String(15, lchar)
    last_name = uchar & String(23, lchar)
    addr1 = uchar & String(39, lchar)
    addr2 = addr1
    city = uchar & String(19, lchar)
    state = uchar & String(9, lchar)
    postal_code = state

End Sub
```

USING THE FILL_IN() METHOD IN THE MAIN LINE

This fill_in() method let's us simplify the main line program. Replace your main() routine in Creator.bas with this code:

```
Public Sub main()

' Create sample object
    Dim p As New People

    p.fill_in 1

' Create ODB
    Dim od As New ODB

    od.create_odb p ' OK

    Dim i As Byte
    For i = 2 To 10
        p.fill_in i
        od.add_obj p
    Next

    od.close_odb ' Success

End Sub
```

THE OBJECT ADD METHOD

The last step is to actually write an add_obj() method. The only trick is to remember that bytes in the file are numbered starting with 1, so you always write to LOF() + 1 to append a new record. Add this routine to the ODB.cls file:

```
Public Sub add_obj(o As Object)

    rec_buf = Chr(13) & Chr(10) & "  " & o.to_string()
    Put file_number, LOF(file_number) + 1, rec_buf
    num_objects = num_objects + 1

End Sub
```

TESTING THE ADD_OBJ() METHOD

With these improvements, you're ready to test. My first test shows that there's an error in my `People` class. Try it yourself and see what you find. (Run the program and use Notepad or your favorite text editor to examine the People.odb file.)

Got it? I wasn't consistent in putting `first_name` in front of `last_name`, so the `to_print()` wasn't quite right. After I saw the problem, I changed `to_print()` to use `first_name` first and `last_name` second.

Figure 7-8 shows me examining a successful run. Make yours look the same.

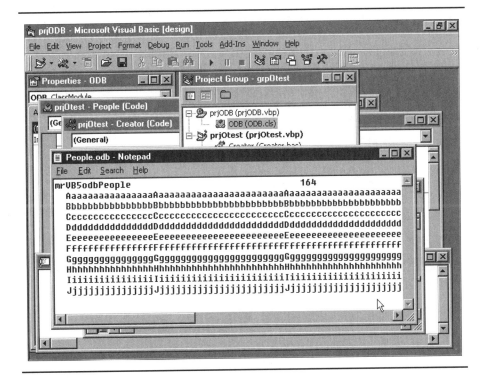

Figure 7-8
The People.odb file is correct.

DELETING OBJECTS IN THE ODB

Because alphabetical order seems as convenient as any other order, we can continue by adding the del_obj() method. To do this, we'll need support routines (private methods) that check the validity of an object number and that correctly locate the start of an object in the ODB. Once those are written, deleting an object is a simple matter of placing an asterisk in the third byte of the object's record prefix. Let's start with the support routines.

General-Purpose Support Routines

Once an object is written to the ODB, we'll need to be able to find it again, given its number. Here you'll have to decide for yourself if you want to number objects from zero or from one. I much prefer counting from zero, which is the way I'll code my routines, but if you have a strong preference for starting with one, go ahead and modify this code appropriately. Both methods work.

Checking the Object Number

Each of the next three methods — del_obj(), get_obj(), and rep_obj() — are called with an object number. A sensible first step is to make sure that this number actually exists. That's a simple check in a private method, like this:

```
Private Function rec_in_file(num As Integer) As Boolean

    ' is num in range 0 to num_objects-1 ?

    rec_in_file = (num > -1) And (num < num_objects)

End Function
```

If you're counting from 1, the range is 1 through num_objects, and the checks are for a number greater than zero and less than or equal to num_objects.

Locating an Object

Our .DBF-style file structure makes it very simple to find an object. This routine does the trick:

```
Private Function oloc(num As Integer)

    ' find object in file
    oloc = header_len + num * rec_len + 1

End Function
```

Don't forget to change this formula if you want to start from one.

 The simplest case would occur if we start counting from zero, and the first byte in the file was byte zero. Lot's of things become simpler when you start from zero.

Deleting an Object

We're not actually going to remove an object physically when it's deleted. That would require rewriting the file from the point of the deletion to its end, which could be a tedious process. Rather, we'll copy Wayne Ratliff's dBASE decision and just mark the object as deleted. The .DBF file Wayne designed used an asterisk to mark a record as deleted, which is a habit I'm going to repeat here.

With our supporting private methods in place, this method is very simple:

```
Public Sub del_obj(num As Integer)

    If Not rec_in_file(num) Then
        err_msgs (ferr_seek)
        Exit Sub
    End If

    Put file_number, oloc(num) + 2, "*"

End Sub
```

Remember that the first two bytes of the record prefix are the carriage return and linefeed pair, so the deletion mark is put at the third byte, `oloc(num) + 2`.

Testing with the Main Line

All that's left is to test our deletions. I've added three tests to my main line code. Two delete actual records, and the third is out of bounds, so it should trigger the error message. My new `main()` routine in Creator.bas looks like this:

```
Public Sub main()

' Create sample object
    Dim p As New People

    p.fill_in 1

' Create ODB
    Dim od As New ODB

    od.create_odb p ' OK

    Dim i As Byte
    For i = 2 To 10
        p.fill_in i
        od.add_obj p
    Next

    od.del_obj 2
    od.del_obj 4
    od.del_obj 14 ' Error!

    od.close_odb ' Success

End Sub
```

When I ran this I received one error message, which was what I wanted. You need to check the valid deletions by looking at the People.odb file, as Figure 7-9 shows.

If you're counting from zero, object 2 is the "C" object.

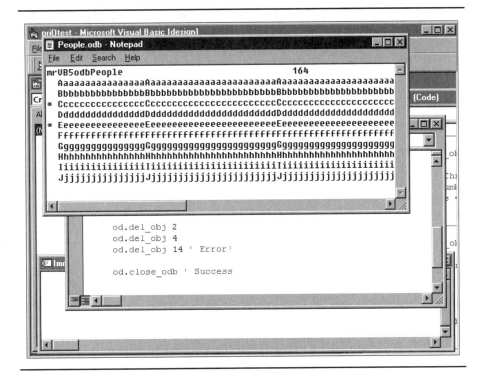

Figure 7-9
Examining the results of object deletions.

RETRIEVING OBJECTS FROM THE ODB

The work we've done so far has resulted in output to the ODB file, so we've been able to check by examining that file. The get_obj() method uses that file for input, not output, so we'll need a different way of checking. The built-in debugger will serve this purpose.

We'll begin by writing the get_obj() method, and then we'll turn to the mainline code to use this new method.

GETTING AN OBJECT FROM THE ODB

The get code is not quite as trivial as the delete code, simply because we need to make an extra check — you should not get an object if it has been deleted. Otherwise, we'll let the subject class's from_string() method do the heavy lifting. We do have to remember to keep our record prefix away from the `from_string()` code, as the `subject` class doesn't know or care about our bookkeeping details.

This is the new code to add to ODB.cls:

```
Public Sub get_obj(num As Integer, ByRef obj As Object)

    If Not rec_in_file(num) Then
        err_msgs (err_seek)
        Exit Sub
    End If

    Get file_number, oloc(num), rec_buf

    If Mid(rec_buf, 3, 1) = "*" Then
        err_msgs (err_getdel)
    Else
        obj.from_string (Right(rec_buf, rec_len - 4))
    End If

End Sub
```

Again, although `ByRef` is the Visual Basic default, I've used the *ByRef* keyword to explicitly remind myself that the routine will be modifying the object passed to it.

Testing the Get from the Main Line

Are you a master of the Visual Basic debugger? If you are, think about how you can use it to make the following checks more efficiently. (Hint: break on change in the Watch window.) This is a straightforward approach for those who might not be debug-meisters.

Add the three calls to the `get_obj()` method that you see here in my extended main line:

```
Public Sub main()

' Create sample object
    Dim p As New People

    p.fill_in 1

' Create ODB
    Dim od As New ODB
```

```
od.create_odb p ' OK

Dim i As Byte
For i = 2 To 10
    p.fill_in i
    od.add_obj p
Next

od.del_obj 2
od.del_obj 4

Call od.get_obj(1, p)
Call od.get_obj(2, p)
Call od.get_obj(3, p)

od.close_odb ' Success

End Sub
```

Remember that object 2 has been deleted, so the middle get should fail with an appropriate message. The other two should succeed.

To check the results, place a breakpoint at each of the three calls to get_obj(). (To place a breakpoint, click the colored area to the left of the line of code in the code editor. You can only place breakpoints in the running code, so lines like Dim won't accept a breakpoint.)

Run the program, and it will stop at the first breakpoint. In the Debug menu, choose Add Watch... and tell it you want to look at the variable p. It will tell you that p is an object of the People class, which you already knew.

If you click the + sign next to p in the Watch window, Visual Basic will expand p to show all its properties. Figure 7-10 shows this, after the first of the get_obj() methods has run.

At the first breakpoint, you should see the J values in p. Press Shift+F8 to run the single line. (F8 without the shift will step into each routine called, which can be invaluable in tracking down trouble. Shift+F8 executes the whole line, which is what you want if you don't have trouble.)

At the second breakpoint, you will have taken object 1 from the ODB. (The break is triggered before the line with the breakpoint runs.) The Watch window will show the p object has been filled with the B values. (If you coded your version to count from one, that would be the A values.)

You can press Shift+F8 or F5 (or click the run icon) to continue because the breakpoints stop execution for you.

Is yours running correctly? We just have one more method to implement, and we're ready to call our ODB class complete.

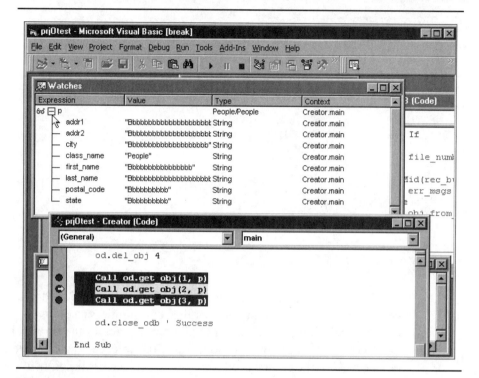

Figure 7-10
Watching at a breakpoint.

REPLACING OBJECTS IN THE ODB

As soon as you create a system that lets users enter data, you'll find that you need to let the users change the data they've entered. The edit process is an integral part of every system I've ever come across. That's the reason we need the rep_obj() method.

In working systems, we'll use Visual Basic forms for data entry and editing. When the user completes the data entry, (clicks OK or whatever) we'll call the add_obj() method. Then when the user navigates back to the record and makes changes, we'll call the rep_obj() method.

Replacing an Object in the ODB

Replacing an object is simple. Again, more code is involved in error checking than in actually doing the work. My version of rep_obj() in ODB.cls looks like this:

```
Public Sub rep_obj(num As Integer, o As Object)

    If Not rec_in_file(num) Then
        err_msgs (err_seek)
        Exit Sub
    End If

    rec_buf = Chr(13) + Chr(10) + "  " + o.to_string()
    Put file_number, oloc(num), rec_buf

End Sub
```

Once more, the `to_string()` method supplied by the storable class is doing the real work.

Testing the rep_obj() Method

We can go back to examining the file to test the results of our `rep_obj()` method. I've modified my main line code so that it replaces object 3 with Ks and object 5 with Ls. It now reads this way:

```
Public Sub main()

' Create sample object
    Dim p As New People

    p.fill_in 1

' Create ODB
    Dim od As New ODB

    od.create_odb p ' OK

    Dim i As Byte
    For i = 2 To 10
        p.fill_in i
        od.add_obj p
    Next

    p.fill_in 11
    Call od.rep_obj(3, p)

    p.fill_in 12
    Call od.rep_obj(5, p)

    od.close_odb ' Success

End Sub
```

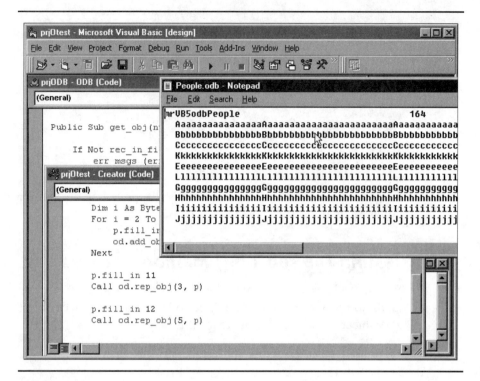

Figure 7-11
People.odb after replacing objects 3 and 5.

Figure 7-11 shows the new People.odb file this main line creates.

THE FULL ODB SYSTEM LISTINGS

If you're having trouble making your ODB class function correctly and your husband has used this book's disk as part of the really cute mobile he made for the baby, Listings 7-2 should help. Listing 7-2a shows the final People.cls, Listing 7-2b shows the final Creator.bas, and Listing 7-2c shows the final ODB.cls.

The disk's 07-02 file also includes the .VBP project files and the .VBG group file.

Listing 7-2a
The storable People class

```
' People.cls — basic data about a person
' Copyright 1997, Martin L. Rinehart

Option Explicit

Const class_name = "People"

' Public data members
    Public first_name As String
    Public last_name As String

    Public addr1 As String
    Public addr2 As String
    Public city As String
    Public state As String
    Public postal_code As String

Public Function get_name()
    get_name = class_name
End Function

Public Function to_string() As String

    to_string = fix_len(first_name, 16) & _
        fix_len(last_name, 24) & _
        fix_len(addr1, 40) & _
        fix_len(addr2, 40) & _
        fix_len(city, 20) & _
        fix_len(state, 10) & _
        fix_len(postal_code, 10)

End Function

Public Sub from_string(s As String)

    first_name = Left(s, 16)
    last_name = Mid(s, 17, 24)
    addr1 = Mid(s, 41, 40)
    addr2 = Mid(s, 81, 40)
    city = Mid(s, 121, 20)
    state = Mid(s, 141, 10)
    postal_code = Right(s, 10)

End Sub
```

(continued)

The storable People class

```
Public Sub fill_in(b As Byte)

    ' if b is 1, fills in with "Aaaaa..."
    ' if b is 2, fills in with "Bbbbb...", etc.

    Dim uchar As String, lchar As Byte

    uchar = Chr(Asc("A") - 1 + b)
    lchar = Asc("a") - 1 + b

    first_name = uchar & String(15, lchar)
    last_name = uchar & String(23, lchar)
    addr1 = uchar & String(39, lchar)
    addr2 = addr1
    city = uchar & String(19, lchar)
    state = uchar & String(9, lchar)
    postal_code = state

End Sub

' end of People.cls
```

Listing 7-2b
The final main line program

```
' Creator.bas — utility to create Object DataBase file
' Copyright 1997, Martin L. Rinehart

Option Explicit

Public Sub main()

' Create sample object
    Dim p As New People

    p.fill_in 1

' Create ODB
    Dim od As New ODB

    od.create_odb p ' OK

    Dim i As Byte
```

```
    For i = 2 To 10
        p.fill_in i
        od.add_obj p
    Next

    p.fill_in 11
    Call od.rep_obj(3, p)

    p.fill_in 12
    Call od.rep_obj(5, p)

    od.close_odb ' Success

End Sub


' end of Creator.bas
```

Listing 7-2c
The completed ODB class

```
' ODB.cls — Object DataBase class
' Copyright 1997, Martin L. Rinehart

' Creates a data file which holds objects of a single
' class.

' The class must provide a get_name() function returning
' a String, suitable for use as a file name.
' It must also provide a to_string() function that returns
' a fixed-length string containing all the property values
' that will be stored. And it must provide a from_string()
' method that extracts the property values from the string
' created by the to_string() operation.

' Format of the ODB file is:
'   Header
'   Object 0 record
'   Object 1 record
'   ...
'   Object n-1 record

' Format of the header is
'   Signature (8 bytes) = "mrVB5odb"
'   Object type name (32 bytes)
'   Record length (8 bytes)
```

(continued)

The completed ODB class

```
' Format of the object record is
'    CR byte (chr(13))
'    LF byte (chr(10))
'    Deleted flag byte ("*" if deleted, " " otherwise)
'    unused byte (pad to dword boundary)
'    obj.to_string()

Option Explicit

Const signature = "mrVB5odb"
Const header_len = 48

' Errors:
    Public Enum err_types
        err_freefile = 0
        err_open
        err_seek
        err_close
        err_getdel
        err_badrec
        err_notgot
        number_of_errors
    End Enum

' Data members
    Public default_drive As String
    Public default_path As String

    Private file_number As Integer
    Private rec_len As Integer
    Private rec_buf As String
    Private path_name As String
    Private num_objects As Integer
    Private current_object_num As Integer

Public Sub close_odb()

    If file_number = 0 Then
        err_msgs (err_close)
        Exit Sub
    End If

    Close file_number
    file_number = 0 ' signal no file open

End Sub
```

```
Public Sub create_odb(first As Object)

    file_number = FreeFile

    path_name = first.get_name
    path_name = _
        default_drive & _
        default_path & _
        path_name & ".odb"

    If Len(Dir(path_name)) Then Kill path_name

    Open path_name For Binary As file_number

    rec_buf = Chr(13) & Chr(10) & "  " & first.to_string
    rec_len = Len(rec_buf)
    Dim header As String

    Dim nm As String
    nm = first.get_name

    header = signature & _
        fix_len(nm, 32) & _
        Right(Space(8) & Str(rec_len), 8)

    Put file_number, , header
    Put file_number, , rec_buf
    current_object_num = 1

End Sub

Public Sub open_odb(pn As String)

' check that a file number is available
    file_number = FreeFile
    If file_number = 0 Then
        err_msgs (err_freefile)
        Exit Sub
    End If

' open the file — if it's 0 long, its new
    Open pn & ".odb" For Binary As file_number
    If LOF(file_number) = 0 Then ' not an ODB!
        Close file_number
        err_msgs (err_open)
        Exit Sub
    End If
```

(continued)

The completed ODB class

```
' create buffer for header, then read header
    Dim header As String
    header = Space(header_len)

    Get file_number, , header

' check for a valid signature
    If Left(header, 8) @@@> signature Then
        Close file_number
        err_msgs (err_open)
        Exit Sub
    End If

' set up private data members
    rec_len = Val(Right(header, 8))
    rec_buf = Space(rec_len)
    path_name = pn

    num_objects = (LOF(file_number) - header_len) / rec_len
    current_object_num = 0

End Sub

Public Sub add_obj(o As Object)

    rec_buf = Chr(13) & Chr(10) & "  " & o.to_string()
    Put file_number, LOF(file_number) + 1, rec_buf
    num_objects = num_objects + 1

End Sub

Public Sub del_obj(num As Integer)

    If Not rec_in_file(num) Then
        err_msgs (err_seek)
        Exit Sub
    End If

    Put file_number, oloc(num) + 2, "*"

End Sub

Public Sub get_obj(num As Integer, ByRef obj As Object)

    If Not rec_in_file(num) Then
        err_msgs (err_seek)
        Exit Sub
    End If
```

```
    Get file_number, oloc(num), rec_buf

    If Mid(rec_buf, 3, 1) = "*" Then
        err_msgs (err_getdel)
    Else
        obj.from_string (Right(rec_buf, rec_len - 4))
    End If

End Sub


Public Sub rep_obj(num As Integer, o As Object)

    If Not rec_in_file(num) Then
        err_msgs (err_seek)
        Exit Sub
    End If

    rec_buf = Chr(13) + Chr(10) + "  " + o.to_string()
    Put file_number, oloc(num), rec_buf

End Sub

Private Function rec_in_file(num As Integer) As Boolean

    ' is num in range 0 to num_objects-1 ?

    rec_in_file = (num > -1) And (num < num_objects)

End Function

Private Function oloc(num As Integer)

    ' find object in file
    oloc = header_len + num * rec_len + 1

End Function

Private Sub err_msgs(errno As Byte)

    Call MsgBox(ferr_msgs(errno), vbCritical, "ODB Error")

End Sub

Private Sub Class_Initialize()
```

(continued)

The completed ODB class

```
        default_drive = ""
        default_path = ""
        file_number = 0 ' 0 = no file open

End Sub

Public Function ferr_msgs(msg_num As Byte)

    ' pseudo class static array

    Select Case msg_num

        Case err_freefile:
            ferr_msgs = "No file number available"

        Case err_open:
            ferr_msgs = "Cannot open file"

        Case err_seek:
            ferr_msgs = "Cannot perform seek"

        Case err_close:
            ferr_msgs = "Cannot close — no file open"

        Case err_getdel:
            ferr_msgs = "Cannot get — record deleted"

        Case err_badrec:
            ferr_msgs = "Cannot get — record damaged"

        Case err_notgot:
            ferr_msgs = _
                "Cannot get — invalid object number"

    End Select

End Function

Public Function fix_len(s As String, _
    num_chars As Integer)

' returns s padded or truncated to num_chars length

    fix_len = Left(s & Space(num_chars), num_chars)

End Function

' end of ODB.CLS
```

SUMMARY

We began this chapter with a look at multiple-project development. Our first job was to eliminate the global .BAS module that we'd used in Chapter 6. Visual Basic doesn't really support classwide data, but we were able to use a method as a fairly good substitute.

We then turned our single-project system into a multiple-project system. This meant creating projects and then using the Add File dialog box to add the component modules back in. We used an ActiveX .DLL project for the class work. After we set its `Instancing` property to `Global MultiUse` and used the Project ⇨ References... dialog box to include the new ActiveX work, we were back in business.

Then we went on to write the code that manipulated the objects in the ODB file. We wrote two support routines to check for a valid object number and to find an object's location in the file, given its number. Then writing the code was straightforward.

For adding, deleting, and replacing objects in the ODB, we were able to test our work by examining the ODB file directly. The method for getting objects out of the ODB required testing with the Visual Basic debugger. The Watch window handled that job nicely.

Now you have a class that you'll be able to use whenever you need a modest amount of data storage. How big did you estimate the finished result would be?

Let's produce a final, ActiveX .DLL, to check its size. This is how: right-click prjODB in the Project Explorer and choose Properties... from the popup menu. On the Compile tab, select Compile to Native Code. For simplicity, ignore all the optimization settings.

Shut the Properties dialog box with an OK click and go to the File menu. This will give you a Make prjODB DLL... choice. Click it and Visual Basic will get to work. A short while later you'll have a native Intel executable .DLL. (Your C++-writing friends will be green with envy!)

My prjODB.DLL is just under 18K. That, I'm sure you'll agree, is a whole lot more reasonable than 3MB if you want something that can be downloaded from a Web page!

In Chapter 8, we'll look at `Property Get` and the other `Property` routines and then we'll start on a schedule that we can use in the MyTime system.

BUILDING A SCHEDULE DISPLAY

*O*ur ODB class will let us store objects on disk, at very little cost in executable size. It's not yet hooked to any visual capability, as the Data Access Object is.

Before we go back to work on that problem, however, I'd like to do some visual programming. Let's build a schedule object that will show our appointment schedule. Once it's built, we can hook it to a small database of appointments. This is a key class for the MyTime system we'll work on, beginning in Chapter 14.

Pause for a moment and think through the implications. We're going to build an object that we can use in a system we haven't even designed, yet. The MyTime system will also use the calendar and ODB classes, too. This is what object-oriented programming is all about: creating classes we can use in systems we haven't even invented yet.

Before we dive into the schedule programming, we'll take a look at the Property statements that Visual Basic provides for controlling access to Private data members. I've already told you that I'm not a big fan of these statements. In fact, I'd just leave them out altogether, but Visual Basic keeps writing them for us, so you should at least understand them.

While we're looking at them, we'll have some fun with a very rude method. That's actually going to be the `rude()` method.

Then we'll move on to building our schedule class. We'll create a project and set up the form. Then we'll add an array of time labels and use program logic to set their positions and captions.

Next we'll put a `TextBox` on top to display the date, and we'll write a very nice date display routine, too.

We'll drop an elevator down the side, but we'll leave it unconnected until Chapter 9, in which we'll thoroughly investigate the strange elevator critter.

Finally, we'll put some buttons on the bottom and add a zoom in and zoom out capability. Let's begin with the `Property` statement family.

PROPERTY STATEMENT PROGRAMMING

`Property` statements provide the external appearance of public properties, but internally they access private properties through subroutines that do whatever checking or other work is involved. We've been doing property-like programming already.

In fact, I'd leave these statements out of my personal toolkit altogether, if only Visual Basic would let me! Its tools, however, seem to think that these extra statements are just the cat's meow. It refuses to stop writing them.

If you use the Wizards, you see `Property` statements. If you use the Add Procedure dialog box, you'll see `Property` statements. If you use `Private` data, you see `Property` procedures, whether you want them or not.

That's right, Microsoft's documentation insists that all access to `Private` data members is through internally created `Property Let` (or `Property Set`) and `Property Get` procedures. Thus, it concludes, you should actually write your own. In other contexts, it sensibly suggests that you use procedures only when you have some work for the procedures to do. (Again, if `Public` access is reasonable for your data, go ahead and make it `Public`.)

Property Let Statements

Those of us who were around when Columbus discovered America remember the `Let` statement, which was used for all BASIC assignments:

```
Let x = 2
Let Y$ = "Hello, World!"
```

Fairly early in the development of the language, the interpreter writers discovered that they could live without the `Let` keyword, and BASIC programmers quickly stopped using it. The Let has now been reincarnated as part of the Property Let statement.

The Functionality Is Already Available

The common use for a Property Let statement is to create public access to a private property. Assume that you have a _foo_ variable that holds a string which must not exceed a maximum length. In Java or C++ you would keep the data member private and provide a public set() routine. In Visual Basic you do that this way:

```
Const max_foo_len = 20
Private prvFoo As String
    ' not to exceed max_foo_len chars long

Public Sub set_foo(s As String)

    If Len(s) <= max_foo_len Then
        prvFoo = s
    Else
        ' Handle error here
    End If

End Sub
```

Then the routines that wanted to assign values to prvFoo would work this way:

```
' bar is an object of the appropriate class

bar.set_foo("String to assign")
```

This is the method I recommend you use because the call to the set_foo() method looks like it's a call to a method that sets the value of a foo property. The Property Let statement begins a property function that can do exactly the same job.

Property Let Does the Same Job

The Property Let statement handles the same job, this way:

```
Const max_foo_len = 20
Private prvFoo As String
    ' not to exceed max_foo_len chars long

Public Property Let pubFoo(s As String)
```

```
    If Len(s) <= max_foo_len Then
        prvFoo = s
    Else
        ' handle error here
    End If

End Property
```

When you do this, that code that uses your object makes assignments to the public name, this way:

```
' This calls the pubFoo method:

bar.pubFoo = "String to assign"
```

It's Really a Method Call

You have no restriction on the code you can include in a Property Let method. Here's a Property Let with a real attitude problem:

```
Public Property Let rude(s As String)

    Dim msgs(4) As String
    msgs(0) = "No way will I assign that"
    msgs(1) = "I said 'No!' and I mean No!"
    msgs(2) = "Forget it, pal"
    msgs(3) = "Go away and don't bother me!"
    msgs(4) = "Absolutely no way will I do that!"

    Static i ' defaults to zero

    If i > 4 Then i = 0

    MsgBox msgs(i)
    i = i + 1


    End Property
```

The rude() method doesn't do any assignment. It cycles through a list of messages saying that it refuses to cooperate. Your calling code can test it this way:

```
bar.rude = "This won't be assigned."
```

Figure 8-1 shows the rude() Property Let in operation.

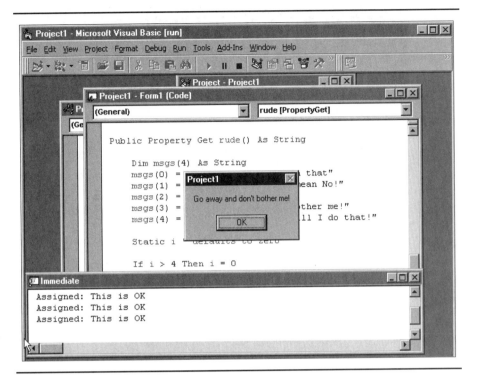

■ **Figure 8-1**
▌ *rude() refuses to help.*

There's a serious point to be made, here. The `Property Let` statement creates a method that is called by a statement that looks like an assignment to a data member. In fact, that *assignment* is really a method call. The method will do whatever job you give it.

Memo to Bill Gates

Bill, what's good about calling methods with code that doesn't look like it's calling a method? Isn't that opposed to all known principles of readable programming?

I don't write `Property Let` methods, and I can't think of a good reason why you should, either. The only possible reason is that you originally created a `Public` property and now you want to replace it with a `Private` one, but you don't want to change the code that uses your class.

Visual Basic is fond of writing `Property` statements, so you'll see a lot of these, even if you don't write your own.

The Property Get Statement

The Property Get statement introduces a method that returns a value, again letting your code look like it's working with a Public data member when it's really calling a method. I don't use the Property Get, but again, Visual Basic is uncommonly fond of this syntax, so you can't avoid it.

Here's a rude() Property Get:

```
Public Property Get rude() As String

    Dim msgs(4) As String
    msgs(0) = "No way will I assign that"
    msgs(1) = "I said 'No!' and I mean No!"
    msgs(2) = "Forget it, pal"
    msgs(3) = "Go away and don't bother me!"
    msgs(4) = "Absolutely no way will I do that!"

    Static i ' defaults to zero

    If i > 4 Then i = 0

    rude = msgs(i)
    i = i + 1


End Property
```

Visual Basic enforces the intent of the Property Let and Get by insisting that they be used as compatible pairs if you have a Let and Get that both use the same name. For example, you can't do this:

```
Public Property Let foo(s As String)

    ' called with: bar.foo = "String"

End Property

' This is a compile error:

Public Property Get foo() As Integer

    ' returns an integer: i = bar.foo

End Property
```

If the Property Let assigns a string, a Property Get of the same name must return a string, or, to put it more exactly, if the Let looks like it assigns a string the Get should announce that it will return a string or the compiler will refuse to compile the class.

The Property Set Statement

Last, and with the same "Don't want it, but can't avoid it" problem, we have Property Set statements. These parallel the Let and Set pair in other assignments:

```
Dim i As Integer
Let i = 2

Dim m As MyClass
Set m = New MyClass
```

The Set statement never made any sense to me. We eliminated the Let early on in our BASIC dialects, so why bring in another assignment keyword? This is perfectly clear code:

```
' This is clear, but it won't work

Dim m As MyClass
m = New MyClass

' A 'Set' is mandatory with objects
```

Memo to Bill Gates

Bill, why do we need another statement when we work with objects? Did somebody think that typing **Set** was more fun than typing **Let**?

You use Property Set to deal with object values. Then your calling code uses Set statements, just as if it were assigning to an object variable. I'll go right on writing my own methods that look like they're methods, thank you.

Sample Property Let and Get Code

I've written my Property Let and Get code in a form-based class. They work the same way in either a .FRM or a .CLS module. All this code and the related project file is in 08-01 if you have the disk.

The sensible `prvFoo` variable is set via the `Public pubFoo` method. As Figure 8-2 shows, this code reports successful operation in the Immediate window, but uses `MsgBox` output for errors.

The Class Code

Listing 8-1a shows the `Form`-based class that contains `Property Let` and `Property Get` methods. The `prvFoo` variable is set with the `pubFoo Property Set` method. A correctly paired `rude()` `Let` and `Get` illustrate the point that these are just methods, in spite of the way they are called.

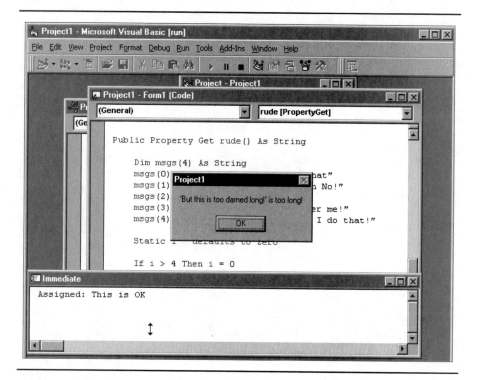

Figure 8-2
Assigning To `prvFoo` *via* `pubFoo`.

Listing 8-1a
A .FRM with Property Let and Get methods

```
Option Explicit

Const max_foo_len = 20
Private prvFoo As String
```

```vb
' not to exceed max_foo_len chars long

Public Property Let pubFoo(s As String)

    If Len(s) <= max_foo_len Then
        prvFoo = s
        Debug.Print "Assigned: " & prvFoo
    Else
        MsgBox "'" & s & "'" & _
            " is too long!"
    End If
End Property

Public Property Let rude(s As String)

    Dim msgs(4) As String
    msgs(0) = "No way will I assign that"
    msgs(1) = "I said 'No!' and I mean No!"
    msgs(2) = "Forget it, pal"
    msgs(3) = "Go away and don't bother me!"
    msgs(4) = "Absolutely no way will I do that!"

    Static i ' defaults to zero

    If i > 4 Then i = 0

    MsgBox msgs(i)
    i = i + 1

End Property

Public Property Get rude() As String

    Dim msgs(4) As String
    msgs(0) = "No way will I assign that"
    msgs(1) = "I said 'No!' and I mean No!"
    msgs(2) = "Forget it, pal"
    msgs(3) = "Go away and don't bother me!"
    msgs(4) = "Absolutely no way will I do that!"

    Static i ' defaults to zero

    If i > 4 Then i = 0

    rude = msgs(i)
    i = i + 1


End Property
```

By the way, I've just copied the block of code that assigns the rude()
values. That's a horrible practice that you'll never do in actual, working
code, right? This is throwaway code. You won't see me do something this
crude in the classes we're building for actual use.

Using Property Let and Get Methods

I created a standard module and, in the Project Properties dialog box, set
the startup to main(), where the calling statements are written. Listing
8-1b shows the calls to pubFoo() and rude().

Listing 8-1b
A .BAS using Property Let and Get methods

```
Option Explicit

Public Sub main()

    Dim f As Form1
    Set f = New Form1

    f.pubFoo = "This is OK"
    f.pubFoo = "But this is too darned long!"

    ' f.prvFoo is not accessible here

    Dim i As Byte
    For i = 0 To 5
        f.rude = "Attitude problem"
    Next

    For i = 0 To 5
        MsgBox f.rude
    Next

End Sub
```

You'll find that the rude() methods live up to their name. Notice how
the calling code looks like it's dealing with a Public data member, even
though it's calling methods. This offends my sense of good software
engineering.

Now you know how to use Property Let, Get, and Set methods, and
why not to. Let's move on to having some fun writing code.

> ### Memo to Bill Gates
>
> Property Let and Get pairs prove that you can allow polymorphism in Visual Basic, Bill. You have two very different routines using the same name. Why not allow this in a more useful way? Letting us write routines with the same name but different parameters would match this very useful capability of C++ and Java.

BEGINNING THE SCHEDULE PROJECT

In our PIM project, I'll want a schedule where I can see my appointments. In my life, I have relatively few appointments, so I'm not going to allow for a lot here. The way I'm building this would be totally inappropriate for, for example, a busy doctor.

You'll see other ways that I fit this project to my personal habits. I like to start working very early in the morning, and I don't want to be interrupted before 9:00 a.m. Therefore, I start my schedule at 9:00. If your day starts with a breakfast meeting, you'll need to start your schedule much earlier.

While you work on your own version of the PIM, don't follow my version too closely. This is a personal project, so make it fit your own life. If you do, you'll have a small, quick PIM that you'll enjoy using.

Create the Directory

As always, the first step is to exit from Visual Basic. Then:

- Create a working directory
- Create your Visual Basic shortcut to that directory
- Launch Visual Basic via your shortcut

Now we're ready to create the project.

Create the Project

The schedule will be a form-based class, so start a new, standard .EXE project. Use Ctrl+N if you're already in Visual Basic.

Then take these steps:

- Name the project prjSched

- Name the form frmSched

- Caption the form Schedule

- Make the form about 4000 twips tall, 5000 wide

Now you're ready to save. Accept the default names: prjSched.vbp and frmSched.frm.

Figure 8-3 shows me ready to start the programming.

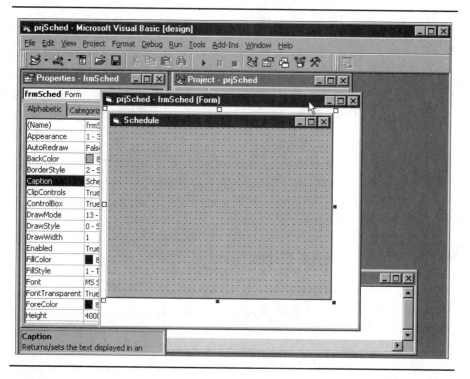

Figure 8-3
It won't be empty for long.

ADDING LABELS AND A TEXTBOX

You have to start by making an important decision: how many time increments will you display? I'm going with nine, which will default to hourly from 9:00 a.m. to 5:00 p.m.

We'll program the schedule so that you can zoom in (down to minute-by-minute, if you insist) and zoom out (hourly is the largest increment I use), but the straightforward way to do labels is to create an array of some fixed size. A lot of items are going to depend on this size.

You could very well go for a larger number than nine. Sixteen would get you from 9:00 a.m. to 4:30 p.m. by half hours, for example. I'll go ahead explaining it the way I've written mine, but I trust you'll be making yours fit your own life.

Adding a Label Array

I'll run the time labels down the left, as Figure 8-4 shows.

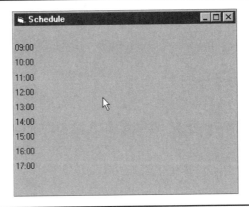

Figure 8-4
Your labels will look like this.

Start by double-clicking a label into the center of your form. Then make these adjustments:

- Change the Name to lblTime
- Change the Caption to 00:00
- Change the Height to 160
- Change the Width to 400

Figure 8-5 shows me making the last of these changes.

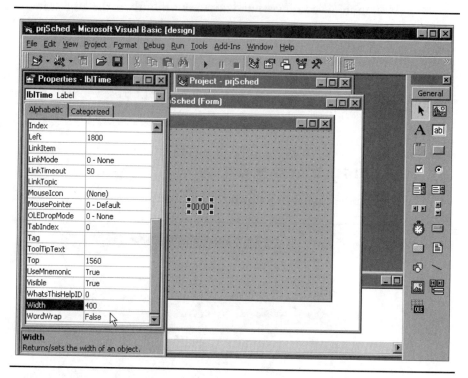

Figure 8-5

Adjusting the default label.

Once you've made these changes, cut (don't copy, cut!) the label to the clipboard. Then paste it back. That moves it to the upper-left corner of your screen.

Then paste the second label. Visual Basic will ask you if you want a control array, which is exactly what we have in mind. Say Yes, and then continue to paste additional labels until you have nine of them.

You can drag them into approximate positions if you like, but I haven't bothered. I'm leaving them in a heap in the corner, as Figure 8-6 shows.

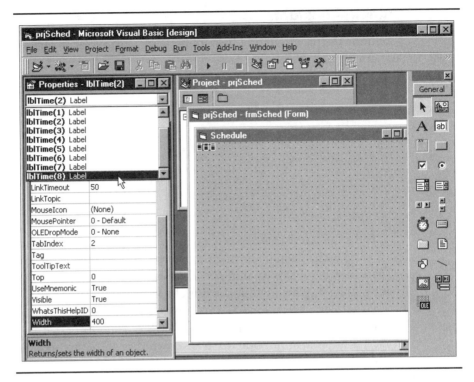

Figure 8-6
Leaving a heap of labels in the corner.

Programming the Time Labels

Because we'll have a resizable schedule, we'll need to set the label's position in the resize() event-handling method. We'll need to assign appropriate captions that will vary as we zoom the schedule in and out. When we zoom in, we'll also reset the captions as we scroll forward or backward during the day.

Before you begin the programming, add appropriate comments for the top and bottom of your program, like these:

```
' frmSched.frm — Appointment Schedule Class
' Copyright 1997, Martin L. Rinehart

' end of frmSched.frm
```

By the way, go right ahead and add your own name to the copyright line if you'll be making even slight changes to my code. If you ever need to defend your work, you'll also want my name there or whomever steals your work will claim that it wasn't yours to begin with.

Adding Constants

Continue the programming by adding these constants to the general declarations section:

```
Const tp_space = 350
Const bt_space = 400
Const lf_space = 460
Const rt_space = 40

Const str_time = 9 * 60 ' 9AM

Const min_width = 3200
Const min_height = 3000
```

The `space` and `min` constants will serve in the `resize()` method. The `str_time` is the default starting time. It will be assigned to the `start_time` private member when we initialize the form. We'll keep time in minutes since midnight, which will make our clock work easy.

Visual Basic keeps time as a fractional number. This works well for scientific applications, but it presents a host of roundoff error problems. I've tried this approach, but practice has shown that counting minutes is far simpler.

Adding Private Data Members

We'll need some data members, too. Add these, just after the constants:

```
Private start_time As Integer
Private stop_time As Integer

Private top_time
Private bottom_time

Private current_date As Date

Private interval As Byte
Private interval_index As Byte ' Range: 0-6
Private intervals(6) As Byte
```

The `start_time` and `stop_time` are your own limits on the extent of your day that you can schedule. I restrict mine to 9:00 a.m. to 5:00 p.m. You could use any other slice, up to the full 24 hours, if you like.

The `top_time` and `bottom_time` record the extent of the time that is visible on the schedule after you've zoomed in.

The `interval` is the amount of time between units shown on the schedule. My default interval is 60 minutes. I keep an array of 7 different intervals: 60, 30, 15, 10, 5, 2, and 1. The `interval_index` points to the element of that array that's currently set. You increment the index to zoom in; decrement it to zoom out.

Initialization Code

I've inserted my initialization in the Form's `Initialize()` event-handling method. This lets the calling code change defaults before it first shows the schedule when the defaults aren't adequate. Add this new code:

```
Private Sub Form_Initialize()

    intervals(0) = 60
    intervals(1) = 30
    intervals(2) = 15
    intervals(3) = 10
    intervals(4) = 5
    intervals(5) = 2
    intervals(6) = 1

    interval_index = 0

    start_time = str_time
    interval = 60 ' intervals(interval_index)
    stop_time = start_time + interval * 8

    current_date = Date
    reset_times

End Sub
```

The `reset_times()` method is the one that takes care of those labels. Add it and the supporting routine that converts a time (remember, our time is in minutes: 600 is 10:00 a.m.) to a string.

These are the new methods:

```
Private Sub reset_times()

    start_time = start_time ' fixup later!
    top_time = start_time

    interval = intervals(interval_index)
    stop_time = start_time * 9
```

```
        Dim i As Integer
        For i = 0 To 8
            lblTime(i).Caption = _
                time_label(top_time + i * interval)
        Next

        bottom_time = top_time + 8 * interval

    End Sub

    Private Function time_label(min As Integer) As String

        Dim mn As Byte, hr As Byte
        hr = Int(min / 60)
        mn = min - (60 * hr)

        time_label = Right(Str(hr + 100), 2) & ":" & _
            Right(Str(mn + 100), 2)

    End Function
```

You have another decision to make here. I'm quite happy using 24-hour times. Right now my watch tells me that it's 13:10. You might prefer that this hour be called 1:10 p.m. That's a simple adjustment to the `time_label` function, provided that your `start_time` and `stop_time` don't span more than 11 hours.

If you schedule from 9:00 to 5:00, the times are unambiguous, but if you schedule from 6:00 a.m. to 9:00 p.m., the time 7:30 could be either morning or evening. This ambiguity becomes serious when you zoom in. I show less than a full hour when the interval is below ten minutes. You'll need to add some a.m. and p.m. indication if this applies to you.

Positioning the Labels

To test this code, you'll need to add the first code to the Form's `resize()` method. Add this code:

```
    Private Sub Form_Resize()

    ' time labels
        Dim vert_space As Integer, vert_start As Integer

        If WindowState = vbMinimized Then Exit Sub

        If Width < min_width Then Width = min_width
        If Height < min_height Then Height = min_height
```

```
        vert_start = tp_space
        vert_space = (Height - tp_space - bt_space - 400) / 9

        Dim i As Byte
        For i = 0 To 8
            lblTime(i).Top = vert_start + vert_space * i
        Next

    End Sub
```

The extra 400 twips subtracted in the line that calculates vertical space is a good approximation of the Form space lost to the title bar and the bottom border. Otherwise, you've seen similar code in the calendar project.

This class is now ready to run for the first time. You should see a nicely arranged set of time labels, as shown in Figure 8-7.

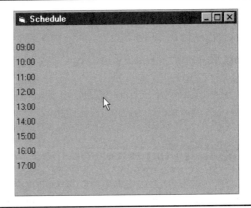

Figure 8-7
Displaying proper time labels.

This finishes this stage for the time labels. Now we can move on to showing the date.

Showing the Date TextBox

Wouldn't it be nice to have one of our popup calendars available to set the date? I think it would. I also would like to go to the toolbar, double-click a calendar icon, and have a calendar component appear on our Form, ready to be dragged into place and have some properties set.

Later on we'll do exactly that. We'll use our calendar class as the base for an ActiveX component that we can keep on our toolbar. You'll be pleasantly surprised to find that you've already done almost all the programming!

Because we're going to be able to do that later, for right now let's just drop a TextBox into place. While we're at it we can make a nicer date display. Later on, we can put the display code into the calendar component.

Setting Up the TextBox

For now, double-click the TextBox and drag one into place at the top of the Form. Set these properties:

- Change the Name to txtDate
- Change the Text to month dd, year
- Change the Top to 0
- Change the Left to 460
- Change the Height to 285
- Change the Width to fit your Form

We'll be setting the actual Width in the resize() method, and we'll be setting the Text property in the code, too.

Programming the resize() Method

We want the txtDate to report the date that our appointment schedule shows, and we want the width adjusted based on the overall width of the schedule. This code in the resize() method achieves those goals:

```
' Date text box
txtDate.Text = niceStr(current_date)
txtDate.Width = Width - rt_space - lf_space - _
   275 - 120
```

In the Width line, the constant 275 is the width we'll use for a vertical elevator. The 120 is the number of twips taken up by the left and right borders of the Form.

The niceStr() method is one that I've added to format a date as a nice string.

The niceStr() Method

We'll eventually move this code into our calendar component. For the moment, though, add it as a `Public` method of the `frmSched`. This is the new code:

```
Public Function niceStr(d As Date)

    ' Spell out date: "January 1, 2000"

    niceStr = monthStr(Month(d)) & _
        Str(Day(d)) & "," & _
        Str(Year(d))

End Function
```

I decided to make this a `Public` method because there's no reason not to. If any other part of the code wants to use it, it's welcome to do so. This code depends on my `monthStr()` function to return the name of the month. I've made this `Private` because its only job is to support `niceStr()`. `Public` would work here, too, if you think that there might be some other use for this routine.

The `monthStr()` method is one of those that I'd prefer to implement as a classwide static data array. Because that construct doesn't exist in Visual Basic, I've written a function that serves the same purpose. This is the code:

```
Private Function monthStr(m As Byte)

    'm must be from 1 thru 12

    Select Case m
        Case 1: monthStr = "January"
        Case 2: monthStr = "February"
        Case 3: monthStr = "March"
        Case 4: monthStr = "April"
        Case 5: monthStr = "May"
        Case 6: monthStr = "June"
        Case 7: monthStr = "July"
        Case 8: monthStr = "August"
        Case 9: monthStr = "September"
        Case 10: monthStr = "October"
        Case 11: monthStr = "November"
        Case 12: monthStr = "December"
    End Select

End Function
```

The colon lets you put multiple statements on a single line. Although I seldom use it, in this function it lets me write very readable, compact code. (Java and C++ use the colon this way as part of their equivalent case syntax.)

You'll adjust the language, of course, to suit your preferences.

With this much code in place, you can run the program. Your result should be similar to that shown in Figure 8-8.

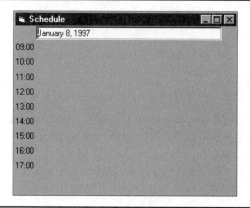

Figure 8-8
Time and date labels installed.

The Full, Interim Listing

Listing 8-2 shows the program to this point.

Listing 8-2
The schedule with lblTime() and txtDate prepared

```
' frmSched.frm — Appointment Schedule Class
' Copyright 1997, Martin L. Rinehart

Option Explicit

Const tp_space = 350
Const bt_space = 400
Const lf_space = 460
Const rt_space = 40

Const str_time = 9 * 60 ' 9AM
```

```
Const min_width = 3200
Const min_height = 3000

Private start_time As Integer
Private stop_time As Integer

Private top_time
Private bottom_time

Private current_date As Date

Private interval As Byte
Private interval_index As Byte ' Range: 0-6
Private intervals(6) As Byte

Private Sub Form_Initialize()

    intervals(0) = 60
    intervals(1) = 30
    intervals(2) = 15
    intervals(3) = 10
    intervals(4) = 5
    intervals(5) = 2
    intervals(6) = 1

    interval_index = 0

    start_time = str_time
    interval = 60 ' intervals(interval_index)
    stop_time = start_time + interval * 8

    current_date = Date
    reset_times

End Sub

Private Sub Form_Resize()

' time labels
    Dim vert_space As Integer, vert_start As Integer

    If WindowState = vbMinimized Then Exit Sub

    If Width < min_width Then Width = min_width
    If Height < min_height Then Height = min_height

    vert_start = tp_space
    vert_space = (Height - tp_space - bt_space - 400) / 9
```

(continued)

The schedule with lblTime() and txtDate prepared (continued)

```
    Dim i As Byte
    For i = 0 To 8
        lblTime(i).Top = vert_start + vert_space * i
    Next

' Date text box
    txtDate.Text = niceStr(current_date)
    txtDate.Width = Width - rt_space - lf_space - _
        275 - 120

End Sub

Private Sub reset_times()

    start_time = start_time ' fixup later!
    top_time = start_time

    interval = intervals(interval_index)
    stop_time = start_time * 9

    Dim i As Integer
    For i = 0 To 8
        lblTime(i).Caption = _
            time_label(top_time + i * interval)
    Next
    bottom_time = top_time + 8 * interval

End Sub

Private Function time_label(min As Integer) As String

    Dim mn As Byte, hr As Byte
    hr = Int(min / 60)
    mn = min - (60 * hr)

    time_label = Right(Str(hr + 100), 2) & ":" & _
        Right(Str(mn + 100), 2)

End Function

Public Function niceStr(d As Date)

    ' Spell out date: "January 1, 2000"

    niceStr = monthStr(Month(d)) & _
        Str(Day(d)) & "," & _
        Str(Year(d))
```

```
End Function

Private Function monthStr(m As Byte)

    'm must be from 1 thru 12

    Select Case m
        Case 1: monthStr = "January"
        Case 2: monthStr = "February"
        Case 3: monthStr = "March"
        Case 4: monthStr = "April"
        Case 5: monthStr = "May"
        Case 6: monthStr = "June"
        Case 7: monthStr = "July"
        Case 8: monthStr = "August"
        Case 9: monthStr = "September"
        Case 10: monthStr = "October"
        Case 11: monthStr = "November"
        Case 12: monthStr = "December"
    End Select

End Function

' end of frmSched.frm
```

ADDING AN ELEVATOR

Elevators often appear automatically at just the right moment. You'll find them in your multiple-line `TextBoxes`, in `ListBoxes`, `ComboBoxes`, and many other places. They snap into place when you have enough data to require scrolling, and the stay out of view otherwise.

Every once in a while, though, you find that you need to add one of your own, which is when the trouble starts. Microsoft's `Scrollbar` objects provide elevators, but they're quite idiosyncratic, and the documentation doesn't do anything to shed light on their operation.

Our next chapter will begin with a thorough analysis of the elevator. We'll turn into scientists who explore it and discover the laws that govern it. It will be fun and useful, too.

For now, though, we'll just drop the elevator onto our frmSched and let it sit there. In Chapter 9 we'll worry about actually hooking it to our schedule.

Begin by double-clicking the vertical scrollbar to place one on your form and then set its properties this way:

- Name it VScroll
- Set its Width to 275
- Set its Top to 350
- Set its Height and Left to look nice

We'll have the program set the Height and Left properties in the resize() process, this way:

```
' Vertical elevator
    VScroll.Left = Width - VScroll.Width - 120
    VScroll.Height = Height - 400 - 350 - _
        VScroll.Top - 50
' Form.Height less:
'    400 twips for Form borders,
'    350 twips for the bottom command buttons' height,
'    It's own top and 50 extra for good looks
```

Good, modern compilers all do a process known as *constant folding.* That means that they do all the arithmetic that can be done at compile time. That line that sets the Height property will be reduced to this by the compiler:

```
    VScroll.Height = Height - VScroll.Top - 800
```

or at least the constants should be folded. If this version of Visual Basic doesn't do that, the next one will. Write for clarity, not to make the compiler's job easy.

By the way, if any of you are really bothered by it, go ahead and call this fellow elvVScroll. VScroll alone looked like a good name to me.

Here's something to think about before you reach Chapter 9. You can set these properties to control the elevator:

- Min: value at the top
- Max: value at the bottom
- Value: current value
- SmallChange: distance to move when the arrows are clicked
- LargeChange: distance to move when the elevator shaft is clicked

LargeChange is the one parallel to pressing PgUp or PgDn on the keyboard, indicated by clicking between the elevators and the elevator car.

The default schedule is showing the full range, from `start_time` to `stop_time`, so we want the initial elevator car to completely fill the elevator shaft. How can you do that without a `CarSize` or similar property?

Chapter 9 will clear up this and other mysteries. For now, Figure 8-9 shows the appearance of our schedule.

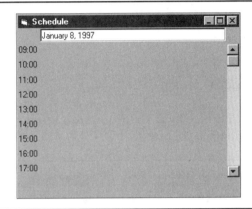

Figure 8-9
The elevator is added, but not connected.

ADDING COMMAND BUTTONS

With the elevator in place, we're ready to finish our border by adding command buttons at the bottom. We'll begin by creating the buttons, and then we'll go on to add code.

Creating the Buttons

Double-click or drag a button onto your form. Set these properties:

- Change the `Name` to `cmdOK`
- Change the `Caption` to `&OK`
- Change the `Height` to `350`

Drag it down to the bottom and center it. We'll have the `resize()` logic actually set its `Top`, `Left`, and `Width` properties.

Now get another button and set these properties:

- Change the Name to `cmdZoomIn`
- Change the Caption to `&Zoom In`
- Change the Height to `350`

Drag this one down to the lower-left and then add the last button, setting these properties:

- Change the Name to `cmdZoomOut`
- Change the Caption to `Zoom Ou&t`
- Change the Height to `350`

Drag this one down to the lower-right. Your form should now look like the one in Figure 8-10.

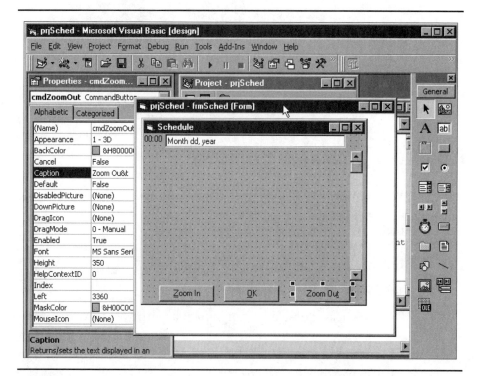

Figure 8-10

The design form looks like this.

We can go on to precise positioning and then add actual functionality.

Programming the Buttons

I'll begin with the sizing and positioning logic. This turns out to be quite a bit of trouble.

Memo to Bill Gates

Bill, have your folks in Visual Basic go talk to the folks in Visual J++ about `LayoutManager` objects. A Java `BorderLayout` would have made all this positioning a piece of cake. We need `LayoutManager` objects in Visual Basic, too.

The resize() Event Handler

Add this code to the `resize()` method:

```
' Bottom command buttons

    Dim btn_width As Integer
    Const between_spacer = 60
    Const side_spacer = 40

    ' 120 is approximate window border width
    btn_width = _
        (Width - (2 * side_spacer) _
            - (2 * between_spacer) _
            - VScroll.Width - 120) / 3

    cmdZoomIn.Left = side_spacer
    cmdZoomIn.Width = btn_width
    cmdZoomIn.Top = Height - 400 - cmdZoomIn.Height

    cmdOK.Left = cmdZoomIn.Left + btn_width + _
        between_spacer
    cmdOK.Width = btn_width
    cmdOK.Top = cmdZoomIn.Top

    cmdZoomOut.Left = cmdOK.Left + btn_width + _
        between_spacer
    cmdZoomOut.Width = btn_width
    cmdZoomOut.Top = cmdZoomIn.Top
```

The OK Button Click

Programming the cmdOK button's click() method is trivial. Double-click the OK button on the form and add the middle line here to the function skeleton that Visual Basic provides:

```
Private Sub cmdOK_Click()
    Hide
End Sub
```

Unfortunately, the zoom-related methods won't be quite this simple.

Programming Zoom

With our interval array (I'll bet it looked like a lot of extra trouble when you first saw it) zooming will be pretty simple. On a Zoom In click we want to increase the interval index and then reset the times. Of course, we want an error check to avoid going to far. This is the code to add to the Zoom In button:

```
Private Sub cmdZoomIn_Click()

    If interval_index < 6 Then
        interval_index = interval_index + 1
        reset_times
    End If

End Sub
```

Zooming out is the reverse process. We adjust the interval downward, unless it's at zero. This is the code:

```
Private Sub cmdZoomOut_Click()

    If interval_index > 0 Then
        interval_index = interval_index - 1
        reset_times
    End If

End Sub
```

Now that wasn't hard, was it? Run the program and you'll be able to zoom in until your schedule is going minute-by-minute (but no farther) and then you can zoom right back out, with a few button clicks. Figure 8-11 shows my schedule zoomed to show quarter hours.

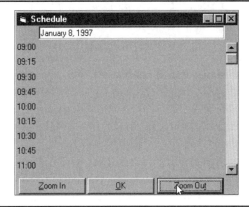

Figure 8-11
The schedule is zoomed to show quarter hours.

Of course, this makes me want to be able to scroll during the day, which we won't be able to do until we get that scrollbar hooked up. Once that works, we'll want to show actual appointments, which means accessing a database of appointments. That's a job we'll start in Chapter 10. For now, we'll take care of one last detail before we draw this chapter to a close.

Setting the Tab Order

By the simple expedient of using ampersands in the button captions, we've provided minimal keyboard access to the command buttons. We can provide the same service for the TextBox if we precede it with a Label.

A Label appears in the tabbing sequence, but it is not a tab stop, so when the appropriate mnemonic key is pressed, control goes to and then right on past the Label. All of which explains why I want to add one more label.

Put another label on your form, and modify it this way:

- Change the `Name` to `lblFor`
- Change the `Caption` to `&For:`
- Change the `Height` to `255`
- Change the `Top` to `50`
- Change the `Width` to `300`
- Change the `Left` to `140`

If you make all these changes in the Properties window, you'll avoid the mess you get into trying to manipulate the label when it's almost squarely on top of the pile of other labels I've left in the upper-left corner.

Now you're ready to set the tab order. I like the OK button to be the default, so select it and set its `TabIndex` property to zero. I've set `Zoom In` to `TabIndex` 1 and `Zoom Out` to `TabIndex` 2.

You can select `lblFor` in the dropdown list at the top of the Properties window to avoid clicking in the pile of labels. I set its `TabIndex` to 3 and the `TextBox`'s `TabIndex` to 4.

Finally, select `VScroll` and set its `TabStop` property to `False`. If a `Scrollbar` is set as a tab stop, you can tab to it and then press PgUp and PgDn to manipulate it. In the meantime, the elevator's thumb blinks annoyingly to indicate that it is the selected tab stop, and very few people will know what to do if the elevator is in the tab sequence. We'll look more closely at this and all the other `Scrollbar` behaviors in Chapter 9.

THE FULL LISTING

If the maid took your disk home with her (maybe she thought it was a computer game?) and your program's not in perfect shape this far, the complete program to this point is shown in Listing 8-3.

Listing 8-3
The complete frmSched.frm to this point

```
' frmSched.frm — Appointment Schedule Class
' Copyright 1997, Martin L. Rinehart

Option Explicit

Const tp_space = 350
Const bt_space = 400
Const lf_space = 460
Const rt_space = 40

Const str_time = 9 * 60 ' 9AM

Const min_width = 3200
Const min_height = 3000

Private start_time As Integer
Private stop_time As Integer

Private top_time
Private bottom_time
```

```
Private current_date As Date

Private interval As Byte
Private interval_index As Byte ' Range: 0-6
Private intervals(6) As Byte

Private Sub cmdOK_Click()
    Hide
End Sub

Private Sub cmdZoomIn_Click()

    If interval_index < 6 Then
        interval_index = interval_index + 1
        reset_times
    End If

End Sub
Private Sub cmdZoomOut_Click()

    If interval_index > 0 Then
        interval_index = interval_index - 1
        reset_times
    End If

End Sub

Private Sub Form_Initialize()

    intervals(0) = 60
    intervals(1) = 30
    intervals(2) = 15
    intervals(3) = 10
    intervals(4) = 5
    intervals(5) = 2
    intervals(6) = 1

    interval_index = 0

    start_time = str_time
    interval = 60 ' intervals(interval_index)
    stop_time = start_time + interval * 8

    current_date = Date
    reset_times

End Sub
```

(continued)

The complete frmSched.frm to this point

```
Private Sub Form_Resize()

' time labels
    Dim vert_space As Integer, vert_start As Integer

    If WindowState = vbMinimized Then Exit Sub

    If Width < min_width Then Width = min_width
    If Height < min_height Then Height = min_height

    vert_start = tp_space
    vert_space = (Height - tp_space - bt_space - 400) / 9

    Dim i As Byte
    For i = 0 To 8
        lblTime(i).Top = vert_start + vert_space * i
    Next
' Date text box
    txtDate.Text = niceStr(current_date)
    txtDate.Width = Width - rt_space - lf_space - _
        275 - 120

' Vertical elevator
    VScroll.Left = Width - VScroll.Width - 120
    VScroll.Height = Height - 400 - 350 - _
        VScroll.Top - 50
    ' Form.Height less:
    '    400 twips for Form borders,
    '    350 twips for the bottom command buttons' height,
    '    It's own top and 50 extra for good looks

' Bottom command buttons

    Dim btn_width As Integer
    Const between_spacer = 60
    Const side_spacer = 40

    ' 120 is approximate window border width
    btn_width = _
        (Width - (2 * side_spacer) _
            - (2 * between_spacer) _
            - VScroll.Width - 120) / 3

    cmdZoomIn.Left = side_spacer
    cmdZoomIn.Width = btn_width
    cmdZoomIn.Top = Height - 400 - cmdZoomIn.Height

    cmdOK.Left = cmdZoomIn.Left + btn_width + _
```

```
            between_spacer
        cmdOK.Width = btn_width
        cmdOK.Top = cmdZoomIn.Top

        cmdZoomOut.Left = cmdOK.Left + btn_width + _
            between_spacer
        cmdZoomOut.Width = btn_width
        cmdZoomOut.Top = cmdZoomIn.Top

End Sub

Private Sub reset_times()

    start_time = start_time ' fixup later!
    top_time = start_time

    interval = intervals(interval_index)
    stop_time = start_time * 9

    Dim i As Integer
    For i = 0 To 8
        lblTime(i).Caption = _
            time_label(top_time + i * interval)
    Next

    bottom_time = top_time + 8 * interval

End Sub

Private Function time_label(min As Integer) As String

    Dim mn As Byte, hr As Byte
    hr = Int(min / 60)
    mn = min - (60 * hr)

    time_label = Right(Str(hr + 100), 2) & ":" & _
        Right(Str(mn + 100), 2)

End Function

Public Function niceStr(d As Date)

    ' Spell out date: "January 1, 2000"

    niceStr = monthStr(Month(d)) & _
        Str(Day(d)) & "," & _
        Str(Year(d))

End Function
```

(continued)

The complete frmSched.frm to this point

```
Private Function monthStr(m As Byte)

    'm must be from 1 thru 12

    Select Case m
        Case 1: monthStr = "January"
        Case 2: monthStr = "February"
        Case 3: monthStr = "March"
        Case 4: monthStr = "April"
        Case 5: monthStr = "May"
        Case 6: monthStr = "June"
        Case 7: monthStr = "July"
        Case 8: monthStr = "August"
        Case 9: monthStr = "September"
        Case 10: monthStr = "October"
        Case 11: monthStr = "November"
        Case 12: monthStr = "December"
    End Select

End Function

' end of frmSched.frm
```

Summary

We began this chapter with a close look at Visual Basic's Property statements: Let, Get, and Set. You can use these to provide public access to private variables. When you do this, the code that uses these statements is actually calling methods but doesn't look like it's calling methods.

For that reason, I prefer to write actual methods that look like methods. It accomplishes the same job in a much more straightforward, readable, and maintainable way. Just to show that the assignment in your calling code is really just a method call, I showed you a rude() method that absolutely refused to do what it was told.

We would have ignored these Property methods altogether, but Visual Basic's code-generating machinery insists on including them.

Then we moved on to our schedule class, beginning by setting up a new, form-based project. After setting up the Form we added an array of Labels to show the times down the left side of the schedule. We programmed these to show different time intervals.

After these, we added a `TextBox` on the top, where eventually we'd like to have a calendar component. Later on we'll rebuild our calendar so that we can drag it off the toolbar. For now, we're using a `TextBox` that just displays a nicely worded date.

We then dropped in an elevator but left hooking it up for Chapter 9. You saw that setting the size appropriately wasn't intuitive.

Finally, we added command buttons that let us zoom in and out and close the schedule. You found out that the earlier work we had done in setting up a time interval array paid off in providing very, very simple zooming code.

Now we're ready to get on to that scrollbar, and to achieve genuine scrolling. Chapter 9 will remove the mystery from the elevator.

SCROLLING THE SCHEDULE

9

We'll need to scroll when we zoom in with our schedule, which means we'll want to hook up a vertical scrollbar. Microsoft doesn't really provide much documentation on this component. In fact, I couldn't figure out how it worked at all until I built a test bench and starting doing experiments.

We'll start this chapter by doing exactly that: we'll build a test bench and hook a scrollbar specimen to a nice range of test equipment. Then we can run experiments and find out how it really works.

You'll see that the secret is in the number of jumps needed to span a range. It's one of those things that makes sense when you understand it. Before you understand it, it's really weird.

By the time we're done, we'll reduce the behavior of this component to mathematical law. That's always a satisfying resolution to a scientific inquiry.

Then we'll jump back to the schedule project and put our new knowledge to practical usc. Along the way, we'll meet and defeat circular event recursion.

If you're the highly skeptical type, try to answer this question: how do you set the elevator car's size? Use the documentation. As a hint, don't bother with the books online; they just refer you back to the language manual. When you're convinced that Microsoft didn't tell you much about scrollbars, come back here and join us while we figure it out.

BUILDING YOUR TEST BENCH

We'll need to test the Scrollbar object, so our first job is to build a test bench. The first thing we'll need is a ruler so that we can take measurements.

Lay out a Ruler

Begin a new, standard .EXE project. You can use the same directory that you're using for the schedule because we'll throw out this entire project after we're done with it.

Make the starting form 4,000 twips tall and 5,000 wide. Figure 9-1 shows this form with the full ruler in place. Add the two lines that form the top and bottom of the ruler. Their width should be about as shown, but the vertical positioning is important. Use the Properties window to position the top line at 500 (Y1 and Y2) and then put the bottom line at 2,500. (Remember, if the Form is 4,000 twips tall, the client area is about 3,600 twips tall.)

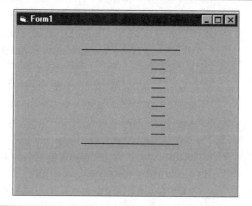

Figure 9-1
The ruler laid out on the form.

For the tic marks, grab one more line, change its name to *tic*, and cut it to the clipboard. Copy it twice, on the second copy accept Visual Basic's kind offer to create a control array, and copy it seven more times for a total of nine.

You could manually position them (this won't be a resizable form), but I think it's easier in code. This is what I added to the load() event handler:

```
Private Sub Form_Load()

    Dim y As Integer
    y = 700

    Dim i As Byte
    For i = 0 To 8

        With Tic(i)
            .X1 = 3000
            .X2 = 3300
            .Y1 = y
            .Y2 = y
        End With

        y = y + 200
    Next

End Sub
```

That gives you the ruler shown in Figure 9-1 when you run it.

Position a Specimen

Now, fellow scientists, we'll need a specimen to measure. Double-click or drag a vertical scrollbar from the toolbar. Position it as Figure 9-2 shows.

You'll want to position the right edge of the elevator against the tic marks, which start at 3,000. Therefore, pick a convenient width (I used 250) and put the left so that left plus width equals 3,000. Then carefully adjust the top and height so that your long lines are right at the start of the elevator shaft. When the elevator car is at the top, you want your top line to appear to separate the car from the arrow at the end of the elevator.

My coordinates are 270 for Top and 2490 for Height. Yours will depend on your equipment and Windows settings. Try to run the program. Drag the car from top to bottom and adjust as needed until you're just splitting the car and the arrows at the ends.

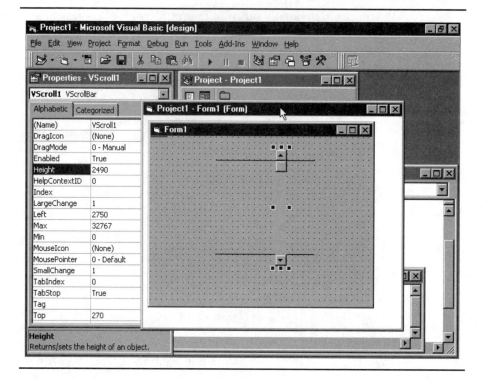

Figure 9-2

Positioning the specimen scrollbar for measurements.

Hooking up the Test Equipment

Now let's hook up some test equipment to measure the important values of our scrollbar specimen. Start with the `Min` and `Max` properties.

Measuring Min and Max

I've added two `TextBox` objects, as Figure 9-3 shows. Add your own and position them similarly.

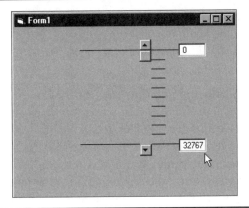

■ Figure 9-3
Displaying the minimum and maximum.

This is the new load() method that sets these boxes to display the Min and Max properties:

```
Private Sub Form_Load()

    Dim y As Integer
    y = 700

    Dim i As Byte
    For i = 0 To 8
        With Tic(i)
            .X1 = 3000
            .X2 = 3300
            .Y1 = y
            .Y2 = y
        End With
        y = y + 200
    Next

    Text1.Text = Str(VScroll1.Min)
    Text2.Text = Str(VScroll1.Max)

End Sub
```

Add the two new lines into your own program, test drive it, return to design mode, and double-click the top TextBox. Visual Basic will give you the skeleton for this routine that lets you set the Min property from this box:

```
Private Sub Text1_Change()

    VScroll1.Min = Val(Text1.Text)

End Sub
```

I originally did just the same for the Max property, but that was a mistake. The problem is that when the focus enters the TextBox, the contents are all selected. That lets a backspace clear the box. Val() of a null string returns 0. When Max is set to 0, Visual Basic reports a runtime error. Most unhelpfully, it offers you the opportunity to debug your program but not to type a reasonable value into the TextBox.

To avoid this situation, the code is just a bit more complex:

```
Private Sub Text2_Change()

    Dim i As Integer
    i = Val(Text2.Text)

    If i > 0 Then
        VScroll1.Max = i
    Else
        VScroll1.Max = VScroll1.Min + 1
    End If

End Sub
```

Now you can test your program again. This time, interesting things happen to the elevator car as you change values. It will expand and shrink and jump up and down, depending on the settings for Min and Max.

If you experiment with it a little, you'll become quite certain that you can't yet see what's happening. You need the rest of the data, which means hooking up more instruments.

Measuring Value

The Value property should be a number not less than Min nor more than Max. The elevator uses this property to position the elevator car. If you manipulate the elevator (drag the car or click the shaft or arrows) you change Value. When Value changes, the elevator raises a change event, just as a TextBox raises a change event when you type in it.

I've dropped a third TextBox on the form and, as Figure 9-4 shows, added a label to its right.

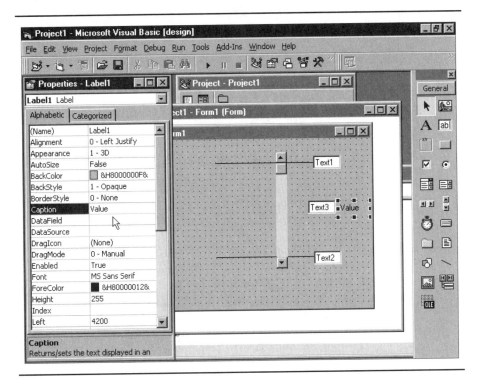

Figure 9-4
Labelling the Value TextBox.

Double-click your elevator, and the code editor will prepare the skeleton for the change event-handling method. Begin by adding this line:

```
Text3.Text = VScroll1.Value
```

Now there's some behavior that I'd really like to understand, which makes me want a different report for Value. Add another line to your form to the left of the elevator. Set its color to white or some other color that will show up when this line is over the top or the bottom line.

What I want to know is exactly where Value lies in relation to the elevator car. I suspect that Value is at the top of the car when Value equals Min, that Value is at the bottom of the car when Value equals Max, and it's in the middle of the car when Value is in the middle of the range.

I want this line to point to Value, so I can see exactly what happens as the car moves. This is the full code I've added to the elevator's change() event handler:

```
Private Sub VScroll_Change()
    Text3.Text = VScroll.Value

    Dim y As Integer, range As Integer
    range = Line2.Y1 - Line1.Y1

    Dim ratio As Double
    ratio = _
        VScroll1.Value / (VScroll1.Max - VScroll1.Min)

    y = Line1.Y1 + range * ratio

    Line3.Y1 = y
    Line3.Y2 = y

End Sub
```

I've added a call to `VScroll1_Change()` in the `Load()` event handler to initialize the `Value` `TextBox` and the `Value` line.

The range is the distance in twips from the top line to the bottom. The ratio is a fraction of the distance that `Value` is from `Min` toward `Max`. Multiplying range by ratio gives you the number of twips to locate the line below the top line.

When you run this code, you'll see a result like the one shown in Figure 9-5.

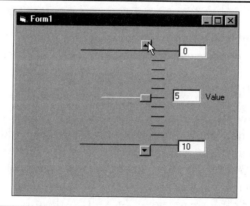

Figure 9-5
Car in mid-range, `Value` in mid-car.

Set a modest range and hold down one of the elevator's arrows. Watch `Value` move as the car moves. You'll see that it moves from the top of the car through the center and down to the bottom of the car as the car moves from the top of the shaft to the bottom.

In fact, Value is the same percentage of the way down the car that the car is down the shaft. That's an interesting result, but we should finish our test bench before we begin to experiment in earnest.

SmallChange and LargeChange

The last two properties of the Scrollbar object that affect the size and position of the car are SmallChange and LargeChange. The SmallChange is the number of units that Value is changed when the user clicks an arrow. It defaults to 1, which you've seen already when you experiment with your specimen elevator.

LargeChange is the amount of change in Value caused by a click on the elevator's shaft, above or below the car. If the elevator gains focus in the tab sequence, you can also change Value by LargeChange via the PgUp and PgDn keys. As we'll see, LargeChange is also critical in sizing the car.

I've added two new TextBoxes and two labels, as Figure 9-6 shows.

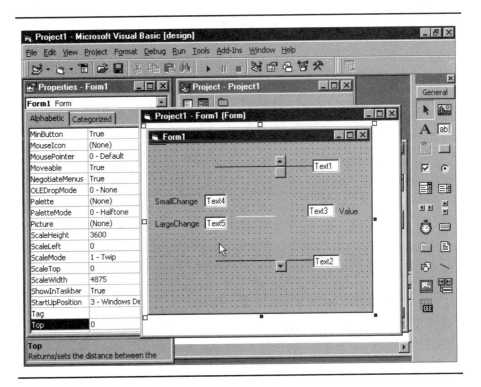

Figure 9-6
Hooking instruments to SmallChange *and* LargeChange.

To initialize the labels, I've added these two lines to the Form's `Load()` handler:

```
Text4.Text = Str(VScroll1.SmallChange)
Text5.Text = Str(VScroll1.LargeChange)
```

Then for setting these values, I've added these two methods:

```
Private Sub Text4_Change()

    Dim i As Integer
    i = Val(Text4.Text)

    If i > 0 Then
        VScroll1.SmallChange = i
    End If

End Sub

Private Sub Text5_Change()

    Dim i As Integer
    i = Val(Text5.Text)

    If i > 0 Then
        VScroll1.LargeChange = i
    End If

End Sub
```

Add those for your own test bench, and you'll be fully equipped to decipher the mysteries of this control. Figure 9-7 shows the test bench launched. Can you figure out why the car doesn't nicely fill the space between our tic marks when, for example, you specify a `LargeChange` of 10 in a range of 0 to 100?

Enabled and Visible Buttons

Before we start serious experiments, let's add one final feature. I'll want to check the behavior of the `Visible` and `Enabled` boolean properties. I'm pretty sure that I know what `Visible` will do, but `Enabled` isn't quite as obvious.

Add the two command buttons you see in Figure 9-8 and set their `Captions` to `Invisible` and `Disable`. Then double-click them to access their click procedures in the code editor. Add routines that flip the elevator's property and the buttons caption, like this:

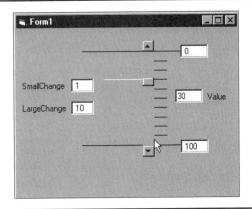

Figure 9-7
Checking a LargeChange setting.

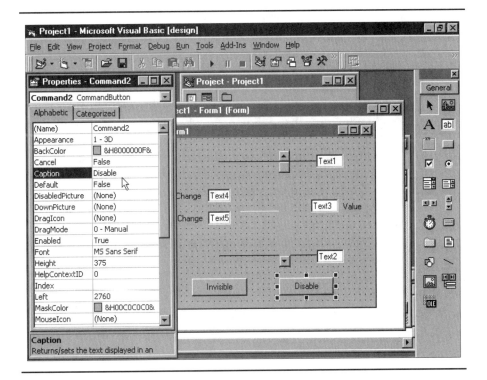

Figure 9-8
Adding buttons for visible and enabled.

```
Private Sub Command1_Click()

    If VScroll1.Visible Then
        VScroll1.Visible = False
        Command1.Caption = "Visible"
    Else
        VScroll1.Visible = True
        Command1.Caption = "Invisible"
    End If

End Sub

Private Sub Command2_Click()

    If VScroll1.Enabled Then
        VScroll1.Enabled = False
        Command2.Caption = "Enable"
    Else

        VScroll1.Enabled = True
        Command2.Caption = "Disable"
    End If

End Sub
```

When you write these routines, the trick is to remember that the button should advertise what will happen when you click it. For a boolean property, that's the opposite of the current state.

When I ran this code, I immediately tested the command buttons. As expected, Invisible makes the elevator disappear entirely. Figure 9-9 shows Disable's effect. The car has gone into hiding, and the arrows at the ends of the elevator are dimmed. I'm sure I'll find a use for this, but I can't think of one just now.

Alright, our test bench is ready; and our specimen is wired. Put your lab coat on, and we can start experimenting.

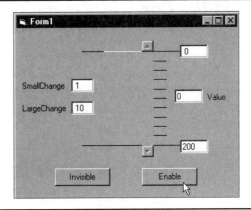

Figure 9-9
Disabling the elevator.

TESTING THE SCROLLBAR

I'd like to know how the various combinations of these properties
determine the size of the car. Let's begin with a SmallChange of 1, a
LargeChange of 10, and a range of 0 to 100. As Figure 9-10 shows, this
gives me a car that doesn't quite fill the space between our tic marks. It
appears to be just under one tenth the size of the shaft.

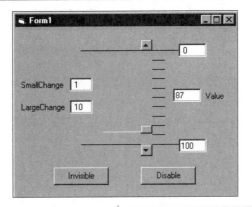

Figure 9-10
The car is less than one-tenth of the shaft..

Resizing the Car with LargeChange

Try changing `LargeChange` and `SmallChange` to see what effect they have. With a little testing, you'll find that `SmallChange` doesn't seem connected to the size of the car. The secret's in `LargeChange`.

As you increase `LargeChange`, the size of the car increases. Figure 9-11 shows a `LargeChange` that's half of the range. Interestingly, the car appears to be three and a third tics tall, or exactly one-third of the shaft size.

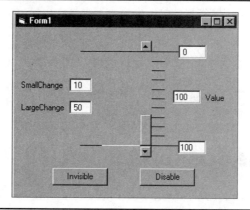

Figure 9-11
The car is one-third of the shaft.

If you increase `LargeChange` to be equal to the full range, you have a car that is exactly half the shaft size, as Figure 9-12 shows.

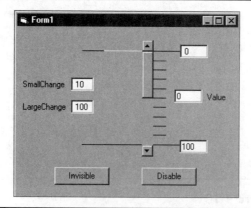

Figure 9-12
The car is one-half of the shaft.

If you continue to increase the LargeChange value, the car keeps expanding, but it doesn't begin to fill the shaft until you approach the absolute maximum value, 32,767. It's size is some function that asymptotically approaches shaft size (call it 1 or 100%) as LargeChange approaches its own version of infinity.

If you want the elevator car to fill the shaft entirely, you have to use a LargeChange of 32767 and a small range. Setting Max to Min+1 will work nicely.

This is good to know, but is there an underlying logic?

The Secret: Counting Jumps

At first I couldn't quite figure it out, but then I realized that it was all a matter of counting jumps.

Set LargeChange to 100 in a range of 100. You'll see a car that fills half the shaft. Click the shaft, and you get a change of 100. If Value was 0, Value becomes 100. You get exactly one jump — top to bottom or bottom to top — from clicking the shaft.

Now try LargeChange of 50. Starting at 0, click the shaft. The Value is incremented to 50, which puts the car dead center. Click again, and you jump to the bottom. So LargeChange of 50 gives you two jumps. The formula is

```
jumps = (Max-Min)/LargeChange
```

That's exactly what LargeChange is supposed to mean, of course, but how does it relate to car size?

Again, you've already seen it. When the LargeChange is half the range the car fills one-third of the shaft (see Figure 9-11). By filling one-third of the shaft, the car can make two complete jumps, from top to bottom. The car fills the top third of the shaft at 0. It fills the middle third at 50 and the bottom third at 100. The formula is

```
car_size = shaft_size / (jumps+1)
```

If you want the car to jump four times from top to bottom, you want it to fill one-fifth of the shaft. Try a LargeChange of 25, as Figure 9-13 shows. Notice how precisely the car fills two tic marks.

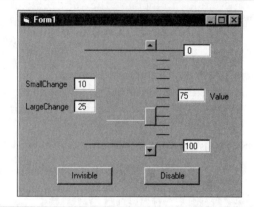

Figure 9-13
When `LargeChange=25` percent the car fills 20 percent of the shaft.

Now you see how the elevator works. If you substitute `Range` for `Max-Min` and combine the two formulas, you get this result:

```
car_size = (LargeChange*Range)/(LargeChange+Range)
```

Congratulations, scientists. You've experimented and found the laws that rule Microsoft's `Scrollbar` object. Now you can leave the scientists' laboratory and go back to the engineering room where we'll put the `Scrollbar` to use in our schedule class.

The Full Test Bench Listing

If your test bench isn't working perfectly and your parakeet is using this book's disk for bombing practice, Listing 9-1 shows the Form1.frm file that creates the elevator test bench.

Listing 9-1
Form1.frm — the elevator test bench

```
VERSION 5.00
Begin VB.Form Form1
   Caption        =   "Form1"
   ClientHeight   =   3600
   ClientLeft     =   60
   ClientTop      =   345
   ClientWidth    =   4875
   LinkTopic      =   "Form1"
```

```
ScaleHeight      =   3600
ScaleWidth       =   4875
StartUpPosition =   3   'Windows Default
Begin VB.CommandButton Command2
   Caption       =   "Disable"
   Height        =   375
   Left          =   2760
   TabIndex      =   10
   Top           =   3000
   Width         =   1215
End
Begin VB.CommandButton Command1
   Caption       =   "Invisible"
   Height        =   375
   Left          =   840
   TabIndex      =   9
   Top           =   3000
   Width         =   1215
End
Begin VB.TextBox Text5
   Height        =   285
   Left          =   1200
   TabIndex      =   8
   Text          =   "Text5"
   Top           =   1560
   Width         =   495
End
Begin VB.TextBox Text4
   Height        =   285
   Left          =   1200
   TabIndex      =   7
   Text          =   "Text4"
   Top           =   1080
   Width         =   495
End
Begin VB.TextBox Text3
   Height        =   285
   Left          =   3480
   TabIndex      =   3
   Text          =   "Text3"
   Top           =   1320
   Width         =   615
End
Begin VB.TextBox Text2
   Height        =   285
   Left          =   3600
   TabIndex      =   2
   Text          =   "Text2"
   Top           =   2400
```

(continued)

Form1.frm — the elevator test bench

```
        Width           =   615
    End
    Begin VB.TextBox Text1
        Height          =   285
        Left            =   3600
        TabIndex        =   1
        Text            =   "Text1"
        Top             =   360
        Width           =   615
    End
    Begin VB.VScrollBar VScroll1
        Height          =   2490
        Left            =   2760
        TabIndex        =   0
        Top             =   270
        Width           =   250
    End
    Begin VB.Label Label3
        Caption         =   "LargeChange  "
        Height          =   255
        Left            =   120
        TabIndex        =   6
        Top             =   1600
        Width           =   975
    End
    Begin VB.Label Label2
        Caption         =   "SmallChange"
        Height          =   255
        Left            =   120
        TabIndex        =   5
        Top             =   1120
        Width           =   975
    End
    Begin VB.Line Line3
        BorderColor     =   &H80000005&
        X1              =   1920
        X2              =   2760
        Y1              =   1560
        Y2              =   1560
    End
    Begin VB.Label Label1
        Caption         =   "Value"
        Height          =   255
        Left            =   4200
        TabIndex        =   4
        Top             =   1380
        Width           =   615
    End
```

```
Begin VB.Line Tic
   Index          =   8
   X1             =   0
   X2             =   360
   Y1             =   0
   Y2             =   0
End
Begin VB.Line Tic
   Index          =   7
   X1             =   0
   X2             =   360
   Y1             =   0
   Y2             =   0
End
Begin VB.Line Tic
   Index          =   6
   X1             =   0
   X2             =   360
   Y1             =   0
   Y2             =   0
End
Begin VB.Line Tic
   Index          =   5
   X1             =   0
   X2             =   360
   Y1             =   0
   Y2             =   0
End
Begin VB.Line Tic
   Index          =   4
   X1             =   0
   X2             =   360
   Y1             =   0
   Y2             =   0
End
Begin VB.Line Tic
   Index          =   3
   X1             =   0
   X2             =   360
   Y1             =   0
   Y2             =   0
End
Begin VB.Line Tic
   Index          =   2
   X1             =   0
   X2             =   360
   Y1             =   0
   Y2             =   0
End
```

(continued)

Form1.frm — the elevator test bench

```
      Begin VB.Line Tic
         Index           =   1
         X1              =   0
         X2              =   360
         Y1              =   0
         Y2              =   0
      End
      Begin VB.Line Tic
         Index           =   0
         X1              =   0
         X2              =   360
         Y1              =   0
         Y2              =   0
      End
      Begin VB.Line Line2
         X1              =   1440
         X2              =   3600
         Y1              =   2500
         Y2              =   2500
      End
      Begin VB.Line Line1
         X1              =   1440
         X2              =   3615
         Y1              =   500
         Y2              =   500
      End
   End
End
Attribute VB_Name = "Form1"
Attribute VB_GlobalNameSpace = False
Attribute VB_Creatable = False
Attribute VB_PredeclaredId = True
Attribute VB_Exposed = False
Option Explicit

Private Sub Command1_Click()

    If VScroll1.Visible Then
        VScroll1.Visible = False
        Command1.Caption = "Visible"
    Else
        VScroll1.Visible = True
        Command1.Caption = "Invisible"
    End If

End Sub

Private Sub Command2_Click()
```

```
        If VScroll1.Enabled Then
            VScroll1.Enabled = False
            Command2.Caption = "Enable"
        Else
            VScroll1.Enabled = True
            Command2.Caption = "Disable"
        End If

End Sub

Private Sub Form_Load()

    Dim y As Integer
    y = 700

    Dim i As Byte
    For i = 0 To 8
        With Tic(i)
            .X1 = 3000
            .X2 = 3300
            .Y1 = y
            .Y2 = y
        End With
        y = y + 200
    Next

    Text1.Text = Str(VScroll1.Min)
    Text2.Text = Str(VScroll1.Max)

    VScroll1_Change

    Text4.Text = Str(VScroll1.SmallChange)
    Text5.Text = Str(VScroll1.LargeChange)

End Sub

Private Sub Text1_Change()

    VScroll1.Min = Val(Text1.Text)

End Sub

Private Sub Text2_Change()

    Dim i As Integer
    i = Val(Text2.Text)
```

(continued)

Form1.frm — the elevator test bench

```
        If i > 0 Then
            VScroll1.Max = i
        Else
            VScroll1.Max = VScroll1.Min + 1
        End If

    End Sub

    Private Sub Text3_Change()

        Dim i As Integer
        i = Val(Text3.Text)

        If i >= VScroll1.Min Then
            VScroll1.Value = i
        Else
            VScroll1.Value = VScroll1.Min
        End If

    End Sub

    Private Sub Text4_Change()

        Dim i As Integer
        i = Val(Text4.Text)

        If i > 0 Then
            VScroll1.SmallChange = i
        End If

    End Sub

    Private Sub Text5_Change()

        Dim i As Integer
        i = Val(Text5.Text)

        If i > 0 Then
            VScroll1.LargeChange = i
        End If

    End Sub

    Private Sub VScroll1_Change()
        Text3.Text = VScroll1.Value

        Dim y As Integer, range As Integer
        range = Line2.Y1 - Line1.Y1
```

```
Dim ratio As Double
ratio = _
    VScroll1.Value / (VScroll1.Max - VScroll1.Min)

y = Line1.Y1 + range * ratio

Line3.Y1 = y
Line3.Y2 = y

End Sub
```

SCROLLING IN THE SCHEDULE

After you've mastered the scrollbar, hooking one to a custom tool, such as our schedule, is a reasonably simple task. It's a matter of three steps, but I'll do it here in five.

We'll create a scrollbar initialization routine. We'll need to call it whenever we zoom in or out, in addition to when we first load the form.

Then we'll do some careful adjusting of the top_time variable, which records the top_time to display on the schedule. This is needed for two reasons.

First, we can create some ugly effects by zooming out without making adjustments. Think about this:

- Zoom in to two minutes
- Scroll to 11:58
- Back out to a 15-minute interval

Without some special adjustment, you'd be looking at this set of times: 11:58, 12:13, 12:28, and so on. These aren't what I had in mind when I chose a 15-minute interval.

The second problem is that you could zoom in, scroll down, and then zoom out. Think about this sequence:

- Zoom in to the 30-minute interval
- Scroll to 12:00
- Zoom out

Without some adjustment, the top time is now too late to cooperate with my specified 5:00 p.m. stop time. You'll see that these adjustments aren't difficult, but they are definitely necessary.

The third step is adding the scrollbar `change()` method. That will be triggered whenever the user manipulates the scrollbar. We have to reset the times the calendar is displaying to respond to these changes.

As a fourth step, we'll take a good look at circular events. Those are any recursive combination, such as an event triggering itself, or event A triggers B and B triggers A. You'll see that we inadvertently created a circular event pattern. Luckily for us it only created a finite and harmless recursion, but we'll eliminate the problem as a matter of good programming technique.

Last, I'm going to leave a bug in the code, so the scrollbar won't work correctly. This is an actual mistake I made when I first wrote this code, and it's instructive enough that I'll leave it for last.

Let's start with the initialization.

Initializing the Scrollbar

We'll need a routine that sets up the scrollbar. We'll need to do these steps when the schedule is first loaded, and then on each zoom, in or out. Thus, we should do this in a separate routine. This is my code:

```
Private Sub set_scrollbar()

    If top_time = start_time And _
        bottom_time = stop_time Then

        VScroll.Visible = False
        Exit Sub

    End If

    With VScroll

        .min = start_time
        .Max = stop_time
        .Value = top_time

        .SmallChange = interval
        .LargeChange = 8 * interval

        .Visible = True

    End With

End Sub
```

You can see that the first job is to hide the scrollbar if we're displaying the entire time range. As a matter of good interface design, you shouldn't show scrollbars if no scrolling will be done. (Look at the Properties window in Visual Basic to see how nice this is when it's done correctly. Look at the code editor in Visual Basic to see how dumb it is when it's not done correctly.)

The main job is to set the five key scrollbar variables and then turn the scrollbar on (in case it was off). The capitalization of min and Max, by the way, was Visual Basic's idea, not mine. Maybe your version will have this little bug eliminated.

We actually haven't handled top_time and bottom_time yet, except to create them as Private properties. In the Form's load() method, add this code after the calculations for start_time and stop_time:

```
top_time = start_time
bottom_time = stop_time
```

Adjusting the Top Time

Our next step is to adjust the top_time so that our scrollbar doesn't do crazy things. It's important in these routines that the little details are taken care of correctly. Here's a routine I've added:

```
Private Sub adjust_top_time()

' round top_time down to a multiple of the interval
    top_time = top_time - (top_time Mod interval)

' back down if too late
    If top_time + 8 * interval > stop_time Then
        top_time = stop_time - (8 * interval)
    End If

End Sub
```

Then you need to call this routine from reset_times before the caller has done any work. You'll see there that reset_times started with a placeholder line with a note that it needed fixup. This is the time. Of the top four lines, delete all but the interval assignment, and add a call to the new adjust_top_time() method. The final routine should look like this:

```
Private Sub reset_times()

    interval = intervals(interval_index)
    adjust_top_time
```

```
Dim i As Integer
For i = 0 To 8
    lblTime(i).Caption = _
        time_label(top_time + i * interval)
Next

bottom_time = top_time + 8 * interval

End Sub
```

With these additions and changes, we're ready to wire in the scrollbar. The reset_times routine is called from both zoom click() methods and in the Form initialization process. After each call to reset_times, add a call to set_scrollbar(). They should all look like this:

```
reset_times
set_scrollbar
```

That's enough to give you a real scrollbar with a real bug. When you first launch this schedule, you'll have no scrollbar. That's correct. Then when you zoom in, the scrollbar appears. This is also correct.

When the scrollbar first appears, though, you're showing half the time (four hours, from 9:00 a.m. to 1:00 p.m.), but the elevator car is only one third the size of the shaft. What's wrong?

This is a real mistake I made. See if you can figure it out. If you can't, I'll give you the solution just before the last listings in this chapter.

Responding to Scrollbar Changes

We now have an output-only scrollbar. It's not hooked up for input yet. That's a matter of programming the scrollbar's change event method. This job could hardly be easier, as this shows:

```
Private Sub VScroll_Change()

    top_time = VScroll.Value

    reset_times

End Sub
```

With that simple addition, you now have a functional, if imperfect, scrollbar. It should look like the one in Figure 9-14.

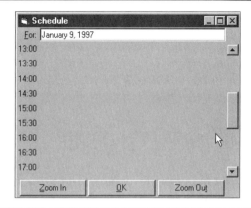

Figure 9-14
The car's too small.

Avoiding Circular Events

We've inadvertently written a circular call in our event handlers. It's a bit sneaky, but the secret is that the change event is raised whenever the Value property changes. We think of it as what happens when the user clicks or drags on the scrollbar, which is true, but the change event is also raised when you explicitly assign the Value property, if your assignment changes Value.

To see the recursion, place a breakpoint at the start of the reset_times() method. Run the program, and you'll stop at this breakpoint when the form is loaded. Click the run icon (or tap F5) to continue.

When the schedule is launched, click Zoom In. You'll stop at your breakpoint. Tap F5 and you'll promptly return to the breakpoint. You need to press F5 again to complete the zoom. That's a typical, mystery recursion.

The Tag property is handy for avoiding these problems. Tag is an empty string attached to all the built-in components. Microsoft doesn't use it; it's for us. You can put anything into a Tag. Because a string can hold just under 64K, the Tag property is fairly commodious. We'll just use it to note when we're making a programmatic assignment to Value so that the change() code can tell the difference between our program and the user's clicks.

Add the two new lines here that set Tag to your set_scrollbar routine:

```
.Tag = "X"
.Value = top_time
.Tag = ""
```

Then add this quick bailout at the very top of your reset_times method:

```
' Don't do this when our code sets Value
    If VScroll.Tag = "X" Then Exit Sub
```

That eliminates the recursion. (To be exact, there's still a recursive call, but the subroutine is smart enough to recognize it and behave accordingly.) One extra call to reset_times remains here, but I'll leave the finding of it to you. The big problem is the size of the elevator's car.

Getting it Right

By now I'm pretty sure that you've either fixed the elevator's car size or you want to know how. The problem is that we haven't assigned the right number to the Max property of the elevator.

We're assigning the elevator's Value to our top_time variable. This means that the elevator's Min and Max should refer not to the total time range but to the range of values we want for top_time. If our interval is 30 minutes, for instance, top_time can vary from 9:00 a.m. through 1:00 p.m. In general, top_time can only come to stop_time minus eight intervals.

This is the corrected line in set_scrollbar:

```
.Max = stop_time - 8 * interval
```

With that change, your scrollbar will behave itself. As Figure 9-15 shows, when half your range is showing, the elevator car politely fills exactly half the elevator shaft.

This is getting pretty slick, no?

Now if it only weren't just a border looking for some contents, we'd actually have an appointment schedule. We'll work on the actual appointment database in Chapter 10.

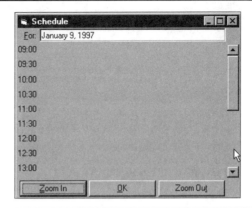

Figure 9-15
Half the time fills half the shaft.

THE FULL LISTING

If you're having trouble with your schedule and your disk is covered with cold cheese from a pizza, Listing 9-2 shows the full `frmSched` code to this point.

Listing 9-2
The schedule code

```
' frmSched.frm — Appointment Schedule Class
' Copyright 1997, Martin L. Rinehart

Option Explicit

Const tp_space = 350
Const bt_space = 400
Const lf_space = 460
Const rt_space = 40

Const str_time = 9 * 60 ' 9AM

Const min_width = 3200
Const min_height = 3000
```

(continued)

The schedule code

```
Private start_time As Integer
Private stop_time As Integer

Private top_time
Private bottom_time

Private current_date As Date

Private interval As Byte
Private interval_index As Byte ' Range: 0-6
Private intervals(6) As Byte

Private Sub cmdOK_Click()
    Hide
End Sub

Private Sub cmdZoomIn_Click()

    If interval_index @@@ 6 Then
        interval_index = interval_index + 1
        reset_times
        set_scrollbar
    End If

End Sub

Private Sub cmdZoomOut_Click()

    If interval_index > 0 Then
        interval_index = interval_index - 1
        reset_times
        set_scrollbar
    End If

End Sub

Private Sub Form_Initialize()

    intervals(0) = 60
    intervals(1) = 30
    intervals(2) = 15
    intervals(3) = 10
    intervals(4) = 5
    intervals(5) = 2
    intervals(6) = 1
```

```
        interval_index = 0

        start_time = str_time
        interval = 60 ' intervals(interval_index)
        stop_time = start_time + interval * 8

        top_time = start_time
        bottom_time = stop_time

        current_date = Date
        reset_times
        set_scrollbar

End Sub

Private Sub Form_Resize()

' time labels
    Dim vert_space As Integer, vert_start As Integer

    If WindowState = vbMinimized Then Exit Sub

    If Width < min_width Then Width = min_width
    If Height < min_height Then Height = min_height

    vert_start = tp_space
    vert_space = (Height - tp_space - bt_space - 400) / 9

    Dim i As Byte
    For i = 0 To 8
        lblTime(i).Top = vert_start + vert_space * i
    Next

' Date text box
    txtDate.Text = niceStr(current_date)
    txtDate.Width = Width - rt_space - lf_space - _
        275 - 120

' Vertical elevator
    VScroll.Left = Width - VScroll.Width - 120
    VScroll.Height = Height - 400 - 350 - _
        VScroll.Top - 50
    ' Form.Height less:
    '    400 twips for Form borders,
    '    350 twips for the bottom command buttons' height,
    '    It's own top and 50 extra for good looks

' Bottom command buttons
```

(continued)

The schedule code

```
    Dim btn_width As Integer
    Const between_spacer = 60
    Const side_spacer = 40

    ' 120 is approximate window border width
    btn_width = _
        (Width - (2 * side_spacer) _
            - (2 * between_spacer) _
            - VScroll.Width - 120) / 3

    cmdZoomIn.Left = side_spacer
    cmdZoomIn.Width = btn_width
    cmdZoomIn.Top = Height - 400 - cmdZoomIn.Height

    cmdOK.Left = cmdZoomIn.Left + btn_width + _
        between_spacer
    cmdOK.Width = btn_width
    cmdOK.Top = cmdZoomIn.Top

    cmdZoomOut.Left = cmdOK.Left + btn_width + _
        between_spacer
    cmdZoomOut.Width = btn_width
    cmdZoomOut.Top = cmdZoomIn.Top

End Sub

Private Sub VScroll_Change()

    top_time = VScroll.Value

    reset_times

End Sub

Private Sub reset_times()

' Don't do this when our code sets Value
    If VScroll.Tag = "X" Then Exit Sub

    interval = intervals(interval_index)
    adjust_top_time

    Dim i As Integer
    For i = 0 To 8
        lblTime(i).Caption = _
            time_label(top_time + i * interval)
    Next
```

```
        bottom_time = top_time + 8 * interval

End Sub

Private Sub adjust_top_time()

' round top_time down to a multiple of the interval
    top_time = top_time - (top_time Mod interval)

' back down if too late
    If top_time + 8 * interval > stop_time Then
        top_time = stop_time - (8 * interval)
    End If

End Sub

Private Function time_label(min As Integer) As String

    Dim mn As Byte, hr As Byte
    hr = Int(min / 60)
    mn = min - (60 * hr)

    time_label = Right(Str(hr + 100), 2) & ":" & _
        Right(Str(mn + 100), 2)

End Function

Public Function niceStr(d As Date)

    ' Spell out date: "January 1, 2000"

    niceStr = monthStr(Month(d)) & _
        Str(Day(d)) & "," & _
        Str(Year(d))

End Function

Private Function monthStr(m As Byte)

        'm must be from 1 thru 12

        Select Case m
            Case 1: monthStr = "January"
            Case 2: monthStr = "February"
            Case 3: monthStr = "March"
            Case 4: monthStr = "April"
            Case 5: monthStr = "May"
            Case 6: monthStr = "June"
            Case 7: monthStr = "July"
```

(continued)

The schedule code

```
                Case 8: monthStr = "August"
                Case 9: monthStr = "September"
                Case 10: monthStr = "October"
                Case 11: monthStr = "November"
                Case 12: monthStr = "December"
            End Select

    End Function

        Private Sub set_scrollbar()

        If top_time = start_time And _
            bottom_time = stop_time Then

            VScroll.Visible = False
            Exit Sub

        End If

        With VScroll

            .min = start_time
            .Max = stop_time - (8 * interval)
            .Tag = "X"
            .Value = top_time
            .Tag = ""

            .SmallChange = interval
            .LargeChange = 8 * interval

            .Visible = True

        End With

    End Sub

    ' end of frmSched.frm
```

SUMMARY

We started by taking a look at a vertical scrollbar. This is a component that just isn't adequately documented, to say the least. We built an experiment-enabling test bench, which is a good way to look at a mystery component.

We brought the key properties — `Min`, `Max`, `Value`, `SmallChange`, and `LargeChange` — out to `TextBoxes` where we could observe them and change them. That made it possible to find out what the elevator was up to.

It turns out that the secret is in the number of jumps required to move `Value` from one end to the other of the range you've specified. If `LargeChange` is 50 in a range of 100, two jumps are required: one click will move `Value` from 0 to 50 and a second click moves it from 50 to 100.

Microsoft leaves space for two jumps by sizing the car to fill a third of the shaft. Clicking from 0 to 50 moves the car from the top third to the middle third. Another click moves it to the bottom.

If you want to fill the shaft entirely with the car, you set a minimal range and specify a maximum `LargeChange` of 32,767. In most applications, however, the scrollbar should disappear rather than be totally filled by the car.

When we completely understood the `Scrollbar` object, we went back to the schedule class and hooked up our elevator. The job was fairly straightforward, once we handled some details about adjusting the `top_time` variable as we zoomed.

We stumbled into a circular event along the way. The scrollbar's `change()` event is raised by user clicks on the elevator, of course, but it's also raised when our program sets the `Value` property of the `Scrollbar` object. We used the do-your-own-thing `Tag` property to hold a flag that the `change()` method read when we didn't want it to run.

Finally, we fixed a bug that came from using the wrong range for the scrollbar. I originally coded it to run from `start_time` to `stop_time`, which seemed sensible but actually wasn't. The real range is determined by how we use `Value`. In our case, it's used to set the `top_time` variable, so the range is the set of possible `top_time` values, which stop eight intervals short of `stop_time`.

With this work done, we've achieved a very nice wrapper, but we have no contents. Our appointments will be displayed from an appointments database, which we'll dive into in Chapter 10.

BUILDING AN APPOINTMENT DATABASE

10

*I*n this chapter we're going to create an appointment database, which we'll need if we want to fill in the contents of the schedule object we were building in the last chapter. There's so much to do here that we won't be able to return to the schedule in this chapter, but we will.

Here we're just going to create an application that will manage our appointment database. In fact, we're going to do this job in a generic way, just as we wrote our ODB to handle any object you can convert to a string.

This will take a lot of work. We'll need to master event programming to do the job. Once we've done it, we'll have general-purpose database code that can easily handle all our other database requirements.

We'll begin with a detailed look at event programming. Visual Basic 5 lets you add your own events. Once you've added them, they're very much like the built-in events — such as `Command1_Click()` — that you're used to programming. They even appear in your code editor's right (procedure) dropdown list.

Once you know how to program your own events, we'll put that knowledge to use in building a four-class database. We'll have an appointment object class, our `ODB` class, and a `frmApp` form-based class. These three will be controlled by an `AppDB` coordinator class. You'll see that having the form raise events lets it communicate fluently with its parent coordinator class.

Let's begin by learning to raise our own events.

EVENT PROGRAMMING

You've been using events tied to Form-based components in all your Visual Basic work. You drop a command button onto your form, double-click it, and the code editor opens a skeleton, like this:

```
Private Sub Command1_Click()

End Sub
```

With Visual Basic 5, you can add your own events. At least you can if you use form-based classes or your own class modules. You can't declare events in a standard (.BAS) module. (That might lead you to think about which sort of modules you'll code, no?)

Programming with events expands the power of your objects, and Visual Basic makes it dead simple.

Events Enable Two-Way Conversation

Think about this little piece of code:

```
Dim kid As MyClass
Set kid = New MyClass
```

That creates an object, *kid,* which is a member of MyClass. Let's say that this code is in a method of an object named *parent.* The parent now owns a kid object. It can call the methods of the kid object.

The kid object doesn't know it has a parent, though. It has no way to call methods of the parent's class. The parent could, if it chose, pass a pointer to itself to enable this sort of two-way conversation, but that's normally a poor design. The kid object shouldn't have to know about its parent.

After all, many different types of parent object could create the kid object. Passing the kid a parent pointer also implies that the kid will know what type of parent it has, what that type's methods are and how to use them.

Compare this to the command button's click() event. The button neither knows nor cares which Form object owns it. The command button knows that its parent wants to be told about user clicks. By raising a click event, it lets its parent know that something has happened. What the parent does with this knowledge is no business of the button.

As you'll see, events can have parameters, like other methods. These can be passed by value or by reference. Passing by reference establishes an additional two-way conversation possibility.

That's getting ahead. Let's begin by creating an object that raises an event.

Raising Your First Event

Open a new standard .EXE project in any convenient directory. Name the form Parent and set its Caption to Parent. Then add a second form and set its name and Caption to Kid. Drop a command button onto the parent and set its Caption to Launch Kid. Then drop a text box onto Kid.

Figure 10-1 shows what this should look like.

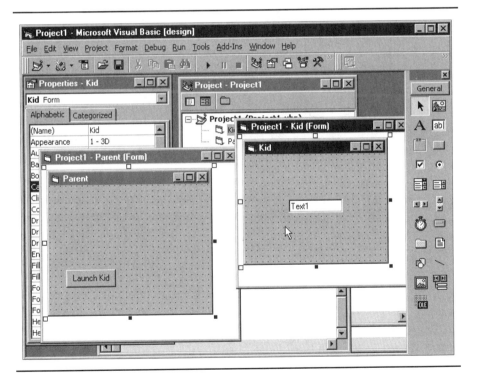

Figure 10-1

Preparing to launch a kid from a parent.

Now we're ready to add some simple code. In Kid, create a Private my_name property. Add this code to handle it:

```
Private my_name As String

Public Sub set_name(nm As String)
    my_name = nm
    Text1.Text = my_name
End Sub

Public Function get_name() As String
    get_name = my_name
End Function
```

In the Parent, add a variable to hold a Kid object, and create, name, and launch the Kid in the button's click() method. This is the code:

```
Private k As Kid

Private Sub Command1_Click()

    Set k = New Kid
    k.set_name "Junior"
    k.Show

End Sub
```

Figure 10-2 shows the Parent and Kid combination at this point.

Ready for the event? You declare an event with an Event statement in the Kid class. A simple event (no parameters) is declared this way:

```
Public Event changeName
```

Put that declaration in the Kid class's declarations section. After you declare an event, you raise it with the RaiseEvent statement, this way:

```
RaiseEvent changeName
```

Use the left (object) dropdown list to select your TextBox, and you'll see a skeleton automatically created for its change() event handler. Add this code:

```
Private Sub Text1_Change()
    my_name = Text1.Text
    RaiseEvent changeName
End Sub
```

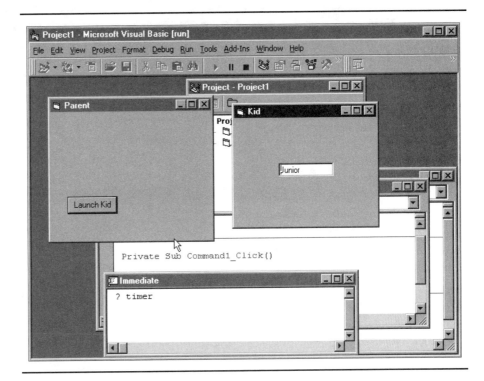

Figure 10-2
The Parent *launches a* Kid.

That's all there is to raising an event. The event source declares it and then uses RaiseEvent to raise it. Any class can declare and raise events this way.

The Public keyword is optional when you declare events. An event is only used when you want to notify other classes. A Private event is an oxymoron, and it's a syntax error.

The magic comes in the Parent that will respond to the events, however.

To respond to events, you must declare the object variable with the WithEvents keyword, this way:

```
Private WithEvents k As Kid
```

When you do that, Visual Basic understands completely. As you see in Figure 10-3, the WithEvents variable is now part of the left (object) dropdown list. It's events (just changeName, in our example) appear in the right dropdown list, and the code editor creates a skeleton event handler for you.

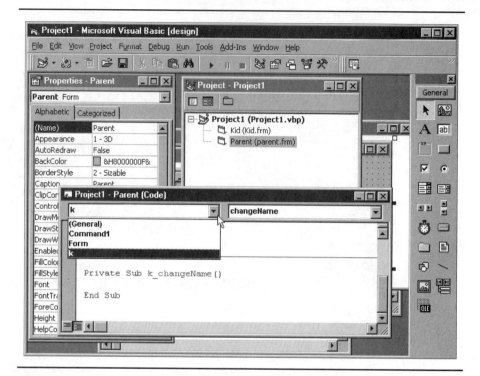

Figure 10-3
Your events become part of the code editor.

At least that's what's supposed to happen. There's a bug in my version of Visual Basic 5. If you don't see the new object in your code editor's dropdown lists, save your project and reopen it. That fixes the problem.

As with programming a button, all you have to do is supply the handling code. Try this:

```
Private Sub k_changeName()
    MsgBox "Kid's name is " & k.get_name()
End Sub
```

Run this program, and you'll see the message box appear when your code makes the assignment to Text1.Text — that raises the Text object's change event which you've used to raise a changeName event.

Then you'll see the message box whenever you make a change in the TextBox. In fact, it's positively annoying because you have to OK the message box after you delete or enter each character in the TextBox, but that's exactly what we programmed.

Adding Message Parameters

What we've done with this event is let the `Kid` call a method in the `Parent`, even though the `Kid` doesn't otherwise know anything about the `Parent`. (To be more exact, the `Kid` raises the event. This will only call a method in `Parent` if `Parent` chooses to handle this event.) As with any method call, you can add parameters. We'll begin with the simple case, providing data to the `Parent`.

Passing Data to the Parent

The declaration of the `Event` is the key to the process. Change your `Event` to return the new name as a parameter, this way:

```
Public Event changeName(new_name As String)
```

Then you pass whatever parameter(s) you specified when you raise the event. Add the parameter to your `RaiseEvents` statement, this way:

```
RaiseEvent changeName(my_name)
```

In the `Parent` class, the `WithEvents` declaration of your object variable doesn't change, but the method is changed. If you delete your `changeName()` method and then use the dropdown lists to return to it you'll see that Visual Basic faithfully copies the parameter information from your declaration into the new skeleton it builds. Add this code:

```
Private Sub k_changeName(new_name As String)
    MsgBox "Kid's name is " & new_name
End Sub
```

Passing Data to the Kid

If you just pass data to the `Parent` this way, you might want to add the optional `ByVal` keyword to the declaration of the parameter. That will prevent the `Parent` from modifying the parameter in the `Kid`.

If you want two-way communication, the default parameter passing is by reference, which provides a bi-directional possibility. If you actually make use of the passing by reference, you should certainly explicitly declare the parameter `ByRef` so that you'll see that the value could be changed in the event handler.

Change the Event declaration to read this way:

```
Public Event changeName(ByRef new_name As String)
```

Next, let's reprogram to accept the name if it's changed by the Parent. Actually, I hope this scares you. It should. I'm so scared I'm just going to say that I've made the change, but I'm not going to really change the TextBox. This is my revised version:

```
Private Sub Text1_Change()
    my_name = Text1.Text
    RaiseEvent changeName(my_name)

' parent may change my_name
    If my_name <> Text1.Text Then
        MsgBox "OK, I'll make it " & my_name
    End If

End Sub
```

Why not just change Text1.Text? Because that's completely recursive! At the point you make that assignment, you trigger another call to Text1_Change(), so your routine is calling itself, which you don't want. If the Parent is always returning the same value the recursion will settle out after one round.

If the Parent returns different values, however, the recursion could easily be infinite. In recursion, *infinite* really means that it runs until the CPU's stack starts to overwrite the code it's running. What happens then is anybody's guess. I hope your disk is backed up!

Now let's change the Parent to be crabby about the name. Again, if you delete your method you'll see that the code editor supplies a skeleton that matches your event declaration. Here's the new routine:

```
Private Sub k_changeName(ByRef new_name As String)
    MsgBox "Kid's name is " & new_name
    new_name = "Junior" ' reset it!
End Sub
```

When you run this code, you'll see that any change is rejected by Parent, who insists on calling Kid Junior, regardless of what you add in the TextBox. Of course, Kid is polite to Parent but doesn't actually do what he's told. (Computers can model real life, can't they?)

Listings 10-1a and 10-1b show the full files Parent.frm and Kid.frm.

Listing 10-1a
The Parent.frm file

```
VERSION 5.00
Begin VB.Form Parent
   Caption         =   "Parent"
   ClientHeight    =   2730
   ClientLeft      =   60
   ClientTop       =   345
   ClientWidth     =   3525
   LinkTopic       =   "Form1"
   ScaleHeight     =   2730
   ScaleWidth      =   3525
   StartUpPosition =   3  'Windows Default
   Begin VB.CommandButton Command1
      Caption      =   "Launch Kid"
      Height       =   375
      Left         =   360
      TabIndex     =   0
      Top          =   1800
      Width        =   1095
   End
End
Attribute VB_Name = "Parent"
Attribute VB_GlobalNameSpace = False
Attribute VB_Creatable = False
Attribute VB_PredeclaredId = True
Attribute VB_Exposed = False
Option Explicit

Private WithEvents k As Kid
Attribute k.VB_VarHelpID = -1

Private Sub Command1_Click()

    Set k = New Kid
    k.set_name "Junior"
    k.Show

End Sub

Private Sub k_changeName(ByRef new_name As String)
    MsgBox "Kid's name is " & new_name
    new_name = "Junior" ' reset it!
End Sub
```

Did you see that the `Attribute` line applicable to your object variable has been introduced into your code? The code editor makes it disappear, so you don't have to worry about it.

Listing 10-1b
The Kid.frm file

```
VERSION 5.00
Begin VB.Form Kid
   Caption        =    "Kid"
   ClientHeight   =    2295
   ClientLeft     =    60
   ClientTop      =    345
   ClientWidth    =    3135
   LinkTopic      =    "Form1"
   ScaleHeight    =    2295
   ScaleWidth     =    3135
   StartUpPosition =   3   'Windows Default
   Begin VB.TextBox Text1
      Height      =      285
      Left        =      960
      TabIndex    =      0
      Text        =      "Text1"
      Top         =      960
      Width       =      1215
   End
End
Attribute VB_Name = "Kid"
Attribute VB_GlobalNameSpace = False
Attribute VB_Creatable = False
Attribute VB_PredeclaredId = True
Attribute VB_Exposed = False
Option Explicit

Public Event changeName(ByRef new_name As String)

Private my_name As String

Public Sub set_name(nm As String)
    my_name = nm
    Text1.Text = my_name
End Sub

Public Function get_name() As String
    get_name = my_name
End Function
```

```
Private Sub Text1_Change()
    my_name = Text1.Text
    RaiseEvent changeName(my_name)

' parent may change my_name
    If my_name <> Text1.Text Then
        MsgBox "OK, I'll make it " & my_name
    End If

End Sub
```

Events in Long Processes

One common use of events is to report progress in long-running processes. You might show a percent completed indicator or otherwise reassure the user that the computer is busy on its appointed tasks. We can simulate a long process with the `Timer()` function.

`Timer()` reports the number of seconds elapsed since midnight. Before we start, I'll point out a bug common to most `Timer`-related code: midnights are problematic. If you routinely work through the midnight hour, create your own cover function for `Timer` that doesn't switch from 86,399 to 0 at midnight. Have it continue at 86,400, and you'll be happy. The code in this section doesn't worry about this problem.

Let's begin by replacing the annoying message box output with a `TextBox` display in `Parent`. While we're making this change, we can eliminate the `ByRef` nature of the `changeName()` event that we added in the last section.

The result will be that we can type in one `TextBox`, and see our input echoed in another. (By the way, that's not so far from where we're going, except that instead of a second `TextBox`, we'll have an `ODB` object in use.)

These are the steps:

- Eliminate the `ByRef` keywords in `Kid` and `Parent`
- Eliminate the logic that reset the parameter in `Parent`
- Eliminate the logic that responded to the reset in `Kid`
- Add a `TextBox` to `Parent`
- Assign the `changeName` parameter to `Text1.Text` in `Parent`

Figure 10-4 shows me entering a new name in `Kid` while `Parent` echoes the name.

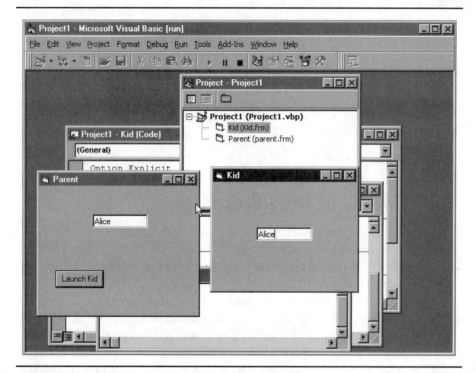

Figure 10-4
Parent's TextBox *echoes* Kid's TextBox.

At this point you could make the two TextBoxes fully bidirectional. You could call the Kid's set_name() routine from the Change() event handler in Parent. (Don't do it, just think about it. If you want to really do it, you'll have to add logic to suppress recursion.)

This illustrates the nature of the event and method relationship. When Parent wants to talk to Kid, Parent calls a method directly. When Kid has something to say to Parent, Kid raises an event. Among the many advantages of events, this leaves the response totally up to the Parent. (You don't want Kid bossing Parent, do you? That's supposed to work the other way!)

Building a Lengthy Process

Let's go ahead and add a lengthy process. In lieu of reading and writing a large data file or some other protracted job, let's just look at our watch repeatedly, waiting for time to pass. The Timer function returns the number of seconds since midnight, so it's perfect for this purpose.

Here's the code that you can add to the Kid class to simulate a lengthy process:

```
Public Sub work_hard(how_long As Integer)

    Dim start As Single
    start = Timer

    While Timer - start @@@ how_long
        ' Kids work is here
    Wend

End Sub
```

With work_hard() available, we need to call it. For this, drop another button onto Parent and set its Caption to Work, Kid! or something similar. (If you're at your job, maybe Begin Process would be better.) Then program the button to have the Kid do a few seconds of work. This is my code:

```
Private Sub Command2_Click()

    k.work_hard (10)

End Sub
```

When you run this program you'll see that you lose control for ten seconds. That's more than long enough to begin wondering if your machine has crashed. You can't click a button or do anything else while Kid wastes the allotted amount of time.

Wouldn't it be nice to have a little sign that something's happening?

Raising a Progress Event

Let's have Kid raise a progress event every second or so. We can report on the progress in Parent's TextBox. Declare another Event in Kid, this way:

```
Option Explicit

Public Event changeName(new_name As String)
Public Event reportProgress(amt_done As Single)
```

Raise this event every second. You can do that by setting another variable (I've called mine now) to track time and comparing it to Timer(). When Timer() exceeds now by more than a second, raise the event and reset now. This won't work, by the way, but trust me. We're going in the right direction.

This is my modified work_hard() code:

```
Public Sub work_hard(how_long As Integer)

    Dim start As Single
    start = Timer

    Dim now As Single
    now = start

    While Timer - start < how_long

        If Timer - now > 1 Then
            RaiseEvent reportProgress(Timer - start)
            now = Timer
        End If

        ' Kids work is here
    Wend

End Sub
```

The remaining job is to respond to the reportProgress event in Parent. I'll do that by reporting in our handy TextBox. You've already declared your object as WithEvents, so you don't have to do that again. You'll see that if you set the object in the left dropdown list, the right dropdown list will have the new event available immediately.

Here's the new code, mostly provided by the code editor. (I added the middle line.)

```
Private Sub k_reportProgress(amt_done As Single)
    Text1.Text = Str(amt_done)
End Sub
```

Again, this won't work, but trust me. When you run this program at this point, you'll have a ten second delay, and then you'll see the last event reported in Parent's TextBox.

This shows that events are not really just like method calls.

Using the DoEvents Function

We've raised our event about ten times, but it wasn't handled until the work_hard() method completed its job. This is because work_hard was monopolizing our application.

The secret to event handling is that Windows does it internally, which broadcasts the results of its work to applications such as our Visual Basic one. If you want true multitasking, wait until we begin building ActiveX .EXE projects in the next chapter. You can launch as many ActiveX .EXEs as you like, all simultaneously. Windows will allocate available resources to all of them, so they can all run at once.

This preemptive multitasking system is very handy when one or more .EXEs are doing jobs that involve mostly waiting. Downloading things from the World Wide Wait is a good example, but Windows doesn't slice into a single executable file, so it doesn't know that our program has been queueing events for itself. Within an executable file, you have to fall back on cooperative multitasking.

The `DoEvents` function lets you surrender control to the operating system so that waiting events can be processed. A good time to insert a `DoEvents` function call is immediately after you `RaiseEvent`. Insert the `DoEvents` function call that you see in the following, and your system will suddenly work just as you want:

```
Public Sub work_hard(how_long As Integer)

    Dim start As Single
    start = Timer

    Dim now As Single
    now = start

    While Timer - start < how_long

        If Timer - now > 1 Then
            now = Timer
            RaiseEvent reportProgress(Timer - start)
            DoEvents
        End If

        ' Kids work is here
    Wend

End Sub
```

Got it? You should now have nine or ten time reports, spaced roughly a second a part. (Actually, a second plus the time that our code takes, as well as time that Windows takes looking around at other programs that might have work for it to handle.) Figure 10-5 shows my `Parent` reporting on the hard work its `Kid` is doing.

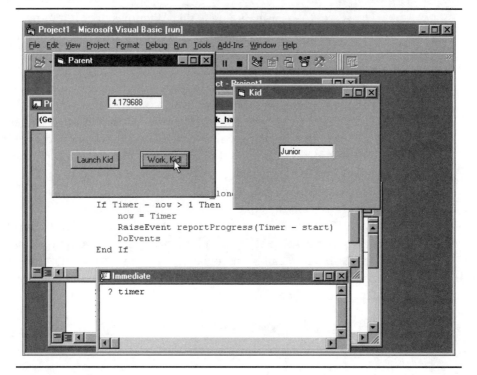

DoEvents should be used as a statement. It returns a value in one
particular version of Visual Basic (see the online language reference for
details) but not in any of the others. This suggests to me that Microsoft
changed its design someplace between releases. The current thinking seems
to be consistent with using DoEvents as a statement.

Listings 10-2a and 10-2b show the editable parts of Parent.frm and
Kid.frm.

Listing 10-2a
The Parent.frm code

```
Option Explicit

Private WithEvents k As Kid
Private Sub Command1_Click()

    Set k = New Kid
    k.set_name "Junior"
    k.Show
```

```
    End Sub

    Private Sub Command2_Click()
        k.work_hard (10)
    End Sub

    Private Sub k_changeName(new_name As String)
        Text1.Text = new_name
    End Sub


    Private Sub k_reportProgress(amt_done As Single)
        Text1.Text = Str(amt_done)
    End Sub
```

Listing 10-2b
The Kid.frm code

```
    Option Explicit

    Public Event changeName(new_name As String)
    Public Event reportProgress(amt_done As Single)

    Private my_name As String

    Public Sub set_name(nm As String)
        my_name = nm
        Text1.Text = my_name
    End Sub

    Public Function get_name() As String
        get_name = my_name
    End Function

    Private Sub Text1_Change()
        my_name = Text1.Text
        RaiseEvent changeName(my_name)
    End Sub

    Public Sub work_hard(how_long As Integer)

        Dim start As Single
        start = Timer

        Dim now As Single
        now = start
```

(continued)

The Kid.frm code

```
While Timer - start < how_long

    If Timer - now > 1 Then
        now = Timer
        RaiseEvent reportProgress(Timer - start)
        DoEvents
    End If

    ' Kids work is here
    Wend

End Sub
```

Event Summary

To raise events, you do two things: declare your events — `Public Event <name>` or `Public Event <name>(<param(s)>)` — and then use the `RaiseEvent` statement whenever you want to raise the event.

To receive an event you do three things. You declare an object variable as `WithEvents`; you create an instance of that object, assigning it to the `WithEvents` variable; and you provide methods that will respond to the events. These methods are named by the object variable and the event name, separated by an underscore. The easy way to get this right is to let the code editor prepare the method skeletons, which it does just as it does for built-in components such as command buttons.

Finally, if your event source is a lengthy process, use the `DoEvents` function after your `RaiseEvent` statements. This will yield control long enough for the operating system to actually handle the events you've raised. Although it's a function, use `DoEvents` as a statement.

Now that you're an event-enabled programmer, you're ready to actually build your appointment database.

A FOUR-CLASS DESIGN

Four classes working together will generally create a reasonable database maintenance program. In this case, we want a database of appointments. Let's call the individual appointment an *app*, which will also be the first class.

In addition to the `app` class, we'll need an `ODB` class to manage the object database. Then a `frmApp` form-based class will provide the actual data-entry form. Finally, an `AppDB` class can tie the first three together.

In the MyTime system, we'll use object stores for appointments, *to do* items, projects, and chores. The *chores* are recurring *to do* items that aren't associated with a single project, such as handling your e-mail or preparing expense reports.

Each of these will have these classes:

! Object class (appointment, project, and so on)

! ODB class

! Data entry form

! Coordinator class

The coordinator's job is to keep everybody working together. For instance, when the user updates an item in the data entry form, it will raise an event for the coordinator. The coordinator will note that the object needs to be updated on disk before moving another object in the class into the form.

In lieu of using the coordinator, you could have the form's TextBoxes call the ODB directly to replace the object with each change() event, but that would mean rewriting the disk copy each time the user tapped a key, which wouldn't be very efficient, to say the least. You'll see that another benefit of this design is that the form's code is completely generic, so we can use it for every object database. All the class-specific code is in the coordinator and the object class.

Now let's take a closer look at each class.

The App Class's Design

Designing the App class is the same job that faces database designers. You have to decide what set of items is adequate. At this point I hope you'll all follow the backpacker's maxim: when in doubt, leave it out.

It's not a lot of trouble to go back to an object and add a new property. If your property list is minimal, you'll have nice, clean data entry forms, easy data entry work, and so on.

Once you're familiar with using ODBs (and particularly when you're fluent with implementing the storable interface, which we'll get to in Chapter 13), you'll find that it's very little trouble to create a utility that expands an existing ODB.

If you're sure you'll need more properties than you can think of at the outset, you can even have your to_string() and from_string() functions provide some extra space for each object. Then you can just use this space when you create additional properties. If your users use disk compression, you'll find that storing extra blank spaces is almost free in terms of disk space used, and even uncompressed disk space doesn't cost very much today.

On the other hand, asking your users (which may be yourself for personal systems like MyTime) to enter superfluous information can be very costly. Your time is valuable, so keep your property set minimal.

The set I've adopted for appointments is this:

- Key (see below)
- Date
- Start time
- End time
- Actual time
- Description

The key field is a `Long` that I'll discuss shortly. I use one automatically for any object that will be stored on disk.

I store each of the time properties as an integer number of minutes since midnight, in RAM. This avoids the roundoff problems you'll get by using Visual Basic's fractional times. Whenever I show a human-readable version, I switch to an HH:MM format.

The date, start, and end times are as scheduled. I record actual time after the fact. If a meeting is scheduled for 10:00 to 11:30 but runs only to 10:45, I'll record 0:45 as the actual time. This is vital for seeing where your time goes. Actual time will default to a zero value until your appointment takes place, so this will let you distinguish between appointments that took place and those that are yet to happen. (If you're like me, you'll find that something scheduled for Tuesday doesn't necessarily happen on Tuesday.)

The description is a field that you can adopt to your own needs. I use it for terse notes like "phone w/Matt" or "Greg re book schedule." You'll see that I discipline myself to be brief, here. You might want more space than I allow.

This gives me a property definition in App.cls that looks like this:

```
' Data members:
    Public key As Long
    Public app_date As Date

    Private start_time As Integer
    Private end_time As Integer
    Private actual_time As Integer

    Public description As String
```

The `get()` and `set()` methods for the time values take care of translating external 00:00 formatted strings to the internal integer format. The other items are stored as provided.

There's nothing really `Public` about, for instance, the key value. I use `Public` because it's only my code that will be updating these values. The key, for example, can't be updated except when the object is created.

Because the `App` class objects will be stored in an `ODB`, they'll need to `to_string()` and `from_string()` methods, which we'll discuss when we start on the code.

The Key Field's Design

Every object must have a unique identity. In RAM, Visual Basic provides a unique object reference identifier for each object. If you are storing objects on disk, you can't depend on Visual Basic to maintain unique identifiers. You have to do it yourself.

The easiest form of unique identifier is also the most robust: each item is given a number one higher than the last as it is written to disk.

In an object database that has no deletions, the key value is also the record number, but it varies once you allow deletions. If the last object is 99 and you add another, it's key is 100. If your maintenance utility deletes 50 of the first 100, the next one you add is still going to be 101. The deleted keys are never reassigned, so you can always read back in objects that have been deleted (from tape backup, for example) without disturbing the current data.

The key update software that I'll show here depends on the last object added never being physically deleted. (Remember, a deleted `ODB` record is marked as deleted, not physically removed from the file.) Any maintenance utility you write must respect this convention.

In a relational database, this field would be called an *abstract primary key*. You can use a key as an object identifier, storing it wherever you need to refer to the object. For example, a `Sales` object might record the key of a `Customer` object (the customer to whom you made the sale in question).

By holding just the key you allow someone to update the customer record without creating redundant data. For example, you could correct the spelling of the customer's name or change the customer's address without changing any `Sales` objects that included the customer key. In relational database terminology you call this a *foreign key*. That's the key in, for example, the sale data that names the customer to whom the sale was made.

The key is created when the object is added to its `ODB`. It is never changed after it is created, so it permanently *points to* or *names* a particular object. The important concepts here are that the key is *never* (absolutely never!) changed and that it is *unique* (absolutely unique!) so a customer key, for instance, will always name exactly one customer and that will always be the same customer.

The frmApp Class's Design

The data entry form must display all the data and provide means for entering it. You can see my data entry form design in Figure 10-6.

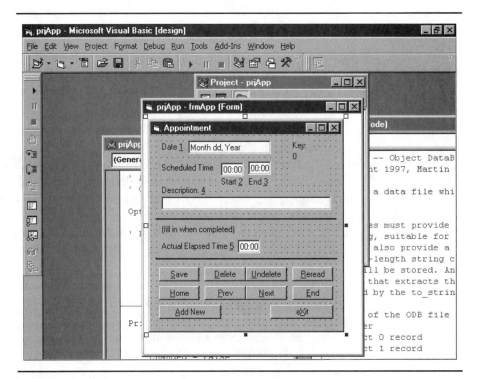

Figure 10-6
The appointment form is designed.

(Hold off on creating your own until we get into the code in the next major section.)

The form needs to_form() and from_form() methods, similar to the App class's to_string() and from_string() methods. We can collect the change() methods of each TextBox into a single, custom event that we'll raise on any change. This will simplify the code for the coordinator object.

Did I say *all* the data? As always (well, *almost* always!), those absolutes get qualified when you look more closely. Some data, such as the object's key, shouldn't be accessible to the end-user. In most systems, I never even show the key on the data entry form.

Because this is a personal system, I'll show the key in a `Label` on the form. This will make debugging easier, but it won't allow manual edits of the key. (Inadvertantly set two keys to the same value, and you destroy the essential uniqueness. You'll have one name for two — or more! — objects.)

The set of buttons at the bottom of this form are generic to all our database objects. We'll also keep the code generic as well. The secret will be raising events in response to the button presses. The coordinator can handle them, providing any object-specific code that's needed.

The ODB Class's Design

We've already built our `ODB` class. When we put it to use here, you'll find that we need some modifications, but basically it will be as already created. I'll try to keep the modifications general so that the improved class will serve our other database needs, as well.

You'll see that we want to launch a single ActiveX .DLL (see Chapter 11) for the `ODB` class. We want it to support all our `ODB` objects.

The Coordinator Class's Design

I've named the coordinator class an `AppDB`. It bundles together the `ODB`, data entry form, and an `App` object. It will use *containment*, containing another object as a data member, as a substitute for object programming's traditional inheritance relationship.

The `AppDB` contains an `ODB`. This lets it use generalized `ODB` methods for work with `App` class objects. We'll cover the design when we start programming, which is what we're about to start.

PROGRAMMING THE MAIN LINE

The coordinator class will be the boss here. It will take care of creating objects of the `App`, `ODB`, and `frmApp` classes, as well as launching the form. We'll need a trivial main line to handle launching an `AppDB` object.

Add a new standard module to your class. Mine's named `MnAppDB`. This is the entire code:

```
' MnAppDB.bas — Mainline for Appointment DataBase
' Copyright 1997, Martin L. Rinehart

Option Explicit

Public Sub main()

    Dim adb As AppDB
    Set adb = New AppDB

End Sub

' end of MnAppDB.bas
```

Unfortunately, the other class modules won't be quite this simple.

PROGRAMMING THE APP CLASS

Begin by creating a working directory and a shortcut that points to it. Then launch Visual Basic and create a new, standard .EXE project. Mine's named `prjApp`. Then add a new class module named `App`.

This is a very simple class that you can program all at once. You've seen that I normally enter and test code in small pieces. This one was an exception. I just wrote it and ran it. After weeding out the inevitable typos, it ran perfectly.

Declaring the Data Members

Start by adding your standard comments to start and end the code and then enter these property declarations:

```
' Data members:
    Public key As Long
    Public app_date As Date

    Private start_time As Integer
    Private end_time As Integer
    Private actual_time As Integer

    Public description As String
```

If you have any questions about this or the other classes, you can see the full code in Listings 10-3a through 10-3e near the end of this chapter.

Get and Set Methods for the Private Properties

The `Private` members need methods to obtain and set their values. In this case, we'll be recording the time internally as an `Integer` (minutes since midnight) and showing it externally as a string in HH:MM format. I call that a `tstring`, for time string. Thus, the `get()` and `set()` methods will take care of calling utility code that does the conversion. This is the code for `start_time`:

```
Public Sub set_start_time(s As String)

    start_time = tstring2int(s)

End Sub

Public Function get_start_time() As String

    get_start_time = int2tstring(start_time)

End Function
```

After you enter that code, make two addtional copies of both routines and edit it to handle the other two time properties.

The Class's Constructor

With one exception, all the values for this class can default to the Visual Basic initial values (zero for numbers and null string for strings.) The exception is the date, which I want to default to today. Because this code won't be called often, I've chosen to explicitly write out each assignment, even though only the date is needed. This is my version:

```
Private Sub Class_Initialize()

    key = 0 ' will be set by ODB
    app_date = Date
    start_time = 0 ' defaults
    end_time = 0
    actual_time = 0
    description = ""

End Sub
```

The get_name(), to_string(), and from_string() Methods

The ODB class depends on having three methods:

- get_name()
- to_string()
- from_string()

The first of this is trivial:

```
Public Function get_name() As String

    get_name = "App"

End Function
```

The to_string() and from_string() methods are the ones that take thoughtful programming. I begin by planning carefully and then writing out my plan. This is the comment that I started with:

```
' string layout:
    ' key:           1-11, pad byte: 12
    ' app_date:      13-20
    ' start_time:    21-26
    ' end_time:      27-32, pad byte: 33
    ' actual_time:   34-39, pad byte: 40
    ' description:   41-80
```

The key is a Long, which takes 11 characters (maximum) to store in a string. We'll use YYYYMMDD to store the date. The times can all be stored in HH:MM format. I'm only using 40 characters for the description. You might want to double that. I've dropped in pad bytes to get to a multiple of four. I've placed them to improve the readability of the ODB file.

The Intel CPU design can transfer one, two, or four bytes at a time. Each mov or other low-level instruction takes about the same number of clock cycles, regardless of the operand size. An instruction such as rep movs, repeated move string, can handle a string that's a multiple of four bytes in one quarter the time that it would take to handle a string one byte at a time. I'm not sure that Visual Basic will correctly optimize this yet, but it probably will some day. Using multiples of four bytes is a good programming habit.

The `to_string()` method looks like this:

```
Public Function to_string() As String

    to_string = _
        ODB.long_str(key) & " " & _
        ODB.date_str(app_date) & _
        ODB.int_str(start_time) & _
        ODB.int_str(end_time) & " " & _
        ODB.int_str(actual_time) & " " & _
        ODB.fix_len(description, 40)

End Function
```

I've used utility functions from the `ODB` class. It already has `fix_len()`, and we'll add the others.

The `from_string()` code looks like this:

```
Public Sub from_string(s As String)

    key = Val(Left(s, 11))
    app_date = ODB.yyyymmdd2date(Mid(s, 13, 8))
    start_time = Val(Mid(s, 21, 6))
    end_time = Val(Mid(s, 27, 6))
    actual_time = Val(Mid(s, 34, 6))
    description = Right(s, 40)

End Sub
```

Utility Methods

Finally, the utility methods convert `tstrings` (HH:MM form) to and from integers. I've kept these with this class because I didn't think they were sufficiently general to go in the `ODB` class. This is the code:

```
Private Function tstring2int(s As String)

' a tstring is "HH:MM" (i.e. "01:00" = 60)

    tstring2int = _
        60 * Val(Left(s, 2)) + _
        Val(Right(s, 2))

End Function

Private Function int2tstring(i As Integer)
```

(continued)

```
' returns "01:00" given 60, "02:30" given 150, etc.

    Dim hr As Byte, mn As Byte
    hr = i / 60
    mn = i - (hr * 60)

    int2tstring = _
        Right(Str(100 + hr), 2) & ":" & _
        Right(Str(100 + mn), 2)

End Function
```

IMPROVING THE ODB CLASS

You've already seen that we'll need some more utility functions in the ODB class. These create fixed-length strings from Long, Integer, and Date data. We'll also need to improve some of the methods we created back in Chapter 7. We'll need to change several Sub methods to Function so that we can return data that the coordinator class will need.

Begin by copying the ODB.cls file from the directory where you built it to the directory you're using for this project. Then add it to your project. That gets you ready to work on the code.

Let's start with the open_odb() method.

The Open_odb Function

When we first wrote the ODB class, we wrote an open_odb() method as a subroutine. For our use now, we'll need that method to return an error code or an OK message. Begin by adding an openOK value to the err_types enum list, this way:

```
Public Enum err_types
    openOK = -1          ' Add this one
    err_freefile = 0
    err_open
    err_seek
```

Then change open_odb() from a Sub to a Function. Visual Basic is very nice about changing the End Sub to an End Function, and any Exit Sub statements change to Exit Function, too. Don't forget to declare its type by adding As Integer.

Once you've made open_odb() a function, you have to assign a value to open_odb. Just before the End Function, you assign it openOK. Before each of the Exit Function statements, assign open_odb the named constant (err_xxxx) that you passed to the error_msgs routine. The completed function looks like this:

```
Public Function open_odb(pn As String) As Integer

' check that a file number is available
    file_number = FreeFile
    If file_number = 0 Then
        err_msgs (err_freefile)
        open_odb = err_freefile
        Exit Function
    End If

' open the file — if it's 0 long, its new
    Open pn & ".odb" For Binary As file_number
    If LOF(file_number) = 0 Then ' not an ODB!
        Close file_number
        err_msgs (err_open)
        open_odb = err_open
        Exit Function
    End If

' create buffer for header, then read header
    Dim header As String
    header = Space(header_len)

    Get file_number, , header

' check for a valid signature
    If Left(header, 8) <> signature Then
        Close file_number
        err_msgs (err_open)
        open_odb = err_open
        Exit Function
    End If

' set up private data members
    rec_len = Val(Right(header, 8))
    rec_buf = Space(rec_len)
    path_name = pn

    num_objects = (LOF(file_number) - header_len) / rec_len
    current_object_num = 0
    open_odb = openOK

End Function
```

The get_obj() Function

We'll want the AppDB class to keep track of the current App object. This means that the get_obj() method has to become a function that returns the number of the object it retrieves. For an error, we can return –1. This won't be important at first, but we'll also want to change the function so that it can skip deleted records and return the first nondeleted record it finds. For this purpose, we'll absolutely need the object number.

Again, change the Sub line to Function and add As Integer to give it a type. Then assign get_obj a –1 value on any error, or assign it the number of the object retrieved on success. The completed code looks like this:

```
Public Function get_obj(num As Integer, _
    ByRef obj As Object) As Integer

    If Not rec_in_file(num) Then
        err_msgs (err_seek)
        get_obj = -1
        Exit Function
    End If

    Get file_number, oloc(num), rec_buf

    If Mid(rec_buf, 3, 1) = "*" Then
        err_msgs (err_getdel)
        get_obj = -1
    Else
        obj.from_string (Right(rec_buf, rec_len - 4))
        get_obj = num
    End If

End Function
```

Adding Utility Functions

Some functions will be generally useful in database work, so I've added them to the ODB class. For example, converting a Long to a String will be commonly useful.

Long to String

A Long holds values between negative and positive 2 billion, approximately. This means the String form could require 10 digits plus an additional character for the negative sign, or a maximum of 11 characters. For use in functions such as `to_string()` (where fixed length is required) you can't use `str()` because that returns a variable length.

This code always returns 11 characters:

```
Public Function long_str(l As Long) As String

' returns 11-byte string

    long_str = Right(Space(10) & Str(l), 11)

End Function
```

If you're very sharp-eyed, you might have noticed that only nine spaces are really needed because the `str()` function automatically supplies a leading space. Of all the languages I know, Visual Basic is the only one that has this quirk. I've ignored it because it might be changed to just return the number.

Integer to String

Integers hold values between plus and minus 32,000, approximately. That could be six characters, when the negative sign is included. This code returns a fixed-length string form:

```
Public Function int_str(i As Integer) As String

' returns 6-byte string

    int_str = Right(Space(5) & Str(i), 6)

End Function
```

Dates to String and Back

The convenient form of a date in a database is YYYYMMDD. This form lets you sort on the date in the string form. This code converts a date to this form:

```
Public Function date_str(d As Date) As String

' returns 8-byte date: YYYYMMDD
```

```
date_str = _
    Right(Str(Year(d)), 4) & _
    Right(Str(100 + Month(d)), 2) & _
    Right(Str(100 + Day(d)), 2)

End Function
```

All conversions need to be two-way. Visual Basic's built-in val() function will return numbers from the string form, so we didn't need to write a String to Long function, for example. However, we do need to supply the reverse conversion for YYYYMMDD strings. This code does the job:

```
Public Function yyyymmdd2date(s As String) As Date

' return date given "YYYYMMDD" string

    yyyymmdd2date = _
        Mid(s, 5, 2) & "/" & _
        Right(s, 2) & "/" & _
        Left(s, 4)

End Function
```

The add_obj() Function

The add_obj() method also needs to become a function, returning the number of the object it adds. This code will do the job:

```
Public Function add_obj(o As Object)

    rec_buf = Chr(13) & Chr(10) & "  " & o.to_string()
    Put file_number, LOF(file_number) + 1, rec_buf
    add_obj = num_objects
    num_objects = num_objects + 1

End Function
```

The final object's number is one less than the number of objects. If you have a hundred objects, for example, they're numbered 0 through 99.

Now we can talk about the form-based class.

BUILDING THE APP FORM CLASS

If your form is still `Form1`, name it `appFrm`. Then add all the buttons, labels, and text boxes you see in Figure 10-7. You see that I've selected the `lblDeleted` label. Because it has no caption, you wouldn't see it otherwise.

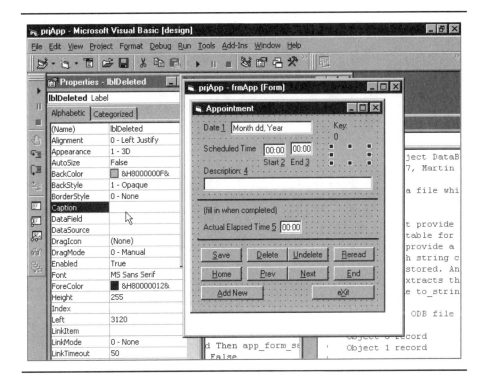

■ **Figure 10-7**
The `frmApp` design, showing `lblDeleted`.

The following list is in tab index order. As you can see in Figure 10-7, the captions follow the names except that I've added numerals to the labels for keyboard access to the text boxes. These are the names I've used:

- `cmdSave`
- `cmdDelete`
- `cmdUndelete`
- `cmdReread`
- `cmdHome`
- `cmdPrev`

- cmdNext
- cmdEnd
- cmdAdd
- cmdExit
- lblDate
- txtDate
- lblScheduledTime
- txtScheduledTime
- lblStart
- txtStart
- lblEnd
- txtEnd
- lblDescription
- txtDescription
- lblActual
- txtActual
- lblKey
- lblKeyNum
- lblDeleted
- Line1
- Line2

The lblKey label has the "Key:" caption. The lblKeyNum label is just under it in the top-right corner, just above the lblDeleted label.

Using underscored letters for keyboard access to the text fields is not a Windows-standard interface. If you can come up with something better, be my guest. I could only think of things that were significantly worse. The buttons use too many of the likely (or even unlikely) letters.

Build the bottom buttons carefully, as we'll reuse them for all our other database needs.

If you need more details, they're on disk in 10-03, and a later version is printed in Appendix B.

Once you've constructed your form, you can get on to the code. You'll see that the code is much simpler than the job of building the form.

Begin the code by adding your standard comments, and then you're ready to do some event programming. It will be completely generic, so we can use it for any database need.

Declaring the Events

Start by adding these declarations:

```
Public Event saveObject()
Public Event deleteObject()
Public Event undeleteObject()
Public Event rereadObject()
Public Event navigate(where As Byte)
Public Event addObject()
Public Event exitButton()
```

As you can see, there's one event for each button, except that the database navigation buttons (Home, Prev, Next, and End) raise the navigate() event passing a parameter. Add this Enum giving the parameter named values:

```
Public Enum navigate_movements
    nav_home
    nav_prev
    nav_next
    nav_end
End Enum
```

Programming the Events

Now you can use the code editor to create skeletons for each button's Click() event handler and fill in middle lines, like this one:

```
Private Sub cmdAdd_Click()

    RaiseEvent addObject

End Sub
```

For the navigation buttons, add the appropriate `enum` name as a parameter, as this example shows:

```
Private Sub cmdHome_Click()

    RaiseEvent navigate(nav_home)

End Sub
```

That's all the programming that this form will get here. Obviously, the work is all done up in the coordinator class, which is our final project in this chapter.

You'll see that we'll add a `change` event later on, but for now we'll concentrate on getting the database running.

PROGRAMMING THE APPDB CLASS

The `AppDB` object is the coordinator that manages the other objects. It will contain an `App`, an `ODB`, and a `frmApp` object. This *containment* construction is sometimes the way you want to design an object, and sometimes it's the way you must design because you don't have inheritance.

Object theorists talk about the *has a* and *is a* relationships. You could say a convertible *has a* fold-down top, but a convertible *is a* car. Your object design would have the convertible inherit all the characteristics of the car class and then add properties for the folding roof.

In Visual Basic, you'd add a car object as a property of the convertible object because you can't inherit from the car class. This isn't as clean as a proper object design, but it works.

The AppDB's Data Members

Begin programming by adding a new class module, called `AppDB`, to your project. Add your standard top and bottom comments. Then you're ready to add these properties:

```
' Properties:
    Private obj_db As ODB
    Private cur_app As App
    Private WithEvents app_form As frmApp

    Private app_num As Integer
    Private changed As Boolean
```

The first three properties are the objects we've been working with up to this point. The final two are bookkeeping data. The `app_num` tells us which App object in the ODB is currently in RAM. You need to know this to navigate in response to the Next and Prev buttons.

The changed boolean tells you if the data has changed. If it has, you'll need to rewrite the disk copy before you navigate to another object and before you exit. (We haven't programmed the `frmApp` class to set `changed` `True` yet. You'll have to remember to press the Save button for now.)

The Class Constructor and Destructor

This class creates its component objects in its constructor. They are automatically released when the `AppDB` object goes out of scope, so all the destructor has to do is unload the form.

This is the code for the constructor:

```
Private Sub Class_Initialize()

    Set cur_app = New App
    Set obj_db = New ODB
    Set app_form = New frmApp

    Dim pn As String ' pathname
    pn = cur_app.get_name

    If Len(Dir(pn & ".ODB")) = 0 Then
        obj_db.create_odb cur_app
    Else
        If obj_db.open_odb(pn) <> openOK Then End
    End If

    app_num = obj_db.get_obj(0, cur_app)
    to_form ' fill in TextBoxes

    changed = False
    app_form.Show 1 ' modal

End Sub
```

This constructor assumes that the database will be in your current directory. I'll leave it up to you to improve on that when you have the time. For now, it lets us focus on the object programming.

The destructor is trivial:

```
Private Sub Class_Terminate()

    Unload app_form

End Sub
```

Going to_form() and from_form()

A key job is moving data from the App object to the frmApp's TextBoxes and back again. I handle this with the to_form() and from_form() methods shown here:

```
Public Sub to_form()

' fill form's text boxes from object

    app_form.lblKeyNum = Str(cur_app.key)
    app_form.txtDate.Text = CStr(cur_app.app_date)
    app_form.txtStart.Text = cur_app.get_start_time
    app_form.txtEnd.Text = cur_app.get_end_time
    app_form.txtActual.Text = cur_app.get_actual_time
    app_form.txtDescription.Text = cur_app.description

End Sub

Public Sub from_form()

' change object as per form
    cur_app.app_date = app_form.txtDate.Text
    cur_app.set_start_time app_form.txtStart.Text
    cur_app.set_end_time app_form.txtEnd.Text
    cur_app.set_actual_time app_form.txtActual.Text
    cur_app.description = app_form.txtDescription.Text

End Sub
```

Responding to Events

At this point, you're ready to run your main line. (Use your project's property sheets to set Sub Main as the startup object.) You'll find that nothing will happen, however.

Use your code editor to create skeletons for all the events that frmApp raises. Start by dropping in a message box for each event, like this:

```
Private Sub app_form_deleteObject()

    MsgBox "delete"

End Sub
```

Then when you test, you'll at least see that the buttons are correctly connected to the frmApp's parent AppDB object. Now all we have to do is implement these event handlers one at a time.

The class constructor takes care of creating the ODB if it doesn't exist. You'll start with a single object, with all default values, in your ODB.

Saving Your Data

The first thing that you might want to do is actually enter some data in the frmApp's TextBoxes and save it to disk. So the first event to correctly program will be the Save button event.

This code shows that we've already done all the hard work:

```
Private Sub app_form_saveObject()

    from_form ' update cur_app
    Call obj_db.rep_obj(app_num, cur_app)

    changed = False ' not changed since saved

End Sub
```

The from_form() method takes the data from frmApp and updates the cur_app App object. Then the ODB's rep_obj() method writes it to disk. All that's left for us is to set the changed variable back to False. (Remember that we haven't actually got anything that sets changed to True. Always click the Save button to save your data.)

Use this much to enter a test appointment, as Figure 10-8 shows.

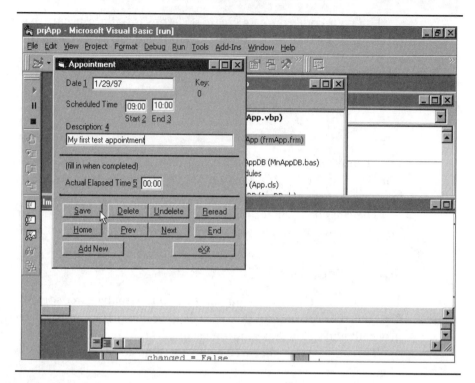

Figure 10-8
Entering starting data.

Erasing Your Work

The Reread button is handy when you decide you don't like the edits you've made. It will also let you see that your ODB is doing its job. This code does the trick:

```
Private Sub app_form_rereadObject()

    Call obj_db.get_obj(app_num, cur_app)
    to_form ' refresh form

    changed = False ' not changed from disk copy

End Sub
```

Now you can run again. Change some of the TextBox values, and then press Reread. Your changes will be replaced by the disk values.

You might want to add bits of dialog like, "Data edited. Overwrite changes?" to these methods. Beginners like this considerate behavior. It can annoy experienced users, though. I prefer speed to caution in this application.

Adding More Records

To check our navigation, we'll need to have more than one object in the ODB, so the next button to implement should be Add New. That raises the addObject event, which you can program this way:

```
Private Sub app_form_addObject()

    If changed Then app_form_saveObject
    changed = False

    Set cur_app = New App
    app_num = obj_db.add_obj(cur_app)
    to_form

End Sub
```

Add a handful of additional appointments. If you use dumb descriptions like, "First app," "Second app," and so on, you'll make testing the navigation buttons much simpler.

Navigating among Your Records

All four navigation keys raise the navigate event with a parameter. Using this parameter in a Select Case switch lets you pick the correct object to navigate to. Then it's just a matter of asking the ODB to fetch that object.

You do have to check that Prev and Next don't navigate past their respective ends of the ODB.

This is the new method:

```
Private Sub app_form_navigate(where As Byte)

    If changed Then app_form_saveObject
    changed = False

    Select Case where

        Case nav_home:
            app_num = 0
```

```
Case nav_prev:
    If app_num > 0 Then
        app_num = app_num - 1
    End If

Case nav_next:
    If app_num < obj_db.get_num_objects - 1 Then
        app_num = app_num + 1
    End If

Case nav_end:
    app_num = obj_db.get_num_objects - 1

End Select

app_num = obj_db.get_obj(app_num, cur_app)
to_form

End Sub
```

The method is careful to save changed data before navigating. We haven't set the changed variable yet, so you'll still have to be careful to click Save.

When you run this, you'll have a correctly navigating object database. Congratulations! (We're still about 3MB smaller than we'd be if we just dropped a data access control into a form.)

We have lots more to do to complete and then polish this application, but I'm going to settle for coding just one more button, eXit. We'll continue working on this application in the next three chapters.

Implementing the eXit Button

The last one's the simplest. Here's the code:

```
Private Sub app_form_exitButton()

    Unload app_form

End Sub
```

We still need to handle deletions, and we need to raise an event when the data changes, and it would be really nice to pop up a calendar to set the date, and those times aren't very nice to type, either.

For now, I'm satisfied. We've mastered the complexities and structured a good, object-oriented application.

THE FULL LISTINGS

If you don't have this book's disk or if it's sticky from the cola your coworker spilled on it, Listings 10-3a through 10-3e show the editable portions of the files through this point. Appendix B shows the non-editable portion of frmApp.frm.

Listing 10-3a
MnAppDB.bas

```
' MnAppDB.bas — Mainline for Appointment DataBase
' Copyright 1997, Martin L. Rinehart

Option Explicit

Public Sub main()

    Dim adb As AppDB
    Set adb = New AppDB

End Sub

' end of MnAppDB.bas
```

Listing 10-3b
App.cls

```
' App.cls — the Appointment class
' Copyright 1997, Martin L. Rinehart

Option Explicit

' Data members:
    Public key As Long
    Public app_date As Date

    Private start_time As Integer
    Private end_time As Integer
    Private actual_time As Integer

    Public description As String

Public Sub set_start_time(s As String)
```

(continued)

App.cls

```
        start_time = tstring2int(s)

    End Sub

    Public Function get_start_time() As String

        get_start_time = int2tstring(start_time)

    End Function

    Public Sub set_end_time(s As String)

        end_time = tstring2int(s)

    End Sub

    Public Function get_end_time() As String

        get_end_time = int2tstring(end_time)

    End Function

    Public Sub set_actual_time(s As String)

        actual_time = tstring2int(s)

    End Sub

    Public Function get_actual_time() As String

        get_actual_time = int2tstring(actual_time)

    End Function

    Private Sub Class_Initialize()

        key = 0 ' will be set by ODB
        app_date = Date
        start_time = 0 ' defaults
        end_time = 0
        actual_time = 0
        description = ""

    End Sub

    Public Function get_name() As String

        get_name = "App"
```

```
End Function

' string layout:
    ' key:          1-11, pad byte: 12
    ' app_date:     13-20
    ' start_time:   21-26
    ' end_time:     27-32, pad byte: 33
    ' actual_time:  34-39, pad byte: 40
    ' description:  41-80

Public Function to_string() As String

    to_string = _
        ODB.long_str(key) & " " & _
        ODB.date_str(app_date) & _
        ODB.int_str(start_time) & _
        ODB.int_str(end_time) & " " & _
        ODB.int_str(actual_time) & " " & _
        ODB.fix_len(description, 40)

End Function

Public Sub from_string(s As String)

    key = Val(Left(s, 11))
    app_date = ODB.yyyymmdd2date(Mid(s, 13, 8))
    start_time = Val(Mid(s, 21, 6))
    end_time = Val(Mid(s, 27, 6))
    actual_time = Val(Mid(s, 34, 6))
    description = Right(s, 40)

End Sub

Private Function tstring2int(s As String)

' a tstring is "HH:MM" (i.e. "01:00" = 60)

    tstring2int = _
        60 * Val(Left(s, 2)) + _
        Val(Right(s, 2))

End Function

Private Function int2tstring(i As Integer)

' returns "01:00" given 60, "02:30" given 150, etc.
```

(continued)

App.cls

```
        Dim hr As Byte, mn As Ryte
        hr = i / 60
        mn = i - (hr * 60)

        int2tstring = _
            Right(Str(100 + hr), 2) & ":" & _
            Right(Str(100 + mn), 2)


    End Function


    ' end of App.cls
```

Listing 10-3c
frmApp.frm

```
' frmApp.frm — Appointment data entry form
' Copyright 1997, Martin L. Rinehart

Option Explicit

Public Event saveObject()
Public Event deleteObject()
Public Event undeleteObject()
Public Event rereadObject()
Public Event navigate(where As Byte)
Public Event addObject()
Public Event exitButton()

Public Enum navigate_movements
    nav_home
    nav_prev
    nav_next
    nav_end
End Enum

Private Sub cmdAdd_Click()

    RaiseEvent addObject

End Sub

Private Sub cmdDelete_Click()

    RaiseEvent deleteObject

End Sub
```

```
Private Sub cmdEnd_Click()

    RaiseEvent navigate(nav_end)

End Sub

Private Sub cmdExit_Click()

    RaiseEvent exitButton

End Sub

Private Sub cmdHome_Click()

    RaiseEvent navigate(nav_home)

End Sub

Private Sub cmdNext_Click()

    RaiseEvent navigate(nav_next)

End Sub

Private Sub cmdPrev_Click()

    RaiseEvent navigate(nav_prev)

End Sub

Private Sub cmdReread_Click()

    RaiseEvent rereadObject

End Sub

Private Sub cmdSave_Click()

    RaiseEvent saveObject

End Sub

Private Sub cmdUndelete_Click()

    RaiseEvent undeleteObject

End Sub

' end of frmApp.frm
```

Listing 10-3d
ODB.cls

```
' ODB.cls — Object DataBase class
' Copyright 1997, Martin L. Rinehart

' Creates a data file which holds objects of a single
' class.

' The class must provide a get_name() function returning
' a String, suitable for use as a file name.
' It must also provide a to_string() function that returns
' a fixed-length string containing all the property values
' that will be stored. And it must provide a from_string()
' method that extracts the property values from the string
' created by the to_string() operation.

' Format of the ODB file is:
'   Header
'   Object 0 record
'   Object 1 record
'   ...
'   Object n-1 record

' Format of the header is
'   Signature (8 bytes) = "mrVB5odb"
'   Object type name (32 bytes)
'   Record length (8 bytes)

' Format of the object record is
'   CR byte (chr(13))
'   LF byte (chr(10))
'   Deleted flag byte ("*" if deleted, " " otherwise)
'   unused byte (pad to dword boundary)
'   obj.to_string()

Option Explicit

Const signature = "mrVB5odb"
Const header_len = 48

' Errors:
    Public Enum err_types
        openOK = -1
        err_freefile = 0
        err_open
        err_seek
```

```
            err_close
            err_getdel
            err_badrec
            err_notgot
            number_of_errors
        End Enum

' Data members
        Public default_drive As String
        Public default_path As String

        Private file_number As Integer
        Private rec_len As Integer
        Private rec_buf As String
        Private path_name As String
        Private num_objects As Integer
        Private current_object_num As Integer

Public Sub close_odb()

        If file_number = 0 Then
            err_msgs (err_close)
            Exit Sub
        End If

        Close file_number
        file_number = 0 ' signal no file open

End Sub

Public Sub create_odb(first As Object)

        file_number = FreeFile

        path_name = first.get_name
        path_name = _
            default_drive & _
            default_path & _
            path_name & ".odb"

        If Len(Dir(path_name)) Then Kill path_name

        Open path_name For Binary As file_number

        rec_buf = Chr(13) & Chr(10) & "  " & first.to_string
        rec_len = Len(rec_buf)
        Dim header As String
```

(continued)

ODB.cls

```
    Dim nm As String
    nm = first.get_name

    header = signature & _
        fix_len(nm, 32) & _
        Right(Space(8) & Str(rec_len), 8)

    Put file_number, , header
    Put file_number, , rec_buf
    current_object_num = 1

End Sub

Public Function open_odb(pn As String) As Integer

' check that a file number is available
    file_number = FreeFile
    If file_number = 0 Then
        err_msgs (err_freefile)
        open_odb = err_freefile
        Exit Function
    End If

' open the file — if it's 0 long, its new
    Open pn & ".odb" For Binary As file_number
    If LOF(file_number) = 0 Then ' not an ODB!
        Close file_number
        err_msgs (err_open)
        open_odb = err_open
        Exit Function
    End If

' create buffer for header, then read header
    Dim header As String
    header = Space(header_len)

    Get file_number, , header

' check for a valid signature
    If Left(header, 8) <> signature Then
        Close file_number
        err_msgs (err_open)
        open_odb = err_open
        Exit Function
    End If

' set up private data members
    rec_len = Val(Right(header, 8))
```

```
        rec_buf = Space(rec_len)
        path_name = pn

        num_objects = (LOF(file_number) - header_len) / rec_len
        current_object_num = 0
        open_odb = openOK

End Function

Public Function add_obj(o As Object)

        rec_buf = Chr(13) & Chr(10) & "  " & o.to_string()
        Put file_number, LOF(file_number) + 1, rec_buf
        add_obj = num_objects
        num_objects = num_objects + 1

End Function

Public Sub del_obj(num As Integer)

        If Not rec_in_file(num) Then
            err_msgs (err_seek)
            Exit Sub
        End If

        Put file_number, oloc(num) + 2, "*"

End Sub

Public Function get_obj(num As Integer, _
        ByRef obj As Object) As Integer

        If Not rec_in_file(num) Then
            err_msgs (err_seek)
            get_obj = -1
            Exit Function
        End If

        Get file_number, oloc(num), rec_buf

        If Mid(rec_buf, 3, 1) = "*" Then
            err_msgs (err_getdel)
            get_obj = -1
        Else
            obj.from_string (Right(rec_buf, rec_len - 4))
            get_obj = num
        End If

End Function
```

(continued)

ODB.cls

```
Public Sub rep_obj(num As Integer, o As Object)

    If Not rec_in_file(num) Then
        err_msgs (err_seek)
        Exit Sub
    End If

    rec_buf = Chr(13) + Chr(10) + "  " + o.to_string()
    Put file_number, oloc(num), rec_buf

End Sub

Private Function rec_in_file(num As Integer) As Boolean

    ' is num in range 0 to num_objects-1 ?

    rec_in_file = (num > -1) And (num @@@ num_objects)

End Function

Private Function oloc(num As Integer)

    ' find object in file
    oloc = header_len + num * rec_len + 1

End Function

Private Sub err_msgs(errno As Byte)

    Call MsgBox(ferr_msgs(errno), vbCritical, "ODB Error")

End Sub

Private Sub Class_Initialize()

    default_drive = ""
    default_path = ""
    file_number = 0 ' 0 = no file open

End Sub

Public Function ferr_msgs(msg_num As Byte)

    ' pseudo class static array

    Select Case msg_num
```

```
            Case err_freefile:
                ferr_msgs = "No file number available"

            Case err_open:
                ferr_msgs = "Cannot open file"

            Case err_seek:
                ferr_msgs = "Cannot perform seek"

            Case err_close:
                ferr_msgs = "Cannot close — no file open"

            Case err_getdel:
                ferr_msgs = "Cannot get — record deleted"

            Case err_badrec:
                ferr_msgs = "Cannot get — record damaged"

            Case err_notgot:
                ferr_msgs = _
                    "Cannot get — invalid object number"

    End Select

End Function

Public Function fix_len(s As String, _
    num_chars As Integer)

' returns s padded or truncated to num_chars length

    fix_len = Left(s & Space(num_chars), num_chars)

End Function

Public Function long_str(l As Long) As String

' returns 11-byte string

    long_str = Right(Space(10) & Str(l), 11)

End Function

Public Function int_str(i As Integer) As String

' returns 6-byte string

    int_str = Right(Space(5) & Str(i), 6)

End Function
```

(continued)

ODB.cls

```
Public Function date_str(d As Date) As String

' returns 8-byte date: YYYYMMDD

    date_str = _
        Right(Str(Year(d)), 4) & _
        Right(Str(100 + Month(d)), 2) & _
        Right(Str(100 + Day(d)), 2)

End Function

Public Function yyyymmdd2date(s As String) As Date

' return date given "YYYYMMDD" string

    yyyymmdd2date = _
        Mid(s, 5, 2) & "/" & _
        Right(s, 2) & "/" & _
        Left(s, 4)

End Function

Public Function get_num_objects() As Integer

    get_num_objects = num_objects

End Function

' end of ODB.CLS
```

The line that reads `Attribute app_form.VB...` in the following listing is added by Visual Basic. It's not visible in the code editor.

Listing 10-3e
AppDB.cls

```
' AppDB.cls — App(ointment) Data Base
' Copyright 1997, Martin L. Rinehart

Option Explicit

' Properties:
    Private obj_db As ODB
    Private cur_app As App
    Private WithEvents app_form As frmApp
    Private app_num As Integer
    Private changed As Boolean
```

```
Private Sub app_form_addObject()

    If changed Then app_form_saveObject
    changed = False

    Set cur_app = New App
    app_num = obj_db.add_obj(cur_app)
    to_form

End Sub

Private Sub app_form_deleteObject()

    MsgBox "delete"

End Sub

Private Sub app_form_exitButton()

    Unload app_form

End Sub

Private Sub app_form_navigate(where As Byte)

    If changed Then app_form_saveObject
    changed = False

    Select Case where

        Case nav_home:
            app_num = 0

        Case nav_prev:
            If app_num > 0 Then
                app_num = app_num - 1
            End If

        Case nav_next:
            If app_num < obj_db.get_num_objects - 1 Then
                app_num = app_num + 1
            End If

        Case nav_end:
            app_num = obj_db.get_num_objects - 1

    End Select
```

(continued)

AppDB.cls

```
        app_num = obj_db.get_obj(app_num, cur_app)
        to_form

End Sub

Private Sub app_form_rereadObject()

        Call obj_db.get_obj(app_num, cur_app)
        to_form ' refresh form

        changed = False ' not changed from disk copy

End Sub

Private Sub app_form_saveObject()

        from_form ' update cur_app
        Call obj_db.rep_obj(app_num, cur_app)

        changed = False ' not changed since saved

End Sub

Private Sub app_form_undeleteObject()

        MsgBox "undelete"

End Sub

Private Sub Class_Initialize()

        Set cur_app = New App
        Set obj_db = New ODB
        Set app_form = New frmApp

        Dim pn As String ' pathname
        pn = cur_app.get_name

        If Len(Dir(pn & ".ODB")) = 0 Then
            obj_db.create_odb cur_app
        Else
            If obj_db.open_odb(pn) @@@> openOK Then End
        End If

        app_num = obj_db.get_obj(0, cur_app)
        to_form ' fill in TextBoxes
```

```
        changed = False
        app_form.Show 1 ' modal

End Sub

Private Sub Class_Terminate()

    Unload app_form

End Sub

Public Sub to_form()

' fill form's text boxes from object

    app_form.lblKeyNum = Str(cur_app.key)
    app_form.txtDate.Text = CStr(cur_app.app_date)
    app_form.txtStart.Text = cur_app.get_start_time
    app_form.txtEnd.Text = cur_app.get_end_time
    app_form.txtActual.Text = cur_app.get_actual_time
    app_form.txtDescription.Text = cur_app.description

End Sub

Public Sub from_form()

' change object as per form
    cur_app.app_date = app_form.txtDate.Text
    cur_app.set_start_time app_form.txtStart.Text
    cur_app.set_end_time app_form.txtEnd.Text
    cur_app.set_actual_time app_form.txtActual.Text
    cur_app.description = app_form.txtDescription.Text

End Sub

' end of AppDB.cls
```

SUMMARY

When you started this chapter, you knew how to program the events that Visual Basic raises, such as `Command1_Click()`. Now you know how to raise and program your own events.

Events let a child object communicate with a parent object without requiring the child to know anything about the specifics of the parent. You raise an event by declaring it in the child, this way: `Public Event <name>` `[(params)]`. You raise it with a `RaiseEvent` statement: `RaiseEvent <name>`.

The parent can respond to custom events by declaring a child object variable as WithEvents, this way: `Dim WithEvents <name> As <child class>`. Once that's done, your code editor handles your own event as if it were a built-in Visual Basic event.

You also used the `DoEvents` function as a statement. By inserting `DoEvents` after a `RaiseEvent` statement, you can interrupt long-running processes to give the operating system a chance to handle the events you raise. Windows 95 handles preemptive multitasking between applications, but you need `DoEvents` to get the same service within a single application.

With event programming mastered, you went on to program a four-class database for appointments. A coordinator class, `AppDB`, contains an `App` (appointment) object, an `ODB`, and a data entry form. The data entry form raises events in response to button presses that the coordinator responds to. The coordinator handles tasks such as getting the correct object from the ODB and then handing the write data to the form's components.

In the next three chapters, we're going to continue working on the appointments database. In Chapter 11, we'll take a good look at ActiveX programming. You'll learn about ActiveX .DLLs (we've already used one) and ActiveX .EXE programs, which we'll use for the appointments database.

In Chapter 12, we'll look at ActiveX control programming. That will let us put our own controls, such as a time control, right onto the toolbar, where we can drag it onto our `frmApp` form in place of the time TextBox we're using now.

For now, take a deep breath and pat yourself on the back. You're really doing serious, object-oriented programming already.

APPOINTMENTS BECOME AN ACTIVEX .EXE

We ended Chapter 9 with a schedule object waiting for some appointments to display. In the last chapter, we built an appointment database but left it, too, incomplete. Don't worry. We're going to finish the database and then the schedule.

Along the way, we're also going to finish our object-oriented programming topics. In this chapter, we'll begin with a long look at ActiveX programming.

In this chapter and the next, the class will have to divide. Some of you have the Standard edition, which omits the ActiveX creation tools. If this is you, read these chapters even though you won't be able to try them out. You'll see that ActiveX programming is object programming plus a few button clicks.

In chapter 13, we'll remove the ActiveX components from the MyTime project so that everyone, Standard or otherwise, can program the whole project in Part II.

We'll start by looking at the ActiveX .DLL, which is also known as an in-process ActiveX server. We'll contrast that with the ActiveX .EXE, which lets you create out-of-process ActiveX objects.

Once you understand the differences, we'll go on to build a sample ActiveX .EXE. You'll see the techniques, including using events to provide asynchronous notification to the application that we could use to launch our databases as out-of-process ActiveX objects. I'll show you how to work on both the application and the ActiveX .EXE at the same time.

With that background, we'll return to the appointment database. We'll use events that raise other events (a key technique for out-of-process ActiveX programming) to handle the change notification. Then we'll complete work on deletions.

Finally, we'll turn the appointment database into an ActiveX .EXE. That, you'll see, takes only a handful of mouse clicks. Of course, only a well-educated Visual Basic programmer will know which mouse clicks. You'll know before the end of this chapter.

ActiveX .EXEs and .DLLs

ActiveX is Microsoft's component specification. *Components* are objects that publish their interfaces in a defined way so that other objects can see what methods they support, what data they make public, what events they can raise, and so on.

ActiveX is only one component specification. It competes head on with, for example, the Java Beans specification. As I write this, both Microsoft and the Java Beans proponents are claiming that they will make their specifications compatible. This would be a welcome change because right now the two specifications are vastly different.

ActiveX grew out of OLE and the .OCX components specification, which in turn grew out of the .VBX specification. The .VBXs were the original Visual Basic components. Ironically, you needed to write them in C or C++. The .VBX was a complex thing, and writing one took a great deal of skill. The .OCX was more complex and required even more skill.

ActiveX is more complex than its predecessors. Visual Basic can now write ActiveX components, and it makes the job almost trivially simple. I'm not sure you should even tell your friends who write C++ how easy it is. They worked very, very hard to write those .VBX and .OCX controls.

In contrast to the complexity of ActiveX, the competing Java Beans specification is quite simple, although it's no less powerful. ActiveX uses the Registry, for example. Beans don't need a Registry. Which should you write?

Again, it's a matter of Windows-specific programming versus multiplatform programming. It's nice to be able to run your program on Solaris and AIX-based computers, as well as on your PCs and Macintoshes. On the other hand, it's nice to be able to use all of Windows. Tooltips, for example, have helped me decipher some otherwise incomprehensible button bars.

If you're using Visual Basic, I assume that your goal is to write Windows programs, so go ahead and use ActiveX. It may be complex under the surface, but Visual Basic 5 makes your job very, very simple.

The ActiveX .DLL

We already programmed an ActiveX .DLL when we started to do multiple-project work. We told Visual Basic that we wanted it to generate an ActiveX .DLL and it did it. We took care of a couple of housekeeping details (selecting Global MultiUse and checking a reference box), and we were on our way, but what is a .DLL?

The acronym *DLL* stands for *Dynamic Link Library*. The .DLL was introduced with Windows. (DOS didn't support .DLLs.) A standard link library was used by C programmers to collect all their commonly used routines. These were linked to the application by the *linker*, a program that collected all the compiled code needed by an application and put it together in a single package.

The problem with static linking was that a routine used by several programs would occur in each of those programs. The routines in a .DLL are loaded into memory by Windows and are then available to any program that wants to use them.

A very well-known example of a .DLL's service is the Windows file open dialog box. Microsoft provides a sophisticated file open dialog box in a .DLL. Every program that needs to open a file can call this dialog box. It will be loaded just once and made available to every program that needs this service.

An ActiveX .DLL is a dynamic link library that also meets the additional specifications for an ActiveX component. It registers itself, publishes its methods, and so on. You don't need to worry about the complexities.

You do, however, need to understand when an ActiveX .EXE should be used, instead of an ActiveX .DLL.

The ActiveX .EXE

In contrast to an ActiveX .DLL, an object launched from an ActiveX .EXE is a standalone executable program. Your other programs can launch ActiveX .EXE objects, but once they are launched they run on their own.

Windows 95 takes charge of multitasking, assuring that your computer's available time is divided between all the running executable files. We'll launch our appointment database, for example, from the MyTime system when the user decides to add or edit appointment data. We can let it run on its own.

An ActiveX .EXE object can raise events, just as any other object can. For example, the appointment database object can raise an event passing the appointment's date whenever data is changed. The parent class can check the date. If it matches the schedule's date, the parent will know that it has to refresh the schedule.

You'll see when we try it out that building an ActiveX .EXE is no more trouble than building an ActiveX .DLL. The job is basically just to tell Visual Basic that we want an ActiveX .EXE and then wait patiently for a second or two while it does all the hard work.

In-Process and Out-of-Process ActiveX

Microsoft uses the term *in-process* to describe an ActiveX .DLL. The term *out-of-process* is used for ActiveX .EXEs. These terms nicely describe the functionality.

An ActiveX .DLL provides subroutines that your process can call just as it calls its own subroutines. They function as another part of the process.

An ActiveX .EXE object, on the other hand, runs as a separate process. A Web browser, for example, could use an out-of-process object to download data. This lets the user continue using the browser while the data is downloaded.

Memo To Bill Gates

Bill, this out-of-process capability is great, but it's not a good substitute for Java-style multithread capability. Separate in-process threads are darned useful, too. I'd like my MyTime system to spawn a separate thread for calculating projects' critical paths, for example.

ActiveX Clients and Servers

Another terminology you'll see occasionally terms ActiveX objects as *servers* and the applications that use them *clients*. This is less than helpful. Fortunately, Microsoft seems to be abandoning these terms.

When you do see these terms, remember that the application is the client. The ActiveX object is the server. You can easily think of examples where this makes sense. You can also, and equally easily, think of examples where the terms *client* and *server* make more sense when you reverse them.

An ActiveX .EXE Example

Let's code a simple ActiveX .EXE. This will be throwaway code, so start your project in any handy directory. Begin by asking for a new project. Figure 11-1 shows me choosing ActiveX .EXE as the project type.

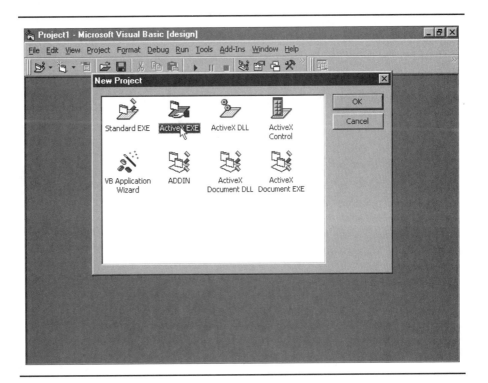

▌ Figure 11-1
Creating an ActiveX .EXE project.

You always see this dialog box when you choose File⇨New Project. It also pops up at startup with a "Don't show this..." checkbox. If you've checked that box, you'll automatically start with a new standard .EXE project.

If you right-click the project in the Project window, you can change the project's type. Figure 11-2 shows me using this technique to create an ActiveX .EXE project.

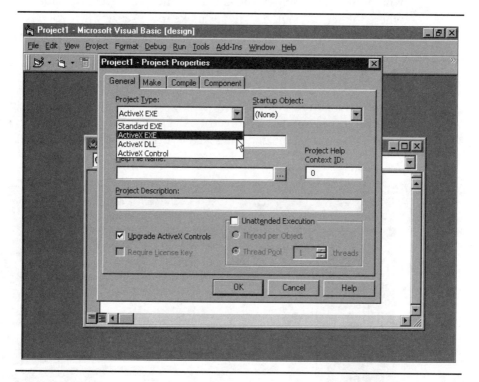

Figure 11-2
Changing the project to ActiveX .EXE.

There is a difference, which you can use to your advantage. The standard .EXE begins with a form. If you begin a new ActiveX .EXE, Visual Basic starts you off with a class module. If you want a form, it's easier to start your ActiveX project as a standard .EXE and then change its type with the Project Properties sheet.

The alternative, which you can use for this project, is to select Class1 in the Project window and right-click to access the popup menu (or use the Project menu after you select Class1) to choose Remove Class1. Then use Add to add a form to your project.

Building the ActiveX .EXE

Ready to create your ActiveX .EXE? It should take about a minute.

Drag two buttons onto your form. Name them `cmdHello` and `cmdGoodbye` and set their captions to `Hello` and `Goodbye`. Figure 11-3 shows my work.

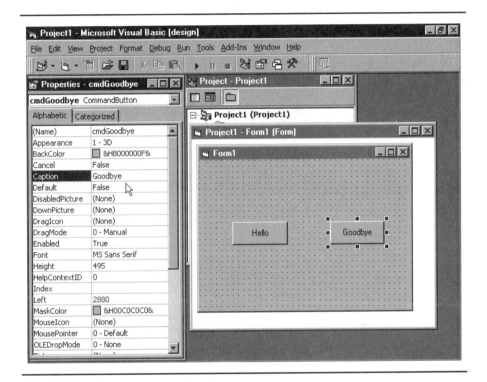

■ Figure 11-3
Creating a simple ActiveX .EXE form.

Now let's program the Hello button to raise a `hi` event. In the declarations section, add this line:

```
Event hi
```

Visual Basic will add empty parentheses to the end of the line.

Now double-click the Hello button and add this line to it's `click()` event handler:

```
RaiseEvent hi
```

Finally, double-click the Goodbye button and add this line:

```
Unload me
```

Name your form `frmAXEXE`, name the project `AXEXE`, and save your work. (That's an important save because the next step will cause a failure.)

Now you can attempt to create your first ActiveX .EXE. On the File menu, choose Make AXEXE. You'll see an error dialog box like the one in Figure 11-4.

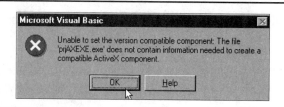

Figure 11-4
A very misleading error.

The problem isn't even related to the error message. You can't have an ActiveX .EXE that uses just a form-based class. You have to have a class module.

Add a class module and name it `clsAXEXE`. You need to know one trick here. This is the class from which your application will instantiate the ActiveX object. It contains the form, but it's not a form. If you want to raise an event for the application, you have to raise it in this class, not in the form.

So how to we get that Hello button to raise a `hi` event? Simple. The class can receive the event from the form and then it will raise its own `hi` event. (Yes, both events can have the same name.) All of this is more trouble to explain than to program.

This is the complete clsAXEXE code:

```
Option Explicit

Event hi()

Private WithEvents f As frmAXEXE

Private Sub Class_Initialize()
    Set f = New frmAXEXE
    f.Show
End Sub
```

```
Private Sub f_hi()
    RaiseEvent hi
End Sub
```

With that code in place, you're ready to build your ActiveX .EXE. This is a complex set of processes involving creating a type library, registering the class, its methods, and events with the Registry, and more. Ready?

From the File menu, choose Make AXEXE. Now listen to Visual Basic and Windows spin your disk. When the disk stops spinning, all the complex work is done.

At least it's finished on your machine. If you want your application to run on another machine, that's another complex process. All you do, though, is use the Setup Wizard. It will do everything for you. Don't let your friends coding C++ know how simple this is, OK?

Building the Test Application

Once your ActiveX .EXE is available, you can go on to build the test program. I've created a form with a button that says Launch, as you can see in Figure 11-5.

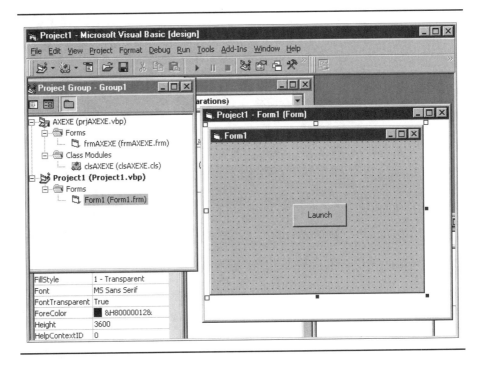

Figure 11-5

Designing the application.

You can see that I've added a second project. You could also just open a new project — the ActiveX .EXE is completed, so Visual Basic could close it down.

This form-based class is trivial. The button's `click()` handler creates a new `clsAXEXE` object. In response to that class's `hi` event, it launches a message box. The only trick is that you have to tell Visual Basic that your project references `AXEXE`. As with the .DLL, you choose References from the Project menu. Figure 11-6 shows me including this reference.

If you have two projects working at once, make sure that you select the new one before you check this reference; otherwise, you'll be telling Visual Basic that `AXEXE` references itself.

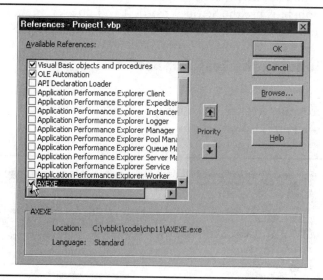

Figure 11-6
Referencing AXEXE *in the application project.*

This is the complete code for the test application:

```
Option Explicit

Public WithEvents c As clsAXEXE

Private Sub Command1_Click()
    Set c = New clsAXEXE
End Sub

Private Sub c_hi()
    MsgBox "Hi!"
End Sub
```

Visual Basic writes all but three of those code lines! Don't overlook the
WithEvents keyword when you declare your clsAXEXE, and be sure to use
the name of the class, not the name of the ActiveX .EXE file.

Figure 11-7 shows the code running after I've clicked Launch and then
Hello on the launched form.

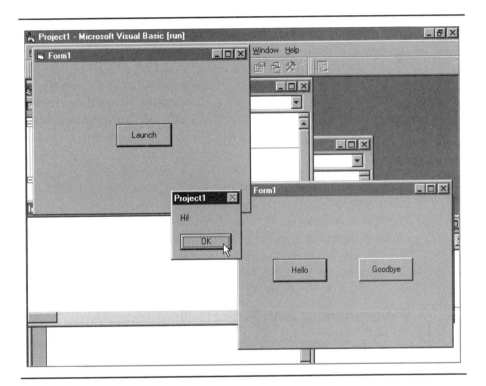

■ **Figure 11-7**
Running the ActiveX .EXE.

If you don't see the message box, try moving your ActiveX dialog box (the
one with Hello and Goodbye buttons). This is the active application following
its button click. The message box will be written in front of the launching
application (Project1, here) but behind the active window (AXEXE).

If you try to move the AXEXE window while the message box is waiting
for a click, you'll see the "Switch to..." dialog box shown in Figure 11-8.

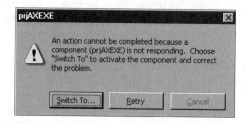

Figure 11-8
One application blocking another.

This will tell you that your AXEXE is not responding, which is not really the case. The problem is that you haven't responded to Project1's modal message box. Choose the Switch to... option and then click OK on the message box and you'll be back in business.

If you get the idea that launching a modal dialog box when you have multiple simultaneous applications is dangerous, you're right! This is fine for a little debugging test dialog box, but avoid it in real applications.

If you want to see how much trouble you can get into, leave the ActiveX form running but close the launching application. In a running system, you want the destructor for the application to close down any forms it has launched, of course.

Programming Both Projects Simultaneously

If you want to work on your ActiveX .EXE while you have the launching application loaded, you have to know a trick.

Microsoft's Books Online tells you to work on both by loading two copies of Visual Basic: one with the ActiveX .EXE and the other with the application. This works, but I don't see any reason for doing it this way. (You'll need tons of RAM or tons of patience. Maybe both.)

This is how you do it. Load both projects. If you're working on the application, work normally. If you're working on the ActiveX .EXE, make your changes and then rebuild using File⇨Make. This forces a complete build so that you won't get stuck in compile errors when your application is already running. Select the application project and click the run icon or press F5 to use them together.

There's just one catch. This works in theory, but in practice you'll see the hostile dialog box shown in Figure 11-9.

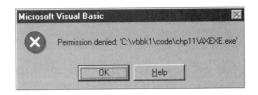

■ **Figure 11-9**
Visual Basic won't rebuild the ActiveX .EXE.

Memo To Bill Gates

This isn't a very nice dialog box, is it Bill? A little hint here as to why access was denied would have saved me hours!

The reason you can't do what you want is that your application project has a reference to the ActiveX .EXE. All you need to do is click the application in the Project Explorer and then choose Project⇨References to uncheck the reference. Then use File⇨Make, and Visual Basic will happily do your bidding.

When your ActiveX .EXE is built, click the application in the Project Explorer and then recheck the reference before you run the application.

In my version of Visual Basic, this technique isn't totally reliable. Sometimes I see the Access Denied dialog box even when I've removed the reference. Apparently the reference leaves a ghost behind. (This only happens rarely.) If this happens to you, reopen the project group, select the ActiveX project again and retry File⇨Make. This seems to be a completely reliable ghost buster.

Using Microsoft's system of opening two copies of Visual Basic, you can actually use the built-in debugger to step into the ActiveX .EXE from the application. You can't do that in the way I'm suggesting. What you can do, however, is run the ActiveX as an in-process .DLL while you're debugging. Switch to an out-of-process executable file when you work the bugs out.

Before we go on, let me mention how far you've come. You have a form-based class object contained in an ActiveX object. The form is raising events, and the ActiveX object is rasing them for the launching application. Your application and your ActiveX object are running in separate threads. This is pretty sophisticated stuff!

The event that's being passed to the application, by the way, is called an *asynchronous* event. Asynchronous events are ones that butt in on the application whenever they feel like it. They are not synchronized with the other work going on in the application. They're handy, for example, for a database application that wants to tell the system that data has been changed.

Now let's get back to our appointment database, which is stacked above our schedule object that we're preparing for the MyTime system.

The Full Listings

Listings 11-1a, 11-1b, and 11-1c show the full files in this project. The disk file 11-01 also has the related group and project files.

Listing 11-1a
frmAXEXE.frm

```
VERSION 5.00
Begin VB.Form frmAXEXE
    Caption         =   "Form1"
    ClientHeight    =   3195
    ClientLeft      =   60
    ClientTop       =   345
    ClientWidth     =   4680
    LinkTopic       =   "Form1"
    ScaleHeight     =   3195
    ScaleWidth      =   4680
    StartUpPosition =   3  'Windows Default
    Begin VB.CommandButton cmdGoodbye
        Caption         =   "Goodbye"
        Height          =   495
        Left            =   2640
        TabIndex        =   1
        Top             =   1320
        Width           =   1215
    End
    Begin VB.CommandButton cmdHello
        Caption         =   "Hello"
        Height          =   495
        Left            =   720
        TabIndex        =   0
        Top             =   1320
        Width           =   1215
    End
End
```

```
Attribute VB_Name = "frmAXEXE"
Attribute VB_GlobalNameSpace = False
Attribute VB_Creatable = False
Attribute VB_PredeclaredId = True
Attribute VB_Exposed = False
Option Explicit

Event hi()

Private Sub cmdGoodbye_Click()
    Unload Me
End Sub

Private Sub cmdHello_Click()
    RaiseEvent hi
End Sub
```

Listing 11-1b: clsAXEXE.cls

```
VERSION 1.0 CLASS
BEGIN
  MultiUse = -1   'True
END
Attribute VB_Name = "clsAXEXE"
Attribute VB_GlobalNameSpace = False
Attribute VB_Creatable = True
Attribute VB_PredeclaredId = False
Attribute VB_Exposed = True
Option Explicit

Event hi()

Private WithEvents f As frmAXEXE
Attribute f.VB_VarHelpID = -1

Private Sub Class_Initialize()
    Set f = New frmAXEXE
    f.Show
End Sub

Private Sub f_hi()
    RaiseEvent hi
End Sub
```

Listing 11-1c
Form1.frm

```
VERSION 5.00
Begin VB.Form Form1
   Caption         =   "Form1"
   ClientHeight    =   3195
   ClientLeft      =   60
   ClientTop       =   345
   ClientWidth     =   4680
   LinkTopic       =   "Form1"
   ScaleHeight     =   3195
   ScaleWidth      =   4680
   StartUpPosition =   3  'Windows Default
   Begin VB.CommandButton Command1
      Caption      =   "Launch"
      Height       =   495
      Left         =   1800
      TabIndex     =   0
      Top          =   1320
      Width        =   1215
   End
End
Attribute VB_Name = "Form1"
Attribute VB_GlobalNameSpace = False
Attribute VB_Creatable = False
Attribute VB_PredeclaredId = True
Attribute VB_Exposed = False
Option Explicit

Public WithEvents c As clsAXEXE
Attribute c.VB_VarHelpID = -1

Private Sub Command1_Click()
    Set c = New clsAXEXE
End Sub

Private Sub c_hi()
    MsgBox "Hi!"
End Sub
```

RAISING CHANGE EVENTS

If you remember, we carefully programmed a changed variable to trigger a data save whenever the data was changed, but we didn't do the disk save until we attempted to change objects or exit. This is the right way to handle buffering the disk-based object, but we didn't finish the job.

As it stands now, the changed variable is never set to True. It should be set whenever one of the data entry TextBoxes raises a change() event.

Changing Changed

The first thing to do is to raise an event that will tell the parent class that a TextBox entry has been changed. We can do this most easily by creating an event in the frmApp form. Then we can have each of the TextBox elements raise this event when their change() events are triggered.

This is the same process we were using to pass events from the ActiveX .EXE's form to the ActiveX .EXE class and then through to the calling application.

Updating the frmApp.frm File

While we make these updates, I'll give you another modification, too. It's simple to do if you trust me to explain it in just a bit. For now, just copy any inexplicable lines.

Begin by adding the two new events you see here:

```
Public Event exitButton()

Public Event change()
Public Event unloading()

Public Enum navigate_movements
```

Next, double-click each of the entry text boxes in turn and add the line shown here:

```
Private Sub txtActual_Change()

    RaiseEvent change

End Sub
```

That handles raising the change event. While you're here, choose the `QueryUnload` event in the right (Property) dropdown list and add the two lines shown here:

```
Private Sub Form_QueryUnload(Cancel As Integer, _
    UnloadMode As Integer)

    RaiseEvent unloading
    DoEvents

End Sub
```

That completes the modifications needed in the form's code.

Modifying the AppDB.cls File

Our form is now raising a change event on any change to the input `TextBox` components. We need to handle this in the `AppDB` class, appropriately updating our changed variable. Except for the exit problem, which I'll cover in the next section, this is trivial.

Click `app_form` in the left (Object) dropdown list of `AppDB`'s code editor and then select change in the right (Property) dropdown list. Add this line:

```
Private Sub app_form_change()

    changed = True

End Sub
```

Now run your program. Change the description of the first appointment. Go to the second appointment, and then return. Your change is still there, right? It was correctly filed. If you want to see a bug, make another change and then close the form.

A bunch of nasty little critters are hanging out in this seemingly simple process.

Making a Well-Behaved Exit

When I first saw this problem, I looked at the `exitButton` event code. It unloads the form. Then it tries to save the updated values to disk. Of course, when the form is unloaded, the values in the `TextBox` components are lost. All that's left are the original values, including "Month dd, year" that was the date's caption. Visual Basic correctly fails when it tries to convert that string to a date.

Obviously, you have to preserve the values in the TextBox components, so change the exitButton event handler to just hide the form, this way:

```
Private Sub app_form_exitButton()

    app_form.Hide

End Sub
```

Then add the change handling code to the class destructor, this way:

```
Private Sub Class_Terminate()

    If changed Then app_form_saveObject
    changed = False

    Unload app_form

End Sub
```

Before you test, can you figure out why this won't work? If you test, you'll see that pressing the eXit button now works correctly. A changed value is written to disk. (You have to rerun the application to see this.)

If you click the upper-right close button, you'll see that it triggers an Unload event before your class_terminate() logic is called, which puts you right back where you were.

The event that you should be using is called QueryUnload(), which is often used for interjecting a query to the user, such as, "Save changes?" QueryUnload is raised before any Unload. It has parameters that you can use to tell Visual Basic *not* to go ahead with the unload, if necessary.

We're ignoring most of the power of QueryUnload and just using it to do our data saving before the actual unload happens. If you go back to the changes we made to the frmApp form, they should now make complete sense.

In the AppDB class, choose app_form in the left dropdown list and choose unloading in the right dropdown list. Here's where you should add the save code:

```
Private Sub app_form_unloading()

    If changed Then app_form_saveObject
    changed = False

End Sub
```

Cut those two lines from the `class_terminate()` event (that's *cut*, not copy) to the clipboard if you really enjoy having your computer do all the work. Paste them into `app_form_unloading()`, where they belong.

Now you should have a program that's very nice about always recording the changes you've made. This returns the Save button to its designed function, saving in the middle of a long set of changes. (Make some changes, Save, mess up some other changes, and press Reread to recover your good work.)

HANDLING DELETIONS

We have more things to take care of before we can go back to the schedule. For example, I'd like to launch a calendar for the date and do something to be sure that times are entered in HH:MM format. To do a really nice job for both those items, what would be really nice would be a new component that we could pick off the toolbar that would be just like the existing components.

Because adding components is the lead topic in Chapter 12, I'm going to wait on those items until we can do a thorough job. That leaves us with the deletion problem to solve before we can move on to turning our database application into an ActiveX .EXE.

The first issue is how we want to handle deletions. Databases typically provide two modes. In the default mode, when you delete a record, it disappears. If you navigate, the database skips deleted records. This is the behavior you probably expect.

The alternative is to show the deleted records but to also show that they are deleted. This is less generally useful but has the distinct advantage of presenting deleted records so that they can be undeleted. I'm going to use this latter approach because it suits my urge to have total control. If you want a tool for typical end users, you'll probably want to make the other choice.

Improving the ODB

To support deletion handling, we'll need to make some improvements to the ODB. We need a new property, improved `get_obj()` and `rep_obj()` methods, a new line in the `del_obj()` routine, and a new `undel_obj()` method.

Add a New, Public Property

Begin by adding the third data member you see here:

```
' Data members
    Public default_drive As String
    Public default_path As String
    Public obj_is_deleted As Boolean
```

Next we'll need to set this property when we get the object from disk.

Improving get_obj()

This is the existing code in get_obj() that's affected:

```
If Mid(rec_buf, 3, 1) = "*" Then
    err_msgs (err_getdel)
    get_obj = -1
Else
    obj.from_string (Right(rec_buf, rec_len - 4))
    get_obj = num
End If
```

Replace that with this code:

```
obj_is_deleted = _
    (Mid(rec_buf, 3, 1) = "*")

obj.from_string (Right(rec_buf, rec_len - 4))
get_obj = num
```

Improving rep_obj()

Next, you need to improve the rep_obj function. It has to check the obj_is_deleted variable to see whether the third character in the record should be an asterisk (deleted) or a space. This is the improved code:

```
Dim del_char As String
If obj_is_deleted Then
    del_char = "*"
Else
    del_char = " "
End If
```

(continued)

```
rec_buf = Chr(13) + Chr(10) + _
    del_char + " " + o.to_string()
Put file_number, oloc(num), rec_buf

End Sub
```

Improving del_obj()

Then we'll need to have the del_obj() method set the obj_is_deleted property. Add this line, just before the end of the method:

```
obj_is_deleted = True
```

Adding undel_obj()

Finally, create an undel_obj function by copying the del_obj function and editing it. Change

- The subroutine's name
- The asterisk becomes a space
- obj_is_deleted is set False

    This is the result:

```
Public Sub undel_obj(num As Integer)

    If Not rec_in_file(num) Then
        err_msgs (err_seek)
        Exit Sub
    End If

    Put file_number, oloc(num) + 2, " "

    obj_is_deleted = False

End Sub
```

Improving AppDB

With those changes, the ODB will support deletions. Now it's up to the AppDB to support deletions.

Displaying the Deleted Status

We'll need to show the deleted status in the `lblDeleted` component that's already waiting for us. Add this routine:

```
Public Sub set_del()

    If obj_db.obj_is_deleted Then
        app_form.lblDeleted = "Deleted"
    Else
        app_form.lblDeleted = ""
    End If

End Sub
```

We can call this routine when we load the other form values. Add this line at the end of your `to_form()` method:

```
set_del
```

Of course, you still won't be able to see anything because none of the objects on file are deleted yet. To make this work, we'll need to program the `app_form_deleteObject()` method. Right now, it's just a message box that rather disingenuously promises to delete something.

Programming the deleteObject() Method

I've programmed for three separate conditions. First, if the object is already deleted we'll do nothing. Second, the object may be changed. If that's true, just set the `Public obj_is_deleted` data member and then replace it with the `rep_obj()` method. Otherwise, calling `del_obj()` does the job.

This is a little bit of extra trouble that I take out of long habit. Disk operations are relatively slow, so I do the minimum. You could probably simplify this code to just a `rep_obj()` followed by `del_obj()` with no noticeable impact on performance. (That assumes, of course, that your computer's not busy doing something else with the disk. If that's the case, this extra trouble might pay off.)

This is the new routine I added:

```
Private Sub app_form_deleteObject()

    If obj_db.obj_is_deleted Then Exit Sub

    If changed Then
        obj_db.obj_is_deleted = True
```

```
              Call obj_db.rep_obj(app_num, cur_app)
              changed = False
          Else
              obj_db.del_obj app_num
          End If

          set_del

      End Sub
```

Programming the undeleteObject() Method

If you copy the contents of app_form_deleteObject() into the
app_form_undeleteObject() method, you can make these changes:

- Make the top test If Not (instead of If)
- Set obj_db.obj_is_deleted to False (not True)
- Call obj_db.undel_obj (not del_obj)

This is the completed routine:

```
      Private Sub app_form_undeleteObject()

          If Not obj_db.obj_is_deleted Then Exit Sub

          If changed Then
              obj_db.obj_is_deleted = False
              Call obj_db.rep_obj(app_num, cur_app)
              changed = False
          Else
              obj_db.undel_obj app_num
          End If

          set_del

      End Sub
```

With those changes, you should be able to delete and undelete objects,
and the ODB should be politely recording (and remembering!) the status of
each object. Now we're ready to relaunch the AppDB as an ActiveX .EXE.

LAUNCHING THE ACTIVEX .EXE

Ready to rebuild this as an out-of-process ActiveX server? OK, let's go.

Begin by deleting the .BAS module. Then use File⟩Add Project to add another standard .EXE project. Visual Basic will open a new form for you. Close the form and then right-click it in the Project Explorer. Choose Remove Form1 to eliminate it.

Another right-click in the Project Explorer will get to the Add menu. Choose a module and select the existing MDAppDB. You should now have the two-project setup shown in Figure 11-10.

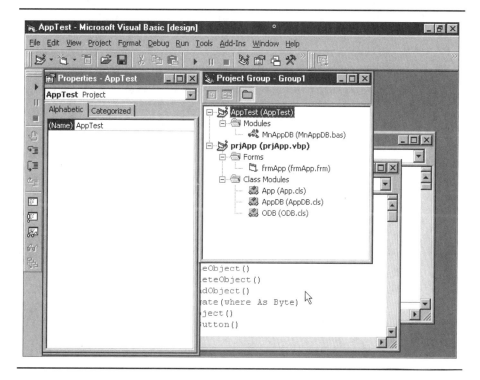

Figure 11-10
The .BAS moved to a separate standard .EXE project.

Right-click the prjApp project in the Project Explorer and select Properties, as you see me doing in Figure 11-11.

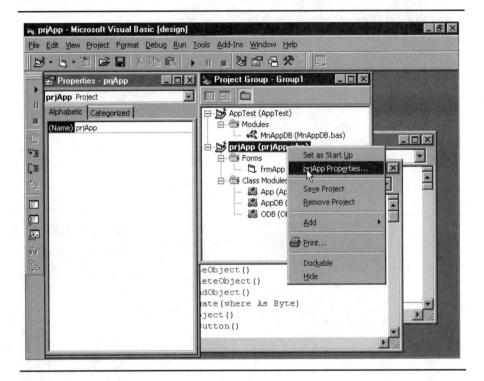

Figure 11-11
Going to work on the ActiveX project.

That launches the Project Properties sheets. Change the type (it was a standard .EXE) to ActiveX .EXE. This gives you an additional startup choice: none. You need to select none as the startup, as you see me doing in Figure 11-12.

Your project's ready to build. Click OK to close the Project Properties. Then choose File⇨Make prjApp, as you see in Figure 11-13.

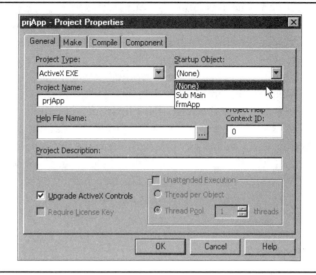

Figure 11-12
Making it an ActiveX .EXE with no startup.

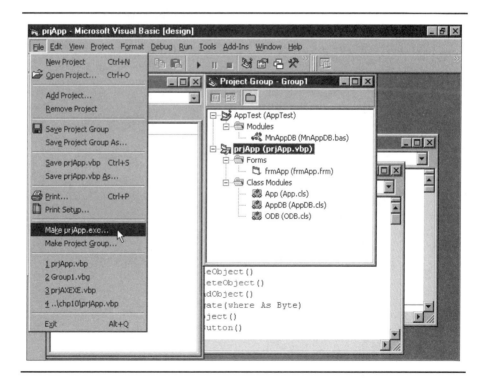

Figure 11-13
Building the ActiveX .EXE.

After Visual Basic builds your ActiveX .EXE, registers it, and whatever else; you're ready to tie it to your main line. Click the main line project in the Project Explorer and then use Project⇨References to access the Reference list. Check prjApp, click OK, and you're ready to run.

Isn't it nice when your computer does all the work for you?

When we assemble our databases into the MyTime system, we'll add events that notify the parent application of changes. The appointment change event, for example, will include the date of the change. That way the schedule can update its object collection if the schedule is affected by the change (the schedule date matches the changed appointment's date).

We won't have an object collection until Chapter 13, so this task will have to wait. You've already written lots of code that handles asynchronous events.

THE FULL LISTINGS

The full listings are on disk in 11-02, along with the project files. If you don't have the book's disk (you *knew* you shouldn't use it for a coffee coaster, didn't you?) Listings 11-2a and 11-2b show the new AppDB.cls and ODB.cls files' editable portions. For the other code files, refer to Listings 10-3.

Listing 11-2a
AppDB.cls

```
' AppDB.cls — App(ointment) Data Base
' Copyright 1997, Martin L. Rinehart

Option Explicit

' Properties:
    Private obj_db As ODB
    Private cur_app As App
    Private WithEvents app_form As frmApp
Attribute app_form.VB_VarHelpID = -1

    Private app_num As Integer
    Private changed As Boolean

Private Sub app_form_addObject()

    If changed Then app_form_saveObject
    changed = False
```

```
        Set cur_app = New App
        app_num = obj_db.add_obj(cur_app)
        to_form

End Sub

Private Sub app_form_change()

    changed = True

End Sub

Private Sub app_form_deleteObject()

    If obj_db.obj_is_deleted Then Exit Sub

    If changed Then
        obj_db.obj_is_deleted = True
        Call obj_db.rep_obj(app_num, cur_app)
        changed = False
    Else
        obj_db.del_obj app_num
    End If

    set_del

End Sub

Private Sub app_form_exitButton()

    app_form.Hide

End Sub

Private Sub app_form_navigate(where As Byte)

    If changed Then app_form_saveObject
    changed = False

    Select Case where

        Case nav_home:
            app_num = 0

        Case nav_prev:
            If app_num > 0 Then
                app_num = app_num - 1
            End If
```

(continued)

AppDB.cls

```
            Case nav_next:
                If app_num < obj_db.get_num_objects - 1 Then
                    app_num = app_num + 1
                End If

            Case nav_end:
                app_num = obj_db.get_num_objects - 1

        End Select

        app_num = obj_db.get_obj(app_num, cur_app)
        to_form

End Sub

Private Sub app_form_rereadObject()

        Call obj_db.get_obj(app_num, cur_app)
        to_form ' refresh form

        changed = False ' not changed from disk copy

End Sub

Private Sub app_form_saveObject()

        from_form ' update cur_app
        Call obj_db.rep_obj(app_num, cur_app)

        changed = False ' not changed since saved

End Sub

Private Sub app_form_undeleteObject()

        If Not obj_db.obj_is_deleted Then Exit Sub

        If changed Then
            obj_db.obj_is_deleted = False
            Call obj_db.rep_obj(app_num, cur_app)
            changed = False
        Else
            obj_db.undel_obj app_num
        End If

        set_del

End Sub
```

```
Private Sub app_form_unloading()

    If changed Then app_form_saveObject
    changed = False

End Sub

Private Sub Class_Initialize()

    Set cur_app = New App
    Set obj_db = New ODB
    Set app_form = New frmApp

    Dim pn As String ' pathname
    pn = cur_app.get_name

    If Len(Dir(pn & ".ODB")) = 0 Then
        obj_db.create_odb cur_app
    Else
        If obj_db.open_odb(pn) <> openOK Then End
    End If

    app_num = obj_db.get_obj(0, cur_app)
    to_form ' fill in TextBoxes

    changed = False
    app_form.Show 1 ' modal

End Sub

Private Sub Class_Terminate()

    Unload app_form

End Sub

Public Sub to_form()

' fill form's text boxes from object

    app_form.lblKeyNum = Str(cur_app.key)
    app_form.txtDate.Text = CStr(cur_app.app_date)
    app_form.txtStart.Text = cur_app.get_start_time
    app_form.txtEnd.Text = cur_app.get_end_time
    app_form.txtActual.Text = cur_app.get_actual_time
    app_form.txtDescription.Text = cur_app.description
```

(continued)

AppDB.cls

```
        set_del

    End Sub

    Public Sub set_del()

        If obj_db.obj_is_deleted Then
            app_form.lblDeleted = "Deleted"
        Else
            app_form.lblDeleted = ""
        End If

    End Sub

    Public Sub from_form()

    ' change object as per form
        cur_app.app_date = app_form.txtDate.Text
        cur_app.set_start_time app_form.txtStart.Text
        cur_app.set_end_time app_form.txtEnd.Text
        cur_app.set_actual_time app_form.txtActual.Text
        cur_app.description = app_form.txtDescription.Text

    End Sub

    ' end of AppDB.cls
```

Listing 11-2b
ODB.cls

```
' ODB.cls — Object DataBase class
' Copyright 1997, Martin L. Rinehart

' Creates a data file which holds objects of a single
' class.

' The class must provide a get_name() function returning
' a String, suitable for use as a file name.
' It must also provide a to_string() function that returns
' a fixed-length string containing all the property values
' that will be stored. And it must provide a from_string()
' method that extracts the property values from the string
' created by the to_string() operation.
```

```
' Format of the ODB file is:
'    Header
'    Object 0 record
'    Object 1 record
'    ...
'    Object n-1 record

' Format of the header is
'    Signature (8 bytes) = "mrVB5odb"
'    Object type name (32 bytes)
'    Record length (8 bytes)

' Format of the object record is
'    CR byte (chr(13))
'    LF byte (chr(10))
'    Deleted flag byte ("*" if deleted, " " otherwise)
'    unused byte (pad to dword boundary)
'    obj.to_string()

Option Explicit

Const signature = "mrVB5odb"
Const header_len = 48

' Errors:
    Public Enum err_types
        openOK = -1
        err_freefile = 0
        err_open
        err_seek
        err_close
        err_getdel
        err_badrec
        err_notgot
        number_of_errors
    End Enum

' Data members
    Public default_drive As String
    Public default_path As String
    Public obj_is_deleted As Boolean

    Private file_number As Integer
    Private rec_len As Integer
    Private rec_buf As String
    Private path_name As String
    Private num_objects As Integer
    Private current_object_num As Integer
```

(continued)

ODB.cls

```
Public Sub close_odb()

    If file_number = 0 Then
        err_msgs (err_close)
        Exit Sub
    End If

    Close file_number
    file_number = 0 ' signal no file open

End Sub

Public Sub create_odb(first As Object)

    file_number = FreeFile

    path_name = first.get_name
    path_name = _
        default_drive & _
        default_path & _
        path_name & ".odb"

    If Len(Dir(path_name)) Then Kill path_name

    Open path_name For Binary As file_number

    rec_buf = Chr(13) & Chr(10) & "  " & first.to_string
    rec_len = Len(rec_buf)
    Dim header As String

    Dim nm As String
    nm = first.get_name

    header = signature & _
        fix_len(nm, 32) & _
        Right(Space(8) & Str(rec_len), 8)

    Put file_number, , header
    Put file_number, , rec_buf
    current_object_num = 1

End Sub

Public Function open_odb(pn As String) As Integer

' check that a file number is available
    file_number = FreeFile
```

```
        If file_number = 0 Then
            err_msgs (err_freefile)
            open_odb = err_freefile
            Exit Function
        End If

' open the file — if it's 0 long, its new
    Open pn & ".odb" For Binary As file_number
    If LOF(file_number) = 0 Then ' not an ODB!
        Close file_number
        err_msgs (err_open)
        open_odb = err_open
        Exit Function
    End If

' create buffer for header, then read header
    Dim header As String
    header = Space(header_len)

    Get file_number, , header

' check for a valid signature
    If Left(header, 8) @@@> signature Then
        Close file_number
        err_msgs (err_open)
        open_odb = err_open
        Exit Function
    End If

' set up private data members
    rec_len = Val(Right(header, 8))
    rec_buf = Space(rec_len)
    path_name = pn

    num_objects = (LOF(file_number) - header_len) / rec_len
    current_object_num = 0
    open_odb = openOK

End Function

Public Function add_obj(o As Object)

    rec_buf = Chr(13) & Chr(10) & "  " & o.to_string()
    Put file_number, LOF(file_number) + 1, rec_buf
    add_obj = num_objects
    num_objects = num_objects + 1

End Function
```

(continued)

ODB.cls

```
Public Sub del_obj(num As Integer)

    If Not rec_in_file(num) Then
        err_msgs (err_seek)
        Exit Sub
    End If

    Put file_number, oloc(num) + 2, "*"

    obj_is_deleted = True

End Sub

Public Sub undel_obj(num As Integer)

    If Not rec_in_file(num) Then
        err_msgs (err_seek)
        Exit Sub
    End If

    Put file_number, oloc(num) + 2, " "

    obj_is_deleted = False

End Sub

Public Function get_obj(num As Integer, _
        ByRef obj As Object) As Integer

    If Not rec_in_file(num) Then
        err_msgs (err_seek)
        get_obj = -1
        Exit Function
    End If

    Get file_number, oloc(num), rec_buf

    obj_is_deleted = _
        (Mid(rec_buf, 3, 1) = "*")

    obj.from_string (Right(rec_buf, rec_len - 4))
    get_obj = num

End Function
```

```
Public Sub rep_obj(num As Integer, o As Object)

    If Not rec_in_file(num) Then
        err_msgs (err_seek)
        Exit Sub
    End If

    Dim del_char As String
    If obj_is_deleted Then
        del_char = "*"
    Else
        del_char = " "
    End If

    rec_buf = Chr(13) + Chr(10) + _
        del_char + " " + o.to_string()
    Put file_number, oloc(num), rec_buf

End Sub

Private Function rec_in_file(num As Integer) As Boolean

    ' is num in range 0 to num_objects-1 ?

    rec_in_file = (num > -1) And (num @@@ num_objects)

End Function

Private Function oloc(num As Integer)

    ' find object in file
    oloc = header_len + num * rec_len + 1

End Function

Private Sub err_msgs(errno As Byte)

    Call MsgBox(ferr_msgs(errno), vbCritical, "ODB Error")

End Sub

Private Sub Class_Initialize()

    default_drive = ""
    default_path = ""
    file_number = 0 ' 0 = no file open

End Sub
```

(continued)

ODB.cls

```
Public Function ferr_msgs(msg_num As Byte)

    ' pseudo class static array

    Select Case msg_num

        Case err_freefile:
            ferr_msgs = "No file number available"

        Case err_open:
            ferr_msgs = "Cannot open file"

        Case err_seek:
            ferr_msgs = "Cannot perform seek"

        Case err_close:
            ferr_msgs = "Cannot close — no file open"

        Case err_getdel:
            ferr_msgs = "Cannot get — record deleted"

        Case err_badrec:
            ferr_msgs = "Cannot get — record damaged"

        Case err_notgot:
            ferr_msgs = _
                "Cannot get — invalid object number"

    End Select

End Function

Public Function fix_len(s As String, _
    num_chars As Integer)

' returns s padded or truncated to num_chars length

    fix_len = Left(s & Space(num_chars), num_chars)

End Function

Public Function long_str(l As Long) As String

' returns 11-byte string

    long_str = Right(Space(10) & Str(l), 11)
```

```
End Function

Public Function int_str(i As Integer) As String

' returns 6-byte string

    int_str = Right(Space(5) & Str(i), 6)

End Function

Public Function date_str(d As Date) As String

' returns 8-byte date: YYYYMMDD

    date_str = _
        Right(Str(Year(d)), 4) & _
        Right(Str(100 + Month(d)), 2) & _
        Right(Str(100 + Day(d)), 2)

End Function

Public Function yyyymmdd2date(s As String) As Date

' return date given "YYYYMMDD" string

    yyyymmdd2date = _
        Mid(s, 5, 2) & "/" & _
        Right(s, 2) & "/" & _
        Left(s, 4)

End Function

Public Function get_num_objects() As Integer

    get_num_objects = num_objects

End Function

' end of ODB.CLS
```

SUMMARY

We began this chapter with an appointment database under construction and a schedule object on hold. We're ending without changing those facts, but we haven't been idle.

We started by discussing the difference between ActiveX .DLLs and ActiveX .EXEs. The .DLL let's you create in-process objects. The .DLL code can be shared by multiple simultaneous applications.

The ActiveX .EXE lets you launch out-of-process objects. These run on their own as independent processes, not as subroutines controlled by the launching application.

We programmed a sample ActiveX .EXE. You added custom events to a form, and you used additional custom events in the ActiveX .EXE class to pass these events to the parent application. This provides for asynchronous (when it happens, it happens) notification to the parent. We'll use asynchronous notification in the MyTime system to have the databases tell MyTime when they've updated data.

We used this double-event (one event triggers another) technique to tell the AppDB object that data has changed on the frmApp form. This let us correctly handle storing data on changes. The QueryUnload() event handler let us correctly handle final changes just before exiting the form.

Then we programmed the ODB and the AppDB objects to handle object deletion and undeletion.

As the last step, we clicked our way through creating an ActiveX .EXE from our AppDB class. Once you know what you're doing, it's very easy.

This leaves us with a nearly completed AppDB class. It's form needs components that are smarter than TextBox components for dates and times. With smarter components, we can call it complete and get back to the schedule, which we'll do in Chapter 13.

In Chapter 12 we'll do a really nice job on the smarter components. We'll actually create a new ActiveX component that we can install on our tool bars.

CREATING
ACTIVEX
COMPONENTS

*R*emember our schedule object? The one that's waiting on our App database? I do. We're going to finish it.

But not in this chapter. Here, we're going to have some real fun and challenges, building ActiveX components. We'll start with a sample and then we'll build a real one that handles time input in the HH:MM format that I'm calling a `tstring`.

Those of you who do not have a Visual Basic edition that supports component creation can read along. Sorry to say, this is going to be more fun for the rest of us. We'll make it up to you, though. In Chapter 13, we'll create functionally equivalent code using only standard objects.

Component programming, like ActiveX .DLL and .EXE programming, is object programming. You're already just a few mouse clicks away from creating your own components, but there's a huge difference between component programming and the other work we've done.

Think about a component: a button, for example. Mentally double-click one onto your form. Now drag a handle to resize it. Watch it draw itself as you shrink or expand it. Think about it. That little critter is running its own `Resize()` code as you shrink or expand it.

That's the difference between components and the work we've been doing. Components have code that runs at design time and code that runs at run time. (Mentally click that button at run time. See it go in and out? Those views are created by MouseDown() and MouseUp() event handlers, working with Paint().

We'll build user controls in this chapter, so you can see exactly how this works. For example, when you create a TextBox, it retrieves a default Text property, like Text1. You see this at design time. If you change it in the Properties box, your change will be saved. The user will see your version.

To keep the process sorted out, Microsoft calls the end-user of your program the *user*. The person who programs the system is called the *developer*. The person who writes the component is called the *author*.

When you develop components, you start at least two projects. One holds the user control. When you work on this, you're the author. The second project uses the control on a form. When you work on this project, you're the developer. When you click the run icon or press F5 to test the form, you're the user.

All of this can be confusing. What's called for, here, is some actual practice. We'll start with a TextBox with a mind of its own. (You can use this on your strictly personal systems.) Then we'll get practical and make that time entry control.

CREATING AN INDEPENDENT CONTROL

Our first control's behavior will be fun. We'll make a nice little control that's like a TextBox but that says something to you whenever you try to change the text.

You can do this by creating an array of sayings and a static byte variable. In the Change event, you can display the saving indexed by the byte and then increment the byte. You reset the byte to zero if it goes past the end of the array. This is the idea:

```
dim sayings(0 to 3) as String
```

```
        sayings(0) = "First saying"
        sayings(1) = "Second saying"
        sayings(2) = "Third saying"
        sayings(3) = "Fourth saying"

' in Change() handler:
        static index as byte
        talker.Text = sayings(byte)

        index = index + 1
        if index > 3 then index = 0
```

That will cycle through your sayings. The sayings you provide will determine the exact personality of this control. Go ahead and make it an unctuous sycophant or give it a bad attitude. It's yours, after all.

Now let's start programming.

Setting up the Projects

Begin by creating or choosing a working directory. Give this some thought when you work on ActiveX. Your controls are going to live here and be registered in your Registry. If you keep all your controls in one directory, you'll avoid lots of problems. If you create Foo.ctl in two different directories, you'll have two separate References entries named Foo. You'll have two separately registered controls in your Registry named Foo. (If that happens, your only hope is to use Regedit.exe to remove all references to Foo and then recompile just one of them.)

You might want to try these examples on a test directory, but remember: compiling controls means registering controls. Visual Basic is smart about reregistering the control when you recompile. It's stupid about registering a new control when a control of the same name is already registered.

Set your shortcut to name this directory and launch Visual Basic. Create a new, standard .EXE project. Name it prjDevel, as you see in Figure 12-1.

Next, create your user control project. Choose File⇨Add Project and then select ActiveX Control, as Figure 12-2 shows.

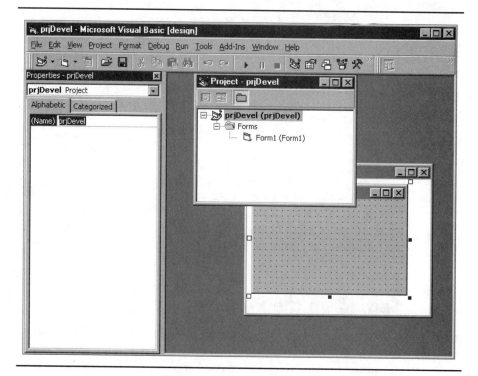

Figure 12-1

Naming the developer project.

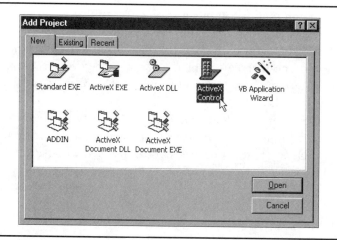

Figure 12-2

Adding an ActiveX Control project.

Name the new project prjAuthr. In this project, you're the author, not the developer. Name your control to reflect its personality. Mine's *Crabby*.

The user control project has a design form that is very similar to the developer's design form, except that it doesn't have a title bar with its associated caption and buttons. Begin by shrinking it drastically. Your design size is the size that the developer will get with a double-click that hops your control off the toolbar onto the developer's form. You don't want it too big. Figure 12-3 shows mine, ready for work.

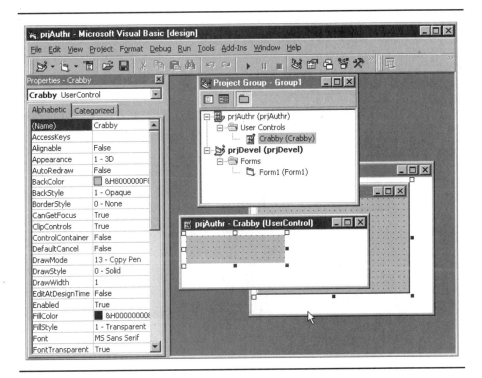

Figure 12-3
Ready to work on the Crabby control.

With this setup, you're ready to start working. We'll start programming for design time. When we get that right, we'll go on to the runtime behavior.

Programming for Design Time

Begin by displaying the tool bar and positioning the user control and the developer's form where you can click them. Then click them alternately while you watch the tool bar.

You should notice two things. The OLE control is dimmed (not available) when your user control has focus. Additionally, a dimmed tool appears following OLE. That dimmed tool is the default tool bar icon for your user control.

Return to the user control. Add a TextBox. Position the TextBox in the upper-left corner as you see in Figure 12-4. Any control except an OLE control can be placed on a UserControl. That includes other UserControls. A control on a UserControl is called a *constituent* control.

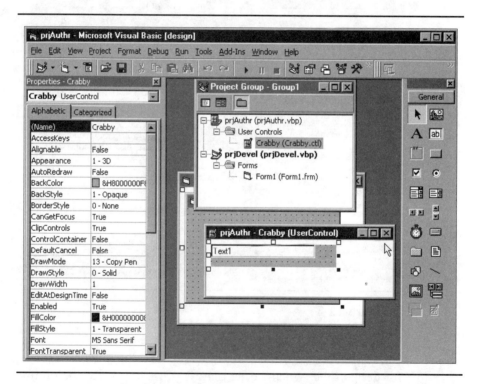

▌ Figure 12-4
The control contains a TextBox.

We're ready to launch this control. Before you do, click the Save icon or press Ctrl+S. Even if you have Visual Basic set to save automatically before you run, that's not enough. That save takes place when you choose run, switching from developer mode to user mode. It does *not* save when you switch from author mode to developer mode.

To switch to developer mode, just close the user control development surface. Go ahead and do that now. When you close it, your user control icon on the tool bar switches from dimmed to available! You have a new component to manipulate.

Go ahead and double-click the new user control onto your developer form. (That's a double-click, please, not click and drag.) Figure 12-5 shows what I have at this point.

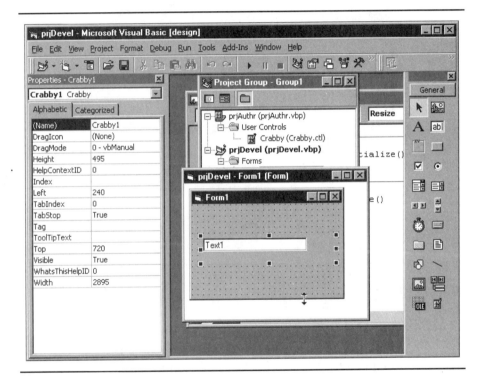

Figure 12-5
A new control on the developer's form.

At this point, the contained TextBox in the user control is the size I wanted. The whole control (the handles are visible) is too large. Now try resizing the control.

When you drag a handle, the control responds appropriately, but the enclosed TextBox isn't changed. The developer has no control over the size of that TextBox, which is not at all what we want. To fix that, return to developing the user control. (Double-click it on the Project Explorer.)

When you return to author mode, you can't manipulate the control on the developer form. Visual Basic draws lines through it to show that it's not available, as Figure 12-6 shows.

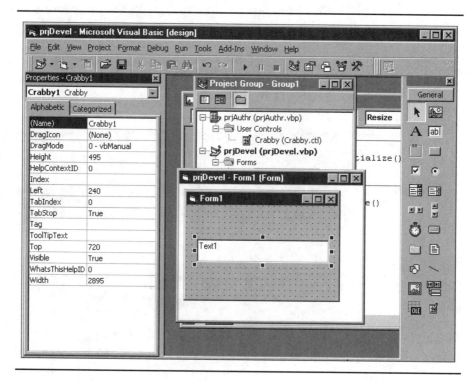

Figure 12-6
The developer's user control is not available.

Double-click the user control surface to launch its code editor. By default, you'll be in the `Initialize()` method. Use the right (procedure) dropdown list and select `Resize()`. Add the two center lines you see here:

```
Private Sub UserControl_Resize()

    Text1.Height = Height
    Text1.Width = Width

End Sub
```

Now save and then return to developer mode (close the user control design tool). Your `TextBox` nicely fills the entire user control. Select it and drag a handle. Your user control stays filled with the `TextBox`. In fact, visually it's a `TextBox` now.

Your code written as author is now running when you manipulate this as the developer. Let's recap.

You've created two projects. One is a standard .EXE where you can test your control and the other is an ActiveX Control project. Displaying the ActiveX control design surface activates author mode. Closing the ActiveX control design surface puts you in developer mode.

With all that knowledge, you've been equipped to write the two lines needed to program your control's behavior at design time.

We're ready to go on to program the runtime behavior.

Programming for Run Time

If you're not there, return to author mode. Double-click your control to launch the control's editor. Click the left (object) dropdown list. You'll have General, Text1, and UserControl objects available. UserControl would be Form in a standard .EXE project.

Start in the general declarations area. Add some appropriate beginning and ending comments. Then declare a private array of strings, this way:

```
' Crabby.ctl — a crabby TextBox control
' Copyright 1997, Martin L. Rinehart

Option Explicit

Private crabs(0 To 4) As String
```

Use as many strings as you like.

The user control's Initialize() method is a good place to initialize this array. (The form is the user control's design surface, when you're in author mode.) Put your control's personality into this method. Here's mine:

```
Private Sub UserControl_Initialize()

    crabs(0) = "No way!"
    crabs(1) = "I won't"
    crabs(2) = "I don't like you"
    crabs(3) = "Definitely not"
    crabs(4) = "Go away"

End Sub
```

The only thing left is to program the TextBox's Change() method. The only wrinkle here is that changing the Text property, which is what we want to do, raises the Change event. You have to add a bit of code to separate the recursive calls from the user-induced changes. This is my routine:

```
Private Sub Text1_Change()
    Static idx As Byte

    If Text1.Tag = "x" Then Exit Sub

    Text1.Tag = "x"
    Text1.Text = crabs(idx)
    Text1.Tag = ""

    idx = idx + 1
    If idx > 4 Then idx = 0

End Sub
```

Be sure that your size check matches the size of your strings array. Ready to test? Go ahead and run the program. Figure 12-7 shows my Crabby control in operation.

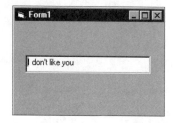

Figure 12-7
Crabby lives up to his name.

The only problem with Crabby is that he launches with Text1 displayed as its Text property. That's not at all what I want. Back in author mode I've changed the TextBox's Text property to Don't touch me!

Of course, you might want the developer to have some control over the initial value in the Text property. Close the author's design surface and select your control in developer mode. Open the property list and see if you can change Text. Figure 12-8 shows what I'm seeing.

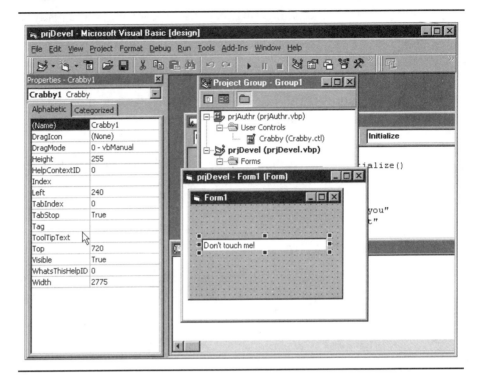

Figure 12-8
There's no Text *property.*

The property list shows the minimal default set that all controls inherit. If the author doesn't provide more, they aren't there. Fortunately, the author (that's you, now) can add Text or any other properties. The author can add events, too.

We'll add Text when we program the time entry control. In the meantime, think about some of the fun little controls you could build like the one you've just made:

■ A Christmas control with cheerful greetings

■ A pest that wants a visitor to leave

■ A stroker that gives you ego-pumping praise

■ An X-rated control for your significant other

Hmmm. We'd better get back to work. Let's build that time control.

First, a word on building the ActiveX control. You're ready to produce your ActiveX control at this point, but I'd recommend against it. I don't want to put too much nonsense into my registry. If you don't mind littering your registry, you just need to choose Make prjAuthr.ocx from the File menu. (Be sure you've selected prjAuthr in the Project Explorer because that's the project you want to make.) Visual Basic will do the rest.

After you OK or change the file name you wait a few moments and your new .OCX is ready.

Don't let a C++ programmer who wrestled with the old .OCX requirements see how trivial this is. Violence might ensue.

The Full Listing

Listing 12-1 shows the full file Crabby.ctl, including the portion not editable with the code editor. On disk, 12-01 also includes the other files in the project, including the test form, Form1.frm, and the project and group files.

Listing 12-1
Crabby.ctl — a Crabby UserControl

```
VERSION 5.00
Begin VB.UserControl Crabby
   ClientHeight    =    480
   ClientLeft      =    0
   ClientTop       =    0
   ClientWidth     =    2760
   PropertyPages   =    "Crabby.ctx":0000
   ScaleHeight     =    480
   ScaleWidth      =    2760
   Begin VB.TextBox Text1
      Height       =    285
      Left         =    0
      TabIndex     =    0
      Text         =    "Don't touch me!"
      Top          =    0
      Width        =    2295
   End
End
```

```
Attribute VB_Name = "Crabby"
Attribute VB_GlobalNameSpace = False
Attribute VB_Creatable = True
Attribute VB_PredeclaredId = False
Attribute VB_Exposed = True
' Crabby.ctl — a crabby TextBox control
' Copyright 1997, Martin L. Rinehart

Option Explicit

Private crabs(0 To 4) As String

Private Sub Text1_Change()
    Static idx As Byte

    If Text1.Tag = "x" Then Exit Sub

    Text1.Tag = "x"
    Text1.Text = crabs(idx)
    Text1.Tag = ""

    idx = idx + 1
    If idx > 4 Then idx = 0

End Sub

Private Sub UserControl_Initialize()

    crabs(0) = "No way!"
    crabs(1) = "I won't"
    crabs(2) = "I don't like you"
    crabs(3) = "Definitely not"
    crabs(4) = "Go away"

End Sub

Private Sub UserControl_Resize()

    Text1.Height = Height
    Text1.Width = Width

End Sub

' end of Crabby.ctl
```

PROGRAMMING A TIME ENTRY CONTROL

The Life of a UserControl

A UserControl is created in author mode, but it's not really alive until you enter developer mode. In developer mode a new UserControl is created and runs in two ways: the developer clicks one from the tool bar or an existing one is loaded with a form.

While developer mode is design time for most controls, a UserControl is running during design time. When the developer presses F5 or clicks start, the design time control dies and a new control is created with all the other controls on the form that is launched in user mode.

When a form with a UserControl is loaded with an existing form, a new one is created and starts running. If you're going to be working extensively with controls, create one and put debug messages into every event, like this:

```
Private Sub UserControl_Initialize()
    debug.print "UC Initialize"
End Sub
```

Your immediate window will tell an interesting tale. This little bit of theory is here to prepare you for writing the time entry control. As author, we'll create a Text property and give it a default value, but we'll want the developer to change the Text property to a different value that will be the default at run time.

For this we'll set our values in the InitProperties() method. This method runs when the initial copy is made as the UserControl is clicked off the toolbar at design time.

The developer's replacements for our default value are saved with the form if we include them in a WriteProperties() method. (The handful of inherited properties are automatically saved. We have to save any that we add.) A ReadProperties() method must be written to return these properties to the form at run time or at a subsequent design time.

Other methods, such as UserControl_Initialize, run when any instance of the control is initialized. Initialize() is run when the developer creates a UserControl by clicking one off the toolbar. It also runs when a control created as a form is loaded at design time, and, of course, it runs when the control is created at run time.

You'll put all of this to use in the time control. Let's begin.

Get Set

We'll begin by preparing our projects. Then we'll program the `Resize()` method. Finally, we'll add the code we'll need to check for a valid `tstring` entry.

Begin by opening a new, standard .EXE project.

Preparing the Projects

The standard .EXE project is the test bed for the ActiveX control. You don't need to give it a name.

Add an ActiveX Control project to your group. I've named mine `prjHH_MM`. Figure 12-9 shows the project at this point.

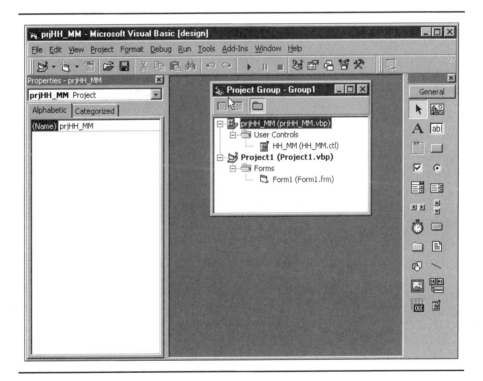

Figure 12-9
New `UserControl` development group created.

Place a `TextBox` constituent control on your `UserControl` at the upper left. Shrink your `UserControl` to something small, as Figure 12-10 shows. Name the `TextBox` `txtHH_MM` and set its `Text` to null.

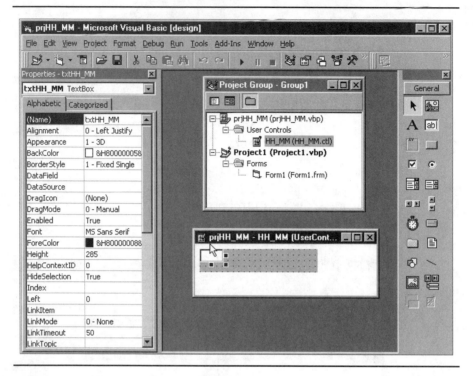

Figure 12-10
Preparing the constituent TextBox.

At this point, you can close the UserControl surface and drag one onto your form in developer mode.

Programming Design Time Resize

There's a problem and a solution to discuss here. The UserControl should be entirely filled with the constituent TextBox, but if you make them the same size at author design time, you can't click one or the other. All clicks would be received by the TextBox. If you want to show the UserControl properties in the properties list or edit the UserControl's code, you can't click the design surface to get there.

The solution is to leave the UserControl oversize here and set its size in the UserControl_InitProperties() event handler. Remember that InitProperties() runs when the developer creates a control from the tool bar. If you set the size in Initialize(), your settings would be applied every time the control is created. That would include at run time. This wouldn't please the developer, whose carefully proportioned controls would always pop back to the author's shape when the user saw the control.

The `InitProperties()` method is also a good place to put your default `Text`. Add the three action lines here:

```
Private Sub UserControl_InitProperties()

    Height = 255
    Width = 510

    txtHH_MM.text = "00:00"

End Sub
```

These sizes work well for the standard 8 pt., MS Sans Serif font. A commercial control should look at the font at user run time.

Now you're ready to add the two lines we used in the Crabby example to fill the `UserControl` with the constituent `TextBox`:

```
Private Sub UserControl_Resize()

    txtHH_MM.Height = Height
    txtHH_MM.Width = Width

End Sub
```

Validating the String

Before we discuss `UserControl`-related programming, put in the `OK_text()` routine and its supporting functions. This returns `True` if a string is in HH:MM format and the HH is less than 24 and the MM is less than 60. (If you use 12-hour time, change the HH check to allow from 1 through 12. 24-hour time runs from 0 through 23.)

These routines do the job:

```
Private Function OK_text(s As String) As Boolean

    OK_text = False
    If Not Len(s) = 5 Then Exit Function

' must have 5 characters before trying this test
    OK_text = _
        is_digit(Left(s, 1)) And _
        is_digit(Mid(s, 2, 1)) And _
        Mid(s, 3, 1) = ":" And _
        is_digit(Mid(s, 4, 1)) And _
        is_digit(Right(s, 1))
```

```
' must have "dd:dd" before trying this test
    If OK_text Then
        OK_text = _
            (Val(Mid(s, 1, 2)) < 24) And _
            (Val(Mid(s, 4, 2)) < 60)
    End If

End Function

Private Function is_digit(s As String) As Boolean

    Dim b As Byte
    b = Asc(s)

    is_digit = is_digitb(b)

End Function

Private Function is_digitb(b As Byte) As Boolean

    Const zero = 48 ' asc("0") is 48
    Const nine = zero + 9

    is_digitb = _
        (b >= zero) And _
        (b <= nine)

End Function
```

Enforcing Correct Values

Before we add the Text property, let's make sure our time control's text is always in HH:MM format when the program uses it. (You have to allow it to be invalid briefly, or the user wouldn't be able to edit it by, for example, deleting a digit.)

If you save the Text string whenever it's known to be valid, you can let the users do whatever they want. If they leave the control with a valid time string, you update your known good copy. If the user leaves an invalid string, you replace it with the last known valid string.

Begin by adding appropriate comments and an old_text Private string property, this way:

```
' HH_MM.ctl — HH:MM time string user control
' Copyright 1997, Martin L. Rinehart

Option Explicit

Private old_text As String
```

Our default string "00:00" is valid. The developer's changes will also be valid (you'll see this below) so we know our starting text is acceptable. This is the initial value for `old_text`:

```
Private Sub UserControl_Initialize()

    old_text = txtHH_MM.text

End Sub
```

Remember, `Initialize()` will run whenever a `UserControl` is created. That's at developer design time and at user run time.

Whenever the control leaves focus, we'll check the final string the user left. If it's not valid, we'll replace it with the `old_text`, this way:

```
Private Sub UserControl_ExitFocus()

    If Not OK_text(txtHH_MM.text) Then

        txtHH_MM.text = old_text

    End If

End Sub
```

Be sure to use `ExitFocus()`, not `LostFocus()`. Your `UserControl` won't fire `GotFocus()` or `LostFocus()` if it has constituent controls that can gain focus. Here, for example, the `TextBox` will fire `GotFocus()` and `LostFocus()`, but the `UserControl` won't. With multiple constituent controls, the `EnterFocus()` fires when the first constituent gains focus and `ExitFocus()` fires after the last constituent loses focus.

Our `ExitFocus()` code ensures that the control's text is only invalid during editing. We can show an invalid condition by setting the control's background color to a warning yellow while the value is invalid. When the user returns to a good string, we'll update the `old_text` value. The logic is all placed in the `Change()` event handler, this way:

```
Private Sub txtHH_MM_Change()

    If txtHH_MM.Tag = "x" Then Exit Sub

    If Len(txtHH_MM.text) > 5 Then
        txtHH_MM.Tag = "x"
        txtHH_MM.text = Left(txtHH_MM.text, 5)
        txtHH_MM.Tag = ""
    End If
```

```
         If Not OK_text(txtHH_MM.text) Then
             txtHH_MM.BackColor = vbYellow
         Else
             txtHH_MM.BackColor = vbWhite
             old_text = txtHH_MM.text
         End If

   End Sub
```

I've guessed that the likely reason for a string being over-length is that the user typed over the minutes digits in insert mode. This will push the old digits to the right, out of view. Chopping them off could restore the string to a valid state.

You can run this code to see that it works. I've added a command button under the UserControl on Form1. This provides a convenient place to give focus. (There's no code in the button's Click(), so it only changes focus.) Figure 12-11 shows my Form1 running.

Figure 12-11
Running the test form.

Now all this needs is a Text property so that I can, for example, set the default text to 09:00 for my first appointment of the day.

Adding a Text Property

You can't just add a Public data member to add a property to the control. You have to use Property Get and Property Let routines. The easy way to get these right is to use Tools⇨Add Procedure. Choose a Public Property and name it text.

You could name the property Text, if you like. I've used the lowercase *text* because I like to see the properties I add distinguished from Visual Basic's intrinsic properties. Suit yourself.

In this case, using a `Property Let` lets you add your validity checking, this way:

```
Public Property Get text() As String

    text = txtHH_MM.text

End Property

Public Property Let text(ByVal s As String)

    If OK_text(s) Then
        txtHH_MM.text = s
    End If

End Property
```

This is live at developer design time, remember. Try this now in developer mode. You'll see that the text property has been added to the properties window and that you can't set it to an invalid string!

Memo To Bill Gates
Bill, this stuff is slick, very slick! Send the folks who did this control stuff to Tahiti for a month. They've earned it.

If you test your control at this point, you'll find it only has one bad habit: it accepts input from the Properties window, but then it forgets and resets the "00:00" initial value.

The problem is that you haven't saved the developer's input. You wouldn't expect the user's input to last from one run to the next, without storing it, would you? As author, the developer is in the same position. You need to take care of filing the developer's changes. That's very simple, but it's done with a whole new object class.

Meet the `PropertyBag` class. With a name like that, what else could it be accept a bag full of properties? It uses a subroutine method, `WriteProperty()`, to put a property into the bag. A function method, `ReadProperty()` grabs the property back out of the bag.

You give both properties a name and a default value. If the developer leaves the default value, the property is not written to the .FRM file, which keeps that file from getting huge and storing every default of every control. The .FRM just stores the nondefault values. You also give the `Write Property()` subroutine a value to store. The `ReadProperty()` function returns the value.

You access the `PropertyBag` by using `ReadProperties()` and `Write Properties()`, which are event-handling methods of the `UserControl`. The respective events are raised at completely reasonable times. For instance, when the developer presses F5, the development `UserControl` fires `WriteProperties()`. The user's runtime `UserControl` fires `ReadProperties()` before it shows itself.

The `UserControl`'s event handlers are plural: `ReadProperties()` and `WriteProperties()`. Each can call the `PropertyBag`'s singular `Read Property()` or `WriteProperty()` as often as it likes, storing or retrieving as many properties as necessary. For some really good news, you can forget almost all of this. If you can just remember *Read* and *Write*, you'll be in business.

Select the `UserControl` in the left (object) dropdown list of your code editor and use the right (procedure) dropdown list to select `ReadProperties`. (You look for *Read*, click, and the whole thing is spelled out for you.)

That will get you a skeleton, like this:

```
Private Sub UserControl_ReadProperties( _
    PropBag As PropertyBag)

End Sub
```

(Actually, it will be like that, but not exactly that. The line wrapping was added to fit this book.) The `PropBag` variable is your `PropertyBag`. It only has two methods, so if you type **propbag.r**, the text editor will fill in the rest of the method name. These routines take very few keystrokes. You may forget that the singular is the `PropertyBag` method, and the plural is the `UserControl` method, but the code editor won't. Let it work for you.

These are the two routines that make your developer's work persistent:

```
Private Sub UserControl_ReadProperties( _
    PropBag As PropertyBag)

    txtHH_MM.text = PropBag.ReadProperty( _
        "Text", "00:00")
```

```
    End Sub


    Private Sub UserControl_WriteProperties( _
        PropBag As PropertyBag)

        PropBag.WriteProperty "Text", _
            txtHH_MM.text, "00:00"

    End Sub
```

As you type these, your code editor will prompt you for the parameters. Name first, then value — if this is `WriteProperties()` — and then default value. This is another one of those things that's more trouble to learn about than it is to do.

Run this version, and you'll see that the developer's value is preserved. It behaves just like any other `Text` property. (If you name it *Text*, your developers won't know that this isn't a Visual Basic intrinsic property, which may be just what you want.)

You can add this control to your App data entry form if you like. Compile it here first. (Select the ActiveX Control project in the Project Explorer, and then use File⇨Make.) Then load your App project and add a reference to your new .OCX. Voilà! A new control appears on the tool bar.

Too bad it appears with that meaningless default icon, isn't it?

Creating an Icon

To put an icon on the toolbar, you have to have an icon. For about $400, you can get Corel Draw 7, which I recommend highly. For $400 less, you can use the Accessory, Microsoft Paint. Paint is all you need for these bitmaps.

Minimize Visual Basic and load Paint. Use Image⇨Attributes to set the size. Visual Basic wants 16 pixels wide by 15 pixels tall for these bitmaps.

From the View⇨Zoom menu choose Custom. In the dialog box that launches, choose 800%, which is the largest possible size. You're now set to go to work. Draw something that looks vaguely representative of your control. Figure 12-12 shows my bitmap.

Some people have a flair for designing these things. I'm not one of those people, as you can see. (Frankly, I wanted to complete an example, here. I didn't intend putting it into regular use, or I would have given it a bit more thought.) This is a chance to show your artistic ability.

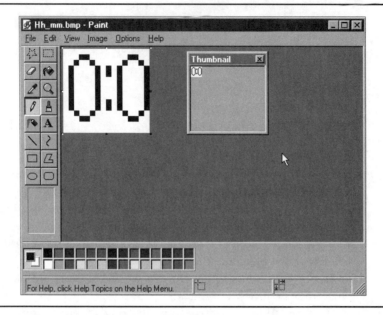

Figure 12-12
Using Paint to create a bitmap.

When you're done, save your work as a .BMP file. I put mine in the same directory as the rest of the project. Minimize Paint and restore Visual Basic. In author design mode, select your `UserControl` and drop the properties list. Go to the `ToolboxBitmap` property. When you select it, you'll see the little "dialog follows" button that my cursor is pointing to in Figure 12-13.

The dialog box is a standard file selection dialog box. Choose your bitmap, and you're in business. Once the bitmap is selected, it is loaded when you change from author mode to developer mode. Try it, and you'll have your very own bitmap on the toolbar from which you can create your very own custom ActiveX controls.

Building your own controls is fun and easy, once you understand the author mode and developer mode differences. On your own, you'll make a few mistakes ("Oh !@#$... I should have used `InitProperties`, not `Initialize`."), but it won't take long before you're a professional control builder.

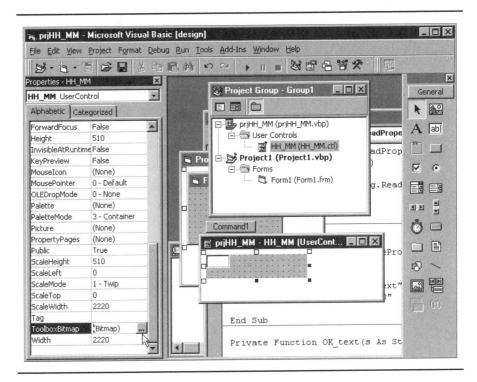

Figure 12-13

Adding your bitmap as the ToolboxBitmap.

Don't go too far this way until you finish this book. Remember, we're going to do MyTime without custom controls, so our Standard edition friends will be included. You'll see how much extra work is involved (not too much), and you'll be able to go back and add custom controls later.

I'm going to replace this HH:MM control with a clock that I can click. At any rate, I am if I get that far down in my wish list.

The Full Listing

If you have the disk, the full listing is in 12-02. That also includes the test form, the project, and group files. If you don't have the disk or if it has your pet piranha's tooth marks in it, the full file (including the parts you can't edit in the code editor) is shown in Listing 12-2.

Listing 12-2

HH_MM.ctl — the time entry control

```
VERSION 5.00
Begin VB.UserControl HH_MM
    ClientHeight    =    510
    ClientLeft      =    0
    ClientTop       =    0
    ClientWidth     =    2220
    PropertyPages   =    "HH_MM.ctx":0000
    ScaleHeight     =    510
    ScaleWidth      =    2220
    Begin VB.TextBox txtHH_MM
        Height       =    285
        Left         =    0
        TabIndex     =    0
        Top          =    0
        Width        =    510
    End
End
Attribute VB_Name = "HH_MM"
Attribute VB_GlobalNameSpace = False
Attribute VB_Creatable = True
Attribute VB_PredeclaredId = False
Attribute VB_Exposed = True
' HH_MM.ctl — HH:MM time string user control
' Copyright 1997, Martin L. Rinehart

Option Explicit

Private old_text As String

Public Property Get text() As String

    text = txtHH_MM.text

End Property

Public Property Let text(ByVal s As String)

    If OK_text(s) Then
        txtHH_MM.text = s
    End If

End Property

Private Sub txtHH_MM_Change()
```

```vb
    If txtHH_MM.Tag = "x" Then Exit Sub

    If Len(txtHH_MM.text) > 5 Then
        txtHH_MM.Tag = "x"
        txtHH_MM.text = Left(txtHH_MM.text, 5)
        txtHH_MM.Tag = ""
    End If

    If Not OK_text(txtHH_MM.text) Then
        txtHH_MM.BackColor = vbYellow
    Else
        txtHH_MM.BackColor = vbWhite
        old_text = txtHH_MM.text
    End If

End Sub

Private Sub UserControl_ExitFocus()

    If Not OK_text(txtHH_MM.text) Then

        txtHH_MM.text = old_text

    End If

End Sub

Private Sub UserControl_Initialize()

    old_text = txtHH_MM.text

End Sub

Private Sub UserControl_InitProperties()

    Height = 255
    Width = 510

    txtHH_MM.text = "00:00"

End Sub

Private Sub UserControl_Resize()

    txtHH_MM.Height = Height
    txtHH_MM.Width = Width

End Sub
```

(continued)

HH_MM.ctl — the time entry control

```
Private Sub UserControl_ReadProperties( _
    PropBag As PropertyBag)

    txtHH_MM.text = PropBag.ReadProperty( _
        "Text", "00:00")

End Sub


Private Sub UserControl_WriteProperties( _
    PropBag As PropertyBag)

    PropBag.WriteProperty "Text", _
        txtHH_MM.text, "00:00"

End Sub

Private Function OK_text(s As String) As Boolean

    OK_text = False
    If Not Len(s) = 5 Then Exit Function

' must have 5 characters before trying this test
    OK_text = _
        is_digit(Left(s, 1)) And _
        is_digit(Mid(s, 2, 1)) And _
        Mid(s, 3, 1) = ":" And _
        is_digit(Mid(s, 4, 1)) And _
        is_digit(Right(s, 1))

' must have "dd:dd" before trying this test
    If OK_text Then
        OK_text = _
            (Val(Mid(s, 1, 2)) @@@ 24) And _
            (Val(Mid(s, 4, 2)) @@@ 60)
    End If

End Function

Private Function is_digit(s As String) As Boolean

    Dim b As Byte
    b = Asc(s)

    is_digit = is_digitb(b)
```

```
End Function

Private Function is_digitb(b As Byte) As Boolean

    Const zero = 48 ' asc("0") is 48
    Const nine = zero + 9

    is_digitb = _
        (b >= zero) And _
        (b <= nine)

End Function

' end of HH_MM.ctl
```

SUMMARY

At this point, our push down stack has the schedule on the bottom, where it waited for us to build a database and then for us to create an appointment class to file in the database. That project was pushed under our exploration of ActiveX, where we created a control that could be used for entering the times of our appointments. In the next chapter, we'll pop the whole stack!

In this chapter, we started by noting that ActiveX controls were no more trouble than ActiveX .DLLs or .EXEs but that they did involve substantial differences. When you build controls, you back up a level from the developer to the author level. From the author's point of view, the developer's design time is the author's runtime.

We started with a fun control that showed a personality. Mine was crabby. I hope yours was personalized. The control was a TextBox that cycled through a list of sayings instead of letting the user actually change the text.

Building it you learned to change from author to developer mode by opening and closing the UserControl's design surface. You saw how the developer design form isn't able to access the control when the author mode is active.

You learned to use Resize() to give the right look when the developer resizes the control. This was your first example of your code running at developer design time. I hope you remembered to save when you left author mode because Visual Basic doesn't save until you enter user run time.

Then we went on to build a time data entry control that kept times in HH:MM format. After setting up, including writing the code that checks the string for validity, we wrote code that enforced validity.

This meant using `Initialize()` to store the default in a variable that always held a valid entry. We replaced an invalid entry with the stored value on `ExitFocus`. (`GotFocus` and `LostFocus` aren't raised for the `UserControl` if they're raised for constituent controls.) We checked for validity in the constituent `TextBox`'s `Change()` event handler.

Then we added a text property. We used `Property Let` and `Property Get` routines for this. The `Let` code enforced validity. When these were added you saw that the same code executing in the `Change` event at runtime would execute as the developer changed the value at design time.

Finally, we hopped out to MS Paint to create a bitmap to display on the toolbar. Even though it's freeware, Paint is adequate for these bitmaps. You have to set the size to 16 pixels wide by 15 tall, and work in maximum zoom. Combine these settings with a bit of talent as an artist and save the results to a .BMP. Back in Visual Basic in author mode, assign the bitmap to your `UserControl`'s `ToolboxBitmap` property and the next time you enter developer mode, it will appear on your toolbar.

This wraps up our tour of ActiveX. Except for the author/developer distinction we've worked with here, you can see that there's really nothing more to ActiveX programming than just object programming, plus a few well-chosen mouse clicks.

In the next chapter, we'll start with our last new learning topic, implementing abstract class interfaces. You'll see that this lets you change some slower late binding to faster early binding. Then we'll modify the ODB to be Standard edition compatible, and we'll finally integrate the schedule and the appointment database. You'll see that it's really a very nice tool.

COLLECTIONS, INTERFACES, AND APPOINTMENTS

13

*I*n this chapter, we'll complete Part I of this book, and we'll get a running start on Part II, where we'll build the MyTime system. In the first two sections of this chapter, we'll complete your OOP education's theoretical work with a study of Collections and interfaces. Then we'll complete the schedule that's been waiting patiently since Chapter 9 for us to add appointments.

The Collection is a fascinating and tremendously useful object. You'll see that it is often easier and more powerful than an array as a tool for organizing your objects.

The interface is an excellent idea that first appeared in Java. When a class *implements* an interface, it provides code for a defined set of properties and methods. This gives us an alternative to inheritance, and it lets the compiler use early binding where it might not be able to otherwise.

Finally, we'll put our knowledge to use. We'll add a Collection to hold the appointments from our App ODB that will be displayed on the schedule. We'll start by modifying the App and ODB classes so that they'll use the simple, Standard edition capabilities that the rest of the MyTime system will use.

To be consistent with the rest of the MyTime system, I'm going to steal the frmApp code from Chapter 16. This is the version that is coded with just Standard edition features. That will let us drop this schedule code right into the MyTime system when we assemble it in Chapter 22.

Finally, we'll dive into the schedule itself, modifying and adding until it is displaying appointments correctly and is ready for use as part of the MyTime system.

USING THE COLLECTION OBJECT

The Collection object is a powerful alternative to arrays. It's particularly useful for storing sets of objects. If you think of a Collection as a bag into which you toss things, you're just about right.

When you drop an object into a Collection, you're not really putting the object into a bag. You're really adding an object reference variable. The object itself is stored in RAM outside the bag. With that fact noted, we can go ahead and use the bag as our mental model.

Creating Collections

The `Collection` is a class that correctly fits the Visual Basic object model. You can create a Collection with standard object creation syntax:

```
Dim app_bag As Collection
Set app_bag = New Collection
```

Once you've created your Collection, you can drop anything you like into it. A Collection can store simple variables (such as integers or booleans), strings, or objects. It can store a messy group of disparate things. I find it most useful, however, for storing groups of a single type of object. When we assemble the schedule, for example, we'll use a Collection to store a bag of App objects.

There is, as yet, no way to tell Visual Basic that you want a Collection to hold just one type of object, as there is with arrays. You could create an array of Apps this way:

```
Dim app_set(20) As App
```

You can't do that with a Collection. If you only want Apps in a Collection, you have to be sure that your code only adds Apps to the Collection. There won't be any help from the compiler.

On the other hand, unlike arrays, a Collection doesn't need to be dimensioned. Which also implies that there's never a need to redimension a

Collection. In addition to this pleasant characteristic, the Collection supports both named and numbered access to its contents.

Collection Keys are Names

When you assign an item to an array, you give it an index number, like this:

```
app_set(16) = some_app_object
```

You need to know that number if you want to retrieve that object later on:

```
some_app_object = app_set(16)
```

You don't need a number to assign an object to a Collection. You use the Add() method. If a Collection had fifteen App objects, this would assign the 16th:

```
app_bag.Add some_app_object
```

If you knew that you had added the 16th item (you could use the Count() method to find out) later you could retrieve a particular App with the Item() method:

```
some_app_object = app_bag.Item(16)
```

Actually, Item() is the default method, so app_bag(16) would work, but don't say I told you so! If you use that shorthand, your Collection will look just like an array. This is only useful if your intent is to write deceptive code. I want my objects to look like objects, thank you.

Memo To Bill Gates

Bill, why did you add this extra feature? It's really bad software engineering to have one thing look like another in source code. Visual Basic shouldn't encourage bad programming practices, should it?

Sometimes you don't have identifiable objects, so a number is all you need. Other times, however, each object is unique and you can use names, instead. Suppose you have an appointment with Fred. This code adds a named object to your collection:

```
app_bag.Add some_app_object, "Fred"
```

When you want to retrieve the object, you can ask for it by name:

```
some_app_object = app_bag.Item("Fred")
```

That capability obviously gives the Collection much more power than a simple array. Visual Basic calls these names *keys*. I think of them as names. There's one more powerful technique you can use with the Collection object.

The For Each Loop

Suppose you have an array of appointment objects and you want to list the description of each appointment. You could loop through the array using an index, this way:

```
Dim i As Integer

For i = 0 To number_of_apps - 1
    Debug.Print app_set(i).description
Next i
```

With a Collection of appointments, the syntax is much more to the point:

```
Dim appntmt As App

For Each appntmt In app_bag
    debug.print appntmt.description
Next
```

You provide a variable of the appropriate type, and the For Each loop will fill it with the first object in the Collection, then the second and so on until it has processed the entire Collection. This code is simple and directly states your intention to process each member of the Collection. You don't need to worry about bookkeeping details such as maintaining a count and working from zero to count minus one.

Memo To Bill Gates

Bill, this one's right! The code does exactly what it looks like it will do. It makes it easy to write readable code. Nice job!

With that introduction, you should be a complete master of Collections after you try your first one. I think you'll find that you'll use a lot more Collections than arrays. Let's try our first example, which, by the way, will lead right into the interface work.

Using a Collection

Launch Visual Basic and create a new, standard .EXE project. Begin by adding a person class to the project. In a real class of people, we'd keep names, addresses, telephone numbers, and so on. Because we're just illustrating the point here, we can keep our class trivially simple. This is mine:

```
' person.cls — trivial class

Option Explicit

Public name As String
' other stuff omitted
```

That's about as simple as a class can be, isn't it? Now let's create a form that lets us show and manipulate a Collection of person objects.

Building a Form

Drop a ListBox and three buttons onto your form. This is throwaway code, so go ahead and leave the default names for everything. My design is shown in Figure 13-1.

With that design, we're ready to write a little code.

Programming the Form

Begin by declaring a Collection object and creating the Collection when the form loads. This code will work:

```
Dim people As Collection

Private Sub Form_Load()

    Set people = New Collection

End Sub
```

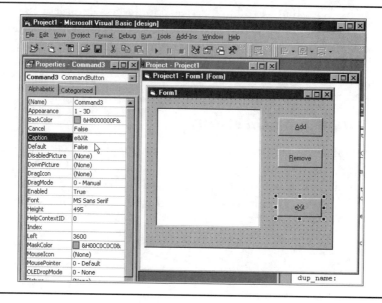

Figure 13-1
Designing a form for a person Collection.

With a Collection, we're ready to add person objects. Double-click the Add button and enter this code:

```
Private Sub Command1_Click()

    Dim s As String * 40
    s = InputBox("Name", "Add Person", s)

    Dim p As New person
    p.name = s

    people.Add p, p.name

    list_names

End Sub
```

All that remains is to program the list_names() method. This code will work:

```
Private Sub list_names()

    empty_list
```

```
        Dim individual As person

        For Each individual In people
            List1.AddItem individual.name
        Next

    End Sub

    Private Sub empty_list()

        Dim i As Integer

        For i = List1.ListCount - 1 To 0 Step -1
            List1.RemoveItem i
        Next

    End Sub
```

The ListBox's list is very similar to a Collection. Unfortunately, it's not a Collection, so the methods and method names aren't quite the same. On the other hand, Visual Basic is so helpful about giving us method lists to pick from (it sure beats typing names from memory!) that this isn't a terribly serious problem.

At this point you can run the project. In Figure 13-2, I've added three people.

So far, we can only add objects. For proper list maintenance, you'll need to be able to delete objects, too. With the Collection's capability to work with objects by name (that's by key, if you like Visual Basic's terminology), this is very simple.

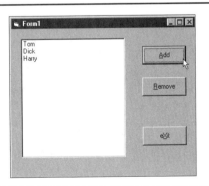

Figure 13-2
Adding people to the Collection.

If a ListBox has an item selected, List(ListIndex) is the selected item. ListIndex is -1 if nothing is selected. This is the code to add to the Remove button:

```
Private Sub Command2_Click()

    If List1.ListIndex = -1 Then ' no one selected
        MsgBox "No one selected", , "Remove who?"
        Exit Sub
    End If

    Dim name As String
    name = List1.list(List1.ListIndex)

    people.Remove name
    list_names

End Sub
```

Because you created the list from the Collection, the list contents are guaranteed to match the key values in the Collection. While we're coding buttons, you can finish the set of three with this code for the eXit button:

```
Private Sub Command3_Click()

    Unload Me

End Sub
```

Now you can add and remove names, almost at will. If you have one person named "Tom," however, what happens when you try to add a second person named "Tom"? Figure 13-3 shows my result:

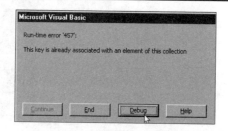

Figure 13-3

Collections refuse duplicate names.

This is not, of course, acceptable in a finished system. Two methods help you avoid this error. You can program your own check and not attempt to use the Add() method until you have assured yourself that the new item is unique. Alternatively, you can let Visual Basic try it and process the error when it finds the problem. Both techniques work. I don't like either, though. This version of the Add button code implements the second technique:

```
Private Sub Command1_Click()

    Dim s As String * 40
    s = InputBox("Name", "Add Person", s)

    Dim p As New person
    p.name = s

    On Error GoTo dup_name
    people.Add p, p.name
    GoTo list

dup_name:
    MsgBox p.name & " already in list", , "No dups!"
list:
    On Error GoTo 0
    list_names

End Sub
```

The way this code hops to labels is just like Intel assembly language. I don't mind this in assembler because that's exactly what the CPU does. I hate it, though, in a higher level language.

On the other hand, programming your own check for uniqueness is wasteful because the Collection will go right ahead and duplicate that work. Your choice is wasteful code or spaghetti code. I use both and like neither.

The Collection Listings

On disk, 13-01 contains Form1.frm and person.cls, as well as the related project and .FRX files. (Visual Basic puts the ListBox's List into an .FRX.) For those who don't have the disk, Listings 13-1a and 13-1b show the form and class files, respectively.

Listing 13-1a
Form1.frm — the person Collection maintenance form

```
VERSION 5.00
Begin VB.Form Form1
   Caption         =   "Form1"
   ClientHeight    =   3945
   ClientLeft      =   60
   ClientTop       =   345
   ClientWidth     =   5070
   LinkTopic       =   "Form1"
   ScaleHeight     =   3945
   ScaleWidth      =   5070
   StartUpPosition =   3  'Windows Default
   Begin VB.CommandButton Command3
      Caption      =   "e&Xit"
      Height       =   495
      Left         =   3600
      TabIndex     =   3
      Top          =   2640
      Width        =   1215
   End
   Begin VB.CommandButton Command2
      Caption      =   "&Remove"
      Height       =   495
      Left         =   3600
      TabIndex     =   2
      Top          =   1320
      Width        =   1215
   End
   Begin VB.CommandButton Command1
      Caption      =   "&Add"
      Height       =   495
      Left         =   3600
      TabIndex     =   1
      Top          =   480
      Width        =   1215
   End
   Begin VB.ListBox List1
      Height       =   3210
      ItemData     =   "Form1.frx":0000
      Left         =   240
      List         =   "Form1.frx":0002
      Sorted       =   -1  'True
      TabIndex     =   0
      Top          =   240
      Width        =   2895
   End
End
```

```
Attribute VB_Name = "Form1"
Attribute VB_GlobalNameSpace = False
Attribute VB_Creatable = False
Attribute VB_PredeclaredId = True
Attribute VB_Exposed = False
Option Explicit

Dim people As Collection

Private Sub Command1_Click()
    Dim s As String * 40
    s = InputBox("Name", "Add Person", s)

    Dim p As New person
    p.name = s

    On Error GoTo dup_name
    people.Add p, p.name
    GoTo list

dup_name:
    MsgBox p.name & " already in list", , "No dups!"

list:
    On Error GoTo 0
    list_names

End Sub

Private Sub Command2_Click()
    If List1.ListIndex = -1 Then ' no one selected
        MsgBox "No one selected", , "Remove who?"
        Exit Sub
    End If

    Dim name As String
    name = List1.list(List1.ListIndex)

    people.Remove name
    list_names

End Sub

Private Sub Command3_Click()

    Unload Me

End Sub

Private Sub Form_Load()
```

(continued)

Form1.frm — the person Collection maintenance form

```
        Set people = New Collection
    End Sub

    Private Sub list_names()

        empty_list

        Dim individual As person

        For Each individual In people
            List1.AddItem individual.name
        Next

    End Sub

    Private Sub empty_list()

        Dim i As Integer

        For i = List1.ListCount - 1 To 0 Step -1
            List1.RemoveItem i
        Next

    End Sub
```

Listing 13-1b

Person.cls — the trivial person class

```
    VERSION 1.0 CLASS
    BEGIN
      MultiUse = -1  'True
    END
    Attribute VB_Name = "person"
    Attribute VB_GlobalNameSpace = False
    Attribute VB_Creatable = True
    Attribute VB_PredeclaredId = False
    Attribute VB_Exposed = False
    ' person.cls — trivial class

    Option Explicit

    Public name As String
    ' other stuff omitted
```

IMPLEMENTING INTERFACES

This section will complete our discussion of new object-oriented concepts in Visual Basic. The last topic is not complex, but it's very new.

The idea of an *abstract* class comes from C++. An abstract class is one that declares data and methods but doesn't define the methods. The declaration determines the names of methods, the types and order of parameters, and the return type of functions. It doesn't supply the actual code, however.

The keyword `implements` and the interface concept come from Java. The idea is that you create an abstract class and then declare that a nonabstract class implements the abstract class, this way:

```
' Concrete.cls — a non-abstract class

implements ab_cls ' implements an abstract class
```

When a class states that it implements an abstract class, it promises to provide code for all the data and code members of the abstract class. It must provide `Property Let` and `Get` methods for the `Public` data members of the abstract class, and it must define the methods declared in the abstract class.

In just a minute, you'll see that the code editor makes this simpler to do than to explain. First, though, what good is an abstract class?

Using Implements Appropriately

Let's pause for a bit of history. C++ added single inheritance, among other things, to the C language. Over time, the call for multiple inheritance grew progressively louder, until finally multiple inheritance was added. The argument over the wisdom of that addition persists even today. Some say multiple inheritance lets you do things that you just couldn't do without it. Others say that the complexities it introduces outweigh the occasional benefits.

Java's designers invented the interface concept as a way of having most of the benefits of multiple inheritance without any of its complexities. In Visual Basic, you can use interfaces to provide some of the benefits of inheritance.

Assume that your organization markets to butchers, bakers, and candlestick makers. You would create a person class and then inherit from that class in, for example, the butcher class if we had inheritance. Lacking inheritance, you can create an abstract person class and then have the `butcher` class implement the person interface. Similarly, your `baker` and `candlestick_maker` classes would implement the person interface.

In addition to being a poor man's substitute for inheritance, the interface can sometimes provide early binding where otherwise you'll have late binding. In our ODB class, for example, we pass the ODB an `Object` reference and the ODB then calls the `Object`'s `get_name()`, `to_string()`, and `from_string()` methods.

Because the compiler only knows that it has an `Object`, the `to_string()` method is late bound — it is looked up at runtime. If we had created a *storable* abstract class that declared the three methods our ODB requires, we could pass the ODB storable objects, this way:

```
Public Sub rep_obj(sobj As storable)

' use the storable methods here

End Sub
```

This lets the compiler use early binding. (More exactly, it gives the compiler the opportunity to use early binding. Whether it does is, of course, up to the compiler implementers.)

The important point here is that objects of a class that implements an abstract class can be used as members of their own class or members of the implemented class. We'll have the `butcher` class implement the person class, and we'll use `butcher` objects as both butchers and as persons.

Let's get to the code so that you can see how this works.

Implements in the Code Editor

Clear out the form and the form code from the last project, but save the person class. The quickest way may be right-clicking in the Project Explorer to first remove Form1 and then to add another form. Begin by extending the person class with a birthdate and a read-only age. This is the new declaration:

```
' Person.cls — an interface definition (abstract) class
' Copyright 1997, Martin L. Rinehart

Option Explicit

Public name As String
Public birthdate As Date

Public Property Get age() As Byte

End Property

' end of Person.cls
```

You can define as many methods as you like. They can be Subs or Functions. Just don't forget the backpackers' motto: when in doubt, leave it out. The most commonly implemented class in Java defines exactly one method. The more extensive your abstract class, the more work it is to implement. Keep it simple and it will be more useful.

Next, add another class and name it Butcher. Immediately after the Option Explicit line, state that it implements person. As you see in Figure 13-4, the code editor is happy to spell out the name after you type two letters.

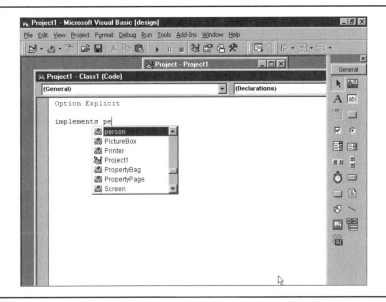

■ **Figure 13-4**
The code editor knows you can implement person.

Before you add the line that says implements person, your left (object) dropdown list includes General and Class objects. As you see in Figure 13-5, adding the implements person line puts a third category, person, into the list.

Next you'll want to create appropriate Property Let and Get statements for the data members. As you see in Figure 13-6, the right (procedure) dropdown list automatically includes all the items defined in your person class when you select person in the left dropdown list.

The quick way to obtain the interface you need is to click your way from top to bottom in this list. This will create skeletons of all the needed methods. Unfortunately, my version of Visual Basic makes all these methods Private, which is not at all what I want. After I generate the skeletons I do a global replace, changing Private to Public.

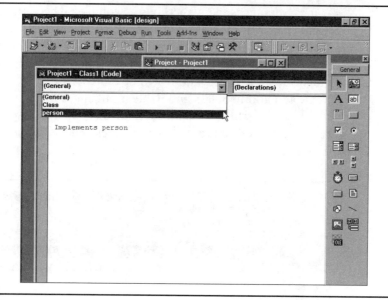

Figure 13-5
Your list of objects includes person.

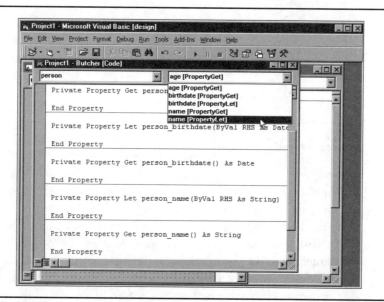

Figure 13-6
The needed methods are listed for you.

This is the result I saw for clicking through person in my `Butcher` class and then changing `Private` to `Public`:

```
' Butcher.cls — a type of person
' Copyright 1997, Martin L. Rinehart

Option Explicit
Implements person

Private pname As String

Public Property Get person_age() As Byte

End Property

Public Property Let person_birthdate(ByVal RHS As Date)

End Property

Public Property Get person_birthdate() As Date

End Property

Public Property Let person_name(ByVal RHS As String)

End Property

Public Property Get person_name() As String

End Property

' end of Butcher.cls
```

The argument name `RHS` comes from *right-hand side*. It will be provided the value of the expression on the right-hand side of the equal sign in the assignment statement.

The implemented class name is added to the property names, separated by an underscore. `Name` becomes `person_name`, and so on. You must *not* use underscores in the names you choose. Visual Basic will become utterly confused if you do.

Memo To Bill Gates

Hey, Bill! That underscore thing costs me hours. If underscores aren't allowed, how about having the compiler tell me so? I was in bug city until I found the underscore thing in some obscure place in the online documents.

Now you're ready to provide implementing code. For our example, programming the name will be adequate. This is a trivial matter of adding the two new lines you see here:

```
Public Property Let person_name(ByVal RHS As String)

    pname = RHS

End Property

Public Property Get person_name() As String

    person_name = pname

End Property
```

Now we're ready to use these new classes.

Memo To Bill Gates

I don't mean to beat a dead horse, Bill, but that name thing really bugs me. In over 30 years of programming, I've never seen a language that didn't have a single, consistent definition of a correct name. Never before. With any luck, never again!

Abstract and Nonabstract Classes

You're probably used to using Sub Main in a .BAS module as a handy main line. If you have a form-based class, you can use the Load() event handler in the same way. This saves you the trouble of adding the .BAS module and telling your project where you want it to start up.

Begin by creating a person in `Form_Load()`, this way:

```
Dim p As New person
p.name = "Fred"
Debug.Print p.name

Unload Me
```

The `Unload Me` statement turns this into the equivalent of a `Sub Main()`.

This will print `Fred`, which proves something that I wish weren't true: you can use the abstract class as a nonabstract class, if you like. In fact, nothing prevents you from adding code to all its methods. This isn't what an abstract class is supposed to be, but Visual Basic doesn't mind.

Memo To Bill Gates

Bill, shouldn't you go all the way with a feature? A class should be abstract or not. The compiler should tell you that your code shouldn't be in an abstract class, shouldn't it? Or it should tell you that you can't implement a class that's not abstract. As it is, it doesn't even care. Not good.

Now let's create a butcher. Add this code, just before `Unload Me`:

```
Dim butch As Butcher
Set butch = New Butcher
butch.person_name = "Butch"
Debug.Print butch.person_name
```

Run this and you'll see `Fred` and `Butch` printed to your Immediate window. Now let's find out what type of objects we have. Add these two lines just above `Unload Me` and predict the result before you run the program:

```
Debug.Print TypeName(p)
Debug.Print TypeName(butch)
```

That will tell you that *p* is a person and *butch* is a Butcher. You probably predicted that result. Now let's add a subroutine that shows you how to use the abstract class in lieu of an Object-class object. This is the routine to add:

```
Private Sub uses_person(p As person)

    Debug.Print TypeName(p) & " " & p.name

End Sub
```

Add these two lines above `Unload Me`:

```
uses_person p
uses_person butch
```

Because `Butcher` implements the person interface, you can pass a `Butcher`-class object to a person-class parameter. (In this example, passing anything other than a person or a `Butcher` will fail to compile, and correctly so.)

When you print the `TypeName()` of these, you may be surprised to find that even though the parameter type is person, the types of the original objects, person, and Butcher are reported.

Full Listings for Implements

On disk, this example is in 13-02. That includes the two classes and the form file, as well as the related project file. For those without the disk, Listing 13-2a shows the person class, Listing 13-2b shows the Butcher class, and Listing 13-2c shows Form1.

Listing 13-2a

person.cls — an abstract person class

```
VERSION 1.0 CLASS
BEGIN
  MultiUse = -1  'True
END
Attribute VB_Name = "person"
Attribute VB_GlobalNameSpace = False
Attribute VB_Creatable = True
Attribute VB_PredeclaredId = False
Attribute VB_Exposed = False
' Person.cls — an interface definition (abstract) class
' Copyright 1997, Martin L. Rinehart

Option Explicit

Public name As String
Public birthdate As Date
```

```
Public Property Get age() As Byte

End Property

' end of Person.cls
```

Listing 13-2b
Butcher.cls — a class that implements person

```
VERSION 1.0 CLASS
BEGIN
  MultiUse = -1  'True
END
Attribute VB_Name = "Butcher"
Attribute VB_GlobalNameSpace = False
Attribute VB_Creatable = True
Attribute VB_PredeclaredId = False
Attribute VB_Exposed = False
' Butcher.cls — a type of person
' Copyright 1997, Martin L. Rinehart

Option Explicit
Implements person

Private pname As String

Public Property Get person_age() As Byte

End Property

Public Property Let person_birthdate(ByVal RHS As Date)

End Property

Public Property Get person_birthdate() As Date

End Property

Public Property Let person_name(ByVal RHS As String)

    pname = RHS

End Property
```

(continued)

Butcher.cls — a class that implements person

```
Public Property Get person_name() As String

    person_name = pname

End Property

' end of Butcher.cls
```

Listing 13-2c
Form1.frm — a main line for testing Butcher and person

```
VERSION 5.00
Begin VB.Form Form1
    Caption         =   "Form1"
    ClientHeight    =   4770
    ClientLeft      =   60
    ClientTop       =   345
    ClientWidth     =   4770
    LinkTopic       =   "Form1"
    ScaleHeight     =   4770
    ScaleWidth      =   4770
    StartUpPosition =   3  'Windows Default
End
Attribute VB_Name = "Form1"
Attribute VB_GlobalNameSpace = False
Attribute VB_Creatable = False
Attribute VB_PredeclaredId = True
Attribute VB_Exposed = False
Option Explicit

Private Sub Form_Load()

    Dim p As New person
    p.name = "Fred"
    Debug.Print p.name

    Dim butch As Butcher
    Set butch = New Butcher
    butch.person_name = "Butch"
    Debug.Print butch.person_name

    Debug.Print TypeName(p)
    Debug.Print TypeName(butch)

    uses_person p
```

```
        uses_person butch

        Unload Me

    End Sub

    Private Sub uses_person(p As person)

        Debug.Print TypeName(p) & " " & p.name

    End Sub
```

IMPROVING THE APP AND ODB CLASSES

Are you ready to finally pop the whole development stack? We've just finished our last theory section and are ready to put this material into practice. The rest of this chapter will help us, at long last, actually see appointments on our schedule.

While we're at it, we'll simplify our database design and eliminate the parts that can't be done with the Standard edition. If you have the Professional or Enterprise edition, feel free to create your own ActiveX components and use them. If you have the Standard edition, you'll appreciate the fact that the rest of the code in this book can be done with just that edition.

Our first job will be to improve the App and ODB classes, with an eye on their use in the MyTime system we'll build in Part II.

Move tstrings to the ODB

We'll begin with the tstring-related functions. We'll need tstrings in many places in the MyTime system, so they should be moved to the ODB where the other parts of the system can use them.

Begin by moving the `int2tstring()` and `tstring2int()` functions from App.cls into ODB.cls. You'll need to change their protection from `Private` to `Public` in the ODB class.

In the App class you'll need to change these:

- `int2tstring` becomes `ODB.int2tstring`
- `tstring2int` becomes `ODB.tstring2int`

The int2tstring has an interesting bug. Visual Basic is too helpful for my taste. It performs floating-point division and then rounds to the nearest integer. (Most languages perform integer division for integer types, which always rounds down.)

This is the fixed version of the calculation of the hour:

```
hr = Int(i / 60)
```

Verifying Time in the ODB

In addition to these functions, we'll need to check the tstrings for validity, rejecting any that aren't in the HH:MM format. Again, most of the MyTime tools will need this capability, so the ODB is a good place to add it. I've added three routines to do a thorough check.

At the lowest level, is_digit() reports True for characters from 0 through 9. This is the is_digit() function:

```
Private Function is_digit(s As String) As Boolean

    Const zero = 48 ' chr("0")
    Const nine = zero + 9

    Dim b As Byte
    b = Asc(s)

    is_digit = _
        (b >= zero) And _
        (b <= nine)

End Function
```

The is_digit() function is used by OK_posint(), which checks to see that a string contains a positive (all digit) integer. This is the code:

```
Public Function OK_posint(s As String) As Boolean

    OK_posint = False

    Dim t As String
    t = Trim(s)
    If Len(t) = 0 Then Exit Function
    Dim i As Byte
```

```
        For i = 1 To Len(t)
            If Not is_digit(Mid(t, i, 1)) Then Exit Function
        Next

        OK_posint = True

    End Function
```

At the highest level, `OK_time()` uses `OK_posint()` to check for a valid time string. This is the top-level logic:

```
    Public Function OK_time(s As String) As Boolean

        OK_time = False
        If Len(s) < 5 Then Exit Function

        Dim s1 As String
        s1 = left(s, 2)
            If Not OK_posint(s1) Then Exit Function
            If Val(s1) > 24 Then Exit Function

        s1 = Mid(s, 4, 2)
            If Not OK_posint(s1) Then Exit Function
            If Val(s1) > 59 Then Exit Function

        OK_time = True

    End Function
```

As I've written this function, it doesn't check the middle character in the HH:MM format. Add a check for the colon, if you want.

Allow Lots of Records

While I was in the ODB, I decided to allow lots of records. Using an integer for the number of objects limits the size of the ODB to 32K (0 through 32K–1) objects. The MyTime system won't need nearly this many, but in looking at it I was pretty sure that sooner or later someone would push past this number. The ODB doesn't have any error handling that would prevent you from running over this limit.

These two data members need to be changed to `Long`:

```
    Private num_objects As Long
    Private current_object_num As Long
```

Additionally, you have to change all the parameters and return values that accept or return an object number from Integer to Long. The simplest method is to change all occurrences of Integer to Long and then search through all the Longs changing the few that should really be integers back to Integer. For example, the open() logic returns an integer result code.

With that change, this nice little tool won't start causing havoc at 32K records. It will start causing havoc at 2G records, which is way past anything that should be put in this ODB. (Add proper error checking if you might ever get there!)

Add Integer Time Functions

As we go forward, you'll see that we frequently want the time as an integer. We could convert tstring back to an integer, but this becomes a little silly. (The class converts the integer to a tstring and the next step is to convert it back to the original integer.) I've added these three iget_xxx() functions:

```
Public Function iget_start_time() As Integer

    iget_start_time = start_time

End Function

Public Function iget_end_time() As Integer

    iget_end_time = end_time

End Function

Public Function iget_actual_time() As Integer

    iget_actual_time = actual_time

End Function
```

Revise the Database Layout

Finally, I found an interesting problem in the database layout. One of the nice things about the ODB file is that you can view it in a normal text editor. You can also do routine maintenance with a text editor, such as physically deleting records marked for deletion. You can easily destroy the ODB this way as it stands now.

The problem is that I put the description last. The description normally is shorter than its full 40 characters. Many text editors will routinely eliminate trailing blanks. This is a handy, unobtrusive feature for dealing with source code and other text, but it is disastrous for a file that depends on having fixed-length records.

I've fixed this by moving the appointment date to the end of the record. Because that's always in YYYYMMDD format, its presence at the end of the record keeps text editors from doing too much damage.

If your text editor insists on converting consecutive blanks to tab characters, you'll still have a problem. Turn that feature off, or use a different text editor.

You can see the revisions in the comments and last two functions in the full listings.

The Full App and ODB Class Listings

On disk the code is in 13-03. For those who don't have the disk and for checking the revised record layout quickly, the complete App.cls and ODB.cls listings follow in Listings 13-3a and 13-3b, respectively.

Listing 13-3a

App.cls — the revised appointment class

```
VERSION 1.0 CLASS
BEGIN
  MultiUse = -1  'True
END
Attribute VB_Name = "App"
Attribute VB_GlobalNameSpace = False
Attribute VB_Creatable = True
Attribute VB_PredeclaredId = False
Attribute VB_Exposed = False
' App.cls — the Appointment class
' Copyright 1997, Martin L. Rinehart

Option Explicit

' Data members:
    Public key As Long
    Public app_date As Date

    Private start_time As Integer
    Private end_time As Integer
    Private actual_time As Integer
```

(continued)

App.cls — the revised appointment class

```
    Public description As String

Public Sub set_start_time(s As String)

    start_time = ODB.tstring2int(s)

End Sub

Public Function iget_start_time() As Integer

    iget_start_time = start_time

End Function

Public Function get_start_time() As String

    get_start_time = ODB.int2tstring(start_time)

End Function

Public Sub set_end_time(s As String)

    end_time = ODB.tstring2int(s)

End Sub

Public Function iget_end_time() As Integer

    iget_end_time = end_time

End Function

Public Function get_end_time() As String

    get_end_time = ODB.int2tstring(end_time)

End Function

Public Sub set_actual_time(s As String)

    actual_time = ODB.tstring2int(s)

End Sub

Public Function get_actual_time() As String

    get_actual_time = ODB.int2tstring(actual_time)
```

```
End Function
Public Function iget_actual_time() As Integer

    iget_actual_time = actual_time

End Function

Private Sub Class_Initialize()

    key = 0 ' will be set by ODB
    app_date = Date
    start_time = 0 ' defaults
    end_time = 0
    actual_time = 0
    description = ""

End Sub

Public Function get_name() As String

    get_name = "App"

End Function

' string layout:
    ' key:          1-11, pad byte: 12
    ' start_time:   13-18
    ' end_time:     19-24
    ' actual_time: 25-30, pad bytes: 31-32
    ' description: 33-72
    ' app_date:     73-80

Public Function to_string() As String

    to_string = _
        ODB.long_str(key) & " " & _
        ODB.int_str(start_time) & _
        ODB.int_str(end_time) & _
        ODB.int_str(actual_time) & "  " & _
        ODB.fix_len(description, 40) & _
        ODB.date_str(app_date)

End Function

Public Sub from_string(s As String)

    key = Val(left(s, 11))
    start_time = Val(Mid(s, 13, 6))
    end_time = Val(Mid(s, 19, 6))
```

(continued)

App.cls — the revised appointment class

```
        actual_time = Val(Mid(s, 25, 6))
        description = Mid(s, 33, 40)
        app_date = ODB.yyyymmdd2date(Right(s, 8))

    End Sub


    ' end of App.cls
```

Listing 13-3b
ODB.cls — the revised Object Database class

```
VERSION 1.0 CLASS
BEGIN
  MultiUse = -1  'True
END
Attribute VB_Name = "ODB"
Attribute VB_GlobalNameSpace = True
Attribute VB_Creatable = True
Attribute VB_PredeclaredId = True
Attribute VB_Exposed = False
' ODB.cls — Object DataBase class
' Copyright 1997, Martin L. Rinehart

' Creates a data file which holds objects of a single
' class.

' The class must provide a get_name() function returning
' a String, suitable for use as a file name.
' It must also provide a to_string() function that returns
' a fixed-length string containing all the property values
' that will be stored. And it must provide a from_string()
' method that extracts the property values from the string
' created by the to_string() operation.

' Format of the ODB file is:
'   Header
'   Object 0 record
'   Object 1 record
'   ...
'   Object n-1 record

' Format of the header is
'   Signature (8 bytes) = "mrVB5odb"
'   Object type name (32 bytes)
'   Record length (8 bytes)
```

```vb
' Format of the object record is
'    CR byte (chr(13))
'    LF byte (chr(10))
'    Deleted flag byte ("*" if deleted, " " otherwise)
'    unused byte (pad to dword boundary)
'    obj.to_string()

Option Explicit

Const signature = "mrVB5odb"
Const header_len = 48

' Errors:
    Public Enum err_types
        openOK = -1
        err_freefile = 0
        err_open
        err_seek
        err_close
        err_getdel
        err_badrec
        err_notgot
        number_of_errors
    End Enum

' Data members
    Public default_drive As String
    Public default_path As String
    Public obj_is_deleted As Boolean

    Private file_number As Integer
    Private rec_len As Integer
    Private rec_buf As String
    Private path_name As String
    Private num_objects As Long
    Private current_object_num As Long

Public Sub close_odb()

    If file_number = 0 Then
        err_msgs (err_close)
        Exit Sub
    End If

    Close file_number
    file_number = 0 ' signal no file open

End Sub
```

(continued)

ODB.cls — the revised Object Database class

```
Public Sub create_odb(first As Object)

    file_number = FreeFile

    path_name = first.get_name
    path_name = _
        default_drive & _
        default_path & _
        path_name & ".odb"

    If Len(Dir(path_name)) Then Kill path_name

    Open path_name For Binary As file_number

    rec_buf = Chr(13) & Chr(10) & "  " & first.to_string
    rec_len = Len(rec_buf)
    Dim header As String

    Dim nm As String
    nm = first.get_name

    header = signature & _
        fix_len(nm, 32) & _
        Right(Space(8) & Str(rec_len), 8)

    Put file_number, , header
    Put file_number, , rec_buf
    current_object_num = 1

End Sub

Public Function open_odb(pn As String) As Integer

' check that a file number is available
    file_number = FreeFile
    If file_number = 0 Then
        err_msgs (err_freefile)
        open_odb = err_freefile
        Exit Function
    End If

' open the file — if it's 0 long, its new
    Open pn & ".odb" For Binary As file_number
    If LOF(file_number) = 0 Then ' not an ODB!
        Close file_number
        err_msgs (err_open)
        open_odb = err_open
```

```
        Exit Function
    End If

' create buffer for header, then read header
    Dim header As String
    header = Space(header_len)

    Get file_number, , header

' check for a valid signature
    If Left(header, 8) <> signature Then
        Close file_number
        err_msgs (err_open)
        open_odb = err_open
        Exit Function
    End If

' set up private data members
    rec_len = Val(Right(header, 8))
    rec_buf = Space(rec_len)
    path_name = pn

    num_objects = (LOF(file_number) - header_len) / rec_len
    current_object_num = 0
    open_odb = openOK

End Function

Public Function add_obj(o As Object)

    rec_buf = Chr(13) & Chr(10) & "  " & o.to_string()
    Put file_number, LOF(file_number) + 1, rec_buf
    add_obj = num_objects
    num_objects = num_objects + 1

End Function

Public Sub del_obj(num As Long)

    If Not rec_in_file(num) Then
        err_msgs (err_seek)
        Exit Sub
    End If

    Put file_number, oloc(num) + 2, "*"

    obj_is_deleted = True

End Sub
```

(continued)

ODB.cls — the revised Object Database class

```
Public Sub undel_obj(num As Long)

    If Not rec_in_file(num) Then
        err_msgs (err_seek)
        Exit Sub
    End If

    Put file_number, oloc(num) + 2, " "

    obj_is_deleted = False

End Sub

Public Function get_obj(num As Long, _
        ByRef obj As Object) As Long

    If Not rec_in_file(num) Then
        err_msgs (err_seek)
        get_obj = -1
        Exit Function
    End If

    Get file_number, oloc(num), rec_buf

    obj_is_deleted = _
        (Mid(rec_buf, 3, 1) = "*")

    obj.from_string (Right(rec_buf, rec_len - 4))
    get_obj = num

End Function


Public Sub rep_obj(num As Long, o As Object)

    If Not rec_in_file(num) Then
        err_msgs (err_seek)
        Exit Sub
    End If

    Dim del_char As String
    If obj_is_deleted Then
        del_char = "*"
    Else
        del_char = " "
    End If

    rec_buf = Chr(13) + Chr(10) + _
        del_char + " " + o.to_string()
```

```
        Put file_number, oloc(num), rec_buf
End Sub

Private Function rec_in_file(num As Long) As Boolean

    ' is num in range 0 to num_objects-1 ?

    rec_in_file = (num > -1) And (num < num_objects)

End Function

Private Function oloc(num As Long)

    ' find object in file
    oloc = header_len + num * rec_len + 1

End Function

Private Sub err_msgs(errno As Byte)

    Call MsgBox(ferr_msgs(errno), vbCritical, "ODB Error")

End Sub

Private Sub Class_Initialize()

    default_drive = ""
    default_path = ""
    file_number = 0 ' 0 = no file open

End Sub

Public Function ferr_msgs(msg_num As Byte)

    ' pseudo class static array

    Select Case msg_num

        Case err_freefile:
            ferr_msgs = "No file number available"

        Case err_open:
            ferr_msgs = "Cannot open file"

        Case err_seek:
            ferr_msgs = "Cannot perform seek"

        Case err_close:
            ferr_msgs = "Cannot close — no file open"
```

(continued)

ODB.cls — the revised Object Database class

```
            Case err_getdel:
                ferr_msgs = "Cannot get - record deleted"

            Case err_badrec:
                ferr_msgs = "Cannot get - record damaged"

            Case err_notgot:
                ferr_msgs = _
                    "Cannot get - invalid object number"

        End Select

    End Function

    Public Function fix_len(s As String, _
        num_chars As Integer)

    ' returns s padded or truncated to num_chars length

        fix_len = Left(s & Space(num_chars), num_chars)

    End Function

    Public Function long_str(l As Long) As String

    ' returns 11-byte string

        long_str = Right(Space(10) & Str(l), 11)

    End Function

    Public Function int_str(i As Integer) As String

    ' returns 6-byte string

        int_str = Right(Space(5) & Str(i), 6)

    End Function

    Public Function date_str(d As Date) As String

    ' returns 8-byte date: YYYYMMDD

        date_str = _
            Right(Str(Year(d)), 4) & _
            Right(Str(100 + Month(d)), 2) & _
            Right(Str(100 + day(d)), 2)

    End Function
```

```
Public Function yyyymmdd2date(s As String) As Date

' return date given "YYYYMMDD" string

    yyyymmdd2date = _
        Mid(s, 5, 2) & "/" & _
        Right(s, 2) & "/" & _
        Left(s, 4)

End Function

Public Function get_num_objects() As Long

    get_num_objects = num_objects

End Function

Public Function tstring2int(s As String)

' a tstring is "HH:MM" (i.e. "01:00" = 60)

    tstring2int = _
        60 * Val(Left(s, 2)) + _
        Val(Right(s, 2))

End Function

Public Function int2tstring(i As Integer)

' returns "01:00" given 60, "02:30" given 150, etc.

    Dim hr As Byte, mn As Byte
    hr = Int(i / 60)
    mn = i - (hr * 60)

    int2tstring = _
        Right(Str(100 + hr), 2) & ":" & _
        Right(Str(100 + mn), 2)

End Function

Public Function OK_time(s As String) As Boolean

    OK_time = False
    If Len(s) < 5 Then Exit Function

    Dim s1 As String
    s1 = Left(s, 2)
        If Not OK_posint(s1) Then Exit Function
        If Val(s1) > 24 Then Exit Function
```

(continued)

ODB.cls — the revised Object Database class

```
    s1 = Mid(s, 4, 2)
        If Not OK_posint(s1) Then Exit Function
        If Val(s1) > 59 Then Exit Function

    OK_time = True

End Function

Public Function OK_posint(s As String) As Boolean

    OK_posint = False

    Dim t As String
    t = Trim(s)
    If Len(t) = 0 Then Exit Function

    Dim i As Byte
    For i = 1 To Len(t)
        If Not is_digit(Mid(t, i, 1)) Then Exit Function
    Next

    OK_posint = True

End Function

Private Function is_digit(s As String) As Boolean

    Const zero = 48  ' chr("0")
    Const nine = zero + 9

    Dim b As Byte
    b = Asc(s)

    is_digit = _
        (b >= zero) And _
        (b <= nine)

End Function

Public Function nice_date(d As Date)

    ' Spell out date: "January 1, 2000"

    nice_date = monthStr(Month(d)) & _
        Str(day(d)) & "," & _
        Str(Year(d))

End Function
```

```
Private Function monthStr(m As Byte)

    'm must be from 1 thru 12

    Select Case m
        Case 1: monthStr = "January"
        Case 2: monthStr = "February"
        Case 3: monthStr = "March"
        Case 4: monthStr = "April"
        Case 5: monthStr = "May"
        Case 6: monthStr = "June"
        Case 7: monthStr = "July"
        Case 8: monthStr = "August"
        Case 9: monthStr = "September"
        Case 10: monthStr = "October"
        Case 11: monthStr = "November"
        Case 12: monthStr = "December"
    End Select

End Function

' end of ODB.CLS
```

REWRITING THE FRMAPP CLASS

The four-file system we used for our App database system worked well. If you recall, we were studying events at the time, so we used an event-raising system. There is, however, a simpler approach that doesn't raise events, and that is completely compatible with the Standard edition of Visual Basic 5.

In Chapter 16, we're going to go into this new approach in detail. For now, I'll just steal the code from that chapter and use it here. This means that the schedule we create here will drop right into the MyTime system at final assembly time in Chapter 22.

On disk the code will be in 13-04. For a full listing, look ahead to Listing 16-3.

SCHEDULING APPOINTMENTS

We finally have the database we needed when we left the schedule class way back in Chapter 9. Now all we have to do is read in a Collection of appointments and write some display code. To keep this from being too simple, I'm going to give you a number of other additions and improvements as we go along.

If you haven't done so yet, copy the frmSched.frm file you created in Chapter 9 into your current working directory and add it to your project. Then we'll begin with the general declarations section.

Improving the Data Members

I've made these improvements and additions to the data members section of frmSched.frm:

- Const rt_space increased from 40 to 45
- Const min_width increased to 4070
- Added Const min_app_height = 240
- Added Const max_apps = 10
- Added Public dont_unload As Boolean
- Added Public boss_cal As Calendar
- Typed top and bottom_time As Integer
- Deleted current_date

Additionally, I've reformatted the section for improved readability and added the last five properties you see here:

```
' frmSched.frm — Appointment Schedule Class
' Copyright 1997, Martin L. Rinehart

Option Explicit

Const tp_space = 350
Const bt_space = 400
Const lf_space = 460
Const rt_space = 45

Const str_time = 9 * 60 ' 9AM

Const min_width = 4070
Const min_height = 3000
Const min_app_height = 240

Const max_apps = 10
```

```
' Data members
    Public dont_unload As Boolean
    Public boss_cal As Calendar ' calendar that sets date

    Private start_time As Integer
    Private stop_time As Integer

    Private top_time As Integer
    Private bottom_time As Integer

    Private interval As Byte
    Private interval_index As Byte ' Range: 0-6
    Private intervals(6) As Byte

    Private app_form As frmApp
    Private app_bag As Collection
    Private app_recnos(1 To max_apps) As Long
    Private todays_date As Date

    Private hi_app As Integer
```

Responding to the Buttons

Add an Edit button. For consistency with the other MyTime tools, I've
changed the OK button to an eXit button. Figure 13-7 shows the new
design form.

Now we're ready to program the clicks.

The Edit button either clicks the Add New button (by sending an Alt+A
through the keyboard) or it sets the ODB to the currently highlighted
appointment (if any). We'll look at the set_odb() later in this section. This
is the Edit code:

```
Private Sub cmdEdit_Click()

    If (app_bag.Count = 0) Then
        SendKeys "%A" ' Press Alt+A to Add New
    Else
        set_odb
    End If

    app_form.Show vbModal
    ' rereads apps via GotFocus()

End Sub
```

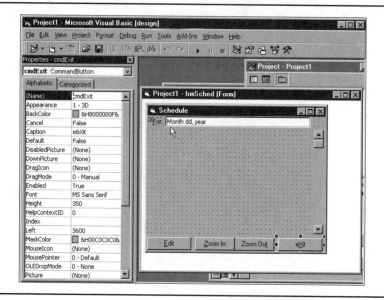

Figure 13-7
Adding an Edit button to the schedule.

Programming the eXit button is simple enough. Add this code:

```
Private Sub cmdExit_Click()

    Unload Me

End Sub
```

Finally, delete the `cmdOK_Click()` routine.

Adding Appointment Labels

In my schedule, I offset the appointments steadily to the right. This doesn't make a lot of sense for consecutive appointments, but it doesn't really hurt either. Figure 13-8 shows consecutive appointments.

Of course, real life is more complicated. Figure 13-9 shows a vital phone call interrupting a staff conference which interrupts a morning meeting. You can see here that the offset makes a lot of sense.

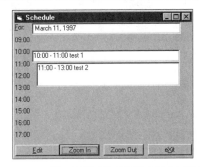

Figure 13-8
One meeting follows another.

Figure 13-9
Meetings may nest, too.

To display the appointments, you'll need a control array of Labels. Start by adding a single label and giving it these properties:

- Name it `lblApp`
- Set its `Caption` to a null string
- Set `BorderStyle` to 1 (Fixed Single)
- Set `BackColor` to white (Palette tab)
- Set `Width` to 2700
- Set `Height` to 1500

Cut it to the clipboard and paste in a copy. Paste another and say Yes when Visual Basic offers to create the control array. Continue pasting until you have as many as you need. (That's `lblApp(0)` through `lblApp(max_apps-1)`.)

Then organize them in the cascade you see in Figure 13-10. The `Left` of `appLbl(0)` is at `480`. For the rest, Visual Basic's default grid spacing works well.

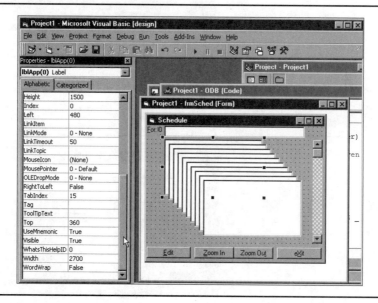

Figure 13-10
Designing a cascade of appointments.

As a final improvement to the form, I found that using a TextBox to display the date looked right but that the user could position the cursor into the box and edit it, even when it wasn't in the tab order. The solution was to replace `txtDate` with a `Label`, `lblDate` and set it up like the appointment labels (`null Caption`, `BorderStyle 1`, `white BackColor`). Globally change all occurences of `txtDate` to `lblDate` in the code. Then go on to handle the lifetime events.

The Lifetime Events

You have to carefully think through the key events that mark the form's lifetime. At birth, the `Initialize()` method will run. During the run,

Activate() will be called whenever the user returns to the schedule. During the run you refuse to unload. When the program ends we'll unload the contained forms.

Modifying the Initialize() Method

When we originally coded this class, we provided the dummy line that set current_date to today's date. Delete that line and then add these new lines at the end of Form_Initialize():

```
' app_form creates and opens the ODB
   Set app_form = New frmApp
   app_form.Visible = False
   app_form.dont_unload = True
   Load app_form

   Set app_bag = New Collection
   hi_app = -1
```

The date setting has to move from Initialize() to Activate() to allow the user to look at today's schedule, click tomorrow in the calendar, and return to the schedule to see how tomorrow's shaping up. (A totally slick version would have the calendar automatically update every other tool when it changed. I'll leave that coding as a challenge for you.)

Setting Up on Activation

Each time the form is activated, we'll need to check the boss calendar's date and read the appointments. To test this as a standalone, we'll not have a boss calendar, so I've commented out the line we'll need for MyTime and added a line for testing.

This event handler does the job:

```
Private Sub Form_Activate()

   ' todays_date = boss_cal.get_hi_date
   todays_date = Date ' use today for testing
   read_apps

End Sub
```

Unload Selectively but Thoroughly

The logic that goes into the QueryUnload() method is very similar to the logic that we added to the data entry form, as you see here:

```
Private Sub Form_QueryUnload(Cancel As Integer, _
    UnloadMode As Integer)

    If dont_unload Then
        Visible = False
        Cancel = -1 ' set bit cancels unload
    Else
        app_form.Visible = False
        app_form.dont_unload = False
        Unload app_form
        Set app_form = Nothing
    End If

End Sub
```

I chose the negative, dont_unload, because booleans default to False. That means that without a parent, dont_unload is automatically set correctly to allow unloading.

Modifying Resize()

Delete the line in Resize() that sets txtDate to current_date. We'll do a better job using boss_cal's date.

I've made some improvements in the section that sets up the buttons and added a new section for the appointments. Use the button section here to replace the existing button section and add the appointments:

```
' Bottom command buttons
    Dim wid As Integer, tp As Integer

    wid = cmdEdit.Width ' all 4 are same width
    tp = VScroll.top + VScroll.Height + 45

    cmdExit.top = tp
    cmdExit.left = Width - wid - 120

    cmdZoomOut.top = tp
    cmdZoomOut.left = cmdExit.left - wid
```

```
        cmdZoomIn.top = tp
        cmdZoomIn.left = cmdZoomOut.left - wid

        cmdEdit.top = tp
        cmdEdit.left = cmdZoomIn.left - wid

' appointment widths
    For i = 0 To max_apps - 1
        lblApp(i).Width = VScroll.left - 60 - _
            lblApp(i).left
    Next
    show_apps
```

Clicking an Appointment

With appointments showing, the user should be able to click one to select it for editing. This new routine supports that feature:

```
    Private Sub lblApp_Click(Index As Integer)

        If hi_app > -1 Then
            lblApp(hi_app).BackColor = vbWhite
        End If

        hi_app = Index

        lblApp(hi_app).BackColor = vbButtonFace

    End Sub
```

Again, this assumes that `vbWhite` and `vbButtonFace` are not the same. For a system written for resale, you'd want to improve this.

Read the Appointments into a Collection

The basic process here is simple. We'll read through all the App objects in the ODB. If the App isn't deleted we'll check the date. If the date matches `todays_date` (as specified by the boss calendar), we'll toss it into the bag.

Unfortunately, this is one of those routines where there's so much bookkeeping and housecleaning going on that the basic work almost gets lost.

It starts by resetting `hi_app` to show nothing highlighted and then empties the bag. After that it checks for an empty ODB, exiting if this is the case. Then it fills the bag by looping over every App in the ODB.

As it fills the bag, it increments num_in_bag, exiting if that reaches the maximum. My maximum is low, by the way. If you have a lot of appointments you'll want to use a larger one.

As each appointment is read, its number in the ODB is returned and saved in recno. This is used to fill in the array app_recnos. This is the array that lets us correctly position the ODB to the selected record when the user highlights an appointment and clicks Edit.

This simple statement tosses appointments into the bag:

```
app_bag.Add a
```

You have to look closely to find it, however.

Finally, the routine calls show_apps() and displays the date. This is the full routine:

```
Private Sub read_apps()

    Dim i As Long

    hi_app = -1 ' nothing highlighted

' empty the collection
    If app_bag.Count > 0 Then

        For i = app_bag.Count To 1 Step -1
            app_bag.Remove (i)
        Next

    End If

' exit if nothing to do
    Dim n As Long
    n = app_form.ob.get_num_objects
    If n = 0 Then Exit Sub

' refill the collection
    Dim a As App, num_in_bag As Integer, recno As Long

    num_in_bag = 0

    For i = 0 To n - 1

        Set a = New App
        recno = app_form.ob.get_obj(i, a)
        If Not app_form.ob.obj_is_deleted Then
            If a.app_date = todays_date Then
```

```
                    app_bag.Add a
                    num_in_bag = num_in_bag + 1
                    If num_in_bag > max_apps Then Exit For
                    app_recnos(num_in_bag) = recno
                End If
            End If

        Next

    ' show the ones that fit
        show_apps

    ' display the new date
        lblDate.Caption = " " & ODB.nice_date(todays_date)

    End Sub
```

Displaying the Appointments

Finally, we come to the rather messy business of actually displaying appointments. This is not trivial. You have to look at your time scale to see where the appointment should be positioned. You have to allow for the fact that part or all of the appointment may be off the visible portion of the schedule. You have to override your own calculations if you need to make the appointment at least tall enough for a line of text.

Let's dive into the code, this time working top down.

Calling the show_apps() Method

The show_apps() method, which we'll talk about shortly, actually displays the appointments. It's called at the end of the appointment reading method, which we'll also look at in detail. Other times, we'll need to call the display code.

We'll need to redisplay the appointments after each zoom, so add the two show_apps() calls you see here:

```
    Private Sub cmdZoomIn_Click()

        If interval_index < 6 Then
            interval_index = interval_index + 1
            reset_times
            set_scrollbar
        End If
```

```
        show_apps

End Sub

Private Sub cmdZoomOut_Click()

    If interval_index > 0 Then
        interval_index = interval_index - 1
        reset_times
        set_scrollbar
    End If

    show_apps

End Sub
```

You'll also need to redisplay the appointments after the user manipulates the elevator, so add this show_apps():

```
Private Sub VScroll_Change()

    top_time = VScroll.Value

    reset_times
    show_apps

End Sub
```

The show_apps() Method

The show_apps() method is a simple controller for a rather complicated process. It just marches through the Collection, displaying all the apps that fit. This is the code:

```
Private Sub show_apps()

    Dim a As App
    Set a = New App

    Dim i As Integer, n As Byte
    n = 0

    For i = 0 To max_apps - 1
        lblApp(i).Visible = False
    Next
```

```
    For i = 1 To app_bag.Count
        Set a = app_bag.Item(i)
        If in_view(a) Then
            display a, n
            n = n + 1
        End If
    Next

End Sub
```

You could convert that loop to a `For Each`. You'll see that it's cleaner that way.

Is the App in View?

The top level stayed simple because it delegated the hard work downstream. First, let's look at the `in_view()` method. This returns `True` if any part of the appointment can show on the schedule, this way:

```
Private Function in_view(a As App) As Boolean

    in_view = _
        (a.iget_start_time < bottom_time) And _
        (a.iget_end_time > top_time)

End Function
```

The appointment shows if its start comes before the bottom time the schedule is showing, and its end comes after the top time the schedule shows.

Displaying the Appointment

The display code uses the `app_loc()` method. Given a time, `app_loc` returns the vertical position, in twips, of that time on the schedule form. Actually, `app_loc()` is not too bright. It may return a negative number (above the top of the schedule) or a positive that is past the end of the schedule. Most of `display()`'s job is to convert `app_loc()`'s answer to a usable position.

If the computed top and bottom aren't far enough apart to show a line of text, the display is widened to a readable size. This widening is usually done downward, leaving the top in the starting position. If that would push the bottom of the appointment below the display area, however, the top will be moved up enough to bring it back into the display.

The scrollbar's top and height are the top and height of the display area. This is the code:

```
Private Sub display(a As App, n As Byte)

    If n >= max_apps Then Exit Sub

' use lblApp(n) to display appointment a
    Dim tp As Integer, bt As Integer, ht As Integer

' to position, get top and bottom locations
    tp = app_loc(a.iget_start_time)
    bt = app_loc(a.iget_end_time)

' if top is above display area, chop off excess
    If tp < VScroll.Top Then tp = VScroll.Top

' show at least tall enough to read text
    ht = bt - tp
    If ht < min_app_height Then ht = min_app_height
    bt = tp + ht

' if bottom is below display area, chop off excess
    Dim vsb As Integer ' vertical scroll bar bottom
    vsb = VScroll.Top + VScroll.Height
    If bt > vsb Then bt = vsb

' adjust top up, if needed, for minimum height
    ht = bt - tp
    If ht < min_app_height Then tp = bt - min_app_height

    With lblApp(n)

        .Top = tp
        .Height = ht
        .Caption = display_str(a)
        .Visible = True

        If n = hi_app Then
            .BackColor = vbButtonFace
        Else
            .BackColor = vbWhite
        End If

    End With

End Sub
```

The `display_str()` method formats the string in the appointment, this way:

```
Private Function display_str(a As App) As String

    display_str = a.get_start_time & _
        " - " & a.get_end_time & _
        " " & a.description

End Function
```

Converting Time to Twips

Given a time (minutes from midnight) the `app_loc()` method returns a vertical location, in twips. It looks at the first time label. The center of this label is the number of twips for the time the label specifies. The distance, in twips, from the top of the first label to the top of the last label is used to calculate the number of twips per minute. An offset of 75 twips (5 pixels) is used as the distance from the top to the center of the time label. This is the code:

```
Private Function app_loc(tim As Integer) As Integer

    Dim tp As Integer, ht As Integer
    tp = VScroll.Top
    ht = VScroll.Height

    '
    Dim twips_per_min As Double
    twips_per_min = _
        (lblTime(8).Top - lblTime(0).Top) / _
        (bottom_time - top_time)

' Use the visual center of the time label's text
    Dim top_time_loc As Integer
    top_time_loc = lblTime(0).Top + 75 ' 5 pixels down

    app_loc = top_time_loc + _
        ((tim - top_time) * twips_per_min)

End Function
```

This whole display process took a long time to program. I tried lots of things before I settled on this approach. The current result is pretty good, but I imagine you could do better. Take a good look at consecutive, hourly appointments (9 to 10, 10 to 11, and so on), and see if you can't make the result look better than mine. I think you could do a better job of adjusting for the pixels used by the borders of the Label components.

Setting the ODB

If the user highlights an appointment and then clicks Edit, we want to edit the highlighted appointment. This is why we saved the record numbers in an array as we filled the Collection with App objects.

If no appointment is highlighted, an Edit click defaults to going to the first appointment of the day. If there aren't any appointments, set_odb() gives up and leaves the ODB alone. This is the method:

```
Private Sub set_odb()

' positions ODB prior to launching data entry form

    If hi_app > -1 Then ' app selected, go to it

        app_form.go_to app_recnos(hi_app + 1)

    Else    ' nothing selected, go to first of the day

        If app_bag.Count > 0 Then
            app_form.go_to app_recnos(1)
        End If

    End If

End Sub
```

Returning a Reference to the ODB

Finally, when the MyTime system is put together the time tool will need references to the other tools' ODBs, including the schedule's App ODB. This routine provides access to that reference:

```
Public Function get_app_db() As ODB

    Set get_app_db = app_form.ob

End Function
```

With this code in place, you can run the schedule and see your appointments!

The Full Schedule Form Listing

On disk, 13-05 contains all the files needed for Project1, which runs the schedule as a standalone program. There is test data in the ODB for March 10 and 11, 1997. If you don't have the disk or if you blew out your CD-ROM drive playing Beethoven's 5th at top volume, Listing 13-4 shows the editable portion of the frmSched.frm file. The portion you don't see in the code editor is included in Appendix D.

Listing 13-4
frmSched.frm — the completed schedule

```
' frmSched.frm — Appointment Schedule Class
' Copyright 1997, Martin L. Rinehart

Option Explicit

Const tp_space = 350
Const bt_space = 400
Const lf_space = 460
Const rt_space = 45

Const str_time = 9 * 60 ' 9AM

Const min_width = 4070
Const min_height = 3000
Const min_app_height = 240

Const max_apps = 10

' Data members
    Public dont_unload As Boolean
    Public boss_cal As Calendar ' calendar that sets date

    Private start_time As Integer
    Private stop_time As Integer

    Private top_time As Integer
    Private bottom_time As Integer

    Private interval As Byte
    Private interval_index As Byte ' Range: 0-6
    Private intervals(6) As Byte

    Private app_form As frmApp
    Private app_bag As Collection
    Private app_recnos(1 To max_apps) As Long
    Private todays_date As Date
```

(continued)

frmSched.frm — the completed schedule

```
    Private hi_app As Integer

Private Sub cmdEdit_Click()

    If (app_bag.Count = 0) Then
        SendKeys "%A" ' Press Alt+A to Add New
    Else
        set_odb
    End If

    app_form.Show vbModal
    ' rereads apps via GotFocus()

End Sub

Private Sub cmdExit_Click()

    Unload Me

End Sub

Private Sub cmdZoomIn_Click()

    If interval_index < 6 Then
        interval_index = interval_index + 1
        reset_times
        set_scrollbar
    End If

    show_apps

End Sub

Private Sub cmdZoomOut_Click()

    If interval_index > 0 Then
        interval_index = interval_index - 1
        reset_times
        set_scrollbar
    End If

    show_apps

End Sub

Private Sub Form_Activate()

    ' todays_date = boss_cal.get_hi_date
```

```
        todays_date = Date
        read_apps
End Sub

Private Sub Form_Initialize()

        intervals(0) = 60
        intervals(1) = 30
        intervals(2) = 15
        intervals(3) = 10
        intervals(4) = 5
        intervals(5) = 2
        intervals(6) = 1

        interval_index = 0

        start_time = str_time
        interval = 60 ' intervals(interval_index)
        stop_time = start_time + interval * 8

        top_time = start_time
        bottom_time = stop_time

        reset_times
        set_scrollbar

' app_form creates and opens the ODB
        Set app_form = New frmApp
        app_form.Visible = False
        app_form.dont_unload = True
        Load app_form

        Set app_bag = New Collection
        hi_app = -1

End Sub

Private Sub Form_QueryUnload(Cancel As Integer, _
        UnloadMode As Integer)

    If dont_unload Then
        Visible = False
        Cancel = -1 ' set bit cancels unload
    Else
        app_form.Visible = False
        app_form.dont_unload = False
        Unload app_form
        Set app_form = Nothing
    End If
```

(continued)

frmSched.frm — the completed schedule

```
End Sub

Private Sub Form_Resize()

' time labels
    Dim vert_space As Integer, vert_start As Integer

    If WindowState = vbMinimized Then Exit Sub

    If Width < min_width Then Width = min_width
    If Height < min_height Then Height = min_height

    vert_start = tp_space
    vert_space = (Height - tp_space - bt_space - 400) / 9

    Dim i As Byte
    For i = 0 To 8
        lblTime(i).Top = vert_start + vert_space * i
    Next

' Date text box
    lblDate.Width = Width - rt_space - lf_space - _
        275 - 120

' Vertical elevator
    VScroll.Left = Width - VScroll.Width - 120
    VScroll.Height = Height - 400 - 350 - _
        VScroll.Top - 50
    ' Form.Height less:
    '    400 twips for Form borders,
    '    350 twips for the bottom command buttons' height,
    '    It's own top and 50 extra for good looks

' Bottom command buttons
    Dim wid As Integer, tp As Integer

    wid = cmdEdit.Width ' all 4 are same width
    tp = VScroll.Top + VScroll.Height + 45

    cmdExit.Top = tp
    cmdExit.Left = Width - wid - 120

    cmdZoomOut.Top = tp
    cmdZoomOut.Left = cmdExit.Left - wid

    cmdZoomIn.Top = tp
    cmdZoomIn.Left = cmdZoomOut.Left - wid
```

```
        cmdEdit.Top = tp
        cmdEdit.Left = cmdZoomIn.Left - wid

' appointment widths
    For i = 0 To max_apps - 1
        lblApp(i).Width = VScroll.Left - 60 - _
            lblApp(i).Left
    Next
    show_apps

End Sub

Private Sub lblApp_Click(Index As Integer)

    If hi_app > -1 Then
        lblApp(hi_app).BackColor = vbWhite
    End If

    hi_app = Index

    lblApp(hi_app).BackColor = vbButtonFace

End Sub

Private Sub VScroll_Change()

    top_time = VScroll.Value

    reset_times
    show_apps

End Sub

Private Sub reset_times()

' Don't do this when our code sets Value
    If VScroll.Tag = "X" Then Exit Sub

    interval = intervals(interval_index)
    adjust_top_time

    Dim i As Integer
    For i = 0 To 8
        lblTime(i).Caption = _
            time_label(top_time + i * interval)
    Next

    bottom_time = top_time + 8 * interval

End Sub
```

(continued)

frmSched.frm — the completed schedule

```
Private Sub adjust_top_time()

' round top_time down to a multiple of the interval
    top_time = top_time - (top_time Mod interval)

' back down if too late
    If top_time + 8 * interval > stop_time Then
        top_time = stop_time - (8 * interval)
    End If

End Sub

Private Function time_label(min As Integer) As String

    Dim mn As Byte, hr As Byte
    hr = Int(min / 60)
    mn = min - (60 * hr)

    time_label = Right(Str(hr + 100), 2) & ":" & _
        Right(Str(mn + 100), 2)

End Function

Private Sub set_scrollbar()

    If top_time = start_time And _
        bottom_time = stop_time Then

        VScroll.Visible = False
        Exit Sub

    End If

    With VScroll

        .min = start_time
        .Max = stop_time - (8 * interval)
        .Tag = "X"
        .Value = top_time
        .Tag = ""

        .SmallChange = interval
        .LargeChange = 8 * interval

        .Visible = True

    End With

End Sub
```

```
Private Sub read_apps()

    Dim i As Long

    hi_app = -1 ' nothing highlighted

' empty the collection
    If app_bag.Count > 0 Then

        For i = app_bag.Count To 1 Step -1
            app_bag.Remove (i)
        Next

    End If

' exit if nothing to do
    Dim n As Long
    n = app_form.ob.get_num_objects
    If n = 0 Then Exit Sub

' refill the collection
    Dim a As App, num_in_bag As Integer, recno As Long

    num_in_bag = 0

    For i = 0 To n - 1

        Set a = New App
        recno = app_form.ob.get_obj(i, a)

        If Not app_form.ob.obj_is_deleted Then
            If a.app_date = todays_date Then
                app_bag.Add a
                num_in_bag = num_in_bag + 1
                If num_in_bag > max_apps Then Exit For
                app_recnos(num_in_bag) = recno
            End If
        End If

    Next

' show the ones that fit
    show_apps

' display the new date
    lblDate.Caption = " " & ODB.nice_date(todays_date)

End Sub
```

(continued)

frmSched.frm — the completed schedule

```
Private Sub show_apps()

    Dim a As App
    Set a = New App

    Dim i As Integer, n As Byte
    n = 0

    For i = 0 To max_apps - 1
        lblApp(i).Visible = False
    Next

    For i = 1 To app_bag.Count
        Set a = app_bag.Item(i)
        If in_view(a) Then
            display a, n
            n = n + 1
        End If
    Next

End Sub

Private Function in_view(a As App) As Boolean

    in_view = _
        (a.iget_start_time < bottom_time) And _
        (a.iget_end_time > top_time)

End Function

Private Sub display(a As App, n As Byte)

    If n >= max_apps Then Exit Sub

' use lblApp(n) to display appointment a
    Dim tp As Integer, bt As Integer, ht As Integer

' to position, get top and bottom locations
    tp = app_loc(a.iget_start_time)
    bt = app_loc(a.iget_end_time)

' if top is above display area, chop off excess
    If tp < VScroll.Top Then tp = VScroll.Top

' show at least tall enough to read text
    ht = bt - tp
    If ht < min_app_height Then ht = min_app_height
    bt = tp + ht
```

```
' if bottom is below display area, chop off excess
    Dim vsb As Integer ' vertical scroll bar bottom
    vsb = VScroll.Top + VScroll.Height
    If bt > vsb Then bt = vsb

' adjust top up, if needed, for minimum height
    ht = bt - tp
    If ht < min_app_height Then tp = bt - min_app_height

    With lblApp(n)

        .Top = tp
        .Height = ht
        .Caption = display_str(a)
        .Visible = True

        If n = hi_app Then
            .BackColor = vbButtonFace
        Else
            .BackColor = vbWhite
        End If

    End With

End Sub

Private Function display_str(a As App) As String

    display_str = a.get_start_time & _
        " - " & a.get_end_time & _
        " " & a.description

End Function

Private Function app_loc(tim As Integer) As Integer

    Dim tp As Integer, ht As Integer
    tp = VScroll.Top
    ht = VScroll.Height

    Dim twips_per_min As Double
    twips_per_min = _
        (lblTime(8).Top - lblTime(0).Top) / _
        (bottom_time - top_time)

' Use the visual center of the time label's text
    Dim top_time_loc As Integer
    top_time_loc = lblTime(0).Top + 75 ' 5 pixels down
```

(continued)

frmSched.frm — the completed schedule

```
        app_loc = top_time_loc + _
            ((tim - top_time) * twips_per_min)

End Function

Private Sub set_odb()

' positions ODB prior to launching data entry form

    If hi_app > -1 Then ' app selected, go to it

        app_form.go_to app_recnos(hi_app + 1)

    Else    ' nothing selected, go to first of the day

        If app_bag.Count > 0 Then
            app_form.go_to app_recnos(1)
        End If

    End If

End Sub

Public Function get_app_db() As ODB

    Set get_app_db = app_form.ob

End Function

' end of frmSched.frm
```

SUMMARY

Congratulations for getting here! You've come to the end of Part I and completed the theoretical work. There's a lot more to learn, such as how an object-oriented system fits together, but it's all just implementing the ideas you've seen here in Part I.

In this chapter, we learned about Collections. The Collection class is a regular part of the Visual Basic object model (not the irregular muddle). You can create a new Collection whenever you like. I use them more often than I use arrays. You don't ever need to dimension or redimension a Collection, and you can store and retrieve objects by name, as well as by index number.

After Collections, we looked at the `implements` keyword and its use with abstract classes and interfaces. An abstract class is one that declares properties and methods but doesn't define (provide code for) the methods. It just shows the methods' parameters and, for functions, return types. A class that implements the interface provides the code for the methods. The code editor writes correct skeletons for the properties (`Property Let` and `Get` methods) and for the methods.

Then we went on to put our knowledge to use. We started by modifying the App and ODB classes. Then we borrowed the frmApp from Chapter 16 to be compatible with the Standard edition and the rest of the MyTime system.

Finally, we modified and extended the frmSched class to be the parent of the App ODB and to display appointments. We used a Collection of appointment objects as a convenient way of holding today's appointments, and we provide the hooks that the MyTime system will use, as we develop it in Part II.

In Part II we'll put all your new mental tools into use building a real, object-oriented system. We'll begin with a look at the design in Chapter 14.

DOING OBJECT- ORIENTED PROGRAMMING

DESIGNING MYTIME

14

*I*n Part I, you learned to use the tools Visual Basic provides for object-oriented programming, and you learned to work around the features that Visual Basic doesn't provide, such as inheritance. With that knowledge, one more question remains unanswered: How do you use these tools?

Experienced programmers new to OOP always get stuck on the same point. Fitting together a system of objects is fundamentally unlike the coding they're used to doing.

If you're used to procedural programming, your code is like the parent of a young child. The parent tells the child what to do, and the child does it. Event-driven, object-oriented programs are like the parent of a teenager. They provide the basic instruction, and then trust the child to respond appropriately when it meets new situations. The parent of the teenager has to accept the fact that the child is out on its own. Object-oriented programmers similarly let code out of their direct control.

In the case of kids, this is a dicey proposition. You do your best, and hope that it was good enough. In the case of programs, it's entirely up to the programmer. You provide the code, and you check the users' inputs to be sure you can handle them. If you've done your job, nothing's at all dicey. Your system will be as solid (or flaky) as any procedural system.

In Part II of this book, we'll put together a system I call MyTime. I use it for managing my own work. It has the features I need. (Definition: if you want it badly enough to program it, it's a feature you need.) It doesn't have any other features, so it's small and loads almost instantly. I can leave it running, and it's not stealing a big chunk of my RAM.

As you work through building this system, you'll see how it uses objects (it's nothing but objects) working together as a system. I also hope that you'll twist it to meet your own needs. This is MyTime. As you learn how it works, make it Your Time.

While we work through MyTime, we'll build many pieces that you can use elsewhere, too. In addition to objects, you'll meet lots of techniques that can solve problems for you, too. In this chapter, we'll look at the design. You won't need your computer until we start programming in Chapter 15.

The entire MyTime system, with one small exception, uses only the Standard edition's features. That exception is the HH_MM ActiveX control. It's on the disk, so you Standard edition folks can use it. If you don't have the disk, just use a TextBox. Write enough error checking to suit yourself. (The ActiveX control version doesn't actually fix errors. It just turns the control yellow so you can see that there's a problem.)

Now let's look at the design.

DESIGN OVERVIEW

I managed my time with a variety of list-based systems. Finally I decided to computerize the process. At the time I was using the Clipper (Xbase compiler) system heavily for other work, so I wrote a Clipper program. When Borland released dBASE IV, I rewrote it with that tool.

I used it for many years. Over time I added this and deleted that. (When it's your own, you can actually delete things! No marketing manager is going to tell you that some customer might still be using it.) Its feature set has been reasonably settled for years.

A while back, I decided that a Windows version was in order because Windows now dominates my professional life. I was working at a C++ version in my spare time. Ironically, I managed that project with a DOS-based, text-mode time management system. I never completed that rewrite.

When I got my hands on my first beta version of Visual Basic 5.0, I thought that the acid test would be to rewrite my time system with it. I did, and now I'm using it. I'd say the code is at beta test stage. I still find bugs, although it's generally useful already.

The design, however, is now about at level 3.0. It works well for me. As you look at it, think about what would be really useful for you. Before you finish this chapter, you'll know enough to leave out features you don't want and add in those that you need.

The Main Menu

Figure 14-1 shows my main menu. (Bear in mind that these figures are shot in VGA — 640×480 — resolution, which reproduces well in print. I hope you'll be running at least 1024×768 or better on your desktop machine.)

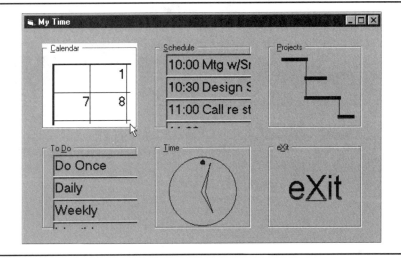

Figure 14-1
The default MyTime main menu.

This is a menu with a bit of a browser feel to it. As you move your mouse pointer over the menu, the tool under the pointer is highlighted. It's a flexible tool, too. Figure 14-2 shows four copies of MyTime launched, with the menus resized to show how flexible this is. Dragging those around is fun!

This flexibility lets you tuck the menu into any convenient corner of your desktop and leave it there.

The menu pads are all toggles. One click brings up the selected item, and a second click hides the item. All the items are loaded at program load time (in under two seconds on my P133+), so the response to a click is nearly instantaneous. On my time test machine (486DX, 33MHz), performance is still a lot nicer than, say, loading your average word processor.

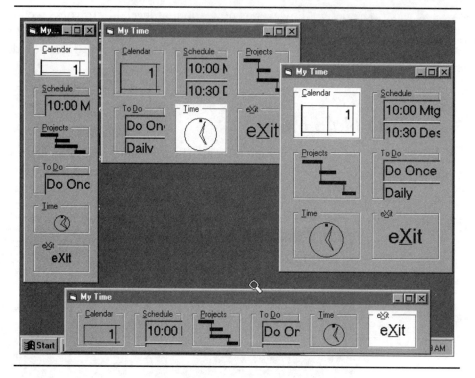

Figure 14-2
The main menu is very flexible.

The MyTime Controls

Two of the menu items, the calendar and eXit, are system controls. The eXit pad performs the expected function. The calendar, shown in Figure 14-3, is the other control. You'll remember this as the first serious object we programmed. (If you look closely, you'll see that I've made some cosmetic improvements. Otherwise, the code's the same.)

The default date is today's date, read from your system. All the date-sensitive tools read this calendar's date. (Internally, the calendar object is known as boss_cal to the other tools.) To view tomorrow's schedule, for example, you just click tomorrow and pick the schedule tool.

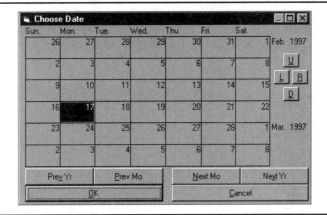

Figure 14-3
The calendar sets the date.

The Schedule

Figure 14-4 shows the schedule. The schedule defaults to showing an eight-hour day by hours (you can tailor this to suit yourself, of course).

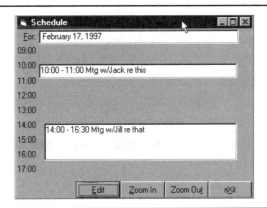

Figure 14-4
The default schedule is hourly.

The zoom buttons let you move in or out to show more or less detail. In Figure 14-5, I've added a third meeting and zoomed in on the morning. It also shows that your schedule just might have overlapping meetings.

You can see that a vertical scroll bar appears appropriately when you zoom in.

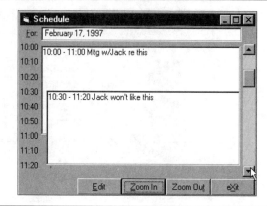

Figure 14-5
The schedule becomes overbooked.

The Project's Cascade

The projects, which are my favorite tools, are implemented as a cascade of lists. Your first project is the root of a tree. When you launch this tool, you see the top level, as Figure 14-6 shows.

A single click selects a project, as you see in Figure 14-6. A second click (or a double-click) drops one level down in the tree, showing the subprojects that compose the higher level project. Figure 14-7 shows the display after a second click on the MyTime project.

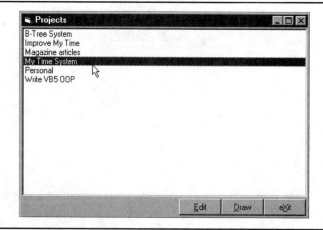

Figure 14-6
The first level of the project tree appears.

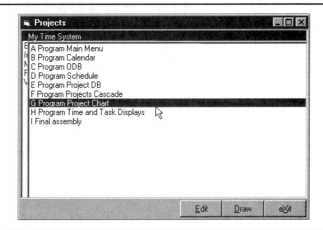

Figure 14-7
Drilling down into the MyTime project.

If you look closely, you'll see that the first list (done with `ListBox` objects) was rearranged before showing the drilldown. The selected project moves to the top of the list so that it shows above the drilldown list. A second click on the Program Project Chart item, as you see in Figure 14-8, drills down to the next level.

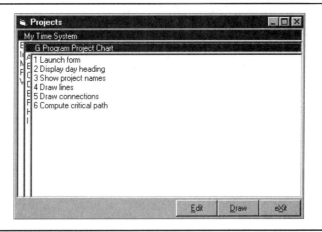

Figure 14-8
Drilling down another level.

I've allowed for ten levels of drilldown. You could have more, but as a practical matter, I don't remember getting past five levels. (My biggest projects are books, such as this one.)

A quick alternative to this board cascade would be to use a standard outline tool. Before you decide to go that way, think about how much information you can show that way. This is like an outline view where you can choose item II-C and items I, II-A, and II-B conveniently hide behind the board you're interested in. It shows a lot more relevant data.

The project items have start and end dates (estimated and actual). The Draw button shows a project chart, as you see in Figure 14-9.

The chart drawing code calculates the project's critical path, which is drawn in red. (This is dramatic on the screen, but it's not effective for a black-and-white book, sorry to say.) The entire lower branch of the tree in Figure 14-9 is in red.

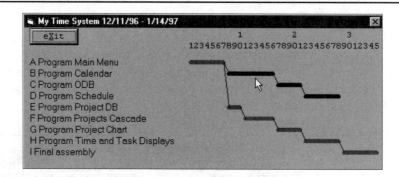

Figure 14-9
Drawing a project chart.

The Tasks Lists

I maintain two separate types of tasks. The to do items are in one list. A separate list handles chores. A *chore* is something that generates a periodic task. For example, handling e-mail is a daily chore. Items in the to do category are not repetitive. Anything that needs to be done but which isn't part of one of the projects is dumped into the to do list. Figure 14-10 shows the tasks tool.

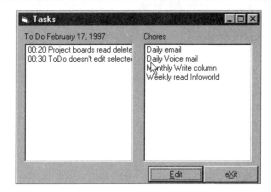

Figure 14-10
Looking at tasks.

The Time List

To find out just how badly overbooked you are, click the clock. That launches the time summary shown in Figure 14-11.

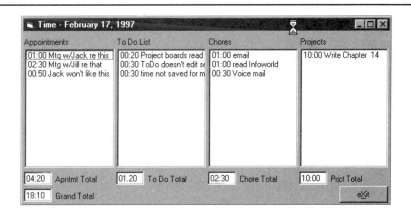

Figure 14-11
Jack and Jill have got to go.

You see that I have 18 hours scheduled between the four classes of time consumers. Fortunately, those meetings aren't real. This is President's Day, so the mail won't come, either. With any luck, I'll reach the end of this chapter.

You'll see when we take a closer look at Projects that there are really two types of tree nodes. If the node takes more than one day, time is not available. For one-day projects, estimated and actual times are available. Your hours here come from these single-day project components.

For each component where both estimated and actual times are available, this schedule gives precedence to actual time, if it's available. When the actual time is zero, the estimated time is used.

This panel is the only one without an Edit button. It summarizes the data from the other tools. I'd like to put an Edit button here, so I could select an item and go straight to it. So far that feature hasn't passed the *needed* feature test: I haven't programmed it.

THE DATA ENTRY PANELS

The three tools that have Edit buttons let you drill down into four object databases: appointments, to do items, chores, and projects. Appointments are edited under the schedule tool, and projects are edited under the project board cascade. The tasks tool lets you edit either to do list items or chores. (Clicking edit defaults to the to do list, but selecting a chore changes that default.)

These data entry panels each have a common array of buttons. If we had inheritance, you'd program a plain data panel class and inherit from it to obtain the specific type of data being handled. Without inheritance, I resorted to old-fashioned code copying.

Memo To Bill Gates
Yeah, Bill, I could've used the Data Access Object, but my .EXE is still under 400K. Even with the code duplication, that's still a lot smaller than a DAO would've been. Inheritance would shrink it further

As luck would have it, I left a nice bug in the eXit button code. It didn't save changes on the last record you edited. Of course, with code copying that meant fixing all four data edit tools. Code copying is a poor substitute for inheritance!

The Chore Data Entry Panel

Figure 14-12 shows the Chore data entry panel. It's the simplest of the four, so it's a good place to start.

The panels each use the ODB access form that we've already programmed. I've adjusted the button size to be consistent with the other buttons in the MyTime system, but otherwise they're the same.

Each panel displays the key at the top left. These use a Label, so there's no danger that the user will change one. The chore uses a dropdown list for the frequency, which also prevents entry of an invalid value.

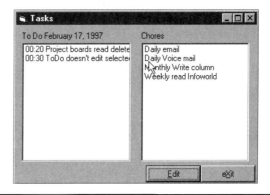

Figure 14-12
Entering a chore.

The To Do List Data Entry Panel

The To Do list data entry panel is shown in Figure 14-13. It's also a straightforward tool.

One feature I want to add here (this one may bubble over the top and get coded soon!) is a way to attach notes. Sometimes I'd like to elaborate a bit or make notes for myself about the item. Our ODB is a fixed-width data tool, however, so adding variable-width notes is going to take some serious work. You could use the DAO, of course, but I like two-second load times.

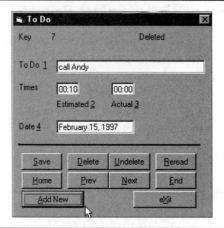

Figure 14-13
Entering To Do list items is simple.

The Appointment Data Entry Panel

The Appointment panel is a bit more sophisticated. Figure 14-14 shows the panel as you see it when you enter an appointment.

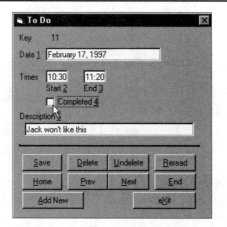

Figure 14-14
Entering an appointment.

When you click the Completed check box, the entry for the time the appointment actually took appears, as you can see in Figure 14-15.

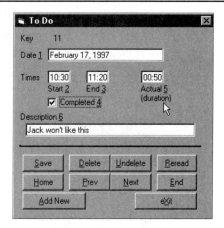

Figure 14-15
Entering time after completing an appointment.

Clicking Completed fills in the Actual time with the difference between your appointment's end and start times. You can modify this if the meeting ran long (or short, but that seems to be an uncommon occurence).

Internally, the appointment object stores only the actual time. If this is zero, the meeting is assumed not to be completed.

The Project Data Entry Panel

The Project data entry panel is more complex, but it does most of the work for you. Figure 14-16 shows a single-day version of this tool.

You can divide projects into arbitrarily small pieces. Each project is a subproject under a parent project, and each project can be a parent to other subprojects. This is a classic tree.

The Part Of area holds the key of the project's parent. To the right, this key is used to look up the Name property of the parent object.

The Begin After area holds the key of this project's precedent project, which is used in drawing the project chart and computing the project's critical path.

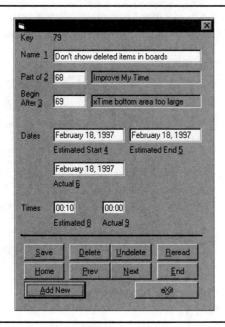

Figure 14-16
Editing a single-day project.

Both these keys are filled in for you, so you seldom need to change them. If you press Add New in this panel, the new entry is given a copy of the visible item's parent key and by default comes after the visible item. This means that if you enter a project's subparts in order, everything happens correctly.

Similarly, if you double-click a project with no subparts, you see a blank board. Pressing Edit here drops you into this data entry panel with a default subproject linked to the correct parent.

If your estimated end date is the same day as the start, you can enter the times, as Figure 14-16 shows. If the project is multiple-day, you'll see the panel as shown in Figure 14-17.

This lets you track actual and estimated durations. I once programmed the dBASE IV version of MyTime to compute multiple-day project times by summing the subprojects. It would work right up the tree. It was impressive to see, but it didn't earn its keep. The problem was that this feature wasn't helpful if you weren't meticulous about plugging in all the actual times. The cost in terms of additional data entry didn't pay for itself.

As it stands now, I won't be able to find out exactly how many hours this book took to write. (Actually, I'm not sure I want to know!) I will, however, know how long, in days, the project was. That meets my needs. You may have your own ideas about what you'll want.

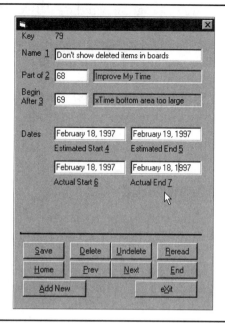

Figure 14-17
Editing a multiple-day project.

THE CODE ARCHITECTURE

You've seen the top-level menu, the second-level tool surfaces, the project chart, and the bottom-level data entry panels. In fact, with the exception of a few message boxes that alert you to errors, you've seen every window in the MyTime system. Now the question is, how are we going to structure the code?

The answer, as always, is the simplest arrangement that does the job. For this project, I've chosen three levels, tied together at the database level.

One problem that you should never forget is that our databases are not programmed for multiple users. It's simple enough to inadvertently become your own multiple user. Do you remember that nice screen shot showing the main menu in four different arrangements?

I launched four copies of MyTime, which gave me each ODB opened four times. If I'd started actually editing data, I would have been in bug city, quickly. (You could tell MyTime that it can't launch multiple copies, of course. If I'd done that, I couldn't have prepared that nice screen shot, however.)

The way we've programmed the ODB lets you do routine database maintenance with any text editor. There's no lock on the door to prevent a tired programmer, working late, from editing the same ODB that MyTime has open. (Can you guess how I know this?)

The ODB, for one example, maintains a count of the objects in the database. If a second process adds or deletes (physically deletes) data, you have a problem. Therefore, you have to design this system with those problems in mind.

The Architect's Levels

I designed a three-level architecture. At the bottom are the ODBs and their data-entry forms. The tool surfaces are the middle level and the main menu is the top level.

At the bottom level there are four forms, one for each database. All access to the data will be through the ODBs that these forms control. (In an early version, I used separate ODBs in the Time tool. That didn't work! Anything added with one of the other tools wasn't reflected in the time tool because the ODB had the original object count.)

The tool surfaces work by rereading the ODB each time they become active. This is less efficient than a more sophisticated system of selective rereading, but it's simple to code and my response time is excellent. (After I accumulate a month's worth of data, I may change this.)

The top level's main job comes at startup time. It creates each of the other surfaces. It distributes information to coordinate their efforts. At run time, the tools are largely independent. It's the user, not the top level, that controls the running program.

The Database Level

At the database level, each disk file is opened by an ODB object. All access is then through the ODB. The ODB is a property of the data entry form that serves the ODB.

These data entry panels are launched as modal windows. I don't like modal windows, but they simplify programming. (If this were a tool I was designing for commercial release, I'd change this. The extra programming would be justified.) In MyTime, the modal data entry prevents lots of conflicts.

For example, the Time surface reads the project ODB to pick up the times from single-day project components that are being done today. What would happen if the Project Editor were changing one of these records at the same time the Time surface was reading it? You'd get an unpredictable result.

The Tool Surface Level

Each tool surface reads all the data it needs, using the ODB of the associated data entry form or forms. Relevant objects are saved in Collections. These collections are discarded and rebuilt after an edit. They're also rebuilt after losing focus to another tool or program.

The tools record the object's database locations as they build their object collections. When you select an item and click edit, this location positions the ODB to the intended record.

The project cascade uses a sorted ListBox object to display project names. This adds another complication: The order of the items in the ListBox doesn't match the order in the collection. You'll see when we see the code that a second index array solves this problem.

The Top Level

The runtime job of the main level is to toggle the Visible property of each of the forms it launches. Its real job occurs at startup. It also has to do shutdown on the eXit command, of course.

At startup time, it creates each surface with code like this:

```
Set objvar = new frmWhateverTool
objvar.Visible = False
objvar.DontUnload = True
Load objvar
```

That gets everything loaded and ready to go when the user clicks one of the menu pads. The DontUnload property is an interesting one. To understand it, take a look at the shutdown code that the eXit pad of the main menu triggers:

```
objvar.Visible = False ' hide it
objvar.DontUnload = False ' allow Unload
Unload objvar
Set objvar = Nothing ' release last reference
```

The DontUnload property is used by the individual object's QueryUnload method. When the user clicks the object's eXit button (or Windows' close button, or Close from the system menu or whatever) the command to unload triggers the `QueryUnload` event. This was designed for dialog boxes like:

```
Data changed. Save file?
```

In our case, we'll look at the `DontUnload` property. If it's true we'll set `Visible` to `False`, and then cancel the unload.

This is an interesting property because the parent sets it. We want the object itself to have read-only access to the property. I don't know any programming language that actually supports this type of protection. I don't know any human parent who doesn't appreciate the need for this sort of protection. (For example, you might like to set `YellVolume` to a reasonably low level, most of the time.)

Without the right protection, we're left with just careful programming. The parent object sets `DontUnload` to `True` at startup and doesn't set it `False` until it shuts down. In the meantime, the object respects the setting.

The Object Structure

The object structure follows the design. The top-level menu is one object. Each of the tool surfaces is another object. The data entry forms are objects, and each of the four types of ODB (project, apppointment, to do list, and chore) is another object class. The data objects' permanent storage is managed by the ODB, which is the final class.

Temporary storage is up to the individual tools. Each tool uses a `Collection` object to hold copies of the relevant subset of the filed data objects. For example, the schedule object includes a `Collection` object holding appointment objects. This collection holds the appointments that are scheduled for today (or the day the calendar chooses).

The project tool maintains one `Collection` of projects for each board (`ListBox`) that is visible. The project chart is a single instance of a separate class. The project cascade object hands the chart a reference to the appropriate collection of project objects when its Draw button is pressed.

At startup time, the main menu is responsible for distributing references that let the objects talk to each other. All the tools except the project's cascade need to know what the calendar says, for example. To facilitate this, the main menu gives the schedule, task list, and time tools a reference variable pointing to the calendar. When they need to know what day it is, they ask, like this:

```
' "today" is the date the calendar is highlighting

todays_date = boss_cal.get_hi_date
```

They call the calendar `boss_cal`, but it's really a peer relationship. The tools and the calendar are all kids of the main menu, but the parent is out of the loop between startup and shutdown.

The schedule, project's cascade, and task lists all contain form-based objects, the editors for their respective ODBs. When they need to pull out a collection of objects from the ODB, they use the ODB indirectly, this way:

```
' frmApp contains an ODB, called "ob"

    Dim n As Long
    n = app_form.ob.get_num_objects
```

This works for the contained object databases. The time tool, however, has to depend on the ODBs contained by the others. For this, the main menu passes the time tool references to those ODBs after they are launched.

There are no large data structures other than the objects, including the Collection objects I've already mentioned. Arrays are used infrequently for occasional jobs. For example, an array stores references to the `Collection` objects maintained in the project's cascade. A collection would work nicely here, but an array is cheaper when you have a fixed number of entries. The number of collections is fixed because the size of the `ListBox` array that displays projects is fixed at design time.

The Code Structure

The code mirrors the object structure. There are form files for each of the tools, the main menu, and the chart. There are four more form files for the ODB controllers, and there is a class file for each class. There are no .BAS modules.

The main menu does its serious work in its `initialize()` method, where it launches one each of its component tools. Then, in its `resize()` method, it does the really hard cosmetic work. (The calendar pad is drawn with one or two rows and one or two days in each row, depending on the space available. The concept's not hard, but it takes a lot of code.) The `unload()` method takes care of unloading everything that the `initialize()` code loaded.

The tools also load their components (data entry forms for all but the time tool and the chart for the project's cascade). They set a `dont_unload` property of each of their children to `True`. They use the `QueryUnload()` event handler to unload what they have loaded.

This pattern is followed throughout. Any form that launches another is responsible for unloading what it has launched.

You'll see as we get into the programming that there's very little here that you haven't seen already. Putting it to use in this project should firmly anchor object-oriented habits in your mental arsenal.

THE PROGRAMMING STRATEGY

I don't begin any project until I've thought out a programming strategy. A good strategy lets you build a small amount of code and then test it. Once it works, you go on to another small amount of code. Coding can progress rapidly, if you get the strategy right.

In MyTime, I decided to start on the main menu. (Did I hear someone raise the *top-down* or *bottom-up* issue? Theorists told us once that *top-down* was the right way to code. In practice, this doesn't work in many situations. You'll see one right here.)

The main menu can be coded as a standalone application. It won't do anything except look good, but then, that's its job. This is a program I use many times each day. It had better look good. After all, its going to remind me of its author every time I see it. This is like smiling into the mirror.

After the main menu, however, you can't proceed top-down. Here we'll have to go back to bottom-up. The tools, of course, can't do anything without data. You need to create the database programs to build small sample databases so that you have somthing to let the tools work with. (Actually, you could write programs specially to create the samples. Then test the tools with the samples. Write the databases last. That will make the top-down purists happy. It will also be a stupid waste of time.)

Thus, we'll create forms and hook them to the ODBs for each of the four databases next. We can use these as standalone programs while we add data. Once they've served their purpose in creating databases, we'll just launch them from the Edit buttons of the appropriate tools. They won't know or care who launches them. If you do your design right, you won't have to change a line of code. (This never works in practice, by the way, but if it's your design target, you can often come very close to this ideal.)

Lastly, we'll create the tools. I created the projects first because the projects cascade is the most challenging tool. Having it running helped me keep track of the rest of the work. The only functionally determined order here is that the time tool comes last because the other tools provide its data.

I brought up each tool in the same order:

- Launch the form
- Program `Resize()` for good looks

- Read the data
- Display the data

In the case of the project's cascade, I programmed it to display a single board. Then I went on to handle the array of boards. The project chart was actually a separate project. It's development sequence is shown in Figure 14-8 on the top board.

Doing the time tool last let me postpone what seemed like a knotty problem: emitting chores to appropriate days given the list of chores. I started the chore panel by simply having it display all the chores. That way I knew that I was reading the database correctly. Then I discovered that the knotty problem was trivial. You'll see when we're there.

As each tool started working, I hung it under the main menu. After doing the first two tools, I actually got the last two to work *without changing a line of code.* In this book, I'll leave that assembly to happen all at once, in the final chapter. It'll be an easy and fun finish to a book that I hope has been fun, but I'm sure it's taken some old-fashioned hard work, too.

Saving the assembly for last is my not-too-sneaky way of showing you how much fun object-oriented programming can be, leaving you remembering this and forgetting that objects take hard work to program correctly.

Summary

This chapter began Part II of this book, where we'll build a serious, object-oriented system. For most procedural programmers, it's not obvious how object techniques can fit together into a complete system. This part will show you how it's done. In this chapter, we looked at the design.

We'll begin our time-management system with a good-looking main menu. It will have a complete resizing capability, displaying six pads in a 1×6 array, or 2×3, 3×2, or 6×1, depending on how the user sizes it. The pads toggle five lower-level tools and the sixth pad is for eXit.

At the next level down, the calendar is a control tool that the others read to set their working date. The project's cascade and schedule show project components and appointments, respectively. The tasks tool handles both to do list items and chores, which are regurlarly recurring to do items. The time tool summarizes your day's appointments, to do items, chores, and projects.

Under the project's cascade, the schedule and the tasks tools are four databases for projects, appointments, to do list items, and chores. Each of these is managed through a data entry panel. The four panels have a consistent set of navigation buttons and custom data entry screens.

The organization of the code parallels the forms in the system. At the bottom level, four classes model appointments, projects, to do list items, and chores. Four ODBs, one for each class, manage the disk-based storage of these objects. Four data entry form-based classes contain these ODBs.

At the next level, the tools provide edit buttons that launch the data entry forms. When the tools are launched and after edits, the tools read the ODBs to gather a collection of appropriate objects for display in ListBoxes. Appointments, for example, are gathered from the undeleted appointment objects in the ODB that match the calendar's selected date. The time tool is an exception in that it does not provide data entry access; it simply reports data.

At the highest level, the main menu provides startup and shutdown services. At runtime, it simply toggles each tools' Visible property. Startup includes launching each tool with a False Visible property. It also includes passing references to relevant sibling objects, such as a reference to the calendar for the schedule tool. Shutdown correctly unloads each loaded form.

The development strategy is part top-down and part bottom-up. We'll begin with the main menu, which we'll code as a standalone tool in the next chapter. Then we'll bring up the individual tools by working bottom up, coding the class and ODB-containing form, first. We'll use these as standalone databases to provide test data for the tools. We'll code each tool as its needed ODB or ODBs are finished.

We'll code the time tool last because it reports on all the othe ODB's contents. As a final step, we'll assemble all the individual tools under the main menu to create the finished system.

In Chapter 15, we'll build the main menu, but we won't worry about hooking its pads up to tools. (When we start final assembly in Chapter 22, you'll see that this is simple.) Chapter 15 is the longest in this book, by far. It's also got the most neat stuff! The main menu is fun to play with, highly visual but small, because its graphics are done with form-based objects, not with bitmaps. You'll really like the way you can resize it.

A Super Main Menu

15

*H*ow should we drive the choices that will be available in the MyTime system?

A classic menu could do the trick, a set of icons would work, but I have something else in mind.

Old-fashioned menus just don't hold much interest for me anymore, and those little icons are almost always too tiny to be helpful until you know a program really well.

The interface of the late '90s is based on browser technology. You have lots of pictures and as you move the mouse pointer around, different pictures are highlighted. You can click a highlighted item when you want to jump into its area. The whole page becomes a menu.

Another thing I like is when you expand or contract a browser page, the whole thing adjusts. I'm going to go further here. After all, this menu is the first thing I see every time I use my MyTime system. I want it to be a thing I take some pride in having written, so I'm going to teach this menu page to reformat itself.

You've probably noticed that this chapter is a long one. I'm deliberately spending more time and more bytes on this front end because I think the starting point should be a showcase for your programming talents. We'll do more work than we need to, but we'll see a super result. This coding is all visual, so it's all fun work.

Take a look at Figure 15-1. I've launched MyTime four different times, so you can see some of the possibilities. What you can't see is how nicely MyTime chooses the best layout as you resize the window. It will change from 1×6 to 2×3, then 3×2, and finally 6×1 as you change the proportions of the window.

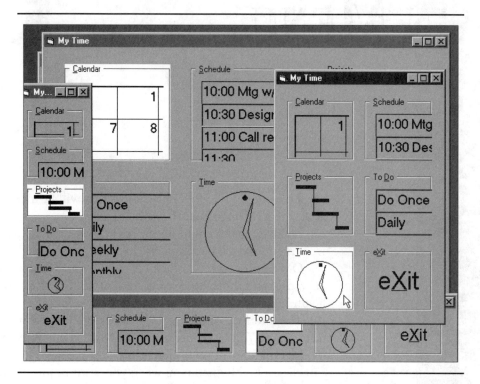

Figure 15-1
Four MyTime menu layouts are on-screen.

Look closely at the calendar drawing in the different views. You can see that this sketch is programmed to vary as the size of its frame varies.

In this chapter we'll begin with code that handles the layout. We'll place six Frames on a Form, and then we'll teach the Form to arrange the Frames to fit the available space.

Then we'll go on to add a draw method for each of the Frames. You'll see that the calendar takes a lot of trouble. I've kept the schedule and to do list options dead simple. The time and project options are in between. The eXit option isn't quite as simple as it looks.

After we've programmed each Frame's picture, we'll go on to add menu functionality. We'll start by teaching the highlight to follow the mouse pointer. We'll also add keyboard operations, which will take a bit of kludging, but will work successfully in the end.

We'll make the eXit option actually exit, but we'll not hook the other options to objects until we reach the last chapter, where we'll do the final assembly.

Before we start any of this work, however, we'll need to take a brief look at the Frame object.

UNDERSTANDING FRAMES

There are two things you need to know about the Frame that may not be obvious at first.

Frames Are Like Forms

First, if you create a component in a Frame, it's part of that Frame, just as objects created in a Form are part of the Form. If you move the object to the edge of the Frame, the part that is outside the Frame is clipped off. Only the part within the Frame shows.

Coordinate addresses of objects in Frames are given relative to the top-left corner of the Frame, just as Form-hosted components are positioned relative to the top-left corner of the Form.

The Frame will contain a component if the component is created in the Frame. That means that you should think when you have Frames on a Form. Do you want the component in the Form or in a Frame? The component's owner is determined when it is born.

That also means that you can't double-click the toolbar to get the component you want as readily as you can without Frames. If the component lands in a Frame, it becomes part of the Frame. If it lands on the Form (or overlapping and not entirely within a Frame) it is part of the Form.

The same goes for pasting from the clipboard. If a Frame happens to be in the upper-left corner, it will contain anything you paste into it. If the Frame you want as a container is not in the upper-left corner, pasting will not put a new component into the Frame.

When you move a component that is not contained in a Frame over the Frame, it may be shown in front of or behind the Frame. You can control this using the Z-order, but it's simpler to put things that should show on a Frame actually in the Frame.

The second point to note about Frame objects is their size.

Frames are Bigger than They Look

Let's call the Frame's available space within its borders its *client area*. This space is smaller than the Frame's Height and Width properties suggest.

First, if the border type is 3-D, the bottom and side borders are three pixels wide. That's 45 twips if you're at the standard 15 twips per pixel.

More importantly, and less obviously, the Frame's top is several pixels above the visible Frame boundary. This allows space to display the Caption property. Figure 15-2 shows a white Frame on a gray background, which reveals this feature.

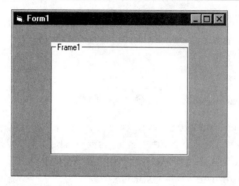

Figure 5-1
The Frame's Top *extends above its top border.*

This is a good approximation of the distance, in twips, from the top of the Frame to the start of the Frame's client area:

```
frame_top = 1.5 * FontSize * Screen.TwipsPerPixelY
```

With a standard setup, that's 180 twips. You'll see that I sometimes calculate this and other times I just throw in a ballpark 200 twips. It's surprising how often those top twips ruin an otherwise good-looking sketch if you don't allow for them.

With these notes on Frames, you'll understand some otherwise mysterious adjustments.

For example, I start the first task in the project sketch at:

```
.Y1 = 200 + ( 0.15 * (ht - 200) )
```

Just using 15 percent of the total height wouldn't work when the `Frame`'s height is small. The task line would overwrite the `Frame`'s caption. That adjustment keeps the task line below the caption.

Let's get started on the `Form` and its layout capability.

LAYING OUT FRAMES ON A FORM

This form-based class begins our work on the MyTime project, so create a directory for that project. As we go along, you'll see that we'll copy the other classes we've created into this directory as they're needed. Point your Visual Basic shortcut to this working directory. You may want to make a copy of the shortcut called MyTime (or something along those lines) that points to your working directory.

Begin with a new standard .EXE project. Name the project prjMyTim and name the Form frmMyTim. Save and accept the default file names.

Dropping in the Frames

Extend the default Form until it's fairly large. I'm using one that's 5,000 twips tall and 8,000 twips wide.

Double-click just one Frame onto the Form. (If you double-click a second one, it will land squarely on top of, and therefore be contained in, the first.) Position it in the upper-left. Size it to fit in a 2 rows, 3 frames across each row arrangement.

The order here will be important if you want to follow my work. If you start in a different position, you won't match my arrangement. That's OK, of course, if it's what you have in mind.

Name the Frame fraOpts, as in *FRA*me menu *OPT*ion*S*. The other properties can all be left at their defaults.

Copy the Frame to the clipboard and paste just one frame back onto the Form. Accept Visual Basic's offer to create a control array. (If you paste again without moving the Frame, the next Frame will be contained by the first because it will paste into exactly the same location.)

Drag `fraOpts(1)` to the top center, and paste another and drag it to the top-right corner. Continue, filling the bottom half of the Form with fraOpts(3), fraOpts(4), and fraOpts(5). Using Format⇨Align is faster than trying to position manually, by the way. Figure 15-3 shows my work at this point.

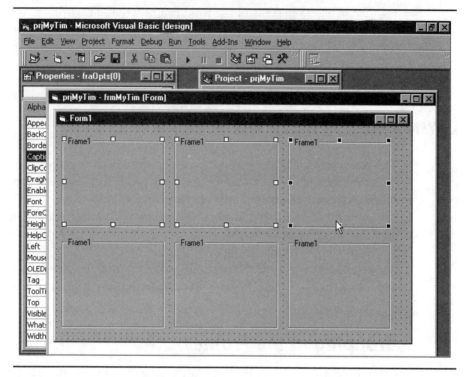

Figure 5-3
Frames in place to start programming.

Starting the Resize Method

This resize() event-handling method will be our most complex yet. We'll start with the code that does the layout magic. This is probably the most fun part.

First, we'll want resize() to adjust the coordinates to preserve a minimum size. Setting Height or Width triggers another resize event, which will call resize() recursively. Because this is a large routine, eliminating this recursion is important. Begin by dropping a recursion preventer into the declarations, this way:

```
' recursion suppresants:
    Private resizing As Boolean
```

While you're in the declarations section, add appropriate starting and ending comments, and add this code to start the `resize()` routine on the right foot:

```
Private Sub Form_Resize()

' outta here if form is minimized
    If frmMyTim.WindowState = vbMinimized Then Exit Sub

' outta here if we're in here
    If resizing Then Exit Sub

    resizing = True

' enforce minimum height
    If Height < 1400 Then Height = 1400

' enforce minimum total size
    If Height + Width < 6000 Then Width = 6000 - Height

    resizing = False

End Sub
```

When you test at this point, you'll see that your minima are enforced and that your Frames are simply truncated because they're fixed in position at design time. That's the first thing we're going to change.

In the following code, we define a constant that we'll use to switch from, for example, 1×6 to 2×3 as the aspect ratio (height to width) of the Form changes. Here I've set it to 3, which changes to 6 rows from 3 when the Form's height is more than 3 times its width. You can experiment with different settings after you add the rest of the code in this section.

This code shows one of the rare times when I think that using the colon to write two statements on a single line is a good idea. It's in the `Select Case` block, here:

```
' layout may be 1x6, 2x3, 3x2 or 6x1
    Dim cols As Byte, rows As Byte

    Dim cli_height As Integer, cli_width As Integer

' client area is smaller than form coordinates
    cli_height = Height - 400
    cli_width = Width - 120
```

```
' round down to a full pixel
cli_height = cli_height / tppY
cli_height = cli_height * tppY

cli_width = cli_width / tppX
cli_width = cli_width * tppX

Dim aspect_ratio As Single
aspect_ratio = cli_height / cli_width

Const key_ratio = 3 ' used to choose layout

' Choose layout
Select Case aspect_ratio

    Case Is > key_ratio
        rows = 6: cols = 1

    Case Is > 1
        rows = 3: cols = 2

    Case Is > (1 / key_ratio)
        rows = 2: cols = 3

    Case Else
        rows = 1: cols = 6

End Select
```

Now that we've computed a layout, all we have to do is size and position the Frames appropriately. This will involve working with the `Screen.TwipsPerPixelX` and `Screen.TwipsPerPixelY` values extensively, so it's both easier and more efficient to read these into `Private` variables. Add this declaration and method:

```
' Useful shorthands:
    Private tppX As Integer, tppY As Integer

Private Sub Form_Initialize()

    tppX = Screen.TwipsPerPixelX
    tppY = Screen.TwipsPerPixelY

End Sub
```

Now we're ready to go back and continue extending the `resize()` method. Do this by deciding how to divide the client area between blank space and Frame space. Again, do that by defining and using a constant that you can adjust when you get the routine running. I'm using 80 percent of the available space for Frames and 20 percent for blank space.

We divide the blank space, horizontally and vertically, into as many pieces as needed. For example, showing two rows requires three blank spaces (above, between, and below the rows). After calculating the size of the blank space, adjust everything carefully to fit exact pixels, as this shows:

```
Dim vert_spacer As Integer, hori_spacer As Integer
Dim fram_width As Integer, fram_height As Integer

Const for_options = 0.8 ' 80% for options, 20% space

fram_width = cli_width * for_options / cols
fram_height = cli_height * for_options / rows

fram_width = fram_width / tppX
fram_height = fram_height / tppY

fram_width = fram_width * tppX
fram_height = fram_height * tppY

vert_spacer = (cli_height - (rows * fram_height)) _
    / (rows + 1)
hori_spacer = (cli_width - (cols * fram_width)) _
    / (cols + 1)

vert_spacer = vert_spacer / tppY
vert_spacer = vert_spacer * tppY

hori_spacer = hori_spacer / tppX
hori_spacer = hori_spacer * tppX
```

Next, set up some variables and hide all the Frames, this way:

```
Dim opt_num As Byte
Dim r As Byte, c As Byte

Dim top As Integer, left As Integer

For c = 0 To 5
    fraOpts(c).Visible = False
Next c
```

Then you're ready to actually position each Frame. That's probably easier than you guessed. Just loop over the rows in an outer loop and over the columns in an inner loop. Keep a running tally of where you are as you go, and your Frames are positioned and sized. This code works:

```
        top = vert_spacer

    For r = 1 To rows

        left = hori_spacer

        For c = 1 To cols

            With fraOpts(opt_num)
                .top = top
                .left = left
                .Height = fram_height
                .Width = fram_width
                .Visible = True
            End With

            left = left + fram_width + hori_spacer
            opt_num = opt_num + 1

        Next c

        top = top + fram_height + vert_spacer
    Next r
```

Last, you'll want to see where everything lands. This code will create an informed Immediate window:

```
        Debug.Print " "
    Debug.Print "Form Ht WD:" & _
        Str(frmMyTim.Height) & Str(frmMyTim.Width)
    Debug.Print "Frame Ht Wd:" & _
        Str(fraOpts(0).Height) & Str(fraOpts(0).Width)
    Debug.Print "Tops" & _
        Str(fraOpts(0).top) & Str(fraOpts(3).top)
    Debug.Print "Lefts" & _
        Str(fraOpts(0).left) & Str(fraOpts(1).left) & _
        Str(fraOpts(2).left)
```

When you get this code running, you'll see the basic functionality come to life. It's fun!

Figure 15-4 shows me playing with the system at this point. (Actually, it doesn't show the fun, which is in the movement. It's like one frame from a movie.)

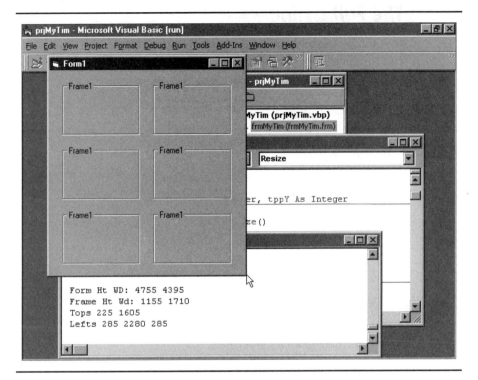

Figure 15-4
Having fun with the Form.

One more step will add some polish to the finished project. When Visual Basic loads your form, it positions the components as the .FRM file suggests. Then it starts to display the form. While it's doing this, it finds that your code's resize() is modifying things, so you see an annoying wiggle on-screen.

To avoid this, have the default calculations set into the .FRM file, so launch your form and then exit the form without manually resizing. Your Immediate window (Ctrl+G) shows the coordinates after your resize() code does its calculations. You have to go back to the Properties window to enter these for the individual components.

This is easier to do, by far, if you select groups of components and enter the values just once. Select all six Frames, for instance, and enter their Height and Width. Then select the three in the top row and enter the first Top value, and so on.

The Full Listing

If you have pizza sauce on the book's disk, Listing 15-1 shows the full editable portion of frmMyTim.frm to this point.

Listing 15-1
The Form with Frames and Layout logic

```
' frmMyTim.frm — main menu for MyTime system
' Copyright 1997, Martin L. Rinehart

Option Explicit

' recursion suppresants:
    Private resizing As Boolean

' Useful shorthands:
    Private tppX As Integer, tppY As Integer

Private Sub Form_Initialize()

    tppX = Screen.TwipsPerPixelX
    tppY = Screen.TwipsPerPixelY

End Sub

Private Sub Form_Resize()

' outta here if form is minimized
    If frmMyTim.WindowState = vbMinimized Then Exit Sub

' outta here if we're in here
    If resizing Then Exit Sub

    resizing = True

' enforce minimum height
    If Height < 1400 Then Height = 1400

' enforce minimum total size
    If Height + Width < 6000 Then Width = 6000 - Height

    resizing = False

' layout may be 1x6, 2x3, 3x2 or 6x1
    Dim cols As Byte, rows As Byte

    Dim cli_height As Integer, cli_width As Integer
```

```
' client area is smaller than form coordinates
    cli_height = Height - 400
    cli_width = Width - 120

    ' round down to a full pixel
    cli_height = cli_height / tppY
    cli_height = cli_height * tppY

    cli_width = cli_width / tppX
    cli_width = cli_width * tppX

    Dim aspect_ratio As Single
    aspect_ratio = cli_height / cli_width

    Const key_ratio = 3 ' used to choose layout

' Choose layout
    Select Case aspect_ratio

        Case Is > key_ratio
            rows = 6: cols = 1

        Case Is > 1
            rows = 3: cols = 2

        Case Is > (1 / key_ratio)
            rows = 2: cols = 3

        Case Else
            rows = 1: cols = 6

    End Select

    Dim vert_spacer As Integer, hori_spacer As Integer
    Dim fram_width As Integer, fram_height As Integer

    Const for_options = 0.8 ' 80% for options, 20% space

    fram_width = cli_width * for_options / cols
    fram_height = cli_height * for_options / rows

    fram_width = fram_width / tppX
    fram_height = fram_height / tppY

    fram_width = fram_width * tppX
    fram_height = fram_height * tppY
```

(continued)

The Form with Frames and Layout logic

```
vert_spacer = (cli_height - (rows * fram_height)) _
    / (rows + 1)
hori_spacer = (cli_width - (cols * fram_width)) _
    / (cols + 1)

vert_spacer = vert_spacer / tppY
vert_spacer = vert_spacer * tppY

hori_spacer = hori_spacer / tppX
hori_spacer = hori_spacer * tppX

Dim opt_num As Byte
Dim r As Byte, c As Byte

Dim top As Integer, left As Integer

For c = 0 To 5
    fraOpts(c).Visible = False
Next c

top = vert_spacer

For r = 1 To rows

    left = hori_spacer

    For c = 1 To cols

        With fraOpts(opt_num)
            .top = top
            .left = left
            .Height = fram_height
            .Width = fram_width
            .Visible = True
        End With

        left = left + fram_width + hori_spacer
        opt_num = opt_num + 1

    Next c

    top = top + fram_height + vert_spacer
Next r

Debug.Print " "
Debug.Print "Form Ht WD:" & _
    Str(frmMyTim.Height) & Str(frmMyTim.Width)
Debug.Print "Frame Ht Wd:" & _
    Str(fraOpts(0).Height) & Str(fraOpts(0).Width)
```

```
        Debug.Print "Tops" & _
            Str(fraOpts(0).top) & Str(fraOpts(3).top)
        Debug.Print "Lefts" & _
            Str(fraOpts(0).left) & Str(fraOpts(1).left) & _
            Str(fraOpts(2).left)

    End Sub

    ' end of frmMyTim.frm
```

PROGRAMMING CALENDAR SKETCHES

Now we're going to begin graphics programming. That is, we're going to use a program in lieu of using other forms of graphics, such as bitmaps.

I like bitmaps and genuine artwork. As the saying goes, a picture is worth a thousand words, but in an executable file, a picture can be a lot bigger than that. A thousand average words will tip the scale at 56K. Using 24-bit color, that's good for a bitmap only about 48 pixels square. Programming graphics can give you the benefit of graphic images that can be as large as you like, without worrying about the executable file's size.

This is a particularly important technique to know for building user-friendly Web sites. No one enjoys waiting for graphics to load. Even off the Web, our gigabyte hard disks are not going empty for long. Bitmapped graphics can eat them up quickly. For example, each screen shot in this book takes as much disk space as the text and listings for half an average chapter.

Programmed sketches will be much smaller and faster than bitmaps, although they'll require some hard work and creativity. The calendar is particularly complex. You'll see in our other sketches that a little bit of creative cheating can make the programming very simple. In the appointment schedule graphic, for instance, as the Frame shrinks less of the graphic shows.

The calendar is done much more creatively. If you look at Figure 15-1 again, you'll see that the larger calendar shows days 1, 7, and 8 with day 1 on Monday. This really suggests a calendar. As the calendar shrinks, however, I move day 1 back to Sunday, showing as little as a single day. This is less suggestive of a calendar, but it's the best we can do with so little space.

Again, this is a slick interface technique. Users will really see that the sketch is a calendar when the program is launched. Then they can reduce the size of this menu as they become more familiar with the program. Let's roll up our sleeves and get going.

We'll start with a pair of lines that will provide coordinates for the rest of the calendar. First, though, let's take care of some bookkeeping.

Preparing for the Calendar

We could do all our drawing in place in the `resize()` routine, but that would become an unwieldy behemoth. I've created a `hide()` and a `draw()` routine for each of the six sketches we're using. You should call the `hide()` method just before you turn off the Frames. The following shows the line to add, in context in the `resize()` routine:

```
Dim top As Integer, left As Integer

hide_cal

For c = 0 To 5
    fraOpts(c).Visible = False
Next c
```

Then add the `draw()` call. This is the line, again in context in the `resize()` routine:

```
Next r

draw_cal fraOpts(on_cal)

Debug.Print " "
```

It's called with a particular frame. I've used an enum to name the frames. Add this `Enum` to your declarations section:

```
Private Enum option_numbers
    on_cal = 0
    on_sched
    on_proj
    on_todo
    on_time
    on_exit
End Enum
```

The names in the `Enum` are consistent with the names of the hide and draw routines, this way:

```
hide_whatever
draw_whatever fraOpts(on_whatever)
```

While you're in the declarations, create this constant:

```
Const cap_width = 900 ' frame size at which captions
    ' are spelled out completely
```

As a last step, add an empty `hide()` and a nearly empty `draw()` routine. These go just above the file-end comment:

```
Private Sub hide_cal()

End Sub

Private Sub draw_cal(ByRef f As Frame)

    If f.Width > cap_width Then
        f.Caption = " &Calendar "
    Else
        f.Caption = "&Cal"
    End If

End Sub
```

You can see that the Frame parameter is clearly labeled `ByRef` because we'll be setting its `Caption` here. That's set, depending on space available, to a full or abbreviated name. The leading and trailing blanks in the full name give a little nicer appearance than you have without them.

You might want to change the design time caption of the top-left frame at this time. Use `" &Calendar "` with the extra blanks. It won't matter at run time, but it might help to remind you.

Now we can go on to adding the top and left lines, which set coordinates for the rest of the calendar.

Add the Calendar's Top and Left Lines

In your top-left `Frame`, add a line for the left edge of the calendar and another for the top. Make these changes in the Properties window:

- Set the left line's `Name` to `linCalLf`
- Set the top line's `Name` to `linCalTp`
- Set both line's `BorderWidth` to 3

Your design should look like Figure 15-5.

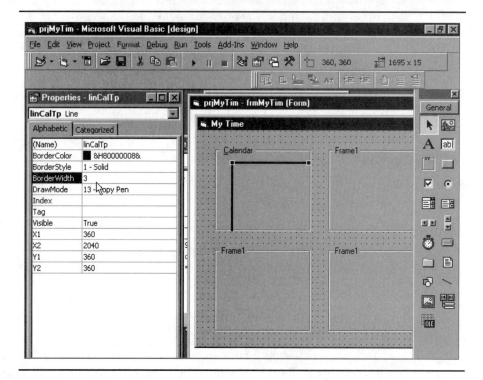

Figure 15-5
The two key lines are positioned and sized.

This code in `cal_draw()` correctly positions and sizes the lines:

```
Dim tp As Integer, ht As Integer
Dim lf As Integer, wd As Integer

' find clear coordinates (losing frame's frame)
    tp = 1.5 * FontSize * tppY
    lf = 3 * tppX

    ht = f.Height - tp - (2 * tppY)
    wd = f.Width - (2 * lf)

    Dim cal_tp As Integer, cal_lf As Integer
    cal_tp = tp + 0.1 * ht
    cal_lf = lf + 0.1 * wd
```

```
With linCalLf
    .X1 = cal_lf
    .X2 = cal_lf
    .Y1 = cal_tp
    .Y2 = (0.95 * ht) + tp
    .BorderWidth = 1 + Int(wd / 1000)
    .Visible = True
End With

With linCalTp
    .X1 = cal_lf
    .X2 = (0.95 * wd) + lf
    .Y1 = cal_tp
    .Y2 = cal_tp
    .BorderWidth = 1 + Int(ht / 1000)
    .Visible = True
End With
```

That adjustment to the `BorderWidth` makes the lines fatter as the space becomes larger. I first left the lines set at the design time value, but this didn't look right in smaller sizes. You can try it yourself by commenting these lines out and then running and shrinking the form.

Add the Grid Lines

We'll show one or two grid lines in each dimension, as space permits. You have to add two vertical and two horizontal lines. I've used these names:

- `linCalGrdHor1`
- `linCalGrdHor2`
- `linCalGrdVer1`
- `linCalGrdVer2`

There aren't any other Properties settings to adjust. Your design should look like the one shown in Figure 15-6.

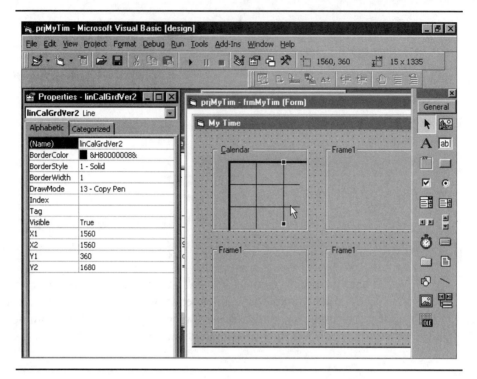

Figure 15-6
Adding calendar grid lines.

These lines are shown with the following logic. It sets constants that determine how wide and tall the frame must be to use the two day or two week display. Below these minima, only one line is displayed; otherwise, we show both. This is the code:

```
Const wd2 = 1200 ' > wd2, show 2 days
Const ht2 = 1200 ' > ht2, show 2 weeks

If ht < ht2 Then ' show 1 week

    With linCalGrdHor1
        .X1 = cal_lf
        .X2 = linCalTp.X2
        .Y1 = cal_tp + 0.75 * ht
        .Y2 = .Y1
        .Visible = True
    End With

Else ' show 2 weeks
```

```
    With linCalGrdHor1
        .X1 = cal_lf
        .X2 = linCalTp.X2
        .Y1 = cal_tp + (0.4 * ht)
        .Y2 = .Y1
        .Visible = True
    End With

    With linCalGrdHor2
        .X1 = cal_lf
        .X2 = linCalTp.X2
        .Y1 = cal_tp + (0.8 * ht)
        .Y2 = .Y1
        .Visible = True
    End With

End If

If wd < wd2 Then ' show 1 day

    With linCalGrdVer1
        .X1 = cal_lf + (0.75 * wd)
        .X2 = .X1
        .Y1 = cal_tp
        .Y2 = linCalLf.Y2
        .Visible = True
    End With

Else ' show 2 days

    With linCalGrdVer1
        .X1 = cal_lf + (0.4 * wd)
        .X2 = .X1
        .Y1 = cal_tp
        .Y2 = linCalLf.Y2
        .Visible = True
    End With

    With linCalGrdVer2
        .X1 = cal_lf + (0.8 * wd)
        .X2 = .X1
        .Y1 = cal_tp
        .Y2 = linCalLf.Y2
        .Visible = True
    End With

End If
```

You can run this and see just how flexible that calendar display really is. When you add the day numbers inside the calendar grid cells does this becomes an unmistakable calendar sketch.

Adding the Day Labels

To complete the calendar, we'll need three day labels. We'll always show day 1 in the top week. If space permits, we'll show it in the second day. If there's room for a second row we'll show day 8 under day 1. We'll show days 7 and 8 if two days fit.

Begin by setting your Form's FontSize property to 14. This will separate our graphic lettering from the normal Windows lettering.

With the FontSize set, add three labels within the calendar Frame. Use the Properties window to set these values:

- Set Names to lblCalDay1, lblCalDay7, and lblCalDay8
- Set each Alignment to 1, Right Justify
- Set Caption to 1, 7, and 8, respectively

Position the labels near the upper-right corners of the calendar grid's cells, positioned for displaying two days and two weeks.

When you add the following code, you'll be able to run and see the effects we're after. There's still a bug. If you shrink the Form, you may see unused labels floating wherever you left them. Don't worry about it. We'll fix that in our cleanup step.

This is the day label code:

```
' Place day labels

    If wd < wd2 Then ' showing one day

        With lblCalDay1
            .top = cal_tp + _
                (tppY * linCalTp.BorderWidth)
            .left = linCalGrdVer1.X1 - 220
            .Height = 350
            .Width = 200
            .Visible = True
        End With

        If ht >= ht2 Then ' showing two weeks

            With lblCalDay8
```

```
                .top = linCalGrdHor1.Y1 + tppY
                .left = linCalGrdVer1.X1 - 320
                .Height = 400
                .Width = 300
                .Visible = True
            End With

        End If

    Else ' Showing two days

        With lblCalDay1
            .top = cal_tp + _
                (tppY * linCalTp.BorderWidth)
            .left = linCalGrdVer2.X1 - 320
            .Height = 400
            .Width = 300
            .Visible = True
        End With

        If ht >= ht2 Then ' showing two weeks

            With lblCalDay1
                .top = cal_tp + _
                    (tppY * linCalTp.BorderWidth)
                .left = linCalGrdVer2.X1 - 320
                .Height = 400
                .Width = 300
                .Visible = True
            End With

            With lblCalDay7
                .top = linCalGrdHor1.Y1 + tppY
                .left = linCalGrdVer1.X1 - 320
                .Height = 400
                .Width = 300
                .Visible = True
            End With

            With lblCalDay8
                .top = linCalGrdHor1.Y1 + tppY
                .left = linCalGrdVer2.X1 - 320
                .Height = 400
                .Width = 300
                .Visible = True
            End With

        End If

    End If
```

Add the Finishing Touch

You now have a really slick calendar sketch that fits itself to the available space. The finishing touch is to hide all the elements before you resize and reposition them. We already have the `hide()` skeleton available. Fill it in this way:

```
Private Sub hide_cal()

    linCalLf.Visible = False
    linCalTp.Visible = False

    linCalGrdHor1.Visible = False
    linCalGrdHor2.Visible = False
    linCalGrdVer1.Visible = False
    linCalGrdVer2.Visible = False

    lblCalDay1.Visible = False
    lblCalDay7.Visible = False
    lblCalDay8.Visible = False

End Sub
```

That leaves a tiny problem. The 1 day label is too tall when you hit the absolute minimum `Frame` height. That's not the height you have if you stretch the `Form` to a wide but short size, showing one row of six sketches. This problem doesn't show up in that arrangement.

The minimum `Frame` height is achieved by finding a 2 row by 3 sketch size at the smallest permissible combination of total height and width. This is the case where the 1 doesn't quite fit.

You could eliminate this glitch by increasing the absolute minimum size permitted. You could make it really elegant by varying the font size to go up and down with the Frames' heights.

You could also say to yourself that the squish was something the user chose. If that's the way the users really want to view these sketches, they'll just have to tolerate a little blemish. I don't normally find this last position acceptable, but I'm going to go with it because this case is uncommon and the damage is minor and only cosmetic. The easy way to fix it is to drag out the corner of the `Form` to a nicer size!

Congratulations. You've built the hardest of the six sketches. Compared to this calendar, the schedule component is just a cheat. It works nicely, though. Listing 15-2 shows the completed `draw_cal()` routine. On disk, 15-02 has the complete .FRM and project files. If you're having trouble with a portion of the file not show here, the full program is available in Listing 15-9 and the noneditable parts of the file are shown in Appendix C.

Listing 15-2
The complete draw_cal() method

```
Private Sub draw_cal(ByRef f As Frame)

    If f.Width > cap_width Then
        f.Caption = " &Calendar "
    Else
        f.Caption = "&Cal"
    End If

    Dim tp As Integer, ht As Integer
    Dim lf As Integer, wd As Integer

' find clear coordinates (losing frame's frame)
    tp = 1.5 * FontSize * tppY
    lf = 3 * tppX

    ht = f.Height - tp - (2 * tppY)
    wd = f.Width - (2 * lf)

    Dim cal_tp As Integer, cal_lf As Integer
    cal_tp = tp + 0.1 * ht
    cal_lf = lf + 0.1 * wd

    With linCalLf
        .X1 = cal_lf
        .X2 = cal_lf
        .Y1 = cal_tp
        .Y2 = (0.95 * ht) + tp
        .BorderWidth = 1 + Int(wd / 1000)
        .Visible = True
    End With

    With linCalTp
        .X1 = cal_lf
        .X2 = (0.95 * wd) + lf
        .Y1 = cal_tp
        .Y2 = cal_tp
        .BorderWidth = 1 + Int(ht / 1000)
        .Visible = True
    End With

    Const wd2 = 1200 ' > wd2, show 2 days
    Const ht2 = 1200 ' > ht2, show 2 weeks

    If ht < ht2 Then ' show 1 week
```

(continued)

The complete draw_cal() method

```
    With linCalGrdHor1
        .X1 = cal_lf
        .X2 = linCalTp.X2
        .Y1 = cal_tp + 0.75 * ht
        .Y2 = .Y1
        .Visible = True
    End With

Else ' show 2 weeks

    With linCalGrdHor1
        .X1 = cal_lf
        .X2 = linCalTp.X2
        .Y1 = cal_tp + (0.4 * ht)
        .Y2 = .Y1
        .Visible = True
    End With

    With linCalGrdHor2
        .X1 = cal_lf
        .X2 = linCalTp.X2
        .Y1 = cal_tp + (0.8 * ht)
        .Y2 = .Y1
        .Visible = True
    End With

End If

If wd < wd2 Then ' show 1 day

    With linCalGrdVer1
        .X1 = cal_lf + (0.75 * wd)
        .X2 = .X1
        .Y1 = cal_tp
        .Y2 = linCalLf.Y2
        .Visible = True
    End With

Else ' show 2 days

    With linCalGrdVer1
        .X1 = cal_lf + (0.4 * wd)
        .X2 = .X1
        .Y1 = cal_tp
        .Y2 = linCalLf.Y2
        .Visible = True
    End With
```

```
        With linCalGrdVer2
            .X1 = cal_lf + (0.8 * wd)
            .X2 = .X1
            .Y1 = cal_tp
            .Y2 = linCalLf.Y2
            .Visible = True
        End With

    End If

' Place day labels

    If wd < wd2 Then ' showing one day

        With lblCalDay1
            .top = cal_tp + _
                (tppY * linCalTp.BorderWidth)
            .left = linCalGrdVer1.X1 - 220
            .Height = 350
            .Width = 200
            .Visible = True
        End With

        If ht >= ht2 Then ' showing two weeks

            With lblCalDay8
                .top = linCalGrdHor1.Y1 + tppY
                .left = linCalGrdVer1.X1 - 320
                .Height = 400
                .Width = 300
                .Visible = True
            End With

        End If

    Else ' Showing two days

        With lblCalDay1
            .top = cal_tp + _
                (tppY * linCalTp.BorderWidth)
            .left = linCalGrdVer2.X1 - 320
            .Height = 400
            .Width = 300
            .Visible = True
        End With

        If ht >= ht2 Then ' showing two weeks
```

(continued)

The complete draw_cal() method

```
            With lblCalDay1
                 .top = cal_tp + _
                    (tppY * linCalTp.BorderWidth)
                 .left = linCalGrdVer2.X1 - 320
                 .Height = 400
                 .Width = 300
                 .Visible = True
            End With

            With lblCalDay7
                 .top = linCalGrdHor1.Y1 + tppY
                 .left = linCalGrdVer1.X1 - 320
                 .Height = 400
                 .Width = 300
                 .Visible = True
            End With

            With lblCalDay8
                 .top = linCalGrdHor1.Y1 + tppY
                 .left = linCalGrdVer2.X1 - 320
                 .Height = 400
                 .Width = 300
                 .Visible = True
            End With

        End If

      End If

  End Sub
```

BUILDING A SCHEDULE

To draw the schedule, add four TextBox objects inside the top-middle Frame. Name the first one txtSched, name the second one the same, and accept Visual Basic's offer to create a control array. Name the other two the same, as well.

Add text that is strongly suggestive of an appointment schedule. Remember that as the window is manipulated this text shrinks to where just the upper-left corner will show. My texts are as follows:

- 10:00 Mtg w/Smith
- 10:30 Design Schedule

- 11:00 Call re Status of Chapter 15
- 11:30

Select all four and then choose these settings in the Properties window:

- Left should be 240
- Choose Button Face as the BackColor (System tab)
- Make Width equal 4000
- Set TabStop to False

You'll probably prefer the default (white) color to Button Face, which is the color of dialog windows. When we have the highlight automatically appear under the mouse pointer, you'll see that this is a necessary choice.

Position the TextBoxes as shown in Figure 15-7. I've deliberately chosen Width to overflow the frame size. Windows truncates these at the frame's border. It will also truncate the bottom TextBox. You may find it easier to position the last one with the Properties window.

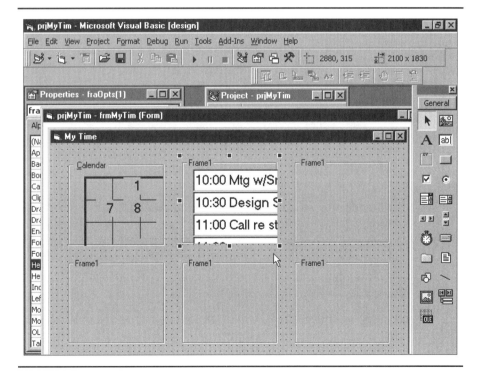

Figure 15-7

Designing the schedule for truncation.

What I'm doing here is simply letting Windows truncate the parts that don't fit. This is the simplest possible way of programming a resizable sketch. When it works, it's delightfully simple. Listing 15-3 shows the entire `hide_sched()` and `draw_sched()` methods.

Listing 15-3
The Schedule code

```
Private Sub hide_sched()

    Dim i As Byte

    For i = 0 To 3
        txtSched(i).Visible = False
    Next i

End Sub


Private Sub draw_sched(ByRef f As Frame)
    Dim i As Byte

    If f.Width > cap_width Then
        f.Caption = " &Schedule "
    Else
        f.Caption = "&Scd"
    End If

    For i = 0 To 3
        txtSched(i).Visible = True
    Next i

End Sub
```

In addition to these routines, which you add just above the file-end comment, don't forget to add calls to these routines. (It works even if you do forget!) The calls go in the `resize()` method after the `hide_cal()` and `draw_cal()` calls.

You might want to change the design `Caption` to `" &Schedule "` before we go on to the project sketch.

ADDING A PROJECT CHART

I've shown a little sketch of a project's dependency chart as my graphic for our projects work. It pretends that we have four subtasks of varying lengths. Tasks 2 and 3 follow task 1, and task 4 follows 3. It's enough to get the idea across.

Like the calendar, it properly squishes and stretches as you resize the Form. Unlike the calendar, it doesn't take a lot of code.

Adding the Lines

If you want, change the design Caption of the upper-right Frame to &Projects and add four lines for the tasks. Name them linTask1 through linTask4. Select all four and change the BorderWidth property to 5.

Now for the connections, add two more lines, call linTaskCon1 and linTaskCon2. You don't need to set any other properties for these last two lines. Figure 15-8 shows the arrangement you want.

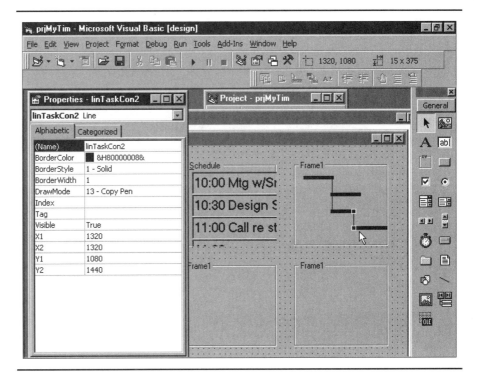

Figure 15-8

Creating a project chart with lines.

Programming the Lines

Listing 15-4 shows the code to position these lines. If you enter the
positioning code a component or two at a time, testing as you go, you
should have this sketch running very quickly.

For example, start with this version:

```
Private Sub draw_proj(ByRef f As Frame)

    If f.Width > cap_width Then
        f.Caption = " &Projects "
    Else
        f.Caption = "&Prj"
    End If

    Dim ht As Integer, wd As Integer
    ht = f.Height
    wd = f.Width

    With linTask1
        .X1 = wd * 0.15
        .X2 = wd * 0.4
        .Y1 = 200 + ((ht - 200) * 0.1)
        .Y2 = .Y1
        .Visible = True
    End With

    With linTask2
        .X1 = wd * 0.4
        .X2 = wd * 0.6
        .Y1 = 200 + ((ht - 200) * 0.35)
        .Y2 = .Y1
        .Visible = True
    End With

End Sub
```

Then add the next two lines this way:

```
    With linTask3
        .X1 = wd * 0.4
        .X2 = wd * 0.75
        .Y1 = 200 + ((ht - 200) * 0.6)
        .Y2 = .Y1
        .Visible = True
    End With
```

```
         With linTask4
             .X1 = wd * 0.75
             .X2 = wd * 0.9
             .Y1 = 200 + ((ht - 200) * 0.85)
             .Y2 = .Y1
             .Visible = True
         End With
```

Your completed routine and the related hide() method look like Listing 15-4.

Listing 15-4
Complete hide() and draw() project sketch methods

```
Private Sub hide_proj()

    linTask1.Visible = False
    linTask2.Visible = False
    linTask3.Visible = False
    linTask4.Visible = False

    linTaskCon1.Visible = False
    linTaskCon2.Visible = False

End Sub

Private Sub draw_proj(ByRef f As Frame)

    If f.Width > cap_width Then
        f.Caption = " &Projects "
    Else
        f.Caption = "&Prj"
    End If

    Dim ht As Integer, wd As Integer
    ht = f.Height
    wd = f.Width

    With linTask1
        .X1 = wd * 0.15
        .X2 = wd * 0.4
        .Y1 = 200 + ((ht - 200) * 0.1)
        .Y2 = .Y1
        .Visible = True
    End With
```

(continued)

Complete hide() and draw() project sketch methods

```
With linTask2
     .X1 = wd * 0.4
     .X2 = wd * 0.6
     .Y1 = 200 + ((ht - 200) * 0.35)
     .Y2 = .Y1
     .Visible = True
End With

With linTask3
     .X1 = wd * 0.4
     .X2 = wd * 0.75
     .Y1 = 200 + ((ht - 200) * 0.6)
     .Y2 = .Y1
     .Visible = True
End With

With linTask4
     .X1 = wd * 0.75
     .X2 = wd * 0.9
     .Y1 = 200 + ((ht - 200) * 0.85)
     .Y2 = .Y1
     .Visible = True
End With

With linTaskCon1
     .X1 = linTask1.X2
     .X2 = .X1
     .Y1 = linTask1.Y2
     .Y2 = linTask3.Y1
     .Visible = True
End With

With linTaskCon2
     .X1 = linTask3.X2
     .X2 = .X1
     .Y1 = linTask3.Y2
     .Y2 = linTask4.Y1
     .Visible = True
End With

End Sub
```

Again, add calls to these routines to your resize() method. After you have it running, go on to the next sketch.

SHOWING THE TO DO LISTS

We're ready to add the to do lists. Here we can take advantage of the fact that names like *Do Once*, *Daily*, and so on are very suggestive. We can use the same technique that produced the appointment sketch here.

Begin by adding four TextBoxes. Create a control array, naming them all txtToDo. I've set the Text properties to these values:

- Do Once
- Daily
- Weekly
- Monthly

Select them all and set these values in the Properties window:

- Left should be 240
- Choose Button Face as the BackColor (System tab)
- Make Width equal 4000
- Set Tabstop to False

The easy way to add the code is to make a copy of the hide() and draw() routines from the appointment schedule and edit them. Your result should be as shown in Listing 15-5.

Listing 15-5
The To Do code

```
Private Sub hide_todo()

    Dim i As Byte

    For i = 0 To 3
        txtToDo(i).Visible = False
    Next i

End Sub

Private Sub draw_todo(ByRef f As Frame)
```

(continued)

The To Do code

```
If f.Width > cap_width Then
    f.Caption = " To &Do "
Else
    f.Caption = "To&Do"
End If

Dim i As Byte

For i = 0 To 3
    txtToDo(i).Visible = True
Next i

End Sub
```

Add calls to these two methods in the `resize()` method and launch the program. Figure 15-9 shows my version at this point.

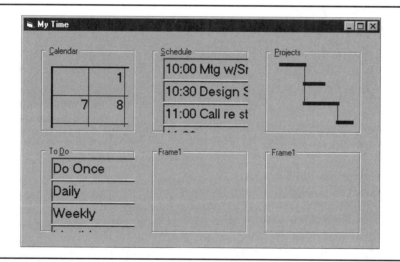

Figure 5-9

Four sketches are complete.

USING AN ICON FOR TIME

I've used a circle, a dot, and four lines to suggest a watch face. (I tried drawing the hands with just two lines, but it didn't look very good.) You probably don't know where I found the dot.

The Windows line drawing routine rounds the ends of lines when the line is over a pixel in width. The line endpoint you specify is actually the center of the line end that Windows draws. This works well if you have, for example, lines meeting at right angles. If your lines aren't too many pixels wide, it looks good.

As a side effect, if you create a line that starts and ends at the same point, you get a dot. For some sizes, the dot is nearly square. In other sizes it's more round. If you make the line very wide, you get an ugly splotch.

Test this in design mode. Add a line to your fifth frame. (You'll need one there anyway.) Using the Properties window, set X1 equal to X2, and Y1 equal to Y2. Then fiddle with BorderWidth. (For small values, you'll need to select something other than your dot, or the handles obscure the dot.) Interesting, no?

Begin by adding the additional pieces.

Adding a Circle, a Dot, and Four Lines

In the fifth Frame, add a shape. Name it shpCircle and set its Shape to 3, Circle. Make it about as large as the Frame. Then put your dot (Line object) up where the 12 would be on a 12-hour clock. Name the dot linDot.

Then add four lines, like the ones you see me adding in Figure 15-10. I've set mine to about 5:05. (Actually, mine's closer to five minutes past 4:45, but it doesn't matter.) Pick a time you like. My hands' lines are named

- linMinLf
- linMinRt
- linHrLf
- linHrRt

You don't need to set any other properties.

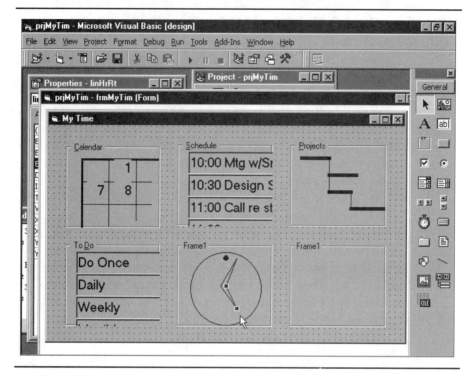

Figure 15-10
Five frames complete.

Programming the Time

Begin by programming the hide_time() method. You need to make
shpCircle, linDot, and the four lines that form the hands all disappear.
Then add this code to draw the watch face:

```
Private Sub draw_time(ByRef f As Frame)

    If f.Width > cap_width Then
        f.Caption = " &Time "
    Else
        f.Caption = "&Time"
    End If

    Dim ht As Integer, wd As Integer
    ht = f.Height
    wd = f.Width
```

```
' Draw a watch face
    Dim Vmid As Integer, Hmid As Integer
    Dim radius As Integer

    With shpCircle
        .top = 1.5 * FontSize * tppY
        .left = 3 * tppX

        .Height = f.Height - .top - (3 * tppY)
        .Width = f.Width - (2 * .left)

        Vmid = .top + (.Height / 2)
        Hmid = .left + (.Width / 2)
        radius = min(.Height, .Width) / 2
        .Visible = True
    End With

End Sub
```

You'll need to add a min() function, like this:

```
Private Function min(a As Integer, b As Integer)

    If a < b Then
        min = a
    Else
        min = b
    End If

End Function
```

Then add calls to hide() and draw() in your resize() method. Run this and you'll have a nicely resizable circle.

Next, add the dot to the draw() method. This code gives you a nicely sized and placed dot:

```
With linDot
    .X1 = Hmid
    .X2 = Hmid
    .Y1 = Vmid - (radius * 0.85)
    .Y2 = .Y1
    .BorderWidth = 2 + radius / 150
    .Visible = True
End With
```

Then add the hands. My hands are done this way:

```
' Draw hands
    With linMinLf
        .X1 = 0.95 * Hmid
        .X2 = 1.15 * Hmid
        .Y1 = Vmid
        .Y2 = linDot.Y1
        .Visible = True
    End With

    With linMinRt
        .X1 = 1.05 * Hmid
        .X2 = linMinLf.X2
        .Y1 = Vmid
        .Y2 = linMinLf.Y2
        .Visible = True
    End With

    With linHrLf
        .X1 = linMinLf.X1
        .X2 = Hmid * 1.2
        .Y1 = linMinLf.Y1
        .Y2 = Vmid + 0.6 * radius
        .Visible = True
    End With

    With linHrRt
        .X1 = linMinRt.X1
        .X2 = linHrLf.X2
        .Y1 = linMinRt.Y1
        .Y2 = linHrLf.Y2
        .Visible = True
    End With
```

You'll have to make your hands point at whatever time you chose, of course. At run time, my hands come up pointing nicely at 5:03. The minute hand isn't arguing with the hour hand, as it is at design time. (As you resize, the argument resumes. Oh well.)

Listing 15-6 shows the hide() and draw() routines. Again, refer to disk file 15-06 for the full file, or look ahead to Listing 15-9.

Listing 15-6
Hide and draw time

```
Private Sub hide_time()

    shpCircle.Visible = False
    linDot.Visible = False
```

```
            linMinLf.Visible = False
            linMinRt.Visible = False

            linHrLf.Visible = False
            linHrRt.Visible = False

End Sub

Private Sub draw_time(ByRef f As Frame)

    If f.Width > cap_width Then
        f.Caption = " &Time "
    Else
        f.Caption = "&Time"
    End If

    Dim ht As Integer, wd As Integer
    ht = f.Height
    wd = f.Width

' Draw a watch face
    Dim Vmid As Integer, Hmid As Integer
    Dim radius As Integer

    With shpCircle
        .top = 1.5 * FontSize * tppY
        .left = 3 * tppX

        .Height = f.Height - .top - (3 * tppY)
        .Width = f.Width - (2 * .left)

        Vmid = .top + (.Height / 2)
        Hmid = .left + (.Width / 2)
        radius = min(.Height, .Width) / 2
        .Visible = True
    End With

    With linDot
        .X1 = Hmid
        .X2 = Hmid
        .Y1 = Vmid - (radius * 0.85)
        .Y2 = .Y1
        .BorderWidth = 2 + radius / 150
        .Visible = True
    End With

' Draw hands
    With linMinLf
```

(continued)

Hide and draw time

```
        .X1 = 0.95 * Hmid
        .X2 = 1.15 * Hmid
        .Y1 = Vmid
        .Y2 = linDot.Y1
        .Visible = True
    End With

    With linMinRt
        .X1 = 1.05 * Hmid
        .X2 = linMinLf.X2
        .Y1 = Vmid
        .Y2 = linMinLf.Y2
        .Visible = True
    End With

    With linHrLf
        .X1 = linMinLf.X1
        .X2 = Hmid * 1.2
        .Y1 = linMinLf.Y1
        .Y2 = Vmid + 0.6 * radius
        .Visible = True
    End With

    With linHrRt
        .X1 = linMinRt.X1
        .X2 = linHrLf.X2
        .Y1 = linMinRt.Y1
        .Y2 = linHrLf.Y2
        .Visible = True
    End With

End Sub
```

The eXit box will complete our sketches.

COMPLETING WITH A TEXT eXIT

In the eXit box we'll show the word *eXit*, showing the action and the shortcut key, simultaneously. Here we'll fiddle with the font to get it right.

Windows defaults to MS Sans Serif, an unexciting but useful choice. Unfortunately, that predates Microsoft's TrueType technology, which means that there are a limited number of font size choices. If you want your font to vary continuously as the size of the Frame varies, you'll need either a TrueType font or another continuously adjustable font.

I've chosen Arial because it's available on almost every Windows computer. Arial is an excellent font, too. Microsoft's font work has been first-class.

Begin by adding a Label to the last Frame. Fill a generous portion of the Frame with it. Set it this way:

- Change the Name to lblExit
- Make Alignment 2, Center
- Make the Caption e&Xit
- Set the font to 24-point Arial

Figure 15-11 shows the completed design.

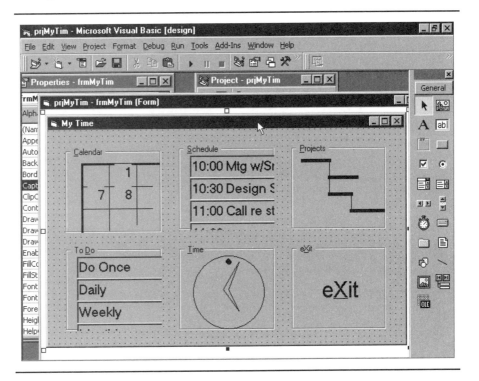

Figure 15-11

All the sketches are designed.

Add the code in Listing 15-7 and add calls to hide() and draw() in your resize() method, and you'll have the full menu. Except, of course, it's not a menu yet; it's just some sketches, but that's what we'll address next.

Listing 15-7
Completing the final sketch

```
Private Sub hide_exit()

    lblExit.Visible = False

End Sub

Private Sub draw_exit(ByRef f As Frame)

    Dim ht As Integer, wd As Integer
    ht = f.Height
    wd = f.Width

    If f.Width > cap_width Then
        f.Caption = " e&Xit "
    Else
        f.Caption = "&Xit"
    End If

    With lblExit

        .left = 0.15 * wd
        .Width = 0.7 * wd

        .Height = ht * 0.4
        .top = (f.Height - .Height) / 2

        .FontSize = min(ht, wd) / 50
        .Visible = True

    End With

End Sub
```

From Sketches to Menu

Have you ever programmed a menu? I don't mean created one using a menu editor, I mean actually programmed the internals. Very few programmers today have ever done this. Mostly you just fire up your favorite programming tool, draw the menu, and you're done.

For those of you who are doing this for the first time, menu programming is a snap. You create a private data member in the menu object to record which menu option is currently highlighted. Then you program a method to highlight a new option.

That method begins by returning the currently highlighted option to normal and then does whatever painting is required to highlight a new option. It then resets the variable that records which option is highlighted.

Two things remain. First, you have to call this highlighting method appropriately. We'll call it with the current `Frame` index whenever we detect mouse movement over a `Frame`. In the last section, we'll go on to add keyboard control — you can ignore that for now.

The last thing is actually to respond to a menu choice. We'll wait for the final chapter to do the final assembly, but we'll hook up the exit option to an exit method, so you can see that it's really no trouble.

Begin with a simple menu setup.

Adding Simple Menu Capability

Start by adding a new `Private` data member to the `frmMyTim` class. Add this line to the declarations section:

```
Private hi_opt As Byte
```

The `hi_opt` variable will get a number from 0 to 5, corresponding to the currently highlighted option. We'll need to set it to a special value when no option is highlighted. You can do this in the `initialize()` method. This is also a good place to highlight the default option, which I've assumed will be zero.

Add these two lines to your `initialize()`:

```
hi_opt = 255 ' Nothing high yet
make_hi 0
```

Then we need to code the `make_hi()` method. That method repaints the currently highlighted option as normal and then highlights the new one. It also updates the `hi_opt` property. For highlighting we can change the `Frame`'s background from `Button Face` to maximum white. (This won't work if the `Button Face` is already high white. If you want to turn this program into a million-copy bestseller, you'd better have your code check this out.)

Add this method after your `min()` function:

```
Public Sub make_hi(onum As Byte)

' Low light old hilighted option

    If hi_opt <> 255 Then ' skip this on initialization
        fraOpts(hi_opt).BackColor = vbButtonFace
    End If

' High light new highlighted option

    fraOpts(onum).BackColor = &HFFFFFF ' hi white
    hi_opt = onum

End Sub
```

You can run this version and your initial option will be highlighted, as Figure 15-12 shows.

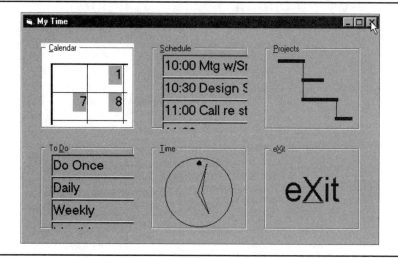

█ Figure 15-12
An option is highlighted.

The figure also shows that leaving the `Labels` colors set to `Button Face` doesn't look too professional. We'll fix that in the next section. For now, let's go on to move the highlight.

For this, pick `fraOpts` in the left (object) dropdown list of the code editor and choose the `MouseMove` event. Then add the simple line shown here:

```
Private Sub fraOpts_MouseMove(Index As Integer, _
    Button As Integer, Shift As Integer, _
    X As Single, Y As Single)

    make_hi (Index)

End Sub
```

I've reformatted the top line to make it fit in this book.

When you run this, you'll see that you've added genuine menuing functionality. It has an annoying flicker and several other not-quite-professional quirks, but the capability's there.

Making the Menu Better

Let's find those quirks. First, the flicker is caused by the repeated MouseMove events calling the make_hi() method. To eliminate it, add this line to the top of your make_hi():

```
If onum = hi_opt Then Exit Sub
```

That's all it takes to change the highlighting from quivering to rock solid.

Now let's do a better job of having the highlight follow the mouse pointer. The problem is that your Labels block the Frame's view of the mouse pointer. Have the mouse pointer enter the schedule Frame over the Labels to see this problem.

Memo To Bill Gates
Bill, ask your Visual Basic folks to take a good look at the Java event handler, OK? They'd code details like unhandled events correctly.

In Java, if a component doesn't handle an event, the event is passed on to a component that *can* handle it. For example, a MouseMove over a Label in our schedule Frame would be passed on to the underlying Frame because the Label doesn't handle MouseMove events. Unfortunately, this doesn't happen in Visual Basic. The event handler passes the event to the top object and then figures its job is done, which really bounces the work right back to us.

Therefore, it's up to us to handle events anywhere we think important. In this application, the two problem areas are the arrays of Labels that mostly cover the schedule and To Do Frames.

A smaller problem is in the eXit Frame. It's possible to move the mouse pointer into this Frame and position it over the eXit Label without Windows triggering a MouseMove as we pass over the bit of Frame that surrounds the label. (Try entering from the left, quickly. It may take a few tries, but you should be able to move the mouse pointer over the Label without highlighting the Frame.)

Fortunately, fixing the problem is simple.

Let your code editor do the heavy lifting involved in adding these three routines (you just add the middle line in each one):

```
Private Sub lblExit_MouseMove(Button As Integer, _
    Shift As Integer, X As Single, Y As Single)

    make_hi (on_exit)

End Sub

Private Sub txtToDo_MouseMove(Index As Integer, _
    Button As Integer, Shift As Integer, _
    X As Single, Y As Single)

    make_hi (on_todo)

End Sub

Private Sub txtSched_MouseMove(Index As Integer, _
    Button As Integer, Shift As Integer, _
    X As Single, Y As Single)

    make_hi (on_sched)

End Sub
```

Now your highlight will do a very nice job of following the mouse pointer. This is becoming fun to use, isn't it?

The last thing I want to handle is the rather ugly color of the Labels in the calendar and eXit boxes when they are highlighted. (The Labels in the schedule and To Do Frames don't change, but I really like the effect. You could change them too, if you like.)

This is a complication we'll add to the make_hi() method. It will handle the Labels as well as the Frames. Add these lines to the highlighting section, after hi_opt has been set to the new value:

```
Select Case hi_opt

    Case on_cal
        lblCalDay1.BackColor = &HFFFFFF
        lblCalDay7.BackColor = &HFFFFFF
        lblCalDay8.BackColor = &HFFFFFF

    Case on_exit
        lblExit.BackColor = &HFFFFFF

End Select
```

When you run this, the labels will be nicely changed when the option is highlighted, but they'll also stay changed when the highlight moves on. For that, we have to add the reverse code to the make_hi() routine. Add this code *before* the value of hi_opt is reset:

```
Select Case hi_opt

    Case on_cal
        lblCalDay1.BackColor = vbButtonFace
        lblCalDay7.BackColor = vbButtonFace
        lblCalDay8.BackColor = vbButtonFace

    Case on_exit
        lblExit.BackColor = vbButtonFace

End Select
```

Listing 15-8 shows the full make_hi() method.

Listing 15-8
The full highlighting method

```
Public Sub make_hi(onum As Byte)

    If onum = hi_opt Then Exit Sub

' Low light old hilighted option

    If hi_opt <> 255 Then ' skip this on initialization
        fraOpts(hi_opt).BackColor = vbButtonFace
    End If

    Select Case hi_opt
```

(continued)

The full highlighting method

```
        Case on_cal
            lblCalDay1.BackColor = vbButtonFace
            lblCalDay7.BackColor = vbButtonFace
            lblCalDay8.BackColor = vbButtonFace

        Case on_exit
            lblExit.BackColor = vbButtonFace

    End Select

' High light new highlighted option

    fraOpts(onum).BackColor = &HFFFFFF ' hi white
    hi_opt = onum

    Select Case hi_opt

        Case on_cal
            lblCalDay1.BackColor = &HFFFFFF
            lblCalDay7.BackColor = &HFFFFFF
            lblCalDay8.BackColor = &HFFFFFF

        Case on_exit
            lblExit.BackColor = &HFFFFFF

    End Select

End Sub
```

With this addition, you should have your highlight smoothly following the mouse pointer. If it only did something, you could really call this a menu. We don't have the components ready for the first five choices, but we can certainly hook up an eXit method. This will show you how an action routine is programmed.

I use the MouseUp event to handle mouse click over a Frame. You could use MouseDown, but looking for MouseUp makes it easier to add a drag capability in the future. This code shows what the action routine will look like:

```
    Private Sub fraOpts_MouseUp(Index As Integer, _
        Button As Integer, Shift As Integer, _
        X As Single, Y As Single)

        Select Case Index
            Case on_cal
            Case on_sched
```

```
                    Case on_proj
                    Case on_todo
                    Case on_time

                    Case on_exit
                        Unload Me

                End Select

        End Sub
```

When you code this action routine, you would normally code a set of action methods, such as `do_cal()`, `do_sched()`, and so on. Exiting is simple enough so that it doesn't need its own routine.

One problem remains. Again, the `Label` masks the event from the `Frame`. If your click is over the `Label`, it's ignored. The solution is the same as before. Add another event handler, hooked to the label. This fixes the problem:

```
        Private Sub lblExit_Click()

            Unload Me

        End Sub
```

INCLUDING THE KEYBOARD

Finally, we should add the keyboard as a second means of controlling this menu. The underscored letters on our `Captions` suggest that we already have such a capability, but we don't.

In fact, I have a rather serious bug in Visual Basic. (It may be fixed by the time you read this, so check.) I have exactly zero tab stops on the `Form`. Visual Basic doesn't know what to do in this situation, so it picks the first potential tab stop that it comes to (the first schedule appointment) and puts the text cursor there. You can edit it right on the menu!

Of course that's not what we want. You'd like to have the mnemonic keys function as they do in any menu, of course. Press X, for example, and you'll move to the eXit option. We'll have to kludge it up.

Adding More TextBoxes

Begin by drawing a new `TextBox` in each `Frame`. Put it at the extreme top left, set in just enough to not interfere with the `Frame`'s visual border. Name them all `txtKey` so that you get a control array. Drop them in order so that `txtKey(0)` is in `fraOpts(0)` and so on.

In the properties window, you can toggle a two-state property (e.g. `BorderStyle`'s 0/1 or `Visible`'s True/False) by double-clicking its value. You can minimize a numeric by blanking out the value. It's good to know these tricks because you'll have to set each `TextBox` separately. Visual Basic won't let you select multiple components if they're in different `Frames`. Set these properties:

- Set `Appearance` to 0, `Flat`
- Set `BackColor` to high white (Palette tab)
- Toggle `BorderStyle` to 0, `None`
- Minimize `Height`
- Set `Left` to 50
- Set `Password Char` to a single space
- Set `Top` to 150
- Blank out `Text`
- Toggle `Visible` to `False`
- Minimize `Width`

The `make_hi()` routine that will set this box in the highlighted `Frame` has to be `Visible`. Every other box will be not `Visible`, so this will be the only available tab stop. That's why we're using the white color: it's only `Visible` when it's highlighted.

The `PasswordChar` is the character that is echoed to the text box when you type in it. If it's blank, the actual keystrokes are entered. If you make it not blank, your choice is echoed. This is useful for echoing blanks or asterisks when the user enters a password. It's also useful to us since we don't want keystrokes appearing in these boxes.

Coding the TextBoxes

Begin by having the `make_hi()` method set one `TextBox` at a time to `Visible`. Add this code to the beginning of the `make_hi()` method, just after the line that forces a quick exit:

```
' Change to new visible key handler
    txtKey(onum).Visible = True
    If hi_opt <> 255 Then txtKey(hi_opt).Visible = False
```

We turn the new box `Visible` before we turn the old one not `Visible`. This ensures that there's always one tab stop for Visual Basic to hand control. If you do it the other way around, there's no telling where Visual Basic will pass control when it doesn't have any tab stops.

With the boxes passing control around nicely, we're ready to respond to a keystroke. We can do this in the `change()` event-handling method of the `txtKey` array. Recursion is a problem here because we'll want to blank out the text, which will call the `change()` method recursively, so add this additional recursion suppressant in the declarations section:

```
Private rekeying As Boolean
```

This code will do the trick:

```
Private Sub txtKey_Change(Index As Integer)

' eliminate recursion
    If rekeying Then Exit Sub

    Dim k As String
    k = UCase(left(txtKey(Index).Text, 1))

    Select Case k
        Case "C": make_hi (on_cal)
        Case "S": make_hi (on_sched)
        Case "P": make_hi (on_proj)
        Case "D": make_hi (on_todo)
        Case "T": make_hi (on_time)
        Case "X": make_hi (on_exit)
    End Select
    rekeying = True
    txtKey(Index).Text = ""
    rekeying = False

End Sub
```

With that code in place, you should be able to run your program and find keyboard sensitivity, or you should find mouse sensitivity. If you try to use both, you're in trouble.

If the mouse cursor is over a Frame when you use the keyboard, the keyboard's make_hi() selects a new highlighted option, and then Windows sends a MouseMove to whatever option the mouse pointer is on. This causes a new make_hi() to hop right back to the mouse's position.

I've added this workaround. In the declarations, include another Private:

```
' critter catcher
    Private ignore_mouse_move As Boolean
```

Then change each of your MouseMove event handlers from this body:

```
make_hi (on_whatever)
```

Change them to this body:

```
If ignore_mouse_move
Then
    ignore_mouse_move = False


Else
    make_hi (on_whatever)
End If
```

Finally, add this final statement to your txtKey_Change() method:

```
ignore_mouse_move = True
```

With that improvement, the MouseMove that is generated without actually moving the mouse is ignored. Real mouse movement is obeyed. We're just about done.

Being More Discrete

The final detail to handle is that big text cursor in our nearly hidden TextBoxes. There's no direct method for turning it off, but there is a simple way to minimize the problem.

You'll see a related problem if you try to shrink your Form to find minimal Frames. The TextBoxes start to interfere with the sketches. The same solution also solves this problem.

The minimum size for a TextBox is large enough to hold a single character, so you simply need to find a smaller character, and then you can shrink the TextBox. Right now it's holding a 14-point character, which is fairly large.

Choose one of the TextBoxes and click the Font dialog box in the Properties window. You can set the FontSize attribute here to as little as 8, which is a step in the right direction.

Try choosing a different font, first. In fact, Small Fonts is an ideal choice because it goes all the way down to a 2-point size.

When you choose 2-point Small Fonts you can again minimize Height and Width. Now Visual Basic will let you go down to 45 by 15 twips: three pixels tall by one pixel wide.

Set each of your txtKey TextBoxes this way and your problem has disappeared. You and I will still see the TextBoxes because we know they're there. No one else will notice, though.

THE FULL LISTING

If your spouse dropped this book's disk into the tank with your pet piranha, Listing 15-9 shows the editable portion of the frmMyTim.frm file.

Listing 15-9
frmMyTim.frm — the main menu for MyTime

```
' frmMyTim.frm — main menu for MyTime system
' Copyright 1997, Martin L. Rinehart

Option Explicit

' recursion suppresants:
    Private resizing As Boolean
    Private rekeying As Boolean
Const cap_width = 900 ' frame size at which captions
    ' are spelled out completely

Private Enum option_numbers
    on_cal = 0
    on_sched
```

(continued)

frmMyTim.frm — the main menu for MyTime

```
            on_proj
            on_todo
            on_time
            on_exit
    End Enum

    ' Useful shorthands:
        Private tppX As Integer, tppY As Integer

    Private hi_opt As Byte

    ' Critter catcher
        Private ignore_mouse_move
    Private Sub Form_Initialize()

        tppX = Screen.TwipsPerPixelX
        tppY = Screen.TwipsPerPixelY
        hi_opt = 255 ' Nothing high yet
        make_hi 0

    End Sub

    Private Sub Form_Resize()

    ' outta here if form is minimized
        If frmMyTim.WindowState = vbMinimized Then Exit Sub

    ' outta here if we're in here
        If resizing Then Exit Sub

        resizing = True

    ' enforce minimum height
        If Height < 1400 Then Height = 1400

    ' enforce minimum total size
        If Height + Width < 6000 Then Width = 6000 - Height

        resizing = False

    ' layout may be 1x6, 2x3, 3x2 or 6x1
        Dim cols As Byte, rows As Byte

        Dim cli_height As Integer, cli_width As Integer
```

```
' client area is smaller than form coordinates
    cli_height = Height - 400
    cli_width = Width - 120

    ' round down to a full pixel
    cli_height = cli_height / tppY
    cli_height = cli_height * tppY

    cli_width = cli_width / tppX
    cli_width = cli_width * tppX

    Dim aspect_ratio As Single
    aspect_ratio = cli_height / cli_width

    Const key_ratio = 3 ' used to choose layout

' Choose layout
    Select Case aspect_ratio

        Case Is > key_ratio
            rows = 6: cols = 1

        Case Is > 1
            rows = 3: cols = 2

        Case Is > (1 / key_ratio)
            rows = 2: cols = 3

        Case Else
            rows = 1: cols = 6

    End Select

    Dim vert_spacer As Integer, hori_spacer As Integer
    Dim fram_width As Integer, fram_height As Integer

    Const for_options = 0.8 ' 80% for options, 20% space

    fram_width = cli_width * for_options / cols
    fram_height = cli_height * for_options / rows

    fram_width = fram_width / tppX
    fram_height = fram_height / tppY

    fram_width = fram_width * tppX
    fram_height = fram_height * tppY
```

(continued)

frmMyTim.frm — the main menu for MyTime

```
vert_spacer = (cli_height - (rows * fram_height)) _
    / (rows + 1)
hori_spacer = (cli_width - (cols * fram_width)) _
    / (cols + 1)

vert_spacer = vert_spacer / tppY
vert_spacer = vert_spacer * tppY

hori_spacer = hori_spacer / tppX
hori_spacer = hori_spacer * tppX

Dim opt_num As Byte
Dim r As Byte, c As Byte

Dim top As Integer, left As Integer

hide_cal
hide_sched
hide_proj
hide_todo
hide_time
hide_exit

For c = 0 To 5
    fraOpts(c).Visible = False
Next c

top = vert_spacer

For r = 1 To rows

    left = hori_spacer

    For c = 1 To cols

        With fraOpts(opt_num)
            .top = top
            .left = left
            .Height = fram_height
            .Width = fram_width
            .Visible = True
        End With

        left = left + fram_width + hori_spacer
        opt_num = opt_num + 1

    Next c
```

```
            top = top + fram_height + vert_spacer
        Next r

        draw_cal fraOpts(on_cal)
        draw_sched fraOpts(on_sched)
        draw_proj fraOpts(on_proj)
        draw_todo fraOpts(on_todo)
        draw_time fraOpts(on_time)
        draw_exit fraOpts(on_exit)

        Debug.Print " "
        Debug.Print "Form Ht WD:" & _
            Str(frmMyTim.Height) & Str(frmMyTim.Width)
        Debug.Print "Frame Ht Wd:" & _
            Str(fraOpts(0).Height) & Str(fraOpts(0).Width)
        Debug.Print "Tops" & _
            Str(fraOpts(0).top) & Str(fraOpts(3).top)
        Debug.Print "Lefts" & _
            Str(fraOpts(0).left) & Str(fraOpts(1).left) & _
            Str(fraOpts(2).left)

End Sub

Private Sub hide_cal()

    linCalLf.Visible = False
    linCalTp.Visible = False

    linCalGrdHor1.Visible = False
    linCalGrdHor2.Visible = False
    linCalGrdVer1.Visible = False
    linCalGrdVer2.Visible = False

    lblCalDay1.Visible = False
    lblCalDay7.Visible = False
    lblCalDay8.Visible = False


End Sub

Private Sub draw_cal(ByRef f As Frame)

    If f.Width > cap_width Then
        f.Caption = " &Calendar "
    Else
        f.Caption = "&Cal"
    End If
```

(continued)

frmMyTim.frm — the main menu for MyTime

```
Dim tp As Integer, ht As Integer
Dim lf As Integer, wd As Integer

' find clear coordinates (losing frame's frame)
tp = 1.5 * FontSize * tppY
lf = 3 * tppX

ht = f.Height - tp - (2 * tppY)
wd = f.Width - (2 * lf)

Dim cal_tp As Integer, cal_lf As Integer
cal_tp = tp + 0.1 * ht
cal_lf = lf + 0.1 * wd

With linCalLf
    .X1 = cal_lf
    .X2 = cal_lf
    .Y1 = cal_tp
    .Y2 = (0.95 * ht) + tp
    .BorderWidth = 1 + Int(wd / 1000)
    .Visible = True
End With

With linCalTp
    .X1 = cal_lf
    .X2 = (0.95 * wd) + lf
    .Y1 = cal_tp
    .Y2 = cal_tp
    .BorderWidth = 1 + Int(ht / 1000)
    .Visible = True
End With

Const wd2 = 1200 ' > wd2, show 2 days
Const ht2 = 1200 ' > ht2, show 2 weeks

If ht < ht2 Then ' show 1 week

    With linCalGrdHor1
        .X1 = cal_lf
        .X2 = linCalTp.X2
        .Y1 = cal_tp + 0.75 * ht
        .Y2 = .Y1
        .Visible = True
    End With

Else ' show 2 weeks
```

```
        With linCalGrdHor1
            .X1 = cal_lf
            .X2 = linCalTp.X2
            .Y1 = cal_tp + (0.4 * ht)
            .Y2 = .Y1
            .Visible = True
        End With

        With linCalGrdHor2
            .X1 = cal_lf
            .X2 = linCalTp.X2
            .Y1 = cal_tp + (0.8 * ht)
            .Y2 = .Y1
            .Visible = True
        End With

    End If

    If wd < wd2 Then ' show 1 day

        With linCalGrdVer1
            .X1 = cal_lf + (0.75 * wd)
            .X2 = .X1
            .Y1 = cal_tp
            .Y2 = linCalLf.Y2
            .Visible = True
        End With

    Else ' show 2 days

        With linCalGrdVer1
            .X1 = cal_lf + (0.4 * wd)
            .X2 = .X1
            .Y1 = cal_tp
            .Y2 = linCalLf.Y2
            .Visible = True
        End With

        With linCalGrdVer2
            .X1 = cal_lf + (0.8 * wd)
            .X2 = .X1
            .Y1 = cal_tp
            .Y2 = linCalLf.Y2
            .Visible = True
        End With

    End If
```

(continued)

frmMyTim.frm — the main menu for MyTime

```
' Place day labels

    If wd < wd2 Then ' showing one day

        With lblCalDay1
            .top = cal_tp + _
                (tppY * linCalTp.BorderWidth)
            .left = linCalGrdVer1.X1 - 220
            .Height = 350
            .Width = 200
            .Visible = True
        End With

        If ht >= ht2 Then ' showing two weeks

            With lblCalDay8
                .top = linCalGrdHor1.Y1 + tppY
                .left = linCalGrdVer1.X1 - 320
                .Height = 400
                .Width = 300
                .Visible = True
            End With

        End If

    Else ' Showing two days

        With lblCalDay1
            .top = cal_tp + _
                (tppY * linCalTp.BorderWidth)
            .left = linCalGrdVer2.X1 - 320
            .Height = 400
            .Width = 300
            .Visible = True
        End With

        If ht >= ht2 Then ' showing two weeks

            With lblCalDay1
                .top = cal_tp + _
                    (tppY * linCalTp.BorderWidth)
                .left = linCalGrdVer2.X1 - 320
                .Height = 400
                .Width = 300
                .Visible = True
            End With
```

```
              With lblCalDay7
                  .top = linCalGrdHor1.Y1 + tppY
                  .left = linCalGrdVer1.X1 - 320
                  .Height = 400
                  .Width = 300
                  .Visible = True
              End With

              With lblCalDay8
                  .top = linCalGrdHor1.Y1 + tppY
                  .left = linCalGrdVer2.X1 - 320
                  .Height = 400
                  .Width = 300
                  .Visible = True
              End With

          End If

      End If

End Sub

Private Sub hide_sched()

    Dim i As Byte

    For i = 0 To 3
        txtSched(i).Visible = False
    Next i

End Sub


Private Sub draw_sched(ByRef f As Frame)
    Dim i As Byte

    If f.Width > cap_width Then
        f.Caption = " &Schedule "
    Else
        f.Caption = "&Scd"
    End If

    For i = 0 To 3
        txtSched(i).Visible = True
    Next i

End Sub
```

(continued)

frmMyTim.frm — the main menu for MyTime

```vb
Private Sub hide_proj()

    linTask1.Visible = False
    linTask2.Visible = False
    linTask3.Visible = False
    linTask4.Visible = False

    linTaskCon1.Visible = False
    linTaskCon2.Visible = False

End Sub

Private Sub draw_proj(ByRef f As Frame)

    If f.Width > cap_width Then
        f.Caption = " &Projects "
    Else
        f.Caption = "&Prj"
    End If

    Dim ht As Integer, wd As Integer
    ht = f.Height
    wd = f.Width

    With linTask1
        .X1 = wd * 0.15
        .X2 = wd * 0.4
        .Y1 = 200 + ((ht - 200) * 0.1)
        .Y2 = .Y1
        .Visible = True
    End With

    With linTask2
        .X1 = wd * 0.4
        .X2 = wd * 0.6
        .Y1 = 200 + ((ht - 200) * 0.35)
        .Y2 = .Y1
        .Visible = True
    End With

    With linTask3
        .X1 = wd * 0.4
        .X2 = wd * 0.75
        .Y1 = 200 + ((ht - 200) * 0.6)
        .Y2 = .Y1
        .Visible = True
    End With
```

```
        With linTask4
            .X1 = wd * 0.75
            .X2 = wd * 0.9
            .Y1 = 200 + ((ht - 200) * 0.85)
            .Y2 = .Y1
            .Visible = True
        End With

        With linTaskCon1
            .X1 = linTask1.X2
            .X2 = .X1
            .Y1 = linTask1.Y2
            .Y2 = linTask3.Y1
            .Visible = True
        End With

        With linTaskCon2
            .X1 = linTask3.X2
            .X2 = .X1
            .Y1 = linTask3.Y2
            .Y2 = linTask4.Y1
            .Visible = True
        End With

End Sub

Private Sub hide_todo()

    Dim i As Byte

    For i = 0 To 3
        txtToDo(i).Visible = False
    Next i

End Sub

Private Sub draw_todo(ByRef f As Frame)

    If f.Width > cap_width Then
        f.Caption = " To &Do "
    Else
        f.Caption = "To&Do"
    End If

    Dim i As Byte

    For i = 0 To 3
        txtToDo(i).Visible = True
    Next i
```

(continued)

frmMyTim.frm — the main menu for MyTime

```
End Sub

Private Sub hide_time()

    shpCircle.Visible = False
    linDot.Visible = False

    linMinLf.Visible = False
    linMinRt.Visible = False

    linHrLf.Visible = False
    linHrRt.Visible = False

End Sub

Private Sub draw_time(ByRef f As Frame)

    If f.Width > cap_width Then
        f.Caption = " &Time "
    Else
        f.Caption = "&Time"
    End If

    Dim ht As Integer, wd As Integer
    ht = f.Height
    wd = f.Width

' Draw a watch face
    Dim Vmid As Integer, Hmid As Integer
    Dim radius As Integer

    With shpCircle
        .top = 1.5 * FontSize * tppY
        .left = 3 * tppX

        .Height = f.Height - .top - (3 * tppY)
        .Width = f.Width - (2 * .left)

        Vmid = .top + (.Height / 2)
        Hmid = .left + (.Width / 2)
        radius = min(.Height, .Width) / 2
        .Visible = True
    End With

    With linDot
        .X1 = Hmid
        .X2 = Hmid
```

```
            .Y1 = Vmid - (radius * 0.85)
            .Y2 = .Y1
            .BorderWidth = 2 + radius / 150
            .Visible = True
        End With

' Draw hands
        With linMinLf
            .X1 = 0.95 * Hmid
            .X2 = 1.15 * Hmid
            .Y1 = Vmid
            .Y2 = linDot.Y1
            .Visible = True
        End With

        With linMinRt
            .X1 = 1.05 * Hmid
            .X2 = linMinLf.X2
            .Y1 = Vmid
            .Y2 = linMinLf.Y2
            .Visible = True
        End With

        With linHrLf
            .X1 = linMinLf.X1
            .X2 = Hmid * 1.2
            .Y1 = linMinLf.Y1
            .Y2 = Vmid + 0.6 * radius
            .Visible = True
        End With

        With linHrRt
            .X1 = linMinRt.X1
            .X2 = linHrLf.X2
            .Y1 = linMinRt.Y1
            .Y2 = linHrLf.Y2
            .Visible = True
        End With

End Sub

Private Sub hide_exit()

    lblExit.Visible = False

End Sub
```

(continued)

frmMyTim.frm — the main menu for MyTime

```
Private Sub draw_exit(ByRef f As Frame)

    Dim ht As Integer, wd As Integer
    ht = f.Height
    wd = f.Width

    If f.Width > cap_width Then
        f.Caption = " e&Xit "
    Else
        f.Caption = "&Xit"
    End If

    With lblExit

        .left = 0.15 * wd
        .Width = 0.7 * wd

        .Height = ht * 0.4
        .top = (f.Height - .Height) / 2

        .FontSize = min(ht, wd) / 50
        .Visible = True

    End With

End Sub

Private Sub fraOpts_MouseMove(Index As Integer, _
    Button As Integer, Shift As Integer, _
    X As Single, Y As Single)

    If ignore_mouse_move Then
        ignore_mouse_move = False
    Else
        make_hi (Index)
    End If

End Sub

Private Sub lblExit_MouseMove(Button As Integer, _
    Shift As Integer, X As Single, Y As Single)

    If ignore_mouse_move Then
        ignore_mouse_move = False
    Else
        make_hi (on_exit)
    End If
```

```
End Sub

Private Sub txtToDo_MouseMove(Index As Integer, _
    Button As Integer, Shift As Integer, _
    X As Single, Y As Single)

    If ignore_mouse_move Then
        ignore_mouse_move = False
    Else
        make_hi (on_todo)
    End If

End Sub


Private Sub txtSched_MouseMove(Index As Integer, _
    Button As Integer, Shift As Integer, _
    X As Single, Y As Single)

    If ignore_mouse_move Then
        ignore_mouse_move = False
    Else
        make_hi (on_sched)
    End If

End Sub

Private Sub fraOpts_MouseUp(Index As Integer, _
    Button As Integer, Shift As Integer, _
    X As Single, Y As Single)

    Select Case Index
        Case on_cal
        Case on_sched
        Case on_proj
        Case on_todo
        Case on_time

        Case on_exit
            Unload Me

    End Select

End Sub

Private Sub lblExit_Click()
```

(continued)

frmMyTim.frm — the main menu for MyTime

```
    Unload Me

End Sub

Private Sub txtKey_Change(Index As Integer)

' eliminate recursion
    If rekeying Then Exit Sub

    Dim k As String
    k = UCase(left(txtKey(Index).Text, 1))

    Select Case k
        Case "C": make_hi (on_cal)
        Case "S": make_hi (on_sched)
        Case "P": make_hi (on_proj)
        Case "D": make_hi (on_todo)
        Case "T": make_hi (on_time)
        Case "X": make_hi (on_exit)
    End Select

    rekeying = True
    txtKey(Index).Text = ""
    rekeying = False

    ignore_mouse_move = True

End Sub

Private Function min(a As Integer, b As Integer)

    If a < b Then
        min = a
    Else
        min = b
    End If

End Function

Public Sub make_hi(onum As Byte)

    If onum = hi_opt Then Exit Sub

' Change to new visible key handler
    txtKey(onum).Visible = True
    If hi_opt <> 255 Then txtKey(hi_opt).Visible = False

' Low light old hilighted option
```

```
        If hi_opt <> 255 Then ' skip this on initialization
            fraOpts(hi_opt).BackColor = vbButtonFace
        End If

        Select Case hi_opt

            Case on_cal
                lblCalDay1.BackColor = vbButtonFace
                lblCalDay7.BackColor = vbButtonFace
                lblCalDay8.BackColor = vbButtonFace

            Case on_exit
                lblExit.BackColor = vbButtonFace

        End Select

    ' High light new highlighted option

        fraOpts(onum).BackColor = &HFFFFFF ' hi white
        hi_opt = onum

        Select Case hi_opt

            Case on_cal
                lblCalDay1.BackColor = &HFFFFFF
                lblCalDay7.BackColor = &HFFFFFF
                lblCalDay8.BackColor = &HFFFFFF

            Case on_exit
                lblExit.BackColor = &HFFFFFF

        End Select

End Sub

' end of frmMyTim.frm
```

SUMMARY

In this chapter, we've created a totally slick main menu. It uses words and pictures to show us what the program's key sections are. It's mouse and keyboard enabled.

We've used program code to create the graphics, so our size is modest compared to using bitmaps. I've compiled my version to native code (set native code in the Project Properties compile tab and use File⇨Make to build). It uses 40K. Using bitmaps here could easily use 400K.

After we looked at some interesting features of the `Frame` component, we started by programming the layout feature. This was a matter of using `resize()` to look at the dimensions of the window and choosing one of four possible layouts. Then we sized our `Frame`s and positioned them.

After that we drew six sketches. Two we didn't resize; we just let them become truncates as the `Frame` shrinks. Three we adjusted, and one, the calendar, we showed in different ways depending on how much space was available. Each of these methods works well for some sketches, less well for others.

After we did the sketches, we added menu functionality, using the `MouseMove` event to find and move a highlight around the menu, following the mouse pointer.

Finally, we added keystroke handling with some nearly invisible `TextBox` objects. We worked around Visual Basic's inability to deal with a `Form` without a tabstop, and we worked around a spurious `MouseMove` event that Windows generates after we use the keyboard. The finished product makes all the trouble worth while.

Our completed MyTime menu is a very nice piece of code. I'm looking forward to using it. I'm particularly looking forward to reducing it to a minimum size and sliding it out of the way where it will be available, but not obtrusive.

Now we need some objects to attach to our beautiful MyTime menu. In the next chapter, we'll begin working on our to do lists.

PROGRAMMING THE APPOINTMENT DATABASE

16

*I*n the last chapter, we worked very hard to make the system look very good. You learned that a graphic look doesn't need a lot of large bitmaps. In this chapter, we're going to hop from top to bottom. As I pointed out in Chapter 14, we can't work in classic top-down style because the middle layers, the tools surfaces, need some data.

We can build the database components with database forms. These will run as standalone programs, letting us enter test data. Then we can incorporate these just about unchanged into the finished tools' surfaces. So this top-down, then bottom-up approach will actually do the job most efficiently.

From this point on, we'll go very quickly. Instead of building the software yourself, one step at a time, just go ahead and use the listings on the disk. Copy them in and run them.

If you don't completely understand any routines, drop breakpoints at their starts and step through them. Visual Basic's debugger is exceptionally well integrated. The feature that shows the value of a variable when you point to it is wonderfully useful.

What I *do* want you to do is to improve my work. You'll really understand this code if you tinker a little. Change it to work better for you and your work style. Make it your own.

We'll begin with the ODB. I've made some key improvements in that bottommost layer, so we'll be ready to put the appointments database form and appointments class on top of it.

IMPROVING THE ODB

You recall that we built the database and planned on having a key capability, but we didn't actually implement one. Well, the time has come. I never thought of a very good programming strategy for this job, by the way. Perhaps you can.

A good programming strategy, of course, is a way that lets you do a little at a time, testing as you go. I couldn't figure out how to do that. If you start with a form working on top of the old ODB, you'll need to rewrite the form to handle the new ODB. Therefore, you might as well rewrite the ODB before you write the form, which is just what I did.

In this section I'm going to discuss the most important changes. This will not include every change, so you'll need to copy the complete file from disk (it's in 16-01). There will be a full listing for those who don't have the disk.

Fixing the Key's Position

First, if you're going to handle the key, you have to know what the key is. That will work in two ways. The one that originally appealed to me was asking the object to provide methods such as get_key() and set_key(). The alternative, which I decided to use, is simply to demand that the key be in a fixed position in the record.

I decided to declare that the key must be the first 11 bytes of the record. (That's the long_str() of the Long key's value.) This reduces the flexibility of the object's design. I couldn't think of a single example where putting the key in some other position actually made any difference, though. First seemed just as good as last or middle.

Doing it this way has the advantage of not adding two new functions — the get_key() and set_key() methods — to the interface definition. (A three-method interface is 40 percent better than a five-method interface.) This was eventually the deciding factor for me. You also save a little overhead by eliminating the extra method calls, but that's hardly a major concern.

Maintaining a Blank Record

After that decision, I decided to standardize on a single waste record to carry the highest key in use. That's the last physical record in the file. We'll make the last record invisible to the calling software. If the ODB tells the application that ten objects are on file, there will really be eleven.

We'll use that blank record just to maintain the key value. Remember, our goal with the key is to make it permanently and immutably unique. It's the name of each object on disk and every object must have its own, permanent name. Other objects that store this value are always guaranteed to refer to the correct object.

When we are asked to add a record to the database, we'll look at the blank record. We'll take the key, increment it, and then use it as the key of a brand new blank record, written to the end of the database. Then the data being appended will simply overwrite the former blank record, using its key.

The order of these operations is important. By writing a new trailing record first, overwriting the former blank will survive even hardware failure. If the hardware fails before you've written the new record, the crash just eliminates the whole append operation. If the hardware fails after the new blank record is added, you have an unused blank record as your last visible record. You can replace this object with the data you wanted to append, and you'll be back in business. Your key system has survived intact.

Let's begin with the code that creates the blank record.

Creating the Blank Record

There will be a difference here between the old and new create methods. In the old method, we added the first record. Now we'll add the record, but it will be the blank record that trails the visible portion of the file. The num_objects property is set to zero after this record is written.

This is the new create_odb() method:

```
Public Sub create_odb(first As Object)

    file_number = FreeFile

    path_name = first.get_name
    path_name = _
        default_drive & _
        default_path & _
        path_name & ".odb"

    If Len(Dir(path_name)) Then Kill path_name
```

```
        Open path_name For Binary As file_number

        rec_buf = Chr(13) & Chr(10) & "  " & first.to_string
        rec_len = Len(rec_buf)
        Dim header As String

        Dim nm As String
        nm = first.get_name

        header = signature & _
            fix_len(nm, 32) & _
            Right(Space(8) & Str(rec_len), 8)

        Put file_number, , header
        Put file_number, , rec_buf

        current_object_num = 0
        num_objects = 0

    End Sub ' create odb
```

Opening the ODB

The open_odb( ) method now has to know about the trailing blank record. Its calculation of the number of objects has to be reduced by one. This is the new code:

```
    Public Function open_odb(pn As String) As Integer

' check that a file number is available
        file_number = FreeFile
        If file_number = 0 Then
            err_msgs (err_freefile)
            open_odb = err_freefile
            Exit Function
        End If

' open the file — if it's 0 long, its new
        Open pn & ".odb" For Binary As file_number
        If LOF(file_number) = 0 Then ' not an ODB!
            Close file_number
            err_msgs (err_open)
            open_odb = err_open
            Exit Function
        End If

' create buffer for header, then read header
        Dim header As String
```

```
        header = Space(header_len)

        Get file_number, , header

' check for a valid signature
    If left(header, 8) <> signature Then
        Close file_number
        err_msgs (err_open)
        open_odb = err_open
        Exit Function
    End If

' set up private data members
    rec_len = Val(Right(header, 8))
    rec_buf = Space(rec_len)
    path_name = pn

    num_objects = ((LOF(file_number) - header_len) / _
        rec_len) - 1
    current_object_num = 0
    open_odb = openOK

End Function
```

Adding Objects

The process of adding an object is substantially changed by the new design. It's also smarter about a subtle point, which I'll mention after you've had a chance to look at the code.

The comments here describe the operation in detail. The code under the increment the key comment handles the key job of creating a new blank record by reading the old one's key, incrementing it, and then writing a new record with the incremented value.

I'll explain the get_obj_priv() method shortly. This is the new code:

```
Public Function add_obj(o As Object) As Long

' A key value is maintained in the final physical record
' This record is invisible to the application. Adding a
' new object is done by reading the hidden record,
' incrementing the key and writing a new hidden record.

' Then the former hidden record is replaced with the
' actual data of the object being added.

' save a copy of the object's data
    Dim save_object As String
    save_object = o.to_string()
```

```
' read the end object
    get_obj priv num_objects, o

' increment the key
    Dim s As String
    s = o.to_string()

    Dim old_key As String, new_key As String
    old_key = left(s, 11)
    new_key = long_str(Val(old_key) + 1)

    s = new_key + Right(s, Len(s) - 11)

' write the new end record
    rec_buf = Chr(13) & Chr(10) & "  " & s
    Put file_number, oloc(num_objects + 1), rec_buf
    add_obj = num_objects
    num_objects = num_objects + 1

' write the added object as the final visible object
    o.from_string (save_object)
    o.key = Val(old_key)
    rep_obj num_objects - 1, o

End Function
```

The improved intelligence is in the calculation of the place to write the record. The old version appended the new record at LOF() + 1. This version calculates the record location. Obviously, I thought the first way would work when I wrote it. To some extent it does work, but there's a problem.

You can edit our ODBs with a simple text editor. This is handy for development, for checking contents during debugging, and for simple file maintenance. However, text editors do funny things at the end of the file. Some think the last line should terminate with a CR/LF pair, and some don't. If you edit the ODB with an editor that adds a trailing CR/LF, the original method fails. Writing at LOF() + 1 is actually writing two bytes past the correct spot.

I thought I was writing dates like "19970216," but I read in dates in years like 9702. I don't want to be unduly pessimistic, but I don't think I'll be around then. Writing to the specific location fixes this problem.

Finding an Object by Key

When you begin to use keys, you'll need a function to find records by key. I added this one that does a simple direct scan. This looks very slow, but in practice it isn't. Remember that these ODB files are small. The operating system reads them by its own buffer sizes. Our program's reads are really just logical disk reads. Windows will return the data that it has in its buffer, if the data was read the last time it read in a buffer.

The operating system's buffers may be larger than our entire ODB. This makes this slow-looking code run just fine. You'll see that I regularly use my text editor to physically delete records. That message box hasn't appeared yet.

Look on the disk for the READ.ME. It will give you the details if I've actually gotten around to writing the better method. A binary search won't be as good as an indexed lookup, but it will be lightning fast for perhaps the first million records. Past that, you'd better think about using the Data Access Object.

This is the new code:

```
Public Function find_obj(num As Long, _
    ByRef obj As Object) As Long

    Dim i As Long, key As Long

    If num_objects > 100 Then
        MsgBox _
            "Program a binary search for ODB.find_obj()"
    End If

    For i = 0 To num

        Get file_number, oloc(i), rec_buf
        key = Val(Mid(rec_buf, 5, 11))
        If key = num Then Exit For

    Next i

    If key = num Then
        find_obj = get_obj_priv(i, obj)
    Else
        find_obj = -1
    End If

End Function
```

The get_obj() Method Splits

The get_obj() method won't carry an object past the end of the database. That means that get_obj() can't read the last, hidden record. The code that appends a new record needs to read this hidden record. To allow for that, I split the get_obj() method into two parts.

The get_obj() method is functionally the same as it was, but its actual working part has moved to get_obj_priv(), a private function. The get_obj_priv() method isn't available outside the ODB, so no one in the outside world will know about our hidden object.

This is the new pair of routines:

```
Public Function get_obj(num As Long, _
    ByRef obj As Object) As Long

    If Not rec_in_file(num) Then
        err_msgs (err_seek)
        get_obj = -1
        Exit Function
    End If

    get_obj = get_obj_priv(num, obj)

End Function

Private Function get_obj_priv(num As Long, _
    ByRef obj As Object) As Long

    Get file_number, oloc(num), rec_buf

    obj_is_deleted = _
        (Mid(rec_buf, 3, 1) = "*")

    obj.from_string (Right(rec_buf, rec_len - 4))
    get_obj_priv = num

End Function
```

Adding Utilities

In addition to these functional improvements, I realized that most of our tools would be able to use utility routines such as nice_date() and int2tstring(). If you don't remember the former, it's the one that returns "January 1, 1997" when given the date "01/01/97."

This is the code that converts an integer to a `tstring`:

```
Public Function int2tstring(i As Integer) As String

' returns "01:00" given 60, "02:30" given 150, etc.

    Dim hr As Byte, mn As Byte
    hr = Int(i / 60)
    mn = i - (hr * 60)

    int2tstring = _
        Right(Str(100 + hr), 2) & ":" & _
        Right(Str(100 + mn), 2)

End Function
```

The general-purpose method for providing utilities in an object-oriented environment is to create a utility object. You might put these in a class called LIB.CLS. Then your code could call them this way:

```
foo = LIB.nice_date("01/01/97")
```

In this project I didn't see the need for a separate LIB.CLS. The ODB seemed quite capable of hosting the small number of utility routines that would be needed, so I've added them at the end of ODB.CLS. You can see them all in Listing 16-1.

To substitute for the ActiveX component, I've added this `OK_time()` method:

```
Public Function OK_time(s As String) As Boolean

    OK_time = False
    If Len(s) < 5 Then Exit Function

    Dim s1 As String
    s1 = left(s, 2)
        If Not OK_posint(s1) Then Exit Function
        If Val(s1) > 24 Then Exit Function

    s1 = Mid(s, 4, 2)
        If Not OK_posint(s1) Then Exit Function
        If Val(s1) > 59 Then Exit Function

    OK_time = True

End Function
```

The Full Listing

For those who don't have the book's disk, Listing 16-1 is the new ODB.CLS file. This is the full file, including the lines above those normally shown in the code editor.

Listing 16-1
ODB.cls — the Object DataBase class

```
VERSION 1.0 CLASS
BEGIN
  MultiUse = -1  'True
END
Attribute VB_Name = "ODB"
Attribute VB_GlobalNameSpace = True
Attribute VB_Creatable = True
Attribute VB_PredeclaredId = True
Attribute VB_Exposed = False
' ODB.cls — Object DataBase class
' Copyright 1997, Martin L. Rinehart

' Creates a data file which holds objects of a single
' class.

' The class must provide a get_name() function returning
' a String, suitable for use as a file name.
' It must also provide a to_string() function that returns
' a fixed-length string containing all the property values
' that will be stored. And it must provide a from_string()
' method that extracts the property values from the string
' created by the to_string() operation.

' The first 11 bytes of the to_string() string must be a
' long_str() representation of a Long integer key. A new
' unique key is assigned by the ODB as each record is
' added. It must never be modified.

' Format of the ODB file is:
'    Header
'    Object 0 record
'    Object 1 record
'    ...
'    Object n-1 record

' Format of the header is
'    Signature (8 bytes) = "mrVB5odb"
'    Object type name (32 bytes)
'    Record length (8 bytes)
```

```
' Format of the object record is
'   CR byte (chr(13))
'   LF byte (chr(10))
'   Deleted flag byte ("*" if deleted, " " otherwise)
'   unused byte (pad to dword boundary)
'   obj.to_string()

' Format of the obj.to_string()
'   long_str() of the key (assigned by ODB)
'   other data as needed

Option Explicit

Const signature = "mrVB5odb"
Const header_len = 48

' Errors:
    Public Enum err_types
        openOK = -1
        err_freefile = 0
        err_open
        err_seek
        err_close
        err_getdel
        err_badrec
        err_notgot
        number_of_errors
    End Enum

' Data members
    Public default_drive As String
    Public default_path As String
    Public obj_is_deleted As Boolean

    Private file_number As Integer
    Private rec_len As Integer
    Private rec_buf As String
    Private path_name As String
    Private num_objects As Long
    Private current_object_num As Long

Public Sub close_odb()

    If file_number = 0 Then
        err_msgs (err_close)
        Exit Sub
    End If
```

(continued)

ODB.cls — the Object DataBase class

```
        Close file_number
        file_number = 0 ' signal no file open

    End Sub

    Public Sub create_odb(first As Object)

        file_number = FreeFile

        path_name = first.get_name
        path_name = _
            default_drive & _
            default_path & _
            path_name & ".odb"

        If Len(Dir(path_name)) Then Kill path_name

        Open path_name For Binary As file_number

        rec_buf = Chr(13) & Chr(10) & "  " & first.to_string
        rec_len = Len(rec_buf)
        Dim header As String

        Dim nm As String
        nm = first.get_name

        header = signature & _
            fix_len(nm, 32) & _
            Right(Space(8) & Str(rec_len), 8)

        Put file_number, , header
        Put file_number, , rec_buf

        current_object_num = 0
        num_objects = 0

    End Sub ' create odb

    Public Function open_odb(pn As String) As Integer

    ' check that a file number is available
        file_number = FreeFile
        If file_number = 0 Then
            err_msgs (err_freefile)
            open_odb = err_freefile
            Exit Function
        End If
```

```
' open the file - if it's 0 long, its new
    Open pn & ".odb" For Binary As file_number
    If LOF(file_number) = 0 Then ' not an ODB!
        Close file_number
        err_msgs (err_open)
        open_odb = err_open
        Exit Function
    End If

' create buffer for header, then read header
    Dim header As String
    header = Space(header_len)

    Get file_number, , header

' check for a valid signature
    If left(header, 8) <> signature Then
        Close file_number
        err_msgs (err_open)
        open_odb = err_open
        Exit Function
    End If

' set up private data members
    rec_len = Val(Right(header, 8))
    rec_buf = Space(rec_len)
    path_name = pn

    num_objects = ((LOF(file_number) - header_len) / _
        rec_len) - 1
    current_object_num = 0
    open_odb = openOK

End Function

Public Function add_obj(o As Object) As Long

' A key value is maintained in the final physical record
' This record is invisible to the application. Adding a
' new object is done by reading the hidden record,
' incrementing the key and writing a new hidden record.

' Then the former hidden record is replaced with the
' actual data of the object being added.

' save a copy of the object's data
    Dim save_object As String
    save_object = o.to_string()
```

(continued)

ODB.cls — the Object DataBase class

```
' read the end object
    get_obj_priv num_objects, o

' increment the key
    Dim s As String
    s = o.to_string()

    Dim old_key As String, new_key As String
    old_key = left(s, 11)
    new_key = long_str(Val(old_key) + 1)

    s = new_key + Right(s, Len(s) - 11)

' write the new end record
    rec_buf = Chr(13) & Chr(10) & "  " & s
    Put file_number, oloc(num_objects + 1), rec_buf
    add_obj = num_objects
    num_objects = num_objects + 1

' write the added object as the final visible object
    o.from_string (save_object)
    o.key = Val(old_key)
    rep_obj num_objects - 1, o

End Function

Public Sub del_obj(num As Long)

    If Not rec_in_file(num) Then
        err_msgs (err_seek)
        Exit Sub
    End If

    Put file_number, oloc(num) + 2, "*"

    obj_is_deleted = True

End Sub

Public Sub undel_obj(num As Long)

    If Not rec_in_file(num) Then
        err_msgs (err_seek)
        Exit Sub
    End If
```

```vb
        Put file_number, oloc(num) + 2, " "

        obj_is_deleted = False

End Sub

Public Function find_obj(num As Long, _
        ByRef obj As Object) As Long

    Dim i As Long, key As Long

    If num_objects > 100 Then
        MsgBox _
            "Program a binary search for ODB.find_obj()"
    End If

    For i = 0 To num

        Get file_number, oloc(i), rec_buf
        key = Val(Mid(rec_buf, 5, 11))
        If key = num Then Exit For

    Next i

    If key = num Then
        find_obj = get_obj_priv(i, obj)
    Else
        find_obj = -1
    End If

End Function

Public Function get_obj(num As Long, _
        ByRef obj As Object) As Long

    If Not rec_in_file(num) Then
        err_msgs (err_seek)
        get_obj = -1
        Exit Function
    End If

    get_obj = get_obj_priv(num, obj)

End Function
```

(continued)

ODB.cls — the Object DataBase class

```
Public Function get_obj_num() As Long

    get_obj_num = current_object_num

End Function

Private Function get_obj_priv(num As Long, _
        ByRef obj As Object) As Long

    Get file_number, oloc(num), rec_buf

    obj_is_deleted = _
        (Mid(rec_buf, 3, 1) = "*")

    obj.from_string (Right(rec_buf, rec_len - 4))
    get_obj_priv = num

End Function

Public Sub rep_obj(num As Long, o As Object)

    If Not rec_in_file(num) Then
        err_msgs (err_seek)
        Exit Sub
    End If

    Dim del_char As String
    If obj_is_deleted Then
        del_char = "*"
    Else
        del_char = " "
    End If

    rec_buf = Chr(13) + Chr(10) + _
        del_char + " " + o.to_string()
    Put file_number, oloc(num), rec_buf

End Sub

Private Function rec_in_file(num As Long) As Boolean

    ' is num in range 0 to num_objects-1 ?

    rec_in_file = (num > -1) And (num < num_objects)

End Function
```

```vb
Private Function oloc(num As Long) As Long

    ' find object in file
    oloc = header_len + num * rec_len + 1

End Function

Private Sub err_msgs(errno As Byte)

    Call MsgBox(ferr_msgs(errno), vbCritical, "ODB Error")

End Sub

Private Sub Class_Initialize()

    default_drive = ""
    default_path = ""
    file_number = 0 ' 0 = no file open

End Sub

Public Function ferr_msgs(msg_num As Byte) As String

    ' pseudo class static array

    Select Case msg_num

        Case err_freefile:
            ferr_msgs = "No file number available"

        Case err_open:
            ferr_msgs = "Cannot open file"

        Case err_seek:
            ferr_msgs = "Cannot perform seek"

        Case err_close:
            ferr_msgs = "Cannot close — no file open"

        Case err_getdel:
            ferr_msgs = "Cannot get — record deleted"

        Case err_badrec:
            ferr_msgs = "Cannot get — record damaged"

        Case err_notgot:
            ferr_msgs = _
                "Cannot get — invalid object number"
```

(continued)

ODB.cls — the Object DataBase class

```
        End Select

End Function

Public Function fix_len(s As String, _
    num_chars As Integer) As String

' returns s padded or truncated to num_chars length

    fix_len = left(s & Space(num_chars), num_chars)

End Function

Public Function long_str(l As Long) As String

' returns 11-byte string

    long_str = Right(Space(10) & Str(l), 11)

End Function

Public Function int_str(i As Integer) As String

' returns 6-byte string

    int_str = Right(Space(5) & Str(i), 6)

End Function

Public Function date_str(d As Date) As String

' returns 8-byte date: YYYYMMDD

    date_str = _
        Right(Str(Year(d)), 4) & _
        Right(Str(100 + Month(d)), 2) & _
        Right(Str(100 + day(d)), 2)

End Function

Public Function yyyymmdd2date(s As String) As Date

' return date given "YYYYMMDD" string

    yyyymmdd2date = _
        Mid(s, 5, 2) & "/" & _
        Right(s, 2) & "/" & _
        left(s, 4)
```

```
End Function

Public Function tstring2int(s As String) As Integer

' a tstring is "HH:MM" (i.e. "01:00" = 60)

    tstring2int = _
        60 * Val(left(s, 2)) + _
        Val(Right(s, 2))

End Function

Public Function int2tstring(i As Integer) As String

' returns "01:00" given 60, "02:30" given 150, etc.

    Dim hr As Byte, mn As Byte
    hr = Int(i / 60)
    mn = i - (hr * 60)

    int2tstring = _
        Right(Str(100 + hr), 2) & ":" & _
        Right(Str(100 + mn), 2)

End Function


Public Function get_num_objects() As Long

    get_num_objects = num_objects

End Function

'Public Function OK_yyyymmdd(s As String) As Boolean
'
'    OK_yyyymmdd = False
'    If Len(s) <> 8 Then Exit Function
'
'    Dim i As Byte
'    For i = 1 To 8
'        If Not is_digit(Mid(s, i, 1)) Then Exit Function
'    Next i
'
'    OK_yyyymmdd = True
'
'End Function
'
```

(continued)

ODB.cls — the Object DataBase class

```
Public Function OK_time(s As String) As Boolean

    OK_time = False
    If Len(s) < 5 Then Exit Function

    Dim s1 As String
    s1 = left(s, 2)
        If Not OK_posint(s1) Then Exit Function
        If Val(s1) > 24 Then Exit Function

    s1 = Mid(s, 4, 2)
        If Not OK_posint(s1) Then Exit Function
        If Val(s1) > 59 Then Exit Function

    OK_time = True

End Function

Public Function OK_posint(s As String) As Boolean

    OK_posint = False

    Dim t As String
    t = Trim(s)
    If Len(t) = 0 Then Exit Function

    Dim i As Byte
    For i = 1 To Len(t)
        If Not is_digit(Mid(t, i, 1)) Then Exit Function
    Next

    OK_posint = True

End Function

Private Function is_digit(s As String) As Boolean

    Const zero = 48 ' chr("0")
    Const nine = zero + 9

    Dim b As Byte
    b = Asc(s)

    is_digit = _
        (b >= zero) And _
        (b <= nine)

End Function
```

```
Public Function nice_date(d As Date) As String

    nice_date = _
        month_str(d) & _
        Str(day(d)) & "," & _
        Str(Year(d))

End Function

Private Function month_str(d As Date) As String

    Select Case Month(d)

        Case 1: month_str = "January"
        Case 2: month_str = "February"
        Case 3: month_str = "March"

        Case 4: month_str = "April"
        Case 5: month_str = "May"
        Case 6: month_str = "June"

        Case 7: month_str = "July"
        Case 8: month_str = "August"
        Case 9: month_str = "September"

        Case 10: month_str = "October"
        Case 11: month_str = "November"
        Case 12: month_str = "December"

    End Select

End Function

' end of ODB.CLS
```

THE APPOINTMENT CLASS

To build the appointment database, we need to start with an appointment class. Mine's APP.CLS. Here I'll highlight the main points. Again, you can see the full listing from 16-02 on disk, or from Listing 16-2 at the end of this section.

We'll start with the data members.

The Declarations

For an appointment, we have to know its date, when it starts, and when it ends. I provide an actual time member, too. This one is filled in after the appointment. Until it's filled in, the class thinks the appointment hasn't taken place (even if it's scheduled for yesterday or last year).

Finally, the appointment gets a description. I've been pretty stingy with my description space. This works for me. If it doesn't work for you, adjust the to_form() and from_form() functions for whatever space you want.

These are the declarations:

```
' Data members:
    Public key As Long
    Public app_date As Date

    Private start_time As Integer
    Private end_time As Integer
    Private actual_time As Integer

    Public description As String
```

You'll see that the times are private not because there is any value checking but because this lets us keep integers (minutes since midnight) internally but show "HH:MM" strings externally.

The Constructor and Destructor

After adding the declarations, I go immediately to the constructor and the destructor. The constructor here sets the default date to today and explicitly sets the zero and null string values that Visual Basic would set anyway. I spell these out as reminders to the programmer (who is me).

There is nothing to do on termination, so there's no destructor. This is the constructor:

```
Private Sub Class_Initialize()

    key = 0 ' will be set by ODB
    app_date = Date
    start_time = 0 ' defaults
    end_time = 0
    actual_time = 0
    description = ""

End Sub
```

Going to and from String

After the constructor and destructor, I take any class designed for ODB use right to the three mandatory functions. The get_name() function just returns App. The to_string() and from_string() functions depend on carefully laying out the record and then typing with the mindset of an accountant.

I always include the record layout as commentary, like this:

```
' string layout:
    ' key:          1-11, pad byte: 12
    ' start_time:   13-18
    ' end_time:     19-24
    ' actual_time:  25-30, pad bytes: 31-32
    ' description:  33-72
    ' app_date:     73-80

Public Function to_string() As String

    to_string = _
        ODB.long_str(key) & " " & _
        ODB.int_str(start_time) & _
        ODB.int_str(end_time) & _
        ODB.int_str(actual_time) & "  " & _
        ODB.fix_len(description, 40) & _
        ODB.date_str(app_date)

End Function

Public Sub from_string(s As String)

    key = Val(left(s, 11))
    start_time = Val(Mid(s, 13, 6))
    end_time = Val(Mid(s, 19, 6))
    actual_time = Val(Mid(s, 25, 6))
    description = Mid(s, 33, 40)
    app_date = ODB.yyyymmdd2date(Right(s, 8))

End Sub
```

The Get() and Set() Methods

The rest of the class consists of get() and set() methods (not Property Gets and Lets). The basic handling of the times is as tstrings, that is, times in HH:MM format, so I get a tstring and return a tstring. Internally, though, I store the integer. For the times, I also provide an `iget()` method that contains the integer value. (The time tool likes the integers, so it can do its calculations.)

This is a sample of the code:

```
Public Sub set_end_time(s As String)

    end_time = ODB.tstring2int(s)

End Sub

Public Function iget_end_time() As Integer

    iget_end_time = end_time

End Function

Public Function get_end_time() As String

    get_end_time = ODB.int2tstring(end_time)

End Function
```

The Full Listing

If you don't have the disk or if your partner's pinned it over the bull's-eye on the dart board and shot badly, Listing 16-2 shows the full file.

Listing 16-2
App.cls — the Appointment class

```
VERSION 1.0 CLASS
BEGIN
  MultiUse = -1  'True
END
Attribute VB_Name = "App"
Attribute VB_GlobalNameSpace = False
Attribute VB_Creatable = True
Attribute VB_PredeclaredId = False
Attribute VB_Exposed = False
' App.cls — the Appointment class
' Copyright 1997, Martin L. Rinehart

Option Explicit

' Data members:
    Public key As Long
    Public app_date As Date
```

```
    Private start_time As Integer
    Private end_time As Integer
    Private actual_time As Integer

    Public description As String

Public Sub set_start_time(s As String)

    start_time = ODB.tstring2int(s)

End Sub

Public Function iget_start_time() As Integer

    iget_start_time = start_time

End Function

Public Function get_start_time() As String

    get_start_time = ODB.int2tstring(start_time)

End Function

Public Sub set_end_time(s As String)

    end_time = ODB.tstring2int(s)

End Sub

Public Function iget_end_time() As Integer

    iget_end_time = end_time

End Function

Public Function get_end_time() As String

    get_end_time = ODB.int2tstring(end_time)

End Function

Public Sub set_actual_time(s As String)

    actual_time = ODB.tstring2int(s)

End Sub
```

(continued)

App.cls — the Appointment class

```
Public Function get_actual_time() As String

    get_actual_time = ODB.int2tstring(actual_time)

End Function

Public Function iget_actual_time() As Integer

    iget_actual_time = actual_time

End Function

Private Sub Class_Initialize()

    key = 0 ' will be set by ODB
    app_date = Date
    start_time = 0 ' defaults
    end_time = 0
    actual_time = 0
    description = ""

End Sub

Public Function get_name() As String

    get_name = "App"

End Function

' string layout:
    ' key:          1-11, pad byte: 12
    ' start_time:   13-18
    ' end_time:     19-24
    ' actual_time:  25-30, pad bytes: 31-32
    ' description:  33-72
    ' app_date:     73-80

Public Function to_string() As String

    to_string = _
        ODB.long_str(key) & " " & _
        ODB.int_str(start_time) & _
        ODB.int_str(end_time) & _
        ODB.int_str(actual_time) & "  " & _
        ODB.fix_len(description, 40) & _
        ODB.date_str(app_date)

End Function
```

```
Public Sub from_string(s As String)

    key = Val(left(s, 11))
    start_time = Val(Mid(s, 13, 6))
    end_time = Val(Mid(s, 19, 6))
    actual_time = Val(Mid(s, 25, 6))
    description = Mid(s, 33, 40)
    app_date = ODB.yyyymmdd2date(Right(s, 8))

End Sub

' end of App.cls
```

THE APPOINTMENT FORM

Figure 16-1 shows the appointment data entry panel. With the Completed box checked, the Actual TextBox and Label are displayed, as we discussed in Chapter 14, only when this box is checked.

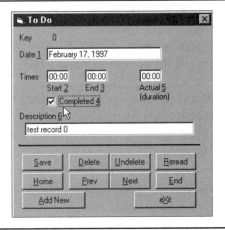

Figure 16-1
The appointment form shows a test record.

The time boxes are TextBox objects, not the ActiveX control we built in Chapter 12. This lets you build the whole project even if you only have the Standard edition of Visual Basic. The error checking function, OK_time() in the ODB class, lets you use these TextBoxes with confidence.

Let's begin by looking at the declarations. Again, we won't discuss routines that are trivial or that you've already seen when we built our first ODB. For the full code, see Listing 16-3.

The Declarations

First, we'll have the `Public dont_unload` data member. This is set by the parent (in the case of the appointment form, the parent is the schedule tool). This class treats `dont_unload` as a read-only property. (You have no way to tell Visual Basic to enforce this; you just have to be careful.)

As long as `dont_unload` is `True`, the `QueryUnload` event handler will cancel attempts to unload. Because all `Boolean`s default to `False`, this will have no effect when you run this code as a standalone program.

Next, there are the three properties you need for an ODB-accessing class. They are a current object, its number, and the ODB itself. These are public here because the parent tool (the schedule) will need access to them. (By the way, that's the kind of thing you don't really discover until you start assembling the finished system. I found out the hard way.)

The changed `Boolean` is the flag that triggers saving the object in the ODB when you change records or exit.

The last three properties are related to the popup calendar. The `adate` stores the date of the appointment (the form will show the `ODB.nice_date()` version of this date). The `popcal` is the popup calendar object and the `im_changing_date` boolean lets you tell the difference between changes made by the user and ones you make in response to the calendar.

This is the code:

```
Public dont_unload As Boolean

Public cur_obj As App
Public cur_obj_num As Long
Public ob As ODB

Private changed As Boolean

Private adate As Date
Private popcal As Calendar
Private im_changing_date As Boolean
```

Going to and from Form

Just as ODB-stored classes supply `to_string()` and `from_string()` methods, ODB-using forms supply `from_form()` and `to_form()` methods. These take the object and display it, or take the display and put its values back into the object's properties.

You'll see that having the `get()` and `set()` time methods work externally with `tstrings` makes them very convenient to use. These are the routines:

```
Public Sub to_form()

    lblKey_num = cur_obj.key
    set_del

    adate = cur_obj.app_date
    im_changing_date = True
        txtDate.Text = ODB.nice_date(adate)
    im_changing_date = False

    txtStart_time.Text = cur_obj.get_start_time
    txtEnd_time.Text = cur_obj.get_end_time
    txtAct_time.Text = cur_obj.get_actual_time

    chkCompleted.Value = IIf( _
        txtAct_time.Text = "00:00", 0, 1)
    set_act

    txtDescription = Trim(cur_obj.description)

End Sub

Private Sub from_form()

    cur_obj.app_date = adate

    cur_obj.set_start_time txtStart_time.Text
    cur_obj.set_end_time txtEnd_time.Text
    cur_obj.set_actual_time txtAct_time.Text

    cur_obj.description = txtDescription.Text

End Sub
```

Making the Look Dynamic

The dynamic effect of having the CheckBox modify the form is basically a matter of setting the Visible property appropriately. Here, there's an additional wrinkle.

When you check the completed box, having the Actual time default to the time you calculate from the start and end times is a great convenience. So I set the "00:00" string when going to not checked and set the default time when the box is checked. This is the code:

```
Private Sub chkCompleted_Click()

    set_act

End Sub

Private Sub set_act()

' Actual time is 0 until appointment is completed
    If chkCompleted.Value = 0 Then

        lblActual.Visible = False
        txtAct_time.Text = "00:00"
        txtAct_time.Visible = False

    Else

        chkCompleted.Value = 1
        lblActual.Visible = True
        txtAct_time.Visible = True

        If txtAct_time.Text = "00:00" Then
            txtAct_time.Text = ODB.int2tstring( _
                ODB.tstring2int(txtEnd_time.Text) - _
                ODB.tstring2int(txtStart_time.Text))
        End If

    End If


    End Sub
```

The CheckBox's Click() event handler calls the set_act() routine that does the real work, which lets this code be called by the to_form() routine, also.

The Command Button Event Handlers

The command buttons' code is basically the same as that we wrote when we built our first ODB. The exit handler has been fixed by the addition of the save line you see here:

```
Private Sub cmdExit_Click()

    If changed Then cmdSave_Click
    Unload Me

End Sub
```

The navigate event has been replaced to eliminate the user-defined event.

Raising that event caused too many page fault crashes in the early versions of Visual Basic that I used. I expect it will be fixed by the time you read this, but some careful checking is in order. That feature is at release level 1.0, even though this is Visual Basic 5.

Now the code calls the go_to() method. As you see here, it does the same thing:

```
Public Sub go_to(onum As Long)

    If onum < 0 Then onum = 0

    If onum >= ob.get_num_objects Then
        onum = ob.get_num_objects - 1
    End If

    If changed Then
        from_form
        ob.rep_obj cur_obj_num, cur_obj
    End If

    cur_obj_num = ob.get_obj(onum, cur_obj)
    changed = False
    to_form

End Sub
```

The Constructor and Destructor

We have both a constructor and a destructor here. The constructor code is in the Initialize() routine, shown here:

```
Private Sub Form_Initialize()

    Set cur_obj = New App
    Set ob = New ODB

    Dim pn As String ' pathname
    pn = cur_obj.get_name

    If Len(Dir(pn & ".ODB")) = 0 Then
        ob.create_odb cur_obj
        ob.add_obj cur_obj
    Else
        If ob.open_odb(pn) <> openOK Then End
    End If

    Set popcal = New Calendar
    popcal.Visible = False
    popcal.dont_unload = True
    Load popcal

    cur_obj_num = ob.get_obj(0, cur_obj)
    to_form ' fill in TextBoxes

    changed = False

End Sub
```

When your constructor creates an object, such as the cur_obj and ob objects that are built here, a reference is assigned to these object variables. When the object of this class goes out of scope, these variables are freed. That removes the reference, which lets Visual Basic free the objects. You don't have to worry about it. That's not true of a form-based object, however.

Forms live forever unless you kill them yourself. If you forget to unload a form that's Visible property is False, you'll see that your program doesn't end but that you have no way to access it. Try running this code in Visual Basic with the Unload statement commented out. Your run will appear to end, but Visual Basic will still highlight the break and end buttons, as it does when a program is running normally.

Memo to Bill Gates

Bill, you know that that's pretty bizarre, don't you? Why not treat a form-based object like any normal object? Free the last reference, and it goes away. That would make our lives a lot easier.

The destructor code is placed in the QueryUnload() handler. This method also has to examine that dont_unload boolean that the parent may hand it and take its status as an order if it's True. This is the code:

```
Private Sub Form_QueryUnload( _
        Cancel As Integer, UnloadMode As Integer)

    If changed Then cmdSave_Click

    If dont_unload Then
        Visible = False
        Cancel = -1 ' cancels the unload
    Else
        popcal.Visible = False
        popcal.dont_unload = False
        Unload popcal
        Set popcal = Nothing
    End If

End Sub
```

The Change() LostFocus() Methods

There are many Change() methods. Most of them have one working line that sets the changed Boolean to True. The time and date boxes are more interesting. This shows the time:

```
Private Sub txtAct_time_change()

    changed = True
    txtAct_time.BackColor = set_bcolor(txtAct_time.Text)

End Sub

Private Sub txtAct_time_LostFocus()

    If Not ODB.OK_time(txtAct_time.Text) Then
        txtAct_time.Text = "00:00"
    End If

End Sub
```

For time, the set_bcolor function returns yellow when the text string isn't in HH:MM format and it returns white when the string is formatted correctly. The LostFocus() event ensures that the string you pass to the object in from_form() is correctly formatted.

This isn't quite as nice as our HH_MM control, which preserved the original value. You can add that feature if you think it's important.

Now look at the date change() handler:

```
Private Sub txtDate_Change()

    If Not im_changing_date Then txtDate_GotFocus

End Sub
```

The user might get into your txtDate TextBox and use normal editing keys on the nice_date() version of the date. You want to prevent this. If the user positions the text cursor inside this box, you immediately want to launch the popup calendar, so the user sets the date with that tool. Once you start using this system, you'll see that this technique is very, very friendly. Clicking the calendar is much faster than entering the data any other way I've tried. The txtDate's GotFocus event has the code that pops up the calendar, checks the date, and assigns the date if it's been changed, which is why you can call it here.

You also need to be able to set this TextBox.Text value in response to the pop-up calendar. Setting txtDate.Text from within the program will also raise a Change() event, so you don't want the calendar popped up a second time if your program is setting the text. That's where im_changing_date comes in. Your program sets that True when it does its job and immediately resets it to False after it's made the change.

Popping up the Calendar

This is the code in the GotFocus() method:

```
Private Sub txtDate_GotFocus()

    Static working As Boolean

    If working Then

' here if just re-entering after calendar pops down
        working = False

    Else
        working = True
        popcal.set_hi_date adate
        popcal.Show vbModal
```

```
Dim d As Date
d = popcal.get_hi_date

If d <> adate Then
    adate = popcal.get_hi_date
    im_changing_date = True
        txtDate.Text = ODB.nice_date(adate)
    im_changing_date = False
    changed = True
End If

txtDate.Visible = False ' lose focus
txtDate.Visible = True

    End If

End Sub
```

It sets the working static boolean when the date TextBox gains focus. Remember that it loses focus when the calendar is popped up and gets focus again when the calendar is closed. The working variable lets you know when you're coming in here to start the process as opposed to the time when you're gaining focus in mid-process.

After showing the calendar, you read its date with its get_hi_date() method. If that's a new value, you reset your adate property and the text in the TextBox.

The final trick, turning Visible to False and then back to True, forces focus out of this TextBox, so the user can't edit your nice_date() string. This means that its theoretically impossible for the Change event to be raised by user action. You take control of popping up the calendar when you get focus, and then forcing focus out.

OK, so comment out the txtDate_Change() method. It's theoretically useless. I bet you'll uncomment it quickly enough. Funnier things than this happen in Windows.

The Full Listing

The full file is available on disk in the 16-03 file. That includes the related project files and a sample database. If you don't have the disk, or if your toddler thought that her Oreo cookie made a neat fit in its center, Listing 16-3 shows the editable portion. Appendix B shows the full list of properties set for the frmApp form.

Listing 16-3
frmApp.frm — the Appointment entry panel

```
' frmApp.frm — Appointment data entry form
' Copyright 1997, Martin L. Rinehart

Option Explicit

Public dont_unload As Boolean

Public cur_obj As App
Public cur_obj_num As Long
Public ob As ODB

Private changed As Boolean

Private adate As Date
Private popcal As Calendar
Private im_changing_date As Boolean

Public Sub to_form()

    lblKey_num = cur_obj.key
    set_del

    adate = cur_obj.app_date
    im_changing_date = True
        txtDate.Text = ODB.nice_date(adate)
    im_changing_date = False

    txtStart_time.Text = cur_obj.get_start_time
    txtEnd_time.Text = cur_obj.get_end_time
    txtAct_time.Text = cur_obj.get_actual_time

    chkCompleted.Value = IIf( _
        txtAct_time.Text = "00:00", 0, 1)
    set_act

    txtDescription = Trim(cur_obj.description)

End Sub

Private Sub from_form()

    cur_obj.app_date = adate

    cur_obj.set_start_time txtStart_time.Text
    cur_obj.set_end_time txtEnd_time.Text
    cur_obj.set_actual_time txtAct_time.Text
```

```
        cur_obj.description = txtDescription.Text

End Sub

Private Sub chkCompleted_Click()

    set_act

End Sub

Private Sub set_act()

' Actual time is 0 until appointment is completed
    If chkCompleted.Value = 0 Then

        lblActual.Visible = False
        txtAct_time.Text = "00:00"
        txtAct_time.Visible = False

    Else

        chkCompleted.Value = 1
        lblActual.Visible = True
        txtAct_time.Visible = True

        If txtAct_time.Text = "00:00" Then
            txtAct_time.Text = ODB.int2tstring( _
                ODB.tstring2int(txtEnd_time.Text) - _
                ODB.tstring2int(txtStart_time.Text))
        End If

    End If


End Sub

Private Sub cmdAdd_Click()

    If changed Then cmdSave_Click

    Set cur_obj = New App
    cur_obj_num = ob.add_obj(cur_obj)

    changed = False
    to_form
```

(continued)

frmApp.frm — the Appointment entry panel

```
        SendKeys "%1" ' Alt+1 starts data entry

    End Sub

    Private Sub cmdDelete_Click()

        If ob.obj_is_deleted Then Exit Sub

        If changed Then
            ob.obj_is_deleted = True
            ob.rep_obj cur_obj_num, cur_obj
            changed = False
        Else
            ob.del_obj cur_obj_num
        End If

        set_del

    End Sub

    Private Sub cmdEnd_Click()

        go_to ob.get_num_objects - 1

    End Sub

    Private Sub cmdExit_Click()

        If changed Then cmdSave_Click
        Unload Me

    End Sub

    Private Sub cmdHome_Click()

        go_to 0

    End Sub

    Private Sub cmdNext_Click()

        go_to cur_obj_num + 1

    End Sub

    Private Sub cmdPrev_Click()
```

```
        go_to cur_obj_num - 1

End Sub

Private Sub cmdReread_Click()

    ob.get_obj cur_obj_num, cur_obj
    to_form
    changed = False

End Sub

Private Sub cmdSave_Click()

    from_form
    ob.rep_obj cur_obj_num, cur_obj
    changed = False

End Sub

Private Sub cmdUndelete_Click()

    If Not ob.obj_is_deleted Then Exit Sub

    If changed Then
        ob.obj_is_deleted = False
        ob.rep_obj cur_obj_num, cur_obj
        changed = False
    Else
        ob.undel_obj cur_obj_num
    End If

    set_del

End Sub

Private Sub Form_Initialize()

    Set cur_obj = New App
    Set ob = New ODB

    Dim pn As String ' pathname
    pn = cur_obj.get_name

    If Len(Dir(pn & ".ODB")) = 0 Then
        ob.create_odb cur_obj
        ob.add_obj cur_obj
```

(continued)

frmApp.frm — the Appointment entry panel

```
    Else
        If ob.open_odb(pn) <> openOK Then End
    End If

    Set popcal = New Calendar
    popcal.Visible = False
    popcal.dont_unload = True
    Load popcal

    cur_obj_num = ob.get_obj(0, cur_obj)
    to_form ' fill in TextBoxes

    changed = False

End Sub

Private Sub Form_QueryUnload( _
        Cancel As Integer, UnloadMode As Integer)

    If changed Then cmdSave_Click

    If dont_unload Then
        Visible = False
        Cancel = -1 ' cancels the unload
    Else
        popcal.Visible = False
        popcal.dont_unload = False
        Unload popcal
        Set popcal = Nothing
    End If

End Sub

Private Sub timEst_time_Change()

    changed = True

End Sub

Private Sub txtName_Change()

    changed = True

End Sub

Private Sub set_del()
```

```
        lblDeleted.Caption = _
            IIf(ob.obj_is_deleted, "Deleted", "")

End Sub

Public Sub go_to(onum As Long)

    If onum < 0 Then onum = 0

    If onum >= ob.get_num_objects Then
        onum = ob.get_num_objects - 1
    End If

    If changed Then
        from_form
        ob.rep_obj cur_obj_num, cur_obj
    End If

    cur_obj_num = ob.get_obj(onum, cur_obj)
    changed = False
    to_form

End Sub

Private Sub txtAct_time_change()

    changed = True
    txtAct_time.BackColor = set_bcolor(txtAct_time.Text)

End Sub

Private Sub txtAct_time_LostFocus()

    If Not ODB.OK_time(txtAct_time.Text) Then
        txtAct_time.Text = "00:00"
    End If

End Sub

Private Sub txtDate_Change()

    If Not im_changing_date Then txtDate_GotFocus

End Sub

Private Sub txtDate_GotFocus()
```

(continued)

frmApp.frm — the Appointment entry panel

```vb
        Static working As Boolean

        If working Then

        ' here if just re-entering after calendar pops down
            working = False

        Else
            working = True
            popcal.set_hi_date adate
            popcal.Show vbModal

            Dim d As Date
            d = popcal.get_hi_date

            If d <> adate Then
                adate = popcal.get_hi_date
                im_changing_date = True
                    txtDate.Text = ODB.nice_date(adate)
                im_changing_date = False
                changed = True
            End If

            txtDate.Visible = False ' lose focus
            txtDate.Visible = True

        End If

    End Sub

    Private Sub txtDescription_Change()

        changed = True

    End Sub

    Private Sub txtEnd_time_change()

        changed = True
        txtEnd_time.BackColor = set_bcolor(txtEnd_time.Text)

    End Sub

    Private Sub txtEnd_time_LostFocus()

        If Not ODB.OK_time(txtEnd_time.Text) Then
            txtEnd_time.Text = "00:00"
        End If
```

```
    End Sub

    Private Sub txtStart_time_change()

        changed = True
        txtStart_time.BackColor = set_bcolor(txtStart_time.Text)

    End Sub

    Private Sub txtStart_time_LostFocus()

        If Not ODB.OK_time(txtStart_time.Text) Then
            txtStart_time.Text = "00:00"
        End If

    End Sub

    Private Function set_bcolor(s As String) As Long

        set_bcolor = IIf(ODB.OK_time(s), vbWhite, vbYellow)

    End Function

    ' end of frmApp.frm
```

THE CALENDAR CLASS

Constructing this code as a project requires the calendar class, which I mention here in the interest of thoroughness. Your existing calendar will work perfectly.

If you want to match mine completely, load the calendar form into Visual Basic and reset all the command buttons' Height properties to 360 twips, which is the height of every MyTime button. You'd be surprised at how much difference it makes to have all these exactly the same.

You'll need to fuss with the Resize() event a bit, mostly adjusting constants, to have the few extra pixels you need for this larger size.

My adjusted Calendar.frm file is also included on disk in 16-03.

SUMMARY

In this chapter, we dove into the code for the new appointment object database. We skipped from developing top-down to working bottom-up because we needed data to serve up to the intermediate surfaces, in this case for the schedule tool.

Starting in this chapter, I'm suggesting that you look at the code and build the project, but not enter and build one step at a time.

I began by recreating an ODB that correctly handled maintaining unique keys. While I was improving the ODB, I added a simple method to find an object given its key.

After looking at the ODB, we moved on to the appointment class. It's a simple, ODB-compliant class that supports the get_name(), to_string(), and from_string() interface. Its only trick was to handle times internally as integers while dealing with the outside world with "HH:MM" strings.

The appointment form completed this project. That was similar to the ODB-based schedule that we had built, but it replaced the four-file structure with a three-file one. This is simpler and avoids some bugs that plagued the prerelease versions of Visual Basic 5.

As a final note, I mentioned some cosmetic improvements I've made in the calendar. In the next chapter, we'll take our new ODB and put it to use in a project database.

PROGRAMMING THE PROJECT DATABASE

17

*I*n the last chapter, we looked at the revised ODB and the appointments database. In this chapter, we're going to look at the project database.

The bad news is that you've seen most of this already, so it won't be as interesting as exploring new ground. The good news is that it won't take very long. In the next chapter, we'll be looking at the project cascade surface, which will be challenging new ground indeed, but we can't start cascading our projects until we've built a database that holds them.

We'll begin with the `Prjct` class, and then go on to the `frmPrjct` class. In each one, we'll look at the routines that will be new to you, and we'll skip the ones that are repetitious. I hope that you'll be tinkering with the project as we go along.

THE PRJCT CLASS

The project, as I'm using it here, makes an interesting object. You can subdivide each project into a set of additional projects, and you can further subdivide each of those. Except for the arbitrary cap we place on this process to keep it within the limitations of our display, this process has no limit.

Every project except the root also has a parent. This is a classic tree. There's no distinction between a node and a leaf except that the latter has no children.

In relational databases, you use *foreign* keys to name records in other tables. A table of projects, on the other hand, uses *foreign* keys as different names within itself. This is self-referential. It's rare in databases, but it works well.

In addition to holding the *name* (key) of its parent project, each project holds the name of its precedent project. That's the one you have to complete before this one can start. (For me, for example, writing the project database code was precedent to writing this chapter.)

More sophisticated project management software allows multiple precedent projects. Go ahead and add more, if you like. I get along fine with just one.

We'll begin by looking at the class's properties.

The Prjct Class's Data Members

Each project begins with a key (required for ODB-storable classes) and a name. Then it includes keys for the foreign keys that name other projects. These are private, of course. It also includes estimated and actual start and end dates and estimated and actual times.

If you recall from Chapter 14, we'll show the times for single-day projects and not show them for multiple-day projects. In practice I use single-day projects as the leaves of my project tree, but the software will be happy to oblige if you want to subdivide single-day projects further.

This is the code:

```
' Data Members
    Public key As Long
    Public Name As String

    Private parent_key As Long
    Private after_key As Long

    Public est_start_date As Date
    Public est_end_date As Date
    Public act_start_date As Date
    Public act_end_date As Date

    Private est_time As Integer
    Private act_time As Integer
```

The Constructor and Destructor

The constructor, in `Class_Initialize()`, assigns a dummy value for the name. It assigns today's date to all four date values and lets the time values default to zero. This is the code:

```
Private Sub Class_Initialize()

    Name = "No_name"
    est_start_date = Date
    est_end_date = est_start_date
    act_start_date = est_start_date
    act_end_date = est_end_date

End Sub
```

An interesting design question is whether the dates should default to today or to the day currently set by the "boss" calendar. The choice I made here is simpler to implement and it runs as a standalone program.

The Storable Interface

As always, the `get_name()` routine is trivial. The other two, along with the associated comments, are shown here:

```
' use full module view; comments below

Public Function to_string() As String

    to_string = _
        ODB.long_str(key) & " " & _
        ODB.fix_len(Name, 40) & _
        ODB.long_str(parent_key) & " " & _
        ODB.long_str(after_key) & " " & _
        ODB.date_str(est_start_date) & _
        ODB.date_str(est_end_date) & _
        ODB.date_str(act_start_date) & _
        ODB.date_str(act_end_date) & _
        ODB.int_str(est_time) & _
        ODB.int_str(act_time)

End Function

' String layout:
    ' key 1-11, pad 12
    ' name 13-52
```

```
' parent_key 53-63, pad 64
' after_key 65-75, pad 76
' est_start_date 77-84
' est_end_date 85-92
' act_start_date 93-100
' act_end_date 101-108
' est_time 109-114
' act_time 115-120

Public Sub from_string(ByVal s As String)

    key = Val(left(s, 11))
    Name = Mid(s, 13, 40)
    parent_key = Val(Mid(s, 53, 11))
    after_key = Val(Mid(s, 65, 11))
    est_start_date = ODB.yyyymmdd2date(Mid(s, 77, 8))
    est_end_date = ODB.yyyymmdd2date(Mid(s, 85, 8))
    act_start_date = ODB.yyyymmdd2date(Mid(s, 93, 8))
    act_end_date = ODB.yyyymmdd2date(Mid(s, 101, 8))
    est_time = Val(Mid(s, 109, 6))
    act_time = Val(Right(s, 6))

End Sub
```

Putting the comments between the two functions lets you view both comments and code, which is absolutely necessary to get these routines implemented robustly. (If they're not perfect, you'll find out quickly!)

As the starting comment points out, if you don't use full module view in the code editor, you'll see comments above, but not below, the current method.

The Data Access Methods

The remainder of this class provides get() and set() routines. The keys are presented to the outside world as strings, this way:

```
Public Function get_parent_key() As String

    get_parent_key = ODB.long_str(parent_key)

End Function

Public Sub set_parent_key(s As String)

    parent_key = Val(s)

End Sub
```

Times are treated as `tstring` objects externally, with an `iget()` provided for instances where the calling code really wants the integer value. (The time surface, for example, totals the times, so it needs the integer.) This is an example:

```
Public Function get_act_time() As String

    get_act_time = ODB.int2tstring(act_time)

End Function

Public Function iget_act_time() As Integer

    iget_act_time = act_time

End Function

Public Sub set_act_time(s As String)

    act_time = ODB.tstring2int(s)

End Sub
```

The Full Listing

Listing 17-1 shows the complete Prjct.cls file, including the part not visible in the code editor.

Listing 17-1
Prjct.cls — the Project class

```
VERSION 1.0 CLASS
BEGIN
  MultiUse = -1  'True
END
Attribute VB_Name = "Prjct"
Attribute VB_GlobalNameSpace = False
Attribute VB_Creatable = True
Attribute VB_PredeclaredId = False
Attribute VB_Exposed = False
' Prjct.cls — The Prjct object
' Copyright 1997, Martin L. Rinehart

Option Explicit
```

(continued)

Prjct.cls — the Project class

```
' Data Members
    Public key As Long
    Public Name As String

    Private parent_key As Long
    Private after_key As Long

    Public est_start_date As Date
    Public est_end_date As Date
    Public act_start_date As Date
    Public act_end_date As Date

    Private est_time As Integer
    Private act_time As Integer


Private Sub Class_Initialize()

    Name = "No_name"
    est_start_date = Date
    est_end_date = est_start_date
    act_start_date = est_start_date
    act_end_date = est_end_date

End Sub

' The storable interface

Public Function get_name() As String

    get_name = "Prjct"

End Function

' use full module view; comments below

Public Function to_string() As String

    to_string = _
        ODB.long_str(key) & " " & _
        ODB.fix_len(Name, 40) & _
        ODB.long_str(parent_key) & " " & _
        ODB.long_str(after_key) & " " & _
        ODB.date_str(est_start_date) & _
        ODB.date_str(est_end_date) & _
        ODB.date_str(act_start_date) & _
        ODB.date_str(act_end_date) & _
        ODB.int_str(est_time) & _
        ODB.int_str(act_time)
```

```
End Function

' String layout:
    ' key 1-11, pad 12
    ' name 13-52
    ' parent_key 53-63, pad 64
    ' after_key 65-75, pad 76
    ' est_start_date 77-84
    ' est_end_date 85-92
    ' act_start_date 93-100
    ' act_end_date 101-108
    ' est_time 109-114
    ' act_time 115-120

Public Sub from_string(ByVal s As String)

    key = Val(left(s, 11))
    Name = Mid(s, 13, 40)
    parent_key = Val(Mid(s, 53, 11))
    after_key = Val(Mid(s, 65, 11))
    est_start_date = ODB.yyyymmdd2date(Mid(s, 77, 8))
    est_end_date = ODB.yyyymmdd2date(Mid(s, 85, 8))
    act_start_date = ODB.yyyymmdd2date(Mid(s, 93, 8))
    act_end_date = ODB.yyyymmdd2date(Mid(s, 101, 8))
    est_time = Val(Mid(s, 109, 6))
    act_time = Val(Right(s, 6))

End Sub

Public Function get_parent_key() As String

    get_parent_key = ODB.long_str(parent_key)

End Function

Public Sub set_parent_key(s As String)

    parent_key = Val(s)

End Sub

Public Function get_after_key() As String

    get_after_key = ODB.long_str(after_key)

End Function

Public Sub set_after_key(s As String)
```

(continued)

Prjct.cls — the Project class

```
        after_key = Val(s)

End Sub

Public Function get_act_time() As String

    get_act_time = ODB.int2tstring(act_time)

End Function

Public Function iget_act_time() As Integer

    iget_act_time = act_time

End Function

Public Sub set_act_time(s As String)

    act_time = ODB.tstring2int(s)

End Sub

Public Function get_est_time() As String

    get_est_time = ODB.int2tstring(est_time)

End Function

Public Function iget_est_time() As Integer

    iget_est_time = est_time

End Function

Public Sub set_est_time(s As String)

    est_time = ODB.tstring2int(s)

End Sub


' end of Prjct.cls
```

THE FRMPRJCT FORM-BASED CLASS

The frmPrjct form is the basic data entry panel at the deepest level of the project cascade. Figure 17-1 shows what we are working on.

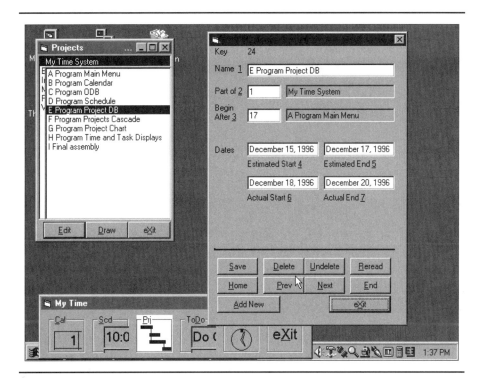

Figure 17-1
The menu launched the cascade which launched the form.

I don't start by building a form, though.

Immediately after I write the class module, I check it. The form module is a handy place to do this, if you do it before you add anything else. You can use `Form_Load()` the same way you would use `Sub Main()` in a standard module.

I write a routine that creates a new whatever and then assigns values to the properties. Then I `to_string()` it and `from_string()` the properties back. If a second `to_string()` still matches the result of the first `to_string()`, you can be confident that you did your job correctly.

I've left this code in place, commented out, so that you (or I) can use it if we need to add or remove properties from the class. This is what my test code looks like:

```
'Private Sub Form_Load()
'
' debugging code — test to/from_string:
'     Dim t As Prjct
'     Set t = New Prjct
'
'     t.Key = 123
'     t.Name = "Test Prjct"
'     t.set_est_time "1:00"
'     t.set_act_time "0:45"
'     t.Prjct_date = "1/1/1999"
'
'     Dim s1 As String, s2 As String
'     s1 = t.to_string
'
'     t.from_string (s1)
'     s2 = t.to_string
'
'     Debug.Print IIf(s1 = s2, "OK", "Error")
'
'End Sub
```

Now let's dive into the class, beginning, as always, with the properties.

The frmPrjct Class's Data Members

The Public properties include the public cur_obj (in this case, a Prjct object) and cur_obj_num, the associated ODB object and the dont_unload property set by the parent (if there is a parent). This is the code:

```
' public properties
    Public cur_obj As Prjct
    Public cur_obj_num As Long
    Public ob As ODB
    Public dont_unload As Boolean
```

The Private properties include a popup calendar and an array of dates. For each date, I could have coded the popup calendar logic separately. By using an array of dates, I only have to code for the array (which functions like a class, with array members being objects of the class). The estimated start date is in prj_dates(0), for example. An enum helps keep the code readable. (Reading prj_dates(dn_est_start) is better than prj_dates(0), isn't it?)

The my_date_change Boolean is used to distinguish between change events directed by the code and change events caused by the user. The changed Boolean is our old friend who signals the need to rewrite the data to the database. This is the code:

```
Private pop_cal As Calendar

Private prj_dates(0 To 3) As Date
Private Enum dnames
    dn_est_start
    dn_est_end
    dn_act_start
    dn_act_end
End Enum

Private my_date_change As Boolean
Private changed As Boolean
```

The Constructor and Destructor

The constructor code is in Form_Initialize. It looks like this:

```
Private Sub Form_Initialize()

    Set cur_obj = New Prjct
    Set ob = New ODB

    Set pop_cal = New Calendar
    Load pop_cal

    Dim pn As String ' pathname
    pn = cur_obj.get_name

    If Len(Dir(pn & ".ODB")) = 0 Then
        ob.create_odb cur_obj
        ob.add_obj cur_obj
    Else
        If ob.open_odb(pn) <> openOK Then End
    End If

    cur_obj_num = ob.get_obj(0, cur_obj)
    to_form ' fill in TextBoxes

    changed = False

End Sub
```

A destructor is needed because without it the popup calendar will not unload, and your program won't end after the last object goes invisible. Query_Unload() provides this service, as well as canceling an unload, if the parent has set dont_unload to True.

This is the code:

```
Private Sub Form_QueryUnload( _
        Cancel As Integer, UnloadMode As Integer)

    If changed Then cmdSave_Click

    If dont_unload Then

        Cancel = 1 ' Cancel the unload
        Visible = False

    Else

        Unload pop_cal
        Set pop_cal = Nothing ' Free Willy

    End If

End Sub
```

Going to_form() and from_form()

The process of going to and from the form should be familiar to you by now. These are the details:

```
Private Sub to_form()

    lblKey_num = cur_obj.key
    set_del

    txtName.Text = Trim(cur_obj.Name)
    txtParent_num.Text = Trim(cur_obj.get_parent_key)
    txtAfter_num.Text = Trim(cur_obj.get_after_key)

    change_date dn_est_start, cur_obj.est_start_date
    change_date dn_est_end, cur_obj.est_end_date
    change_date dn_act_start, cur_obj.act_start_date
    change_date dn_act_end, cur_obj.act_end_date

    txtEst_time.Text = cur_obj.get_est_time
    txtAct_time.Text = cur_obj.get_act_time
```

```
        set_form_display
        lookup_parent
        lookup_precedent

    End Sub
```

The `change_date` routine takes care of setting both the correct date variable and the text display. The `lookup_parent` and `lookup_precedent` routines provide the respective project names, given the keys that are part of the object.

The `from_form()` routine is simpler:

```
    Private Sub from_form()

        cur_obj.Name = txtName.Text
        cur_obj.set_parent_key txtParent_num.Text
        cur_obj.set_after_key txtAfter_num.Text

        cur_obj.est_start_date = prj_dates(dn_est_start)
        cur_obj.est_end_date = prj_dates(dn_est_end)
        cur_obj.act_start_date = prj_dates(dn_act_start)
        cur_obj.act_end_date = prj_dates(dn_act_end)

        cur_obj.set_est_time txtEst_time.Text
        cur_obj.set_act_time txtAct_time.Text

    End Sub
```

The Command Button Click() Handlers

You know about all the command button handling because you wrote your own with our first ODB, and revisited the handlers in the last chapter. The `cmdAdd_Click()` method is much fancier here than it's been elsewhere.

This code sets the current project as the added project's precedent. In practice, this is right most of the time. It also sets the new project's parent to be the same as the current project, which is also right most of the time.

It also taps Alt+1, which starts data entry for you. This is the code:

```
    Private Sub cmdAdd_Click()

        If changed Then cmdSave_Click

        Dim old_parent As Long, old_key As Long
        old_parent = cur_obj.get_parent_key
```

```
        old_key = cur_obj.key

        Dim part_of As Long, begin_after As Long
        part_of = cur_obj.get_parent_key
        begin_after = cur_obj.get_after_key

        Set cur_obj = New Prjct
        cur_obj_num = ob.add_obj(cur_obj)

        cur_obj.set_parent_key Str(old_parent)
        cur_obj.set_after_key Str(old_key)
        changed = True

        to_form

        SendKeys "%1" ' press Alt+1

    End Sub
```

Handling the Dates as a Component Array

Dates are implemented as an array, which cuts down on the code. A control array's event handlers apply to every member of the array, just as a class's methods apply to every object instantiated from the class.

This leads to more efficient code, since you don't have to code, for example, txtAct_date_Change and txtEst_date_Change. On the other hand, you have to refer to txtDates(Index), which is less readable. In practice, I prefer the more readable code for up to two or three controls. At four, though, an array seems appropriate. Consider the dates_Change routine:

```
    Private Sub dates_Change(Index As Integer)

        If Not my_date_change Then

            my_date_change = True
            dates(Index).Text = ODB.nice_date(prj_dates(Index))
            my_date_change = False

            dates_GotFocus Index

        End If

    End Sub
```

This routine adds the "January 1, 1997" form of the date to the visible TextBox's Text. That fixes whatever damage the user did through changing the text. It sets my_date_change to True before it makes that change so that it doesn't call itself recursively. (It actually does call itself, but at the first recursive level it just returns immediately.) Finally, it calls the GotFocus() method, which pops up the calendar that we want the user to manipulate.

The GotFocus() method is similar to the ones we worked with before, except that it is adjusted to handle the array. This is the code:

```
Private Sub dates_GotFocus(Index As Integer)

    Static working As Boolean ' initially False
    If working Then

        working = False

    Else

        working = True

        pop_cal.set_hi_date prj_dates(Index)
        pop_cal.Show vbModal

        Dim d As Date
        d = pop_cal.get_hi_date

        If d <> prj_dates(Index) Then

            changed = True
            change_date (Index), d

            Select Case Index
                Case 0: Est_start_Change
                Case 1: Est_end_Change
                Case 2: Act_start_Change
                Case 3: Act_end_Change
            End Select

        End If

    End If

End Sub
```

Date Changing Methods

The array handling is complemented by individual date handlers that take care of special cases. For example, the end date handlers check the start date. If it's not on or before the end date, they back up the start date. This is an example:

```
Private Sub Act_end_Change()

    changed = True

    If prj_dates(dn_act_end) < _
            prj_dates(dn_act_start) Then

        change_date dn_act_start, prj_dates(dn_act_end)

    End If

End Sub
```

The actual date changing is done by the change_date() method, which takes care to change both the date in the date array and the text on the display. Changing the text is done with the my_date_change Boolean preventing excess recursion, this way:

```
Private Sub change_date(date_num As Byte, new_date As Date)

    prj_dates(date_num) = new_date

    my_date_change = True
    dates(date_num).Text = ODB.nice_date(new_date)
    my_date_change = False

End Sub
```

Handling Foreign Keys

A really robust handling of foreign keys will never let the user get his or her hands on the key. In this system, for example, we could pop up list boxes that listed project names. When one was selected, we could fill in the key in the object, but display the name for the user.

My treatment isn't completely robust, but it meets my needs and doesn't take too much code. The `txtAfter_num_Change()` routine handles the process for the precedent project key, this way:

```
Private Sub txtAfter_num_Change()

    Dim ok_num As Boolean
    ok_num = OK_key(txtAfter_num.Text)

    If ok_num Then

        txtAfter_num.BackColor = vbWhite
        lookup_precedent

    Else

        txtAfter_num.BackColor = vbYellow

    End If

    changed = True

End Sub
```

The job is done the same way for the parent key. Both routines depend on this `lookup_parent()` method:

```
Private Sub lookup_parent()

    txtParent_name.Text = lookup_key_string( _
        txtParent_num.Text)

End Sub
```

That method in turn depends on `lookup_key_string()`, which actually searches the database. It lets the `ODB.find_obj()` routine do the hard work, this way:

```
Private Function lookup_key_string(s As String) As String

' find lookup name
' (called after checking for valid number)

    Dim this_obj_num As Long
    this_obj_num = cur_obj_num

    Dim lookup_obj_num As Long
    lookup_obj_num = Val(s)
```

```
cur_obj_num = ob.find_obj(lookup_obj_num, cur_obj)

If cur_obj_num > -1 Then
    lookup_key_string = cur_obj.Name
Else
    lookup_key_string = ""
End If

cur_obj_num = ob.get_obj(this_obj_num, cur_obj)

End Function
```

These routines are only called with valid keys. A valid key is a positive integer less than the current key, or, in the special case where the current key is zero, zero is the only valid foreign key. OK_key() handles the job:

```
Private Function OK_key(s As String) As Boolean

Dim ok_num As Boolean
ok_num = ODB.OK_posint(s)

If ok_num Then

    If cur_obj.key > 0 Then
        OK_key = Val(s) < cur_obj.key
    Else
        OK_key = Val(s) = 0
    End If

End If

End Function
```

Making the Display Dynamic

There are two forms of the display. Figure 17-2 shows them side by side.

I took that screen shot by launching MyTime twice, by the way. Kids, don't try this at home! I now have two ODBs each thinking that it is in charge of a single file. That's just one file, of course. (I clicked eXit on everything that was available and breathed a sigh of relief when it didn't trash the file.)

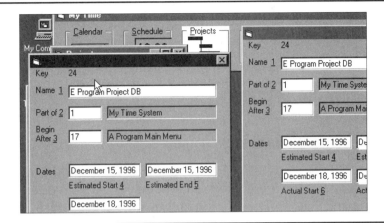

Figure 17-2
Single-day and multi-day versions of one form.

The `set_form_display()` method handles changing between multiple-day and single-day displays. This code shows that it doesn't just change Visible properties, although that's the bulk of the job. It also changes the label of the `Actual` date. (Calling it *Start* isn't appropriate if it's the only day.) Figure 17-2 shows the effect of this small bit of added code:

```
Private Sub set_form_display()

If prj_dates(dn_est_start) = _
        prj_dates(dn_est_end) Then

    lblAct_start_date.Caption = "Actual &6"
    lblAct_end_date.Visible = False
    dates(dn_act_end).Visible = False
    lblTime.Visible = True
    lblEst_time.Visible = True
    lblAct_time.Visible = True
    txtEst_time.Visible = True
    txtAct_time.Visible = True

Else

    lblAct_start_date.Caption = "Actual Start &6"
    lblAct_end_date.Visible = True
    dates(dn_act_end).Visible = True
    lblTime.Visible = False
    lblEst_time.Visible = False
    lblAct_time.Visible = False
    txtEst_time.Visible = False
    txtAct_time.Visible = False
```

```
        End If

    End Sub
```

In addition to these routines, many others exist, such as `Change()` routines for every control. You can refer to Listing 17-2 for the details.

The Full Listing

Disk file 17-02 contains the Prjct.cls file and the frmPrjct.frm files. It also contains a project file and the other classes needed to run this as a standalone program. (Calendar.frm and ODB.cls are used here, unchanged from their previous versions.)

If you don't have the disk or if your grandmother's been using it for those stencils she's painting, Listing 17-2 shows the portion of frmPrjct.frm that's visible in the code editor. The rest of the file, which details all the properties set building the form, is in Appendix D.

Listing 17-2
frmPrjct.frm — the Project data entry form

```
' frmPrjct.frm — Project data entry form
' Copyright 1997, Martin L. Rinehart

Option Explicit

' public properties
    Public cur_obj As Prjct
    Public cur_obj_num As Long
    Public ob As ODB
    Public dont_unload As Boolean

' private
    Private pop_cal As Calendar

    Private prj_dates(0 To 3) As Date
    Private Enum dnames
        dn_est_start
        dn_est_end
        dn_act_start
        dn_act_end
    End Enum

    Private my_date_change As Boolean
    Private changed As Boolean
```

```
Private Sub to_form()

    lblKey_num = cur_obj.key
    set_del

    txtName.Text = Trim(cur_obj.Name)
    txtParent_num.Text = Trim(cur_obj.get_parent_key)
    txtAfter_num.Text = Trim(cur_obj.get_after_key)

    change_date dn_est_start, cur_obj.est_start_date
    change_date dn_est_end, cur_obj.est_end_date
    change_date dn_act_start, cur_obj.act_start_date
    change_date dn_act_end, cur_obj.act_end_date

    txtEst_tiee.Text = cur_obj.get_est_time
    txtAct_time.Text = cur_obj.get_act_time

    set_form_display
    lookup_parent
    lookup_precedent

End Sub

Private Sub from_form()

    cur_obj.Name = txtName.Text
    cur_obj.set_parent_key txtParent_num.Text
    cur_obj.set_after_key txtAfter_num.Text

    cur_obj.est_start_date = prj_dates(dn_est_start)
    cur_obj.est_end_date = prj_dates(dn_est_end)
    cur_obj.act_start_date = prj_dates(dn_act_start)
    cur_obj.act_end_date = prj_dates(dn_act_end)

    cur_obj.set_est_time txtEst_time.Text
    cur_obj.set_act_time txtAct_time.Text

End Sub

Private Sub cmdAdd_Click()

    If changed Then cmdSave_Click

    Dim old_parent As Long, old_key As Long
    old_parent = cur_obj.get_parent_key
    old_key = cur_obj.key

    Dim part_of As Long, begin_after As Long
```

(continued)

frmPrjct.frm — the Project data entry form

```
        part_of = cur_obj.get_parent_key
        begin_after = cur_obj.get_after_key

        Set cur_obj = New Prjct
        cur_obj_num = ob.add_obj(cur_obj)

        cur_obj.set_parent_key Str(old_parent)
        cur_obj.set_after_key Str(old_key)
        changed = True

        to_form

        SendKeys "%1" ' press Alt+1

    End Sub

    Private Sub cmdDelete_Click()

        If ob.obj_is_deleted Then Exit Sub

        If changed Then
            ob.obj_is_deleted = True
            replace cur_obj_num, cur_obj
            changed = False
        Else
            ob.del_obj cur_obj_num
        End If

        set_del

    End Sub

    Private Sub cmdEnd_Click()

        go_to ob.get_num_objects - 1

    End Sub

    Private Sub cmdExit_Click()

        If changed Then cmdSave_Click
        changed = False

        Unload Me

    End Sub

    Private Sub cmdHome_Click()
```

```
        go_to 0

End Sub

Private Sub cmdNext_Click()

    go_to cur_obj_num + 1

End Sub

Private Sub cmdPrev_Click()

    go_to cur_obj_num - 1

End Sub

Private Sub cmdReread_Click()

    ob.get_obj cur_obj_num, cur_obj
    to_form
    changed = False

End Sub

Private Sub cmdSave_Click()

    from_form
    replace cur_obj_num, cur_obj
    changed = False

End Sub

Private Sub cmdUndelete_Click()

    If Not ob.obj_is_deleted Then Exit Sub

    If changed Then
        ob.obj_is_deleted = False
        replace cur_obj_num, cur_obj
        changed = False
    Else
        ob.undel_obj cur_obj_num
    End If

    set_del

End Sub
```

(continued)

frmPrjct.frm — the Project data entry form

```
Private Sub dates_Change(Index As Integer)

    If Not my_date_change Then

        my_date_change = True
        dates(Index).Text = ODB.nice_date(prj_dates(Index))
        my_date_change = False

        dates_GotFocus Index

    End If

End Sub

Private Sub dates_GotFocus(Index As Integer)

    Static working As Boolean ' initially False
    If working Then

        working = False

    Else

        working = True

        pop_cal.set_hi_date prj_dates(Index)
        pop_cal.Show vbModal

        Dim d As Date
        d = pop_cal.get_hi_date

        If d <> prj_dates(Index) Then

            changed = True
            change_date (Index), d

            Select Case Index
                Case 0: Est_start_Change
                Case 1: Est_end_Change
                Case 2: Act_start_Change
                Case 3: Act_end_Change
            End Select

        End If

    End If

End Sub
```

```
Private Sub Form_Initialize()

    Set cur_obj = New Prjct
    Set ob = New ODB

    Set pop_cal = New Calendar
    Load pop_cal

    Dim pn As String ' pathname
    pn = cur_obj.get_name

    If Len(Dir(pn & ".ODB")) = 0 Then
        ob.create_odb cur_obj
        ob.add_obj cur_obj
    Else
        If ob.open_odb(pn) <> openOK Then End
    End If

    cur_obj_num = ob.get_obj(0, cur_obj)
    to_form ' fill in TextBoxes

    changed = False

End Sub

'Private Sub Form_Load()
'
' debugging code — test to/from_string:
'    Dim t As Prjct
'    Set t = New Prjct
'
'    t.Key = 123
'    t.Name = "Test Prjct"
'    t.set_est_time "1:00"
'    t.set_act_time "0:45"
'    t.Prjct_date = "1/1/1999"
'
'    Dim s1 As String, s2 As String
'    s1 = t.to_string
'
'    t.from_string (s1)
'    s2 = t.to_string
'
'    Debug.Print IIf(s1 = s2, "OK", "Error")
'
'End Sub

Private Sub Form_LostFocus()
```

(continued)

frmPrjct.frm — the Project data entry form

```
        If changed Then cmdSave_Click
        changed = False

    End Sub

    Private Sub Form_QueryUnload( _
            Cancel As Integer, UnloadMode As Integer)

        If changed Then cmdSave_Click

        If dont_unload Then

            Cancel = 1 ' Cancel the unload
            Visible = False

        Else

            Unload pop_cal
            Set pop_cal = Nothing ' Free Willy

        End If

    End Sub

    Private Sub txtPrjct_date_Change()

        changed = True

    End Sub

    Private Sub Act_end_Change()

        changed = True

        If prj_dates(dn_act_end) < _
                prj_dates(dn_act_start) Then

            change_date dn_act_start, prj_dates(dn_act_end)

        End If

    End Sub

    Private Sub Act_start_Change()

        changed = True
```

```
        If prj_dates(dn_act_start) > _
                prj_dates(dn_act_end) Then

            change_date dn_act_end, prj_dates(dn_act_start)

        End If

End Sub

Private Sub Est_end_Change()

    changed = True

    If prj_dates(dn_est_end) < _
            prj_dates(dn_est_start) Then

        change_date dn_est_start, prj_dates(dn_est_end)

    End If

    set_form_display

End Sub

Private Sub Est_start_Change()

    changed = True

    If prj_dates(dn_est_start) > _
            prj_dates(dn_est_end) Then

    change_date dn_est_end, prj_dates(dn_est_start)

    End If

    set_form_display

End Sub

Private Sub change_date(date_num As Byte, new_date As Date)

    prj_dates(date_num) = new_date

    my_date_change = True
    dates(date_num).Text = ODB.nice_date(new_date)
    my_date_change = False

End Sub
```

(continued)

frmPrjct.frm — the Project data entry form

```
Private Sub txtAfter_num_Change()

    Dim ok_num As Boolean
    ok_num = OK_key(txtAfter_num.Text)

    If ok_num Then

        txtAfter_num.BackColor = vbWhite
        lookup_precedent

    Else

        txtAfter_num.BackColor = vbYellow

    End If

    changed = True

End Sub

Private Sub txtAct_time_Change()

    changed = True

    txtAct_time.BackColor = set_bcolor(txtAct_time.Text)

End Sub

Private Sub txtEst_time_Change()

    changed = True

    txtEst_time.BackColor = set_bcolor(txtEst_time.Text)

End Sub

Private Function set_bcolor(s As String) As Long

    set_bcolor = IIf(ODB.OK_time(s), vbWhite, vbYellow)

End Function

Private Sub txtAct_time_LostFocus()

    If Not ODB.OK_time(txtAct_time.Text) Then
        txtAct_time.Text = "00:00"
    End If
```

```
End Sub

Private Sub txtEst_time_LostFocus()

    If Not ODB.OK_time(txtEst_time.Text) Then
        txtEst_time.Text = "00:00"
    End If

End Sub

Private Sub txtName_Change()

    changed = True

End Sub

Private Sub txtParent_num_Change()

    Dim ok_num As Boolean
    ok_num = OK_key(txtParent_num.Text)

    If ok_num Then

        txtParent_num.BackColor = vbWhite
        lookup_parent

    Else

        txtParent_num.BackColor = vbYellow

    End If

    changed = True

End Sub

Private Sub set_form_display()

    If prj_dates(dn_est_start) = _
            prj_dates(dn_est_end) Then

        lblAct_start_date.Caption = "Actual &6"
        lblAct_end_date.Visible = False
        dates(dn_act_end).Visible = False
        lblTime.Visible = True
        lblEst_time.Visible = True
        lblAct_time.Visible = True
```

(continued)

frmPrjct.frm — the Project data entry form

```
                    txtEst_time.Visible = True
                    txtAct_time.Visible = True

            Else

                    lblAct_start_date.Caption = "Actual Start &6"
                    lblAct_end_date.Visible = True
                    dates(dn_act_end).Visible = True
                    lblTime.Visible = False
                    lblEst_time.Visible = False
                    lblAct_time.Visible = False
                    txtEst_time.Visible = False
                    txtAct_time.Visible = False

            End If

    End Sub

    Private Sub go_to(onum As Long)

        If onum < 0 Then onum = 0

        If onum >= ob.get_num_objects Then
            onum = ob.get_num_objects - 1
        End If

        If changed Then
            from_form
            ob.rep_obj cur_obj_num, cur_obj
        End If

        cur_obj_num = ob.get_obj(onum, cur_obj)
        changed = False
        to_form

    End Sub

    Private Sub replace(num As Long, obj As Object)

        If obj.Name = "" Then obj.Name = "No_name"
        ob.rep_obj num, obj

    End Sub

    Private Sub lookup_parent()

        txtParent_name.Text = lookup_key_string( _
            txtParent_num.Text)
```

```
End Sub

Private Sub lookup_precedent()

    txtAfter_name.Text = lookup_key_string( _
        txtAfter_num.Text)

End Sub

Private Function lookup_key_string(s As String) As String

' find lookup name
' (called after checking for valid number)

    Dim this_obj_num As Long
    this_obj_num = cur_obj_num

    Dim lookup_obj_num As Long
    lookup_obj_num = Val(s)

    cur_obj_num = ob.find_obj(lookup_obj_num, cur_obj)

    If cur_obj_num > -1 Then
        lookup_key_string = cur_obj.Name
    Else
        lookup_key_string = ""
    End If

    cur_obj_num = ob.get_obj(this_obj_num, cur_obj)

End Function

Private Function OK_key(s As String) As Boolean

    Dim ok_num As Boolean
    ok_num = ODB.OK_posint(s)

    If ok_num Then

        If cur_obj.key > 0 Then
            OK_key = Val(s) < cur_obj.key
        Else
            OK_key = Val(s) = 0
        End If

    End If
```

(continued)

frmPrjct.frm — the Project data entry form

```
End Function

Private Sub set_del()

    lblDeleted.Caption = _
        IIf(ob.obj_is_deleted, "Deleted", "")

End Sub

Public Sub new_cur(new_key As Long)

' May not have anything to do
    If new_key = cur_obj.key Then Exit Sub

    If changed Then cmdSave_Click

    If new_key >= 0 Then

        cur_obj_num = ob.find_obj(new_key, cur_obj)

        If cur_obj_num = -1 Then ' not found
            Set cur_obj = New Prjct
            cur_obj_num = ob.add_obj(cur_obj)
        End If

    Else

        Set cur_obj = New Prjct
        cur_obj_num = ob.add_obj(cur_obj)

    End If

    to_form

End Sub

Public Sub new_parent_key(new_key As Long)

    cur_obj.set_parent_key Str(new_key)
    to_form
    changed = True

End Sub

' end of frmPrjct.frm
```

SUMMARY

We've built another database, here. (Well, OK, I built it. You studied it.)

It shows you how to use foreign keys that name other objects in the database. The lookups here give good visual feedback to the user, although dropdown lists would be a better solution.

You saw how these keys can be intelligently initialized when adding new records. Extra logic in the cmdAdd_Click() method guesses the user's intent correctly more often than not.

Using a control array for dates took advantage of that feature's class-like behavior. By using single methods for an array of controls, a significant amount of code is eliminated.

I'm pretty sure that you're impatient to go on to that project cascade. I know I was. That's the subject of Chapter 18.

The Project
Boards Cascade

*T*he project boards cascade is my favorite tool in the
MyTime system. It took some work to program, but the
work's paying off. I'm using this system right now to keep me
on track writing this book.

In this chapter, we'll start with a look at the design, so you
know exactly where we're going. I'll include a discussion of the
theory behind this design. The boards cascade is another way
of looking at a tree. I argue that it's better than other, more
common, views for many applications.

Then we'll dive into the code. We'll begin with a look at
the properties and continue with the constructor and
destructor code. That will be familiar to you.

After that, we'll go on to unfamiliar territory, beginning
with handling the collections. Did I mention that our project
revolves around an array of collections of objects? Actually, I
think that if I'd brought that up earlier it would have scared
about half of you away from learning about Visual Basic
object-oriented programming. Here you'll see that it's actually
quite simple to code.

After the collections, we'll go on to the boards themselves.
These are an array of `ListBox`es. I do some tricky work with
the names to make the board cascade show the whole
drilldown. You'll see how its done, here.

Finally, we'll take a look at the event handlers that respond to mouse clicks, double clicks, and button clicks.

I'll skip routines like `Resize()`. If you wrote the calendar `Resize()`, you know far more than enough to handle that one on your own.

We'll start with a look at the design.

DESIGNING THE CASCADE

In this section, we'll start by looking at the design concept, and then we'll look at the design time form and we'll finish with a look at a snippet of `Resize()` code. (If arguing about code editors bores you, try asserting that coding `resize()` routines is part of the design process. It is, isn't it?)

The Design Concept

Figure 18-1 shows my first project board. The names shows you that we are looking at four subprojects at the first level. If you look at the data (on disk it's in 18-01), you'll see that the real root is project zero. The name of project zero is displayed as the `Caption` of this form. (18-01 runs without full compile.)

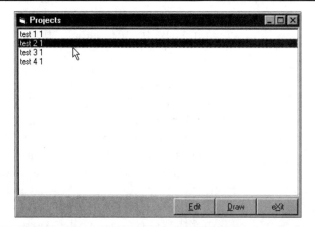

Figure 18-1
The cascade's first board.

I've clicked on the second item. That project is broken down into four more subprojects. If you click a second time on a selected item, or if you double-click, you cause its breakdown to appear. Figure 18-2 shows the breakdown of "test 2 1" into its components.

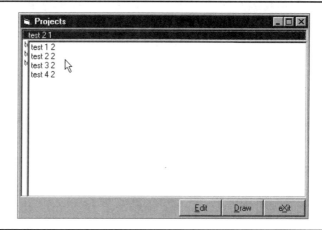

Figure 18-2

Looking at the second board in the cascade.

Look carefully at the small bit of the first board that is showing above and left of the second board. You'll see that I've taken the selected project ("test 2 1" here) and moved its name to the top. If you look more carefully, you'll see that I've inserted spaces on the left of the name.

The trick here is that this is a sorted list, so prepending spaces causes the selected item to sort first. I've kept the selected item highlighted, which keeps the color of the drilldown consistent, starting with the form's caption. Figure 18-3 shows the third level of the cascade.

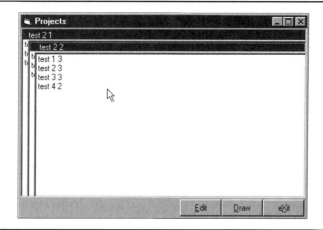

Figure 18-3

Looking at a breakdown of a breakdown.

Again, you see that I've popped the highlighted name on the second board to the top by prepending spaces.

You back out of the drilldown by clicking one of the deeper boards. You return right back to the top level with one click, no matter how deeply your boards are nested. This makes the tool very quick and very handy.

Memo to Bill Gates

Bill, you should have some of your designers take a serious look at this tool. It would make a dynamite version of My Computer, wouldn't it? The Theory section that follows explains why.

The Design Time Form

The boards themselves are members of a control array of `ListBox` objects. Figure 18-4 shows the design time form.

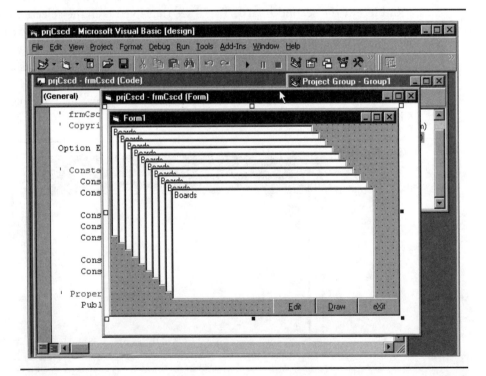

Figure 18-4
Designing an Array of ListBoxes.

The design time lasso (position the pointer over the form and drag out a rectangle to select everything within or touched by the rectangle) is a big help in working with arrays like this. Figure 18-5 shows me selecting the entire array.

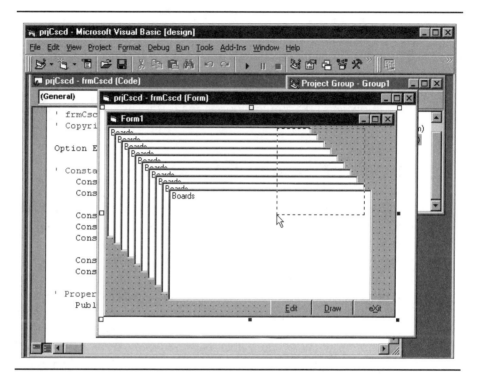

Figure 18-5
Selecting the entire boards array.

All the design time properties are listed in Appendix E.

The Resize Code

The real layout of the boards is done in the Resize() method, not at design time. This fragment of that method positions the boards:

```
For i = 0 To last_board

    Boards(i).top = (i * text_line_height)
    Boards(i).left = i * board_indent

    Boards(i).Height = Height - 300 - btm_space - _
        Boards(i).top ' 20 pixels border
```

```
            Boards(i).Width = Width - 120 - _
                Boards(i).left ' 7 pixels border

            Boards(i).Visible = i <= top_board

        Next i
```

This indents each successive board by the `board_indent` constant and drops each one down an additional `text_line_height`. That is another constant. (A better treatment would be to use the actual height of the text. This treatment works for personal software.)

Now let's take a quick look at what this cascade is really doing.

THE THEORY OF BOARD CASCADES

The board cascades I used for projects were one of my ideas that really worked. After I'd used them for a long time (this was back in DOS, in text mode), I realized just what I'd done. I'll explain that here. You'll see that this is an idea you can apply in a lot of situations.

First, we've already said that the projects' list is a tree. At the root is project 0, which is the one you start with, of course. Every other project has a parent and any project can have kids. There's no limit on the number of kids per parent. (As a practical matter, you might remind yourself that psychologists say we can remember only about seven things in a list.)

Each subproject can also have subprojects. The mechanics of my first implementation suggested a depth limit of 10. (That was on an Intel 386-based computer.) If you had five projects at the first level and averaged just five subprojects under each project, filling the tree ten deep would get you to almost 10 million entries. With six items per level, ten deep nets you to 60 million. Long before that, you'd better invest in some serious project management software!

This is supposed to be small and fast. A book like this one only gets me to five or six levels deep, dividing everything down to the under-one-day level. Therefore, I've not bothered expanding that limit of ten deep. If you want to, make sure your minimum height is adequate. (You'll crash with a bad property value message, trying to set a negative height, if you don't have enough space. That crash happens in `Form_Initialize`, so you'll see it before the cascade loads. Can you guess why I know this?)

An Outline Is a Tree

You probably haven't looked at it this way, but an outline is just another way of displaying a tree. Consider this:

```
Outline of Whatever

I. Big one
     A. One A
     B. One B
     C. One C
II. Big two
     A. Two A
     B. Two B
          1. Two B 1
          2. Two B 2
          3. Two B 3
III. Big three
     A. Three A
     B. Three B
```

You could also display that same relationship, maintaining the connections, this way:

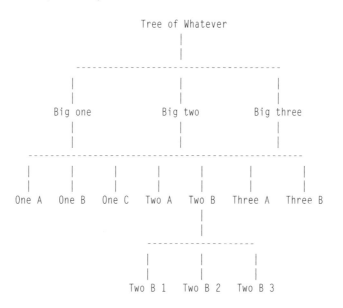

Of course, you can look at it the other way, too. If an outline is a tree, a tree is an outline. These are two ways of visualizing the same information.

A Cascade Is an Outline View

Our projects cascade gives us one view of the projects tree. Because a tree is an outline, the cascade is another outline view.

Now compare the cascade outline view to the standard outline view (for example, directory tree, Windows Explorer-type outline).

Again, consider this outline:

```
Outline of Whatever

I. Big one
    A. One A
    B. One B
    C. One C
II. Big two
    A. Two A
    B. Two B
        1. Two B 1
        2. Two B 2
        3. Two B 3
III. Big three
    A. Three A
    B. Three B
```

Suppose that you are interested in the Two B group. Let's close up this outline so that we can look at just what interests us. I'll add + and - signs that show how I conceptually clicked. (The + shows that the topic is closed.)

```
- Outline of Whatever
  + I. Big one
  - II. Big two
    + A. Two A
    - B. Two B
        1. Two B 1
        2. Two B 2
        3. Two B 3
  + III. Big three
```

Now let's put the same information into project boards. These are the five boards:

```
I. Big one       A. One A     A. Two A
II. Big two      B. One B     B. Two B
III. Big three   C. One C
```

```
1. Two B 1    A. Three A
2. Two B 2    B. Three B
3. Two B 3
```

As separate boards, you lose the visual connection between the parts. You can mentally reconstruct it here because of the names I chose. With other names, the relationship is lost. That's why I thought of the drilldown where each board overlays its parent with the relevant parent item name popped to the top. This is the detail of the same drilldown we featured in the collapsed outline view:

```
Whatever
   II. Big two
      B. Two B
         1. Two B 1
         2. Two B 2
         3. Two B 3
```

This brings us to the fundamental laws of the physics of collapsed outline and board cascade views. In the board cascade view, you see the board you're interested in and one parent item at each higher level in the tree. In other words, you see the drilldown to the board of interest and nothing else.

In the collapsed outline view, you cannot collapse further than showing every board in the drilldown. Look at the collapsed outline again:

```
- Outline of Whatever
  + I. Big one
  - II. Big two
    + A. Two A
    - B. Two B
        1. Two B 1
        2. Two B 2
        3. Two B 3
  + III. Big three
```

You're looking at the items in three full boards:

```
+ I. Big one      + A. Two A    1. Two B 1
- II. Big two     - B. Two B    2. Two B 2
+ III. Big three                3. Two B 3
```

More rigorously, you're looking at four full boards. The first board is the root (*Whatever* in this example). The root is treated like a title (or *is* the title) in both views, so you can ignore it.

What we have here is a better outline view. At least it's better when the information about your parent's siblings isn't relevant to the item you're seeing.

Going four levels deep in a tree with five items at each level, the board cascade will show the five items you're focusing on plus the parent, grandparent, and great-grandparent (seven items). The maximally collapsed outline view will show 20 items (five at each level).

Can't some outlines or trees be improved with a board cascade view? Think carefully about this, especially if your software will be used on laptop computers.

Now let's look at the code, beginning with the properties.

THE DATA MEMBERS

Let's look at the constants and data members, a group at a time. We'll begin with the number of boards:

```
Const max_depth = 10
Const last_board = max_depth - 1
```

The `max_depth`, as its name suggests, is the maximum depth of the cascade. That's actually the number of levels not including the root. The `last_board` constant is a convenience. The board array runs from zero to `last_board`.

These are the constants that `Resize()` uses to make things look good:

```
Const board_indent = 150 ' twips for left offset
Const pixels_between_boards = 4
Const btm_space = 510

Const min_height = 3300
Const min_width = 3000
```

Now we come to the properties. First is our friend `dont_unload`, which is the control value set by the parent.

```
Public dont_unload As Boolean
    ' False unless parent resets it
```

The `top_board` value is the index of the board (`ListBox` object) that is currently on top of the cascade:

```
Private top_board As Byte
```

Next, this object contains a frmPrjct object, an ODB, and a Prjct object, for data access:

```
Private proj_form As frmPrjct
Private ob As ODB
Private p As Prjct
```

Then we have the array of Collection objects. Each Collection is a bag of Prjct objects, corresponding to the board in the cascade. This is the declaration:

```
Private project_colls(0 To max_depth - 1) As Collection
```

When we pop up board 1, for example, the highlighted name on board zero is moved to the top of the board. The old_listindices array records the ListIndex of the highlighted item as it originally appeared:

```
Private old_listindices(0 To max_depth - 1) As Integer
```

Finally, when we move the names in the ListBox, its change event will be raised. This Boolean lets us distinguish our program's fiddling from the user's fiddling:

```
Private from_mouse As Boolean
```

In addition to the property declarations, one routine provides access to the ODB. (The time surface will need this to gather a bag of today's projects.) This is that code:

```
Public Function get_prjct_db() As ODB

    Set get_prjct_db = proj_form.ob

End Function
```

CONSTRUCTOR AND DESTRUCTOR

As in the schedule tool, the Form_Initialize() event handler contains the constructor code and the Form_QueryUnload() event handler contains the destructor code.

The Constructor

The constructor creates a frmPrjct object. As you saw in Chapter 17, that object creates an ODB object accessing the projects on disk. This form is loaded but not visible. (Explicitly setting Visible to False isn't necessary because that's the default value. I link to keep reminding myself, regardless.)

The ODB picks the first item in the file for its default object. This lets us grab its name for our Caption. After setting top_board to zero (again, it's just a reminder), the constructor fills the project_colls array with new Collection objects. Then it calls read_coll() with the key of the current object (object 0, unless you physically delete it) to fill board zero.

The set_list routine takes the data from the Collection of Prjct objects and uses it to fill the board's list with project names.

Finally, the from_mouse() Boolean is set to True because any further changes to the list will be done by the user's clicks. This is the code:

```
Private Sub Form_Initialize()

' proj_form creates the ODB
    Set proj_form = New frmPrjct
    proj_form.Visible = False
    Load proj_form
    proj_form.dont_unload = True

    Caption = proj_form.cur_obj.Name
    top_board = 0

    Dim i As Byte
    For i = 0 To max_depth - 1
        Set project_colls(i) = New Collection
    Next

    read_coll proj_form.cur_obj.key, top_board

    set_list top_board
    from_mouse = True ' source of click event

End Sub
```

The Destructor

The destructor code is the same as the schedule's destructor:

```
Private Sub Form_QueryUnload(Cancel As Integer, _
    UnloadMode As Integer)
```

```
      If dont_unload Then
          Visible = False
          Cancel = -1 ' set bit cancels unload
      Else

          proj_form.Visible = False
          proj_form.dont_unload = False
          Unload proj_form
          Set proj_form = Nothing ' Free Willy

      End If

  End Sub
```

HANDLING THE COLLECTIONS

Three routines handle the Collections. One empties a Collection, another fills a Collection, and the third is a utility to find a particular object in the Collection. Two of these are simple methods. Filling the collection isn't simple.

Empty the Bag

I back down from the last object to the first, discarding the objects (actually, object references) on a last-in, first-out basis. This is the code:

```
Private Sub empty_coll(n As Byte)

    If (project_colls(n).Count) = 0 Then Exit Sub

    Dim i As Integer
    For i = project_colls(n).Count To 1 Step -1
        project_colls(n).Remove i
    Next

End Sub
```

Fill the Bag

This routine is too long, and it's too deeply indented. I want to rewrite it every time I look at it. Then I remind myself that it's doing a difficult job with complete reliability. "If it ain't broke, don't fix it" is one of my favorite sayings, so I don't fix it.

Let's start by looking at the overview, omitting all the details. This is the process:

```
Loop over all projects in the ODB

    Create a new project
    read values into it from ODB

    If the object's parent_key matches the parent's key
        put it in the bag
    end if

end loop
```

That's the job in concept. The devil's in the details. Look at the innermost level of indentation where the actual item is inserted. This is the code that does the insertion:

```
While name_in( _
    project_colls(board_num), p2.Name)

    MsgBox "Name '" & p2.Name & _
        "' already in use.", _
        vbCritical, _
        "Duplicate Name Error"

    p2.Name = "New_name" & _
            Trim(Str(suffix))
    suffix = suffix + 1

Wend

project_colls(board_num).Add _
        p2, p2.Name
```

The critical point here is that you generate a runtime error if you are inserting into a `Collection` using a key and you attempt to add an item that has the same key as one already in the bag. In that case, after a suitable warning this loop tries changing the name (in the bag, not on disk) to New_name0. If that fails it will try New_name1 and so on, until it finally finds one that's not already in the bag. Then it lets the code actually Add() the object.

There's lots of housekeeping besides this. The bag has to be emptied before you start. You don't want deleted objects. You have to stop if you find 255 objects. I record and restore the position of the ODB so that I don't disturb some other code that may be looking at the ODB. Here is the full method:

```
Private Sub read_coll( _
        parent_key As Long, board_num As Byte)

    empty_coll board_num

    Dim odb_num As Long, old_odb_num As Long
    Dim p As Prjct, p2 As Prjct
    Set p = New Prjct

    With proj_form.ob

' save original database position
        old_odb_num = .get_obj_num

' locate parent in database
        odb_num = .find_obj(parent_key, p)
        If odb_num = -1 Then Exit Sub ' empty odb

' search rest of database for kids
        odb_num = odb_num + 1
        Do While odb_num < .get_num_objects

            odb_num = .get_obj(odb_num, p)
            If Not .obj_is_deleted Then

                If p.get_parent_key = parent_key Then

                    ' add kids to collection
                    Set p2 = New Prjct

                    .get_obj odb_num, p2

                    Dim suffix As Integer
                    suffix = 0

                    While name_in( _
                        project_colls(board_num), p2.Name)

                        MsgBox "Name '" & p2.Name & _
                            "' already in use.", _
                            vbCritical, _
                            "Duplicate Name Error"

                        p2.Name = "New_name" & _
                                Trim(Str(suffix))
                    suffix = suffix + 1
```

```
                              Wend

                        project_colls(board_num).Add _
                              p2, p2.Name

                        ' limit collections to byte-sized
                        If project_colls(board_num).Count = _
                              255 Then Exit Do
                  End If

            End If

            odb_num = odb_num + 1

      Loop

' restore original database position
      .get_obj old_odb_num, p

      End With

End Sub
```

Fortunately, the rest of this system doesn't have another method as long or as deeply indented as this one. Nobody else is even close.

Find a Name in the Bag

You can use On Error to handle duplicate names in the Collection.Add() method. I don't like the spaghetti code that always seems to involve, so I wrote my own checker. It loops through each object in the Collection. It exits, reporting True, as soon as it finds the name. If it doesn't find the name, it reports False. This is the code:

```
Private Function name_in( _
      c As Collection, s As String) As Boolean

   name_in = False
   If c.Count = 0 Then Exit Function

   Dim i As Integer
   For i = 1 To c.Count

      If c.Item(i).Name = s Then
         name_in = True
         Exit For
      End If
```

```
        Next

    End Function
```

HANDLING THE BOARDS

Handling the boards also means having a method to empty one and a method to fill one. You'll find this fill code vastly simpler than the collection's fill code.

Empty a Board

I empty a list the same way I empty a collection. This code calls RemoveItem() on a last-in, first-out basis:

```
Private Sub empty_list(n As Byte)

    If Boards(n).ListCount = 0 Then Exit Sub

    Dim i As Integer
    For i = Boards(n).ListCount - 1 To 0 Step -1
        Boards(n).RemoveItem i
    Next

End Sub
```

Fill a Board

The board fill process is as clean as the Collection fill is messy. This is the routine:

```
Private Sub set_list(n As Byte)

    empty_list n

    Dim i As Byte

    With project_colls(n)

        For i = 1 To .Count
            Boards(n).AddItem .Item(i).Name
        Next

    End With
```

```
        old_listindices(n) = -1

End Sub
```

Changing Boards

You change boards in two directions. You drill down or you go back up.
Neither process is complex.

Drill Down

Drilling down is simple. You increment the top_board index, fill a
Collection, and then fill the new top board. Last, Visible is set to True,
so you can see the result of your work. This is the whole method:

```
Private Sub add_board(key As Long)

    If top_board = last_board Then Exit Sub

    top_board = top_board + 1
    read_coll key, top_board
    set_list top_board
    Boards(top_board).Visible = True

End Sub
```

Back Up

Backing up is even simpler than drilling down. You set Visible to False,
decrement top_board, and reset its name. (We'll cover name handling in
the next section.) This is the whole method:

```
Private Sub drop_board()

' drops the current top board
    If top_board = 0 Then Exit Sub

    Boards(top_board).Visible = False
    top_board = top_board - 1
    reset_name

End Sub
```

Handling Names

Two routines handle the process of resetting the name. The first calls the second.

Reset the Name

When you drill down, you remove the highlighted name from the ListBox's List array. Then you add it back, but with spaces prepended. Because the ListBox's Sorted property is True, this inserts it at the top with no further trouble on your part. Setting ListIndex to zero highlights it.

The reverse process is not quite so simple. First I grab the name from the board (.list(.ListIndex) is the highlighted name). Then I trim the prepended spaces. The added logic allows the prepend routine to not add the normal amount of left-hand spaces when the list is narrow.

Then, setting from_mouse to False, the top name is removed, and the revised version is added back. Finally, the highlight is reset. This is the method:

```
Private Sub reset_name()

' called with top_board showing selected name with spaces
' prepended at top of list

    Dim Name As String

    With Boards(top_board)

        Name = .list(.ListIndex)

        Dim slen As Byte
        slen = 2 * (top_board + 1)

        If left(Name, slen) = Space(slen) Then
            Name = Right(Name, Len(Name) - slen)
        Else
            Name = LTrim(Name)
        End If

        from_mouse = False
        .RemoveItem 0
        .AddItem Name
        .ListIndex = find_name(Name)
        from_mouse = True

    End With

End Sub
```

Find a Name

When you add a name to a board, the `ListBox` inserts it in sorted order into the `List` array. This routine lets you find it:

```
Private Function find_name(nm As String) As Byte

' finds a name in the current top_board's .List array

    With Boards(top_board)

        Dim i As Byte
        i = 0

        Do While nm <> .list(i)
            If i = .ListIndex Then Exit Do
            i = i + 1
        Loop

        find_name = i

    End With

End Function
```

RESPONDING TO THE USER

We have two categories of clicks to think about: clicks on the names and button clicks. We'll start with clicks on the names.

Clicks on Names

One of the more annoying things about Windows is that it raises a `Click` event and then raises a double-click event if the user double-clicks. Many other systems raise a click event for single clicks and a double-click event (not a single-click event) for double clicks.

In this case, however, I was able to design around that problem. I treat a second single-click event on a highlighted name as if it were a double-click on that name. Let's start with the single-click handler.

The Single Click Event Handler

This handler takes care of three separate cases:

- Clicks on a board not on top
- Clicks on a top item not highlighted
- Clicks on the highlighted item

Going backwards in the cascade is just a matter of calling the drop_board() method. A click on an item not highlighted just inserts the highlighted item's number in the old_listindices array. The second click on a highlighted item calls the DblClick() method, as this code shows

```
Private Sub Boards_Click(Index As Integer)

' changing .ListIndex raises this event
    If Not from_mouse Then Exit Sub

    If Index <> top_board Then

        While Index < top_board
            drop_board
        Wend

    Else

        With Boards(top_board)

            If .ListIndex = _
                    old_listindices(top_board) Then
                Boards_DblClick (Index)
            Else
                old_listindices(top_board) = .ListIndex
            End If

        End With

    End If

End Sub
```

The Double Click

This method is called by the single-click handler when the click is on a highlighted item. It's also called by Visual Basic when Windows detects a double-click by the user.

The user could double-click on an empty board (`ListIndex - -1`).

The `Prjct` objects were put into the collection, keyed by their name. That lets you get the right `Prjct` back from the collection with this line:

```
Set p = project_colls(top_board).Item(Name)

' project_colls(top_board) is the Collection
' project_colls(top_board).Item(Name) is the Prjct
```

Collections are handy, aren't they? Once you've found the project, it's easy to remove it from the `List`, prepend spaces, and add it back to the `List`. This is the code:

```
Private Sub Boards_DblClick(Index As Integer)

' double-click not defined over covered boards
    If Index <> top_board Then Exit Sub

    With Boards(top_board)
        If .ListIndex = -1 Then Exit Sub

        Dim Name As String
        Name = .list(.ListIndex)

        Dim p As Prjct
        Set p = project_colls(top_board).Item(Name)

' move the selected name to the top
        from_mouse = False

        .RemoveItem .ListIndex
        Name = Space(2 * (top_board + 1)) & Name
        .AddItem Name, 0
        .ListIndex = 0

        from_mouse = True

    End With

    add_board p.key

End Sub
```

Clicks on Buttons

The last topic for which we'll look closely at the code is the clicks on buttons. There are three of them:

- Edit
- Draw
- eXit

The eXit code is trivial, but Edit and Draw are not.

The Edit Button

When the user clicks Edit, you launch the project form, let the user do whatever editing he or she wants, and then you reread the top board (because its data was probably changed). It sounds easy, right? Again, the devil's in the details.

First, rereading empties the List and then refills it. Nothing will be selected (ListIndex = -1). Because we don't want editing to effectively unselect the edited item, the hilite_saver variable is introduced. That's used to restore the selection after an edit.

Restoring the highlight wouldn't be too hard if the user promised not to delete the highlighted item, not to delete enough items so that the highlight is past the end of the reread list and not to change the name of the highlighted item (which will move it in the list). This method isn't nice about the latter (it just keeps the highlight in the same place). It has to handle the others to avoid errors.

Suppose you drill down from a project and come to a blank board (project has no subprojects). If you then press Edit, it's obvious that you want to add items. The parent key of these items should be set to point to the highlighted subproject on the previous board, shouldn't it?

The high_key() function returns the database key of the highlighted item on the top board, by the way. We'll talk about that function next.

With that background, this code should make sense:

```
Private Sub cmdEdit_Click()

    proj_form.new_cur high_key

    Dim hilite_saver As Integer
    hilite_saver = Boards(top_board).ListIndex

' no item selected? new item follows previous hi item
```

```
                  If hilite_saver = -1 Then

                      If top_board > 0 Then

                          top_board = top_board - 1
                          proj_form.new_parent_key high_key
                          top_board = top_board + 1

                          ' top board defaults to 0 for ODB item 0

                      End If

                  End If

                  proj_form.Show vbModal
                  reread

          ' restore list selection (reread erases it)
              If hilite_saver <> -1 Then

                  ' deletion(s) may have shortened or emptied the list

                      Dim max_items As Integer
                      max_items = Boards(top_board).ListCount

                      If max_items > 0 Then
                          If hilite_saver > max_items - 1 Then _
                              hilite_saver = max_items - 1

                          Boards(top_board).ListIndex = hilite_saver
                      End If

                  End If

              End Sub
```

The high_key() routine returns the key of the currently highlighted
project or -1 if nothing is selected.
I first wrote it this way:

```
high_key = project_colls(top_board).Item( _
    LTrim(.List(.ListIndex))).key
```

I think you'll agree that this version is a lot more readable:

```
Private Function high_key() As Long

    ' gets key of currently highlighted item
```

```
    With Boards(top_board)

        If .ListIndex = -1 Then
            high_key = -1
            Exit Function
        End If

        Dim c As Collection
        Set c = project_colls(top_board)

        Dim nm As String
        nm = .list(.ListIndex)
        nm = LTrim(nm)

        Dim p As Prjct
        Set p = c.Item(nm)

        high_key = p.key

    End With

End Function
```

The `reread()` function is called after the user stops using the data entry form. You don't have any way of knowing what the user edited, and the `frmPrjct` object doesn't have any knowledge of what is on your boards. The simple solution is to do a complete reread. The only trick to the reread is that you need to look at the second-to-top board to retrieve its `high_key()` value. That's the parent for which you're constructing this board.

This is the method:

```
Private Sub reread()

' Called after edit to refresh top board

    Dim p As Prjct
    Set p = New Prjct

    With proj_form.ob

        If top_board = 0 Then
            ' do caption, too
            .get_obj 0, p
            Caption = p.Name
        End If

    End With
```

```
Dim key As Long
If top_board = 0 Then
    key = 0
Else
    top_board = top_board - 1
    key = high_key()
    top_board = top_board + 1
End If

read_coll key, top_board
set_list top_board

End Sub
```

The Draw Button

The Draw button will generate an error if you click it. We don't have a project charting routine yet. (That's coming in Chapter 19.) This code will launch after we program it:

```
Private Sub cmdDraw_Click()

' can't draw an empty project
    If project_colls(top_board).Count = 0 Then Exit Sub

    Dim f As frmChart
    Set f = New frmChart
    f.set_coll project_colls(top_board)

    If Not f.too_wide Then

        If top_board = 0 Then
            f.set_name Trim(Caption)
        Else
            f.set_name Trim(Boards(top_board - 1).list(0))
        End If

        f.Show vbModal

    End If

    ' f discarded here

End Sub
```

The Exit Button

This is the final button, and the final bit of code to examine. Compared to the others, it's a mental vacation:

```
Private Sub cmdExit_Click()

    Unload Me

End Sub
```

THE FULL LISTING

Disk file 18-01 contains the frmCscd.frm file. It also contains a project file and the other classes needed to run this as a standalone program. (Calendar.frm, ODB.cls, and frmPrjct.frm are used here, unchanged from their previous versions.)

If you don't have the disk or if your nephew tucked it into his disc player before he went out Roller Blading, Listing 18-1 shows the portion of frmCscd.frm that's visible in the code editor. The rest of the file, which details all the properties set building the form, is in Appendix E.

Listing 18-1
frmCscd.frm — The project boards cascade

```
' frmCscd.frm — Cascading project lists
' Copyright 1997, Martin L. Rinehart

Option Explicit

' Constants
    Const max_depth = 10
    Const last_board = max_depth - 1

    Const board_indent = 150 ' twips for left offset
    Const pixels_between_boards = 4
    Const btm_space = 510

    Const min_height = 3300
    Const min_width = 3000

' Properties
    Public dont_unload As Boolean
        ' False unless parent resets it
```

(continued)

frmCscd.frm — The project boards cascade

```vb
        Private top_board As Byte
        Private proj_form As frmPrjct
        Private ob As ODB
        Private p As Prjct
        Private project_colls(0 To max_depth - 1) As Collection
        Private old_listindices(0 To max_depth - 1) As Integer
        Private from_mouse As Boolean

    Private Sub Boards_Click(Index As Integer)

    ' changing .ListIndex raises this event
        If Not from_mouse Then Exit Sub

        If Index <> top_board Then

            While Index < top_board
                drop_board
            Wend

        Else

            With Boards(top_board)

                If .ListIndex = _
                        old_listindices(top_board) Then
                    Boards_DblClick (Index)
                Else
                    old_listindices(top_board) = .ListIndex
                End If

            End With

        End If

    End Sub

    Private Sub Boards_DblClick(Index As Integer)

    ' double-click not defined over covered boards
        If Index <> top_board Then Exit Sub

        With Boards(top_board)
            If .ListIndex = -1 Then Exit Sub

            Dim Name As String
            Name = .list(.ListIndex)
```

```
        Dim p As Prjct
        Set p = project_colls(top_board).Item(Name)

' move the selected name to the top
        from_mouse = False

        .RemoveItem .ListIndex
        Name = Space(2 * (top_board + 1)) & Name
        .AddItem Name, 0
        .ListIndex = 0

        from_mouse = True

    End With

    add_board p.key

End Sub

Private Sub reset_name()

' called with top_board showing selected name with spaces
' prepended at top of list

    Dim Name As String

    With Boards(top_board)

        Name = .list(.ListIndex)

        Dim slen As Byte
        slen = 2 * (top_board + 1)

        If left(Name, slen) = Space(slen) Then
            Name = Right(Name, Len(Name) - slen)
        Else
            Name = LTrim(Name)
        End If

        from_mouse = False
        .RemoveItem 0
        .AddItem Name
        .ListIndex = find_name(Name)
        from_mouse = True

    End With

End Sub
```

(continued)

frmCscd.frm — The project boards cascade

```
Private Function find_name(nm As String) As Byte

' finds a name in the current top_board's .List array

    With Boards(top_board)

        Dim i As Byte
        i = 0

        Do While nm <> .list(i)
            If i = .ListIndex Then Exit Do
            i = i + 1
        Loop

        find_name = i

    End With

End Function

Private Sub add_board(key As Long)

    If top_board = last_board Then Exit Sub

    top_board = top_board + 1
    read_coll key, top_board
    set_list top_board
    Boards(top_board).Visible = True

End Sub

Private Sub drop_board()

' drops the current top board
    If top_board = 0 Then Exit Sub

    Boards(top_board).Visible = False
    top_board = top_board - 1
    reset_name

End Sub

Private Sub cmdDraw_Click()

' can't draw an empty project
    If project_colls(top_board).Count = 0 Then Exit Sub
```

```
    Dim f As frmChart
    Set f = New frmChart
    f.set_coll project_colls(top_board)

    If Not f.too_wide Then

        If top_board = 0 Then
            f.set_name Trim(Caption)
        Else
            f.set_name Trim(Boards(top_board - 1).list(0))
        End If

        f.Show vbModal

    End If

    ' f discarded here

End Sub

Private Sub cmdEdit_Click()

    proj_form.new_cur high_key

    Dim hilite_saver As Integer
    hilite_saver = Boards(top_board).ListIndex

' no item selected? new item follows previous hi item
    If hilite_saver = -1 Then

        If top_board > 0 Then

            top_board = top_board - 1
            proj_form.new_parent_key high_key
            top_board = top_board + 1

        ' top board defaults to 0 for ODB item 0

        End If

    End If

    proj_form.Show vbModal
    reread

' restore list selection (reread erases it)
    If hilite_saver <> -1 Then
```

(continued)

frmCscd.frm — The project boards cascade

```
    ' deletion(s) may have shortened or emptied the list

        Dim max_items As Integer
        max_items = Boards(top_board).ListCount

        If max_items > 0 Then
            If hilite_saver > max_items - 1 Then _
                hilite_saver = max_items - 1

            Boards(top_board).ListIndex = hilite_saver
        End If

    End If

End Sub

Private Function high_key() As Long

' gets key of currently highlighted item

    With Boards(top_board)

        If .ListIndex = -1 Then
            high_key = -1
            Exit Function
        End If

        Dim c As Collection
        Set c = project_colls(top_board)

        Dim nm As String
        nm = .list(.ListIndex)
        nm = LTrim(nm)

        Dim p As Prjct
        Set p = c.Item(nm)

        high_key = p.key

    End With

End Function

Private Sub cmdExit_Click()

    Unload Me

End Sub
```

```
Private Sub Form_Initialize()

' proj_form creates the ODB
    Set proj_form = New frmPrjct
    proj_form.Visible = False
    Load proj_form
    proj_form.dont_unload = True

    Caption = proj_form.cur_obj.Name
    top_board = 0

    Dim i As Byte
    For i = 0 To max_depth - 1
        Set project_colls(i) = New Collection
    Next

    read_coll proj_form.cur_obj.key, top_board

    set_list top_board
    from_mouse = True ' source of click event

End Sub

'Private Sub Form_Load()
'
'' Debugging initialization code
'    Dim i As Byte
'
'    For i = 0 To 4
'        Boards(i).AddItem "Board" & Str(i) & _
'            " Sample Text 1"
'        Boards(i).AddItem "Board" & Str(i) & _
'            " Text sample 2"
'        Boards(i).AddItem "Board" & Str(i) & _
'            " Another sample"
'        Boards(i).AddItem "Board" & Str(i) & _
'            " Yet another text"
'    Next
'
'    For i = 0 To last_board
'        Boards(i).Visible = False
'    Next
''
'End Sub

Private Sub Form_QueryUnload(Cancel As Integer, _
        UnloadMode As Integer)
```

(continued)

frmCscd.frm — The project boards cascade

```
        If dont_unload Then
            Visible = False
            Cancel = -1 ' set bit cancels unload
        Else

            proj_form.Visible = False
            proj_form.dont_unload = False
            Unload proj_form
            Set proj_form = Nothing ' Free Willy

        End If

End Sub

Private Sub Form_Resize()

    If Tag = "x" Then Exit Sub

    Tag = "x"

        If Height < min_height Then Height = min_height
        If Width < min_width Then Width = min_width

    Tag = ""

    Dim text_line_height As Integer
    text_line_height = TextHeight("Ag") + _
        (pixels_between_boards * Screen.TwipsPerPixelY)

    Dim i As Byte

    For i = 0 To last_board

        Boards(i).top = (i * text_line_height)
        Boards(i).left = i * board_indent

        Boards(i).Height = Height - 300 - btm_space - _
            Boards(i).top ' 20 pixels border
        Boards(i).Width = Width - 120 - _
            Boards(i).left ' 7 pixels border

        Boards(i).Visible = i <= top_board

    Next i

    Dim tp As Integer, lf As Integer, wd As Integer
    tp = Boards(0).Height + 30
```

```
        wd = cmdEdit.Width ' all 3 buttons have same width
        lf = Width - (3 * wd) - 150

        cmdEdit.top = tp
        cmdEdit.left = lf

        cmdDraw.top = tp
        cmdDraw.left = lf + wd

        cmdExit.top = tp
        cmdExit.left = lf + 2 * wd

        cmdExit.top = tp

End Sub

Private Sub empty_coll(n As Byte)

    If (project_colls(n).Count) = 0 Then Exit Sub

    Dim i As Integer
    For i = project_colls(n).Count To 1 Step -1
        project_colls(n).Remove i
    Next

End Sub

Private Sub read_coll( _
        parent_key As Long, board_num As Byte)

    empty_coll board_num

    Dim odb_num As Long, old_odb_num As Long
    Dim p As Prjct, p2 As Prjct
    Set p = New Prjct

    With proj_form.ob

' save original database position
        old_odb_num = .get_obj_num

' locate parent in database
        odb_num = .find_obj(parent_key, p)
        If odb_num = -1 Then Exit Sub ' empty odb

' search rest of database for kids
        odb_num = odb_num + 1
        Do While odb_num < .get_num_objects
```

(continued)

frmCscd.frm — The project boards cascade

```
        odb_num = .get_obj(odb_num, p)
        If Not .obj_is_deleted Then

            If p.get_parent_key = parent_key Then

                ' add kids to collection
                Set p2 = New Prjct

                .get_obj odb_num, p2

                Dim suffix As Integer
                suffix = 0

                While name_in( _
                    project_colls(board_num), p2.Name)

                    MsgBox "Name '" & p2.Name & _
                        "' already in use.", _
                        vbCritical, _
                        "Duplicate Name Error"

                    p2.Name = "New_name" & _
                        Trim(Str(suffix))
                    suffix = suffix + 1

                Wend

                project_colls(board_num).Add _
                    p2, p2.Name

                ' limit collections to byte-sized
                If project_colls(board_num).Count = _
                    255 Then Exit Do
            End If

        End If

        odb_num = odb_num + 1

    Loop

' restore original database position
        .get_obj old_odb_num, p

    End With

End Sub
```

```vbnet
Private Function name_in( _
    c As Collection, s As String) As Boolean

    name_in = False
    If c.Count = 0 Then Exit Function

    Dim i As Integer
    For i = 1 To c.Count

        If c.Item(i).Name = s Then
            name_in = True
            Exit For
        End If

    Next

End Function

Private Sub empty_list(n As Byte)

    If Boards(n).ListCount = 0 Then Exit Sub

    Dim i As Integer
    For i = Boards(n).ListCount - 1 To 0 Step -1
        Boards(n).RemoveItem i
    Next

End Sub

Private Sub set_list(n As Byte)

    empty_list n

    Dim i As Byte

    With project_colls(n)

        For i = 1 To .Count
            Boards(n).AddItem .Item(i).Name
        Next

    End With

    old_listindices(n) = -1

End Sub
```

(continued)

frmCscd.frm — The project boards cascade

```
Private Sub reread()

' Called after edit to refresh top board

    Dim p As Prjct
    Set p = New Prjct

    With proj_form.ob

        If top_board = 0 Then
            ' do caption, too
            .get_obj 0, p
            Caption = p.Name
        End If

    End With

    Dim key As Long
    If top_board = 0 Then
        key = 0
    Else
        top_board = top_board - 1
        key = high_key()
        top_board = top_board + 1
    End If

    read_coll key, top_board
    set_list top_board

End Sub

Public Function get_prjct_db() As ODB

    Set get_prjct_db = proj_form.ob

End Function

'' debugging code
'Private Sub dump_colls()
'
'    Dim i As Byte, j As Byte
'    For i = 0 To last_board
'
'        Debug.Print "Collection" & Str(i)
'        With project_colls(i)
'
'            j = 1
```

```
'              Do While j <= .Count
'                  Debug.Print "    " & Str(j) & _
'                      " " & .Item(j).name
'                  j = j + 1
'              Loop
'
'          End With
'      Next
'
'End Sub

' end of frmCscd.frm
```

SUMMARY

We began with a look at the design. After looking at the details, the design time form and a bit of Resize() code, I talked about the theory. This cascade is another way of viewing a tree or outline. It's more focused than the standard outline view because it omits parent's siblings.

Then we went on to the code. We looked first at the data: constants and properties, as well as one routine that provides access to the private ODB.

Then we went on to the constructor and destructor. The destructor code is in QueryUnload(), where it can respect the parent's setting of the dont_unload Boolean.

The code that handles the Collection objects came next. The routine that fills a Collection with Prjct objects is by far the worst in the system, measuring either length or indentation levels, but it works.

After the Collection's fill routine, the code that handles the boards appeared a model of elegant simplicity. The only minor complication is the fussing I do, putting the name of the selected item on top when a new board appears, and replacing it when its board returns to the topmost position.

Finally, we looked at the code that responds to clicks. Clicking on names selects items, drills down, or backs up in the cascade. Clicking on Edit launches the data entry tool, which can edit any data in the ODB. Because of this, we have to reread the data after an edit, which is made more complex by an attempt to restore the highlight to the selected item.

Clicking the Draw button will cause the tool to crash because we haven't started drawing yet. That is the subject of Chapter 19.

THE PROJECT CHART

*A*t the end of the last chapter, we had a really nice project capability, except that the Draw button was worse than useless: it would crash the project. In this chapter, I'll present the code that turns that button into a powerful tool.

Whenever I start drawing a project chart and calculating the critical path, someone always wants to rush out and buy a commercial project management package. If you have big project management needs, these packages are wonderful. If you're planning the next war or the next launch of a major Microsoft operating sytem, you need some serious help. This won't work.

I have more modest needs. What's important for me is that I can keep organized lists of steps that a project requires. I like to list the main points at first and then break each one down as I come to it. This is project management software for the rest of us: for all of you who really *don't* want to rush out and buy a commercial project management package.

We'll begin by designing the chart. Then we'll move right into the code.

We'll dispense with the preliminaries quickly. That will include the data members, constructor, and destructor code. Then we'll march through the code in the order I built it:

- Day labels across the top
- Row labels down the left
- Project lines
- Project connection lines
- Critical path calculation
- Finishing touches

Let's start by looking at the design.

DESIGNING THE PROJECT CHART

Here we'll cover the design of the chart. I'll show you pictures of some of its behavior. If you run the project (it's in 19-01 on disk), you'll be able to fiddle with it yourself. Then we'll take a quick look at the controls on the design-time chart.

The Chart's Behavior

Figure 19-1 shows the project chart for a simple set of test data. (The test data is also included on disk in 19-01.)

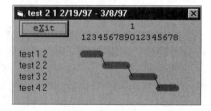

Figure 19-1
Drawing a simple chart.

If you're sharp-eyed and have a good memory, you'll notice that these lines are fatter than the ones you looked at in Chapter 14. That's because I've made a modification in the code, just for this chapter.

The fat lines show the critical path. They're in red, but I'm not going to know how clear the difference between red and black will be until this book is printed. Then it will be too late, of course, so I've added fatness as a critical path feature.

In Figure 19-2, I've added three new subprojects that are not in the critical path.

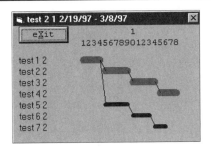

Figure 19-2
Clearly showing the critical path.

These are not in the critical path because a one-day extension of any one of them would not cause a one-day extension to the final completion date.

In my design, the date an item ends is fully taken by that item. A following item will start the following day. The critical path calculation assumes that projects all start the day after the completion of their precedent project, unless their scheduled start is still later. This means that your connection lines will all go down and to the right, as you see here, right?

Not at all right! If your scheduled dates are screwy, your chart will be screwy. Figure 19-3 shows a typical example.

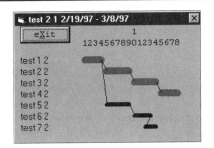

Figure 19-3
This project is in trouble.

If you like, you could ask the computer to reschedule things automatically. A nice touch would be to have the critical path calculation put into the data entry, so the computer would suggest the earliest possible start date as the default estimated start date.

I just make manual adjustments to screwball charts, but before I fix this data, let me show you another feature. Figure 19-4 shows a critical path that doesn't appear to be critical.

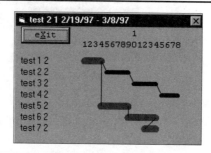

Figure 19-4
This project's in big trouble.

Is the chart program wrong? Well, it might have bugs, but this isn't one of them. The critical path algorithm calculates the earliest possible start date as the day after the completion of the precedent project. It uses this date in place of the actual start date if the calculated date is later.

Figure 19-5 shows the same project with the tasks done as the critical path demands.

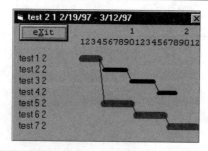

Figure 19-5
This is the critical path truth.

There is no law that says your project's pieces have to be displayed in time order. They're being displayed in alphabetical order. Because project names and orders don't normally cooperate so nicely, I usually prefix the names with a number or letter, like this:

a Do this

b Do that

c Do the other

Without the preceding letter, those three would sort to "Do that," "Do the other," and "Do this." That's not the way I wanted them. The chart, however, doesn't care. Supposing that I rename the top project to "test 4.5 2." That will sort it between 4 and 5. Figure 19-6 shows the result.

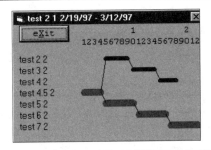

Figure 19-6
Projects don't always go top down.

Figure 19-7 shows what happens with a little more renaming.

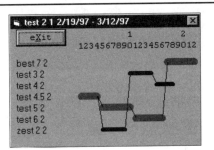

Figure 19-7
Is there method in this madness?

You can see that making one the "best" and giving another some "zest" really shakes things up. This chart doesn't try to make sense. It just draws what you give it. That may not be helpful enough for you. It's just what I want, though.

Before we go on to the form design, let me draw your attention to the caption of the chart form. It's the title of the parent project followed by the start and end dates of the project.

The Design Time Form

Figure 19-8 shows the design form. It has four controls:

- `cmdExit`: The eXit button
- `lblDayTop`: Top line of the day labels
- `lblDayBtm`: Bottom line of the day labels
- `txtPnames`: TextBox for the project names

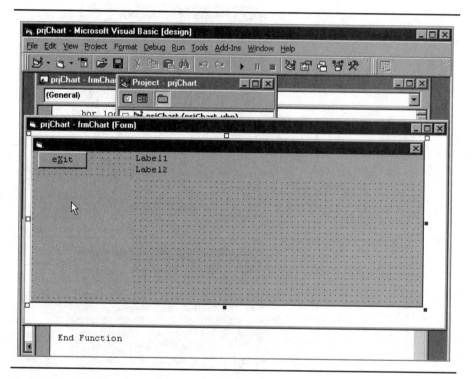

Figure 19-8
The design time project chart form.

From this sparse set you can see that the code will handle most of the work.

Now we can dive into the code and see how this happens.

PROGRAMMING PRELIMINARIES

If you've done all your Visual Basic programming with the standard components, you'll find this interesting. We'll draw the chart right on the form. That's right — it's not built with Line objects. We get out our computer's pen and ruler and start to draw. (If you don't think the computer's pen can leak ink all over a nice drawing, you haven't debugged one of these things yet.)

Before we get there, though, we'll quickly dispense with the preliminaries, starting with the declarations section.

The Data Members

If you check the full listing below, you'll see constants like `min_form_width` and properties like:

```
Private finish As Date
```

I'll skip these obvious ones and discuss the main structures. These are the big ones:

```
Private coll As Collection ' collection of Prjcts

Private coll_loc() As Integer ' will redim
Private chart_loc() As Integer
Private critical() As Boolean
Private follows() As Integer
```

The `coll` is the `Collection` object. It's a bag of `Prjct` objects in whatever order they appear in the database. The `coll_loc()` and `chart_loc()` arrays are used to translate between bag order and chart order. If item 1 in the collection is the fourth line on the chart, `chart_loc(1)` will be 4. In that case, `coll_loc(4)` would be 1.

The `critical()` array is `True` if the item is in the critical path and the `follows()` array holds the number of the precedent project. In our test data, `follows(2)` was 1 and `follows(5)` was also 1.

Three arrays are used in the critical path calculation. They are

```
Private sched_start() As Integer
Private sched_days() As Integer
Private calc_done() As Integer
```

We'll cover them when we discuss that calculation.
There's one public data member:

```
Public too_wide As Boolean
```

If the data won't fit (see the various constants) the chart refuses to even try. It pops up a message box explaining what went wrong, sets `too_wide` to `True`, and returns.

The Constructor and Destructor

There is no true constructor; there's no destructor at all. All the work of initialization gets done in the `form_load()` method:

```
Private Sub Form_Load()

    set_day_labels
    set_order
    set_pnames

    compute_form_size
    compute_follows
    compute_critical_path

End Sub
```

We'll look at the `compute_form_size()` routine here and then examine the others in the order I programmed them. (This was one project that neatly divided itself into small steps.) I'll show the routine here, but I'll intersperse my comments just before the applicable lines of code.
This is the start of the routine:

```
Private Sub compute_form_size()
```

The first thing that needs to be done is to create a copy of the form's font name and size. These are the ones that the user has picked (presumably) and which Windows supplies as defaults. We'll be setting others, so it's only polite to restore these:

```
' temporarily change font, to get correct sizes
    Dim save_name As String, save_size As Integer
    save_name = Font.Name
    save_size = Font.Size
```

Memo to Bill Gates

Bill, this is a nuisance. It's no big deal, but if you have a spare moment it would be nice to have a TextHeight and TextWidth for all the objects that have Text properties. Thanks.

Next, we'll use the `TextHeight` method to obtain the size of the text in the `TextBox`. You'll see later that this has already been filled with the names of the projects.

The `TextHeight()` method is a method of the form. Unfortunately, if you want to know the height of the text in a `TextBox`, you have to first assign the `TextBox`'s `Font.Name` and `Font.Size` to the form and then ask for `TextHeight()` to evaluate your text:

```
' compute height
    Font.Name = txtPnames.Font.Name
    Font.Size = txtPnames.Font.Size

    Dim txt_hgt As Integer
    txt_hgt = TextHeight(txtPnames.Text)
```

Then I compute the height we need. The `txtPnames` obtains the height of the text plus a bit of margin. The form retrieves this height plus the top, 300 twips to allow for the form's caption, and another margin at the bottom:

```
    txtPnames.Height = txt_hgt + margin_height
    Height = txtPnames.top + 300 + _
        txtPnames.Height + margin_height
```

The `TextWidth()` method works the same way as `TextHeight()`. If you have multiple lines, it returns the width of the widest line:

```
' setup left-side space
    txtPnames.Width = TextWidth(txtPnames.Text) + _
        margin_width

    If txtPnames.Width < min_pname_width Then
        txtPnames.Width = min_pname_width
    End If
```

The day labels are positioned to start over the drawing area. The left side of this area is a `margin_width` past the right side of the `txtPnames` project names `TextBox`:

```
lblDayTop.left = txtPnames.left + _
    txtPnames.Width + margin_width
lblDayBtm.left = lblDayTop.left
```

The day labels use a fixed-width font. You have to do this to place the digits in the top row to line up over the zeros in the bottom row, this way:

```
         1         2
12345678901234567890123
```

Code that we'll meet later has already assigned the captions to these labels. If the project were 23 days long, they would be exactly the two strings above.

Here's the same two lines, but set in this book's highly readable font:

```
1       2
12345678901234567890123
```

So again, we have to pull the Font.Name and Font.Size from these labels, assign them to the form, and then use the form's TextWidth() method:

```
' compute width
    Font.Name = lblDayTop.Font.Name
    Font.Size = lblDayTop.Font.Size
```

Now we can set the width of the day labels to be just wide enough to accommodate the contents of the bottom line:

```
Dim lbl_wid As Integer
lbl_wid = TextWidth(lblDayBtm.Caption)
lblDayTop.Width = lbl_wid
lblDayBtm.Width = lbl_wid
```

Then the form's width becomes calculable at this point:

```
Width = lblDayTop.left + margin_width + _
    TextWidth(lblDayBtm.Caption)

If Width < min_form_width Then
    Width = min_form_width
End If
```

The next four variables are private data member Integers:

```
' setup picture area
    pic_area_top = txtPnames.top
```

```
    pic_area_lft = lblDayBtm.left
    pic_area_hgt = txtPnames.Height
    pic_area_wid = lblDayBtm.Width
```

Finally, we restore the font and we're done:

```
' reset original font
    Font.Name = save_name
    Font.Size = save_size


End Sub
```

That was simple enough, wasn't it? Now you know why calculating the form's size wasn't the first thing we did. You can't size the form until the day labels and row labels are set up because you don't know how much space you need.

When I developed the system, I started with a dummy form size routine that just made an oversized form. Then I wrote the code that set up the day labels and row labels, and I replaced the dummy code with the code you see here.

Now that we've sized the form, we're ready to look at two more setup routines.

Other Setup Code

Filling the Bag

Filling the bag is no trouble at all. The parent calls this public method, passing a `Collection` object. (More exactly, passing a reference to a collection object.) This code then calculates the length of the project and displays a message if it is too long.

This is the code:

```
Public Sub set_coll(c As Collection)

    Set coll = c
    compute_width

    If ndays > max_days Then

        MsgBox "Too many days —" & Str(ndays) & _
            " — in project", vbCritical, _
            Str(max_days) & " day limit exceeded"
```

```
        too_wide = True

    End If

End Sub
```

All the date data we'll use is reduced to integer numbers of days, with the earliest day being day 1. You'll see that this will keep some of the later calculations as simple as possible.

Calculating the Project's Length

The length calculation grabs a start and finish date from the actual dates of the first project. It then looks through the rest of the `Prjct` objects in the collection. For each one it checks to see if it starts before the trial start or ends after the trial end. The start and finish dates are reset if needed. This is the code:

```
Private Function compute_width() As Integer

    start = coll.Item(1).act_start_date
    finish = coll.Item(1).act_end_date

    Dim i As Integer
    For i = 2 To coll.Count

        With coll.Item(i)

            If .act_start_date < start Then _
                start = .act_start_date
            If .act_end_date > finish Then _
                finish = .act_end_date

        End With

    Next

    ndays = finish - start + 1

End Function
```

This finishes the bookkeeping and brings us to the more interesting parts.

SETTING THE DAY LABELS

After launching the form, I went to work immediately on the day labels. I did these very simply. (One of these days I'm going to replace this code with code that does something like this):

```
2    3 Nov.   1    1
5    0    5    0    5
```

Wouldn't that be nicer? The current version sets a string of digits "1234567890" into the bottom label and repeats it as often as needed. The top label places nine spaces and a single digit above the bottom label, which combines to count out the days.

The loop counter j is incremented once for each block of ten days. The top label gets only the right-hand digit of the str() form of j. At 100, for example, the day will be labelled "00." That should be enough to suggest the full truth on really wide charts.

As a final step, any days less than ten are tagged onto the lower label. This is the code:

```
Private Sub set_day_labels()

    Dim i As Integer, j As Integer
    i = Int(ndays / 10)

    lblDayTop.Caption = ""
    lblDayBtm.Caption = ""

    For j = 1 To i
        lblDayTop.Caption = lblDayTop.Caption & _
            Space(9) & Right(Str(j), 1)
        lblDayBtm.Caption = lblDayBtm.Caption & _
            "1234567890"
    Next

    i = ndays Mod 10
    If i > 0 Then

        lblDayBtm.Caption = lblDayBtm.Caption & _
            left("123456789", i)

    End If

End Sub
```

SETTING THE ROW LABELS

The basic job here is to march through the list of items appending each `Prjct.Name` to the `txtPnames.Text`. For all but the last name, you append a carriage return and linefeed pair. There's one wrinkle here, however.

You want the chart to appear not in the collection's order, but in alphabetical order, so here we don't say:

```
coll.Item(i).Name
```

Rather, we use the `coll_loc()` function to translate `i`, the location on the chart, to the location in the bag:

```
coll.Item(coll_loc(i)).Name
```

This is the full method:

```
Private Sub set_pnames()

    Dim crlf As String
    crlf = Chr(13) & Chr(10)

    With txtPnames

        .Text = ""

        Dim i As Integer
        For i = 1 To coll.Count

            .Text = .Text & _
                Trim(coll.Item(coll_loc(i)).Name)

            If i < coll.Count Then
                .Text = .Text & crlf
            End If

        Next

    End With

End Sub
```

That brings us to the fun part.

DRAWING

The form's `Paint()` method is provided for drawing directly on the form. It will be called when the form is first displayed after resizing and as needed to repaint after, for instance, an overlapping window is moved.

We have two sets of lines to draw. One will serve to show the projects and the other is the thin lines for the connections between the projects.

My `Form_Paint()` could hardly be simpler:

```
Private Sub Form_Paint()

    draw_projects
    draw_connections

End Sub
```

Before we talk about those routines, lets look at two hard-working members of the supporting cast. The `hor_loc()` function returns the horizontal location, in twips, of a day. Similarly, `ver_loc()` returns a vertical location, in twips, given a row number.

The `hor_loc()` calculates the twips for a single day by dividing the length of the day `Label` by the total number of day's. Then it multiplies this by the number of days.

At least that's the idea. The actual calculation multiplies by one less than the number of days and then adds half a day's width to get to the center of the given day, this way:

```
Private Function hor_loc(day As Integer) As Integer

    Dim day_wid As Integer

    day_wid = lblDayTop.Width / ndays
    hor_loc = lblDayTop.left + _
        ((day - 1) * day_wid) + (day_wid / 2)

End Function
```

The vertical calculation is similar. It uses the height of the `txtPnames` `TextBox`, adjusted for the margin, divided by the number of rows as the height of a single row. This is the code:

```
Private Function ver_loc(row As Integer) As Integer

    Dim row_hgt As Integer

    row_hgt = (txtPnames.Height - margin_height) / _
```

```
                    coll.Count
            ver_loc = txtPnames.top + _
                    ((row - 1) * row_hgt) + (row_hgt / 2)

        End Function
```

Now that we can find X and Y coordinates for any day and row, we're ready to do the drawing.

Drawing the Projects

Drawing the projects is handled by two methods. The `draw_projects()` method loops over the rows. For each row it picks the appropriate `Prjct` from the bag and finds its start and end date. It adjusts these to the appropriate day numbers and then calls the `draw_proj()` method, which does the actual drawing.

It also saves the existing `DrawWidth` and sets the project line's `DrawWidth` (in pixels) to 6. It restores the original `DrawWidth` when the drawing is done. This is the code:

```
    Private Sub draw_projects()

        Dim save_width As Integer
        save_width = DrawWidth

        DrawWidth = 6

        Dim pstart As Integer, pstop As Integer

        Dim i As Integer
        For i = 1 To coll.Count

            With coll.Item(coll_loc(i))
                pstart = .act_start_date - start + 1
                pstop = .act_end_date - start + 1
            End With

            draw_proj i, pstart, pstop
        Next

        DrawWidth = save_width

    End Sub
```

The actual work of drawing is done with a `Line` statement. The simple form is this:

```
    Line (x1, y1)-(x2, y2)
```

Memo to Bill Gates

Bill, you have to tell those folks to cool it with the weird syntax. Each one, like this one, makes individual sense, but before you're done you have a huge language where we all have to look up anything we don't use all the time. A simple function call — Line(x1, y1, x2, y2) — would've been better here.

We'll use the form that adds a color:

```
Line(x1, y1)-(x2, y2), color
```

This was the code:

```
Private Sub draw_proj(row As Integer, _
        from_day As Integer, to_day As Integer)

    Dim x1 As Integer, x2 As Integer, Y As Integer
    x1 = hor_loc(from_day)
    x2 = hor_loc(to_day)
    Y = ver_loc(row)

    Line (x1, Y)-(x2, Y), _
        IIf(critical(coll_loc(row)), vbRed, vbBlack)

End Sub
```

That worked well, but for the screen shots in this chapter I wanted fat lines for the critical path. This is the revised version:

```
Private Sub draw_proj(row As Integer, _
        from_day As Integer, to_day As Integer)

    Dim x1 As Integer, x2 As Integer, Y As Integer
    x1 = hor_loc(from_day)
    x2 = hor_loc(to_day)
    Y = ver_loc(row)

    Dim save_width As Integer
    save_width = DrawWidth

    If critical(coll_loc(row)) Then _
        DrawWidth = save_width + 4

    Line (x1, Y)-(x2, Y), _
        IIf(critical(coll_loc(row)), vbRed, vbBlack)
```

```
        DrawWidth = save_width

    End Sub
```

Drawing the Connections

Once I placed the project lines on the form, I was rolling. The connections would be simple, right?

Wrong. They aren't simple at all. First, we need to know what project each Prjct follows. We have keys of the precedent project, but these have to be converted to locations in the Collection.

Who Follows Whom?

One way to break down a complex process is to write the top level and just pretend you have the exact routine that you need. This is where I started:

```
        Private Sub compute_follows()

            ReDim follows(1 To coll.Count)

            Dim i As Integer
            For i = 1 To coll.Count

                follows(i) = whos_before(i)

            Next

        End Sub
```

Of course, that doesn't solve the problem. It just postpones it. Just isolating the exact algorithm, though, (don't worry about every Prjct in the Collection, just worry about a single Prjct) makes the next step easier.

This step is to go through the whole collection one at a time, looking for a Prjct.Key that matches our target's Prjct.After_key. We'll return zero when there's no match. (For the purpose of our chart, if the precedent project isn't in the bag it doesn't exist.) This is the code:

```
        Private Function whos_before(n As Integer) As Integer

        ' if follows(i) = n, then coll(i) follows coll(n)
        ' if follows(i) = 0, then it has no precedent

            Dim my_key As Long
            my_key = coll.Item(n).get_after_key
```

```
        whos_before = 0

    Dim i As Integer
    For i = 1 To coll.Count

        If i <> n Then

            If coll.Item(i).key = my_key Then
                whos_before = i
                Exit For
            End If

        End If

    Next

End Function
```

Collection and Chart Locations

With the `follows()` array calculated, we're ready to look at two more routines. These are done long before we get to drawing connections. The `coll_loc()` array was also used in drawing the project lines, but they're used most heavily in the connection drawing, so I'm covering them here.

Our goal is to have two arrays, `coll_loc()` and `chart_loc()`. The `coll_loc()` array gives the index of an item in the `Collection` given its chart location. The `chart_loc()` array provides the opposite translation.

These are both computed by a call to the `set_order()` method. It begins by appropriately dimensioning these arrays. Then it sets `coll_loc(1)` to 1. If there are more items in the `Collection`, it passes each item to the `insert()` method. That method finds the right place in the array for the new item and inserts it, moving the others as needed.

Last, the `set_order()` routine calls `set_chart_loc`, which builds the `chart_loc()` array. This is the method:

```
Private Sub set_order()

' coll_loc(chart_row) = location in coll
' chart_loc(location in coll) = chart_row

    ReDim coll_loc(1 To coll.Count) As Integer
    ReDim chart_loc(1 To coll.Count) As Integer

    coll_loc(1) = 1
    If coll.Count = 1 Then Exit Sub

    Dim i As Integer
```

```
        For i = 2 To coll.Count

            insert i

        Next

        set_chart_loc

    End Sub
```

The insert( ) function is called with an integer, n. When it is called, there are n-1 items in sorted order in the coll_loc array. It compares the new item to the existing set, working from n-1 back down to 1. When the new item comes after an existing one, it shifts the higher items down one and inserts itself into the vacated position.

If you know your sorts, this is the classic bubble sort. It's terribly slow for large, unsorted collections of data, but if you've entered your project in time order (which is the normal case), this is very fast.

Here's the code:

```
    Private Sub insert(n As Integer)

    ' coll_loc 1 through n-1 are sorted
    ' add coll.item(i)

    ' find location for insert
        Dim i As Integer
        For i = n - 1 To 1 Step -1

            If after(n, coll_loc(i)) Then Exit For

            If i = 1 Then
                i = 0
                Exit For
            End If

        Next

        Dim insert_loc As Integer
        insert_loc = i + 1

    ' shift higher items down
        If insert_loc < n Then

            For i = n - 1 To insert_loc Step -1
                coll_loc(i + 1) = coll_loc(i)
```

```
        Next

      End If

' insert new item
      coll_loc(insert_loc) = n

End Sub
```

A separate function performs the actual comparison. Any C programmer knows this trick. By keeping the comparison code separate from the rest of the sort code, it's trivially easy to sort in some other order. You might want to sort by completion date, for instance.

To make that change, you just substitute a different middle line in this function:

```
Private Function after( _
         i As Integer, j As Integer) As Boolean

' true iff coll.item(i) comes after coll.item(j)
     after = coll.Item(i).Name >= coll.Item(j).Name

End Function
```

All that trouble was needed to order the names correctly. Finally, we're ready to compute the reverse array that returns chart location given an index in the Collection. That's done by nested loops.

The outer loop processes each item in the collection. For each item, the inner loop searches for its number in the coll_loc array. This is the code:

```
Private Sub set_chart_loc()

    Dim bag As Integer, chrt As Integer

    For chrt = 1 To coll.Count

        bag = 1
        Do Until coll_loc(chrt) = bag
            bag = bag + 1
        Loop

        chart_loc(bag) = chrt

    Next

End Sub
```

Actually Drawing the Connections

With the infrastructure in place, we're actually ready to draw the connections. The structure here is similar to the project drawing structure. An outer routine, `draw_connections()` loops over all the items. It calls the `draw_conn()` method to actually do the drawing, but only for those items that have a connection.

It also handles setting `DrawWidth`, preserving whatever other value that property starts with. This is the method:

```
Private Sub draw_connections()

    Dim save_width As Integer
    save_width = DrawWidth

    DrawWidth = 1

    Dim i As Integer
    For i = 1 To coll.Count

        If follows(i) > 0 Then
            draw_conn i
        End If

    Next

    DrawWidth = save_width

End Sub
```

The connection is drawn by `draw_conn()`. This was a nasty little thing to debug! It's complicated by the need to translate between chart and `Collection` indexes.

The x1, y1 point is the endpoint of the precedent project. The x2, y2 location is the start point of the target project. The x1 and x2 values are computed entirely from the `Collection` data, using `Collection` indexes. The y1 and y2 values are determined from the chart indexes.

By naming the target index "in_coll" and naming the chart index for the same `Prjct` "on_chart," I've managed to make this code somewhat readable, but it wins no prizes in that regard. This is the best I could muster:

```
Private Sub draw_conn(in_coll As Integer)

    Dim x1 As Integer, x2 As Integer
```

```
Dim y1 As Integer, y2 As Integer

Dim on_chart As Integer
on_chart = chart_loc(in_coll)

x1 = hor_loc( _
    coll.Item(follows(in_coll)).act_end_date - _
    start + 1)
y1 = ver_loc(chart_loc(follows(in_coll)))

x2 = hor_loc(coll.Item(in_coll).act_start_date - _
    start + 1)
y2 = ver_loc(on_chart)

Line (x1, y1)-(x2, y2), vbBlack

End Sub
```

COMPUTING THE CRITICAL PATH

When I programmed the drawing, I dummied up a critical path routine. It dimensioned the array and assigned True to the second and fourth items. That let me get the drawing tested. Making this work was, except for some finishing touches, the last piece of the chart that I programmed.

It works with an outer routine, compute_critical_path(), and an inner one, calc_cp(). The inner routine takes the collection and computes the completion date of the project. It doesn't allow any project to start until the later of its scheduled start date or the day after its precedent project is finished. This may give a finish date that's significantly different from the date we call "finish."

The outer routine has a fairly simple job. It calls calc_cp to find out when the project will be completed. Then it loops over all the component projects. For each one, it sets its completion date one day later and calls calc_cp again. If calc_cp reports that the project's finish is a day later, the item is in the critical path. If the project's finish doesn't change, the item isn't in the critical path.

This is the outer code:

```
Private Sub compute_critical_path()

    ReDim critical(1 To coll.Count)

' These arrays are normalized to integers.
' First day of project is 1. All dates are
' offsets from day 1.
```

```
        ReDim sched_start(1 To coll.Count)
        ReDim sched_days(1 To coll.Count)
        ReDim calc_done(1 To coll.Count)

' Initialize calculation arrays
        Dim i As Integer
        For i = 1 To coll.Count

            With coll.Item(i)
                sched_start(i) = .act_start_date - start + 1
                sched_days(i) = _
                    .act_end_date - .act_start_date + 1
            End With

        Next


' Compute critical path length
        Dim length As Integer
        length = calc_cp()
        If length = 0 Then Exit Sub ' not computable

' A task is critical if an increase in its length
' delays completion of the project.

' Algorithm:
' for each task
'     add one day to its length
'     recalculate the project
'     if project length is increased, task is critical
' next task

        Dim new_length As Integer

        For i = 1 To coll.Count

        ' stretch one task
            sched_days(i) = sched_days(i) + 1

        ' calculate new total length
            new_length = calc_cp()

        ' critical if total length increases
            critical(i) = new_length > length

        ' reset for next pass
            sched_days(i) = sched_days(i) - 1

        Next

End Sub
```

Calculating the completion date of a project involves one messy problem. That's the order of completion of the components. You can't compute the completion date of a component until you've calculated the completion date of its precedent component.

The routine as written includes extensive comments. I'll present it here, interspersed with additional remarks.

For starters, the routine includes the algorithm it uses, in comments. This is the start of the method:

```
Private Function calc_cp() As Integer

' algorithm:
' mark every task as not completed
' until every task is completed
'    for each task not marked completed
'       if task has no precedent or a completed precedent
'          compute completion
'          mark task as completed
'       end if
'    next task
```

It will make an indefinite but finite number of passes over the entire list of projects. On each pass, it calculates the completion dates of any projects for which the data's available.

On the first pass, it will calculate completion dates for the projects that have no precedents. (Remember that having a precedent project that's not in the collection is the same as having no precedent for our chart's purpose.)

On the second pass, it calculates completion dates for the projects that it processed in the first pass. The third pass calculates completion for projects that depended on those found in the second pass, and so on.

The calc_done() array records the date of completion as an integer number of days. (1 is the start date of the whole project.) It's initialized to zeros. If calc_done(i) is zero, the project's not complete.

This code provides all "not completed" values:

```
' if calc_done = 0 the task is not complete

    Dim complete As Boolean, i As Integer
    Dim project_done As Integer, num_completed As Integer

' if calc_done = 0, task is NOT completed
    For i = 1 To coll.Count
        calc_done(i) = 0
    Next

    project_done = 0
```

Then the multiple-pass loop starts. The complete Boolean is set `True` here. If any project is found that can't be completed, this will be set `False`:

```
Do Until complete

    num_completed = 0
    complete = True
```

The inner loop makes a pass over every project. It ignores all the ones that have been completed

```
For i = 1 To coll.Count
    If calc_done(i) = 0 Then
```

If there is no precedent project, the completion happens as scheduled

```
If follows(i) = 0 Then
    calc_done(i) = sched_start(i) + _
        sched_days(i) - 1
    num_completed = num_completed + 1
Else
```

Otherwise, the completion happens at the later of schedule or the project's length after the completion of the precedent project:

```
If calc_done(follows(i)) > 0 Then
    calc_done(i) = cp_comp( _
        sched_start(i), _
        calc_done(follows(i)), _
        sched_days(i))
    num_completed = num_completed + 1
End If
End If

End If
```

Then we reset complete, if necessary, and extend the final completion date, also if necessary:

```
' If calc_done(i) = 0 Then complete = False
complete = complete And calc_done(i) > 0

If calc_done(i) > project_done Then
    project_done = calc_done(i)
End If

Next
```

This algorithm will always complete at last one item on each pass, if the data is valid. In the case of circular precedence relationships, however, the project won't be able to be calculated. (A follows B and B follows A is the simplest circle.)

This check is made after completing the pass:

```
If num_completed = 0 Then ' circular reference

    MsgBox "Cannot calculate critical path " & _
        "completion date.", vbCritical,
        "Circular Reference In Project"

    project_done = 0
    complete = True

End If
```

Finally, we're done:

```
Loop

    calc_cp = project_done

End Function
```

The cp_comp() method is a little function that actually sets the completion of an individual project. The completion date comes length=1 days after the start. (If start is 3 and length is 4, days 3, 4, 5, and 6 are needed.) The start is the greater of the scheduled start or the day following completion of the precedent project. This is the code:

```
Private Function cp_comp(my_start As Integer, _
        follows_done As Integer, length As Integer) _
        As Integer

' start date is the greater of the scheduled start
' or the day after the completion of the precedent task

    cp_comp = IIf(my_start > follows_done, _
        my_start, follows_done + 1) + length - 1

End Function
```

That concludes the critical path code. If you understood it all, you're entitled to congratulations. If you thought the methods were complex, I agree. The algorithms are not trivial. If you're tired, rest assured that nothing remains that's as complex as this.

FINISHING TOUCHES

We've nothing left to do except set the `Caption` and program the eXit button. This routine sets the `Caption`:

```
Public Sub set_name(s As String)

    proj_name = s

    Caption = proj_name & " " & CStr(start) & _
        " - " & CStr(finish)

End Sub
```

If that's not simple enough, I'm sure you'll agree that the eXit button code is as simple as a method can be:

```
Private Sub cmdExit_Click()

    Unload Me

End Sub
```

THE FULL LISTING

On disk, the 19-01 includes the frmChart.frm file as well as the other form and class files used in this project. It also includes the project file and the sample ODB. If you supply your own ODB, you'll need good data to produce a good chart.

If you don't have the disk or if the cat scratched it when she jumped off your desk, the full listing follows in Listing 19-1. Appendix F shows the portion that is not editable with your code editor.

You can use it to set the properties of the design time form.

Listing 19-1
frmChart.frm — Project chart form

```
' frmChart.frm — Project chart form
' Copyright 1997, Martin L. Rinehart

Option Explicit

Const max_days = 180
```

```
Const margin_width = 150
Const margin_height = 150
Const min_pname_width = 1200
Const min_form_width = 4200


' Properties:
    Private coll As Collection ' collection of Prjcts
    Private ndays As Integer ' # of days to chart

    Private start As Date
    Private finish As Date

    Private coll_loc() As Integer ' will redim
    Private chart_loc() As Integer
    Private critical() As Boolean
    Private follows() As Integer

    Private pic_area_top As Integer
    Private pic_area_lft As Integer
    Private pic_area_hgt As Integer
    Private pic_area_wid As Integer

    Private sched_start() As Integer
    Private sched_days() As Integer
    Private calc_done() As Integer

    Public too_wide As Boolean

    Private proj_name As String

Public Sub set_name(s As String)

    proj_name = s

    Caption = proj_name & " " & CStr(start) & _
        " - " & CStr(finish)

End Sub

Public Sub set_coll(c As Collection)

    Set coll = c
    compute_width

    If ndays > max_days Then

        MsgBox "Too many days -" & Str(ndays) & _
            " - in project", vbCritical, _
            Str(max_days) & " day limit exceeded"
```

(continued)

frmChart.frm—Project chart form

```vb
            too_wide = True

        End If

    End Sub

    Private Function compute_width() As Integer

        start = coll.Item(1).act_start_date
        finish = coll.Item(1).act_end_date

        Dim i As Integer
        For i = 2 To coll.Count

            With coll.Item(i)

                If .act_start_date < start Then _
                    start = .act_start_date
                If .act_end_date > finish Then _
                    finish = .act_end_date

            End With

        Next

        ndays = finish - start + 1

    End Function

    Private Sub cmdExit_Click()

        Unload Me

    End Sub

    Private Sub Form_Load()

        set_day_labels
        set_order
        set_pnames

        compute_form_size
        compute_follows
        compute_critical_path

    End Sub
```

```
Private Sub Form_Paint()

    draw_projects
    draw_connections

End Sub

Private Sub compute_form_size()

' temporarily change font, to get correct sizes
    Dim save_name As String, save_size As Integer
    save_name = Font.Name
    save_size = Font.Size

' compute height
    Font.Name = txtPnames.Font.Name
    Font.Size = txtPnames.Font.Size

    Dim txt_hgt As Integer
    txt_hgt = TextHeight(txtPnames.Text)

    txtPnames.Height = txt_hgt + margin_height
    Height = txtPnames.top + 300 + _
        txtPnames.Height + margin_height

' setup left-side space
    txtPnames.Width = TextWidth(txtPnames.Text) + _
        margin_width

    If txtPnames.Width < min_pname_width Then
        txtPnames.Width = min_pname_width
    End If

    lblDayTop.left = txtPnames.left + _
        txtPnames.Width + margin_width
    lblDayBtm.left = lblDayTop.left

' compute width
    Font.Name = lblDayTop.Font.Name
    Font.Size = lblDayTop.Font.Size

    Dim lbl_wid As Integer
    lbl_wid = TextWidth(lblDayBtm.Caption)
    lblDayTop.Width = lbl_wid
    lblDayBtm.Width = lbl_wid

    Width = lblDayTop.left + margin_width + _
```

(continued)

frmChart.frm—Project chart form

```
        TextWidth(lblDayBtm.Caption)

    If Width < min_form_width Then
        Width = min_form_width
    End If

' setup picture area
    pic_area_top = txtPnames.top
    pic_area_lft = lblDayBtm.left
    pic_area_hgt = txtPnames.Height
    pic_area_wid = lblDayBtm.Width

' reset original font
    Font.Name = save_name
    Font.Size = save_size

End Sub

Private Sub compute_follows()

    ReDim follows(1 To coll.Count)

    Dim i As Integer
    For i = 1 To coll.Count

        follows(i) = whos_before(i)

    Next

End Sub

Private Function whos_before(n As Integer) As Integer

' if follows(i) = n, then coll(i) follows coll(n)
' if follows(i) = 0, then it has no precedent

    Dim my_key As Long
    my_key = coll.Item(n).get_after_key

    whos_before = 0

    Dim i As Integer
    For i = 1 To coll.Count

        If i <> n Then

            If coll.Item(i).key = my_key Then
                whos_before = i
```

```
                    Exit For
                End If

            End If

        Next

End Function

Private Sub compute_critical_path()

    ReDim critical(1 To coll.Count)

' These arrays are normalized to integers.
' First day of project is 1. All dates are
' offsets from day 1.

    ReDim sched_start(1 To coll.Count)
    ReDim sched_days(1 To coll.Count)
    ReDim calc_done(1 To coll.Count)

' Initialize calculation arrays
    Dim i As Integer
    For i = 1 To coll.Count

        With coll.Item(i)
            sched_start(i) = .act_start_date - start + 1
            sched_days(i) = _
                .act_end_date - .act_start_date + 1
        End With

    Next

' Compute critical path length
    Dim length As Integer
    length = calc_cp()
    If length = 0 Then Exit Sub ' not computable

' A task is critical if an increase in its length
' delays completion of the project.

' Algorithm:
' for each task
'     add one day to its length
'     recalculate the project
'     if project length is increased, task is critical
' next task
```

(continued)

frmChart.frm—Project chart form

```vb
        Dim new_length As Integer

        For i = 1 To coll.Count

        ' stretch one task
            sched_days(i) = sched_days(i) + 1

        ' calculate new total length
            new_length = calc_cp()

        ' critical if total length increases
            critical(i) = new_length > length

        ' reset for next pass
            sched_days(i) = sched_days(i) - 1

        Next

    End Sub

    Private Function calc_cp() As Integer

    ' algorithm:
    ' mark every task as not completed
    ' until every task is completed
    '   for each task not marked completed
    '     if task has no precedent or a completed precedent
    '         compute completion
    '         mark task as completed
    '       end if
    '   next task

    ' if calc_done = 0 the task is not complete

        Dim complete As Boolean, i As Integer
        Dim project_done As Integer, num_completed As Integer

    ' if calc_done = 0, task is NOT completed
        For i = 1 To coll.Count
            calc_done(i) = 0
        Next

        project_done = 0

        Do Until complete

            num_completed = 0
            complete = True
```

```
For i = 1 To coll.Count
    If calc_done(i) = 0 Then

        If follows(i) = 0 Then
            calc_done(i) = sched_start(i) + _
                sched_days(i) - 1
            num_completed = num_completed + 1
        Else
            If calc_done(follows(i)) > 0 Then
                calc_done(i) = cp_comp( _
                    sched_start(i), _
                    calc_done(follows(i)), _
                    sched_days(i))
                num_completed = num_completed + 1
            End If
        End If

    End If

    ' If calc_done(i) = 0 Then complete = False
    complete = complete And calc_done(i) > 0

    If calc_done(i) > project_done Then
        project_done = calc_done(i)
    End If

Next

If num_completed = 0 Then ' circular reference

    MsgBox "Cannot calculate critical path " & _
        "completion date.", vbCritical, _
        "Circular Reference In Project"

    project_done = 0
    complete = True

End If
Loop

calc_cp = project_done

End Function

Private Function cp_comp(my_start As Integer, _
    follows_done As Integer, length As Integer) _
    As Integer
```

(continued)

frmChart.frm—Project chart form

```
' start date is the greater of the scheduled start
' or the day after the completion of the precedent task

    cp_comp = IIf(my_start > follows_done, _
        my_start, follows_done + 1) + length - 1

End Function

Private Sub set_order()

' coll_loc(chart_row) = location in coll
' chart_loc(location in coll) = chart_row

    ReDim coll_loc(1 To coll.Count) As Integer
    ReDim chart_loc(1 To coll.Count) As Integer

    coll_loc(1) = 1
    If coll.Count = 1 Then Exit Sub

    Dim i As Integer
    For i = 2 To coll.Count

        insert i

    Next

    set_chart_loc

End Sub

Private Sub set_chart_loc()

    Dim bag As Integer, chrt As Integer

    For chrt = 1 To coll.Count

        bag = 1
        Do Until coll_loc(chrt) = bag
            bag = bag + 1
        Loop

        chart_loc(bag) = chrt

    Next

End Sub
```

```
Private Sub insert(n As Integer)

' coll_loc 1 through n-1 are sorted
' add coll.item(i)

' find location for insert
    Dim i As Integer
    For i = n - 1 To 1 Step -1

        If after(n, coll_loc(i)) Then Exit For

        If i = 1 Then
            i = 0
            Exit For
        End If

    Next

    Dim insert_loc As Integer
    insert_loc = i + 1

' shift higher items down
    If insert_loc < n Then

        For i = n - 1 To insert_loc Step -1
            coll_loc(i + 1) = coll_loc(i)
        Next

    End If

' insert new item
    coll_loc(insert_loc) = n

End Sub

Private Function after( _
        i As Integer, j As Integer) As Boolean

' true iff coll.item(i) comes after coll.item(j)
    after = coll.Item(i).Name >= coll.Item(j).Name

End Function

Private Sub set_pnames()

    Dim crlf As String
    crlf = Chr(13) & Chr(10)

    With txtPnames
```

(continued)

frmChart.frm—Project chart form

```
        .Text = ""

        Dim i As Integer
        For i = 1 To coll.Count

            .Text = .Text & _
                Trim(coll.Item(coll_loc(i)).Name)

            If i < coll.Count Then
                .Text = .Text & crlf
            End If

        Next

    End With

End Sub

Private Sub set_day_labels()

    Dim i As Integer, j As Integer
    i = Int(ndays / 10)

    lblDayTop.Caption = ""
    lblDayBtm.Caption = ""

    For j = 1 To i
        lblDayTop.Caption = lblDayTop.Caption & _
            Space(9) & Right(Str(j), 1)
        lblDayBtm.Caption = lblDayBtm.Caption & _
            "1234567890"
    Next

    i = ndays Mod 10
    If i > 0 Then

        lblDayBtm.Caption = lblDayBtm.Caption & _
            left("123456789", i)

    End If

End Sub

Private Sub draw_projects()

    Dim save_width As Integer
    save_width = DrawWidth
```

```
    DrawWidth = 6

    Dim pstart As Integer, pstop As Integer

    Dim i As Integer
    For i = 1 To coll.Count

        With coll.Item(coll_loc(i))
            pstart = .act_start_date - start + 1
            pstop = .act_end_date - start + 1
        End With

        draw_proj i, pstart, pstop
    Next

    DrawWidth = save_width

End Sub

Private Sub draw_proj(row As Integer, _
        from_day As Integer, to_day As Integer)

    Dim x1 As Integer, x2 As Integer, Y As Integer
    x1 = hor_loc(from_day)
    x2 = hor_loc(to_day)
    Y = ver_loc(row)

    Line (x1, Y)-(x2, Y), _
        IIf(critical(coll_loc(row)), vbRed, vbBlack)

End Sub

Private Sub draw_connections()

    Dim save_width As Integer
    save_width = DrawWidth

    DrawWidth = 1

    Dim i As Integer
    For i = 1 To coll.Count

        If follows(i) > 0 Then
            draw_conn i
        End If

    Next

    DrawWidth = save_width
```

(continued)

frmChart.frm—Project chart form

```
End Sub

Private Sub draw_conn(in_coll As Integer)

    Dim x1 As Integer, x2 As Integer
    Dim y1 As Integer, y2 As Integer

    Dim on_chart As Integer
    on_chart = chart_loc(in_coll)

    x1 = hor_loc( _
        coll.Item(follows(in_coll)).act_end_date - _
        start + 1)
    y1 = ver_loc(chart_loc(follows(in_coll)))

    x2 = hor_loc(coll.Item(in_coll).act_start_date - _
        start + 1)
    y2 = ver_loc(on_chart)

    Line (x1, y1)-(x2, y2), vbBlack

End Sub

Private Function hor_loc(day As Integer) As Integer

    Dim day_wid As Integer

    day_wid = lblDayTop.Width / ndays
    hor_loc = lblDayTop.left + _
        ((day - 1) * day_wid) + (day_wid / 2)

End Function

Private Function ver_loc(row As Integer) As Integer

    Dim row_hgt As Integer

    row_hgt = (txtPnames.Height - margin_height) / _
            coll.Count
    ver_loc = txtPnames.top + _
            ((row - 1) * row_hgt) + (row_hgt / 2)

End Function

' end of frmChart.frm
```

SUMMARY

In this chapter, you saw the project chart code that creates the form your project cascade's Draw button requires. This chart gives you a visual representation of the contents of a project board in the cascade.

We looked at the design and saw that this tool only provides a chart. It's up to you to make the data sensible.

Then we went on to looking at the code, beginning with some preliminary items. These included the data, the constructor code, and the routines that received the collection and calculated the number of days in the project.

Then we continued through the code in the same order that I implemented it. I put the day labels on first and then added the row labels.

The project itself is drawn with lines in the form's `Paint()` event handler. Drawing the project lines was simple compared to drawing the connections. The latter required some nontrivial work to set arrays that cross-reference the rows of the chart and the order of `Prjct` objects in the `Collection`.

The algorithms needed to calculate the critical path were even more complex. You saw that calculating the finish date of the project was significantly complicated by the fact that there is no easy way to decide what to do first, second, and so on.

Once that work was done, however, completing the chart's `Caption` and eXit button was trivial.

In the next chapter, we'll build databases for to do lists and for chores. If you thought the code here was challenging, you'll find the databases will be simple. We'll breeze right on through so that we can reach the fun part, creating tool surfaces, in Chapter 21.

THE TO DO LIST AND CHORES DATABASES

We've completed the projects portion of the MyTime system. When I designed my first time management system, it was all projects. That didn't work too well. My projects, programming, and writing consume most of my time, but you have lots of other little things to keep organized, too. There are scheduled appointments, recurring chores, and random to do list items. We've built our appointments and schedule, so now it's time to complete the final two items.

Again, a *chore* is a process that recurs on some regular frequency. You have to tend to your e-mail daily, for example. Expense reports are filed monthly, and so on. A *to do list item* is anything that's going to take some of your time but doesn't otherwise fit into this system.

For example, I showed my older daughter the MyTime system. As luck would have it, it was just after 5:00 when she saw it. The clock on the wall matched the clock on the menu. She thought that was totally cool. I confessed that it was totally coincidental, but I promised her that if she looked up the formula for a circle, we would make the clock's hands actually tell time. She understood that formula, so that's on my to do list for today. (If we get it working, I'll put it on the disk somewhere.)

We'll start with a look at the design of the databases, including their related data entry forms. Then we'll look at both databases' code, together. We'll cover the class modules first and then the form modules. I'll skip over the code that you've already seen. Most of the forms' button click handlers are already familiar to you, for instance. You can refer to the complete listings for any details that interest you.

Let's start with the database design.

DESIGNING THE DATABASES

In this section, we'll look first at the design of the databases themselves. Then we'll look at the data entry forms that support these databases.

The ODBs

Both these ODBs are simpler than the projects and appointments we've already discussed. We'll start with the to do list ODB and then move to the chore ODB. (The latter is the simplest of all.)

To Do List ODB

We only need to know these items for a to do list object:

- key — to provide a unique, permanent name
- name — a descriptive string
- est_time — how long we guess it will take
- act_time — how long it really took
- todo_date — the day we'll do it

Chore ODB

The chore ODB needs to track even fewer items:

- key — to provide a unique, permanent name
- name — a descriptive string

- est_time — how long it normally takes
- chore_frequency — daily, weekly, or monthly

Data Entry Forms

The data entry forms are copies of our other data entry forms' buttons with unique top parts.

To Do List Entry Form

Figure 20-1 shows the to do list's data entry form.

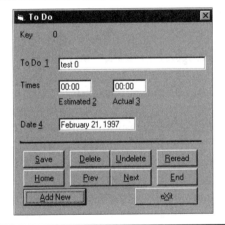

Figure 20-1
Handling to do list items.

The exact design time settings of the properties on this form are available in Appendix G. The frmToDo.frm file is included on disk in 20-02.

Chore Entry Form

Figure 20-2 shows the chore's data entry form.

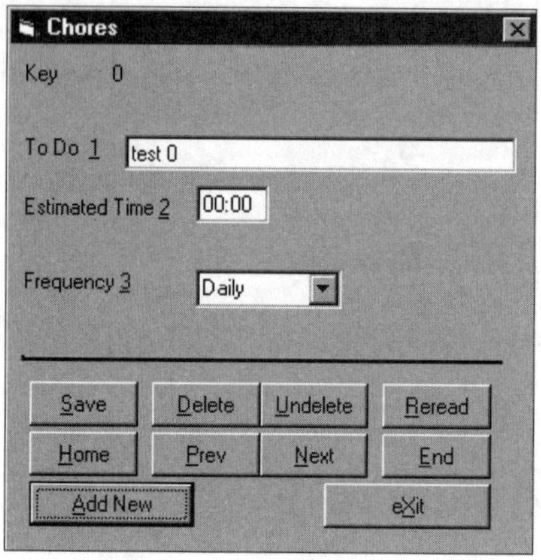

Figure 20-2
Handling chores.

The exact design-time settings of the properties on this form are available in Appendix H. The frmChore.frm file is also included on disk in 20-02.

My version of Visual Basic put the combo box's list values into a file and then lost track of the file when I moved the code from one directory to another. (It should have put the full path into the file.) If you encounter a load problem, check the combo box's List property at design time. Enter **Daily**, **Weekly**, and **Monthly** for list items zero, one, and two, respectively, and you'll be back in business.

As with appointments and projects, these to do lists and chores are implemented with a class module and a form module. We'll start with the class modules.

THE CLASS MODULES

In this section, we'll look at the data members first, and then we'll look at the constructors (they're trivial) and the storable interfaces where the records are carefully laid out.

Data Members

The data members of these classes are completely straightforward. These are the ToDo class members:

```
' Data Members
    Public key As Long
    Public Name As String
    Private est_time As Integer
    Private act_time As Integer
    Public todo_date As Date
```

and these are the Chore class members:

```
' Data Members
    Public key As Long
    Public Name As String
    Private est_time As Integer
    Public chore_frequency As Byte
```

The Chore class also provides an Enum for the possible frequencies:

```
Public Enum chore_frequencies
    chore_daily
    chore_weekly
    chore_monthly
End Enum
```

Constructors and Destructors

The constructors are even simpler. This is the ToDo class constructor:

```
Private Sub Class_Initialize()

    todo_date = Date

End Sub
```

and this is the Chore class constructor:

```
Private Sub Class_Initialize()

    chore_frequency = chore_daily

End Sub
```

Storable Interface

As always in an ODB-capable class, laying out the record and writing
to_string() and from_string() routines is the really hard work. We have
so few data members in these classes that the work wasn't really hard at all.

The get_name() methods return ToDo and Chore, respectively. We'll
look at the record routines here.

To Do List Storable Interface

The ToDo class stores its data members this way:

```
' String layout:
    ' Key 1-11, pad 12
    ' Name 13-52
    ' est_time 53-58
    ' act_time 59-64
    ' todate 65-72

Public Function to_string() As String

    to_string = _
        ODB.long_str(key) & " " & _
        ODB.fix_len(Name, 40) & _
        ODB.int_str(est_time) & _
        ODB.int_str(act_time) & _
        ODB.date_str(todo_date)

End Function

Public Sub from_string(ByVal s As String)

    key = Val(left(s, 11))
    Name = Mid(s, 13, 40)
    est_time = Val(Mid(s, 53, 6))
    act_time = Val(Mid(s, 59, 6))
    todo_date = ODB.yyyymmdd2date(Right(s, 8))

End Sub
```

Chore Storable Interface

The Chore class stores its data members this way:

```
' String layout:
    ' Key 1-11, pad 12
```

```
' Name 13-52
' est_time 53-58, pad 59
' frequency 60

Public Function to_string() As String

    to_string = _
        ODB.long_str(key) & " " & _
        ODB.fix_len(Name, 40) & _
        ODB.int_str(est_time) & " " & _
        Chr(Asc("0") + chore_frequency)

End Function

Public Sub from_string(ByVal s As String)

    key = Val(left(s, 11))
    Name = Mid(s, 13, 40)
    est_time = Val(Mid(s, 53, 6))
    chore_frequency = Val(Right(s, 1))

End Sub
```

The Data Access Methods

Both classes provide Public access to the name and get() and set()
functions for the times and dates. As our other classes have done, time is
treated externally as a string in HH:MM format but stored internally as an
Integer. The classes both provide iget() functions for direct read access
to the integer.

The Full Listings

Listings 20-1a and 20-1b show the full files, including the portions not
editable in the code editor.

Listing 20-1a
ToDo.cls

```
VERSION 1.0 CLASS
BEGIN
  MultiUse = -1  'True
END
```

(continued)

ToDo.cls

```
Attribute VB_Name = "todo"
Attribute VB_GlobalNameSpace = False
Attribute VB_Creatable = True
Attribute VB_PredeclaredId = False
Attribute VB_Exposed = False
' ToDo.cls - The ToDo List item object
' Copyright 1997, Martin L. Rinehart

Option Explicit

' Data Members
    Public key As Long
    Public Name As String
    Private est_time As Integer
    Private act_time As Integer
    Public todo_date As Date

Private Sub Class_Initialize()

    todo_date = Date

End Sub

' The storable interface

Public Function get_name() As String

    get_name = "ToDo"

End Function

' String layout:
    ' Key 1-11, pad 12
    ' Name 13-52
    ' est_time 53-58
    ' act_time 59-64
    ' todate 65-72

Public Function to_string() As String

    to_string = _
        ODB.long_str(key) & " " & _
        ODB.fix_len(Name, 40) & _
        ODB.int_str(est_time) & _
        ODB.int_str(act_time) & _
        ODB.date_str(todo_date)

End Function
```

```
Public Sub from_string(ByVal s As String)

    key = Val(left(s, 11))
    Name = Mid(s, 13, 40)
    est_time = Val(Mid(s, 53, 6))
    act_time = Val(Mid(s, 59, 6))
    todo_date = ODB.yyyymmdd2date(Right(s, 8))

End Sub

Public Function get_act_time() As String

    get_act_time = ODB.int2tstring(act_time)

End Function

Public Function iget_act_time() As Integer

    iget_act_time = act_time

End Function

Public Sub set_act_time(s As String)

    act_time = ODB.tstring2int(s)

End Sub

Public Function get_est_time() As String

    get_est_time = ODB.int2tstring(est_time)

End Function

Public Function iget_est_time() As Integer

    iget_est_time = est_time

End Function

Public Sub set_est_time(s As String)

    est_time = ODB.tstring2int(s)

End Sub

' end of ToDo.cls
```

Listing 20-1b
Chore.cls

```
VERSION 1.0 CLASS
BEGIN
   MultiUse = -1  'True
END
Attribute VB_Name = "Chore"
Attribute VB_GlobalNameSpace = False
Attribute VB_Creatable = True
Attribute VB_PredeclaredId = False
Attribute VB_Exposed = False
' Chore.cls — The Chore object
' Copyright 1997, Martin L. Rinehart

Option Explicit

Public Enum chore_frequencies
    chore_daily
    chore_weekly
    chore_monthly
End Enum

' Data Members
    Public key As Long
    Public Name As String
    Private est_time As Integer
    Public chore_frequency As Byte

Private Sub Class_Initialize()

    chore_frequency = chore_daily

End Sub

' The storable interface

Public Function get_name() As String

    get_name = "Chore"

End Function

' String layout:
    ' Key 1-11, pad 12
    ' Name 13-52
    ' est_time 53-58, pad 59
    ' frequency 60

Public Function to_string() As String
```

```
        to_string = _
            ODB.long_str(key) & " " & _
            ODB.fix_len(Name, 40) & _
            ODB.int_str(est_time) & " " & _
            Chr(Asc("0") + chore_frequency)

End Function

Public Sub from_string(ByVal s As String)

    key = Val(left(s, 11))
    Name = Mid(s, 13, 40)
    est_time = Val(Mid(s, 53, 6))
    chore_frequency = Val(Right(s, 1))

End Sub

Public Function get_est_time() As String

    get_est_time = ODB.int2tstring(est_time)

End Function

Public Function iget_est_time() As Integer

    iget_est_time = est_time

End Function

Public Sub set_est_time(s As String)

    est_time = ODB.tstring2int(s)

End Sub

Public Function get_freq_name() As String

    Select Case chore_frequency

        Case chore_daily: get_freq_name = "Daily"
        Case chore_weekly: get_freq_name = "Weekly"
        Case chore_monthly: get_freq_name = "Monthly"

    End Select

End Function

' end of Chore.cls
```

FORM MODULES

In this section, we'll look at the form modules for both classes, skipping over the familiar parts. We'll look at the data members first, followed by the constructors, the command button click handlers, and then the other routines.

Data Members

Both form modules have straightforward property lists. We'll start with the frmToDo form's data members.

To Do List Data Members

The frmToDo data resembles our other ODB-containing forms. Because the to do list items are dated, they include a Calendar object, a Private date, and an im_changing_date Boolean that suppresses the handling of the Change event by the TextBox that shows the date. This is the code:

```
' Properties:
    Public dont_unload As Boolean

    Public cur_obj As todo
    Public cur_obj_num As Long
    Public ob As ODB

    Private popcal As Calendar
    Private tdate As Date

    Private im_changing_date As Boolean
    Private changed As Boolean
```

Chore Data Members

The frmChore database doesn't include a date, so its property list is even simpler:

```
' Properties
    Public dont_unload As Boolean

    Public cur_obj As Chore
    Public cur_obj_num As Long
    Public ob As ODB

    Private changed As Boolean
```

Constructors and Destructors

Both classes include a constructor in the `Form_Initialize()` method. The `frmToDo` class also includes a destructor because its constructor launches a form.

The To Do List Form's Constructor

The `frmToDo` constructor creates a new `ToDo` object and uses it to create its ODB. It opens or creates the ODB and puts the first `ToDo` object in the ODB onto the form. Then it creates and loads an invisible `Calendar` object. This is the method:

```
Private Sub Form_Initialize()

    Set cur_obj = New todo
    Set ob = New ODB

    Dim pn As String ' pathname
    pn = cur_obj.get_name

    If Len(Dir(pn & ".ODB")) = 0 Then
        ob.create_odb cur_obj
        ob.add_obj cur_obj
    Else
        If ob.open_odb(pn) <> openOK Then End
    End If

    cur_obj_num = ob.get_obj(0, cur_obj)
    to_form ' fill in TextBoxes

    changed = False

    Set popcal = New Calendar
    popcal.Visible = False
    popcal.dont_unload = True
    Load popcal

End Sub
```

The To Do List Form's Destructor

The destructor code refuses to unload if a parent has set `dont_unload` to `True`. When it does unload, it first takes care of removing the calendar that it created. This is the routine:

```
Private Sub Form_QueryUnload( _
        Cancel As Integer, UnloadMode As Integer)
```

```
        If changed Then cmdSave_Click

        If dont_unload Then
            Visible = False
            Cancel = -1 ' set bit cancels unload
        Else
            popcal.Visible = False
            popcal.dont_unload = False
            Unload popcal
            Set popcal = Nothing
        End If

    End Sub
```

The Chore Form's Constructor

The `frmChore` constructor takes care of creating an initial object and ODB, opening or creating the ODB, and initializing the form with the properties of the first object. It has no calendar because `Chore` objects have a frequency, not a date:

```
    Private Sub Form_Initialize()

        Set cur_obj = New Chore
        Set ob = New ODB

        Dim pn As String ' pathname
        pn = cur_obj.get_name

        If Len(Dir(pn & ".ODB")) = 0 Then
            ob.create_odb cur_obj
            ob.add_obj cur_obj
        Else
            If ob.open_odb(pn) <> openOK Then End
        End If

        cur_obj_num = ob.get_obj(0, cur_obj)
        to_form ' fill in TextBoxes

        changed = False

    End Sub
```

The `frmChore` uses `QueryUnload` to ensure that the last object is saved if it has been changed. I hesitate to call that a destructor.

To and From Form Methods

Both forms provide to_form() and from_form() methods. The frmToDo methods are slightly more involved than the frmChore methods, but neither is complex.

To and From the To Do List Form

Because the underlying ToDo object handles time as tstring Strings externally, the to_form and from_form methods are quite simple. The only complication is the setting of im_changing_date to suppress change event handling in the date TextBox. This is the code:

```
Private Sub to_form()

    lblKey_num = cur_obj.key
    set_del

    txtName.Text = Trim(cur_obj.Name)
    txtEst_time.Text = cur_obj.get_est_time
    txtAct_time.Text = cur_obj.get_act_time
    tdate = cur_obj.todo_date
    im_changing_date = True
        txtToDo_date.Text = ODB.nice_date(tdate)
    im_changing_date = False

End Sub

Private Sub from_form()

    cur_obj.Name = txtName.Text
    cur_obj.set_est_time txtEst_time.Text
    cur_obj.set_act_time txtAct_time.Text
    cur_obj.todo_date = tdate

End Sub
```

To and From the Chore Form

The frmChore code is even simpler:

```
Private Sub to_form()

    lblKey_num = cur_obj.key
    set_del
```

```
        txtName.Text = Trim(cur_obj.Name)
        txtEst_time.Text = cur_obj.get_est_time
        cmbChore_frequency.ListIndex = cur_obj.chore_frequency

    End Sub

    Private Sub from_form()

        cur_obj.Name = txtName.Text
        cur_obj.set_est_time txtEst_time.Text
        cur_obj.chore_frequency = cmbChore_frequency.ListIndex

    End Sub
```

The way the Enum values for chore_frequency map to the ListIndex of the combo box make this delightfully simple code.

Command Button Click Handlers

The command button click handling code, which is the largest part of both frmToDo.frm and frmChore.frm, is completely standard except that the specific object type has to be included in the cmdAdd_Click method. This is the version in frmToDo:

```
    Private Sub cmdAdd_Click()

        If changed Then cmdSave_Click

        Set cur_obj = New todo
        cur_obj_num = ob.add_obj(cur_obj)

        changed = False
        to_form

        SendKeys "%1" ' press Alt+1

    End Sub
```

Late in testing, I added the SendKeys statement. This is a kludge to start the data entry process immediately after the Add New button is clicked. It makes using the form a bit nicer.

Other Routines

Both form modules include a range of other routines such as Change routines. All the Change routines set the value of changed to True. The date Change code in frmToDo has the same complications you saw in the project database, so we won't repeat it here. The other routines, such as set_del() and go_to() are the same as in our other data-entry forms.

The Full Listings

On disk, the file 20-2 includes everything you need to make and run both these form modules as standalone projects. That includes a form file, the class file, the ODB class, and the calendar form for the to do list database.

If you don't have the disk or if your mother-in-law has ruined your CD-ROM drive by trying to read floppy disks with it, the full listings of the portions you edit with the code editor are included here. The to do list file is in Listing 20-2a and the chore file is in Listing 20-2b. Appendices G and H contain the respective lists of properties set at design time.

Listing 20-2a
frmToDo.frm — the to do list data entry form

```
' frmToDo.frm — To Do list data entry form
' Copyright 1997, Martin L. Rinehart

Option Explicit

' Properties:
    Public dont_unload As Boolean

    Public cur_obj As todo
    Public cur_obj_num As Long
    Public ob As ODB

    Private popcal As Calendar
    Private tdate As Date

    Private im_changing_date As Boolean
    Private changed As Boolean

Private Sub to_form()

    lblKey_num = cur_obj.key
    set_del
```

(continued)

frmToDo.frm — the to do list data entry form

```
            txtName.Text = Trim(cur_obj.Name)
            txtEst_time.Text = cur_obj.get_est_time
            txtAct_time.Text = cur_obj.get_act_time
            tdate = cur_obj.todo_date
            im_changing_date = True
                txtToDo_date.Text = ODB.nice_date(tdate)
            im_changing_date = False

        End Sub

        Private Sub from_form()

            cur_obj.Name = txtName.Text
            cur_obj.set_est_time txtEst_time.Text
            cur_obj.set_act_time txtAct_time.Text
            cur_obj.todo_date = tdate

        End Sub

        Private Sub cmdAdd_Click()

            If changed Then cmdSave_Click

            Set cur_obj = New todo
            cur_obj_num = ob.add_obj(cur_obj)

            changed = False
            to_form

            SendKeys "%1" ' press Alt+1

        End Sub

        Private Sub cmdDelete_Click()

            If ob.obj_is_deleted Then Exit Sub

            If changed Then
                ob.obj_is_deleted = True
                ob.rep_obj cur_obj_num, cur_obj
                changed = False
            Else
                ob.del_obj cur_obj_num
            End If

            set_del

        End Sub
```

```
Private Sub cmdEnd_Click()

    go_to ob.get_num_objects - 1

End Sub

Private Sub cmdExit_Click()

    If changed Then cmdSave_Click
    Unload Me

End Sub

Private Sub cmdHome_Click()

    go_to 0

End Sub

Private Sub cmdNext_Click()

    go_to cur_obj_num + 1

End Sub

Private Sub cmdPrev_Click()

    go_to cur_obj_num - 1

End Sub

Private Sub cmdReread_Click()

    ob.get_obj cur_obj_num, cur_obj
    to_form
    changed = False

End Sub

Private Sub cmdSave_Click()

    from_form
    ob.rep_obj cur_obj_num, cur_obj
    changed = False

End Sub

Private Sub cmdUndelete_Click()
```

(continued)

frmToDo.frm — the to do list data entry form

```
        If Not ob.obj_is_deleted Then Exit Sub

        If changed Then
            ob.obj_is_deleted = False
            ob.rep_obj cur_obj_num, cur_obj
            changed = False
        Else
            ob.undel_obj cur_obj_num
        End If

        set_del

End Sub

Private Sub Form_Initialize()

    Set cur_obj = New todo
    Set ob = New ODB

    Dim pn As String ' pathname
    pn = cur_obj.get_name

    If Len(Dir(pn & ".ODB")) = 0 Then
        ob.create_odb cur_obj
        ob.add_obj cur_obj
    Else
        If ob.open_odb(pn) <> openOK Then End
    End If

    cur_obj_num = ob.get_obj(0, cur_obj)
    to_form ' fill in TextBoxes

    changed = False

    Set popcal = New Calendar
    popcal.Visible = False
    popcal.dont_unload = True
    Load popcal

End Sub

Private Sub Form_Load()

' debugging code — test to/from_string:
'    Dim t As todo
'    Set t = New todo
'
'    t.Key = 123
'    t.Name = "Test todo"
```

```
'      t.set_est_time "1:00"
'      t.set_act_time "0:45"
'      t.todo_date = "1/1/1999"
'
'      Dim s1 As String, s2 As String
'      s1 = t.to_string
'
'      t.from_string (s1)
'      s2 = t.to_string
'
'      Debug.Print IIf(s1 = s2, "OK", "Error")
'
End Sub

Private Sub Form_QueryUnload( _
        Cancel As Integer, UnloadMode As Integer)

    If changed Then cmdSave_Click

    If dont_unload Then
        Visible = False
        Cancel = -1 ' set bit cancels unload
    Else
        popcal.Visible = False
        popcal.dont_unload = False
        Unload popcal
        Set popcal = Nothing
    End If

End Sub

Private Sub txtAct_time_LostFocus()

    If Not ODB.OK_time(txtAct_time.Text) Then
        txtAct_time.Text = "00:00"
    End If

End Sub

Private Sub txtEst_time_LostFocus()

    If Not ODB.OK_time(txtEst_time.Text) Then
        txtEst_time.Text = "00:00"
    End If

End Sub

Private Sub txtToDo_date_Change()

    If im_changing_date Then Exit Sub
```

(continued)

frmToDo.frm — the to do list data entry form

```
        txtToDo_date_GotFocus

End Sub

Private Sub txtToDo_date_GotFocus()

    Static working As Boolean

    If working Then

        working = False

    Else

        working = True
        popcal.set_hi_date tdate
        popcal.Show √bModal

        Dim d As Date
        d = popcal.get_hi_date
        If d <> tdate Then

            changed = True
            tdate = d

            im_changing_date = True
                txtToDo_date.Text = ODB.nice_date(tdate)
            im_changing_date = False

        End If

        txtToDo_date.Visible = False ' lose focus
        txtToDo_date.Visible = True

    End If

End Sub

Private Sub txtAct_time_Change()

    changed = True
    txtAct_time.BackColor = set_bcolor(txtAct_time.Text)

End Sub
```

```
Private Sub txtEst_time_Change()

    changed = True
    txtEst_time.BackColor = set_bcolor(txtEst_time.Text)

End Sub

Private Function set_bcolor(s As String) As Long

    set_bcolor = IIf(ODB.OK_time(s), vbWhite, vbYellow)

End Function

Private Sub txtName_Change()

    changed = True

End Sub

Private Sub set_del()

    lblDeleted.Caption = _
        IIf(ob.obj_is_deleted, "Deleted", "")

End Sub

Public Sub go_to(onum As Long)

    If changed Then cmdSave_Click

    If onum < 0 Then onum = 0

    If onum >= ob.get_num_objects Then
        onum = ob.get_num_objects - 1
    End If

    If changed Then
        from_form
        ob.rep_obj cur_obj_num, cur_obj
    End If

    cur_obj_num = ob.get_obj(onum, cur_obj)
    changed = False
    to_form

End Sub

' end of frmToDo.frm
```

Listing 20-2b
frmChore.frm — the chore data entry form

```
' frmChore.frm — To Do list data entry form
' Copyright 1997, Martin L. Rinehart

Option Explicit

' Properties
    Public dont_unload As Boolean

    Public cur_obj As Chore
    Public cur_obj_num As Long
    Public ob As ODB

    Private changed As Boolean

Private Sub to_form()

    lblKey_num = cur_obj.key
    set_del

    txtName.Text = Trim(cur_obj.Name)
    txtEst_time.Text = cur_obj.get_est_time
    cmbChore_frequency.ListIndex = cur_obj.chore_frequency

End Sub

Private Sub from_form()

    cur_obj.Name = txtName.Text
    cur_obj.set_est_time txtEst_time.Text
    cur_obj.chore_frequency = cmbChore_frequency.ListIndex

End Sub

Private Sub cmbChore_frequency_Change()

' Note: -1 for ListIndex means user edited a frequency

    If cmbChore_frequency.ListIndex = -1 Then

        cmbChore_frequency.ListIndex = _
            cur_obj.chore_frequency

    Else

        changed = True

    End If
```

```
End Sub

Private Sub cmdAdd_Click()

    If changed Then cmdSave_Click

    Set cur_obj = New Chore
    cur_obj_num = ob.add_obj(cur_obj)

    changed = False
    to_form

    SendKeys "%1" ' press Alt+1

End Sub

Private Sub cmdDelete_Click()

    If ob.obj_is_deleted Then Exit Sub

    If changed Then
        ob.obj_is_deleted = True
        ob.rep_obj cur_obj_num, cur_obj
        changed = False
    Else
        ob.del_obj cur_obj_num
    End If

    set_del

End Sub

Private Sub cmdEnd_Click()

    go_to ob.get_num_objects - 1

End Sub

Private Sub cmdExit_Click()

    Unload Me

End Sub

Private Sub cmdHome_Click()

    go_to 0

End Sub
```

(continued)

frmChore.frm — the chore data entry form

```
Private Sub cmdNext_Click()

    go_to cur_obj_num + 1

End Sub

Private Sub cmdPrev_Click()

    go_to cur_obj_num - 1

End Sub

Private Sub cmdReread_Click()

    ob.get_obj cur_obj_num, cur_obj
    to_form
    changed = False

End Sub

Private Sub cmdSave_Click()

    from_form
    ob.rep_obj cur_obj_num, cur_obj
    changed = False

End Sub

Private Sub cmdUndelete_Click()

    If Not ob.obj_is_deleted Then Exit Sub

    If changed Then
        ob.obj_is_deleted = False
        ob.rep_obj cur_obj_num, cur_obj
        changed = False
    Else
        ob.undel_obj cur_obj_num
    End If

    set_del

End Sub

Private Sub Form_Initialize()

    Set cur_obj = New Chore
    Set ob = New ODB
```

```
    Dim pn As String ' pathname
    pn = cur_obj.get_name

    If Len(Dir(pn & ".ODB")) = 0 Then
        ob.create_odb cur_obj
        ob.add_obj cur_obj
    Else
        If ob.open_odb(pn) <> openOK Then End
    End If

    cur_obj_num = ob.get_obj(0, cur_obj)
    to_form ' fill in TextBoxes

    changed = False

End Sub

Private Sub Form_Load()

' debugging code — test to/from_string:
'    Dim t As Chore
'    Set t = New Chore
'
'    t.Name = "Test Chore"
'    t.set_est_time "1:00"
'    t.chore_frequency = 1
'
'    Dim s1 As String, s2 As String
'    s1 = t.to_string
'
'    t.from_string (s1)
'    s2 = t.to_string
'
'    Debug.Print IIf(s1 = s2, "OK", "Error")
'
End Sub

Private Sub Form_QueryUnload( _
        Cancel As Integer, UnloadMode As Integer)

    If changed Then cmdSave_Click

End Sub

Private Sub txtChore_date_Change()

    changed = True

End Sub
```

(continued)

frmChore.frm — the chore data entry form

```vb
Private Sub txtEst_time_time_Change()

    changed = True

End Sub

Private Sub txtEst_time_Change()

    changed = True
    txtEst_time.BackColor = IIf( _
            ODB.OK_time(txtEst_time.Text), _
            vbWhite, vbYellow)

End Sub

Private Sub txtEst_time_LostFocus()

    If Not ODB.OK_time(txtEst_time.Text) Then
        txtEst_time.Text = "00:00"
    End If

End Sub

Private Sub txtName_Change()

    changed = True

End Sub

Private Sub set_del()

    lblDeleted.Caption = _
        IIf(ob.obj_is_deleted, "Deleted", "")

End Sub

Public Sub go_to(onum As Long)

    If onum < 0 Then onum = 0

    If onum >= ob.get_num_objects Then
        onum = ob.get_num_objects - 1
    End If

    If changed Then
        from_form
        ob.rep_obj cur_obj_num, cur_obj
```

```
        End If

        cur_obj_num = ob.get_obj(onum, cur_obj)
        changed = False
        to_form

    End Sub

    ' end of frmChore.frm
```

SUMMARY

That was easy, wasn't it? It's simple because by now you know exactly how these ODB-storable classes work. It's also simple because your ODB class is getting a very healthy dose of reuse.

We looked at the design of the databases and the forms that allow data entry.

Then we went on to look at the class modules. These contained the normal data members, constructors, the storable interface's three functions, and data access routines.

After looking at the class modules, we went on to the forms. Again we looked at data members, constructors and destructors, button click handlers, and other methods. They were very similar to our other data entry handling classes.

Now that we have the infrastructure built, we're ready to go on to the design surfaces, which are visual and generally a lot more fun.

If you hadn't noticed — and I suspect that you had — we're only one chapter away from putting the entire MyTime system together. When we get there, I'm going to ask you to roll up your sleeves and build the system yourself.

Chapter 21, though, will finish your time as a mere reader of this code.

TASKS AND TIME

*I*n this chapter, we'll look at the code for the last two tools. The tasks and the time surfaces are similar and both are simpler than the other tools we've already built. Their job is to display the facts you've entered. The tasks tool gives you access to the To Do and Chore ODBs.

The time tool tells you how hopelessly overbooked your schedule is. Its job is to summarize everything your system knows about your time. I consider it absolutely essential, but not always welcome.

Before we start, I'm going to tell you that real life isn't always like books. Using an object-oriented approach has let us build necessary pieces that ran on their own. We built the projects database and then we built the cascade object. In the next chapter, we'll use that as part of the whole system.

But that doesn't always work so neatly. For example, the tasks object lists To Do objects for a given date. In the finished system, the calendar will provide that date. When I built tasks, I just used today's date to run and debug the object. The calendar date waited for final assembly.

Sometimes you can find convenient, temporary solutions, like using today's date in lieu of the calendar date. On the other hand, sometimes you can't. The time object needs access to the ODBs of the other surfaces. The parent MyTime menu object will take care of handing it references to these ODBs. That means that it can't work until after final assembly.

To develop this project, you'd have to assemble all the other pieces first and then build the time surface under the running system. Build most of the pieces; put them together; build pieces that don't work independently. Real systems work like that.

This book, however, will be better organized than real life. We'll finish all the components here, and then in the last chapter we'll put them together.

We'll look at the tasks tool first.

TASKS

In this section we'll take another look at the design of the tasks tool, and then we'll dive right into the code. This is a simple tool, and the code is correspondingly simple. If you really enjoyed studying those tough algorithms in Chapter 20, you'll be disappointed here. If you're hoping that we'll quickly and easily get on with the job so that you can put the whole project together (we'll do that in the next chapter), you'll be delighted.

I'll skip routines such as `resize()` and the ones that return references to ODBs. The former is large but does nothing unusual. The latter are trivial.

The Tasks Design

Figure 21-1 shows the tasks tool. On the left, you have today's (or the date set by the calendar) to do list items. On the right you have all your chores.

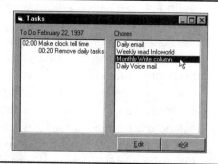

Figure 21-1
The tasks tool shows to do list items and chores.

When a `ToDo` object is completed, it's shown indented. (Completion is indicated by a nonzero actual time.)

You can highlight any item because these panels are ListBox objects. When you click Edit, the corresponding ODB is positioned to the highlighted item, and the appropriate data entry form is launched.

If nothing is selected, the last ODB you work with opens by default. If you've made no selection, the ToDo ODB is used by default. If the ToDo list is empty, the ODB is launched with a new ToDo added, automatically.

Figure 21-2 shows the tasks tool at design time.

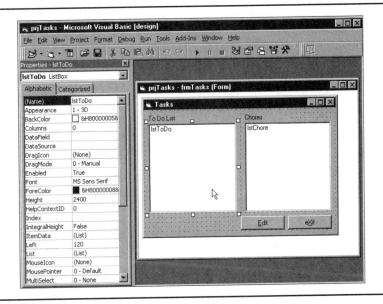

Figure 21-2
Designing the tasks tool.

You can see that it's built with two Labels, two ListBoxes, and two CommandButtons. The components are

- lblToDo
- lblChore
- lstToDo
- lstChore
- cmdEdit
- cmdExit

Now that we've looked at the design, we're ready to look at the code.

Tasks Data

The `frmTask` data section begins with constants used by the `Resize()` method. You can refer to the full listing for these constants and that method. These are the other constants:

```
Const max_chores = 100
Const max_todos = 100 ' max for a single day

Private Enum list
    list_todo
    list_chore
End Enum
```

The maxima are ones that are about ten times what I think I'll ever use. The `Enum` is used in deciding which ODB to use when the Edit button is clicked.

These are the data members:

```
' Data members
    Public dont_unload As Boolean
    Public boss_cal As Calendar ' sets todays_date

    Private dont_resize As Boolean
    Private todo_form As frmToDo
    Private chore_form As frmChore

    Private todays_date As Date
    Private todo_bag As Collection
    Private chore_bag As Collection

    Private hi_list As Byte

    Private todo_recnos(1 To max_todos) As Long
    Private chore_recnos(1 To max_chores) As Long
```

As we've done with projects and appointments, we'll read both `ToDo` objects into one `Collection`, and `Chore` objects into another `Collection`. As we read them, we'll record their record numbers in the two recnos arrays. This will eliminate the need for a search when an item is selected and Edit is clicked.

Tasks' Constructor and Destructor

This is the constructor code:

```
Private Sub Form_Initialize()

    Set todo_form = New frmToDo
    todo_form.Visible = False
    todo_form.dont_unload = True
    Load todo_form

    Set chore_form = New frmChore
    chore_form.Visible = False
    chore_form.dont_unload = True
    Load chore_form

    hi_list = list_todo

    Set todo_bag = New Collection
    Set chore_bag = New Collection

End Sub
```

This creates new form-based objects for the two ODBs. (The frmToDo object creates the ToDo ODB object, which opens the file.) The hi_list is the list that corresponds to a highlighted ListBox item. Here it is assigned the to do list as its default.

The destructor code has to clean up the forms:

```
Private Sub Form_QueryUnload(Cancel As Integer, _
        UnloadMode As Integer)

    If dont_unload Then

        Visible = False
        Cancel = -1 ' Don't cancel if bit set

    Else

        todo_form.Visible = False
        todo_form.dont_unload = False
        Unload todo_form
        Set todo_form = Nothing
```

```
        chore_form.Visible = False
        chore_form.dont_unload = False
        Unload chore_form
        Set chore_form = Nothing

    End If

End Sub
```

Filling the Tasks Lists

The tasks are read in whenever the tool is activated, by this routine:

```
Private Sub Form_Activate()

    todays_date = Date
    read_todos
    read_chores

End Sub
```

In Chapter 22, we'll take care of replacing that date assignment with one that actually uses the calendar's date.

Getting the ToDo Objects

The read_todos() method does the actual work. It empties the bag and then refills it. It reads in every ToDo that matches the todays_date, provided it's not deleted. If it ever reaches the maximum (which I don't anticipate), it simply stops reading. You might want to improve this with, at a minimum, a warning message.

This is the code:

```
Private Sub read_todos()

    Dim i As Long

' empty the collection
    If todo_bag.Count > 0 Then

        For i = todo_bag.Count To 1 Step -1
            todo_bag.Remove (i)
        Next

    End If
```

```
' exit if nothing to do
    Dim n As Long
    n = todo_form.ob.get_num_objects
    If n = 0 Then Exit Sub

' refill the collection
    Dim a As todo, num_in_bag As Integer, recno As Long

    num_in_bag = 0

    For i = 0 To n - 1

        Set a = New todo
        recno = todo_form.ob.get_obj(i, a)

        If Not todo_form.ob.obj_is_deleted Then
            If a.todo_date = todays_date Then
                todo_bag.Add a
                num_in_bag = num_in_bag + 1
                If num_in_bag > max_todos Then Exit For
                todo_recnos(num_in_bag) = recno
            End If
        End If

    Next

' show the ones that fit
    show_todos

' display the new date
    lblToDo.Caption = "To Do " & ODB.nice_date(todays_date)

End Sub
```

Getting the Chore Objects

The chores are read in almost the same fashion. The difference is that chores don't have a date, so we read all the nondeleted chores, this way:

```
Private Sub read_chores()

    Dim i As Long

' empty the collection
    If chore_bag.Count > 0 Then
```

```
            For i = chore_bag.Count To 1 Step -1
                chore_bag.Remove (i)
            Next

        End If

    ' exit if nothing to do
        Dim n As Long
        n = chore_form.ob.get_num_objects
        If n = 0 Then Exit Sub

    ' refill the collection
        Dim a As Chore, num_in_bag As Integer, recno As Long

        num_in_bag = 0

        For i = 0 To n - 1

            Set a = New Chore
            recno = chore_form.ob.get_obj(i, a)

            If Not chore_form.ob.obj_is_deleted Then
                chore_bag.Add a
                num_in_bag = num_in_bag + 1
                If num_in_bag > max_chores Then Exit For
                chore_recnos(num_in_bag) = recno
            End If

        Next

    ' show the ones that fit
        show_chores

    End Sub
```

In rereading these methods, I don't particularly like the way they go on to call the display routines. Those calls should be moved up to the calling level. A routine called read_chores() should read chores, shouldn't it? My time tool is telling me that if I want to make improvements, however, today's not the day. Oh well.

Displaying Tasks

The show_todos() and show_chores() methods do the display. Their basic job is to fill the ListBox.List.

Displaying ToDo Objects

The ToDo items are shown with their estimated or actual times. Items with nonzero actual times are also indented.

These lists are *not* sorted.

This is the code:

```
Private Sub show_todos()

    Dim i As Integer, s As String, tim As Integer

    With lstToDo

    ' empty list
        For i = .ListCount - 1 To 0 Step -1
            .RemoveItem i
        Next

    ' refill list
        For i = 1 To todo_bag.Count
            tim = todo_bag.item(i).iget_act_time
            If tim > 0 Then
                s = Space(10) & _
                        todo_bag.item(i).get_act_time
            Else
                s = todo_bag.item(i).get_est_time
            End If

            s = s & " " & todo_bag.item(i).Name
            .AddItem s
        Next

    End With

End Sub
```

Displaying Chore Objects

Chores are shown with their frequency name in front of their names. This is the method:

```
Private Sub show_chores()

    Dim i As Integer, s As String

    With lstChore
```

```
        'empty list
            For i = .ListCount - 1 To 0 Step -1
                .RemoveItem i
            Next

        ' refill list
            For i = 1 To chore_bag.Count
                s = chore_bag.item(i).get_freq_name & _
                    " " & chore_bag.item(i).Name
                .AddItem s
            Next

        End With

    End Sub
```

Responding to Clicks

You can click on either ListBox or on either of the two buttons. Clicks on the listbox don't really do anything directly, but they set the selection for the Edit button. We'll look at these first.

ListBox Clicks

When a ListBox is clicked, the hi_list is set to the appropriate enum value. GotFocus also does this, for times when you tab to the ListBox. The ListBox object takes care of setting ListIndex to the appropriate item number.

This is the ToDo code:

```
    Private Sub lstToDo_Click()

        hi_list = list_todo

    End Sub

    Private Sub lstToDo_GotFocus()

        hi_list = list_todo

    End Sub
```

The lstChore() methods do the same work for chores.

The Edit Button

The Edit button sets up the ODB and then launches the appropriate data entry form. This is the routine:

```
Private Sub cmdEdit_Click()

    set_odb
    If hi_list = list_todo Then
        todo_form.Show vbModal
    Else
        chore_form.Show vbModal
    End If

End Sub
```

The set_odb() method calls the appropriate form's go_to() method with the object number that it stored in the array when it filled the Collection. If the ListIndex is -1, however, (nothing selected) it skips this task. This is the code:

```
Private Sub set_odb()

    Dim item As Integer

    If hi_list = list_todo Then

        item = lstToDo.ListIndex
        If item > -1 Then todo_form.go_to _
            todo_recnos(item + 1)

    Else

        item = lstChore.ListIndex
        If item > -1 Then chore_form.go_to _
            chore_recnos(item + 1)

    End If

End Sub
```

The eXit Button

The eXit button has the normal, trivial job:

```
Private Sub cmdExit_Click()

    Unload Me

End Sub
```

The Full Listing

The disk file 21-01 has the full frmTasks.frm, as well as all the other files needed to run tasks as a standalone program. This includes the project file and all the other supporting .FRM and .CLS modules, none of which are changed from their previous versions.

For those of you who don't have the disk or if your little sister dropped her peanut buttered toast on it (and it landed peanut butter side down, of course), the full listing of the portion you see in the code editor is here in Listing 21-1. The properties portion of the file is listed in Appendix I.

Listing 21-1
frmTask.frm — the tasks tool

```
' frmTasks.frm — To Do and Chore lists
' Copyright 1997, Martin L. Rinehart

Option Explicit

Const top_space = 450
Const btm_space = 345
Const side_space = 120
Const between_space = 210
Const below_space = 75

Const min_height = 3000
Const min_width = 4000

Const max_chores = 100
Const max_todos = 100 ' max for a single day

Private Enum list
    list_todo
    list_chore
End Enum

' Data members
    Public dont_unload As Boolean
    Public boss_cal As Calendar ' sets todays_date

    Private dont_resize As Boolean
    Private todo_form As frmToDo
    Private chore_form As frmChore

    Private todays_date As Date
    Private todo_bag As Collection
    Private chore_bag As Collection
```

```vb
        Private hi_list As Byte

        Private todo_recnos(1 To max_todos) As Long
        Private chore_recnos(1 To max_chores) As Long

Private Sub cmdEdit_Click()

        set_odb
        If hi_list = list_todo Then
            todo_form.Show vbModal
        Else
            chore_form.Show vbModal
        End If

End Sub

Private Sub cmdExit_Click()

        Unload Me

End Sub

Private Sub Form_Activate()

        todays_date = Date
        read_todos
        read_chores

End Sub

Private Sub Form_Initialize()

        Set todo_form = New frmToDo
        todo_form.Visible = False
        todo_form.dont_unload = True
        Load todo_form

        Set chore_form = New frmChore
        chore_form.Visible = False
        chore_form.dont_unload = True
        Load chore_form

        hi_list = list_todo

        Set todo_bag = New Collection
        Set chore_bag = New Collection

End Sub
```

(continued)

frmTask.frm — the tasks tool

```
Private Sub Form_QueryUnload(Cancel As Integer, _
    UnloadMode As Integer)

    If dont_unload Then

        Visible = False
        Cancel = -1 ' Don't cancel if bit set

    Else

        todo_form.Visible = False
        todo_form.dont_unload = False
        Unload todo_form
        Set todo_form = Nothing

        chore_form.Visible = False
        chore_form.dont_unload = False
        Unload chore_form
        Set chore_form = Nothing

    End If

End Sub

Private Sub Form_Resize()

    If dont_resize Then Exit Sub

    If Width < min_width Then
        dont_resize = True
        Width = min_width
        dont_resize = False
    End If

    If Height < min_height Then
        dont_resize = True
        Height = min_height
        dont_resize = False
    End If

    Dim col_wid As Integer
    col_wid = (Width - (2 * side_space) - _
        between_space - 150) / 2

    Dim lft As Integer, rgt As Integer

    lft = side_space
    rgt = lft + col_wid + between_space
```

```
        lstToDo.left = lft
        lstChore.left = rgt

        lblToDo.left = lft
        lblChore.left = rgt

        lstToDo.Width = col_wid
        lstChore.Width = col_wid

        lstToDo.Height = Height - 400 - top_space - btm_space
        lstChore.Height = lstToDo.Height

        cmdExit.top = lstChore.top + _
            lstChore.Height + below_space
        cmdExit.left = Width - cmdExit.Width - 135

        cmdEdit.top = cmdExit.top
        cmdEdit.left = cmdExit.left - cmdEdit.Width

End Sub

Private Sub lstChore_Click()

    hi_list = list_chore

End Sub

Private Sub lstChore_GotFocus()

    hi_list = list_chore

End Sub

Private Sub lstToDo_Click()

    hi_list = list_todo

End Sub

Private Sub lstToDo_GotFocus()

    hi_list = list_todo

End Sub

Private Sub read_todos()

    Dim i As Long
```

(continued)

frmTask.frm — the tasks tool

```vb
' empty the collection
    If todo_bag.Count > 0 Then

        For i = todo_bag.Count To 1 Step -1
            todo_bag.Remove (i)
        Next

    End If

' exit if nothing to do
    Dim n As Long
    n = todo_form.ob.get_num_objects
    If n = 0 Then Exit Sub

' refill the collection
    Dim a As todo, num_in_bag As Integer, recno As Long

    num_in_bag = 0

    For i = 0 To n - 1

        Set a = New todo
        recno = todo_form.ob.get_obj(i, a)

        If Not todo_form.ob.obj_is_deleted Then
            If a.todo_date = todays_date Then
                todo_bag.Add a
                num_in_bag = num_in_bag + 1
                If num_in_bag > max_todos Then Exit For
                todo_recnos(num_in_bag) = recno
            End If
        End If

    Next

' show the ones that fit
    show_todos

' display the new date
    lblToDo.Caption = "To Do " & ODB.nice_date(todays_date)

End Sub

Private Sub read_chores()

    Dim i As Long

' empty the collection
    If chore_bag.Count > 0 Then
```

```
            For i = chore_bag.Count To 1 Step -1
                chore_bag.Remove (i)
            Next

        End If

' exit if nothing to do
    Dim n As Long
    n = chore_form.ob.get_num_objects
    If n = 0 Then Exit Sub

' refill the collection
    Dim a As Chore, num_in_bag As Integer, recno As Long

    num_in_bag = 0

    For i = 0 To n - 1

        Set a = New Chore
        recno = chore_form.ob.get_obj(i, a)

        If Not chore_form.ob.obj_is_deleted Then
            chore_bag.Add a
            num_in_bag = num_in_bag + 1
            If num_in_bag > max_chores Then Exit For
            chore_recnos(num_in_bag) = recno
        End If

    Next

' show the ones that fit
    show_chores

End Sub

Private Sub show_todos()

    Dim i As Integer, s As String, tim As Integer

    With lstToDo

    ' empty list
        For i = .ListCount - 1 To 0 Step -1
            .RemoveItem i
        Next

    ' refill list
        For i = 1 To todo_bag.Count
            tim = todo_bag.item(i).iget_act_time
```

(continued)

frmTask.frm — the tasks tool

```vb
            If tim > 0 Then
                s = Space(10) & _
                        todo_bag.item(i).get_act_time
            Else
                s = todo_bag.item(i).get_est_time
            End If

            s = s & " " & todo_bag.item(i).Name
            .AddItem s
        Next

    End With

End Sub

Private Sub show_chores()

    Dim i As Integer, s As String

    With lstChore

    'empty list
        For i = .ListCount - 1 To 0 Step -1
            .RemoveItem i
        Next

    ' refill list
        For i = 1 To chore_bag.Count
            s = chore_bag.item(i).get_freq_name & _
            " " & chore_bag.item(i).Name
            .AddItem s
        Next

    End With

End Sub

Private Sub set_odb()

    Dim item As Integer

    If hi_list = list_todo Then

        item = lstToDo.ListIndex
        If item > -1 Then todo_form.go_to _
            todo_recnos(item + 1)
```

```
            Else

                item = lstChore.ListIndex
                If item > -1 Then chore_form.go_to _
                    chore_recnos(item + 1)

            End If

        End Sub

        Public Function get_todo_db() As ODB

            Set get_todo_db = todo_form.ob

        End Function

        Public Function get_chore_db() As ODB

            Set get_chore_db = chore_form.ob

        End Function

        ' end of frmTasks.frm
```

TIME

The time panel is twice the size of the tasks panel, which makes it more extensive. On the other hand, there's no Edit button to program, which simplifies it considerably.

The Time Design

Figure 21-3 shows the time tool.

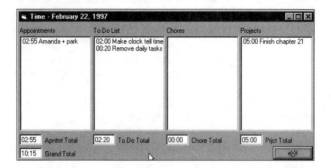

Figure 21-3
The time tool summarizes everything.

The full name of that item that starts "Remove daily tasks" is "Remove daily tasks from weekend." On Saturday morning, this tool was annoying me with reminders to check my mail. You'll see in the code that this doesn't happen anymore.

The projects that are shown are the single-day ones for which you provide time data. All times are actual times, unless that is zero. With no actual time, the estimated time is used.

Figure 21-4 shows the time tool at design time.

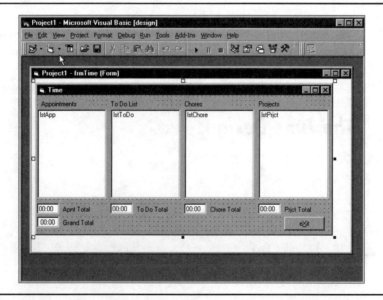

Figure 21-4
Designing the time tool.

The large rectangles are ListBoxes. The times are shown in TextBoxes. Item names regularly use App, ToDo, Chore, and Prjct. For example, the label over the appointments is lblApp; the ListBox for appointments is lstApp.

Again, when we go through the code, I'll omit the trivial and typical data and methods.

Time Data

The data begins with a set of size constants used by the Resize() code. Then it comes to these properties:

```
' Properties
    Public dont_unload As Boolean
    Public boss_cal As Calendar

    Public app_db As ODB ' these are set by the parent
    Public todo_db As ODB
    Public chore_db As ODB
    Public prjct_db As ODB

    Private todays_date As Date

    Private app_bag As Collection
    Private todo_bag As Collection
    Private chore_bag As Collection
    Private prjct_bag As Collection

    Private app_total As Integer
    Private todo_total As Integer
    Private chore_total As Integer
    Private prjct_total As Integer
    Private grand_total As Integer

    Private dont_resize As Boolean
```

The parent MyTime menu passes frmTime references to each of the ODB objects created by the other objects. These are used, of course, to read the data. Again, Collections are used to hold the four different types of objects. Integers hold the times that are displayed in tstring format.

Time's Constructor and Destructor

The constructor only needs to create the contained `Collection` objects:

```
Private Sub Form_Initialize()

    Set app_bag = New Collection
    Set todo_bag = New Collection
    Set chore_bag = New Collection
    Set prjct_bag = New Collection

End Sub
```

There isn't any destructor code. `QueryUnload` just respects its parent's order regarding unloading:

```
Private Sub Form_QueryUnload(Cancel As Integer, _
    UnloadMode As Integer)

    If dont_unload Then

        Visible = False
        Cancel = -1 ' set bit cancels unload

    End If

End Sub
```

Filling the Time Lists

Whenever the form is activated, it rereads all the data. (It has no way of knowing what might be changed.) This is controlled by the `Activate()` event handler:

```
Private Sub Form_Activate()

    todays_date = boss_cal.get_hi_date
    Caption = "Time - " & ODB.nice_date(todays_date)

    read_apps
    read_todos
    read_chores
    read_prjcts
```

```
        show_apps
        show_todos
        show_chores
        show_prjcts

    End Sub
```

Each of these methods use the `empty_coll()` method to empty their `Collection` objects. We'll look at that method at the end of this section.

Reading the App Objects

The `read_apps()` method empties the app_bag `Collection`. Then it refills it with all appointments for `todays_date` (the date the calendar sets) that are not deleted. This is the code:

```
    Private Sub read_apps()

        Dim i As Long

        empty_coll app_bag

' exit if nothing to do
        Dim n As Long
        n = app_db.get_num_objects
        If n = 0 Then Exit Sub

' refill the collection
        Dim a As App

        For i = 0 To n - 1

            Set a = New App
            app_db.get_obj i, a

            If Not app_db.obj_is_deleted Then
                If a.app_date = todays_date Then
                    app_bag.Add a
                End If
            End If

        Next

    End Sub
```

Reading the ToDo Objects

The read_todos() method is very similar to read_apps(). This is its code:

```
Private Sub read_todos()

    Dim i As Long

    empty_coll todo_bag

' exit if nothing to do
    Dim n As Long
    n = todo_db.get_num_objects
    If n = 0 Then Exit Sub

' refill the collection
    Dim t As todo

    For i = 0 To n - 1

        Set t = New todo
        todo_db.get_obj i, t

        If Not todo_db.obj_is_deleted Then
            If t.todo_date = todays_date Then
                todo_bag.Add t
            End If
        End If

    Next

End Sub
```

Reading the Chore Objects

Chores have no dates, of course. Time is the tool that decides what chores are done when. The read_chores() method calls a do_today() function that determines whether a particular chore gets done on todays_date. This is the method:

```
Private Sub read_chores()

    Dim i As Long

    empty_coll chore_bag
```

```
' exit if nothing to do
    Dim n As Long
    n = chore_db.get_num_objects
    If n = 0 Then Exit Sub

' refill the collection
    Dim c As Chore
    For i = 0 To n - 1

        Set c = New Chore
        chore_db.get_obj i, c

        If Not chore_db.obj_is_deleted Then
            If do_today(c) Then chore_bag.Add c
        End If

    Next

End Sub
```

The do_today() function uses these arbitrary rules. You may want to replace them with your own rules:

- Daily chores are done Monday through Friday
- Weekly chores are done on Mondays
- Monthly chores are done on the last day of each month

This is the function:

```
Private Function do_today(c As Chore) As Boolean

    Select Case c.chore_frequency

        Case chore_daily
            do_today = _
                (Weekday(todays_date) <> vbSaturday) And _
                (Weekday(todays_date) <> vbSunday)

        Case chore_weekly
            do_today = (WeekDay(todays_date) = vbMonday)

        Case chore_monthly
            do_today = Month(todays_date) <> _
                Month(todays_date + 1)

    End Select

End Function
```

The original code for chore_daily just said:

```
Case chore_daily
    do_today = True
```

You can see that this no longer annoys me on weekends.

Reading the Prjct Objects

The read_prjcts() method uses a boolean function, one_day(), to decide if the project is the type that is entered on the time display. This is the code:

```
Private Sub read_prjcts()

    Dim i As Long

    empty_coll prjct_bag

' exit if nothing to do
    Dim n As Long
    n = prjct_db.get_num_objects
    If n = 0 Then Exit Sub

' refill the collection
    Dim p As Prjct

    For i = 0 To n - 1

        Set p = New Prjct
        prjct_db.get_obj i, p

        If Not prjct_db.obj_is_deleted Then

            If p.est_start_date = todays_date Then
                If one_day(p) Then prjct_bag.Add p
            End If

        End If

    Next

End Sub
```

This is the one_day() function:

```
Private Function one_day(p As Prjct) As Boolean

    one_day = (p.est_start_date = p.est_end_date)

End Function
```

Emptying a Collection

Emptying the collections is done by the empty_coll() routine shown here:

```
Private Sub empty_coll(ByRef coll As Collection)

    If coll.Count > 0 Then

        Dim i As Integer
        For i = coll.Count To 1 Step -1
            coll.Remove (i)
        Next

    End If

End Sub
```

Displaying Tasks

The display routine's basic job is to show the length of time each item requires along with its name. They all take each object from a Collection, format a string, and add it to the appropriate ListBox. Each display routine uses the empty_list() method that we'll look at at the end of this section.

Displaying App Objects

In addition to the basic job, each display routine handles its own total time. The total is set to zero initially and then increased with the time for each item. This is the show_apps() method:

```
Private Sub show_apps()

    Dim i As Integer, n As Byte, _
            tim As Integer, s As String
    n = 0
    app_total = 0
    empty_list lstApp
```

```
For i = 1 To app_bag.Count

    With app_bag.item(i)

        tim = .iget_actual_time
        If tim = 0 Then
            tim = .iget_end_time - .iget_start_time
        End If

        app_total = app_total + tim

        s = ODB.int2tstring(tim) + " " + .description
        lstApp.AddItem s

    End With

Next

txtTotal_app.Text = ODB.int2tstring(app_total)

End Sub
```

Displaying ToDo Objects

ToDo objects are displayed by show_todos(). This is the code:

```
Private Sub show_todos()

    Dim i As Integer, n As Byte, tim As Integer
    n = 0
    todo_total = 0

    empty_list lstToDo

    For i = 1 To todo_bag.Count

        With todo_bag.item(i)

            tim = .iget_act_time
            If tim = 0 Then tim = .iget_est_time

            todo_total = todo_total + tim
            lstToDo.AddItem ODB.int2tstring(tim) & _
                " " & Trim(.Name)

        End With
    Next
```

```
        txtTotal_todo.Text = ODB.int2tstring(todo_total)

    End Sub
```

Displaying Chore Objects

Chores do not have an actual time, so the time handling is simply a matter of retrieving the estimated time. This routine displays the chores:

```
    Private Sub show_chores()

        Dim i As Integer, n As Byte, tim As Integer
        n = 0
        chore_total = 0

        empty_list lstChore

        For i = 1 To chore_bag.Count

            With chore_bag.item(i)

                tim = .iget_est_time

                chore_total = chore_total + tim
                lstChore.AddItem ODB.int2tstring(tim) & _
                    " " & Trim(.Name)

            End With
        Next

        txtTotal_chore.Text = ODB.int2tstring(chore_total)

    End Sub
```

Displaying Prjct Objects

Being last in the chain, the project display routine was assigned the additional job of handling the grand total. Otherwise it's similar to the appointment and to do list display routines. This is the code:

```
    Private Sub show_prjcts()

        Dim i As Integer, n As Byte, tim As Integer
        n = 0
        prjct_total = 0
```

```
        empty_list lstPrjct

        For i = 1 To prjct_bag.Count

            With prjct_bag.item(i)

                tim = .iget_act_time
                If tim = 0 Then tim = .iget_est_time

                prjct_total = prjct_total + tim
                lstPrjct.AddItem ODB.int2tstring(tim) & _
                    " " & Trim(.Name)

            End With
        Next

        txtTotal_prjct.Text = ODB.int2tstring(prjct_total)
        Dim gtot As Integer
        gtot = app_total + todo_total + chore_total + prjct_total

        txtGrand_total.Text = ODB.int2tstring(gtot)

    End Sub
```

Emptying a List

The empty_list() method does just what its name suggests for each of the ListBox objects. It works on a last-in, first-out basis, this way:

```
    Private Sub empty_list(ByRef ls As ListBox)

        If ls.ListCount = 0 Then Exit Sub

        Dim i As Integer
        For i = ls.ListCount To 1 Step -1
            ls.RemoveItem i - 1
        Next

    End Sub
```

Because you have no clicks to worry about, other than the eXit button, that brings us to the end of our tour of the time tool. The eXit button has the normal trivial click event handler.

The Full Listing

The full frmTime.frm file is on disk in 21-02. It is not accompanied by project and other files because it cannot be run as a standalone program. (It needs the ODBs that the other tools create.)

For those who do not have the disk or if your baby brother dropped his cupcake (icing side down, of course) on your disk, the full listing of the portion you can edit with the code editor is in Listing 21-2. The properties set at design time are shown in Appendix J.

Listing 21-2
frmTime.frm — the time tool

```
' frmTime.frm — Daily Time Summary
' Copyright 1997, Martin L. Rinehart

Option Explicit

Const top_space = 450
Const btm_space = 660
Const side_space = 15
Const between_space = 30
Const below_space = 75

Const min_height = 3000
Const min_width = 6300

' Properties
    Public dont_unload As Boolean
    Public boss_cal As Calendar

    Public app_db As ODB ' these are set by the parent
    Public todo_db As ODB
    Public chore_db As ODB
    Public prjct_db As ODB

    Private todays_date As Date

    Private app_bag As Collection
    Private todo_bag As Collection
    Private chore_bag As Collection
    Private prjct_bag As Collection

    Private app_total As Integer
    Private todo_total As Integer
    Private chore_total As Integer
    Private prjct_total As Integer
    Private grand_total As Integer
```

(continued)

frmTime.frm — the time tool

```
        Private dont_resize As Boolean

    Private Sub cmdExit_Click()

        Unload Me

    End Sub

    Private Sub Form_Activate()

        todays_date = boss_cal.get_hi_date
        Caption = "Time - " & ODB.nice_date(todays_date)

        read_apps
        read_todos
        read_chores
        read_prjcts

        show_apps
        show_todos
        show_chores
        show_prjcts

    End Sub

    Private Sub Form_Initialize()

        Set app_bag = New Collection
        Set todo_bag = New Collection
        Set chore_bag = New Collection
        Set prjct_bag = New Collection

    End Sub

    Private Sub Form_QueryUnload(Cancel As Integer, _
        UnloadMode As Integer)

        If dont_unload Then

            Visible = False
            Cancel = -1 ' set bit cancels unload

        End If

    End Sub

    Private Sub Form_Resize()

        If dont_resize Then Exit Sub
```

```
If Width < min_width Then
    dont_resize = True
    Width = min_width
    dont_resize = False
End If

If Height < min_height Then
    dont_resize = True
    Height = min_height
    dont_resize = False
End If

Dim col_wid As Integer
col_wid = (Width - (2 * side_space) - _
    (3 * between_space) - 120) / 4

Dim lft As Integer, lcntr As Integer, _
    rcntr As Integer, rgt As Integer

lft = side_space
lcntr = lft + col_wid + between_space
rcntr = lcntr + col_wid + between_space
rgt = rcntr + col_wid + between_space

lstApp.left = lft
lstToDo.left = lcntr
lstChore.left = rcntr
lstPrjct.left = rgt

lblApp.left = lft
lblToDo.left = lcntr
lblChore.left = rcntr
lblPrjct.left = rgt

lstApp.Width = col_wid
lstToDo.Width = col_wid
lstChore.Width = col_wid
lstPrjct.Width = col_wid

lstApp.Height = Height - 400 - top_space - btm_space
lstToDo.Height = lstApp.Height
lstChore.Height = lstApp.Height
lstPrjct.Height = lstApp.Height

txtTotal_app.left = lft
txtTotal_todo.left = lcntr
txtTotal_chore.left = rcntr
txtTotal_prjct.left = rgt
```

(continued)

frmTime.frm — the time tool

```
        txtTotal_app.top = lstApp.top + _
            lstApp.Height + below_space

        Dim tta_top As Integer
        tta_top = txtTotal_app.top

        txtTotal_todo.top = tta_top
        txtTotal_chore.top = tta_top
        txtTotal_prjct.top = tta_top

        Dim twid As Integer
        twid = txtTotal_app.Width + 75

        lblTotal_app.left = lft + twid
        lblTotal_todo.left = lcntr + twid
        lblTotal_chore.left = rcntr + twid
        lblTotal_prjct.left = rgt + twid

        lblTotal_app.top = tta_top + 60
        lblTotal_todo.top = tta_top + 60
        lblTotal_chore.top = tta_top + 60
        lblTotal_prjct.top = tta_top + 60

        txtGrand_total.top = tta_top + _
            txtTotal_app.Height + below_space
        lblGrand_total.top = txtGrand_total.top + 60

        txtGrand_total.left = lft
        lblGrand_total.left = lft + twid

        cmdExit.top = txtGrand_total.top - _
            (cmdExit.Height - txtGrand_total.Height) + 30
        cmdExit.left = Width - side_space - cmdExit.Width - 120

    End Sub

    Private Sub read_apps()

        Dim i As Long

        empty_coll app_bag

    ' exit if nothing to do
        Dim n As Long
        n = app_db.get_num_objects
        If n = 0 Then Exit Sub
```

```
' refill the collection
    Dim a As App

    For i = 0 To n - 1

        Set a = New App
        app_db.get_obj i, a

        If Not app_db.obj_is_deleted Then
            If a.app_date = todays_date Then
                app_bag.Add a
            End If
        End If

    Next

End Sub

Private Sub read_todos()

    Dim i As Long

    empty_coll todo_bag

' exit if nothing to do
    Dim n As Long
    n = todo_db.get_num_objects
    If n = 0 Then Exit Sub

' refill the collection
    Dim t As todo

    For i = 0 To n - 1

        Set t = New todo
        todo_db.get_obj i, t

        If Not todo_db.obj_is_deleted Then
            If t.todo_date = todays_date Then
                todo_bag.Add t
            End If
        End If

    Next

End Sub
```

(continued)

frmTime.frm — the time tool

```vb
Private Sub read_chores()

    Dim i As Long

    empty_coll chore_bag

' exit if nothing to do
    Dim n As Long
    n = chore_db.get_num_objects
    If n = 0 Then Exit Sub

' refill the collection
    Dim c As Chore
    For i = 0 To n - 1

        Set c = New Chore
        chore_db.get_obj i, c

        If Not chore_db.obj_is_deleted Then
            If do_today(c) Then chore_bag.Add c
        End If

    Next

End Sub

Private Function do_today(c As Chore) As Boolean

    Select Case c.chore_frequency

        Case chore_daily
            do_today = True

        Case chore_weekly
            do_today = (WeekDay(todays_date) = vbMonday)

        Case chore_monthly
            do_today = Month(todays_date) @@@> _
                Month(todays_date + 1)

    End Select

End Function

Private Sub read_prjcts()

    Dim i As Long

    empty_coll prjct_bag
```

```
' exit if nothing to do
    Dim n As Long
    n = prjct_db.get_num_objects
    If n = 0 Then Exit Sub

' refill the collection
    Dim p As Prjct

    For i = 0 To n - 1

        Set p = New Prjct
        prjct_db.get_obj i, p

        If Not prjct_db.obj_is_deleted Then

            If p.est_start_date = todays_date Then
                If one_day(p) Then prjct_bag.Add p
            End If

        End If

    Next

End Sub

Private Function one_day(p As Prjct) As Boolean

    one_day = (p.est_start_date = p.est_end_date)

End Function

Private Sub show_apps()

    Dim i As Integer, n As Byte, _
            tim As Integer, s As String
    n = 0
    app_total = 0

    empty_list lstApp

    For i = 1 To app_bag.Count

        With app_bag.item(i)

            tim = .iget_actual_time
            If tim = 0 Then
                tim = .iget_end_time - .iget_start_time
            End If
```

(continued)

frmTime.frm — the time tool

```
                app_total = app_total + tim

                s = ODB.int2tstring(tim) + " " + .description
                lstApp.AddItem s

          End With

    Next

    txtTotal_app.Text = ODB.int2tstring(app_total)

End Sub

Private Sub show_todos()

    Dim i As Integer, n As Byte, tim As Integer
    n = 0
    todo_total = 0

    empty_list lstToDo

    For i = 1 To todo_bag.Count

        With todo_bag.item(i)

            tim = .iget_act_time
            If tim = 0 Then tim = .iget_est_time

            todo_total = todo_total + tim
            lstToDo.AddItem ODB.int2tstring(tim) & _
                " " & Trim(.Name)

        End With
    Next

    txtTotal_todo.Text = ODB.int2tstring(todo_total)

End Sub

Private Sub show_chores()

    Dim i As Integer, n As Byte, tim As Integer
    n = 0
    chore_total = 0

    empty_list lstChore

    For i = 1 To chore_bag.Count
```

```
        With chore_bag.item(i)

            tim = .iget_est_time

            chore_total = chore_total + tim
            lstChore.AddItem ODB.int2tstring(tim) & _
                " " & Trim(.Name)

        End With
    Next

    txtTotal_chore.Text = ODB.int2tstring(chore_total)

End Sub

Private Sub show_prjcts()

    Dim i As Integer, n As Byte, tim As Integer
    n = 0
    prjct_total = 0

    empty_list lstPrjct

    For i = 1 To prjct_bag.Count

        With prjct_bag.item(i)

            tim = .iget_act_time
            If tim = 0 Then tim = .iget_est_time

            prjct_total = prjct_total + tim
            lstPrjct.AddItem ODB.int2tstring(tim) & _
                " " & Trim(.Name)

        End With
    Next

    txtTotal_prjct.Text = ODB.int2tstring(prjct_total)
    Dim gtot As Integer
    gtot = app_total + todo_total + chore_total + prjct_total

    txtGrand_total.Text = ODB.int2tstring(gtot)

End Sub

Private Sub empty_coll(ByRef coll As Collection)

    If coll.Count > 0 Then
```

(continued)

frmTime.frm — the time tool

```
        Dim i As Integer
        For i = coll.Count To 1 Step -1
            coll.Remove (i)
        Next

    End If

End Sub

Private Sub empty_list(ByRef ls As ListBox)

    If ls.ListCount = 0 Then Exit Sub

    Dim i As Integer
    For i = ls.ListCount To 1 Step -1
        ls.RemoveItem i - 1
    Next

End Sub

' end of frmTime.frm
```

SUMMARY

In this chapter, we looked at the tasks and time tools' design and code. These are display panels, which are fundamentally simpler than the projects and schedule tools we've been using. The two-panel tasks tool was actually more complex than the four-panel time tool because the latter didn't have an Edit button to consider.

Both tools work in a similar fashion. They gather their data into a `Collection` and then format strings for each object that are displayed by a `ListBox`'s `List`.

The tasks tool creates arrays of ODB object numbers that it uses to immediately access the correct object with the data entry form. It also has added work in the constructor and destructor to create and free the form.

This brings us to the final chapter, where we can put all these objects together in the MyTime system. I hope you're beginning to see how an object-oriented system is built. If it assembles easily (it will!), I think you'll agree that objects have definitely made our programming simpler and more modular.

ASSEMBLING THE COMPLETE SYSTEM

22

*I*n this chapter, we're going to pull the whole system together. You'll see that the tools all work independently of the main menu. It's job is to fully equip each of the component objects and then to let each go off on its own. The main menu literally functions as nothing more than a way of toggling its piece's Visible properties. The pieces do everything on their own.

We'll build sibling relationships where we need them. For example, everyone except the project's cascade has to know what date the calendar is showing. That's a simple matter of calling the calendar's get_hi_date() method, but the pieces need a reference to the calendar so that they can call the method.

Similarly, the time panel needs to be able to call all the ODBs. It could gain this access indirectly if it had a reference to each of its siblings. The code is easier, however, when the time panel has references directly to the ODBs. The parent main menu sets this up when it launches the time panel.

I'd like you to build this for yourself. I'll give you step-by-step instructions, beginning with setting up the project. Then we'll march across the main menu, attaching one tool at a time. When we attach the time tool, we'll have a complete, working system.

Ready? Turn your computer on and let's begin.

GETTING STARTED

First we'll create a directory and populate it with class and form modules. Then we'll launch Visual Basic and open a project. If you have Visual Basic running, close it down.

Creating a Directory

Pick or create a directory for the complete project, and use your favorite file moving tool to populate it with the following class modules:

- ODB.cls
- App.cls
- Prjct.cls
- ToDo.cls
- Chore.cls

Then put the following form files into it:

- frmMyTim.frm
- frmApp.frm
- frmPrjct.frm
- frmToDo.frm
- frmChore.frm
- frmSched.frm
- frmCscd.frm
- frmChart.frm
- frmTasks.frm
- frmTime.frm

If you're particularly fond of any of your existing ODBs, add any of these you like:

- App.ODB
- Prjct.ODB
- ToDo.ODB
- Chore.ODB

If you don't have them, the ODB object will create empty files for you. This might be more convenient than using your test data. It's up to you.

Creating a Project

Now create a shortcut to Visual Basic that specifies the directory you just populated as Visual Basic's working directory. Launch Visual Basic and create a new, standard .EXE project.

Remove `Form1` to empty the project. Then add `frmMyTim.frm` to it. Run it, and Visual Basic will tell you that you must have a startup form or `Sub Main`. Conveniently, it will load the project's property pages, so you can specify MyTime.frm without any trouble.

Your `frmMyTim` will continue to be ready to run as soon as you click OK on the property page. If you have set Visual Basic to save before running, it will ask you if you would like to save the project in MyTime.vbp. I think that's a fine idea. If Visual Basic isn't doing this automatically, don't forget to do it manually.

At this point, my main menu ran, just as we left it at the end of Chapter 15. That's complete with debugging output in the Immediate window. Use your code editor to remove all references to the debug object so that your run is clean.

At this point, you should have a simple project like the one shown in Figure 22-1.

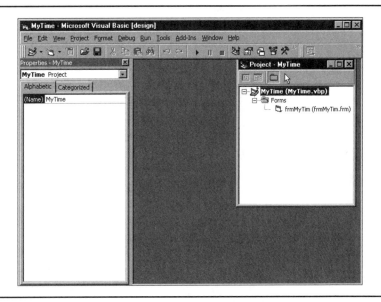

Figure 22-1

We begin with a simple project.

LAUNCHING THE CALENDAR

The first problem we have to solve is programming the MyTime system to respond to mouse clicks on the menu items. Once it handles that, we can add keypress logic. Then we can actually go ahead and launch the calendar. Conveniently, that's the simplest of the tools to launch. Everybody else needs to know about the calendar, but it doesn't need to know about anyone else.

Begin with the clicks.

Responding to Mouse Clicks

The menu is built on an array of Frame objects, fraOpts. We have a skeleton fraOpts_MouseUp() routine that responds to a click on the eXit pad. Add a simple message box to each of the other pads, but don't try to run this until you read the next paragraph. This is what the routine should look like:

```
Private Sub fraOpts_MouseUp(Index As Integer, _
    Button As Integer, Shift As Integer, _
    X As Single, Y As Single)

    Select Case Index
        Case on_cal: MsgBox "Calendar"
        Case on_sched: MsgBox "Schedule"
        Case on_proj: MsgBox "Projects' cascade"
        Case on_todo: MsgBox "To Do list"
        Case on_time: MsgBox "Time tool"

        Case on_exit
            Unload Me

    End Select

End Sub
```

This won't work if you don't click on the Frame object. For example, clicking on the TextBoxes that hold the text in the schedule pad and tasks pad won't work. Clicking over the numbers in the calendar won't work. Only clicking directly on the Frames works. Go ahead and give it a try.

In Java, events not handled at the top layer are passed through to lower layers. That means that eventually the Frame would see the mouse click. Not so in Visual Basic. If we want an intervening component to pass a click along, we have to program that behavior ourselves.

To do this, dropdown the left (objects) combo box in the code editor. Pick lblCalDay1. Your code editor will open the default Click() event handler. Add the pass-along line shown here:

```
Private Sub lblCalDay1_Click()
    fraOpts_MouseUp on_cal, 0, 0, 0, 0
End Sub
```

Test again. This time, when you click over the 7 or 8 on the calendar, nothing happens. If you click over the 1, the "Calendar" message appears, so go back and add these click pass-along methods to lblCalDay7 and lblCalDay8, too.

Next, pick txtSched from the objects' dropdown list and choose Click in the right-hand (procedure) combo box. Add the middle line shown here:

```
Private Sub txtSched_Click(Index As Integer)
    fraOpts_MouseUp on_sched, 0, 0, 0, 0
End Sub
```

Finally, do the same with the txtToDo object, adding this line:

```
Private Sub txtToDo_Click(Index As Integer)
    fraOpts_MouseUp on_Todo, 0, 0, 0, 0
End Sub
```

If you're cutting and pasting the added line, be sure that txtSched passes the on_sched argument and txtToDo passes on_todo.

Give this a final test. You should now respond to mouse clicks anywhere on the form.

Responding to Key Presses

At this point we highlight the appropriate Frame in response to a keypress. I like to launch the selected item as well. That means that the one-line cases in the txtKey_Change() method become two-line cases, as shown here:

```
Private Sub txtKey_Change(Index As Integer)

' eliminate recursion
    If rekeying Then Exit Sub

    Dim k As String
    k = UCase(left(txtKey(Index).Text, 1))
    Select Case k
        Case "C":
```

```
            make_hi (on_cal)
            fraOpts_MouseUp on_cal, 0, 0, 0, 0

        Case "S":
            make_hi (on_sched)
            fraOpts_MouseUp on_sched, 0, 0, 0, 0

        Case "P":
            make_hi (on_proj)
            fraOpts_MouseUp on_proj, 0, 0, 0, 0

        Case "D":
            make_hi (on_todo)
            fraOpts_MouseUp on_todo, 0, 0, 0, 0

        Case "T":
            make_hi (on_time)
            fraOpts_MouseUp on_time, 0, 0, 0, 0

        Case "X":
            make_hi (on_exit)
            ' fraOpts_MouseUp on_exit, 0, 0, 0, 0

    End Select

    rekeying = True
    txtKey(Index).Text = ""
    rekeying = False

    ignore_mouse_move = True

End Sub
```

The final call in the `on_exit` case is commented out. That's because it doesn't work in my version of Visual Basic. It doesn't unload the form, which leaves a flying, invisible form. I have no idea why this happens after a change event but not after a mouse event. Maybe your version of Visual Basic won't have that problem.

With this work done, all that's left now is to march down the list of message boxes, replacing them with the actual objects we want.

Sending the Calendar Up

To attach a calendar, you need a calendar. Copy Calendar.cls into your working directory and add it to the project. Then you'll be ready to think about the code.

Launching a calendar encompasses four steps. First, we need to declare a calendar variable. Then we need to create a calendar object. We have to add destructor code to eliminate the object because it's form-based. Finally, we have to replace the message box that promises a calendar with the real calendar.

Creating a Calendar Variable

In the general declarations section, add the new line shown here to declare a calendar variable:

```
Option Explicit
    Private form_cal As New Calendar
```

Creating a Calendar Object

Select the form's `Initialize()` method in your code editor. Add the five calendar lines shown here:

```
Private Sub Form_Initialize()
    tppX = Screen.TwipsPerPixelX
    tppY = Screen.TwipsPerPixelY
    hi_opt = 255 ' Nothing high yet
    make_hi 0

    Set form_cal = New Calendar
    form_cal.Visible = False
    form_cal.dont_unload = True
    form_cal.Height = 5400
    Load form_cal

End Sub
```

The line that sets `Height` is a personal choice. I like a slightly larger calendar than we use for data entry. Adjust the height (and width, too, if you like) to suit yourself.

Add Destructor Code

Forms sail forever if you don't add destructor code. Add the new lines shown here to the form's `QueryUnload()` method:

```
Private Sub Form_QueryUnload(Cancel As Integer, _
    UnloadMode As Integer)
    form_cal.Visible = False
```

```
form_cal.dont_unload = False
Unload form_cal
Set form_cal = Nothing

End Sub
```

Replace the Message Box

The final step is to reprogram the `fraOpts_MouseUp()` event to show a calendar. All this takes is toggling the `Visible` property. Change the line as shown here and you've attached your first tool to the main menu:

```
Case on_cal: form_cal.Visible = Not form_cal.Visible
```

That's the entire relationship between our main menu and our calendar between creation and destruction. We toggle the `Visible` property. These objects live a very independent existence, don't they?

At this point, your system should correctly raise and drop the calendar in response to clicks. It will raise it with a *c* keypress, too. (An Alt+X keypress drops the calendar. Pressing *c* doesn't work when the calendar has focus.) Figure 22-2 shows my calendar launched from the main menu.

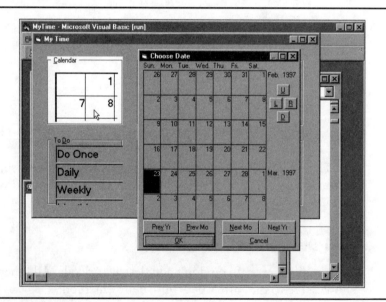

Figure 22-2
Our main menu launches its first tool.

Are you pleased? You should be! These pieces work together nicely. Now it's time to launch the schedule, which has to know about the calendar. It's simple.

LAUNCHING THE SCHEDULE

The calendar is the simplest of the tools because it needs no knowledge of any siblings. Its siblings, however, need to know about it. The schedule that we finished back in Chapter 13 only knows how to show you today's schedule. When we put these pieces together, we need to have it respond to the calendar's selection. You'll see that this is less trouble in practice than in theory!

Create a Schedule Variable

You'll need to expand your project at this point. Begin by adding the forms `frmSched.frm` and `frmApp.frm` (the schedule and the appointment data entry form). Then add `ODB.cls` and `App.cls`. Figure 22-3 shows the Project Explorer at this point.

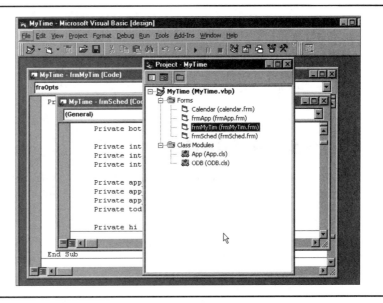

Figure 22-3

Expanding the project.

Now you're ready to add that variable. Add the new line shown here in your general declarations section:

```
Option Explicit
    Private form_cal As New Calendar
    Private form_sched As New frmSched
```

Launch a Schedule Object

With the variable defined, you next need to have the constructor create and load a nonvisible form. This is the new version of Form_Initialize():

```
Private Sub Form_Initialize()

    tppX = Screen.TwipsPerPixelX
    tppY = Screen.TwipsPerPixelY
    hi_opt = 255 ' Nothing high yet
    make_hi 0

    Set form_cal = New Calendar
    form_cal.Visible = False
    form_cal.dont_unload = True
    form_cal.Height = 5400
    Load form_cal

    Set form_sched = New frmSched
    form_sched.Visible = False
    form_sched.dont_unload = True
    Load form_sched

End Sub
```

Destroy the Schedule

By now you are in the habit of adding destructor code immediately after you launch a form, aren't you? Good. This is the new QueryUnload() method:

```
Private Sub Form_QueryUnload(Cancel As Integer, _
    UnloadMode As Integer)
```

```
form_cal.Visible = False
form_cal.dont_unload = False
Unload form_cal
Set form_cal = Nothing

form_sched.Visible = False
form_sched.dont_unload = False
Unload form_sched
Set form_sched = Nothing
```

```
End Sub
```

Display the Schedule

Finally, the fraOpts_MouseUp() method gets a new toggle, and you are ready to test. This is that method:

```
Private Sub fraOpts_MouseUp(Index As Integer, _
    Button As Integer, Shift As Integer, _
    X As Single, Y As Single)

    Select Case Index
        Case on_cal: form_cal.Visible = Not form_cal.Visible
        Case on_sched: form_sched.Visible = Not _
            form_sched.Visible
        Case on_proj: MsgBox "Projects' cascade"
        Case on_todo: MsgBox "To Do list"
        Case on_time: MsgBox "Time tool"

        Case on_exit
            Unload Me

    End Select

End Sub
```

At this point, you can run your system. It should show and hide the schedule tool, but you're still stuck on today. The final step is to make the schedule aware of the calendar.

Link the Schedule to the Calendar

We have to do two things for this link. We have to pass a reference to the calendar to the schedule, and then we need to tell the schedule how to use that reference. This will take a grand total of two lines of code.

First, you have to set the public `boss_cal` variable. This is one of those publics in the child that is set by the parent and is read-only by the child. (It's read-only only because you've avoided writing any code that would change it. There's no support for this in the theory or practice of object-oriented programming that I've ever met. Haven't any of these people ever raised a child?)

Add the line that sets `boss_cal` in the `sched` block of the constructor:

```
Set form_sched = New frmSched
form_sched.Visible = False
form_sched.dont_unload = True
Set form_sched.boss_cal = form_cal ' Add this one
Load form_sched
```

While we often think that our variables, like `form_cal`, *are* objects, that's not true, of course. The objects live on their own. The variable is simply a reference to that object. Setting `boss_cal` this way simply passes a reference to the calendar object to the schedule.

Now you have access to all the public data and methods of the calendar in the schedule. The only one that concerns us is the `get_hi_date()` method. Replace the `date()` function in the `Form_Activate()` method of the schedule with this polite request for the currently highlighted date in the calendar:

```
Private Sub Form_Activate()

    todays_date = boss_cal.get_hi_date ' modified
    read_apps

End Sub
```

That's all there is to it. Figure 22-4 shows my system at this point. You'll need to add a test meeting or two to your own system to see this proved out.

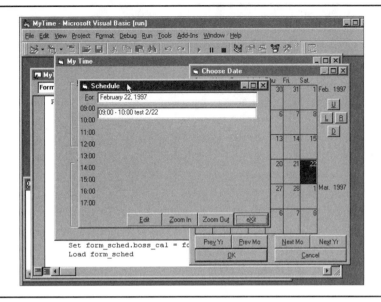

Figure 22-4
Checking another day's schedule.

LAUNCHING THE PROJECT'S CASCADE

Ready to try one on your own? Go ahead and add the projects cascade.
Don't forget the chart.

You can double-check your work against these step-by-step instructions,
but you'll learn more from a mistake or two than from simply following me.
I'll provide the detailed instructions for those who don't feel up to it, yet.

Add a Project's Cascade Variable

Before you can add the variable, you have to add the new forms and classes
to your project. In this case, you'll need `frmCscd.frm`, `frmPrjct.frm`, and
`frmChart.frm` (the cascade, project data entry form, and form chart).
You'll also need `Prjct.cls`. Figure 22-5 shows the system at this point.

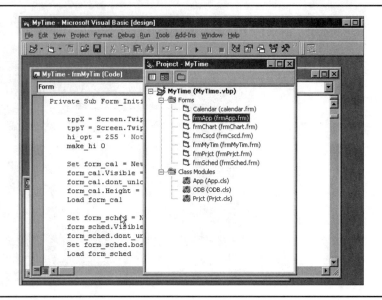

Figure 22-5
Exploring a growing system.

Create a Project's Cascade Object

Declare form_cscd as a frmCscd variable in the declarations section. With the variable prepared, you next add the creation code to the constructor. This is a fragment from the bottom of Form_Initialize():

```
        Load form_sched

        Set form_cscd = New frmCscd ' these are new
        form_cscd.Visible = False
        form_cscd.dont_unload = True
        Load form_cscd

    End Sub ' end of Form_Initialize()
```

You don't need (or have a place for) the calendar for the project's cascade.

Destroy the Project's Cascade Object

The destructor code follows the same pattern. This is a new addition to the end of `QueryUnload()`:

```
Set form_sched = Nothing

form_cscd.Visible = False ' these are new
form_cscd.dont_unload = False
Unload form_cscd
Set form_cscd = Nothing

End Sub ' end of Form_QueryUnload()
```

Show the Project's Cascade

Last, you replace the message box in `fraOpts_MouseUp` with a `Visible` toggle. This is the revised method:

```
Private Sub fraOpts_MouseUp(Index As Integer, _
    Button As Integer, Shift As Integer, _
    X As Single, Y As Single)

    Select Case Index
        Case on_cal: form_cal.Visible = Not form_cal.Visible
        Case on_sched: form_sched.Visible = Not _
            form_sched.Visible
        Case on_proj: form_cscd.Visible = Not form_cscd.Visible
        Case on_todo: MsgBox "To Do list"
        Case on_time: MsgBox "Time tool"

        Case on_exit
            Unload Me

    End Select

End Sub
```

Did it launch? Figure 22-6 shows my version with a pair of test `Prjct` objects. When you add data, don't forget to set the name of `Prjct` zero. That's the one in the `Caption` of your cascade form.

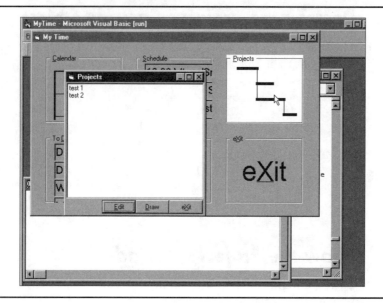

Figure 22-6
The project's cascade is launched.

Check the chart, too. I've set the estimated and actual dates of my two test Prjcts, as you can see in Figure 22-7.

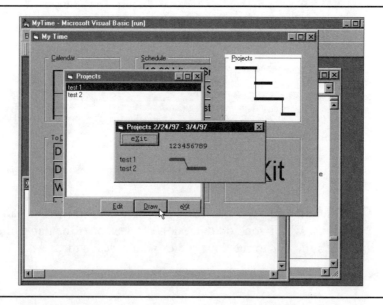

Figure 22-7
Charting a test project.

That wasn't hard, was it?

LAUNCHING THE TASKS LISTS

Before you start on the tasks, be aware of a problem. If you build a dropdown box and enter data into its list, Visual Basic puts that data in a file. It puts the file's relative path (relative to the working directory at the time you made the list) into the .FRM file. If you move the .FRM to a different directory, you'll lose the file. Therefore, when you load frmChore, you may see "errors during" load messages. Just reenter the Daily, Weekly, and Monthly frequencies in the list, save, and you're back in business.

With that word of advice, go ahead and launch the tasks panel. Remember that it deals with two ODBs, so you'll have two data entry forms and two corresponding class modules. It will also need to know the calendar's date. I'll carry on with the step-by-step explanation here, but I hope no one uses it.

Add a Tasks Variable

You begin by adding the needed forms and class modules to your project. The forms are frmTask.frm, frmToDo.frm, and frmChore.frm. The classes are ToDo.cls and Chore.cls. Figure 22-8 shows the project at this point.

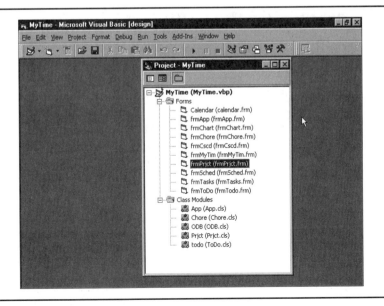

Figure 22-8
The Project Explorer fills up.

Then you're ready to add the actual variable. This shows the new line to add to the general declarations section of frmMyTim.frm:

```
Option Explicit
    Private form_cal As New Calendar
    Private form_sched As New frmSched
    Private form_cscd As New frmCscd
    Private form_tasks As New frmTasks
```

Create a Tasks Object

The constructor code is similar to the schedule's constructor code. This shows the new end to frmMyTim.frm's Form_Initialize() method:

```
    Load form_cscd

    Set form_tasks = New frmTasks ' new block
    form_tasks.Visible = False
    form_tasks.dont_unload = True
    Set form_tasks.boss_cal = form_cal
    Load form_tasks

End Sub ' Form_Initialize()
```

Destroy the Tasks Object

The destructor code requires a new block for this Tasks object. This shows the block, added to the end of the frmMyTim.frm's Form_QueryUnload() method:

```
    Set form_cscd = Nothing

    form_tasks.Visible = False ' new block
    form_tasks.dont_unload = False
    Unload form_tasks
    Set form_tasks = Nothing

End Sub ' Form_QueryUnload()
```

Replace the Message Box

I was beginning to really dislike the fraOpts_MouseUp() routine. It was badly in need of some decent formatting. When I added the new Visible toggle, I also took the time to decently lay out the rest of the code. This is my result:

```
Private Sub fraOpts_MouseUp(Index As Integer, _
    Button As Integer, Shift As Integer, _
    X As Single, Y As Single)

    Select Case Index
        Case on_cal:
            form_cal.Visible = Not form_cal.Visible

        Case on_sched:
            form_sched.Visible = Not form_sched.Visible

        Case on_proj:
            form_cscd.Visible = Not form_cscd.Visible

        Case on_todo:
            form_tasks.Visible = Not form_tasks.Visible

        Case on_time: MsgBox "Time tool"

        Case on_exit
            Unload Me

    End Select

End Sub
```

Linking Tasks to the Calendar

Again, that takes one more line in the constructor code in frmMyTim.frm. We added it with the rest of the constructor. Then you need to modify the Form_Activate() method of frmTasks.frm. This is the new version:

```
Private Sub Form_Activate()

    todays_date = boss_cal.get_hi_date
    read_todos
    read_chores

End Sub
```

With that in place, your tasks panel is part of your MyTime system. Figure 22-9 shows my version running.

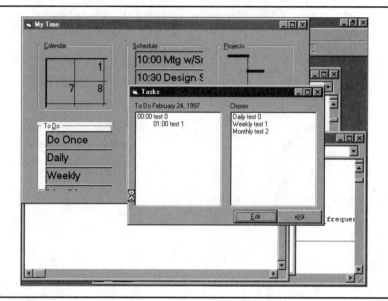

■ Figure 22-9
Launching the tasks panel.

LAUNCHING THE TIME TOOL

If you did tasks on your own, congratulations. If you skipped right to here, take a moment to spruce up fraOpts_MouseUp() in frmMyTim.frm. Mine was pretty ugly, but now it's quite nice. Ugly code has a habit of being buggy code. Good-looking code usually runs the way it looks like it will run. Writing solid code isn't quite as simple as just writing good-looking code, but that's part of it.

Now let's talk about the time tool. It needs references to the ODBs that the other tools create. We've built methods into those tools that get references to the ODBs, and we have convenient variables to hold them ready in the time tool.

If you're feeling bold, try this on your own. In the constructor, set the time panel object's app_db variable to the reference returned by the schedule object's get_app_db() method. The other variables are prjct_db, todo_db, and chore_db. They're each returned by a get() method from their parent objects.

If you're not feeling bold, follow these steps.

Create a Time Variable

Before you reach the code, add the `frmTime.frm` to your project's list of forms. Figure 22-10 shows the final list in the Project Explorer.

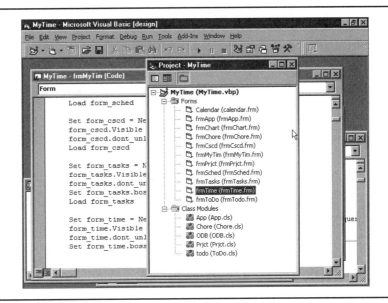

■ Figure 22-10
A good-sized list at last.

You don't need to add any other forms or classes since time relies on the ODBs provided by the other tools.

In the general declarations section of your `frmMyTim.frm` file add the final variable declaration shown here:

```
Option Explicit
    Private form_cal As New Calendar
    Private form_sched As New frmSched
    Private form_cscd As New frmCscd
    Private form_tasks As New frmTasks
    Private form_time As New frmTime
```

Create a Time Object

The constructor code has to provide the needed ODB references to the time panel object. You could do this by handing the time object references to its siblings and letting it query them directly. I think it's simpler to just assign

the references. These are two new blocks of code to add to the
`Form_Initialize()` constructor method:

```
Load form_tasks

Set form_time = New frmTime ' new starting here
form_time.Visible = False
form_time.dont_unload = True
Set form_time.boss_cal = form_cal
Load form_time

Set form_time.app_db = form_sched.get_app_db
Set form_time.prjct_db = form_cscd.get_prjct_db
Set form_time.todo_db = form_tasks.get_todo_db
Set form_time.chore_db = form_tasks.get_chore_db

End Sub ' Form_Initialize()
```

This time tool has to be created last, of course. The constructors for the
other objects create the ODBs to which `frmTime` is getting references.

Destroy the Time Object

The destructor code is no different than the code for the other blocks. This
is the new block at the end of `Form_QueryUnload()` in `frmMyTim.frm`:

```
Set form_tasks = Nothing

form_time.Visible = False ' new block
form_time.dont_unload = False
Unload form_time
Set form_time = Nothing

End Sub ' Form_QueryUnload()
```

Replace the Message Box

Now we're ready to launch the new tool. This is the final
`fraOpts_MouseUp()` method in `frmMyTim.frm`:

```
Private Sub fraOpts_MouseUp(Index As Integer, _
    Button As Integer, Shift As Integer, _
    X As Single, Y As Single)
```

```
Select Case Index
    Case on_cal:
        form_cal.Visible = Not form_cal.Visible

    Case on_sched:
        form_sched.Visible = Not form_sched.Visible

    Case on_proj:
        form_cscd.Visible = Not form_cscd.Visible

    Case on_todo:
        form_tasks.Visible = Not form_tasks.Visible

    Case on_time:
        form_time.Visible = Not form_time.Visible

    Case on_exit
        Unload Me

End Select

End Sub
```

With that done, your system is complete! Figure 22-11 shows my time tool running with test data.

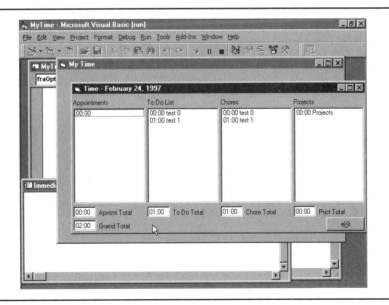

Figure 22-11

The final piece is in place.

If yours is working like mine (like mine, that is, excepting where you've made yours better), you've become an object-oriented Visual Basic programmer.

A PARTIAL LISTING

The complete project is on disk in 22-01. This includes the project file, eleven form files, and five other class files. The ODB class will create .ODB files for you.

All the changes made to frmMyTim.frm were made in the declarations section, the Form_Initialize() method, the Form_QueryUnload() method, and the fraOpts_MouseUp method. These are shown in Listing 22-1. For the rest of the file, refer to Listing 15-9.

There are also one-line modifications made to frmSched.frm and frmTasks.frm noted in the text above. Refer to Chapter 13 and Chapter 21 for those files' full listings.

Listing 22-1

frmMyTim.frm — changed routines only

```
' frmMyTim.frm — main menu for MyTime system
' Copyright 1997, Martin L. Rinehart

Option Explicit
    Private form_cal As New Calendar
    Private form_sched As New frmSched
    Private form_cscd As New frmCscd
    Private form_tasks As New frmTasks
    Private form_time As New frmTime

' recursion suppresants:
    Private resizing As Boolean
    Private rekeying As Boolean

Const cap_width = 900 ' frame size at which captions
    ' are spelled out completely

Private Enum option_numbers
    on_cal = 0
    on_sched
    on_proj
    on_todo
    on_time
    on_exit
End Enum
```

```
' Useful shorthands:
    Private tppX As Integer, tppY As Integer

Private hi_opt As Byte

' Critter catcher
    Private ignore_mouse_move

Private Sub Form_Initialize()

    tppX = Screen.TwipsPerPixelX
    tppY = Screen.TwipsPerPixelY
    hi_opt = 255 ' Nothing high yet
    make_hi 0

    Set form_cal = New Calendar
    form_cal.Visible = False
    form_cal.dont_unload = True
    form_cal.Height = 5400
    Load form_cal

    Set form_sched = New frmSched
    form_sched.Visible = False
    form_sched.dont_unload = True
    Set form_sched.boss_cal = form_cal
    Load form_sched

    Set form_cscd = New frmCscd
    form_cscd.Visible = False
    form_cscd.dont_unload = True
    Load form_cscd

    Set form_tasks = New frmTasks
    form_tasks.Visible = False
    form_tasks.dont_unload = True
    Set form_tasks.boss_cal = form_cal
    Load form_tasks

    Set form_time = New frmTime
    form_time.Visible = False
    form_time.dont_unload = True
    Set form_time.boss_cal = form_cal
    Load form_time

    Set form_time.app_db = form_sched.get_app_db
    Set form_time.prjct_db = form_cscd.get_prjct_db
    Set form_time.todo_db = form_tasks.get_todo_db
    Set form_time.chore_db = form_tasks.get_chore_db

End Sub
```

(continued)

frmMyTim.frm — changed routines only

```
Private Sub Form_QueryUnload(Cancel As Integer, _
    UnloadMode As Integer)

    form_cal.Visible = False
    form_cal.dont_unload = False
    Unload form_cal
    Set form_cal = Nothing

    form_sched.Visible = False
    form_sched.dont_unload = False
    Unload form_sched
    Set form_sched = Nothing

    form_cscd.Visible = False
    form_cscd.dont_unload = False
    Unload form_cscd
    Set form_cscd = Nothing

    form_tasks.Visible = False
    form_tasks.dont_unload = False
    Unload form_tasks
    Set form_tasks = Nothing

    form_time.Visible = False
    form_time.dont_unload = False
    Unload form_time
    Set form_time = Nothing

End Sub

Private Sub fraOpts_MouseUp(Index As Integer, _
    Button As Integer, Shift As Integer, _
    X As Single, Y As Single)

    Select Case Index
        Case on_cal:
            form_cal.Visible = Not form_cal.Visible

        Case on_sched:
            form_sched.Visible = Not form_sched.Visible

        Case on_proj:
            form_cscd.Visible = Not form_cscd.Visible

        Case on_todo:
            form_tasks.Visible = Not form_tasks.Visible

        Case on_time:
```

```
                form_time.Visible = Not form_time.Visible

            Case on_exit
                Unload Me

        End Select

    End Sub
```

SUMMARY

We built objects. Way back in Chapter 2 we started with a cute little tugboat example, but from there on we built serious objects. Remember the calendar? What a `Resize()` that has!

The calendar was a lot of trouble, but it's certainly worth it. Clicking a date makes short work of data entry. (It makes me want a clickable clock for time entry.)

Then we built a schedule object. Remember dissecting the poor scrollbar? But we have that working nicely.

Before we could use the schedule, it needed some data. To save three megabytes in the executable file (I like fast loads, don't you?), we created our own object database. Four of those ODBs are running here.

For those of you with the Professional and Enterprise editions, we visited each of the three main ActiveX objects along the way: ActiveX .DLLs, ActiveX .EXEs, and ActiveX Controls.

For those of you who have the Standard edition, we built the MyTime system without ActiveX components. By the time we reached Part II, where we built MyTime, we'd created lots of its pieces.

Some of our objects were reused a lot in this one project. Do you know how many calendar objects MyTime uses? I haven't counted, but it has to be a lot.

In Chapter 14, we looked at the design. In Chapter 15, we built a main menu as our front end. This is a menu to be proud of!

Then we added the remaining components. We built a projects database, the project's cascade and finally a chart tool. The tasks tool handles to do lists and recurring chores. The time panel summarizes our overbooked days.

In this chapter, we pulled it all together. This went very smoothly. (When you do your own, you'll find that there's always something you forgot that needs to be added. There was in MyTime the first time I built it, too.)

You've seen the way our objects encapsulate their behaviors. A calendar pops up and serves the user. When the user is finished with it the calendar disappears. The calendar's parent just uses its `get_hi_date()` method to find out what the user wanted. The parent hasn't a clue about how the calendar might know the user's intent. It just does.

You've seen object reuse. Our ODB is serving four different types of storable objects. The calendar works happily as a main tool, and it serves equally as a data entry component for individual fields in our data entry forms.

You've seen that siblings can work together, but they don't have to be tangled up with each other. The MyTime system has almost 10,000 lines of code, but none of the pieces is particularly large. Only the critical path calculations used by the chart tool are complicated. They're complex because the subject is complex, not because our code is tangled.

You've also seen that although Visual Basic can't yet claim to be an object-oriented system, you can use it successfully to build object-oriented systems. You contain when you can't inherit and you copy code when even containership doesn't work. It's not ideal, but it can work for you. For most jobs, I like Visual Basic better than Visual C++, despite its limitations.

Now go on to build your own object-oriented systems. Once you start working with objects you'll never go back to programming without them. Thanks for letting me show you how.

APPENDICES

THE CALENDAR CLASS' PROPERTIES

*T*his appendix lists the form properties stored in Calendar.frm. The portion you can edit in the code editor is shown in Chapter 4, Listing 4-5c.

The Calendar.frm File Above Editable Portion

```
VERSION 5.00
Begin VB.Form Calendar
   Caption         =   "Choose Date"
   ClientHeight    =   3285
   ClientLeft      =   60
   ClientTop       =   345
   ClientWidth     =   4380
   LinkTopic       =   "Form1"
   MinButton       =   0   'False
   ScaleHeight     =   3285
   ScaleWidth      =   4380
   Begin VB.CommandButton btnCancel
      Caption      =   "&Cancel"
      Height       =   240
      Left         =   2400
      TabIndex     =   9
      Top          =   2960
      Width        =   1800
End
```

(continued)

```
Begin VB.CommandButton btnOK
   Caption        =   "&OK"
   Height         =   240
   Left           =   100
   TabIndex       =   0
   Top            =   2960
   Width          =   1800
End
Begin VB.CommandButton btnNextYr
   Caption        =   "Ne&xt Yr"
   Height         =   240
   Left           =   3300
   TabIndex       =   8
   Top            =   2700
   Width          =   900
End
Begin VB.CommandButton btnNextMo
   Caption        =   "&Next Mo"
   Height         =   240
   Left           =   2400
   TabIndex       =   7
   Top            =   2700
   Width          =   900
End
Begin VB.CommandButton btnPrevMo
   Caption        =   "&Prev Mo"
   Height         =   240
   Left           =   1000
   TabIndex       =   6
   Top            =   2700
   Width          =   900
End
Begin VB.CommandButton btnPrevYr
   Caption        =   "Pre&v Yr"
   Height         =   240
   Left           =   120
   TabIndex       =   5
   Top            =   2700
   Width          =   900
End
Begin VB.CommandButton btnDown
   Caption        =   "&D"
   Height         =   300
   Left           =   3800
   TabIndex       =   4
   Top            =   1320
   Width          =   350
End
```

```
Begin VB.CommandButton btnRight
   Caption          =    "&R"
   Height           =    300
   Left             =    4000
   TabIndex         =    3
   Top              =    960
   Width            =    350
End
Begin VB.CommandButton btnLeft
   Caption          =    "&L"
   Height           =    300
   Left             =    3600
   TabIndex         =    2
   Top              =    960
   Width            =    350
End
Begin VB.CommandButton btnUp
   Caption          =    "&U"
   Height           =    300
   Left             =    3800
   TabIndex         =    1
   Top              =    600
   Width            =    350
End
Begin VB.Label bot_mo_label
   Caption          =    "Mon. 9999"
   Height           =    255       Left          =    3600
   TabIndex         =    60
   Top              =    1800
   Width            =    795
End
Begin VB.Label top_mo_label
   Caption          =    "Mon. 9999"
   Height           =    250
   Left             =    3600
   TabIndex         =    59
   Top              =    240
   Width            =    800
End
Begin VB.Label col_labels
   Caption          =    "Sun."
   Height           =    200
   Index            =    0
   Left             =    100
   TabIndex         =    10
   Top              =    0
   Width            =    400
End
```

(continued)

```
Begin VB.Label day_labels
```

```
        Alignment       =   1  'Right Justify
        Caption         =   "0"
        Height          =   375
        Index           =   41
        Left            =   0
        TabIndex        =   58
        Top             =   0
        Visible         =   0    'False
        Width           =   495
    End
    Begin VB.Label day_labels
        Alignment       =   1  'Right Justify
        Caption         =   "0"
        Height          =   375
        Index           =   40
        Left            =   0
        TabIndex        =   57
        Top             =   0
        Visible         =   0    'False
        Width           =   495
    End
    Begin VB.Label day_labels
        Alignment       =   1  'Right Justify
        Caption         =   "0"
        Height          =   375
        Index           =   39
        Left            =   0
        TabIndex        =   56
        Top             =   0
        Visible         =   0    'False
        Width           =   495
    End
    Begin VB.Label day_labels
        Alignment       =   1  'Right Justify
        Caption         =   "0"
        Height          =   375
        Index           =   38
        Left            =   0
        TabIndex        =   55
        Top             =   0
        Visible         =   0    'False
        Width           =   495
    End
    Begin VB.Label day_labels
        Alignment       =   1  'Right Justify
        Caption         =   "0"
        Height          =   375
        Index           =   37
        Left            =   0
        TabIndex        =   54
```

```
      Top             =    0
      Visible         =    0    'False
      Width           =    495
   End
   Begin VB.Label day_labels
      Alignment       =    1    'Right Justify
      Caption         =    "0"
      Height          =    375
      Index           =    36
      Left            =    0
      TabIndex        =    53
      Top             =    0
      Visible         =    0    'False
      Width           =    495
   End
   Begin VB.Label day_labels
      Alignment       =    1    'Right Justify
      Caption         =    "0"
      Height          =    375
      Index           =    35
      Left            =    0
      TabIndex        =    52
      Top             =    0
      Visible         =    0    'False
      Width           =    495
   End
   Begin VB.Label day_labels
      Alignment       =    1    'Right Justify
      Caption         =    "0"
      Height          =    375
      Index           =    34
      Left            =    0
      TabIndex        =    51
      Top             =    0
      Visible         =    0    'False
      Width           =    495
   End
   Begin VB.Label day_labels
      Alignment       =    1    'Right Justify
      Caption         =    "0"
      Height          =    375
      Index           =    33
      Left            =    0
      TabIndex        =    50
      Top             =    0
      Visible         =    0    'False
      Width           =    495
   End
```

(continued)

```
   Begin VB.Label day_labels
```

```
              Alignment       =   1   'Right Justify
              Caption         =   "0"
              Height          =   375
              Index           =   32
              Left            =   0
              TabIndex        =   49
              Top             =   0
              Visible         =   0   'False
              Width           =   495
           End
           Begin VB.Label day_labels
              Alignment       =   1   'Right Justify
              Caption         =   "0"
              Height          =   375
              Index           =   31
              Left            =   0
              TabIndex        =   48
              Top             =   0
              Visible         =   0   'False
              Width           =   495
           End
           Begin VB.Label day_labels
              Alignment       =   1   'Right Justify
              Caption         =   "0"
              Height          =   375
              Index           =   30
              Left            =   0
              TabIndex        =   47
              Top             =   0
              Visible         =   0   'False
              Width           =   495
           End
           Begin VB.Label day_labels
              Alignment       =   1   'Right Justify
              Caption         =   "0"
              Height          =   375
              Index           =   29
              Left            =   0
              TabIndex        =   46
              Top             =   0
              Visible         =   0   'False
              Width           =   495
           End
           Begin VB.Label day_labels
              Alignment       =   1   'Right Justify
              Caption         =   "0"
              Height          =   375
              Index           =   28
              Left            =   0
              TabIndex        =   45
```

```
      Top            =    0
      Visible        =    0    'False
      Width          =    495
   End
   Begin VB.Label day_labels
      Alignment      =    1    'Right Justify
      Caption        =    "0"
      Height         =    375
      Index          =    27
      Left           =    0
      TabIndex       =    44
      Top            =    0
      Visible        =    0    'False
      Width          =    495
   End
   Begin VB.Label day_labels
      Alignment      =    1    'Right Justify
      Caption        =    "0"
      Height         =    375
      Index          =    26
      Left           =    0
      TabIndex       =    43
      Top            =    0
      Visible        =    0    'False
      Width          =    495
   End
   Begin VB.Label day_labels
      Alignment      =    1    'Right Justify
      Caption        =    "0"
      Height         =    375
      Index          =    25
      Left           =    0
      TabIndex       =    42
      Top            =    0
      Visible        =    0    'False
      Width          =    495
   End
   Begin VB.Label day_labels
      Alignment      =    1    'Right Justify
      Caption        =    "0"
      Height         =    375
      Index          =    24
      Left           =    0
      TabIndex       =    41
      Top            =    0
      Visible        =    0    'False
      Width          =    495
   End
```

(continued)

```
   Begin VB.Label day_labels
```

```
          Alignment       =    1   'Right Justify
          Caption         =    "0"
          Height          =    375
          Index           =    23
          Left            =    0
          TabIndex        =    40
          Top             =    0
          Visible         =    0    'False
          Width           =    495
     End
     Begin VB.Label day_labels
          Alignment       =    1   'Right Justify
          Caption         =    "0"
          Height          =    375
          Index           =    22
          Left            =    0
          TabIndex        =    39
          Top             =    0
          Visible         =    0    'False
          Width           =    495
     End
     Begin VB.Label day_labels
          Alignment       =    1   'Right Justify
          Caption         =    "0"
          Height          =    375
          Index           =    21
          Left            =    0
          TabIndex        =    38
          Top             =    0
          Visible         =    0    'False
          Width           =    495
     End
     Begin VB.Label day_labels
          Alignment       =    1   'Right Justify
          Caption         =    "0"
          Height          =    375
          Index           =    20
          Left            =    0
          TabIndex        =    37
          Top             =    0
          Visible         =    0    'False
          Width           =    495
     End
     Begin VB.Label day_labels
          Alignment       =    1   'Right Justify
          Caption         =    "0"
          Height          =    375
          Index           =    19
          Left            =    0
          TabIndex        =    36
```

```
                  Top         =   0
                  Visible     =   0    'False
                  Width       =   495
               End
               Begin VB.Label day_labels
                  Alignment   =   1    'Right Justify
                  Caption     =   "0"
                  Height      =   375
                  Index       =   18
                  Left        5   0
                  TabIndex    =   35
                  Top         =   0
                  Visible     =   0    'False
                  Width       =   495
               End
               Begin VB.Label day_labels
                  Alignment   =   1    'Right Justify
                  Caption     =   "0"
                  Height      =   375
                  Index       =   17
                  Left        =   0
                  TabIndex    =   34
                  Top         =   0
                  Visible     =   0    'False
                  Width       =   495
               End
               Begin VB.Label day_labels
                  Alignment   =   1    'Right Justify
                  Caption     =   "0"
                  Height      =   375
                  Index       =   16
                  Left        =   0
                  TabIndex    =   33
                  Top         =   0
                  Visible     =   0    'False
                  Width       =   495
               End
               Begin VB.Label day_labels
                  Alignment   =   1    'Right Justify
                  Caption     =   "0"
                  Height      =   375
                  Index       =   15
                  Left        =   0
                  TabIndex    =   32
                  Top         =   0
                  Visible     =   0    'False
                  Width       =   495
               End

               Begin VB.Label day_labels
```

(continued)

```
            Alignment       =   1  'Right Justify
            Caption         =   "0"
            Height          =   375
            Index           =   14
            Left            =   0
            TabIndex        =   31
            Top             =   0
            Visible         =   0    'False
            Width           =   495
         End
         Begin VB.Label day_labels
            Alignment       =   1  'Right Justify
            Caption         =   "0"
            Height          =   375
            Index           =   13
            Left            =   0
            TabIndex        =   30
            Top             =   0
            Visible         =   0    'False
            Width           =   495
         End
         Begin VB.Label day_labels
            Alignment       =   1  'Right Justify
            Caption         =   "0"
            Height          =   375
            Index           =   12
            Left            =   0
            TabIndex        =   29
            Top             =   0
            Visible         =   0    'False
            Width           =   495
         End
         Begin VB.Label day_labels
            Alignment       =   1  'Right Justify
            Caption         =   "0"
            Height          =   375
            Index           =   11
            Left            =   0
            TabIndex        =   28
            Top             =   0
            Visible         =   0    'False
            Width           =   495
         End
         Begin VB.Label day_labels
            Alignment       =   1  'Right Justify
            Caption         =   "0"
            Height          =   375
            Index           =   10
            Left            =   0
            TabIndex        =   27
```

```
      Top            =   0
      Visible        =   0    'False
      Width          =   495
   End
   Begin VB.Label day_labels
      Alignment      =   1    'Right Justify
      Caption        =   "0"
      Height         =   375
      Index          =   9
      Left           =   0
      TabIndex       =   26
      Top            =   0
      Visible        =   0    'False
      Width          =   495
   End
   Begin VB.Label day_labels
      Alignment      =   1    'Right Justify
      Caption        =   "0"
      Height         =   375
      Index          =   8
      Left           =   0
      TabIndex       =   25
      Top            =   0
      Visible        =   0    'False
      Width          =   495
   End
   Begin VB.Label day_labels
      Alignment      =   1    'Right Justify
      Caption        =   "0"
      Height         =   375
      Index          =   7
      Left           =   0
      TabIndex       =   24
      Top            =   0
      Visible        =   0    'False
      Width          =   495
   End
   Begin VB.Label day_labels
      Alignment      =   1    'Right Justify
      Caption        =   "0"
      Height         =   375
      Index          =   6
      Left           =   0
      TabIndex       =   23
      Top            =   0
      Visible        =   0    'False
      Width          =   495
   End
```

(continued)

```
   Begin VB.Label day_labels
```

```
      Alignment       =    1   'Right Justify
      Caption         =    "0"
      Height          =    375
      Index           =    5
      Left            =    0
      TabIndex        =    22
      Top             =    0
      Visible         =    0    'False
      Width           =    495
   End
   Begin VB.Label day_labels
      Alignment       =    1   'Right Justify
      Caption         =    "0"
      Height          =    375
      Index           =    4
      Left            =    0
      TabIndex        =    21
      Top             =    0
      Visible         =    0    'False
      Width           =    495
   End
   Begin VB.Label day_labels
      Alignment       =    1   'Right Justify
      Caption         =    "0"
      Height          =    375
      Index           =    3
      Left            =    0
      TabIndex        =    20
      Top             =    0
      Visible         =    0    'False
      Width           =    495
   End
   Begin VB.Label day_labels
      Alignment       =    1   'Right Justify
      Caption         =    "0"
      Height          =    375
      Index           =    2
      Left            =    0
      TabIndex        =    19
      Top             =    0
      Visible         =    0    'False
      Width           =    495
   End
   Begin VB.Label day_labels
      Alignment       =    1   'Right Justify
      Caption         =    "0"
      Height          =    375
      Index           =    1
      Left            =    0
      TabIndex        =    18
```

```
    Top          =   0
    Visible      =   0    'False
    Width        =   495
End
Begin VB.Label day_labels
    Alignment    =   1    'Right Justify
    Caption      =   "0"
    Height       =   135
    Index        =   0
    Left         =   720
    TabIndex     =   17
    Top          =   720
    Visible      =   0    'False
    Width        =   255
End
Begin VB.Label col_labels
    Caption      =   "Sat."
    Height       =   195
    Index        =   6
    Left         =   3000
    TabIndex     =   16
    Top          =   0
    Width        =   405
End
Begin VB.Label col_labels
    Caption      =   "Fri."
    Height       =   195
    Index        =   5
    Left         =   2520
    TabIndex     =   15
    Top          =   0
    Width        =   405
End
Begin VB.Label col_labels
    Caption      =   "Thu"
    Height       =   195
    Index        =   4
    Left         =   2040
    TabIndex     =   14
    Top          =   0
    Width        =   405
End
Begin VB.Label col_labels
    Caption      =   "Wed."
    Height       =   195
    Index        =   3
    Left         =   1560
    TabIndex     =   13

    Top          =   0
```

(continued)

```
      Width          =   405
   End
   Begin VB.Label col_labels
      Caption         =   "Tue."
      Height          =   195
      Index           =   2
      Left            =   1080
      TabIndex        =   12
      Top             =   0
      Width           =   405
   End
   Begin VB.Label col_labels
      Caption         =   "Mon."
      Height          =   195
      Index           =   1
      Left            =   600
      TabIndex        =   11
      Top             =   0
      Width           =   405
   End
   Begin VB.Line Vlines
      Index           =   7
      Visible         =   0   'False
      X1              =   3480
      X2              =   3480
      Y1              =   240
      Y2              =   2400
   End
   Begin VB.Line Vlines
      Index           =   6
      Visible         =   0   'False
      X1              =   3000
      X2              =   3000
      Y1              =   240
      Y2              =   2400
   End
   Begin VB.Line Vlines
      Index           =   5
      Visible         =   0   'False
      X1              =   2520
      X2              =   2520
      Y1              =   240
      Y2              =   2400
   End
   Begin VB.Line Vlines
      Index           =   4
      Visible         =   0   'False
      X1              =   2040
      X2              =   2040
      Y1              =   240
```

```
   Y2              =    2400
End
Begin VB.Line Vlines
   Index           =    3
   Visible         =    0    'False
   X1              =    1560
   X2              =    1560
   Y1              =    240
   Y2              =    2400
End
Begin VB.Line Vlines
   Index           =    2
   Visible         =    0    'False
   X1              =    1080
   X2              =    1080
   Y1              =    240
   Y2              =    2400
End
Begin VB.Line Vlines
   Index           =    1
   Visible         =    0    'False
   X1              =    600
   X2              =    600
   Y1              =    240
   Y2              =    2400
End
Begin VB.Line Vlines
   Index           =    0
   Visible         =    0    'False
   X1              =    120
   X2              =    120
   Y1              =    240
   Y2              =    2400
End
Begin VB.Line Hlines
   Index           =    6
   Visible         =    0    'False
   X1              =    120
   X2              =    3480
   Y1              =    2400
   Y2              =    2400
End
Begin VB.Line Hlines
   Index           =    5
   Visible         =    0    'False
   X1              =    120
   X2              =    3480

   Y1              =    2040
```

(continued)

```
         Y2              =     2040
      End
      Begin VB.Line Hlines
         Index           =     4
         Visible         =     0     'False
         X1              =     120
         X2              =     3480
         Y1              =     1680
         Y2              =     1680
      End
      Begin VB.Line Hlines
         Index           =     3
         Visible         =     0     'False
         X1              =     120
         X2              =     3480
         Y1              =     1320
         Y2              =     1320
      End
      Begin VB.Line Hlines
         Index           =     2
         Visible         =     0     'False
         X1              =     120
         X2              =     3480
         Y1              =     960
         Y2              =     960
      End
      Begin VB.Line Hlines
         Index           =     1
         Visible         =     0     'False
         X1              =     120
         X2              =     3480
         Y1              =     600
         Y2              =     600
      End
      Begin VB.Line Hlines
         Index           =     0
         Visible         =     0     'False
         X1              =     120
         X2              =     3495
         Y1              =     240
         Y2              =     240
      End
   End
End
Attribute VB_Name = "Calendar"
Attribute VB_GlobalNameSpace = False
Attribute VB_Creatable = False
Attribute VB_PredeclaredId = True
Attribute VB_Exposed = False
```

THE APPOINTMENT DATA ENTRY FORM'S PROPERTIES

B

*T*his appendix lists the form properties stored in frmApp.frm. The portion you can edit in the code editor is shown in Chapter 13, Listing 13-4.

The frmApp.frm File Above Editable Portion

```
VERSION 5.00
Begin VB.Form frmApp
   BorderStyle     =   3  'Fixed Dialog
   Caption         =   "To Do"
   ClientHeight    =   4065
   ClientLeft      =   45
   ClientTop       =   330
   ClientWidth     =   4365
   LinkTopic       =   "Form1"
   LockControls    =   -1  'True
   MaxButton       =   0   'False
   MinButton       =   0   'False
   ScaleHeight     =   4065
   ScaleWidth      =   4365
   ShowInTaskbar   =   0   'False
   StartUpPosition =   2  'CenterScreen
   Begin VB.TextBox txtAct_time
      Height       =   300
      Left         =   2760
      TabIndex     =   8
      Text         =   "00:00"
```

(continued)

```
      Top             =    915
      Width           =    615
   End
   Begin VB.TextBox txtEnd_time
      Height          =    300
      Left            =    1560
      TabIndex        =    6
      Text            =    "00:00"
      Top             =    915
      Width           =    615
   End
   Begin VB.TextBox txtStart_time
      Height          =    300
      Left            =    720
      TabIndex        =    4
      Text            =    "00:00"
      Top             =    915
      Width           =    615
   End
   Begin VB.CheckBox chkCompleted
      Caption         =    "Completed &4"
      Height          =    255
      Left            =    720
      TabIndex        =    9
      Top             =    1470
      Width           =    1215
   End
   Begin VB.TextBox txtDescription
      Height          =    300
      Left            =    240
      TabIndex        =    11
      Top             =    2040
      Width           =    3735
   End
   Begin VB.TextBox txtDate
      Height          =    300
      Left            =    720
      TabIndex        =    2
      Top             =    435
      Width           =    2655
   End
   Begin VB.CommandButton cmdSave
      Caption         =    "&Save"
      Height          =    360
      Left            =    180
      TabIndex        =    13
      Top             =    2715
      Width           =    900
   End
```

```
Begin VB.CommandButton cmdHome
    Caption         =   "&Home"
    Height          =   360
    Left            =   180
    TabIndex        =   17
    Top             =   3120
    Width           =   900
End
Begin VB.CommandButton cmdPrev
    Caption         =   "&Prev"
    Height          =   360
    Left            =   1200
    TabIndex        =   18
    Top             =   3120
    Width           =   900
End
Begin VB.CommandButton cmdNext
    Caption         =   "&Next"
    Height          =   360
    Left            =   2100
    TabIndex        =   19
    Top             =   3120
    Width           =   900
End
Begin VB.CommandButton cmdEnd
    Caption         =   "&End"
    Height          =   360
    Left            =   3120
    TabIndex        =   20
    Top             =   3120
    Width           =   900
End
Begin VB.CommandButton cmdDelete
    Caption         =   "&Delete"
    Height          =   360
    Left            =   1200
    TabIndex        =   14
    Top             =   2715
    Width           =   900
End
Begin VB.CommandButton cmdUndelete
    Caption         =   "&Undelete"
    Height          =   360
    Left            =   2100
    TabIndex        =   15
    Top             =   2715
    Width           =   900
End
```

(continued)

```
Begin VB.CommandButton cmdReread
   Caption         =    "&Reread"
   Height          =    360
   Left            =    3120
   TabIndex        =    16
   Top             =    2715
   Width           =    900
End
Begin VB.CommandButton cmdAdd
   Caption         =    "&Add New"
   Height          =    360
   Left          . =    180
   TabIndex        =    0
   Top             =    3525
   Width           =    1380
End
Begin VB.CommandButton cmdExit
   Caption         5    "e&Xit"
   Height          =    360
   Left            =    2640
   TabIndex        =    12
   Top             =    3525
   Width           =    1380
End
Begin VB.Label lblDescription
   Caption         =    "Description &6"
   Height          =    255
   Left            =    120
   TabIndex        =    10
   Top             =    1800
   Width           =    1095
End
Begin VB.Label lblActual
   Caption         =    "Actual &5 (duration)"
   Height          =    495
   Left            =    2760
   TabIndex        =    7
   Top             =    1230
   Width           =    855
End
Begin VB.Label lblEnd
   Caption         =    "End &3"
   Height          =    255
   Left            =    1560
   TabIndex        =    5
   Top             =    1230
   Width           =    495
End
```

```
Begin VB.Label lblStart
   Caption        =   "Start &2"
   Height         =   255
   Left           =   720
   TabIndex       =   3
   Top            =   1230
   Width          =   615
End
Begin VB.Label lblTimes
   Caption        =   "Times"
   Height         =   255
   Left           =   120
   TabIndex       =   24
   Top            =   960
   Width          =   495
End
Begin VB.Label lblDate
   Caption        =   "Date &1"
   Height         =   255
   Left           =   120
   TabIndex       =   1
   Top            =   480
   Width          =   615
End
Begin VB.Label lblDeleted
   Height         =   255
   Left           =   2760
   TabIndex       =   23
   Top            =   120
   Width          =   1335
End
Begin VB.Label lblKey_num
   Height         =   255
   Left           =   840
   TabIndex       =   22
   Top            =   120
   Width          =   855
End
Begin VB.Label lblKey
   Caption        =   "Key"
   Height         =   255
   Left           =   120
   TabIndex       =   21
   Top            =   120
   Width          =   375
End
```

(continued)

```
            Begin VB.Line Line2
                BorderWidth     =   2
                X1              =   120
                X2              =   4095
                Y1              =   2520
                Y2              =   2535
            End
        End
    End
    Attribute VB_Name = "frmApp"
    Attribute VB_GlobalNameSpace = False
    Attribute VB_Creatable = False
    Attribute VB_PredeclaredId = True
    Attribute VB_Exposed = False
```

THE MAIN MENU FORM'S PROPERTIES

This appendix lists the form properties stored in frmMyTim.frm. The portion you can edit in the code editor is shown in Chapter 15, Listing 15-9.

The frmMyTim.frm File Above Editable Portion

```
VERSION 5.00
Begin VB.Form frmMyTim
    Caption         =   "My Time"
    ClientHeight    =   4590
    ClientLeft      =   60
    ClientTop       =   345
    ClientWidth     =   7875
    BeginProperty Font
        Name            =   "MS Sans Serif"
        Size            =   13.5
        Charset         =   0
        Weight          =   400
        Underline       =   0   'False
        Italic          =   0   'False
        Strikethrough   =   0   'False
    EndProperty
    LinkTopic       =   "Form1"
    ScaleHeight     =   4590
    ScaleWidth      =   7875
    StartUpPosition =   3   'Windows Default
    Begin VB.Frame fraOpts
```

(continued)

```
Caption          =    " e&Xit "
BeginProperty Font
   Name          =    "MS Sans Serif"
   Size          =    8.25
   Charset       =    65
   Weight        =    400
   Underline     =    0    'False
   Italic        =    0    'False
   Strikethrough =    0    'False
EndProperty
Height           =    1830
Index            =    5
Left             =    5370
TabIndex         =    5
Top              =    2460
Width            =    2100
Begin VB.TextBox txtKey
   Appearance    =    0    'Flat
   BackColor     =    &H00FFFFFF&
   BorderStyle   =    0    'None
   BeginProperty Font
      Name       =    "Small Fonts"
      Size       =    2.25
      Charset    =    0
      Weight     =    400
      Underline  =    0    'False
      Italic     =    0    'False
      Strikethrough = 0    'False
   EndProperty
   Height        =    45
   Index         =    5
   Left          =    50
   PasswordChar  =    " "
   TabIndex      =    23
   Top           =    150
   Visible       =    0    'False
   Width         =    15
End
Begin VB.Label lblExit
   Alignment     =    2 'Center
   Caption       =    "e&Xit"
   BeginProperty Font
      Name       =    "Arial"
      Size       =    24
      Charset    =    0
      Weight     =    400
      Underline  =    0    'False
      Italic     =    0    'False
```

```
            Strikethrough    =    0    'False
        EndProperty
        Height           =    615
        Left             =    120
        TabIndex         =    17
        Top              =    720
        Width            =    1935
    End
End
Begin VB.Frame fraOpts
    Caption          =    " &Time"
    BeginProperty Font
        Name             =    "MS Sans Serif"
        Size             =    8.25
        Charset          =    65
        Weight           =    400
        Underline        =    0    'False
        Italic           =    0    'False
        Strikethrough    =    0    'False
    EndProperty
    Height           =    1830
    Index            =    4
    Left             =    2880
    TabIndex         =    4
    Top              =    2460
    Width            =    2100
    Begin VB.TextBox txtKey
        Appearance       =    0    'Flat
        BackColor        =    &H00FFFFFF&
        BorderStyle      =    0    'None
        BeginProperty Font
            Name             =    "Small Fonts"
            Size             =    2.25
            Charset          =    0
            Weight           =    400
            Underline        =    0    'False
            Italic           =    0    'False
            Strikethrough    =    0    'False
        EndProperty
        Height           =    45
        Index            =    4
        Left             =    50
        PasswordChar     =    " "
        TabIndex         =    22
        Top              =    150
        Visible          =    0    'False
        Width            =    15
    End
```

(continued)

```
Begin VB.Line linHrRt
    X1              =   1080
    X2              =   1320
    Y1              =   960
    Y2              =   1440
End
Begin VB.Line linHrLf
    X1              =   960
    X2              =   1320
    Y1              =   960
    Y2              =   1440
End
Begin VB.Line linMinRt
    X1              =   1080
    X2              =   1320
    Y1              =   960
    Y2              =   360
End
Begin VB.Line linMinLf
    X1              =   960
    X2              =   1320
    Y1              =   960
    Y2              =   360
End
Begin VB.Shape shpCircle
    Height          =   1575
    Left            =   120
    Shape           =   3   'Circle
    Top             =   240
    Width           =   1935
End
Begin VB.Line linDot
    BorderWidth     =   8
    X1              =   1080
    X2              =   1095
    Y1              =   360
    Y2              =   375
End
End
Begin VB.Frame fraOpts
    Caption         =   " To &Do "
    BeginProperty Font
        Name            =   "MS Sans Serif"
        Size            =   8.25
        Charset         =   65
        Weight          =   400
        Underline       =   0   'False
        Italic          =   0   'False
        Strikethrough   =   0   'False
    EndProperty
```

```
Height          =    1830
Index           =    3
Left            =    390
TabIndex        =    3
Top             =    2460
Width           =    2100
Begin VB.TextBox txtKey
   Appearance      =    0   'Flat
   BackColor       =    &H00FFFFFF&
   BorderStyle     =    0   'None
   BeginProperty Font
      Name          =    "Small Fonts"
      Size          =    2.25
      Charset       =    0
      Weight        =    400
      Underline     =    0     'False
      Italic        =    0     'False
      Strikethrough =    0     'False
   EndProperty
   Height          =    45
   Index           =    3
   Left            =    50
   PasswordChar    =    " "
   TabIndex        =    21
   Top             =    150
   Visible         =    0   'False
   Width           =    15
End
Begin VB.TextBox txtToDo
   BackColor       =    &H8000000F&
   Height          =    480
   Index           =    3
   Left            =    240
   TabIndex        =    16
   TabStop         =    0    'False
   Text            =    "Monthly"
   Top             =    1680
   Width           =    4000
End
Begin VB.TextBox txtToDo
   BackColor       =    &H8000000F&
   Height          =    480
   Index           =    2
   Left            =    240
   TabIndex        =    15
   TabStop         =    0    'False
   Text            =    "Weekly"
   Top             =    1200
   Width           =    4000
End
```

(continued)

```
Begin VB.TextBox txtToDo
   BackColor       =    &H8000000F&
   Height          =    480
   Index           =    1
   Left            =    240
   TabIndex        =    14
   TabStop         =    0    'False
   Text            =    "Daily"
   Top             =    720
   Width           =    4000
End
Begin VB.TextBox txtToDo
   BackColor       =    &H8000000F&
   Height          =    480
   Index           =    0
   Left            =    240
   TabIndex        =    13
   TabStop         =    0    'False
   Text            =    "Do Once"
   Top             =    240
   Width           =    4000
End
End
Begin VB.Frame fraOpts
   Caption         =    " &Projects "
   BeginProperty Font
      Name            =    "MS Sans Serif"
      Size            =    8.25
      Charset         =    65
      Weight          =    400
      Underline       =    0    'False
      Italic          =    0    'False
      Strikethrough   =    0    'False
   EndProperty
   Height          =    1830
   Index           =    2
   Left            =    5370
   TabIndex        =    2
   Top             =    315
   Width           =    2100
   Begin VB.TextBox txtKey
      Appearance      =    0    'Flat
      BackColor       =    &H00FFFFFF&
      BorderStyle     =    0    'None
      BeginProperty Font
         Name            =    "Small Fonts"
         Size            =    2.25
         Charset         =    0
```

```
               Weight         =    400
            Underline         =    0    'False
               Italic         =    0    'False
         Strikethrough        =    0    'False
         EndProperty
         Height        =    45
         Index         =    2
         Left          =    50
         PasswordChar  =    " "
         TabIndex      =    20
         Top           =    150
         Visible       =    0    'False
         Width         =    15
      End
      Begin VB.Line linTaskCon2
         X1            =    1320
         X2            =    1320
         Y1            =    1080
         Y2            =    1440
      End
      Begin VB.Line linTaskCon1
         X1            =    840
         X2            =    840
         Y1            =    360
         Y2            =    1080
      End
      Begin VB.Line linTask4
         BorderWidth   =    5
         X1            =    1320
         X2            =    2040
         Y1            =    1440
         Y2            =    1440
      End
      Begin VB.Line linTask3
         BorderWidth   =    5
         X1            =    840
         X2            =    1320
         Y1            =    1080
         Y2            =    1080
      End
      Begin VB.Line linTask2
         BorderWidth   =    5
         X1            =    840
         X2            =    1440
         Y1            =    720
         Y2            =    720
      End
```

(continued)

```
            Begin VB.Line linTask1
               BorderWidth    =    5
               X1             =    240
               X2             =    840
               Y1             =    360
               Y2             =    360
            End
         End
         Begin VB.Frame fraOpts
            Caption          =    " &Schedule "
            BeginProperty Font
               Name           =    "MS Sans Serif"
               Size           =    8.25
               Charset        =    65
               Weight         =    400
               Underline      =    0    'False
               Italic         =    0    'False
               Strikethrough  =    0    'False
            EndProperty
            Height           =    1830
            Index            =    1
            Left             =    2880
            TabIndex         =    1
            Top              =    315
            Width            =    2100
            Begin VB.TextBox txtKey
               Appearance     =    0    'Flat
               BackColor      =    &H00FFFFFF&
               BorderStyle    =    0    'None
               BeginProperty Font
                  Name        =    "Small Fonts"
                  Size        =    2.25
                  Charset     =    0
                  Weight      =    400
                  Underline   =    0    'False
                  Italic      =    0    'False
                  Strikethrough =  0    'False
               EndProperty
               Height         =    45
               Index          =    1
               Left           =    50
               PasswordChar   =    " "
               TabIndex       =    19
               Top            =    150
               Visible        =    0    'False
               Width          =    15
            End
```

```
Begin VB.TextBox txtSched
   BackColor      =   &H8000000F&
   Height         =   480
   Index          =   3
   Left           =   240
   TabIndex       =   12
   TabStop        =   0   'False
   Text           =   "11:30"
   Top            =   1680
   Width          =   4000
End
Begin VB.TextBox txtSched
   BackColor      =   &H8000000F&
   Height         =   480
   Index          =   2
   Left           =   240
   TabIndex       =   11
   TabStop        =   0   'False
   Text           =   "11:00 Call re status of Chapter 15"
   Top            =   1200
   Width          =   4000
End
Begin VB.TextBox txtSched
   BackColor      =   &H8000000F&
   Height         =   480
   Index          =   1
   Left           =   240
   TabIndex       =   10
   TabStop        =   0   'False
   Text           =   "10:30 Design Schedule"
   Top            =   720
   Width          =   4000
End
Begin VB.TextBox txtSched
   BackColor      =   &H8000000F&
   Height         =   480
   Index          =   0
   Left           =   240
   TabIndex       =   9
   TabStop        =   0   'False
   Text           =   "10:00 Mtg w/Smith"
   Top            =   240
   Width          =   4000
End
End
```

(continued)

```
Begin VB.Frame fraOpts
   Caption         =   " &Calendar "
   BeginProperty Font
      Name            =   "MS Sans Serif"
      Size            =   8.25
      Charset         =   0
      Weight          =   400
      Underline       =   0   'False
      Italic          =   0   'False
      Strikethrough   =   0   'False
   EndProperty
   Height          =   1830
   Index           =   0
   Left            =   390
   TabIndex        =   0
   Top             =   360
   Width           =   2100
   Begin VB.TextBox txtKey
      Appearance      =   0   'Flat
      BackColor       =   &H00FFFFFF&
      BorderStyle     =   0   'None
      BeginProperty Font
         Name            =   "Small Fonts"
         Size            =   2.25
         Charset         =   0
         Weight          =   400
         Underline       =   0   'False
         Italic          =   0   'False
         Strikethrough   =   0   'False
      EndProperty
      Height          =   45
      Index           =   0
      Left            =   50
      PasswordChar    =   " "
      TabIndex        =   18
      Top             =   150
      Visible         =   0   'False
      Width           =   15
   End
   Begin VB.Label lblCalDay8
      Alignment       =   1   'Right Justify
      Caption         =   "8"
      Height          =   375
      Left            =   1080
      TabIndex        =   8
      Top             =   840
      Width           =   375
   End
```

```
Begin VB.Label lblCalDay7
    Alignment       =   1 'Right Justify
    Caption         =   "7"
    Height          =   375
    Left            =   480
    TabIndex        =   7
    Top             =   840
    Width           =   375
End
Begin VB.Label lblCalDay1
    Alignment       =   1  'Right Justify
    Caption         =   "1"
    Height          =   375
    Left            =   1080
    TabIndex        =   6
    Top             =   360
    Width           =   375
End
Begin VB.Line linCalGrdHor2
    X1              =   360
    X2              =   1920
    Y1              =   1320
    Y2              =   1320
End
Begin VB.Line linCalGrdHor1
    X1              =   360
    X2              =   1920
    Y1              =   840
    Y2              =   840
End
Begin VB.Line linCalGrdVer2
    X1              =   1560
    X2              =   1560
    Y1              =   360
    Y2              =   1680
End
Begin VB.Line linCalGrdVer1
    X1              =   960
    X2              =   960
    Y1              =   360
    Y2              =   1800
End
Begin VB.Line linCalTp
    BorderWidth     =   3
    X1              =   360
    X2              =   2040
    Y1              =   360
    Y2              =   360
End
```

(continued)

```
        Begin VB.Line linCalLf
            BorderWidth     =   3
            X1              =   360
            X2              =   360
            Y1              =   360
            Y2              =   1800
        End
    End
End
Attribute VB_Name = "frmMyTim"
Attribute VB_GlobalNameSpace = False
Attribute VB_Creatable = False
Attribute VB_PredeclaredId = True
Attribute VB_Exposed = False
```

THE PROJECT FORM'S PROPERTIES

*T*his appendix lists the form properties stored in frmPrjct.frm. The portion you can edit in the code editor is shown in Chapter 17, Listing 17-2.

The frmPrjct.frm File Above Editable Portion

```
VERSION 5.00
Begin VB.Form frmPrjct
   BorderStyle     =   3  'Fixed Dialog
   ClientHeight    =   5925
   ClientLeft      =   45
   ClientTop       =   330
   ClientWidth     =   4365
   LinkTopic       =   "Form1"
   MaxButton       =   0    'False
   MinButton       =   0    'False
   ScaleHeight     =   5925
   ScaleWidth      =   4365
   ShowInTaskbar   =   0    'False
   StartUpPosition =   2  'CenterScreen
   Begin VB.TextBox txtAct_time
      Height       =     300
      Left         =     1920
      TabIndex     =     34
      Text         =     "00:00"
      Top          =     3615
      Width        =     600
End
```

(continued)

```
Begin VB.TextBox txtEst_time
   Height          =   300
   Left            =   840
   TabIndex        =   33
   Text            =   "00:00"
   Top             =   3615
   Width           =   600
End
Begin VB.TextBox dates
   Height          =   300
   Index           =   3
   Left            =   2520
   TabIndex        =   14
   Top             =   2760
   Width           =   1575
End
Begin VB.TextBox dates
   Height          =   300
   Index           =   2
   Left            =   840
   TabIndex        =   12
   Top             =   2760
   Width           =   1575
End
Begin VB.TextBox dates
   Height          =   300
   Index           =   1
   Left            =   2520
   TabIndex        =   10
   Top             =   2040
   Width           =   1575
End
Begin VB.TextBox dates
   Height          =   300
   Index           =   0
   Left            =   840
   TabIndex        =   8
   Top             =   2040
   Width           =   1575
End
Begin VB.TextBox txtAfter_name
   BackColor       =   &H8000000F&
   Height          =   285
   Left            =   1680
   TabIndex        =   32
   TabStop         =   0   'False
   Text            =   "Precedent project name"
   Top             =   1320
   Width           =   2415
End
```

```
Begin VB.TextBox txtAfter_num
   Height          =   300
   Left            =   840
   TabIndex        =   6
   Text            =   "0"
   Top             =   1320
   Width           =   735
End
Begin VB.TextBox txtParent_name
   BackColor       =   &H8000000F&
   Height          =   285
   Left            =   1680
   TabIndex        =   17
   TabStop         =   0   'False
   Text            =   "Parent name"
   Top             =   810
   Width           =   2415
End
Begin VB.TextBox txtParent_num
   Height          =   300
   Left            =   840
   TabIndex        =   4
   Text            =   "0"
   Top             =   810
   Width           =   735
End
Begin VB.CommandButton cmdSave
   Caption         =   "&Save"
   Height          =   360
   Left            =   180
   TabIndex        =   21
   Top             =   4515
   Width           =   900
End
Begin VB.CommandButton cmdHome
   Caption         =   "&Home"
   Height          =   360
   Left            =   180
   TabIndex        =   25
   Top             =   4920
   Width           =   900
End
Begin VB.CommandButton cmdPrev
   Caption         =   "&Prev"
   Height          =   360
   Left            =   1200
   TabIndex        =   26
   Top             =   4920
   Width           =   900
End
```

(continued)

```
Begin VB.CommandButton cmdNext
   Caption         =   "&Next"
   Height          =   360
   Left            =   2100
   TabIndex        =   27
   Top             =   4920
   Width           =   900
End
Begin VB.CommandButton cmdEnd
   Caption         =   "&End"
   Height          =   360
   Left            =   3120
   TabIndex        =   28
   Top             =   4920
   Width           =   900
End
Begin VB.CommandButton cmdDelete
   Caption         =   "&Delete"
   Height          =   360
   Left            =   1200
   TabIndex        =   22
   Top             =   4515
   Width           =   900
End
Begin VB.CommandButton cmdUndelete
   Caption         =   "&Undelete"
   Height          =   360
   Left            =   2100
   TabIndex        =   23
   Top             =   4515
   Width           =   900
End
Begin VB.CommandButton cmdReread
   Caption         =   "&Reread"
   Height          =   360
   Left            =   3120
   TabIndex        =   24
   Top             =   4515
   Width           =   900
End
Begin VB.CommandButton cmdAdd
   Caption         =   "&Add New"
   Height          =   360
   Left            =   180
   TabIndex        =   29
   Top             =   5325
   Width           =   1380
End
```

```
Begin VB.CommandButton cmdExit
   Caption          =   "e&Xit"
   Height           =   360
   Left             =   2640
   TabIndex         =   0
   Top              =   5325
   Width            =   1380
End
Begin VB.TextBox txtName
   Height           =   285
   Left             =   840
   TabIndex         =   2
   Top              =   360
   Width            =   3255
End
Begin VB.Label lblBegin
   Caption          =   "Begin After &3"
   Height           =   495
   Left             =   120
   TabIndex         =   5
   Top              =   1200
   Width            =   615
End
Begin VB.Label lblAct_time
   Caption          =   "Actual &9"
   Height           =   255
   Left             =   1920
   TabIndex         =   16
   Top              =   3960
   Width            =   735
End
Begin VB.Label lblEst_time
   Caption          =   "Estimated &8"
   Height           =   255
   Left             =   840
   TabIndex         =   15
   Top              =   3960
   Width            =   855
End
Begin VB.Label lblAct_end_date
   Caption          =   "Actual End &7"
   Height           =   255
   Left             =   2520
   TabIndex         =   13
   Top              =   3120
   Width            =   1455
End
```

(continued)

```
Begin VB.Label lblAct_start_date
   Caption         =   "Actual Start &6"
   Height          =   255
   Left            =   840
   TabIndex        =   11
   Top             =   3120
   Width           =   1575
End
Begin VB.Label lblTime
   Caption         =   "Times"
   Height          =   255
   Left            =   120
   TabIndex        =   18
   Top             =   3645
   Width           =   615
End
Begin VB.Label lblEstimated_end
   Caption         =   "Estimated End &5"
   Height          =   255
   Left            =   2520
   TabIndex        =   9
   Top             =   2400
   Width           =   1455
End
Begin VB.Label lblEst_start
   Caption         =   "Estimated Start &4"
   Height          =   255
   Left            =   840
   TabIndex        =   7
   Top             =   2400
   Width           =   1575
End
Begin VB.Label lblDates
   Caption         =   "Dates "
   Height          =   255
   Left            =   120
   TabIndex        =   19
   Top             =   2100
   Width           =   615
End
Begin VB.Label lblParent
   Caption         =   "Part of &2"
   Height          =   255
   Left            =   120
   TabIndex        =   3
   Top             =   840
   Width           =   615
End
```

```
         Begin VB.Label lblDeleted
            Height          =   255
            Left            =   2760
            TabIndex        =   20
            Top             =   0
            Width           =   1335
         End
         Begin VB.Label lblKey_num
            Height          =   255
            Left            =   840
            TabIndex        =   31
            Top             =   0
            Width           =   855
         End
         Begin VB.Label lblKey
            Caption         =   "Key"
            Height          =   255
            Left            =   120
            TabIndex        =   30
            Top             =   0
            Width           =   375
         End
         Begin VB.Line Line2
            BorderWidth     =   2
            X1              =   120
            X2              =   4095
            Y1              =   4320
            Y2              =   4335
         End
         Begin VB.Label lblName
            Caption         =   "Name  &1"
            Height          =   255
            Left            =   120
            TabIndex        =   1
            Top             =   360
            Width           =   615
         End
      End
End
Attribute VB_Name = "frmPrjct"
Attribute VB_GlobalNameSpace = False
Attribute VB_Creatable = False
Attribute VB_PredeclaredId = True
Attribute VB_Exposed = False
```

THE CASCADE FORM'S PROPERTIES

This appendix lists the form properties stored in frmCscd.frm. The portion you can edit in the code editor is shown in Chapter 18, Listing 18-1.

The frmCscd.frm File Above Editable Portion

```
VERSION 5.00
Begin VB.Form frmCscd
    Caption         =   "Form1"
    ClientHeight    =   4035
    ClientLeft      =   60
    ClientTop       =   345
    ClientWidth     =   6330
    BeginProperty Font
        Name            =   "MS Sans Serif"
        Size            =   8.25
        Charset         =   0
        Weight          =   400
        Underline       =   0   'False
        Italic          =   0   'False
        Strikethrough   =   0   'False
    EndProperty
    LinkTopic       =   "Form1"
    ScaleHeight     =   4035
    ScaleWidth      =   6330
    StartUpPosition =   3   'Windows Default
    Begin VB.CommandButton cmdDraw
```

(continued)

```
        Caption         =   "&Draw"
        Height          =   360
        Left            =   4530
        TabIndex        =   12
        Top             =   3720
        Width           =   930
    End
    Begin VB.CommandButton cmdExit
        Caption         =   "e&Xit"
        Height          =   360
        Left            =   5460
        TabIndex        =   11
        Top             =   3720
        Width           =   930
    End
    Begin VB.CommandButton cmdEdit
        Caption         =   "&Edit"
        Height          =   360
        Left            =   3600
        TabIndex        =   10
        Top             =   3720
        Width           =   930
    End
    Begin VB.ListBox Boards
        BeginProperty Font
            Name            =   "MS Sans Serif"
            Size            =   8.25
            Charset         =   65
            Weight          =   400
            Underline       =   0   'False
            Italic          =   0   'False
            Strikethrough   =   0   'False
        EndProperty
        Height          =   2400
        Index           =   9
        IntegralHeight  =   0   'False
        Left            =   1350
        Sorted          =   -1  'True
        TabIndex        =   9
        Top             =   1350
        Visible         =   0   'False
        Width           =   4500
    End
    Begin VB.ListBox Boards
        BeginProperty Font
            Name            =   "MS Sans Serif"
            Size            =   8.25
            Charset         =   65
            Weight          =   400
            Underline       =   0   'False
```

```
         Italic          =    0    'False
         Strikethrough   =    0    'False
      EndProperty
      Height             =    2400
      Index              =    8
      IntegralHeight     =    0    'False
      Left               =    1200
      Sorted             =   -1    'True
      TabIndex           =    8
      Top                =    1200
      Visible            =    0    'False
      Width              =    4500
   End
   Begin VB.ListBox Boards
      BeginProperty Font
         Name            =    "MS Sans Serif"
         Size            =    8.25
         Charset         =    65
         Weight          =    400
         Underline       =    0    'False
         Italic          =    0    'False
         Strikethrough   =    0    'False
      EndProperty
      Height             =    2400
      Index              =    7
      IntegralHeight     =    0    'False
      Left               =    1050
      Sorted             =   -1    'True
      TabIndex           =    7
      Top                =    1050
      Visible            =    0    'False
      Width              =    4500
   End
   Begin VB.ListBox Boards
      BeginProperty Font
         Name            =    "MS Sans Serif"
         Size            =    8.25
         Charset         =    65
         Weight          =    400
         Underline       =    0    'False
         Italic          =    0    'False
         Strikethrough   =    0    'False
      EndProperty
      Height             =    2400
      Index              =    6
      IntegralHeight     =    0    'False
      Left               =    900
      Sorted             =   -1    'True
      TabIndex           =    6
```

(continued)

```
            Top             =    900
            Visible         =    0    'False
            Width           =    4500
         End
         Begin VB.ListBox Boards
            BeginProperty Font
               Name            =    "MS Sans Serif"
               Size            =    8.25
               Charset         =    65
               Weight          =    400
               Underline       =    0    'False
               Italic          =    0    'False
               Strikethrough   =    0    'False
            EndProperty
            Height          =    2400
            Index           =    5
            IntegralHeight  =    0    'False
            Left            =    750
            Sorted          =    -1   'True
            TabIndex        =    5
            Top             =    750
            Visible         =    0    'False
            Width           =    4500
         End
         Begin VB.ListBox Boards
            BeginProperty Font
               Name            =    "MS Sans Serif"
               Size            =    8.25
               Charset         =    65
               Weight          =    400
               Underline       =    0    'False
               Italic          =    0    'False
               Strikethrough   =    0    'False
            EndProperty
            Height          =    2400
            Index           =    4
            IntegralHeight  =    0    'False
            Left            =    600
            Sorted          =    -1   'True
            TabIndex        =    4
            Top             =    600
            Visible         =    0    'False
            Width           =    4500
         End
         Begin VB.ListBox Boards
            BeginProperty Font
               Name            =    "MS Sans Serif"
               Size            =    8.25
               Charset         =    65
               Weight          =    400
```

```
            Underline      =    0    'False
            Italic         =    0    'False
            Strikethrough  =    0    'False
         EndProperty
         Height         =    2400
         Index          =    3
         IntegralHeight =    0    'False
         Left           =    450
         Sorted         =    -1   'True
         TabIndex       =    3
         Top            =    450
         Visible        =    0    'False
         Width          =    4500
      End
      Begin VB.ListBox Boards
         BeginProperty Font
            Name           =    "MS Sans Serif"
            Size           =    8.25
            Charset        =    65
            Weight         =    400
            Underline      =    0    'False
            Italic         =    0    'False
            Strikethrough  =    0    'False
         EndProperty
         Height         =    2400
         Index          =    2
         IntegralHeight =    0    'False
         Left           =    300
         Sorted         =    -1   'True
         TabIndex       =    0
         Top            =    300
         Visible        =    0    'False
         Width          =    4500
      End
      Begin VB.ListBox Boards
         BeginProperty Font
            Name           =    "MS Sans Serif"
            Size           =    8.25
            Charset        =    65
            Weight         =    400
            Underline      =    0    'False
            Italic         =    0    'False
            Strikethrough  =    0    'False
         EndProperty
         Height         =    2400
         Index          =    1
         IntegralHeight =    0    'False
         Left           =    150
         Sorted         =    -1   'True
```

(continued)

```
        TabIndex       =    2
        Top            =    150
        Visible        =    0    'False
        Width          =    4500
     End
     Begin VB.ListBox Boards
        BeginProperty Font
           Name        =    "MS Sans Serif"
           Size        =    8.25
           Charset     =    65
           Weight      =    400
           Underline   =    0    'False
           Italic      =    0    'False
           Strikethrough =  0    'False
        EndProperty
        Height         =    2400
        Index          =    0
        IntegralHeight =    0    'False
        Left           =    0
        Sorted         =    -1   'True
        TabIndex       =    1
        Top            =    0
        Visible        =    0    'False
        Width          =    4500
     End
  End
  Attribute VB_Name = "frmCscd"
  Attribute VB_GlobalNameSpace = False
  Attribute VB_Creatable = False
  Attribute VB_PredeclaredId = True
  Attribute VB_Exposed = False
```

THE CHART FORM'S PROPERTIES

*T*his appendix lists the form properties stored in frmChart.frm. The portion you can edit in the code editor is shown in Chapter 19, Listing 19-1.

The frmChart.frm File Above Editable Portion

```
VERSION 5.00
Begin VB.Form frmChart
   BorderStyle     =   3  'Fixed Dialog
   ClientHeight    =   3195
   ClientLeft      =   45
   ClientTop       =   330
   ClientWidth     =   8610
   BeginProperty Font
      Name         =   "MS Sans Serif"
      Size         =   8.25
      Charset      =   0
      Weight       =   400
      Underline    =   0   'False
      Italic       =   0   'False
      Strikethrough =  0   'False
   EndProperty
   LinkTopic       =   "Form1"
   MaxButton       =   0   'False
   MinButton       =   0   'False
   ScaleHeight     =   3195
   ScaleWidth      =   8610
```

(continued)

```
ShowInTaskbar    =   0   'False
StartUpPosition  =   2   'CenterScreen
Begin VB.TextBox txtPnames
   Appearance       =   0   'Flat
   BackColor        =   &H8000000F&
   BorderStyle      =   0   'None
   BeginProperty Font
      Name          =   "MS Sans Serif"
      Size          =   9.75
      Charset       =   0
      Weight        =   400
      Underline     =   0   'False
      Italic        =   0   'False
      Strikethrough =   0   'False
   EndProperty
   Height           =   2415
   Left             =   120
   MultiLine        =   -1  'True
   TabIndex         =   3
   TabStop          =   0   'False
   Top              =   600
   Width            =   2055
End
Begin VB.CommandButton cmdExit
   Caption          =   "e&Xit"
   BeginProperty Font
      Name          =   "Courier New"
      Size          =   9.75
      Charset       =   0
      Weight        =   400
      Underline     =   0   'False
      Italic        =   0   'False
      Strikethrough =   0   'False
   EndProperty
   Height           =   360
   Left             =   120
   TabIndex         =   2
   Top              =   0
   Width            =   1095
End
Begin VB.Label lblDayBtm
   Caption          =   "Label2"
   BeginProperty Font
      Name          =   "Courier New"
      Size          =   9.75
      Charset       =   0
      Weight        =   400
      Underline     =   0   'False
      Italic        =   0   'False
```

```
            Strikethrough   =   0    'False
         EndProperty
         Height          =   255
         Left            =   2280
         TabIndex        =   1
         Top             =   240
         Width           =   7455
      End
      Begin VB.Label lblDayTop
         Caption         =   "Label1"
         BeginProperty Font
            Name            =   "Courier New"
            Size            =   9.75
            Charset         =   0
            Weight          =   400
            Underline       =   0    'False
            Italic          =   0    'False
            Strikethrough   =   0    'False
         EndProperty
         Height          =   255
         Left            =   2280
         TabIndex        =   0
         Top             =   0
         Width           =   7455
      End
   End
End
Attribute VB_Name = "frmChart"
Attribute VB_GlobalNameSpace = False
Attribute VB_Creatable = False
Attribute VB_PredeclaredId = True
Attribute VB_Exposed = False
```

THE TO DO LIST DATA ENTRY FORM'S PROPERTIES

G

This appendix lists the form properties stored in frmToDo.frm. The portion you can edit in the code editor is shown in Chapter 20, Listing 20-2a.

The frmToDo.frm File Above the Editable Portion

```
VERSION 5.00
Begin VB.Form frmToDo
    BorderStyle     =   3  'Fixed Dialog
    Caption         =   "To Do"
    ClientHeight    =   4065
    ClientLeft      =   45
    ClientTop       =   330
    ClientWidth     =   4365
    LinkTopic       =   "Form1"
    LockControls    =   -1  'True
    MaxButton       =   0  'False
    MinButton       =   0  'False
    ScaleHeight     =   4065
    ScaleWidth      =   4365
    ShowInTaskbar   =   0  'False
    StartUpPosition =   2  'CenterScreen
    Begin VB.TextBox txtAct_time
        Height          =   285
        Left            =   2160
        TabIndex        =   7
        Text            =   "00:00"
```

(continued)

```
      Top             =   1200
      Width           =   735
   End
   Begin VB.TextBox txtEst_time
      Height          =   285
      Left            =   960
      TabIndex        =   5
      Text            =   "00:00"
      Top             =   1200
      Width           =   735
   End
   Begin VB.CommandButton cmdSave
      Caption         =   "&Save"
      Height          =   360
      Left            =   180
      TabIndex        =   11
      Top             =   2715
      Width           =   900
   End
   Begin VB.CommandButton cmdHome
      Caption         =   "&Home"
      Height          =   360
      Left            =   180
      TabIndex        =   15
      Top             =   3120
      Width           =   900
   End
   Begin VB.CommandButton cmdPrev
      Caption         =   "&Prev"
      Height          =   360
      Left            =   1200
      TabIndex        =   16
      Top             =   3120
      Width           =   900
   End
   Begin VB.CommandButton cmdNext
      Caption         =   "&Next"
      Height          =   360
      Left            =   2100
      TabIndex        =   17
      Top             =   3120
      Width           =   900
   End
   Begin VB.CommandButton cmdEnd
      Caption         =   "&End"
      Height          =   360
      Left            =   3120
      TabIndex        =   18
      Top             =   3120
```

```
      Width          =    900
   End
   Begin VB.CommandButton cmdDelete
      Caption        =    "&Delete"
      Height         =    360
      Left           =    1200
      TabIndex       =    12
      Top            =    2715
      Width          =    900
   End
   Begin VB.CommandButton cmdUndelete
      Caption        =    "&Undelete"
      Height         =    360
      Left           =    2100
      TabIndex       =    13
      Top            =    2715
      Width          =    900
   End
   Begin VB.CommandButton cmdReread
      Caption        =    "&Reread"
      Height         =    360
      Left           =    3120
      TabIndex       =    14
      Top            =    2715
      Width          =    900
   End
   Begin VB.CommandButton cmdAdd
      Caption        =    "&Add New"
      Height         =    360
      Left           =    180
      TabIndex       =    0
      Top            =    3525
      Width          =    1380
   End
   Begin VB.CommandButton cmdExit
      Caption        =    "e&Xit"
      Height         =    360
      Left           =    2640
      TabIndex       =    10
      Top            =    3525
      Width          =    1380
   End
   Begin VB.TextBox txtToDo_date
      Height         =    285
      Left           =    960
      TabIndex       =    9
      Top            =    2010
      Width          =    1695
   End
```

(continued)

```
Begin VB.TextBox txtName
   Height          =    285
   Left            =    960
   TabIndex        =    2
   Top             =    720
   Width           =    3255
End
Begin VB.Label lblDeleted
   Height          =    255
   Left            =    2760
   TabIndex        =    21
   Top             =    120
   Width           =    1335
End
Begin VB.Label lblKey_num
   Height          =    255
   Left            =    840
   TabIndex        =    20
   Top             =    120
   Width           =    855
End
Begin VB.Label lblKey
   Caption         =    "Key"
   Height          =    255
   Left            =    120
   TabIndex        =    19
   Top             =    120
   Width           =    375
End
Begin VB.Line Line2
   BorderWidth     =    2
   X1              =    120
   X2              =    4095
   Y1              =    2520
   Y2              =    2535
End
Begin VB.Label lbl_ToDo_date
   Caption         =    "Date &4"
   Height          =    255
   Left            =    120
   TabIndex        =    8
   Top             =    2040
   Width           =    615
End
Begin VB.Label lblAct_time
   Caption         =    "Actual &3"
   Height          =    255
```

```
        Left            =    2160
        TabIndex        =    6
        Top             =    1560
        Width           =    975
     End
     Begin VB.Label lblEst_time
        Caption         =    "Estimated &2"
        Height          =    255
        Left            =    960
        TabIndex        =    4
        Top             =    1560
        Width           =    855
     End
     Begin VB.Label lblTime
        Caption         =    "Times"
        Height          =    255
        Left            =    120
        TabIndex        =    3
        Top             =    1200
        Width           =    615
     End
     Begin VB.Label lblName
        Caption         =    "To Do  &1"
        Height          =    255
        Left            =    120
        TabIndex        =    1
        Top             =    720
        Width           =    735
     End
  End
End
Attribute VB_Name = "frmToDo"
Attribute VB_GlobalNameSpace = False
Attribute VB_Creatable = False
Attribute VB_PredeclaredId = True
Attribute VB_Exposed = False
```

The Chore Data Entry Form's Properties

*T*his appendix lists the form properties stored in frmChore.frm. The portion you can edit in the code editor is shown in Chapter 20, Listing 20-2b.

The frmChore.frm File Above the Editable Portion

```
VERSION 5.00
Begin VB.Form frmChore
   BorderStyle     =   3  'Fixed Dialog
   Caption         =   "Chores"
   ClientHeight    =   4065
   ClientLeft      =   45
   ClientTop       =   330
   ClientWidth     =   4365
   LinkTopic       =   "Form1"
   LockControls    =   -1 'True
   MaxButton       =   0    'False
   MinButton       =   0    'False
   ScaleHeight     =   4065
   ScaleWidth      =   4365
   ShowInTaskbar   =   0    'False
   StartUpPosition =   2  'CenterScreen
   Begin VB.TextBox txtEst_time
      Height       =   300
      Left         =   1560
      TabIndex     =   4
      Text         =   "00:00"
```

(continued)

```
         Top             =    1125
         Width           =    600
      End
      Begin VB.ComboBox cmbChore_frequency
         Height          =    315
         ItemData        =    "frmChore.frx":0000
         Left            =    1560
         List            =    "frmChore.frx":000D
         TabIndex        =    6
         Text            =    "Daily"
         Top             =    1800
         Width           =    1215
      End
      Begin VB.CommandButton cmdSave
         Caption         =    "&Save"
         Height          =    360
         Left            =    180
         TabIndex        =    8
         Top             =    2715
         Width           =    900
      End
      Begin VB.CommandButton cmdHome
         Caption         =    "&Home"
         Height          =    360
         Left            =    180
         TabIndex        =    12
         Top             =    3120
         Width           =    900
      End
      Begin VB.CommandButton cmdPrev
         Caption         =    "&Prev"
         Height          =    360
         Left            =    1200
         TabIndex        =    13
         Top             =    3120
         Width           =    900
      End
      Begin VB.CommandButton cmdNext
         Caption         =    "&Next"
         Height          =    360
         Left            =    2100
         TabIndex        =    14
         Top             =    3120
         Width           =    900
      End
      Begin VB.CommandButton cmdEnd
         Caption         =    "&End"
         Height          =    360
         Left            =    3120
         TabIndex        =    15
```

```
      Top             =    3120
      Width           =    900
   End
   Begin VB.CommandButton cmdDelete
      Caption         =    "&Delete"
      Height          =    360
      Left            =    1200
      TabIndex        =    9
      Top             =    2715
      Width           =    900
   End
   Begin VB.CommandButton cmdUndelete
      Caption         =    "&Undelete"
      Height          =    360
      Left            =    2100
      TabIndex        =    10
      Top             =    2715
      Width           =    900
   End
   Begin VB.CommandButton cmdReread
      Caption         =    "&Reread"
      Height          =    360
      Left            =    3120
      TabIndex        =    11
      Top             =    2715
      Width           =    900
   End
   Begin VB.CommandButton cmdAdd
      Caption         =    "&Add New"
      Height          =    360
      Left            =    180
      TabIndex        =    0
      Top             =    3525
      Width           =    1380
   End
   Begin VB.CommandButton cmdExit
      Caption         =    "e&Xit"
      Height          =    360
      Left            =    2640
      TabIndex        =    7
      Top             =    3525
      Width           =    1380
   End
   Begin VB.TextBox txtName
      Height          =    285
      Left            =    960
      TabIndex        =    2
      Top             =    720
      Width           =    3255
   End
```

(continued)

```
Begin VB.Label lblDeleted
   Height          =   255
   Left            =   2760
   TabIndex        =   18
   Top             =   120
   Width           =   1335
End
Begin VB.Label lblKey_num
   Height          =   255
   Left            =   840
   TabIndex        =   17
   Top             =   120
   Width           =   855
End
Begin VB.Label lblKey
   Caption         =   "Key"
   Height          =   255
   Left            =   120
   TabIndex        =   16
   Top             =   120
   Width           =   375
End
Begin VB.Line Line2
   BorderWidth     =   2
   X1              =   120
   X2              =   4095
   Y1              =   2520
   Y2              =   2535
End
Begin VB.Label lblChore_frequency
   Caption         =   "Frequency &3"
   Height          =   255
   Left            =   120
   TabIndex        =   5
   Top             =   1800
   Width           =   1095
End
Begin VB.Label lblTime
   Caption         =   "Estimated Time &2"
   Height          =   255
   Left            =   120
   TabIndex        =   3
   Top             =   1200
   Width           =   1455
End
```

```
      Begin VB.Label lblName
         Caption         =   "To Do  &1"
         Height          =   255
         Left            =   120
         TabIndex        =   1
         Top             =   720
         Width           =   735
      End
   End
End
Attribute VB_Name = "frmChore"
Attribute VB_GlobalNameSpace = False
Attribute VB_Creatable = False
Attribute VB_PredeclaredId = True
Attribute VB_Exposed = False
```

THE TASK FORM'S PROPERTIES

*T*his appendix lists the form properties stored in frmTasks.frm. The portion you can edit in the code editor is shown in Chapter 21, Listing 21-1.

The frmTasks.frm File Above the Editable Portion

```
VERSION 5.00
Begin VB.Form frmTasks
    Caption         =   "Tasks"
    ClientHeight    =   3360
    ClientLeft      =   60
    ClientTop       =   345
    ClientWidth     =   5310
    LinkTopic       =   "Form1"
    LockControls    =   -1  'True
    ScaleHeight     =   3360
    ScaleWidth      =   5310
    StartUpPosition =   3   'Windows Default
    Begin VB.CommandButton cmdEdit
        Caption     =   "&Edit"
        Height      =   360
        Left        =   2640
        TabIndex    =   5
        Top         =   2880
        Width       =   1215
    End
```

(continued)

```
      Begin VB.CommandButton cmdExit
         Caption         =   "e&Xit"
         Height          =   360
         Left            =   3960
         TabIndex        =   4
         Top             =   2880
         Width           =   1215
      End
      Begin VB.ListBox lstChore
         Height          =   2400
         IntegralHeight  =   0    'False
         Left            =   2760
         TabIndex        =   2
         Top             =   360
         Width           =   2415
      End
      Begin VB.ListBox lstToDo
         Height          =   2400
         IntegralHeight  =   0    'False
         Left            =   120
         TabIndex        =   0
         Top             =   360
         Width           =   2415
      End
      Begin VB.Label lblChore
         Caption         =   "Chores"
         Height          =   255
         Left            =   2760
         TabIndex        =   3
         Top             =   120
         Width           =   1215
      End
      Begin VB.Label lblToDo
         Caption         =   "To Do List"
         Height          =   255
         Left            =   120
         TabIndex        =   1
         Top             =   120
         Width           =   2415
      End
   End
Attribute VB_Name = "frmTasks"
Attribute VB_GlobalNameSpace = False
Attribute VB_Creatable = False
Attribute VB_PredeclaredId = True
Attribute VB_Exposed = False
```

The Time Form's Properties

This appendix lists the form properties stored in frmTime.frm. The portion you can edit in the code editor is shown in Chapter 21, Listing 21-2.

The frmTime.frm File Above the Editable Portion

```
VERSION 5.00
Begin VB.Form frmTime
   Caption         =    "Time"
   ClientHeight    =    3675
   ClientLeft      =    60
   ClientTop       =    345
   ClientWidth     =    8100
   LinkTopic       =    "Form1"
   ScaleHeight     =    3675
   ScaleWidth      =    8100
   StartUpPosition =    3  'Windows Default
   Begin VB.ListBox lstPrjct
      Height          =    2400
      IntegralHeight  =    0    'False
      Left            =    6120
      TabIndex        =    18
      Top             =    360
      Width           =    1935
   End
```

(continued)

```
Begin VB.TextBox txtTotal_prjct
   Height          =   285
   Left            =   6120
   TabIndex        =   15
   Text            =   "00:00"
   Top             =   2880
   Width           =   615
End
Begin VB.CommandButton cmdExit
   Caption         =   "e&Xit"
   Height          =   360
   Left            =   6840
   TabIndex        =   14
   Top             =   3240
   Width           =   1095
End
Begin VB.TextBox txtGrand_total
   Height          =   285
   Left            =   0
   TabIndex        =   12
   Text            =   " 00:00"
   Top             =   3240
   Width           =   615
End
Begin VB.TextBox txtTotal_chore
   Height          =   285
   Left            =   4080
   TabIndex        =   8
   Text            =   "00:00"
   Top             =   2880
   Width           =   615
End
Begin VB.TextBox txtTotal_todo
   Height          =   285
   Left            =   2040
   TabIndex        =   7
   Text            =   "00:00"
   Top             =   2880
   Width           =   615
End
Begin VB.TextBox txtTotal_app
   Height          =   285
   Left            =   0
   TabIndex        =   6
   Text            =   "00:00"
   Top             =   2880
   Width           =   615
End
```

```
Begin VB.ListBox lstChore
   Height          =   2400
   IntegralHeight  =   0    'False
   Left            =   4080
   TabIndex        =   2
   Top             =   360
   Width           =   1935
End
Begin VB.ListBox lstToDo
   Height          =   2400
   IntegralHeight  =   0    'False
   Left            =   2040
   TabIndex        =   1
   Top             =   360
   Width           =   1935
End
Begin VB.ListBox lstApp
   Height          =   2400
   IntegralHeight  =   0    'False
   Left            =   0
   TabIndex        =   0
   Top             =   360
   Width           =   1935
End
Begin VB.Label lblPrjct
   Caption         =   "Projects"
   Height          =   255
   Left            =   6120
   TabIndex        =   17
   Top             =   120
   Width           =   1215
End
Begin VB.Label lblTotal_prjct
   Caption         =   "Prjct Total"
   Height          =   240
   Left            =   6840
   TabIndex        =   16
   Top             =   2940
   Width           =   975
End
Begin VB.Label lblGrand_total
   Caption         =   "Grand Total"
   Height          =   255
   Left            =   720
   TabIndex        =   13
   Top             =   3300
   Width           =   1455
End
```

(continued)

```
Begin VB.Label lblTotal_chore
   Caption        =   "Chore Total"
   Height         =   240
   Left           =   4800
   TabIndex       =   11
   Top            =   2940
   Width          =   975
End
Begin VB.Label lblTotal_todo
   Caption        =   "To Do Total"
   Height         =   240
   Left           =   2760
   TabIndex       =   10
   Top            =   2940
   Width          =   975
End
Begin VB.Label lblTotal_app
   Caption        =   "Apntmt Total"
   Height         =   240
   Left           =   720
   TabIndex       =   9
   Top            =   2940
   Width          =   1335
End
Begin VB.Label lblChore
   Caption        =   "Chores"
   Height         =   255
   Left           =   4080
   TabIndex       =   5
   Top            =   120
   Width          =   1215
End
Begin VB.Label lblToDo
   Caption        =   "To Do List"
   Height         =   255
   Left           =   2040
   TabIndex       =   4
   Top            =   120
   Width          =   1215
End
Begin VB.Label lblApp
   Caption        =   "Appointments"
   Height         =   255
   Left           =   120
   TabIndex       =   3
   Top            =   120
   Width          =   1215
End
```

```
End
Attribute VB_Name = "frmTime"
Attribute VB_GlobalNameSpace = False
Attribute VB_Creatable = False
Attribute VB_PredeclaredId = True
Attribute VB_Exposed = False
```

INDEX

P

IDG BOOKS WORLDWIDE, INC.
END-USER LICENSE AGREEMENT

Read This. You should carefully read these terms and conditions before opening the software packet(s) included with this book ("Book"). This is a license agreement ("Agreement") between you and IDG Books Worldwide, Inc. ("IDGB"). By opening the accompanying software packet(s), you acknowledge that you have read and accept the following terms and conditions. If you do not agree and do not want to be bound by such terms and conditions, promptly return the Book and the unopened software packet(s) to the place you obtained them for a full refund.

1. **License Grant.** IDGB grants to you (either an individual or entity) a nonexclusive license to use one copy of the enclosed software program(s) (collectively, the "Software") solely for your own personal or business purposes on a single computer (whether a standard computer or a workstation component of a multiuser network). The Software is in use on a computer when it is loaded into temporary memory (i.e., RAM) or installed into permanent memory (e.g., hard disk, CD-ROM, or other storage device). IDGB reserves all rights not expressly granted herein.

2. **Ownership.** IDGB is the owner of all right, title, and interest, including copyright, in and to the compilation of the Software recorded on the CD-ROM. Copyright to the individual programs on the CD-ROM is owned by the author or other authorized copyright owner of each program. Ownership of the Software and all proprietary rights relating thereto remain with IDGB and its licensors.

3. **Restrictions on Use and Transfer.**

   (a) You may only (i) make one copy of the Software for backup or archival purposes, or (ii) transfer the Software to a single hard disk, provided that you keep the original for backup or archival purposes. You may not (i) rent or lease the Software, (ii) copy or reproduce the Software through a LAN or other network system or through any computer subscriber system or bulletin-board system, or (iii) modify, adapt, or create derivative works based on the Software.

   (b) You may not reverse engineer, decompile, or disassemble the Software. You may transfer the Software and user documentation on a permanent basis, provided that the transferee agrees to accept the terms and conditions of this Agreement and you retain no copies. If the Software is an update or has been updated, any transfer must include the most recent update and all prior versions.

4. **Restrictions on Use of Individual Programs.** You must follow the individual requirements and restrictions detailed for each individual program. These limitations are contained in the individual license agreements recorded on the CD-ROM. These restrictions may include a requirement that after using the program for the period of time specified in its text, the user must pay a registration fee or discontinue use. By opening the Software packet(s), you will be agreeing to abide by the licenses and restrictions for these individual programs. None of the material on this disk(s) or listed in this Book may ever be distributed, in original or modified form, for commercial purposes.

5. <u>Limited Warranty</u>.

   (a) IDGB warrants that the Software and CD-ROM are free from defects in materials and workmanship under normal use for a period of sixty (60) days from the date of purchase of this Book. If IDGB receives notification within the warranty period of defects in materials or workmanship, IDGB will replace the defective CD-ROM.

   (b) **IDGB AND THE AUTHORS OF THE BOOK DISCLAIM ALL OTHER WARRANTIES, EXPRESS OR IMPLIED, INCLUDING WITHOUT LIMITATION IMPLIED WARRANTIES OF MERCHANTABILITY AND FITNESS FOR A PARTICULAR PURPOSE, WITH RESPECT TO THE SOFTWARE, THE PROGRAMS, THE SOURCE CODE CONTAINED THEREIN, AND/OR THE TECHNIQUES DESCRIBED IN THIS BOOK. IDGB DOES NOT WARRANT THAT THE FUNCTIONS CONTAINED IN THE SOFTWARE WILL MEET YOUR REQUIREMENTS OR THAT THE OPERATION OF THE SOFTWARE WILL BE ERROR FREE.**

   (c) This limited warranty gives you specific legal rights, and you may have other rights which vary from jurisdiction to jurisdiction.

6. <u>Remedies</u>.

   (a) IDGB's entire liability and your exclusive remedy for defects in materials and workmanship shall be limited to replacement of the Software, which may be returned to IDGB with a copy of your receipt at the following address: Disk Fulfillment Department, Attn: Visual Basic 5 Power OOP, IDG Books Worldwide, Inc., 7260 Shadeland Station, Ste. 100, Indianapolis, IN 46256, or call 1-800-762-2974. Please allow 3–4 weeks for delivery. This Limited Warranty is void if failure of the Software has resulted from accident, abuse, or misapplication. Any replacement Software will be warranted for the remainder of the original warranty period or thirty (30) days, whichever is longer.

   (b) In no event shall IDGB or the author be liable for any damages whatsoever (including without limitation damages for loss of business profits, business interruption, loss of business information, or any other pecuniary loss) arising from the use of or inability to use the Book or the Software, even if IDGB has been advised of the possibility of such damages.

   (c) Because some jurisdictions do not allow the exclusion or limitation of liability for consequential or incidental damages, the above limitation or exclusion may not apply to you.

7. <u>U.S. Government Restricted Rights</u>. Use, duplication, or disclosure of the Software by the U.S. Government is subject to restrictions stated in paragraph (c) (1) (ii) of the Rights in Technical Data and Computer Software clause of DFARS 252.227-7013, and in subparagraphs (a) through (d) of the Commercial Computer—Restricted Rights clause at FAR 52.227-19, and in similar clauses in the NASA FAR supplement, when applicable.

8. <u>General</u>. This Agreement constitutes the entire understanding of the parties and revokes and supersedes all prior agreements, oral or written, between them and may not be modified or amended except in a writing signed by both parties hereto which specifically refers to this Agreement. This Agreement shall take precedence over any other documents that may be in conflict herewith. If any one or more provisions contained in this Agreement are held by any court or tribunal to be invalid, illegal, or otherwise unenforceable, each and every other provision shall remain in full force and effect.

CD-ROM Installation Instructions

The *Visual Basic 5 Power OOP* CD-ROM contains the tutorial and demonstration files for this book. The files are divided into chapter tutorial files and sample demonstration files.

A Note about Performance

The *Visual Basic 5 Power OOP* CD-ROM is designed for Windows 95 and Windows NT systems. While running this software on Windows NT systems, you may experience system problems. These problems are inherent to the current implementation of Visual Basic 5 in the Windows NT environment and are unrelated to the code of *Visual Basic 5 Power OOP*. At the time of publication, Microsoft was aware of the performance problems of Visual Basic 5 but had not released a solution. We suggest checking www.microsoft.com for the latest updates of Visual Basic 5 for Windows NT.

Tutorial Files

The chapter tutorial files allow you to try the code from the book as you read along. All of the code for the chapters is in the CD-ROM directory Chapters. In that directory, the code is organized by chapters and stages, as cited in *Visual Basic 5 Power OOP*. For example, the directory Chapters\Chap02 contains directories 02-01, 02-02, and so on. Where code is improved from stage to stage in a chapter, the same file name is repeated in the corresponding chapter stage directories.

To use a tutorial file from the *Visual Basic 5 Power OOP* CD-ROM, copy the file from the CD-ROM to your hard drive and follow the corresponding instructions in the chapter.

Sample Application

It's easy to try a finished version of MyTime, the sample application that is built in *Visual Basic 5 Power OOP*. In Windows Explorer, go to the *Visual Basic 5 Power OOP* CD-ROM's MyTime\Installation Files directory and double-click Setup.exe (or Setup, if your system is configured to conceal file extensions). MyTime will be installed on your hard drive.

IDG BOOKS WORLDWIDE REGISTRATION CARD

Visit our Web site at http://www.idgbooks.com

Title of this book: **Visual Basic® 5 Power OOP**

My overall rating of this book: ❑ Very good [1] ❑ Good [2] ❑ Satisfactory [3] ❑ Fair [4] ❑ Poor [5]

How I first heard about this book:

❑ Found in bookstore; name: [6]

❑ Advertisement: [8]

❑ Word of mouth; heard about book from friend, co-worker, etc.: [10]

❑ Book review: [7]

❑ Catalog: [9]

❑ Other: [11]

What I liked most about this book:

What I would change, add, delete, etc., in future editions of this book:

Other comments:

Number of computer books I purchase in a year: ❑ 1 [12] ❑ 2-5 [13] ❑ 6-10 [14] ❑ More than 10 [15]

I would characterize my computer skills as: ❑ Beginner [16] ❑ Intermediate [17] ❑ Advanced [18] ❑ Professional [19]

I use ❑ DOS [20] ❑ Windows [21] ❑ OS/2 [22] ❑ Unix [23] ❑ Macintosh [24] ❑ Other: [25]_____

(please specify)

I would be interested in new books on the following subjects:

(please check all that apply, and use the spaces provided to identify specific software)

❑ Word processing: [26]

❑ Data bases: [28]

❑ File Utilities: [30]

❑ Networking: [32]

❑ Other: [34]

❑ Spreadsheets: [27]

❑ Desktop publishing: [29]

❑ Money management: [31]

❑ Programming languages: [33]

I use a PC at (please check all that apply): ❑ home [35] ❑ work [36] ❑ school [37] ❑ other: [38] _____

The disks I prefer to use are ❑ 5.25 [39] ❑ 3.5 [40] ❑ other: [41]_____

I have a CD ROM: ❑ yes [42] ❑ no [43]

I plan to buy or upgrade computer hardware this year: ❑ yes [44] ❑ no [45]

I plan to buy or upgrade computer software this year: ❑ yes [46] ❑ no [47]

Name: _____ Business title: [48] _____ Type of Business: [49] _____

Address (❑ home [50] ❑ work [51]/Company name: _____)

Street/Suite#

City [52]/State [53]/Zipcode [54]: _____ Country [55]

❑ **I liked this book!** You may quote me by name in future
IDG Books Worldwide promotional materials.

My daytime phone number is _____

IDG
BOOKS
WORLDWIDE
THE WORLD OF
COMPUTER
KNOWLEDGE®

☐ YES!

Please keep me informed about IDG Books Worldwide's World of Computer Knowledge. Send me your latest catalog.